Praise for

The Bitter Road to Freedom

"A remarkable work of history that also sheds light on present-day debates about the merits and the costs of liberating people by force."

—*Foreign Affairs*

"Conveys the pity of war and its aftermath with integrity and proper sympathy. Inevitably the book raises awkward questions about the fate of civilians in the firing line; the current tensions in Gaza lend it an awful relevance."

—*The Guardian*

"Undertaken for the best of motives, Europe's liberation was essentially honorable. But it had a dark side overlooked until recently. *The Bitter Road to Freedom* completes the liberation's master story in compelling fashion."

—*World War II* magazine

"In a history that jars with images of grateful civilians showering soldiers with flowers, William I. Hitchcock's vivid account of post-war Europe paints a violent and chaotic picture of liberation and recovery. It should be essential reading for any leader hankering for regime change."

—*The Independent* (London)

"Deeply moving."

—*The Times* (London)

"[T]he first book I have read that explicitly addresses the plight of civilians during the 'crusade for Europe.' . . . [T]his tale vividly demonstrates that there was no cause for triumphalism in the condition of Europe following the defeat of Hitler."

—Max Hastings, *Sunday Times* (London)

"Remarkable. . . . [U]nderlines that the liberation of Europe was both a major military triumph and a human tragedy of epic proportions."

—*Irish Times*

"A powerful and important new work of history. . . . [A] thorough, passionate corrective to any simple telling of the terrible last year of this war."

—*Financial Times*

"*The Bitter Road to Freedom* is an eloquent presentation of what are too often called war's 'collateral effects.' Chaos, destruction, and suffering are not collateral. They are fundamental."

—*History Book Club*

"An assiduous researcher, historian Hitchcock emphasizes personal stories, an effective tool for humanizing events that enveloped millions upon millions of traumatized survivors of Nazi brutality. Hitchcock successfully recovers the less enlightened acts and attitudes of the liberators toward the liberated, without, however, compromising the basic rightness of the Allied cause. This is history mined and written at a high level of quality, worthy of inclusion in any WWII collection."

—*Booklist*

"The war in Europe was not just an honorable struggle to liberate a continent from a vile dictatorship; Hitchcock reminds us that it was also a disaster that cost millions of people everything they had."

—*Library Journal*

"[Hitchcock] provides a balance to the rosier accounts of this era without compromising the justice of the Allied cause."

—*Jewish Book World*

THE
BITTER ROAD TO FREEDOM

A New History of the Liberation of Europe

WILLIAM I. HITCHCOCK

FREE PRESS
New York   Toronto   London   Sydney

Free Press
A Division of Simon & Schuster, Inc.
1230 Avenue of the Americas
New York, NY 10020

First Free Press trade paperback edition October 2009

FREE PRESS and colophon are trademarks of Simon & Schuster, Inc.

For information about special discounts for bulk purchases, please contact
Simon & Schuster Special Sales at 1-866-506-1949 or
business@simonandschuster.com

The Simon & Schuster Speakers Bureau can bring authors
to your live event. For more information or to book an event
contact the Simon & Schuster Speakers Bureau at
1-866-248-3049 or visit our website at www.simonspeakers.com.

Maps by Chris Robinson
Book design by Ellen R. Sasahara

Library of Congress Cataloging-in-Publication Data

Hitchcock, William I.
The bitter road to freedom: a new history of the liberation of Europe /
William I. Hitchcock.
p. cm.
Includes bibliographical references and index.
1. World War, 1939–1945—Europe—End. 2. World War, 1939–1945—
Social aspects—Europe. I. Title.
D755.7.H56 2008
940.53'14—dc22
2008002344

ISBN 978-0-7432-7381-7
ISBN 978-1-4391-2330-0 (pbk)

for Benjamin and Emma

my little ones

Contents

Preface: A Cemetery in Luxembourg   *1*

PART I: LIBERATION IN THE WEST

Prologue: D-Day   11

1. "Too Wonderfully Beautiful": Liberation in Normandy   *19*
2. Blood on the Snow: The Elusive Liberation of Belgium   *60*
3. Hunger: The Netherlands and the Politics of Food   *98*

PART II: INTO GERMANY

Prologue: Armies of Justice   125

4. Red Storm in the East: Survival and Revenge   *131*
5. A Strange, Enemy Country: America's Germany   *170*

PART III: MOVING BODIES

Prologue: "They Have Suffered Unbearably"   211

6. Freedom from Want: UNRRA and the Relief Effort to Save Europe   *215*
7. "A Tidal Wave of Nomad Peoples": Europe's Displaced Persons   *249*

PART IV: TO LIVE AGAIN AS A PEOPLE

Prologue: "We Felt Ourselves Lost" 283

8. A Host of Corpses: Liberating Hitler's Camps   287

9. Americans and Jews in Occupied Germany   310

10. Belsen and the British   339

Conclusion: The Missing Liberation   367

Acknowledgments   375

Notes   379

Bibliography   415

Index   431

I lift up my eyes to the hills.
From whence does my help come?

—Psalms 121:1

Preface

A Cemetery in Luxembourg

T HE LUXEMBOURG AMERICAN Military Cemetery in Hamm, three miles east of Luxembourg City, serves as the final resting place for 5,076 Americans killed in the battles of the Ardennes and Rhineland in late 1944 and early 1945. Like all the American war cemeteries that dot the European countryside, from the British Isles to France, Italy, Belgium, and Holland, it is a beautiful, serene, melancholy place. Perfect rows of white crosses and Stars of David are pegged out on an immaculate, emerald lawn. American flags snap in the wind. One of the great soldiers of the Second World War, General George S. Patton, Jr., is buried here, though he died just after the war, in December 1945, in a road accident. His tomb stands at the head of the soldiers, facing them, eternally reviewing the troops. But his barking exhortations to battle have long faded. It is always quiet here.

This cemetery is more than a memorial. It aims to educate as well. Upon entering the grounds, visitors come to a series of large engraved maps that visually lay out the last year of the Second World War in Europe in exquisitely bold, enameled colors, with flashing red and blue arrows indicating the knifing progress of the Allied armies across the continent. Visitors also encounter a monumental tablet that narrates the war's final year. Small groups gather here, with necks craning upward and eyes squinting against the bright granite. They read a story about the liberation of Europe that is literally inscribed in stone. "On 6 June 1944," the text begins, "preceded by airborne units and covered by naval and air bombardment, United States and British Commonwealth forces landed on the coast of Normandy. Pushing southward, they established a beachhead some 20 miles in depth. On 25 July, in the wake of paralyzing air bombardment, the US First Army broke out of the beachhead and was soon joined by the US Third Army." The text tells readers that the British and American forces eventually "crushed" the Germans in a great pincer movement in Normandy and "the enemy retreated across the Seine." The Allied armies, "sustained by the Herculean achievements of Army and Navy supply personnel," pursued the enemy "vigorously." At the borders of Germany, progress was slow and the "fighting bitter." But inevitably, "the superb fighting qualities of American soldiers" won out. The Americans turned back the last desperate German attack in the Ardennes in December 1944. "Sweeping across Germany, the Allies met the advancing troops of the USSR to force the complete surrender of the enemy on 8 May 1945, 337 days after the initial landings in France." There, the text concludes.

The brief synopsis on this imposing stone slab might be considered emblematic of a great deal of historical writing about the last year of the war in Europe. Quite naturally, given its location in an American cemetery, this text emphasizes the actions of American armed forces. It deploys muscular, active verbs like *land, repulse, break out, pursue, seize*. Air bombardments are *paralyzing,* the efforts of supply personnel are *Herculean,* armies do not move but *sweep*. This text, like so many popular historical accounts, depicts the Allied armies as irresistible, constantly on the move toward victory. The tablet neatly assigns a precise number of days between start and finish: 337.

The hushed, dignified confines of a military cemetery are no place for a detailed prose account of the human experience of war; in any case, the five thousand headstones laid out row after row offer an enduring, wordless testimonial to that. Yet too often, when Americans think about the liberation of Europe, we take our cues from such monuments. We have fixed our gaze upon battles and armies, and taken refuge in a well-worn and predictable narration of the war that stresses the ennobling quality of the fight for freedom. In doing so, we often overlook the fact that for European people, liberation came hand in hand with unprecedented violence and brutality. Desirable as it was, liberation proved also to be a bitter chapter in the war's history.

To understand this paradox, we must look beyond the military history of the war into the experiences of the liberated peoples themselves. In the pages that follow, I have tried to give voice to those who were on the receiving end of liberation, moving them from the edge of the story to the center. This history of liberation gives detailed attention to the interactions of soldiers and civilians, to the experiences of noncombatants, to the trauma of displacement and loss, and to the unprecedented destruction that liberation required. This book, I believe, offers a new history of liberation, told largely from the ground up. It is a surprising story, often jarring and uncomfortable, and it is one that does not appear in our monuments or our history books.

The keynote of this European story of liberation is violence. However much we wish to assign it a benevolent nature, liberation came to Europe in a storm of destruction and death. On D-Day alone, Allied bombing killed about 3,000 French civilians in Normandy—roughly the same number of American servicemen who would die on that day. And the civilian death toll only mounted during the last year of the war. To liberate Europe from the extremely powerful, well-trained, and superbly equipped German army, the Allied powers were obliged to use massive, overwhelming, and lethal force to destroy and kill Germans in large numbers. Because these Germans occupied towns, cities, farms, schools, hospitals, hotels, railway stations, ports, bridges, and other strategic points across the European continent, much of Europe was churned into rubble by American, British, and Soviet military force. Allied armies made little effort to spare civilian lives. They shelled, bombed, strafed, and attacked towns and cities in full knowledge that civilians would die. This was a consciously accepted dimension of the war of liberation that the Allied armies waged. Liberation was therefore both a glorious chapter in military history and a human tragedy of enormous scope.

European accounts of liberation also have much to say about liberating soldiers themselves. Contrary to what we might expect, liberated civilians viewed their liberators with anxiety and even, at times, fear. Of course, some western capital cities like Paris and Brussels saw their fair share of kissing and delirious flag-waving as liberating troops arrived. But if we dig a bit deeper, we find a more troubling story. The young American, British, or Russian soldiers who defeated the Germans were seldom as virtuous in their behavior as the cause for which they fought. They frequently abused their power and authority, making life for liberated civilians something close to misery. "Deliver us from our liberators!" was the cry on the lips of the residents of one Belgian town, where Americans were still encamped in the fall of 1945, after the war had ended. The power that liberating soldiers possessed over the civilians whom they freed opened up enticing avenues of privilege and temptation for these young, male troopers. Even the best of the "greatest generation" consumed scarce food and drink, billeted themselves in homes and private dwellings, and were capable of profligate waste, drunkenness, carousing, and vandalism. Some soldiers went further, and looted homes, seized property as trophies, and sexually assaulted women of all ages. For all the elation that oppressed Europeans felt at the demise of the Nazi regime, they often found it difficult to comprehend the destructiveness and rapacious acquisitiveness of their liberators.

Europeans who lived in central and eastern Europe tell of a liberation denied. Nineteen forty-five brought no liberation to Poland: that woeful nation saw its borders redrawn by Stalin's imperious demands, and millions of Poles were incorporated into Soviet Belorussia and Ukraine. Poland endured half a century of Communist rule that made a mockery of the promises of liberation that had issued from Soviet propagandists throughout the war. In eastern Germany, the arrival of the Red Army occasioned such fear and panic among Germans that about five million people fled, on foot, rushing away from the wrath of the Soviets. They were wise to do so, for those that remained behind were mistreated, abused, raped, or murdered by rampaging Red Army troops. Millions of Germans were expelled from a large swath of Germany that was in turn transferred to Poland, while millions of *Volksdeutsche,* the ethnic Germans long settled in borderland communities in Poland, Czechoslovakia, Hungary, Romania, and Yugoslavia, were forcibly removed from their homes and pushed westward. In the east, then, the abiding symbol of liberation was the open cattle car slowly rattling along the rails of Europe, bearing a cargo of frightened civilians away from their homes.

In the western part of Germany, life among the liberators was far more tolerable, so much so that many European observers came to think of the Allied occupation of western Germany in bitterly ironic terms. After four years of trying very hard to kill Germans and to destroy German cities and towns, American soldiers who set foot on German soil in the late fall of 1944 quickly grew fond of the German people. They were, in the parlance of the GIs, "just like us." The girls were pretty, the women looked something like Mom, the houses—those not burnt in Allied bombing—were clean and invariably full of such comforts as feather mattresses, books, preserved foods, wine, and spirits. Germans in the western part of the country quickly tried to turn American good nature to their advantage, and thanked these troops for "liberating" Germany. British and American leaders struggled mightily over this problem. They knew that Hitler had won full-throated acclaim from the racist, aggressive German population, yet in their guise as benevolent liberators, they did not wish to be seen as punitive, repressive, or unduly harsh. Within months after the end of the war, British and American armies of occupation had transformed themselves into massive social and humanitarian agencies, caring for Germans, doling out medicine, food rations, clothing, and shoes, while working overtime to restart water pumps, electricity generators, coal mines, and railways. By the fall of 1945, British and American military officials, rejecting the idea that they were occupiers, set themselves the goal of winning "the battle of winter" on behalf of the hungry and cold German people. The Anglo-American forces were indeed magnanimous in victory. But it remains a startling irony that the western Allies worked harder on behalf of the defeated enemy than they ever did for the liberated people of France, Belgium, the Netherlands, or Italy.

Europe's Jews also have a liberation story to tell us. It is as pointed as it is poignant. It has become common for American readers, or at least American viewers of made-for-television war dramas, to assume that the greatest generation fought World War II to rescue Europe's Jews from destruction. Sadly, nothing could be further from the truth. The discovery of the German concentration camps by American GIs in the last weeks of the war occasioned revulsion and pity among the soldiers, as well as anger. But at no point was the cause in Europe framed as a bid to save European Jewry. That may help explain why American and British officers and soldiers in Germany at the close of the war had little knowledge of the plight of the Jews, and failed to treat the survivors they found there with anything like the sensitivity or sympathy they deserved. At first, the surviving remnant of Jews that Allied armies freed from concentration camps was seen simply as another group of wayward "political prisoners," their predicament no worse than that of others who had suffered. Only after extensive and energetic appeals from incarcerated Jews, and from international humanitarian agencies on their behalf, did the U.S. and British armies begin to comprehend and respond to the crisis of Jewish survivors. These forlorn Jews, now homeless, without resources, bereft of family or kinship networks, remained in Germany, dependent on an unfeeling military bureaucracy for aid and help. They ended up in barbed-wire encampments, often in the very same places in which the Nazis had incarcerated them, desperately awaiting a transfer to Palestine. Over 250,000 Jews spent time in camps in Germany after the war, and some remained in these temporary shelters for as long as five years. Jewish survivors who talk about liberation therefore speak with some bitterness about a liberation deferred.

An account of liberation would be incomplete without the voices of liberating soldiers, and this book presents their perceptions as well. These men speak little of heroism, or of their "Crusade in Europe," as General Dwight D. Eisenhower's postwar memoir was called. Instead, they offer cautious, humble, at times evasive accounts of their experiences. Reading through countless memoirs, diaries, letters, and oral testimonies of British and American soldiers who fought in Europe, the historian can immediately perceive the profound ambivalence of these young men in combat. They understood the importance of the job they had been asked to do, but seemed to hate every minute of it. Fighting on behalf of others, in a faraway land of foreign customs and languages, amid filth, death, and destruction, occasioned in most liberating soldiers a profound distaste and disgust with the whole business of war. Few soldiers in combat were motivated by idealistic objectives. Most fought simply because they had to fight in order to end the war and go home. As Sergeant John Babcock of the 78th Infantry Division put it in his memoir, "our bunch of GIs was not fighting for mother, country, and apple pie. Bullshit. We wanted to live. Our ties were to those unfortunates fighting next to us, sharing the same fate."[1] This would seem to be a more honest assessment of the soldier's experience than the hortatory text on the monument in Luxembourg.

THE MATERIAL PRESENTED in these pages bears directly on our own times. When I began this research in 2003, Americans and Europeans were then embroiled in a bitter dispute about the proper role of military force in the world, and the responsibilities of wealthy, democratic nations to use their armies to wage war on repressive nations. At that time, many American leaders, drawing on popular conceptions of the liberation of Europe during the Second World War, argued that the United States had an obligation to use its power to advance the cause of democracy and freedom in the world. As in World War II, the argument ran, when America had led the world in a war against fascism and won the world's gratitude, so in our own times could America overthrow dictators, free oppressed peoples, and bring the blessings of liberty to others. Some American leaders even implied that war itself, while undesirable, might offer a test in which we could measure ourselves against previous generations of honored warriors.

Europeans generally viewed these claims with skepticism, and I now know why. They began from a different premise than Americans, for they had lived through liberation, and still carry the scars. The year 1945 taught Europeans a lesson they have never forgotten: that a war of liberation is still a war, and no matter how noble the cause, mothers and children will die, houses of worship will be burned, disease will spread, refugees will tramp the roads; and then, after all these horrors are over, liberators and liberated alike will still face the hard work of constructing freedom and restoring human dignity. Liberation in 1945 entailed such destruction and social upheaval that it came to be seen by those who were liberated as a time of cruel paradoxes—a time of high hopes and profound disappointment, of cherished freedom and new threats, of full-throated celebration and echoing silences. This is why those who have lived through liberation are often slow to wish the experience on others.

Of course, Europeans remain enormously grateful to Americans for the liberation they helped secure. To see the sincerity of this gratitude, one need only visit the humble coastal towns of Normandy in early June upon the anniversary of the D-Day landings. There, one can admire the hundreds of Allied flags unfurled in the sea breeze, witness the warm reception accorded to the proud, elderly veterans who return to these hallowed precincts, and bask in the genuine sense of trans-Atlantic solidarity that these ceremonials evoke, year after year. These people who ritually gather and shake hands and march to the fading strains of martial tunes are bound by a common project, a common commitment to those four simple freedoms Franklin Roosevelt had named in 1941—freedom of speech and religion, freedom from want and fear.

But those who lived through these times have no illusions about war. They recall all too well the terrible destruction, the countless deaths, and the appalling violence of the Second World War. They know, too, that military victory over Nazism was only a preliminary act in the longer struggle to restore peace to Europe, to rebuild order and stability, and revive the civic, humane traditions that the Nazis had trampled in the dust. They have a clear memory that liberation was a time of valor, but also a time of unceasing toil, bitterness, and death. As these aging witnesses now pass from the scene, we will have to rely on other sources to inform us about this war. If we want to recover the reality of the final stages of the war, in all its ugliness and its ecstasy, we shall have to turn our eyes away from maps and monuments, and explore the lives of ordinary men and women, Europeans and Americans, civilians and soldiers, as they struggled to survive these tragic hours of liberation.

LIBERATION IN THE WEST

I

Prologue

D-Day

THE LIBERATION OF Europe may have begun as early as November 1942, on the banks of the Volga river at Stalingrad, when the Soviet Red Army checked Nazi Germany's advance into Central Asia and began the long, murderous fight that would expel the German invaders from the Soviet Union and bring the Russians across 1,500 bloody miles to Berlin. Or it may have begun with the Anglo-American landings in North Africa, also in November 1942, a deft operation that pointed the blade of the Allied spearhead into Germany's southern flank and opened the way to the invasion of southern Italy in July 1943. Perhaps the liberation began in earnest when the Red Army crossed the prewar Polish border in January 1944, or when American troops entered Rome in June 1944. These are all plausible candidates for the status of "starting point," for the liberation of Europe was a global process, the pressing inward toward Berlin of millions of soldiers, from all directions, gradually tightening a choke hold on the Third Reich. Yet in popular imagination, and most historical writing, the liberation of Europe commenced on that wet gray morning in the rolling surf off the coast of Normandy on June 6, 1944. Here, in France, came the long-awaited, long-planned Second Front, designed to complement the massive thrusts of the Red Army into Germany from the east. This was the moment that European civilians, suffering under German occupation, had awaited for years, the moment when the decisive battle against Germany would be opened, the start of a continental campaign that would bring about the final defeat of the malevolent, depraved Nazi regime. This is where our story of liberation begins.

The great Allied armada that set out across the English Channel on June 6 comprised some 5,000 vessels of all sorts, from hulking, monstrous battleships, cruisers, and destroyers to a vast array of small landing craft. On board, they carried over 100,000 soldiers—American, English, Welsh, Scotch, Irish, Canadians, Poles, and a few Belgians, Dutch, French, and Norwegians—

to landing sites along twenty miles of coastline in the French *départements* (departments) of Calvados and Manche. The overall supreme commander of Operation Overlord was General Dwight D. Eisenhower; the ground commander of the landing forces was an Englishman, General Sir Bernard Law Montgomery. On June 6, the landing forces were all grouped together in the 21st Army Group under Montgomery's command. The British Second Army, commanded by Lieutenant-General Sir Miles Dempsey, took aim at three beaches, code-named Sword, Juno, and Gold, running from the villages of Ouistreham in the east to Arromanches in the west. The Anglo-Canadian forces that splashed ashore here faced moderate resistance but within a few hours had established three beachheads and made contact with the British 6th Airborne Division, which had been dropped across the Orne river to secure the eastern flanks. The British suffered approximately 1,000 casualties on Gold beach and the same number on Sword; 600 airborne troops were killed or wounded, and 600 more were missing; 100 glider pilots also became casualties. The Canadians at Juno beach suffered 340 killed, 574 wounded, and 47 taken prisoner. Twenty-four hours after the landings, British forces had taken the town of Bayeux almost unopposed and were pushing on toward the city of Caen.

To the west, Lieutenant General Omar Bradley's U.S. First Army landed on two beaches, Omaha and Utah. Utah beach was on the western flank of the Allied assault, running along the coast of the Cotentin peninsula. The beach here was thinly defended; three regimental combat teams of the 4th Division faced negligible fire from the German positions and they moved inland in search of the 82nd and 101st Airborne divisions with whom they were supposed to link up. These airborne landings, which had commenced late at night on the 5th, had been badly scattered and it was some days before any cohesion came to this sector; yet the losses sustained on Utah were relatively small. The picture on Omaha beach was far more serious. The 1st and 29th divisions of Bradley's landing force, hitting the beaches between Port-en-Bessin and Vierville-sur-Mer, ran straight into the teeth of well-defended German batteries that had not been softened up by the preliminary air and naval bombardments. The cliffs along Omaha, running up from a stony beach, rise some hundred to two hundred feet, and provided excellent cover for the defenders, who had created extensive trenches and concrete pillbox firing positions; moreover, 27 out of 32 of the "swimming" amphibious DD tanks that were meant to provide armor support for the infantry sank in choppy seas during the landing. The beach and waters were packed with obstacles and mines on which landing craft snagged, blocking the way for those behind. Many heavily burdened soldiers whose craft spilled them into the water sank and drowned. With extraordinary courage, small numbers of soldiers, realizing that to remain on the beach under German fire would surely get them killed, began to fight their way up the craggy hillside and into the narrow ravines that led from the beaches up the hills. Slowly they gained a foothold. The horror on Omaha, which had seemed an eternity to those pinned down there, had lasted less than four hours; by 11:00 A.M. Vierville was in American hands. At the end of the day, a narrow beachhead had been established, but it had cost the Americans dearly. While there had been but 197 casualties on Utah, over 2,000 men were wounded or killed on Omaha beach. Overall, 1,465 American soldiers were killed on D-Day, 3,184 were wounded, 1,928 were listed as missing, and 26 were captured.[1]

The view of Omaha beach from an American landing craft,
June 6, 1944. *FDR Library*

The Omaha landings had been something close to a catastrophe, and the broad territorial objectives of the Allied landings had not been attained anywhere on any beach on D-Day. Even so, the overall strategic picture twenty-four hours after D-Day was good. The landings successfully created a beachhead that could be defended against counterattack, and the planned buildup of additional Allied forces could proceed apace. Casualties, totaling some 10,000 men, had been far smaller than General Eisenhower had anticipated. But over the following weeks and months, the realities of the huge task that lay ahead began to sink in. The first disappointments came on the eastern flank, where the British, whose landings had gone so well, were unable to seize the city of Caen, which lay on the axis that the Allies had hoped to follow farther into France. In the three days after the landings, Canadian and British forces were badly mauled by the 12th SS Panzer Division, which tried desperately to push the invaders back into the sea; by June 10, the Germans, bolstered by the swift arrival of the Panzer Lehr Division and the 21st Panzer Division, took up defensive positions in front of Caen. In the coming weeks, repeated efforts by Montgomery's forces to outflank Caen, at Tilly-sur-Seulles and Villers-Bocage, failed and the struggle for Caen turned into a desperate yard-by-yard fight that many likened to the western front in the First World War. The daring and surprise of the D-Day landings had been completely lost.

The picture was only marginally better on the western flank. After consolidating the Utah and Omaha beachheads, the American VII Corps under Major General J. Lawton Collins attacked westward to cut the Cotentin peninsula in half, then thrust north to capture the port of Cherbourg on June 27. Despite this success, the picture across Normandy was discouraging for General Eisenhower. The Germans had systematically, expertly reduced Cherbourg to rubble, which interfered with the logistical supply plan. By late June, conditions on the ground had settled into a bloody stalemate, as the Germans made superb use of the defensive advantages they possessed, particularly the thick, ancient hedgerows that divided the countryside up into nearly impenetrable squares. The Americans found themselves fighting for every yard across a landscape that looked something like a gigantic ice-cube tray: each square had to be penetrated and seized, one by one. This slow, costly fighting made June and July "a difficult period for all of us," General Eisenhower wrote later.[2] Yet gradually, two elements in the Allied arsenal began to tell in the battle: the steady buildup of men and materiel through the massive Anglo-American naval forces that continued to pour supplies through the beachheads; and the punishing blows delivered daily to the Germans by the dominant Allied air forces. By July 2, there were about one million Allied soldiers in Normandy, including thirteen American, eleven British, and one Canadian division. Over 560,000 tons of supplies had been landed along with 171,000 vehicles.[3] While the Germans proved able to outfight the Allies on the ground in Normandy, they could not easily replace the men and materiel they lost; nor could they hide from the Allied tactical air attack. The battle in Normandy settled into a long, slow battle of attrition, just what the Germans could not afford.

By late July, the allies fielded 1.4 million soldiers in Normandy, about twice the number of German soldiers engaged in the battle, yet were still stuck in positions they had planned to occupy just five days after D-Day. The battle had been far slower and bloodier than expected, with the terrain of Normandy inhibiting Allied maneuvers. But on July 25, with the bulk of the German forces engaged in the Caen area, the American First Army, deployed along a line running west from Saint-Lô to the coast, staged the great breakout that would change the dynamic of the campaign, and the war. Following a colossal (and sloppy) carpet bombing of the German defensive positions just west of Saint-Lô, the Americans ripped open a gap in the German line and plunged forward, rushing south and west toward Avranches, thus opening the way into Brittany and, more importantly, threatening to envelop the German army in Normandy. Fending off a ferocious German counteroffensive at Mortain between August 7 and 12, the U.S. First and Third armies punched eastward and caught the Germans in a massive pincer, between the Anglo-Canadian forces in the north, at Falaise, and their own troops in the south at Argentan. Under sustained air and ground attack, the German army was caught in a rapidly constricting pocket and brutally pummeled. The Germans lost 10,000 men killed in the furnace of Falaise, and another 50,000 were captured. But brilliant German defensive fighting kept the Falaise pocket open just long enough to allow perhaps 100,000 Germans to slip away and escape across the Seine river. They joined a massive exodus of all German forces in France, some 240,000 troops, who rushed headlong through France and Belgium on into Germany itself, where they would regroup behind the Siegfried Line and fight another day. Though victory in Normandy had not brought about the *total* destruction of the German army in France, it dealt it a severe blow and clearly signaled that the liberation of Europe was at hand.

By August 25, when the Allied forces reached the river Seine and marched into Paris, the American and British commanders could look with satisfaction on the victory they had achieved since the landings in early June. The Germans had lost 1,500 tanks, 3,500 guns, and 20,000 vehicles. There were 240,000 German soldiers dead or wounded, and another 200,000 had been taken prisoner. More than forty German divisions had been destroyed, and Hitler could not make good this scale of loss. By the first of September, virtually all of France had been cleared of the German forces and on September 4, the Belgian capital Brussels and vital port city of Antwerp were liberated. The Allies paid for their victory in Normandy with the lives of 36,976 of their own soldiers.

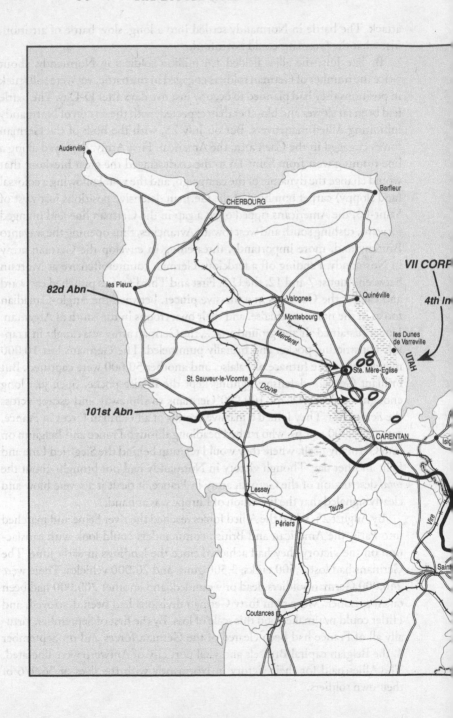

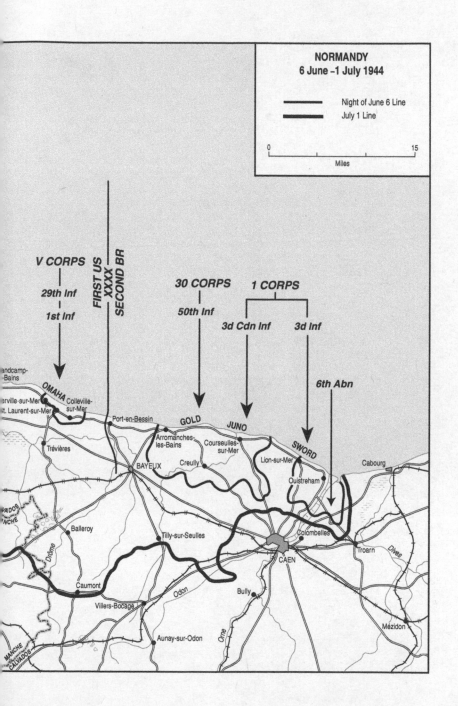

NORMANDY
6 June –1 July 1944

Night of June 6 Line
July 1 Line

0   15
Miles

I

"Too Wonderfully Beautiful": Liberation in Normandy

ABOUT TEN DAYS after the Allied landings on the beaches of Normandy, Ernie Pyle, the legendary American war correspondent, took a jeep ride through the Norman countryside. "It was too wonderfully beautiful to be the scene of a war," he wrote. "Someday I would like to cover a war in a country that is as ugly as war itself." Of course, Pyle saw more than the gently rolling pastures, the wheat fields, and the fruit trees: the region had been shattered by heavy bombardments before and during the D-Day invasion, and he wrote about the ruined hamlets and towns eloquently. But he also told stories that neatly framed the basic American understanding of what the war was really about. Arriving at an old school that was being used as a prison for German POWs, he got out to have a look around.

> At this time the French in that vicinity had been "liberated" less than twelve hours, and they could hardly encompass it in their minds. They were relieved, but they scarcely knew what to do. As we left the prison enclosure and got into the jeep we noticed four or five French country people—young farmers in their twenties, I took them to be—leaning against a nearby house. We were sitting in the jeep getting our gear adjusted when one of the farmers walked toward us, rather hesitantly and timidly. Finally he came up and smilingly handed me a rose. I couldn't go around carrying a rose in my hand all afternoon, so I threw it away around the next bend. But little things like that do sort of make you feel good about the human race.[1]

Ernie Pyle's newspaper columns for the Scripps-Howard syndicate, written from North Africa, Italy, and France, sketched out for avid readers in the

United States detailed portraits of average American soldiers—their concerns and their personalities, their uncomplicated nature and basic kindness. Pyle was honest enough a reporter to write about screw-ups, about wrecked French towns, about how frightened soldiers under fire normally were, and about the moment he found himself caught under the massive American bombing run near Saint-Lô on July 25 that inadvertently killed over a hundred GIs. But Pyle became treasured for his ability to paint moving portraits of these "good boys" and the cause for which they fought. He traveled with these young soldiers, slept out in the cold with them, cooked eggs for them, shared anxieties with them, and in April 1945, while in the Pacific, Pyle died with them, the victim of a Japanese sniper's bullet. He was mourned by the nation precisely because his writing reflected a tone that American readers found comforting: unpretentious, gently ironic, and filled with quiet assurance that the cause was just and that democracy would win through in the end. Pyle, in writing the rose story, told Americans that the liberators had been welcomed to France warmly and that through the horrors of war, one could glimpse some basic human decency still alive in Europe.

And yet, Pyle doesn't tell us much about that young man who offered him the rose. What had become of his family? Had his home been damaged in the invasion? What became of him after the Americans had passed through? Was he, indeed, a Norman? Pyle might not have known if this young farmer was a refugee from any one of the cities nearby that had been evacuated during the fighting, or even if he had been a Pole, or a Russian, transported into France to labor on behalf of the German occupiers as they built up their now-breached Atlantic Wall. In fact, Pyle didn't write much about French civilians in Normandy. In his articles, civilians remain, like that farmer, mute, decent, but alien. Pyle offered no insight into how civilians in the region viewed these gun-toting American boys who arrived in such huge numbers, or how they dealt with the soldiers' petty thefts, periodic looting, and frequent drunkenness; nor did he write much about the shocking violence of the battles that left thousands of French civilians dead. Pyle didn't mention a feature of the battlefield that almost every war diary written by soldiers in Normandy stresses repeatedly: the overwhelming stench of rotting flesh, both from unburied livestock killed in the heavy and constant bombing as well as from decomposing human remains that carpeted great swaths of Normandy for months after the D-Day landings. And Pyle, like the bulk of the Allied soldiers, moved out of Normandy in August and pushed eastward toward Paris, so he never was able to see what life was like in Caen and Saint-Lô and Falaise and dozens of other "liberated" towns that had been ground to powder by Allied bombing. If he had gone there and talked to the inhabitants, he probably would have found very few who, in the summer of 1944, felt "good about the human race."

Of course, Ernie Pyle can be excused: like all war correspondents in World War II, he wrote under the constraints of censorship, and could not truly depict the awful face of war. But even long after these restrictions had been lifted, American writers and scholars who wrote about the D-Day battles continued to give pride of place to soldiers and to events on the battlefield, and neglected the complex experience of the liberated peoples. In the richly detailed official histories produced by the Army, or the many moving journalistic accounts, or the anecdotal histories that have always been popular to American tastes, little if any attention has been given to the local peoples of Normandy.[2] Instead, popular writers of military history return like salmon to the rich breeding grounds of Ernie Pyle's language and imagery. By far the most popular kind of writing about Normandy has long been those that give a picture of combat "As Told By Those Who Were There," to use the inaccurate subtitle of one such work—for these accounts rarely include French voices.[3]

It is possible to write military history without attending to the experiences of noncombatants. But we cannot write the history of liberation without paying attention to the voices, experiences, and travails of the liberated people themselves. For liberation is more than victory on the battlefield: it is a forcible, often brutal destruction of one kind of political order, and its replacement with another. Historical accounts of liberation that start and stop with the soldiers' experience all too easily ignore the social and political aspects of the war, the complex interactions between soldiers and civilians, and especially the after-battle conditions that liberating armies leave behind. They also overlook the patient daily work of recovery that transforms victory at arms into something that looks like peace.

Not surprisingly, the French have their own ways of talking about the events in Normandy: they tend to emphasize the civilian experience because the role of organized French military force was minimal in Normandy in 1944. Drawing on detailed local analyses of casualties, French scholars have determined that about 20,000 French people were killed in Normandy during its liberation, most as a result of Allied bombing. This represents 29 percent of the 70,000 French people killed in Allied bombing attacks in France during the entire Second World War.[4] Along with the deaths, civilians endured a profound social upheaval. In Normandy, hundreds of thousands of townspeople and farmers were displaced by the fighting; they fled the scene of their liberation bearing tattered bundles in rickety wheelbarrows, trying to avoid shells and bullets, while all around them the armies churned up fields, leveled homes and barns, killed off cattle, ruined crops, destroyed roads and bridges, and cut off electricity and water and sewage and basic services, making life a misery not just in June and July but for years to come. French writers of memoirs and contemporary accounts likened the dolorous scene to Calvary—the setting of the Crucifixion—and frequently invoked the "martyrdom" of their villages and towns. The emphasis here has been on loss, death, destruction, and the bittersweet recovery of freedom after the horrible ordeal of German occupation. Even today, in the Norman *départements*, local residents cannot tell the story of the liberation of France without bowing their heads, and grimacing.[5]

"IT WAS RATHER a shock," wrote Corporal L. F. Roker of the Highland Light Infantry in his wartime diary, "to find that we were not welcomed ecstatically as 'Liberators' by the local people, as we were told we should be . . . They saw us as bringers of destruction and pain." Fellow soldiers concurred: Ivor Astley of the 43rd Wessex Infantry Division noted in his memoirs that, far from waving flags and handing out bottles of bubbly, "the French peasants to whom the shell-torn villages and ruined farmlands belonged" were "sullen and silent; if we had expected a welcome, we certainly failed to find it. Some of the people looked utterly bewildered." Major Edward Elliot of the Glasgow Highlanders, whose diary is studded with acute observations, noted that "the French are having a pretty thin time at present. First the Germans dig holes all over the place and pull down houses, then we shell and bomb their homes and drive their vehicles all over the fields. Naturally their attitude to us is inclined to be a bit stiff; however, I think they are mostly for us, though they are desperately tired of the war and the misery it has caused them." In Creully on June 16, Major M. H. Cooke of the Royal Scots noted that "the people came out in force, but for the most part they stood gravely and seriously watching us. Many nodded, and once or twice there was a little clapping, and once a Frenchwoman rushed forward crying, 'Welcome, Messieurs, welcome to France.' It was still a little disappointing."[6]

Why such a chilly reception? Some observers tried to explain this French reticence as typical of the Norman character. A. J. Liebling, the war correspondent for *The New Yorker*, noted the "foolish talk in the British newspapers . . . about the Normans' lack of enthusiasm," and chalked up such stories to "correspondents who acquired their ideas of Frenchmen from music-hall turns and comic drawings. One might as well expect public demonstrations of emotions in Contoocook, New Hampshire or in Burrillville, Rhode Island, as in Normandy, where the people are more like New Englanders than they are like, for instance, Charles Boyer."[7] A British Civil Affairs officer also relied on such typologies to explain the surly civilians: "Taking into account the naturally reserved disposition of the Norman, we have received an enthusiastic welcome."[8]

But there may have been something else behind the diffidence that Allied soldiers encountered among the liberated peoples of Normandy. Though Normandy looked to Ernie Pyle like a peaceful rural idyll, this was an area that had endured four years of a bitter occupation.[9] Consider the *département* of Calvados, home to four of the landing beaches (Sword, Juno, Gold, and Omaha). A productive region of cider, apples, brandy, butter, and milk, Calvados had some 400,000 inhabitants at the start of the war. It was one of the most politically conservative parts of France, and Calvadosiens were known for their independence, their dislike of state intervention, their pro-business attitudes, and strong Catholic traditions. In the national elections of 1936, when France voted for a left-center Popular Front government, Calvados bucked the trend and went further rightward. The department actually became a recruiting ground for the far-right Croix de Feu, which strongly opposed the rise of the Popular Front. Whatever the prewar inclinations of the region, however, opinion in Calvados during the war was firmly anti-German and grew distinctly more so as the war went on. The reason for this was geographic: Calvados, like all the northern coastal departments, was heavily invested with German soldiers whose role was to prepare for an expected cross-channel Allied attack. By the fall of 1941, the Germans had stationed 15,000–20,000 troops in Calvados alone, and this number had trebled by June 1944. This meant that throughout the war, local inhabitants lived literally side by side with the occupiers. Germans took over hotels, public buildings, and schools for barracks and headquarters and requisitioned furnishings, beds, and all manner of domestic equipment; their soldiers were billeted upon the population, taking up living rooms, barnyards, and stables and displacing local families. German requisitions of food for their troops and forage for their animals hurt the economy, as did military maneuvers through the heavily agricultural countryside.[10]

To the depredations of the foreign troops were added the indignities of France's own policy of collaboration. The Vichy-based government of Marshal Henri-Philippe Pétain pursued an obsequious policy toward the Germans through which, in exchange for integrating France into Hitler's New Order as a vassal state, the French authorities gained a measure of independence in running internal affairs. But the burden of this policy fell upon the French people. The attitude of Calvadosiens, who like many of their countrymen had

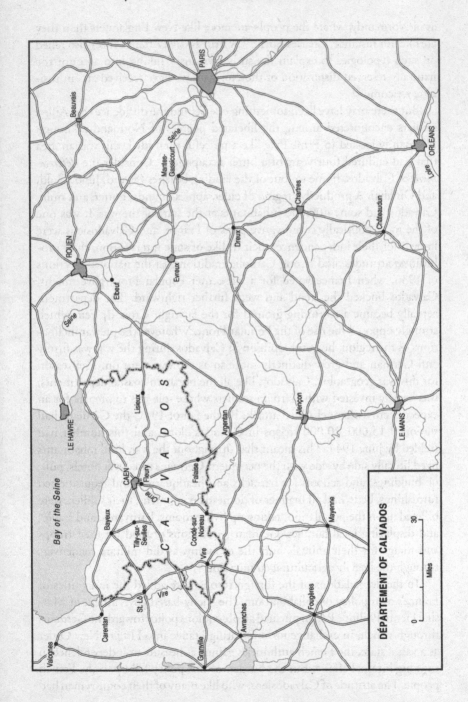

DÉPARTEMENT OF CALVADOS

once admired Pétain as a war hero and a man of steadfast patriotism, sharply deteriorated after the June 1942 announcement of "*la relève*." This program, initiated by Vichy, sought to secure the release of one French prisoner of war from German camps in exchange for every three French civilian workers that could be delivered to German hands. It was blackmail and was met with stupefaction and shame in France. Worse, Calvadosiens quickly learned that the Germans had reneged on their end of the deal: in exchange for six hundred volunteers from the Calvados, the Germans returned only eleven POWs to the department. The *relève* was only one form of conscription: in addition to labor in Germany, the occupation authorities sought French labor for work on the Atlantic Wall. The Todt Organization, under the direction of Albert Speer, started work in the middle of 1942 on a defensive wall running from Brittany to Holland, with particular strength in the Pas-de-Calais, the region considered most likely to be assaulted by the Allies. From October to December 1942, the German headquarters demanded 2,450 workers from Calvados alone to be set to work on building these defensive ramparts. Workers had to be withdrawn from construction and agricultural sectors. They worked directly under German overseers in deplorable conditions alongside Russian and Polish POWs, living in harsh work camps with little medical care. Combined with workers sent into Germany, Calvados had lost 4,500 workers by the end of December 1942, and an additional 1,679 workers were called up by the Germans in April 1943. The local skilled workforce was being systematically stripped bare.[11]

In the context of growing German labor demands and an improvement in the fortunes of the Allied war effort in Africa and Italy, the year 1943 was decisive for the growth of the local Resistance: 40 percent of those who would join a Calvados underground network did so in that year. The Resistance was never large in Calvados. No more than 2,000 people were formally associated with Resistance networks by the start of 1944, precisely because the German military presence was so heavy there, and reprisals against civilians were severe and frequent. Yet Resistance networks played an important role in aiding downed Allied pilots and sheltering young men who were in hiding from forced labor conscription. Resistance networks also acted as a means of promoting periodic civilian acts of defiance, from tearing down of German posters to the scrawling of the "V" sign in public places.[12]

As the prospect of an Allied invasion of France neared, the German occupation of Calvados intensified, with profound consequences for the local inhabitants. Field Marshal Gerd von Rundstedt, commanding the German armies in the west, possessed sixty German divisions, and he deployed four in Calvados. Added to other occupation authorities and labor services, this meant there were 60,000–70,000 foreigners in the department by June 1944, all of whom had to be fed and housed. From the late fall of 1943, the Germans massively increased the pace of defensive preparations along the coast: mines, obstacles, tank traps, barbed wire, and concrete gun emplacements popped up all along the coastline. The Germans laced local fields with mines and flooded lowlands. Open areas were studded with "Rommel's asparagus," tall poles designed to shred any troop-carrying Allied aircraft that might attempt a landing. The Germans banned commercial fishing so they could control all sea-based activity, and halted all local building so that supplies could be channeled toward the construction of defensive positions on the beaches. Thirty thousand hectares, or 7 percent of the arable land of Calvados, was taken out of cultivation by flooding, mines, or defensive preparations. The Germans made still further demands for local labor details, forcing village mayors to produce able-bodied men between eighteen and fifty years old to work on the fortifications. In February 1944, Vichy passed a law making women between eighteen and forty-five subject to immediate labor for the Germans. Inevitably, economic life of the region ground to a halt as the fevered work on the Atlantic Wall sucked in local labor and materials; in the fields, labor disappeared, crops were not sown, and horses were requisitioned by the Germans to pull wagons. The countryside, one of the richest and most productive regions of France, was largely abandoned. Cereals and grain supplies that Calvados relied on could not be transported into the department because the train lines were now given over exclusively to military use. By the spring of 1944, Calvados, normally an abundant supplier of meat, faced a severe shortage of this staple; even the meager official meat ration of a hundred grams per week per person could not be filled, largely the result of the lack of fodder and the heavy demands made by German troops. The black market became the only way to secure sufficient supplies of butter and meat, and prices soared. This in turn heightened social tensions, as farmers naturally hoarded their goods to get a better price and assure their own needs; workers in the towns and cities went increasingly without. The Vichy-controlled prefect reported a sharp rise in morbidity due to typhoid, tuberculosis, diphtheria, and scarlet fever.[13]

The behavior of the Germans toward the civilian population worsened with the likelihood of an Allied invasion. In January 1944, Hitler's chief of conscript labor, Fritz Sauckel, demanded that France produce yet another million laborers to be deployed for the German war effort, but virtually no one complied. In Calvados, of the 1,370 men called up, a mere 104 responded to the order. The desperate Germans resorted to the use of roundups and arrests in cinemas and public places to secure recalcitrant labor conscripts, and shipped off their quarry to camps in Germany. Prisons bulged with civilians arrested on the least pretext. In response to stepped up Resistance attacks on local officials, collaborators, and German soldiers, the Germans violently cracked down. In March 1944, all radios were ordered to be surrendered so that BBC emissions could not be heard. Through arrests, torture, and infiltration by collaborators, the Germans managed to crack open many of the local Resistance networks; over 200 resisters were killed in the six months before the D-Day invasion.[14]

And as if these travails were not enough, the Anglo-American bombing of France, as part of the preliminary preparations for the invasion, intensified throughout the spring of 1944, making life a constant misery for millions of people in towns from the Pas-de-Calais to Normandy. Rouen, a city on the Seine and a rail junction that Allied planners knew the Germans would use to reinforce Normandy, was devastated by repeated attacks: on April 19, 1944, there were 900 people killed in Rouen by British bombing, and in the first week of June a series of attacks by American bombers killed an additional 200 people there. In Calvados, the prefect's reports reveal the constant and enervating presence of Allied aircraft in the skies: air attacks struck the department on March 2, 13, 26, 27; April 9, 11, 20, 23, 25, 27 (twice), and 29; May 9, 15, 19, 21, 22, 23, and 27; and June 1. The ostensible targets were railway junctions, barracks, airfields, and crossroads. But these preparatory attacks killed many French people. The attack of April 27 on the coastal village of Ouistreham killed 17 people and wounded 40. Between March 1 and June 5, 130 people were killed in Calvados by these bombings.[15] It is perhaps no wonder that the Normans, who yearned for liberation, had the appearance of a broken, tired people when the Allied soldiers splashed ashore on June 6, 1944.

WHEN LIBERATION DID arrive, it came not all at once but in a series of devastating, prolonged, murderous blows, delivered by air, sea, and ground bombardment and by the lethal weapons of the Allied soldiers. On D-Day, 1,300 civilians were killed in Calvados alone; on June 7, another 1,200 died. Added to the deaths in other Norman departments, it appears that 3,000 civilians were killed on June 6–7. Thus, roughly the same number of French civilians died in the first twenty-four hours of the invasion of Normandy as did Allied soldiers. And the killing had only just begun: between June 6 and August 25, Normandy would be chewed into a bloody, unrecognizable mess. In the five northern departments that saw the most fighting—Calvados,

Manche, Orne, Eure, and Seine-Maritime—19,890 French civilians paid for liberation with their lives.[16]

Calvados got its first taste of liberation a few minutes before midnight on June 5, when 946 aircraft of the Royal Air Force (RAF) struck targets along the coast of the landing beaches. The RAF dropped five thousand tons of bombs on German defensive positions in ten towns, seven of which were in Calvados: Maisy, Saint-Pierre-du-Mont (the location of the massive guns perched on the promontory of la Pointe du Hoc), Longues-sur-Mer, le Mont Fleury, Ouistreham, Merville, and Houlgate. This was the largest tonnage of bombs yet dropped in a single night in the entire war.[17] Fortunately, these sparsely populated towns had been largely evacuated in the weeks before the landings by order of the Germans and of local authorities. The Germans wished to defend against any Resistance activity by the local population, while many civilians, after the bombings of the early spring, had fled of their own initiative. Even so, these initial bombardments killed at least forty civilians. At dawn on the 6th, 1,083 B-17s and B-24s of the United States Eighth and Ninth Air Forces took their turn, hammering the general vicinity of what was to be Omaha beach. Many of the bombs were dropped too far inland, leaving the coastal batteries on Omaha untouched, while Port-en-Bessin, the coastal village on the far eastern flank of Omaha, was struck hard, as were most of the surrounding hamlets. Naval gunnery joined in, aiming at German batteries but inevitably hitting the surrounding villages. Vierville, Bernières, Courseulles, Saint-Aubin, Lion-sur-Mer, Ouistreham: These are towns that ring down the ages as the site of great heroics by invading Allied soldiers who wrested them from the Germans on June 6 and after. Yet they also ran with the blood of at least 100 noncombatants.[18] Throughout the two days of June 6 and June 7, many Norman communities received devastating bombardments from both air and sea. The purpose of these assaults was obviously to kill Germans and to impede the movement of any reinforcements from the Pas-de-Calais, where large concentrations of Germans had been placed in anticipation of Allied landings there. Yet air power was at best a crude tool: Allied aircraft did not possess the accuracy required to destroy a bridge, a railyard, a crossroads, a telegraph station, or an artillery position without also destroying a great deal of the surrounding area. The results were predictably awful: dozens upon dozens of hamlets were heavily bombed, and their lovely lyrical French names are now as synonymous with death in the minds of Normans as places like Coventry, Dresden, and Hiroshima are dolorous place-names for the British, Germans, and Japanese: Argentan, Aunay-sur-Odon, Avranches, Colombelles, Condé-sur-Noireau, Coutances, Dives-sur-Mer, Évrecy, Falaise, Lisieux, Mézidon, Mondeville, Montebourg,

Ouistreham, Saint-Lô, Thury-Harcourt, Tilly-sur-Seulles, Valognes, Villers-Bocage, Villers-le-Sec, Vire . . .

More than any single location in Normandy, however, the city of Caen offers testimony to the brutality of Normandy's liberation.[19] Caen was the chief target of the British and Canadian landings on D-Day, but for a number of reasons that still stir controversy, General Bernard Montgomery's men failed to take the city.[20] Partly it was because the German 21st Panzer Division put up a stubborn defense just north of Caen, partly it was because the British tanks got bottled up on the beaches, partly it was because the plan was simply too ambitious an objective for units that had crossed the channel and undertaken an unprecedented amphibious landing the same day. Yet it was not for lack of trying. From June 6 to June 8, Anglo-Canadian forces tried to bash their way into Caen, and the skies filled with bombers to help them. At 1:30 P.M. and 4:30 P.M. on June 6, and 2:30 A.M. on June 7, Caen was pummeled from the air by RAF and U.S. Eighth Air Force bombers in an effort to destroy the city's bridges across the Orne and slow German reinforcements from moving through the city. Yet for all the bombing, at least one bridge over the Orne was still intact, while concentrations of German troops were not hit. The 21st Panzers were already established north of the city and were soon joined by the 12th Panzer Division. On June 9, the Panzer Lehr Division arrived in the field and now there was a strong defensive shield to the north and west of Caen. There had been little military value in the air attack on Caen. The rubble in the streets impeded passage of military vehicles, yet even the jaunty official history by the U.S. Air Force admitted the bombing was insignificant: "the effect upon the enemy was small," it concluded, "since detours were easily established."[21] Caen did not see any liberating soldiers for another month.

The effect of the bombing upon the enemy may have been small, but the effect upon the 60,000 inhabitants of Caen was great indeed. In a matter of thirty-six hours, the city was shattered. The attacks on June 6 killed 600 people. The attacks on June 7 left 200 more dead. Thousands were wounded. The city lay in ruins, ablaze. Thirty-nine-year-old Bernard Goupil, a member of one of the *défense passive* (civil defense) teams in the city, recalled just after the war in a detailed account that he and his family, who had built an air raid shelter in his garden, heard the initial bombing on the coast in the early hours of June 6. He reported to his command post, with his helmet and white armband at the ready, only to spend most of the morning in anxious anticipation of liberating soldiers. When none came, he returned home for lunch. At 1:30, he heard "a powerful throbbing"; running into the garden and looking up he cried, "the bombers are coming at us!" Before he could get his family into the shelter, "the terrifying, thunderous explosions crashed upon us. Our poor little dining room shuddered, the chandelier fell onto the table, the door of the house was blown in from the force of the blast. The sounds of the neighboring houses, crashing down under the bombs, followed the great hammer blows from these horrible engines of death. All around us was nothing but violence and infernal noise . . . Clutching one another, we prayed." Goupil, conscious of his duty, tried to return to his civil defense post in the rue des Carmes, but at 4:30 another wave of bombers struck the town and he ran for shelter in a stout eighteenth-century stone building. In the evening he made it to his post, saw after the wounded, and helped transfer them to the Bon Sauveur hospital. In the eerie, smoke-filled evening, in the ruins of a burning city, Goupil wondered if it was over: "There were already enough ruins and victims. Hadn't the allies attained their objectives with these savage bombings? Could they not now leave things to the ground forces? We hoped, in short, that the city would now be taken by the Allies a few hours after the landings." It was not to be. At 2:30 in the morning of June 7 came the heaviest attack yet. "How can I describe with words my experiences in this infernal noise, the shrieking of the falling bombs, the incredible shaking of the ground and of the buildings? The explosions kept coming. Through the doors and windows we saw the flashes and felt the brutal blows. We felt nearby the falling of roofs and material of all sorts in a great deafening cascade. The walls against which we had gathered truly moved under the shock of the bombs." Then at 3:00 in the morning, the bombers disappeared, the skies emptied, and a sinister quiet settled upon the town. Quiet, except for the sounds of the wounded.[22]

One of the most powerful accounts of these two awful days was written by the deputy mayor of Caen, Joseph Poirier. "Nothing had prepared us for the swiftness of the attack," he wrote six months after the liberation of the city. "We knew well that our deliverance was at hand, that the hour of liberation had sounded, but selfishly we thought that the landings would happen elsewhere and that our region would be spared. Providence had decided otherwise." The first bombing raid at 1:30 P.M. struck the central quarters of the city. "It was of an unprecedented violence . . . There was general consternation about the suddenness of the attack." Despite later, and wholly ineffectual, attempts by the Allied command to warn the citizens of impending bombing, no warning had been given on June 6. "The raid had lasted no more than ten minutes but the damage was enormous. The Monoprix stores were shattered and at least ten fires burned in the downtown." The next attack, at 4:30 P.M., struck the prefecture headquarters, and other municipal buildings in the center of town as well as the church of Saint-Jean. Some of the buildings of Le Bon Sauveur, the twenty-acre Benedictine hospital complex in the northwestern quarter of the city, were hit by shells; one nun was killed, trapped under falling stones. By now a quarter of the city was in flames.

The attack of 2:30 A.M. on June 7 proved even more devastating. The first bombload fell on the central fire station, killing the chief, his deputy, and 17 firefighters. More than twenty bombs hit the town hall, in whose basement Poirier had sheltered. The hospital clinic of La Miséricorde, located on the rue des Carmes in the center of town, took a direct hit. Seventy-two people, mostly nuns and their patients, were killed, their bodies buried under the rubble; 171 others were wounded. Emerging into a nightscape illuminated by dozens of fires, Poirier saw dead bodies in feeble air raid trenches, body parts, dead children, the corpse of a close friend on the ground, headless. The electricity, telephone, and water lines were cut, making it difficult to coordinate aid to the wounded. The firefighting equipment was destroyed. "The population was literally crazed, seized by panic, and trying to flee the city into the countryside. People were running about in nightshirts, bare-foot, without having had the time to put on the least clothing. The city was enveloped in a yellowish smoke and dust from all the shattered buildings. It was an infernal scene." The best he and his civil defense teams could do was try to get the wounded to Le Bon Sauveur, and gather up the horribly mutilated corpses and pile them up at the Central Commissariat. "Where, when, how would we bury them?"[23]

Had the liberating troops arrived in Caen on June 9 or 10, with offers of aid, food, medicine, bulldozers to clear rubble, manpower to restore public services, then perhaps Caen's liberation would have gone down as merely one of many sad chapters in a war that took so many civilian lives. But Caen's travails were far from over. By June 10, the Anglo-Canadian troops north of Caen were no closer to taking the city than they had been at midday on June 6. Indeed, with the Germans pouring reinforcements into Normandy, and especially north and west of Caen, the city lay just behind an ever-strengthening German perimeter. With the Americans heavily engaged in the Cotentin peninsula, where they were trying to seize the port of Cherbourg, the British slugged it out with the Germans for every inch of ground around Caen. After the initial assault of June 6–8 had failed, General Montgomery directed another major attack in an attempt to outflank Caen, aiming his tanks at Villers-Bocage, a small town some 12 miles southwest of the city. Historian Max Hastings has called this battle a "wretched episode," in which the British were thoroughly outfought by the German defenders; but Monty tried again on June 26, sending three divisions—60,000 men and 600 tanks—crashing into the German line west of Caen, running out toward Tilly-sur-Seulles. This was Operation Epsom. It too failed.[24]

The implications of these military operations on the western outskirts of Caen were grave indeed for the civilians in the city. German concentrations in and around the city were under assault from the air or from artillery, and the city endured near-constant fire. Thousands of the city's inhabitants sought shelter in the hospital of Le Bon Sauveur and other points designated as welcome centers (*centres d'accueil*) by the city authorities; the thick walls of the old churches like Saint-Etienne offered shelter to thousands of citizens, sprawled amidst the pews on beds of straw. But operations to provide basic services, shelter, and medical care were severely compromised by the shelling. Aid workers painted red crosses on the grounds and buildings of Le Bon Sauveur and on the Lycée Malherbe, a school across the street whose cafeteria had been turned into a hospital ward. Even so, on June 9–10, two hundred artillery shells, intended for German positions on the outskirts of town, landed on Le Bon Sauveur and fifty-seven hit the Lycée; more than 50 people were killed. On June 12, a huge artillery shell struck the superb steeple of the church of Saint-Pierre, a beloved landmark in the center of town. It crashed down in pieces, a Gothic masterpiece wiped out in a flash. On June 13 and 14, the shopping districts, cafés, and hotels of the center of town were all set ablaze, and without water the firefighters had no hope of containing the flames. Le Bon Sauveur, which in normal times handled 1,200 patients with a staff of 120 nuns, was now packed with 2,000 refugees and 1,700 wounded. Working around the clock with few supplies, no electricity, and only what water could be pumped manually from the wells, a handful of doctors tried to treat the worst cases. They achieved great things, conducting some 2,300 operations between June 6 and August 15, relying on a patched-together staff of 31 doctors, 22 interns, 114 nurses, and 46 French Red Cross personnel. Across the street in the Lycée Malherbe, over 500 wounded people and thousands of homeless refugees, installed on makeshift pallets in the hallways and basements, received basic treatment from a skeletal staff of twelve doctors and a handful of Red Cross workers.

As residents fled the city, Caen's population dwindled to about 17,000 by mid-June. In a search for shelter from the bombing, thousands of people made for the large stone quarries two miles to the south of the city in the suburb of Fleury. Here opened up another astonishing chapter in this saga of Caen's destruction. During June and July, as many as 12,000 people huddled in the extensive networks of vacant caves in the old quarries, where the pale yellow limestone, used to build many of Caen's churches, had been quarried since the eleventh century. The Germans, in mid-July, tried halfheartedly to evacuate the caves, perhaps to prepare them as a defensive redoubt for their own troops. Yet thousands of homeless Caennais took little notice and continued to dwell in the dark, dank network of caverns. Small villages sprang up overnight: the ill and elderly were grouped together in makeshift beds, women set up laundry and cooking facilities, the men took on heavy labor on a rotating timetable: digging potatoes in the fields, hauling water, sawing lumber for the communal kitchens, gathering supplies from the nearby villages. Bakers and butchers from Fleury delivered supplies of bread, meat, and occasional vegetables. But the conditions of life in the close, airless caves were dreadful. There was no electric light. The floors of the caves, which had been used lately for the cultivation of mushrooms, were constantly damp and muddy; there were no toilets or running water. Within days, fleas and bedbugs infested everyone; food was always in short supply; and the tension of living underground during constant bombing took a toll on the refugees. One young girl who, with her family, sought shelter in the caves at Fleury recalled the misery of it all: "apart from the fleas, our heads were alive with lice, scratch-scratch all day. Hygiene was non-existent; there were no toilets in the caves. We had to make do with corners or heaps of stones."[25] Yet there was protection from the incessant shelling, and there was communal solidarity. Five hundred homeless refugees actually remained in the caves for two weeks after the complete liberation of Caen, since the city itself had become a shambles.[26]

As the people of Caen clung to life in and around their besieged city, the British Second Army continued its efforts to break through the German line blocking its advance into the interior of France. Having tried twice to outflank Caen, Montgomery now thought he might go straight at it. He called on the RAF to lay down an intense bombardment of German defensive positions and artillery to the north of Caen to open the way for an assault by I Corps directly into the city. What followed was "one of the most futile air attacks of the war," according to historian Max Hastings.[27] Although it was well-known that most of the Germans were deployed north of the city, Bomber Command, in its care not to hit the closely engaged British troops, altered the plan and moved the bombing area farther into Caen itself. With dreadful precision, RAF Mosquitoes and Pathfinders flew in first and dropped their smoke-bomb markers on the northern half of the already ruined city—a city quite free of German units. On July 7, under a clear evening sky, and facing little flak, 456 Lancasters and Halifaxes dumped 2,276 tons of bombs on Caen. "It was afterwards judged," concludes one laconic account, "that the bombing should have been aimed at the original targets. Few Germans were killed in the area actually bombed."[28]

The sight of so many friendly aircraft in the skies over Caen was a great morale booster to the thousands of British soldiers in the field who had been badly beaten up by the Germans for over a month now. "What a lovely sight we saw at about 10:00 p.m.," wrote one soldier in his diary. "Hundreds of Lancasters passing over on way home. Could see them on their bombing run somewhere over Caen in more or less single file. One can now understand the term 'They queued up to bomb.' Could see the flak—a grand sight which inspires confidence." Of the same raid, Captain W. G. Caines of the 43rd Wessex wrote, with boyish enthusiasm: "On the hillside which we were occupying we had an excellent grandstand view of the raid, bombers just flew in, unloaded their deadly cargo and turned and made off across the Channel. This was indeed a pleasant sight for us, the sky was literally black with bombers." Gunner J. Y. White of the Royal Artillery was no less animated in his diary: "July 7: This evening about 1,000 of our brave bombers came over in a continual stream and bombed Caen. The bombs could be seen leaving the planes through field glasses. It was a grand and awe inspiring sight to watch our bombers passing overhead for over an hour in a continuous stream, right through the heavy flak, drop their load, circle around and make for home."[29]

One can hardly blame these beleaguered soldiers for the pleasure they took in seeing someone else take a turn at plastering the Germans; they could not know that few Germans were actually being hit. Still, it is quite unimaginable that words such as *lovely, grand,* and *pleasant* would have occurred to the citizens of Caen at that moment. From within the buildings of the Lycée Malherbe, Joseph Poirier too saw the bombers overhead, "blocking out the sky." He was then thrown against a wall by the force of the explosions. He tried to calm the screaming women and children in the Lycée, "but what can you do to calm these poor people who had already experienced the bombings of June 6–7 and who, for a month, had been living the lives of soldiers on the firing line?" As reports came in, Poirier learned that the university and its wonderful library were in flames. The church of Saint-Julien was destroyed. The battered remains of the town hall were crushed. A shelter on the rue Vaugueux, near the church of Saint-Julien, took a direct hit: 54 people, including many of the church staff, were killed. Fires erupted across the city. "I feared that I would lose my mind in the face of such a calamity," Poirier wrote. Another 250 names were added that night to the lengthening rolls of the dead.

On the morning of July 9, Poirier noticed a new development: the few Germans still in the city were withdrawing. This was an organized retreat to higher ground south and east of the city; but for those Caennais in the northern quarter around Le Bon Sauveur, this marked the start of their liberation. In the afternoon, along the rue Guillaume le Conquérant, Poirier encountered a column of Canadian infantry—French Canadians—who handed out sweets and cigarettes to the bedraggled citizens of the quarter. In a gesture indicative of the continuity between pre- and postwar France that most local officials insisted upon, Poirier now withdrew from safekeeping his tricolored sash, the symbol of his municipal office, and put it on so as to be prepared to greet the British commanders. "I was overcome by emotion, for I recalled at this instant that on the morning of 18 June 1940, it was I that had the sad privilege of greeting the first German officer who arrived in Caen. . . . But today, the man who would soon present himself was our ally, one of the determined British who never lost faith in victory and who now returned to us the right to wave our flag and to sing the Marseillaise." Poirier greeted the commander of 201 Civil Affairs Detachment. They shook hands warmly, and Poirier acknowledged that they both had tears in their eyes. Yet the meeting took on a tragic-comic air when, after a long discussion about the desperate civilian needs in the city, the British major asked if Monsieur Poirier could suggest a good hotel where he might have a hot bath. Poirier, stunned, gathered his composure and gently informed the good major that there were virtually no buildings at all left standing in the city.

The liberation of the dead and ruined city of Caen now unfolded over the course of ten days. The British Second Army pushed up to the northern bank of the Orne, but then stopped, as the Germans had strategically redeployed in a fortified line to the south, on higher ground, and were able to shell, with perfect accuracy, the center of Caen. For the civilians in the northern half of the city, this was finally the time to evacuate, and Poirier, along with the wounded and refugees of the Bon Sauveur and other shelters, were transferred by the Anglo-Canadians to Bayeux and elsewhere in liberated territory. Not until July 18 did the British, deploying carpet bombing on the German positions to the east and south of the city, manage to push the Germans out of Caen altogether. Again, the scale of the bombing was titanic: 2,100 aircraft from the RAF and U.S. Eighth and Ninth Air Forces dropped more than eight thousand tons of bombs on the German lines, following which British VIII Corps managed to push the stunned German defenders a few miles south. Though the Germans remained entrenched along the Bourguebus Ridge, from which they would not be dislodged until early August, the city of Caen was at last free. It was also a largely uninhabited, stinking, burning wreck. By the time the Canadians entered the northern part of the city on July 9, the survivors of Caen were unable to show a great deal of warmth for their liberators. Caen had "suffered an undeserved fate," said one clergyman.[30] "The Canadian and British armies have been received in Caen without great enthusiasm," wrote one of the Benedictine sisters of the Abbaye of Nôtre Dame de Bon Sauveur. "The residents have been too shaken by the memory of days of agony and mourning which we have experienced, and by all the civilian dead, by all the grief. There was not on this day the joy that we might have had if these 'friends' had saved the women, the children, the old people. There has been too much suffering."[31]

———————

CAEN WAS THE largest city in Normandy to be destroyed, but dozens of smaller towns and villages met a similar fate. Some were badly hit on D-Day itself; others, like Falaise, would be chewed to pieces toward the end of the Normandy campaign as the Germans were slowly, brutally hammered during their retreat eastward. The extent of the destruction in Normandy profoundly shaped the way that soldiers—those sent to France to liberate civilians—came to understand the war. It was impossible, after some of the things these men saw, to think about the war as "a great crusade," as General Eisenhower had called it on D-Day; or to speak of killing Germans, as Monty had done on D-Day, as "good hunting." Those soldiers who wrote diaries, letters, and memoirs—and thousands did so—uniformly avoided such clichés. The experience was simply too lugubrious for any but direct and accurate description.

A British soldier carries a girl through the wrecked streets of Caen, July 10, 1944. *Imperial War Museum*

"Villers-Bocage was a sight I'll never forget," wrote one British trooper. "There was just enough room for two lorries to pass through between two heaps of rubble which once were houses; the whole place was absolutely razed to the ground and just outside, in the fields, was a complete mass of bomb holes." The once lovely town of Lisieux, home to a glorious cathedral and a site of many religious pilgrimages, was "absolutely flat, words can't describe the destruction, Coventry and London are nothing compared with this. . . . If a bomb had been placed in every house the damage could not have been greater."[32] Lisieux had suffered the second-highest death toll in Calvados after Caen: 781 killed. "We traveled by jeep through Tilly-sur-Seulles," recalled another soldier, "now not so much a village as a scrap heap with every house and shop shattered." The once well-tended land was filled with "orchard trees broken, blackened and stripped of foliage, the ground blasted, buildings razed and carcasses of horses and cows lying in the open, grossly inflated, putrescent, and beset by swarms of blood-avid flies, feeding on their exposed flesh and tender parts." In village after village, "roofs gape, houses lie in amorphous heaps and church spires, reduced to skeletal shapes, stand out like interrogation marks above surrounding debris. Streets are choked until bulldozers force a track through them, shoveling the rubble aside, temporarily blocking entrances to alleys and side streets." Villers-Bocage "appeared dead,

A British soldier lends a helping hand to an elderly resident in the ruins of Caen. *Imperial War Museum*

mutilated and smothered, a gigantic sightless rubble heap so confounded by devastation as to suggest an Apocalypse." The small hamlet of Aunay-sur-Odon, where 145 people—9 percent of the population—had been killed by Allied bombing, had "no civilized shape," and was "little more than a succession of crumpled ruins."[33] Sgt. R. T. Greenwood saw only "a barren wilderness of destruction [that] resembles the battlefields of the last war. A few gaunt trees standing up, leafless, lifeless."[34]

An American jeep snakes through the remains of Saint-Lô,
which was obliterated during the assault of July 11–18, 1944.
U.S. National Archives

For sheer carnage, nothing matched the twenty-mile stretch of ground known as the Falaise pocket in which the retreating Germans had been nearly encircled. Between Falaise and Argentan, the RAF's murderous Typhoon fighter-bombers, with rocket projectiles and machine guns, had laid waste to the penned-in Germans. The town of Falaise itself was churned into rubble: of 1,637 homes in the town, 950 were destroyed.[35] A few miles to the southeast, between Guêprei and Villedieu, K. W. Morris saw "the terrible results of the Allies' saturation bombing and fierce fighting. The Germans had suffered heavy casualties: thousands of prisoners had been captured but many more lay dead in the fields, hedgerows, and woods.

Animals too had suffered. Cows, rigid and bloated, lay as they had fallen in the fields. Much of the German transport had been horse drawn. Dead horses still in their traces, sometimes with fearful injuries and intestines blown apart, blocked every road, the contents of their wagons strewn in the ditches. The stench of death was dreadful."[36] Captain W. G. Caines passed through the same area

> where mass slaughters had taken place by Typhoon fighter bombers. . . . We traveled along one road and actually our vehicles traveled over the top of many hundreds of crushed German dead bodies and horses. Vehicles of all types of German transport littered the whole area. I could never express here on this page or many others how that lot looked and stunk, dead bodies were running over with maggots and flies, it was indeed a ghastly sight seeing these dead Nazis bursting in the blistering heat of the day. This road was about a mile and a half long, and never before had I smelled anything like it.[37]

The nearby village of Chambois "stank of dead men and cattle," recalled Lieutenant William Greene. "Our Typhoons and guns had wrought havoc all along the road which led through the smashed village . . . German dead were being buried. Stiffened corpses lay in the roadside fields, awaiting burial. Dead horses and cows cluttered up the farmyards. And down the road, unmoved by the carnage, three small girls wandered in their Sunday clothes. I thought of my own little girl at home and thanked God she had been spared this sight and experience."[38]

In this environment of devastating war damage and upheaval, soldiers tended to see civilians as simply another feature of a foreign, strange, and frequently bizarre world. In no sense did civilians put a human face on the events of liberation; on the contrary, the sufferings of civilians only made Normandy all the more inhuman and weird. In the midst of heavy shelling in the Falaise gap, A. G. Herbert recalled a surreal encounter with

> two women, barefoot and dressed only in nightclothes, their hair streaming in the wind as they ran. As they drew near I could see the leading woman was carrying a large picture of Christ in a frame still complete with glass. They were both hysterical, and clutched at my uniform, begging to know where to go out of the fighting. Although I spoke no French I was able to point out the way down and said "La Roguerie!" At that moment, a tank had made its way up the hill and was in the act of forcing a passage up the narrow track when it ran over

a donkey which had followed the women down. The noise of the tank and the sight of the squashed donkey caused the women's hysteria to rise to a new crescendo. They took to their heels, and in a moment were out of sight, running like the wind.[39]

No less chilling was this scene near Falaise: "By the roadside, one small boy stood alone on a dead horse, flies from the carcass around his mouth, a national flag in his hand, stunned by the desolate scene."[40] In Caen a few days after its liberation, "a few elderly women in funereal black moved around the debris, some accompanied by children whose faces appeared equally ashen or dust grey."[41] To these Allied soldiers, civilians were dirty, strange, and mostly unwelcoming. Roscoe Blunt of the U.S. 84th Infantry Division noted that in every bombed-out village he entered, the villagers were "suspicious, their faces sullen and silent." Even the friendly ones were off-putting because of their filth: Blunt was stunned to find a family of Norman farmers dwelling in a home with a dirt floor, no plumbing, no electricity, and a pit in the ground for a toilet. "I had never been in such a barren home and I felt a slight twinge of sympathy," he wrote later.[42] Civilians were also distanced from liberating soldiers by their vulnerability. From June 6 onwards, at least

Refugees, having fled the intense fighting in the Mortain area,
rest on the roadside in Saint-Pois, August 10, 1944.
U.S. National Archives

100,000 Calvadosiens fled their homes and flowed along the roads and dirt tracks of the countryside, seeking safety from the fighting. To the liberating soldiers, this only diminished them: they looked "dispirited" and "frightful." Wrote Sergeant Greenwood of these refugees, "some had prams containing all their worldly goods: others had wheelbarrows. Two very old ladies were being wheeled in these things. Three tiny babies and a few children included. . . . Some of them had been trekking for three weeks."[43] Soldiers felt pity but also disgust for this wretched refuse of war.

Soldiers and civilians, in short, had little use for one another, except as sources of exchange: soldiers constantly sought to barter soap, cigarettes, or tinned bully beef for eggs, butter, poultry, potatoes, or fresh meat. But bartering was certainly not the only way to secure desirable French luxuries. The theft and looting of Norman households and farmsteads by liberating soldiers began on June 6 and never stopped during the entire summer. David Kenyon Webster, who parachuted into Normandy on D-Day with the U.S. 101st Airborne Division, recalled stealing a fifth of Hennessy cognac from a farmhouse within hours of landing.[44] In Colombières, a town just a few miles from the landing beaches that was liberated on D-Day, one woman recalled that her house was thoroughly looted by Canadians. "It was an onslaught throughout the village," she recalled. "With wheelbarrows and trucks, the men stole, pillaged, sacked everything, and as the Germans had abandoned everything there were large stocks. There were disputes about who got what. They snatched clothing, boots, provisions, even money from our strong box. My father was unable to stop them. The furniture disappeared; they even stole my sewing machine." This went on for a number of days, and had a predictable effect:

> the enthusiasm [for the liberators] is diminishing, the soldiers are looting, breaking everything and going into houses everywhere on the pretext of looking for Germans. A soldier who came into our rooms while we were eating searched the rooms, and my gold watch was stolen. The locks on the cupboards were all broken, the doors busted open, the closets emptied and underclothes stolen, all the contents thrown on the floor, the towels stolen. And all the time, they drink our Calvados and Champagne, which they haven't tasted since the start of the war.[45]

On August 8, to the south of Caen, Major A. J. Forrest saw the 7th Battalion of the Green Howards infantry regiment looting and ransacking a farmhouse, sawing up furniture for firewood and feasting on every living creature

Probably staged by the photographer, a crowd of children gathers
around a young French girl who is sewing an American flag
on July 4, 1944. *U.S. National Archives*

in the place, from hens to rabbits, ducks and even pigeons. "A disgraceful
business," he thought. "Three hundred Germans, apparently, had lived here-
abouts and respected the owner's property, livestock and goods. How would
he, on his return, react to this outrage except to curse his liberators?"[46] In
fact, this sort of behavior continued right on through 1945, in Belgium, Holland, and Germany; looting and theft were constant features of the liberated
landscape.

Within days of the massacre in the Falaise pocket, U.S. and British divisions were moving rapidly east, across the Seine river and toward Paris; on
August 25, they, along with the French 2nd Armored Division under the
command of the dazzling lieutenant general Philippe Leclerc, entered Paris.
In a mere two weeks more they would be on the Belgian border. At this point
in the grand narrative of the Liberation of Europe, historical works normally

shift their focus and follow the Allied armies into the grateful, delirious capital city and down the Champs-Elysées. And why not? The arrival in Paris
signaled a new phase of the war: Paris, symbol of civilization and romance,
had been freed unharmed, and its people gave the weary American, British,
and French soldiers an unforgettable welcome. The same warmth met the
liberators across northern France right up to the Belgian border, where the
fighting had been light or had passed by altogether, and where the infantry
was at last riding in trucks, moving forty miles a day and more. Here, at last,
liberation began to look and feel the way it was always supposed to be: flowers, girls, crowds, cheers. "The battalion stopped at the village of La Fertie [La
Ferté, to the east of Paris]," recalled A. G. Herbert. "We now felt at last that
we had left Normandy and were meeting the real French people for the first
time. Unlike the people of Normandy, these folk made us feel welcome, and
it seemed worth fighting for their freedom." Major G. Ritchie reveled in the
change from Normandy: "I have never before been treated as these French
peasants are treating us, and it is a rather amazing sensation and rather brings
a lump to one's throat. Everyone without exception waves to you, flowers are
thrown into the vehicles, and I remember particularly the sight of one oldish
man standing at his gate with his family waving his arms and shouting 'merci!
merci!' At every little cottage I have stayed, when the inhabitants have been
there, they have produced everything of the best, wine, cider, etc., and given
it away liberally to the troops. This appears to be the true spirit of France."
Major Edward Elliot vividly recalled the rapturous welcome:

> Wherever we stopped crowds ran forward to shake our hands and
> clamor for autographs. Fruit and flowers were thrown into jeeps and
> carriers as we drove past dense and enthusiastic people; in return we
> threw out cigarettes and sweets onto the pavements where they were
> immediately seized upon by an arguing swarm of townsfolk. The win-
> dows and shops were bedecked with colors and flags and patriotic slo-
> gans hung across the main street of every town and hamlet. . . . This
> was Victory indeed. Now for the first time we understood why the
> British Western Expeditionary Force had been renamed the British
> Army of Liberation! At first, it had sounded a little cynical to us, toil-
> ing and fighting amongst the frigid Normans who only half seemed to
> appreciate our presence among them. Now we understood full; it was
> as if a veil draping the inner soul of France and hiding her true visage
> had suddenly been lifted to reveal a shining and cheerful countenance;
> a menace which had hung over her life for four long weary years was
> gone—gone they hoped for ever.[47]

NORMANDY'S COUNTENANCE, HOWEVER, could not have been described as cheerful or shining during and after the summer of 1944. An initial assessment of Caen found that, in this city that had once housed 60,000 people, there was habitation left for a mere 8,000 and that returning refugees would have to be evacuated again. Meanwhile, the area between Tilly, Falaise, Argentan, and Vire had only one-fifth of its previous houses left standing. As one somber report by a British official put it on August 30, "there will be no greater war problem in the whole of France than exists in Calvados at the moment."[48] About 125,000 people in this department alone were designated *sinistrés*, or war victims; of those, 76,000 had lost everything they owned, including their homes. By the end of August, over one thousand civilians had been hurt or killed by stepping on buried mines. Allied military authorities set up temporary refugee camps to try to limit civilian movement in the war-torn areas, but refugees avoided them, only desiring to be allowed to return to their towns and assess the scale of the damage. They did so "regardless of whether their homes still existed, of the danger of booby traps, and of the availability of food."

Normandy, a region of ancient traditions and habits, had not changed much in the previous century; yet in the summer of 1944, two million foreign soldiers laid waste to its once-placid precincts. Caen and Lisieux and Vire and Falaise were permanently altered; the familiar markings of an ancient countryside—the church spires, the schoolhouses and civic halls, the roads, the trees, the parks and the extensive farmland—all had been ground into dust, and were literally unrecognizable. One survey of the damage to the cultural heritage of Lower Normandy connected the loss of these familiar buildings with a loss of communal orientation, as if some sort of cultural compass had been knocked off course: "The church spires which sprang from the midst of our gray houses and rose straight up to the heavens, like prayers rising from the dried lips of our ancient ancestors, have disappeared by the dozens." A "return to normal" in such circumstances was quite obviously impossible, for large parts of Normandy could never be recovered.[49]

The task that French and American authorities set themselves was to restore order as quickly as possible. The Anglo-American military authorities had made the restoration of political order a principal aim of the liberation, and it had occupied a good deal of the preinvasion planning. An entire military echelon was created and labeled G-5, or Civil Affairs; within each division, Civil Affairs officers were tasked with the work of imposing order:

that is, finding reliable local political authorities; identifying police forces and empowering them to keep order; enrolling men into labor brigades to clear roads and port facilities; and militarizing all local transportation, fuel, food, and medical supplies. Even the official history of the British Civil Affairs effort noted that this treatment seemed quite similar to German behavior during the occupation.[50]

The French did not warm immediately to such robust foreign political intrusion, even at this time of desperate need. Planning for Civil Affairs in France was hampered by the extreme touchiness of the Free French leader, General Charles de Gaulle. In fact, a formal agreement between de Gaulle's provisional government and General Eisenhower's Supreme Headquarters was not signed until late August 1944—almost three months after the invasion of France. This document settled the large political questions of sovereignty and control of liberated territory: the French agreed to do nothing to inhibit the powers of the Supreme Commander to prosecute the war on French soil, while the Allied armies agreed to restore French political control over liberated territory promptly and to cede political control to French authorities.[51]

If de Gaulle's Free French had worried that the Anglo-American military forces sought to gain a permanent political control in France, they were soon put at ease by the practical work that Civil Affairs officers undertook. British units set up command posts in Ouistreham and in Bayeux with little difficulty, and began to grapple with the basic problems of food distribution, rationing, and the search for fuel to get water pumps going again. The Civil Affairs detachments in Bayeux tried to sort out refugees, arranged for hospitals to accept civilian casualties, and directed emergency medical supplies from the beachheads to the clinics where they were needed. Within three weeks of the landings, the Civil Affairs units had arranged for the publication of the *Renaissance du Bessin*—France's first postliberation newspaper, written by Allied publicity staff. American units of Civil Affairs, some of whom dropped into Normandy with the 82nd Airborne, followed similar procedures in Sainte-Mère-Eglise and other towns on the Cotentin peninsula. Not the least urgent of their first tasks was the "procurement of civilian labor for grave digging . . . and the disposition of cattle killed during combat activities."[52]

Cherbourg, liberated by the Americans on June 27, offers an excellent example of the convergence of thinking between the French and Americans. Civil Affairs Detachment A1A1 of the U.S. Army VII Corps quickly went to work with the city mayor and other French officials who "were all at their posts" and gave "wholehearted cooperation to the detachment." Although the port facilities had been wrecked by the Germans, the American engineers got quickly to work to prepare the quays to receive off-loaded military supplies. Another daunting problem was the state of public health. The Civil Affairs medical officers found sanitation in the city to be "deplorable," lacking basics like potable water and adequate sewage. The American soldiers in the city "made it worse by indiscriminate dumping" of their trash, which added to "a fly nuisance and a rat nuisance." The hospital facilities used by the Germans were, by the time the Americans arrived, in a disastrous state: "same old story," according to Major Harry Tousley of the 298th General Hospital in Cherbourg: "toilets flooded with crap, no water, cockroaches black on the walls and floors."[53] The Civil Affairs team restored power to the water pumping system by July 3. The enormous stocks of food that the German garrison had piled up in Cherbourg were duly distributed. Civil Affairs got the local cinema opened up, put out a newspaper, and even launched Radio Cherbourg. Civil Affairs officers helped arrange the resumption of train service, obtained coal to run the power plants, organized road traffic, seized motorized transport, assured adequate supply of French currency in circulation, and tried to restore telephone service. Of course, they also imposed controls and restrictions on civilian life, such as blackouts, curfews, travel passes, and limits on telephone usage, all of which prompted the frequent complaint that the Americans were far more interfering than the Germans had been. But such friction was inevitable. Cherbourg was being refitted to serve as a major supply and transport base to funnel goods from the port to the armies in the field, and in this effort, the Civil Affairs officers needed and found partners among the French authorities who themselves were eager to restore order. Civil Affairs men acted as a spark to revive the confidence of local authorities and "galvanized into action all available Municipal Services and Prefectural Services" by identifying and gathering judges, teachers, administrators, and town officials and providing them the tools to govern. A British Civil Affairs official felt that after forty-eight hours, the detachment could have left Cherbourg altogether, so well had French authority been reestablished.[54]

IS THERE MORE to be said, however, about the nature of the order that French and Allied authorities imposed on liberated Normandy? The events of July 14, 1944, in Cherbourg, offer intriguing hints of the various ways order could be imposed on liberated space.

On that day, July 14, Bastille Day, and France's national holiday, Allied and French military and civilian officials arranged for a handsome public ceremony designed to consecrate the alliance and the transfer of power from Vichy to Gaullist France. According to the American commander of the Civil Affairs unit who was present at the ceremony, "salvos of artillery and ringing

In the main square of Cherbourg, townspeople attend a ceremony of
allied unity. Hastily made flags bedeck the town hall. July 14, 1944.
U.S. National Archives

of church bells took place at intervals during the day. In the afternoon a big
parade assembled in the Place Napoléon made up of French military, naval
and civilian services, US Army units and British RAF and Army. This parade
marched to the public garden to [pay respects at] the Memorial of the Dead.
It was accompanied by M. François Coulet [the political representative of the
Free French], Admiral Georges Thierry d'Argenlieu, and all the notables of
the city." These Frenchmen were presented by the Allied soldiers with hastily
made national flags that the soldiers had sewn from the cloth of parachutes.
"Next on the program was the renaming of the Place Pétain [Cherbourg's
town square] to Place Général de Gaulle"—a symbolic gesture to indicate the
clear break with France's wartime past. There followed a public concert on
the square that featured "many of the old songs and tunes of France which
had been prohibited for four years."[55] The people of the city turned out in
large numbers, waving hats and singing with all the pent-up gusto that a liberated people naturally felt after such a prolonged period of bondage.

Not far from these official celebrations on July 14, at precisely the same time, another kind of public ceremony was unfolding. About twelve women, publicly accused of consorting with the German occupiers, were dragged into a public square, where they were harangued by a number of self-appointed judges from Resistance groups. Then their hair was shaved off, as smirking young men gazed on with evident satisfaction. The women were placed into the back of a truck and paraded through the town, under a sign that read "The Collaborationist Wagon." As the truck rolled through the streets of the town, a man sat on the cab of the truck, beating a drum to call attention to these shorn captives.

The public shearing of adulterous women in this manner was an ancient tradition, though kept alive more in folklore than in practice. The Resistance members had whispered such threats to the French girlfriends of German

As grinning men and boys of Cherbourg look on, a Frenchman clips
the hair of a woman alleged to have consorted with German soldiers
during the occupation. July 14, 1944. *U.S. National Archives*

soldiers during the war and now they made good on the threat. These women had, according to their persecutors, smiled gaily as they paraded down the streets arm in arm with their foreign masters; now their world was to be turned upside down. Their treachery had been public; their humiliation too would be put on display. Such was the power of the ceremony that it was repeated across liberated France in August and September: as historian Fabrice Virgili has shown, in the summer of '44, some twenty thousand French women felt the cold steel of the shears slice across their scalps, and watched as their tangled locks fell at their feet.[56]

In a public square renamed for the conservative Catholic nationalist General Charles de Gaulle, American and French officials asserted their claim to shape the political order. In the back of a truck, amidst tears and curls, Cherbourg's men and boys asserted their claim to shape the social order. French women who had once used access to Germans as a form of social power were made once again subservient to French men. The new order was marked out in public, on the bodies of these unfortunate women. Both ceremonies occurred on the first postliberation Bastille Day in the first liberated city in the country.

Heads newly shorn, these women of Cherbourg are paraded through the streets in the bed of a truck, beneath a sign that reads "The Collaborators' Wagon." July 14, 1944. *U.S. National Archives*

The new order in liberated Normandy also reflected racial prejudices both of the local French people and of the liberating American army. After the bulk of the Allied combat units left Normandy, on their way to Belgium and Germany, the Americans established large supply operations in Cherbourg, on the Normandy beachheads, and in Le Havre, and linked these supply bases via road to the front lines. This was an enormous operation that grew steadily during the fall of 1944 right until the end of the war. Most of the materiel shipped to Normandy from Britain and the United States was loaded onto trucks and transported across northern France to Paris, Brussels, Liège, and on to the front. This logistical supply effort fell onto the shoulders of support troops, many of whom were African-American soldiers who were generally barred from combat duty. In the famous Red Ball Express, the trucking route that ran from Saint-Lô to the front lines, many of the drivers—as many as 70 percent in some trucking units—were African-American, and were in frequent contact with local French civilians.[57]

Calvados was, politically and socially, a conservative region of France; it was also rural, distant from any major city, and had little contact with people of African descent. The evidence from the Calvados archives suggests that French civilians, and certainly the French police, found the presence of African-American soldiers in their community unsettling. Indeed, the Calvados police reports reveal anxiety not only about black soldiers of the U.S. Army, but about North African soldiers in the French army, who were also being used as support troops in Normandy. French people of rural Calvados would have perceived black and North African men as exotic and foreign, normally visible only as colonial subjects. But French preconceptions of these men of color as exotic strangers were surely reinforced by the way the U.S. Army treated its own black soldiers. French officials observed American racial prejudice on display in liberated Normandy in the division of labor that relegated black servicemen to subordinate roles and segregated them from whites. This atmosphere of racial tension and hostility that emanated from both American and French authorities became a common point of understanding for those officials charged with creating "order" in Normandy. This mutually reinforcing view of an appropriate racial order had grave consequences when local French and American authorities addressed questions of law, order, and punishment.

U.S. Army soldiers, black and white, who were in rear support units, and far from the imminent danger of the battle lines, tended to misbehave in ways that ranged from the predictable—carousing, drunkenness, shouting at women, and so on—to the brutal and revolting, including robbery, sexual assault, gang rapes, and murder. However, African-American troops were more frequently punished for these acts than whites. Evidence from U.S. Army records shows conclusively that although blacks were a small statistical minority of U.S. troops in the European Theater—less than 10 percent—they were targeted, by French and American authorities alike, as the scapegoats for widespread American misbehavior and sexual violence. Black American soldiers were charged and convicted and punished for crimes against French people in numbers vastly disproportionate to their statistical presence in the American Army. White soldiers, by contrast, were far less likely to be the subject of official scrutiny and punishment.

The monthly French police reports that local authorities compiled invariably described *official* French-Allied relations as "correct and cordial." Yet exceptions to such cordiality always, in local police reports, involved alleged misbehavior of black troops. Does this mean that white soldiers behaved well while black soldiers did not? No—the Army's own records show plainly that white soldiers repeatedly were brought up on charges of all kinds. Rather, local French sources show that the comportment of black soldiers was monitored by the French police far more than the comportment of whites.

A local French police report from Trouville, near the Deauville logistics headquarters, said "the proprietors of the cafés and restaurants have been informed not to serve alcohol and food to American soldiers and especially to soldiers of the Negro race [*race nègre*]." A police report by the departmental police command noted that "the attitude of the allied military is correct except as concerns the black Americans, who seem to need greater supervision." In Vire, through which the Red Ball Express ran, and where a large contingent of black troops was based, one police report named various incidents involving black soldiers, and concluded by saying "there is no longer a unit of Military Police in Vire, and it would be desirable, if the blacks continue to be stationed here in the area, that MPs be placed here as a means of dealing with such situations." Another regional overview of Calvados declared wryly in March 1945 that "the comportment of the black American soldiers has improved—we note only one rape, in Breuil-en-Bessin; the victim was 82 years old." But in Mézidon, according to another report, "black American soldiers have become the scourge of the region. They get drunk and run after the women who no longer dare to set foot outside after nightfall." And the town of Vire remained a constant trouble spot, according to police: "The people of Vire continue to complain about the actions of colored American troops stationed in the vicinity."[58]

The emphasis by French authorities upon race when discussing public disorder was not limited to African-American soldiers. From April 1945 on through the summer, police reports, while emphasizing the continued cordiality between Allied and French authorities, reported extensive complaints about the behavior of French North African soldiers in Calvados. "The French units stationed in the region now number at least 1,500 men; most of them are North African soldiers. If the general relations between the civilians and the soldiers are correct, and even sometimes cordial, the same cannot be said of the relations between the population and the North African troops." Such incidents included the following transgressions, according to one report in mid-April: a melee between a woman "of loose morals" and a Moroccan soldier resulted in the knife stabbing of a civilian onlooker; North African soldiers brandished firearms in public to rob locals of wine, leading to scuffles and injuries among civilians and soldiers; in Caen, a North African, described as "un soldat indigène," stabbed a passerby in the neck with a razor after being refused a cigarette; gendarmes stopped and searched two North African soldiers because they "looked suspicious" and found they were carrying two English bayonets under their uniforms. Another report depicted a full-fledged conflict between French police and North African soldiers, triggered by an incident in a bar. Two North African soldiers felt they were not served quickly enough and slapped the daughter of the proprietor in the face; the mother and father intervened but at this moment one of the soldiers drew a knife and pursued the daughter into the bakery next door. While the baker was fending off the soldier, an officer of the gendarmerie arrived and helped the baker overpower and disarm the soldier. As the two soldiers were being arrested, however, a truck bearing a dozen North African soldiers arrived, and these men used force to free their comrades. The police called reinforcements but could not prevail upon the soldiers to surrender the two soldiers; so the police followed the truckload of soldiers back to their base. There, after a serious scuffle that led to injuries to the police, the men were overwhelmed and arrested, with the aid of other soldiers at the base. Clearly, public disorder involving African-American and North African troops occurred in Calvados. Yet it also appears that French police were far more likely to report incidents involving soldiers of color than incidents involving white British or American soldiers. French police, it seems, saw armed black and Arab men, even if wearing American or French military uniforms, as threats to their efforts to restore "order" to Normandy—an order in which nonwhite people did not figure.[59]

The French police may have emphasized the racial dimension of public disorder to establish a point of solidarity with the purveyors of American military justice. Indeed, one of the reasons why French and Allied relations at the top levels of official authority were so "correct and cordial" was their shared racial prejudices, especially when dealing with allegations against black troops. The records of the Army's Judge Advocate General show plainly that while less than 10 percent of American troops in the entire European Theater of Operations (ETO) were African-American, 22 percent of all criminal offenses brought before the courts were attributed to black soldiers.[60] More telling, 42 percent of all offenses involving sexual assault were attributed to black soldiers, and in France 77 percent of the soldiers charged with rape were African-American.[61] Furthermore, black men accused of sexual assault received far harsher punishment than whites. Of the 151 soldiers in the ETO who were actually condemned to death by courts-martial for the offense of rape, 65 percent were black. Still more astonishing: of the 151 capital sentences for rape, only 29 were actually carried out—but of those, 25 soldiers were black, while a mere 4 were white. Put another way, 87 percent of the U.S. soldiers hanged on the charge of raping women in the ETO were black. All these numbers, and others relating to other crimes, can be summed up fairly simply by stating that of the 70 men the U.S. Army hanged for crimes in Europe, 55 were African-American.[62]

Executions of US Soldiers in ETO through October 31, 1945

	Total	Murder	Rape	Murder + Rape	Desertion
White	15 (21.4%)	6 (21.4%)	4 (13%)	4 (33.3%)	1 (100%)
African-American	55 (78.6%)	22 (78.6%)	25 (87%)	8 (66.6%)	—
Total	**70 (100%)**	**28 (40%)**	**29 (41.4%)**	**12 (17.7%)**	**1 (1.4%)**

Source: U.S. Army, History Branch Office of the Judge Advocate General, 18 July 1942–1 November 1945, vol. I, p. 10.

The evidence presented at the courts-martial sheds light on the hidden underside of the liberation and occupation of northern France. It is plain from these records that some American soldiers—how many can never be known—assaulted French people, in some cases with sadistic and lethal force. The evidence shows that sexual violence against women in liberated France was common; it also shows that black soldiers convicted of such awful acts received very severe punishments, while white soldiers received lighter sentences.[63]

Why the disparity in sentencing? Simply, it was much easier for a condemned white man to get a capital sentence reduced than it was for a condemned black man to receive the same leniency. This is because the Army, at the express request of General Eisenhower and the War Depart-

French North African soldiers offer a bag of candies to African-American soldiers. African-Americans were strictly segregated from white troops in the U.S. Army. *U.S. National Archives*

ment, gave weight to an accused soldier's combat record during sentencing. The War Department in an order of August 2, 1945, stated that "while a creditable combat record does not endow the individual with any special immunity, neglect to give it due weight is equally an injustice and an impairment of public respect for the Army's administration of military justice." Yet not only a creditable combat record was required; even combat fatigue and "exhaustion on the battlefield" were considered as mitigating circumstances. Since African-American troops rarely saw action in the front line, they usually had no combat record to shield them.[64]

A second reason for the severity of sentences toward black troops is that Army justice saw sexual violence by African-American troops as dangerous and threatening not simply to French women but to the moral order that the Army wished to establish in France. The Judge Advocate General Board of Review, in considering the conviction for rape by two privates of a woman in Bricquebec, near Cherbourg, just three weeks after D-Day, made plain its opinion that the rape of French women by "colored American soldiers" was part of "a pattern which has made its unwelcome appearance with increasing frequency." This alleged pattern was denounced by the provost marshall of the Normandy Base Section as well: "the reputation of American troops was badly besmirched at this time by the misbehavior of a small percentage of troops," and he noted that "most of these undisciplinary attacks were caused by colored troops and great efforts were made to bring this situation under control, with special attention to the colored units." In short, black soldiers were targeted for special measures, to deflect scrutiny away from white soldiers' misbehavior and to deflect criticisms aimed at the American army.[65]

In the context of liberation, this evidence, when placed alongside police reports from French archives, suggests a broader conclusion: that French and American authorities collaborated to impose a racial order onto liberated Normandy. Some American soldiers pillaged, robbed, raped, and murdered French people during 1944 and 1945, but black men paid a far higher price for such transgressions, and French and U.S. authorities found a degree of common cause in exacting that bloody toll.

AS THE WAR moved onward through France and into Belgium and to Germany itself, the interest of the Allied armies in Normandy's fate waned and the citizens of Calvados felt bereft. The region's housing shortage was severe, and food was still strictly rationed in Caen, with bread down to 100 grams per day and 120 grams of meat per week. A particular grievance of the locals was that the 12,000 German POWs in Calvados, who were put to work on road-building crews, were given better rations and clothing by the Allies than the French themselves enjoyed. "People compare their appearance when the two groups [French and German laborers] arrive for work at the various public works," wrote the prefect of the department. "The Germans arrive by car or truck, clothed in raincoats, with good shoes. The French arrive on foot, with bad shoes and an assortment of cast-off clothing, some civilian, some military." With no summer and fall harvest, cattle lacked fodder and straw and in December, the subprefect of Bayeux termed the condition of livestock in the region "critical." Petty theft and looting of emptied or damaged houses was a constant problem for municipal police, as the crime blotter in the daily newspapers reveals. Basic services such as streetcars, buses, and trains, and electricity were not in place until December and even then were intermittent at best. The region was beset by a criminal racket that trafficked in stolen military goods, which the police found impossible to control, since Allied soldiers were deeply involved. And prostitution—a trade that was legal in France when practiced in licensed houses with regular inspections—had become a major public health problem; women had begun to ply their trade secretly among a desperately eager military clientele, leading to rampant venereal disease.[66]

Caen residents wondered why they had been forsaken. Drawing on a vocabulary rich in suggestive overtones of Christian suffering, an editorial in the Caen-based newspaper *Liberté de Normandie,* one of the first dailies of liberated Normandy, cried out that "Martyred Calvados Must Not Be Forgotten." "For the success of our allies," the paper wrote, "Calvados has paid an unbearable tribute. Entire villages have been pulverized, towns razed, cities wiped out. . . . We do not complain. Fate determined that we should become the ransom for Liberty, and we have strong enough hearts to accept this holocaust with pride. We only ask that we not be forgotten. And yet, we are being forgotten." The editorial appealed for aid from the rest of the country: "We, in our murdered towns, we have nothing; liberated France, which has happily avoided our tragic condition, will you not come to our aid?" Caen, it seemed, had suffered so that France might be resurrected; but there had been no recognition of the sacrifice.[67]

Two girls play on the turret of what was once a tank of the U.S. Third Armored Division, near Mortain. This photograph was taken one year after the Normandy invasion. *U.S. National Archives*

In October, General de Gaulle made his first visit to Caen, and promised immediate aid to "Caen mutilé." "Caen, mutilated in the service of the nation," he said, "Caen, more proud and resolute than ever, I give you my word, you will have the support of the public authorities." Yet in December, Raoul Dautry, the minister of reconstruction, visited the region to inform local leaders that due to shortages across the country, it would be "many years" before Calvados would be rebuilt. Indeed, in January 1945, six months after D-Day, the local director of the office for refugees and war victims described the desperate plight of the homeless in the department, and begged for an immediate delivery to the region of 50,000 blankets, 20,000 cots and mattresses, 40,000 suits of clothing, and an equal number of shoes.[68]

The face of liberation in Normandy, then, was ugly and bruised. Local authorities and their Allied patrons worked diligently to impose their ideas of order on this liberated space, but they operated in an environment they themselves had violently uprooted. Not only had liberation shattered the long-settled Norman countryside, demolished hallowed churchyards, and razed towns, but the presence of millions of armed soldiers, with enormous power and few constraints, unsettled the local inhabitants and invited criminal misbehavior of all kinds. In the wake of liberation, Normandy remained disoriented, disfigured, and disordered.

SIX DECADES AFTER the liberation of Normandy, few visible traces of the trauma of war remain; the green fields and small towns have long been put to rights. The natural beauty of the land is evident at every turn, and Ernie Pyle's description of Normandy as "too wonderfully beautiful to be the scene of a war" seems more apt than ever. Caen, so badly mauled in June and July 1944, is today a quiet, tidy city of 117,000 people. Its inhabitants make their living in a variety of industries, including auto manufacturing, electrical engineering, and, of course, agriculture. The steeples of three handsome churches rise up above a modern cityscape of straight boulevards and pedestrian walkways, and the thick walls of William the Conqueror's castle—which withstood the bombing of 1944—dominate the town center. The river Orne still bisects the town, running slowly northeast on its path toward Ouistreham and the sea. A series of low, stout bridges cross the river, and restaurants and cafés crowd along the riverfront boulevards. Everything seems perfectly normal, and it is, even though the Caen of today is entirely a modern fabrication. The historic town of small, wooden Norman homes and ancient churches died in June 1944. Caen today is a city of absences.

One year after D-Day, a couple strolls along Omaha beach next to a rusting landing craft. In the background are visible the sunken hulks of old ships used to create a breakwater. *U.S. National Archives*

The city's haunting character is emphasized each June, as hundreds of thousands of British and American tourists, many of them veterans or the families of men who fought in Normandy in the summer of 1944, come to the city, fill up the hotels, and make their pilgrimages to the D-Day beaches and the cemeteries that dot the countryside. The American cemetery at Colleville-sur-Mer is a popular destination. In 2005, 1.4 million people, half a million of them Americans, visited this immaculate ground, which overlooks Omaha beach. Here, amid tall, gracefully arched pines and the sound of the rolling surf below, 9,387 Americans lie buried. An additional 1,557 names have been engraved on a semicircular wall in the Garden of the Missing. Yet all is not quiet. Every hour, a loudspeaker plays an eerie, warbling recording of "Stars and Stripes Forever" and "God Bless America." Even in death, the Americans are cheered along to the strains of patriotic songs.

In Caen itself, many small plaques affixed to city walls honor French men and women who assisted the wounded, or who died fighting the German occupiers. The principal site of memory, however, is called "Le Mémorial de Caen." It was erected in 1988 and opened by President François Mitterrand, himself a former member of the French Resistance. Though its original purpose was, like the Colleville cemetery, to honor the sacrifices made during the liberation of 1944, the Caen memorial has emerged as something altogether different: "un musée pour la paix"—a peace museum. The museum is surrounded by the flags of all the nations who fought in the battle, including the German flag; indoors, the central galleries are dedicated to images and ideas of world peace. A Hall of Peace asks visitors to contemplate how world civilizations across time have thought about peace and tolerance; to examine "fractures" to that peace brought about by nations and hate groups; and one corridor offers tribute to all the winners of the Nobel Peace Prize. Rotating exhibits feature, for example, discussions of the geopolitics of oil, and the violent practice of civilian hostage taking in various global conflicts. Monthly seminars are held on moral philosophy, and adult education courses examine human rights law. One might, of course, see the construction of this sophisticated peace museum as a sign that the people of Caen do not wish to dwell too much on their past, or do not wish to be associated only with the tragedies of D-Day. Yet the epigrammatic words engraved in stone on the outside of the building suggest not so much a turning away from the past as a particular stance toward it: "La douleur m'a brisée, La fraternité m'a relevée; De ma blessure a jailli un fleuve de liberté." *Sorrow broke me, Brotherhood has raised me up again; From my wound has sprung a river of freedom.*

The Caen memorial has come under fire in recent years from Anglo-American veterans groups for its peacenik pretensions and its apparent abandonment of its role as a memorial to the battle of Normandy.[69] But museums and memorials tell us more about how and what we choose to remember than about historical events themselves. On these now-placid, verdant Norman fields, Americans come to pay homage to their soldiers amidst the somber grandeur of a military cemetery; the people of Caen prefer to gather in a museum of glass and steel and consider the human cost not just of their liberation but of all wars. Both sites are fitting tributes to the varieties of liberation, and the universality of mourning.

2

Blood on the Snow:
The Elusive Liberation of Belgium

"OUR JOURNEY INTO Belgium," wrote Sgt. Richard Greenwood of the 9th Battalion, Royal Tank Regiment, "was an interesting experience. I felt that here, we were really welcome. But at Brussels! It is difficult to describe the scene. It may have been a royal procession, so great was the acclamation. We passed through the principal streets of the city at a time when there were many business people about, 6:00 P.M., and what a contrast with France! Here there were well dressed civilians, fine shops, cleanliness, order, and intelligent looking people. And girls! There were so many, so clean, healthy, fine looking. What a sight for our lads. The city was a blaze of color: every shop, every house, every window carried a flag. . . . We were bombarded with fruits and flowers, on a greater scale than ever." Major Edward Elliot of the Glasgow Highlanders concurred: "The contrast between Belgium and France struck me at once. The people dressed better, clothes seemed more plentiful, everyone looked clean and healthy, whereas France gave one the impression that everyone was shoddy and tired. The enthusiasm for our cause seemed more genuine and spontaneous in Belgium than anywhere else we had been." A rapturous welcome, yes: yet the reality of the war hung over the proceedings like a shroud. Major Maurice Cooke of the Royal Scots recalled that he and his second in command were billeted with a Belgian family in Courtrai (Kortrijk), just a dozen miles from the French border.

> Troughton and I were invited into a big house, beautifully furnished, whose owner speaking English fluently invited us into his drawing room and opened a bottle of red wine. We noticed a couple dressed heavily in black, and our host explained that his brother and sister in law had lost their three young sons when the RAF had destroyed the

station area earlier in the year. It was a most embarrassing situation—our host was most kind, but the atmosphere was strained. We departed to bed early to find pictures of the three little boys, aged 7, 9, and 11, and a family biography of them on mourning cards on the mantel-piece.

An apt summary of the experience of liberation: a warm welcome mixed with the bitter taste of loss.[1]

After the trauma of Normandy, Allied soldiers basked in the glories of Belgium's apparent peace and prosperity. The British and American forces that dashed across France from the Seine river to the Belgian border entered Brussels, Antwerp, and Liège on September 3, 4, and 7 respectively. They frequently spoke not only of the joy of the liberated Belgians and of the welcome they received, but of the abundance they found in the country. "One got the impression," wrote one British captain, all too aware of the severe shortages Britain had suffered through, "that the Belgians felt they had done their bit by eating their way through the war." A bemused GI, after seeing the flags along the main boulevards, the handsome shop-fronts and well-dressed citizens in Brussels, remarked "one would hardly think they were having a war."[2] We cannot rely, however, upon these soldiers' first impressions. To be sure, Belgians had not experienced the kind of punishing, murderous occupation policies that the Germans had imposed in Eastern Europe, and they had fared better than the French, on balance, but the country had hardly escaped unscathed. Defeated in May 1940 after a battle against the Germans that lasted only eighteen days, Belgium suffered from the systematic German economic exploitation that drained the country's finances, requisitioned food, coal, and textiles, and siphoned off a most valuable commodity: human labor. By 1943, 542,000 Belgians were working in Germany and France for the German war effort. Starting in mid-1943, the insatiable Germans intensified their demands for labor, and hunted men down in the streets, the movie houses, the parks, churches, and in their homes. Thousands of so-called *réfractaires* (defaulters) went into hiding. Wartime reports concluded that "the population is suffering intensely from what it considers a reduction to slavery." And for one group of people in Belgium, their fate was even worse than that: 26,000 Jews, or 45 percent of the Jews in Belgium at the start of the war, were deported to German extermination camps; a mere 1,200 survived.[3]

The liberation too—despite its first flush of glory—was stained with blood. Even as the residents of Brussels were throwing flowers and fruits into the jeeps and trucks of the British troops during the glorious early days of

Citizens of Belgium's capital city, Brussels, greet the arrival of British troops, September 4, 1944. *Imperial War Museum*

September, a number of ghastly events were unfolding in the eastern part of the country that made plain how much brutality the retreating Germans still had in them, and augured ill for the final stages of the war. On September 2–3, along the road that runs from the French town of Valenciennes to the Belgian city of Mons, thousands of Germans in full retreat encountered harassing fire from small bands of ill-equipped and no doubt overconfident Belgian partisans. The Germans responded with typical ferocity: around the villages of Ghlin, along the Mons Canal, and in the towns of Jemappes and Quaregnon, through which their main axis of retreat ran, Wehrmacht and SS soldiers set fire to civilian homes along the route, and killed some sixty civilians. On the same day, just a few miles to the north, in the village of Quevaucamps, Belgian partisans fired upon a column of retreating Germans, killing one soldier; the Germans determined to exact reprisals. They killed two resistance fighters whom they caught, then rounded up seventeen civilians in the town and shot them. By the 4th of September, the Germans were tumbling headlong eastward, across the Meuse river, through the Ardennes, toward Aachen, and toward the shelter of the West Wall—what the Americans called the Siegfried Line—the vast row of concrete fortifications and gun emplacements designed to keep the Allies out of Germany. But as they went, they spread death and destruction along the way, and many Belgians found September 4 to be a day marked by atrocity rather than liberation. In the small hamlet of Sovet, some six miles east of Dinant and the Meuse, a few Belgian partisans unwisely sprayed retreating SS soldiers of the Hitlerjugend and Prinz Eugen divisions with gunfire, wounding two of them; immediately, the Germans organized a manhunt in the town for partisans. In Sovet, they went from house to house, gathering groups of villagers, killing them, and setting their homes ablaze. The home of the village priest, Vicar Beusart, was set alight, and as he was running to rescue his possessions, he was shot dead, his body left to be engulfed by the flames. By the end of the rampage, eighteen people, including three women, were dead.

Not all such German atrocities were provoked by resistance activity. On the same day, in Anhée, a small village on the left bank of the Meuse, a battalion of retreating SS Panzer Grenadiers massacred 13 civilians, pillaged the homes of the village, and set fire to fifty-eight buildings in the town. The victims were mostly men in their sixties—one was eighty-two years old—and none of them had resistance connections of any kind. Just a few hundred yards up the road, soldiers of the 3rd Regiment, Hitlerjugend Division, crossed the Meuse between Dinant and Namur, established a command post, and then deliberately recrossed the river again to pillage and destroy the local villages. In the small riverfront villages of Godinne, Bouillon, Hun, Warnant, and Rivière, the Germans robbed, then set ablaze, numerous homes and shot five civilians to death. Two women, Jeanne Féraille, twenty-one years old, and Elze Hubrecht, thirty-seven, both of nearby Annevoie, were repeatedly raped. Yet the Germans reserved their most vicious treatment for captured resistance men. On September 7, in Failon, eighteen miles east of Dinant, German soldiers arrested seven men, four of whom were civilians, three of whom were members of the local gendarmerie. The Germans considered them all likely resistance members, or "terrorists." The prisoners were transferred to Bonsin the next morning, where they were murdered. A medical examination of the bodies by a local physician the following day revealed that the men had been badly beaten, tortured, and mutilated. One of the victims had his sexual organs cut off. And in December and January 1944–45, this sort of violence and atrocity started up all over again, when these same Germans returned to

Belgium during their ill-fated attack in what became the Battle of the Bulge. The images so many Allied soldiers carried with them of the glory days of September have done much to create a legend about Belgium's "easy war." But liberation in Belgium—a prolonged, uncertain period that ran from September 1944 until January 1945—would prove to be every bit as traumatic as in Normandy. The Belgians would have their war, after all.[4]

WITH THE DEPARTURE of the Germans in early September, Belgians and their liberators grappled with the challenge of restoring the political order. General Eisenhower, the Supreme Allied Commander, appointed a Briton, Major-General George W. E. J. Erskine, to head the mission to Belgium from Supreme Headquarters Allied Expeditionary Force (SHAEF). Erskine's appointment reflected Britain's military control of Brussels and Antwerp, while the Americans occupied southeastern Belgium, from Liège to the Ardennes. Erskine was not meant to rule with an iron fist: his job was to resurrect Belgian political institutions, impose calm in the streets, and ensure the prompt resumption of industrial production on behalf of the Allied armies. He was all too eager to delegate politics to the Belgians themselves. Yet, unlike France, where Charles de Gaulle strode forward to take up his role as the "man of destiny" at the crucial hour, Belgians lacked a national figure to whom they could turn. Belgium's king, Leopold III, had been shamed by his wartime behavior. In May 1940, after the German invasion and the defeat of the Belgian army, Leopold refused to leave the country (as the Dutch sovereign, Queen Wilhelmina, had done) and sued for peace with the Germans. The prime minister, Hubert Pierlot, and his cabinet decided instead to flee the country into France, and soon made their way to London, there to join other forlorn governments-in-exile that had been chased off the continent by the Nazis. King Leopold, meanwhile, remained in his sumptuous palace outside Brussels, claiming that he would share the fate of his people under German rule. He dwelt in royal comfort while the German military, along with the remarkably cooperative Belgian industrialists, bureaucrats, and administrators, ran the country. Leopold met Hitler at Berchtesgaden in November 1940, but failed to win concessions and autonomy from the German Führer; then he withdrew behind his palace walls until June 1944, when the Germans seized him and deported him to Germany, a worthless and unmissed hostage. The Allies therefore accorded recognition to Pierlot's government, set its members up in a house in Eaton Square in London, and ignored them—until the swift, almost miraculously speedy, liberation of Belgium occurred, taking only a few days. On September 8, 1944, a British aircraft flew a dozen Belgian cabinet ministers, led by Pierlot, into Brussels. Upon their arrival at the Brussels airfield, no one met them at the airport. Pierlot, whom the British ambassador said was characterized "by a certain lack of vigorous initiative," was a man very much of the old regime: he was sixty-four years old, a twenty-year veteran of the parliament, a Catholic centrist, a former minister of interior and foreign affairs, and a lawyer. Upon his arrival in Brussels, he installed himself in the Ministry of the Interior, and on September 9 he led a delegation to the World War I memorial to lay a wreath. Spectators on the streets stared mutely; there was no applause. On September 20, the brother of the king, Prince Charles, was appointed by a joint session of parliament to act as regent until the king's fate could be determined. Pierlot resigned, only to be asked by Prince Charles to form a new government. Thus a collection of men from the prewar regime with no connections to the internal Belgian resistance took up the reins of power with full British support; continuity and control were the watchwords of the moment.[5]

Materially, Belgium in 1944 had certain advantages over France, since its infrastructure had not been severely damaged by the war. Though they had wrecked the telephone and telegraph exchange in Brussels, the retreating Germans had not had time to sabotage the rail and transport network. The country's fall harvest was intact, the coal mines had not been destroyed, and even Antwerp's port facilities had not yet been seriously harmed. Even so, the large cities faced a serious bread shortage in the weeks after liberation, and conditions in the country worsened throughout the fall. This was chiefly due to a shortage of coal, oil, and electricity to run trains, fuel trucks, and fire the bakeries. Belgium had been self-sufficient in coal before the war, but at the time of the liberation, coal production had fallen to a mere tenth of prewar production. There was a shortage of labor, since 500,000 workers had been shipped to Germany to work inside the Reich as forced labor. The train system was malfunctioning because the Germans had wrecked the telegraph network, making a shambles of the train timetables. Perhaps most important, the collapse of the German occupation had left little or no centralized Belgian bureaucracy to deal with coal transport and distribution. A good deal of the coal that was mined was sold on the black market at astronomical prices, and it was not until December that the British army agreed to place soldiers on every coal train coming out of the mines to ensure that the coal reached its assigned destination without being detoured and ransacked. Belgians also had to compete with the Allied armies, which since November had gobbled up 900,000 tons of Belgian coal (along with tons of local vegetables, fruits, and potatoes).[6] Without reliable coal supplies for civilian consumption, the country came to a near halt. In mid-October, electricity was shut off between 7:00 A.M. and 8:00 P.M. in an effort to conserve coal; the bread lines grew. By the end of October, the temperature in the main cities among a harassed public rose to dangerous levels, and demonstrations began to form in front of the government offices.

To complaints about shortages, the public added criticism of Prime Minister Pierlot for his dilatory policy toward collaborators. The Allies estimated that some 400,000 Belgians had in some way worked for the German occupation, and the new government initially arrested as many as 60,000 people. But by the end of 1944, thousands had been released while only 495 people had been given capital sentences (mostly in absentia); only one senior administrator had been convicted of crimes against the state. Most received far more lenient punishments. An astute British observer likened "the fierce and bitter hatred of collaborators" to "a religious fervor," and the press excoriated the government ministers, who had spent the war safely in London, for their failure to avenge the injustices suffered at the hands of collaborators during the war. A Belgian who had worked for the BBC in London during the war returned in November to find that Belgians cared more about the purges than any other issue, including food. "Worse than anything," he wrote of the wartime experiences of his countrymen, "was the treason of the Belgians themselves," yet these traitors now went unpunished. "Although the people will exercise great patience," he concluded, "they will never permit that the guilty should slip through the fingers of the law.... The country is beginning to ferment."[7]

The food shortage and the failure of the purges provided the backdrop to a major political crisis in the country in November that required the full intervention of the Allied military authorities. Throughout the war, Belgium had not had a large underground resistance, but as German labor roundups increased in intensity, the resistance grew. By the end of the war, there were 90,000 members of the resistance, most of them armed. The most significant groups were the Armée Secrète, led by former officers of the Belgian army, which tended to have royalist sympathies; and the Front de l'Indépendence (FI), organized and controlled by the Belgian Communist Party. These units harassed the retreating Germans, played a small part in the liberation of the country, and now refused to be marginalized by Pierlot's government, which they viewed as a sad continuation of the prewar gerontocracy. One British senior official described the resistance fighters as "a very motley array.... Members of these guerrilla forces are now to be seen in all parts of the country, bearing distinguishing armlets and carrying Sten guns, revolvers, and sometimes only knives." They engaged in "arbitrary acts of requisition" from the civilians, and indeed were more numerous and "better armed than the Belgian police."[8] In order to protect the Belgian government and to secure public order, General Eisenhower on October 2 ordered that the Belgian resistance groups surrender their weapons, while he complimented them for their "devoted heroism."[9]

Yet they did not readily obey. Instead, upset over the failure of the purges and spurred on by hungry, embittered civilians, elements of the FI arranged a serious challenge to the government. On October 21, the prime minister alerted SHAEF that he had information about a Communist uprising in the country, centered around striking miners and other disaffected laborers; SHAEF responded by swiftly arming the Belgian police with 7,500 weapons and stepping up demands for the disarmament of the resistance. (Some of the weapons had to be parachuted into Belgium by British secret services.) General Erskine published an open letter stressing his support for Pierlot and his determination to use force to put down any political uprising. On November 25, the FI and Communist union members staged a large demonstration in Brussels and marched to government offices; when it appeared they might try to enter the government precincts, police fired on the marchers, wounding over forty demonstrators. Three days later, tramway employees ordered a strike in Brussels and called another large demonstration that was broken up by police. But at midday, the Pierlot government was alerted to the imminent arrival in the capital of truckloads of armed demonstrators en route from Mons. Pierlot made an official appeal to General Erskine, who called out British troops to surround the government buildings; meanwhile, Belgian police stopped the strikers before they could reach the city, and disarmed them. Pierlot later claimed to have information proving that the Communists had clearly stockpiled fifteen tons of weapons and intended to seize control of the government. In the first three months of the liberation, then, food shortages had worsened, the justice system had failed to tackle the purge of collaborators, and the British army had turned the capital city into an armed camp. Belgians had precious little to show for their liberation.[10]

While politics occupied the citizens of Brussels, the realities of the war continued to weigh heavily on the residents of Antwerp and Liège. The Americans had stormed into Liège on September 7, and quickly taken over this eastern city, which sits just twenty miles from Aachen and the German border. This was a front-line town, and the Americans demanded blackouts of all civilian homes at night, reserved certain key road routes for military traffic only, and ran large convoys through the neighboring towns all day and night, endangering pedestrians. The Army naturally requisitioned property, and laid claim to any German war booty or materiel, including buildings and furniture, that had previously been used by the German occupiers. The presence of a large U.S. army in Liège made it a target for German V-1 and V-2 bombs. The *Vergeltungswaffe*, or "reprisal weapon," was a self-propelled rocket that Hitler launched against cities in Britain, France, and Belgium, starting in June 1944. These began to fall on Liège on November 19, 1944. Up to December 31, 86 V-1s and 254 V-2s fell on Liège; 231 people were killed, 365 were wounded. In January, another 49 V-1s hit Liège, killing 170 persons. These attacks caused alarm and panic among civilians in the city as well as widespread damage to homes and public services.[11]

The city that took the greatest brunt of the German V-weapons—other than London, which suffered 2,419 hits and 6,184 deaths—was Antwerp, the great Belgian port city into which British forces had rolled on September 4. From that date until March 1945, Antwerp was under a constant barrage of rocket attacks, usually three or so per day, which killed 3,700 people and injured 6,000 more. In October, before the attacks intensified, the British authorities did not think the V-weapon attacks likely to shake the morale of the stalwart residents of Antwerp. In fact, General Erskine seemed to think the rockets not at all a bad thing: "On its present scale, it is rather a healthy reminder that the war is not yet over," he told SHAEF.[12] But the attacks became very unhealthy indeed in November and December. The worst single attack occurred on the afternoon of December 16, 1944. Belgian civilians as well as many Allied soldiers on leave had just settled in at Antwerp's Rex cinema on the avenue De Keyserlei to see a recent release from Hollywood: *The Plainsman*, starring Gary Cooper and Jean Arthur. The cinema was packed with 1,200 people. At 3:20 P.M., a blinding flash of light cut through the darkened cinema, followed by a defeaning crash and roar. The entire theater exploded into pieces, sending bricks, mortar, wood, and bodies into the air. The cinema had been struck by a V-2 rocket. The ceiling collapsed, the walls caved in, and the balcony fell onto the viewers beneath. There were 567 people killed, 291 injured; 296 of the dead were Allied servicemen.[13]

In the eyes of both British and Belgian observers, Belgium in the late fall of 1944 looked like a dangerously fragile country, beset by shortages, weak leadership, threats of leftist violence, and constant V-rocket attacks. General Erskine used various metaphors, likening Belgium to "a tender plant needing much material and moral nourishment," or an ill patient "which is now convalescent." Nand Geersens of the Belgian branch of the BBC was less sanguine about the country's prospects for recovery: once the joy of liberation had worn off, he said, Belgians faced "the ugly disillusioning reality" that their country had been defeated, occupied, and betrayed by greedy, selfish collaborators that had welcomed Nazi overlords. "The general morality of the country," he felt, "has naturally suffered through all this. . . . Our people, to a certain extent, are sick." He worried that "it will take a long, a very long time before our whole people will once more be healthy."[14]

THE ELECTRIFYING DASH of the Allied armies from the Seine across France and into Belgium was "the headiest and most optimistic advance of the European war," General Omar Bradley, commander of 12th U.S. Army Group, recalled. The Germans had collapsed in France; they turned tail and ran in Belgium; on September 13, tanks from the American 3rd Armored Division of VII Corps kicked through the first belt of the Siegfried Line just south of Aachen. And this was no pin-prick: along a five-hundred-mile front, the powerful Allied armies, numbering fifty-four divisions, seemed poised to crash into Hitler's Germany, cross the Rhine, and drive for Berlin. Inevitably, there was talk, both in the newspapers and in Bradley's headquarters, "of getting home by Christmas."[15]

Then the advance came to a shuddering halt. In the next weeks and months, the clash of armies in the west shifted from a high-gear race across hundreds of miles to a slow, pitched battle for every square yard of turf. The reason is simple: the Allied armies were running out of everything, most crucially, ammunition, gasoline, and men. The joy of gobbling up all those miles of territory between the Normandy beachheads and the German border hid the serious danger of overextended lines. The Germans had made this risk more grave by ordering besieged garrisons in key port cities—Brest, Le Havre, Boulogne-sur-Mer, Calais, Dunkerque—to hold out as long as possible and to sabotage all port facilities. Months after the D-Day landings, Allied forces were still unloading supplies in Normandy and Marseilles, both many miles away from the front, then trucking those supplies across the narrow, rutted, muddy roads of France toward the front—a laborious and inefficient process. And it simply could not be done fast enough to supply the gigantic force of men and vehicles that now massed along the German border.[16]

The Allies actually made their logistics problem worse through a strategic blunder in mid-September that must rank as one of the worst of the European war. On September 4, the British had entered Antwerp. But the port was useless to them as long as the Germans controlled the banks of the watery approaches to the city known as the Scheldt estuary, and in particular Walcheren Island, which sits at the mouth of the Scheldt. Rather than concentrating on the essential task of clearing the approaches to Antwerp when the Germans were still disorganized, Eisenhower approved of a plan

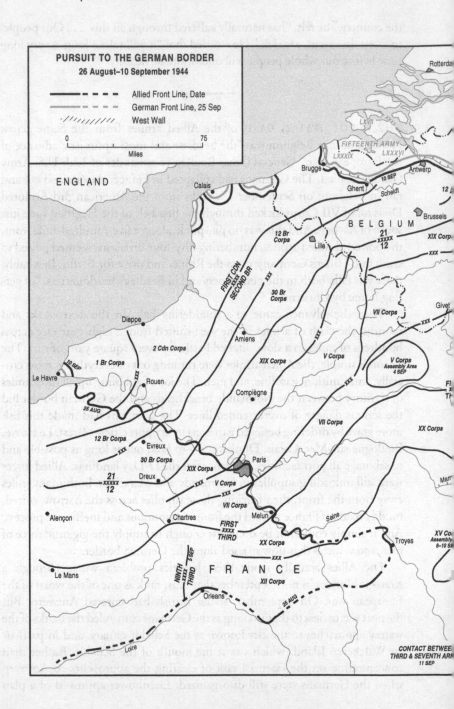

PURSUIT TO THE GERMAN BORDER
26 August–10 September 1944

Allied Front Line, Date
German Front Line, 25 Sep
West Wall

0   75
Miles

hatched by General Montgomery for an airborne assault into Holland in an attempt to seize a bridgehead across the Rhine at Arnhem—Operation Market Garden. Had it worked, it could have outflanked the concrete dragon's teeth of the Siegfried Line and opened up a path into the heart of Germany. But it failed: the Germans were well prepared for the attack, and the British paratroopers took too long to get to the bridge, giving the Germans time to respond. The American 101st Airborne and 82nd Airborne divisions did their part, crossing the river Waal and taking the bridges at Nijmegen, but the operation failed to cross the Rhine and seize the proverbial "bridge too far" at Arnhem. In the meantime, the German Fifteenth Army, recently in flight from the Pas-de-Calais, dug in along the Scheldt, thus denying Antwerp to Allied shipping. Not until November 26 did the British and Canadians manage to clear the German hold on this vital waterway and begin unloading supplies in Belgium. While the Allied armies started to ration their ammunition, the Germans, so bloodied and disorganized after their retreat from France, swiftly resupplied their forces and prepared to defend their homeland. The war that looked as if it might be over by Christmas settled into a stalemate with no end in sight.[17]

Like a long electrified wire snaking through northwest Europe from the North Sea down to Switzerland, the western front continually crackled with lethal violence throughout the fall of 1944. Eisenhower and Bradley agreed that even without adequate supplies, they must continue to put pressure on the Germans without letup, if only because time would allow the Germans to recover further from their reverses of the summer. Talk of darting to Berlin was forgotten, to be replaced by the simple ambition of killing as many German soldiers as possible along as wide a front as possible, thus to deplete the German army and bleed it to death. The heaviest fighting from mid-September to mid-December was located on Walcheren Island by the mouth of the Scheldt; around Aachen and its hinterland; in the Hürtgen Forest and the western bank of the river Roer; in Lorraine, through the French cities of Metz, Nancy, and toward the Saar basin; and in the Vosges mountains of Alsace on toward Strasbourg, right up against the Franco-German border and the Rhine river.[18] For hundreds of thousands of American soldiers this was a time they would never forget, for these battles would prove to be the most difficult, prolonged, and costly of the war. Battle casualties spiked in November, reaching 62,437; they rose in December to 77,726, and in January, the Americans sustained a further 69,119 casualties: these were the three highest monthly totals for the entire European campaign.[19] General Bradley wrote later that he had "to comb the ETO for emergency replacements. But, though truckloads of hastily trained riflemen were bundled off to the front, they could not offset the litter cases that passed them headed rearward." Most of the men being carried out on stretchers were the riflemen of the infantry, the front-line troops. Despite replacements, by December 15, Bradley's 12th Army Group was short 17,000 riflemen, and the rate of loss in the rifle platoons was over 90 percent. If this was a war of attrition, it appeared to be draining the Americans of blood as effectively as it was killing Germans.[20]

The stalemate in the west was broken on December 16, 1944, though not in the manner anticipated by the Americans. Unbeknownst to the huge American force strung out across the western front, the Germans had massed thirty divisions, in total secrecy, just to the east of the Ardennes—precisely the weakest point in the American line. Here, a mere four U.S. divisions occupied an eighty-mile front. Two of them, the 99th and the 106th, had just been deployed and were filled with green troops; the other two, the 4th and the 28th, had recently been withdrawn from the carnage of the Hürtgen Forest, and were refitting and recuperating. Hitler's goal—and this offensive was very much Hitler's idea—was to slice through the wooded Ardennes, race to the Meuse, seize Liège, and head for Antwerp, in the process splitting the Allied armies in two.

The German attack succeeded in creating a menacing "bulge" in the American lines. The two divisions that took the brunt of the attack, the 106th and the 28th, virtually disintegrated, and thousands of men from these divisions would spend the next five months in a brutal captivity behind enemy lines. Yet the advantage of surprise and local superiority in forces lasted only a few days. The Americans showed remarkable resilience in recovering from the initial shock. General Eisenhower, once he grasped the scale and reckless ambition of the attack, ordered the 10th Armored Division into the southern shoulder of the Bulge, and called on the 7th Armored Division to push onto the northern shoulder, thereby holding the German salient to a fairly narrow front. He also sent the 101st Airborne Division into the road junction town of Bastogne, determined to block the Germans there. General Patton's Third Army, previously engaged to the south, wheeled northward and crashed into the German salient, heading toward Bastogne. Meanwhile, Lieutenant General Courtney Hodges sent his VII Corps toward Houffalize in an effort to pinch the Bulge. The Germans, running out of fuel, and pounded by relentless Allied air attack (the poor weather that had shielded the Germans cleared on December 23), stopped and by early January had begun a withdrawal. The attack had been a costly failure for Hitler: 12,652 soldiers killed, 38,600 wounded, and 30,000 missing. The Germans also lost half their tanks and guns they had committed to battle. For the Americans, the Battle of the Bulge was a decisive victory, but it had been extremely costly: 10,276 men were killed, 47,493 were wounded, and 23,218 were missing. Nearly 7,000 soldiers of the 106th Infantry Division were taken prisoner.[21]

"THERE WERE MANY dead and many wounded," wrote war correspondent Martha Gellhorn of the Battle of the Bulge, "but the survivors contained the fluid situation and slowly turned it into a retreat, and finally, as the communiqué said, the bulge was ironed out. This was not done fast or easily; and it was not done by those anonymous things, armies, divisions, regiments. It was done by men, one by one." Gellhorn had seen the Battle of the Bulge up close—as close as a war reporter could see it—and had become well acquainted with the fear, mud, and death that the western front offered. Writing for *Collier's* magazine, she insisted that Americans on the home front attend to the experiences of the common soldier in the field. Gellhorn wanted to remind her readers that beneath the maps, the colored lines, and the flags set out on planning tables, there was a human tragedy unfolding, in which men were dying in awful ways, in large numbers. Like Ernie Pyle, Gellhorn could only hint at the reality of what she saw. We now can look in greater detail, with the benefit of memoirs and oral histories, into what one company commander called "the dread, gnawing daily diet of war." This kind of attention to the human experience of war is necessary not only so that posterity can marvel at the bravery and perhaps even more at the endurance of these soldiers. A close exploration of the physical and mental toll that this fighting took on American soldiers also shows us that the brutalization of the average soldier, which historians readily agree became a feature of the German-Soviet war in the east, occurred in the west as well, with consequences for the liberators and liberated alike.[22]

Many of the men who fought in the ETO in the fall and winter of 1944 were teenagers. Paul Fussell (himself a nineteen-year-old rifleman in 1944) stressed this point in his excellent brief chronicle of the infantry soldier, which he deliberately entitled *The Boys' Crusade*. Captain Charles MacDonald, a company commander in the 2nd Infantry Division who led over 120 men in battle, was twenty-one years old during the Battle of the Bulge. Donald Burgett, a member of the 82nd Airborne Division, went into battle in the Ardennes as a nineteen-year-old—and he was considered "one of the old men who had survived both operations," that is, both the landings of D-Day and Market Garden. Sergeant Spencer Wurst, of the 101st Airborne, also fought in Holland as a nineteen-year-old; on December 19, his twentieth birthday, he was fighting in the Ardennes and killed three men. Being very young, most of these men had seen little of the world before being shipped to Europe, had

Two muddy and tired soldiers from the 110th Regiment, 28th Division.
The regiment performed valiantly outside of Bastogne on December 16–18, 1944,
and slowed the German assault on that vital town. Most of the men in the
regiment were killed, wounded, or captured. *U.S. National Archives*

not held a steady job, started families, or in some cases even finished high
school. They knew little of the cause for which they fought: in the summer of
1943, over a third of a sample of three thousand men in the United States had
never heard of the Four Freedoms, and only 13 percent could actually name
three or four of them. This was a war that men could not avoid; once in combat, they fought to stay alive, and to kill Germans so the war would end.[23]

The conditions in which the men fought in the winter campaign were notoriously difficult. Above all, soldiers recall the cold they were forced to endure.
Daytime temperatures hovered near the freezing mark; at night they fell into
the twenties and teens. Wind, snow, and rain prevailed.[24] George Neill, posted
in Belgium with the 99th Infantry Division, remembered that it snowed on
November 9, 1944—the first snow of the season—and the snowfall "ushered
in a condition of extreme discomfort that was to plague us for the next four
months." Fires were not allowed as they would attract enemy shelling. After just
one night outdoors in below-freezing weather, "with our tent and clothing wet

and half frozen, I felt numb to the point of almost not caring what happened to me." After four days, he and his men were "cold, wet, dirty, and extremely fatigued," and had already started to exhibit "the unforgettable blank look of infantrymen manning the front line." The exposure to the cold was made worse by the soldier's need to shelter in a foxhole. The foxhole was four to five feet in depth, usually difficult to dig because of the frozen topsoil, and invariably full of frozen water and mud. "As darkness descended," Neill wrote, "the temperature moved well below freezing. The half-frozen slush in the bottom of the hole froze solid." Sleeping in such a place was almost impossible. "We just lay there in a fetal position and shivered and swore to ourselves. . . . Words cannot convey the awfulness of this ordeal to the reader. My buddies and I agreed it would be impossible to exaggerate how hopeless, miserable and depressed we felt." Incredibly, the men had no winter equipment. "No earmuffs, no hood, no face covering, no scarf," recalled Lieutenant George Wilson of the 4th Infantry Division. "Our hands also suffered with only wool finger gloves. No mittens, no outer shells. Of course, none of our things were fur lined." And on their heads they wore ice-cold steel helmets. American troops did not receive even rudimentary winter clothing until late January 1945. At the Bulge, they would fight wearing uniforms suitable for summertime.[25]

Prolonged exposure to such cold led directly to the trench foot crisis, which affected tens of thousands of soldiers along the western front. Standing in slush, snow, and ice in a foxhole for many hours while wearing wet leather boots had devastating effects on the soldiers' feet. Rocky Blunt of the 84th Infantry Division recalled that one especially cold night, he fell asleep— lost consciousness is probably more apt—in his foxhole with his feet in the slush. When he awoke, "my feet were encased in a block of ice up to my ankles in the bottom of the hole. Everett [a member of his unit] pounded on my legs but there was absolutely no feeling or movements. He and another nearby GI chipped away the ice with their bayonets, lifted me out of my hole and dragged me across the frozen ground. . . . When circulation returned to my legs, excruciating pain that had been dulled by the numbness gradually became almost unbearable." In a field hospital he almost had his feet amputated but was given a last-minute reprieve. "Both feet had been reduced to ugly, purplish-blue mutations with large blistering pieces of torn skin peeling off them." The only way to deal with trench foot was to remove the wet boots and socks, rub the feet to restore circulation, and find dry socks and shoes— two very rare commodities. Sergeant John Babcock said that his men "learned to sit facing each other [in a foxhole] so as to hold and massage each other's bare feet while heavy, leather combat boots dried out. That rubbing someone else's stinking feet might be distasteful was overridden by sheer necessity."[26]

Other illnesses beset the infantrymen. Donald Burgett of the 101st Airborne endured what he called "trench mouth." After two months in combat in Holland, "pus oozed from my gums. My teeth became so loose that I could move them freely with my tongue, and blood would run out of my mouth from the light pressure of the razor when I shaved." Dysentery was more common. Charles MacDonald, after nine days at the front with virtually no sleep, "became conscious of pains in my stomach, and a wave of nausea came over me. I put my hand to my forehead and realized for the first time that I had a burning fever. I excused myself and walked outside to climb the incline to the latrine. An intense cold had combined with the K-ration diet to give me a violent case of dysentery." This condition afflicted most front-line soldiers. "Since we rarely had hot water and soap for cleaning our mess gear, we used snow and ice water from the river," writes George Neill. "This did nothing to eliminate the grease accumulating after each meal, which set us up for chronic diarrhea." Diarrhea made life in a foxhole difficult—Neill uses the apt word "torture"—not least because exiting the foxhole, undressing, defecating, re-dressing, and returning to the foxhole all had to be done in the dark and in total silence so as to avoid alerting the enemy to one's presence. And this demeaning routine might have to be repeated many times each night. In combat, one might not be able to leave the foxhole at all. "Trapped in a foxhole," writes Rocky Blunt, "when a man had to defecate, he did it in his K-ration box and threw it over the side; when he had to urinate, he did it in a C-ration can or his helmet or in the bottom of his hole." And of course these soldiers were unable to bathe, going for two months and more without a change of clothes or a shower. "Perhaps there's a medical term" for the depressing effect of living in such awful conditions, wrote Lieutenant George Wilson, "but I think the word 'misery' will do."[27]

These cold and frequently ill men were also afraid. They feared death, of course, but even more they feared wounds—mostly in the abdomen, eyes, brain, or genitals. The German 88 mm artillery piece was widely considered the most frightening weapon, since it was astonishingly accurate and powerful, and a blast could instantly shred a human body. Fear induced physical effects such as an accelerated heart rate, muscular tension, dry mouth, and trembling. (And sometimes worse: one-fifth of the men in a division in the Pacific Theater acknowledged that, during combat, fear had led them to lose control of their bowels.) And seeing fear in other men tended to induce fear in the beholder. After the initial German breakthrough in the Ardennes, said Donald Burgett, "fear reigned. Once fear strikes, it spreads like an epidemic, faster than wildfire. Once the first man runs, others soon follow. Then it's all over; soon there are hordes of men running, all of them wild-eyed and driven by fear." Leaders were not immune: Captain MacDonald, facing a German counterattack, recalled that "the paroxysm of fear that gripped me left my body trembling. I was not so much afraid of what was happening as I was of the horrible visions my mind had dreamed up of what would happen should we fail to repulse the attack. . . . [He told himself:] *Quit shaking, dammit. Stop trembling all over. Get control of yourself. Act like a soldier, goddammit! At least you can impersonate an officer!*" Most men felt terrible fear before assaulting an enemy position. But once in the fight, the fear was overtaken by an instinct to survive. "I always got a sick feeling in the pit of my stomach when I started a running attack into frontal fire, knowing that at any moment an enemy bullet might tear through my body, face, or limbs . . . But once we started, there was no turning back. There was only one option as far as I was concerned: run forward and kill."[28]

More even than filth, illness, and fear, men on the front line had to confront death, or to be more precise, dead bodies. These were daily, constant companions. In their first days in the battle zone, infantrymen found the presence of corpses difficult to take, and tried to avert their eyes. Charles MacDonald recalled seeing his first dead American: "I stumbled and looked down at my feet. An American soldier, fully clothed even to his helmet, lay on his back with glassy eyes turned skyward, his arms outstretched. His body was almost twice its normal size. I shuddered involuntarily. The shock of almost stepping upon the body before seeing it left me weak inside." MacDonald also recounted that in the forests of the Ardennes, wild boars frequently made nocturnal forays into the battlefield, with ghastly results:

> Long stopped us to call my attention to a man digging a foxhole to my left.
>
> "What do you think of that, Cap'n?" he asked.
>
> I looked in the direction which he indicated. Five feet from the hole where the soldier dug indifferently lay a dead German, his chest and stomach bare and his stomach a mass of clotted blood and intestines.
>
> "The hogs have been eatin' on him," Long said.[29]

In a short time, dead bodies became simply part of the surreal landscape, and could be objects of perverse interest. Donald Burgett "found the remains of an American trooper who had been killed in the attack. During the night the tanks had run in single file over his body. Just by chance, while going to the truck to refill our canteens with water I noticed a dog tag protruding from the remains, which had been ground into the snow and dirt. I probed with my trench knife and fished out a crumpled pack of Lucky Strike cigarettes from among the flesh and splintered bone. I hung one of the dog tags on a limb near the body in hopes the medics would find it." Soldiers saw so many dead men that they adopted a casual attitude toward corpses and indeed toward death. Rocky Blunt writes with shocking indifference of seeing a GI take a direct hit from a German 88 mm artillery shell. "The man disintegrated, leaving only patches and puddles of flesh and bone spattered in the mud. Graves registration would never find this one, not even his dog tags. Another unknown soldier. I sat and ate my food. I had not known him." After the Battle of the Bulge, Sergeant John Babcock discovered he had his limits. "I could tolerate viewing a dead body, but found very unnerving the sight of parts—a hand, arm, headless torso, entrails, genitals, exposed bones, or the worst, an unidentifiable chunk of human flesh that resembled some kind of roast in a meat market display case." Rocky Blunt, by contrast, found himself compelled to stare at a German soldier who, after an artillery barrage, "had been disemboweled and his mouth, nose and jaw had been blown away. How, I don't know, but he was still alive and as I stared at him, his eyes followed my every movement. With each breath, foamy blood drooled from his mouth onto what had once been his chest. Only a foot-wide gaping hole of bloody meat remain[ed] of what had been his upper chest and his intestinal tract lay stretched out on the gravel like long twisted links of sausage. I could not take my eyes off this macabre scene."[30]

By their own accounts, infantrymen went through a process of psychological brutalization during this kind of warfare. After a short time in combat, men became inured to killing and developed intense animosity toward the German soldiers. Young infantrymen spoke of going into battle as "stacking bodies," or "putting meat on the table." Hatred toward the German soldier increased with every long, bitter hellish day in the front lines. "'Those goddamned Krauts,'" Donald Burgett muttered to himself. "'Those dirty rotten goddamned Krauts. They've lost the damned war and they know it. Why don't they give it up so we can all go home? The hard headed bastards. We're going to have an ass-kicking party when we get up there and they are going to supply the ass.'" Sergeant Babcock disputed the idea that American soldiers did not demonstrate hatred toward the enemy. "A lot of combat reports indicate that our fine soldiers didn't really hate the enemy, nor really take personally the grim battles between our forces. Not so with what was left of A Company. We had grown to hate the Krauts with a vengeance. Each slaughtered comrade added to our venom." And the result of this hatred meant that soldiers adopted a "code" of behavior toward the enemy: "Kill. No half measures. Eliminate the enemy in any way possible. Shoot, blow up, bludgeon, stab, show no mercy. Just one mission: kill."[31]

Some Americans mistreated German prisoners and wounded. On the front line, wounded Germans were left to die, since there was often no medical care available. Beatings and death threats, or deliberate exposure of the bare feet to snow, were techniques used to extract information from captured Germans. And after word got out that the Germans had killed 86 American POWs on a crossroads near Malmédy on December 17, "American feelings toward Germans hardened into vindictive hate. Chances of survival for newly caught German POWs diminished greatly."[32] When a German soldier surrendered to Donald Burgett, one of Burgett's fellow GIs shot him in the belly anyway. Burgett then thought it "merciful" to finish off this unfortunate man. He "was in terrible pain and dying. I knew he wouldn't recover. I knew he would die a horrible death. Lying gut shot and exposed in the woods at ten below zero. Another shot rang out and a bullet tore through his head. Bits of brains spattered the snow in a wide arc behind his body. Tiny puffs of steam drifted up from every spot where they had landed. The German was dead. It had been quick and merciful."[33] Most wartime memoirs mention that the shooting of POWs, while frowned upon, was common.[34] So was the mutilation of corpses. According to Babcock, one dead German near his outpost was stripped of his watch "before he was cold. I had his little blackout flashlight. After a few days, someone looted his wedding ring by neatly snipping off his ring finger." Rocky Blunt came across a mutilated German corpse that had already been dismembered by another GI. "I sat and stared at it for a while and then, totally without provocation, sent the head skimming across the snow with a savage kick." He then kicked it around the ice, "playing soccer. During the whole episode, I felt nothing but macabre elation. Eventually tiring of the sport . . . I sat down beside the mutilated remains of the German and ate a K-ration."[35]

IF COMBAT TRAUMATIZED and brutalized American soldiers—young men who had the benefit of training, group solidarity and, of course, weapons to defend themselves—how much worse might this sort of warfare have been for the civilians caught in this maelstrom? The evidence from Belgian records is quite eloquent: it was every bit as awful for them, and indeed even worse, as these were people who had few means to protect themselves. They were subject not just to violence from their enemies, the Germans, but also from the Americans who, precisely because of their own trauma, often behaved with callous indifference toward civilians and their property, or killed civilians by mistake. And of course for local Belgians the stakes were even higher than for soldiers: the violence of the war threatened their lives, their families, their livelihoods, their homes, villages, cities, and indeed their very sense of place and identity. For the people of the Belgian Ardennes and surrounding areas, the winter of 1944–45 was a time of catastrophe, suffering, and displacement. Over 3,000 civilians died in the Battle of the Bulge. The liberation that had gleamed so brightly in September was to be suffused in a midwinter bloodbath.[36]

"We'll be back," some German soldiers had sneered as they withdrew from Belgium in early September 1944. And so they were, nowhere with more vengeance than in the Amblève valley. The residents of the small town of Stavelot, which straddles the shallow, narrow Amblève river, knew the Germans were coming. On December 17, residents observed anxious, not to say panic-stricken, American soldiers moving westward through town, away from the front. Laurent Lombard, professor at the Athénée Royal de Stavelot, recalled that on the afternoon of the 17th refugees from Lingeuville, six miles to the east, arrived in Stavelot with word that they had seen the German tanks on their way. The residents were stunned, unbelieving: surely the Americans had not been turned back? At 5 P.M., refugees from Malmédy began to trickle into town, bearing the same ill tidings: "The Germans are coming back to Stavelot! For the villagers, this was the most terrifying prospect one could imagine—the return of a nightmare." The word spread fast. A wave of panic and fear spread through the town. Young people made preparations to flee; old people, unable or unwilling to join the flood of refugees, nervously awaited their fate. "The night [of 17 December] passed in a torment of agitation. . . . Few of us slept that night."[37]

Had they known what was coming, they all might have made greater efforts to flee. Stavelot lay in the path of the 100 tanks and 4,000 soldiers of *Kampfgruppe* Peiper, named for its SS-*Obersturmbannführer* (or colonel), Joachim Peiper, part of the 1st SS Leibstandarte Adolf Hitler Panzer Division. Peiper's unit had proven its ruthlessness in Russia, and now was assigned a vital breakthrough role in the Ardennes: along with the rest of the division, Peiper was to penetrate quickly to the Meuse, and hold open the door as the rest of the German invasion rushed through the Ardennes. Colonel Peiper, a mere twenty-nine years old yet battle-hardened and fanatical, let his soldiers know what was expected of them: total commitment, fearlessness, and brutality, including the killing of prisoners and civilians, partly in retribution for Allied bombing of Germany, and partly because this was the SS way—to kill and sow fear.[38] Early in the morning of December 17, immediately upon its penetration through an almost nonexistent American line at Losheim and Lanzerath, Peiper's men had an opportunity to show their zeal: in the village of Honsfeld, they rounded up a few stray, sleepy Americans from small units of the 99th Division—perhaps sixty men in all—and shot them. Another 250 or so prisoners were herded down the road toward the rear, jeered at, beaten, and mistreated by the Germans along the way. Peiper's tanks rolled northwestward into Büllingen, filled up at a captured American gasoline depot, and then stretched out for Stavelot and Trois Ponts, where they planned to cross the Amblève river and race to the Meuse. In the afternoon of the 17th, just south of Malmédy at a road junction at the hamlet of Baugnez, the *Kampfgruppe* surprised a small, ill-equipped American battery of the 285th Field Artillery Observation Battalion. These soldiers, along with men from other scattered units that had been overwhelmed—perhaps 113 men—were herded into an open field, stripped of gloves, clothing, and other items, and shot. Though over 40 Americans survived the shootings by feigning death and later secreting themselves in the nearby woods, 72 men lay dead in the field; another dozen would be rooted out of hiding places and killed in the subsequent hours. The Malmédy massacre, rightly infamous, was the worst atrocity against American troops in the European war.[39]

Belgians flee the advancing German army at the start of the Battle of the Bulge. December 16, 1944. *U.S. National Archives*

The Malmédy massacre is well-known today because it was immediately publicized by the commander of the First U.S. Army, Lieutenant General Courtney Hodges; he learned of it that very day from a few distraught survivors who made it back to American lines and told the grisly tale. The story of this German atrocity spread through American ranks and certainly led to reprisals upon German POWs by Americans. In 1946, seventy-three German soldiers, including Peiper, were put on trial for the murders, and all of them were convicted. Yet less well-known is the fact that Peiper's battle group had not finished its lethal work. After its harvest of death at Baugnez, the *Kampfgruppe* rolled onward to the west, pausing for the night on the outskirts of Stavelot. Early the next morning, the murderous column jerked into life and set out toward the town, where hundreds of terrified citizens huddled in basements and barns, awaiting the return of the Germans. The Germans rolled into town from the southeast, crossed the short bridge into the northern half of Stavelot, and moved west along the road toward Trois Ponts, spitting out gunfire as they went. José Gengoux, fourteen years old, was standing in his family's kitchen at 9:00 A.M. when a bullet hit him in the stomach and felled him. Joseph Alibert, who lived on the Trois Ponts road, had taken shelter in his basement. German soldiers entered his house, interrogated him about the whereabouts of the Americans, and shot him dead. M. and Mme. Lambert, also on the Trois Ponts road, were accosted by passing troops, and obliged to bring beer, wine, and cognac; he was shot and killed in return. On the 19th of December, as the long column continued into Trois Ponts, atrocities mounted. Five Germans entered the Georgin home, to find five people huddled there. The soldiers shot one of them, Louis Nicolay, and summoned M. Georgin outside to meet the same fate. But Georgin ran, made it to the river in a hail of bullets, and dove in. His arm was mangled by gunfire; it would be amputated three days later. The three souls left behind in the house during Georgin's escape—his wife and two members of the Nicolay family—were slaughtered, as were his neighbors, M. and Mme. Burnotte, Mme. Corbisier, and Oscar and Gustave Job—all shot with a bullet to the head.

What happened next was certainly conditioned by the military context. After the Germans had crossed the bridge at Stavelot and begun to move west toward Trois Ponts, the 117th Infantry Regiment of the U.S. 30th Division retook the town of Stavelot and blew up the bridge across the Amblève. This had the effect of cutting off supplies to Peiper's column coming up from the rear; and it also cut off Peiper's line of retreat. That was significant because farther down the line, at Trois Ponts, La Gleize, and Stoumont, all towns along the Amblève, Americans put up stiff resistance to Peiper's attack and managed to pen him in behind the Amblève. Peiper's column, bristling with tanks and soldiers, could not break out across the river or continue its advance westward. The fighting here was emerging as one of the most important engagements of the Battle of the Bulge: American resistance now formed a line that emerged as the northern shoulder of the "bulge." The Americans diverted the Germans away from Liège and into a narrow, compressed westward movement, making them vulnerable to counterattack. Peiper knew this perfectly well, which is why his soldiers fought like caged animals clawing for an exit; inevitably it was the local civilians that felt the sting of this fury.

On December 19, at about 8:00 P.M., twelve SS soldiers appeared in front of the Legaye house on the Trois Ponts road in Stavelot. Inside, twenty-six people huddled in the basement, where they had spent the previous night during the heavy fighting in the town. The Germans, who claimed that shots had been fired at them from the house, rousted out the civilians inside by throwing two grenades into the basement. Madame Regine Grégoire, who knew some German (she was originally from Manderfeld, right on the German border about twenty miles east of Stavelot), and her two children were among the group that now was herded into the garden of the Legaye house. Mme. Grégoire and her children were set to one side, perhaps because of their German ethnicity. The other twenty-three people, almost all women, children, and elderly, were lined up against a hedgerow. After an hour or so, two young SS soldiers drew their weapons and methodically shot them all in the head, using a pistol and rifle. Mme. Grégoire was told directly that the civilians, however innocent, must pay for the crimes of the guilty—presumably the alleged "terrorists" who had been shooting at the Germans. These were not isolated acts but part of a systematic campaign by Peiper's men to exact reprisals. In Parfondruy, a hamlet on the outskirts of Stavelot, a similar atrocity: a dozen women and young children were forced into a garage and shot dead. On December 19, in nearby Renardmont, twenty-one prisoners—nineteen men and two women, one of whom was seventy-five years old—were marched to the Legrand farm, gathered into the large washhouse there, and shot to death. The building was then set ablaze; miraculously one man, Achille André, survived to bear witness. But the owner of the farm, Marcel Legrand, suffered a bitter loss: he was hiding in his granary while the Germans were busy with their murderous activities. After dark, he emerged, only to find in his home the lifeless corpses of his mother-in-law, wife, and two children, aged five and eight. They had all been shot in the head. All told, in Stavelot and the neighboring hamlets during the period of December 17 to 23, about 130 civilians were murdered in cold blood by the soldiers of *Kampfgruppe* Peiper.[40]

IT IS RIGHT to insist that the brutal crimes of the Germans inflicted upon Belgian civilians be remembered, and condemned. What happened in Stavelot, and in Bande, where on December 24, thirty-four civilians were summarily shot, one by one, in the back of the head, ought to be held up as vivid testimony of the true nature of German soldiers.[41] Yet it must not be forgotten that in the Ardennes, as in all of Europe in 1944–45, the liberators also took many lives. This harvest of innocent life by the liberators was not malevolent, as the atrocities described above were. But it was deliberate, because the Allied leaders reluctantly accepted civilian deaths as part of the price to be paid for achieving victory. In Saint Vith, Houffalize, and a dozen other Belgian towns, the once-radiant face of liberation turned ugly, like a bruise.

Just to the south of the icy Amblève river, around Saint Vith, some of the heaviest fighting of the German offensive took place, which boded ill for the people of the town. The 18th and 62nd Volksgrenadier Divisions swallowed up two American infantry regiments on the opening day of the campaign and took thousands of prisoners; the German tanks then moved toward Saint Vith, beyond which lay the Salm river and the road to the Meuse. The Americans, pushed back from the original line of defense near Losheim, drew up an improvised defense around Saint Vith and formed a horseshoe-shaped defensive ring; but waves of German tanks swept down on the town and threatened to surround this salient. On the evening of the 22nd, the Americans began a planned withdrawal across the Salm river. The 106th Division, which had arrived in the line just two weeks earlier, full of green recruits, had been virtually wiped out; the 7th Armored Division had been badly mauled; overall, the Americans had suffered some 5,000 casualties in the Saint Vith sector. German soldiers stormed into Saint Vith hungry, cold, and exhausted; they pillaged the town for food, abandoned American rations, warm clothing, and valuables. The Americans at Saint Vith had successfully delayed the Germans and badly upset their timetable; but this was incontestably a defeat.[42]

These military events caused inevitable human tragedy for residents of Saint Vith. Although the town was in the German-speaking part of Belgium, few civilians there welcomed the return of the Germans. Young men feared either being shot as resistance fighters or enrolled into the German army. On December 16, when the battle began, Saint Vith was shelled by the Germans and this was the signal for many of the townspeople to flee. Those who did not were all but compelled to do so when, on December 25, the American Ninth Air Force bombed the town; one day later, the RAF followed suit. The town was set ablaze by the use of phosphorous bombs, and hundreds of residents were incinerated in their basement shelters. In the midst of battle, fleeing the town was no easy matter. The roads were under constant attack, and to the north, the forces of *Kampfgruppe* Peiper had closed off that escape route. Many refugees choked the road going west to Vielsalm and across the Salm river, adding to the tangled traffic jam of American units that were withdrawing. Mme. Elly Meurer of Saint Vith fled the town at the start of the battle, and wandered from farm to farm, sleeping among cattle in barns or basements amidst other despairing refugees. After walking in the bitter cold through heavy artillery and air bombardment, she and her sister took shelter in a disused railway tunnel a couple of miles outside Saint Vith. For over a month, they slept on the ground without blankets, drank melted snow, and managed to hold out until the Americans returned to town on January 24. When the Americans asked the ladies to tell them their story, "we couldn't," Mme. Meurer recalled. "We could not stop crying." These women stayed in the railway tunnel until February 8, chiefly because their town was uninhabitable. Saint Vith had been utterly crushed during the fighting. When Belgian authorities arrived in early February to survey the scene, they found that "the commune of St. Vith is totally destroyed. There is not a single building standing. . . . The area is completely empty of civilian inhabitants." Ominously, American military authorities had no information on the whereabouts of the population, and the Belgian High Commission for State Security urged that "an investigation should be undertaken immediately to determine the whereabouts of the residents of St. Vith." A town of 2,800 people had vanished. The mayor estimated that there were 400 civilian casualties (later studies suggest 250 townspeople died); and he reported that 200 people were living in "deplorable" conditions in the basements of a few buildings and the town's battered stone convent. They lacked everything: clothing, shoes, food, coal, or wood; medicine; even potable water. The U.S. Army opened a distribution point to give out dry rations to the few bedraggled civilians that turned up. Otherwise, Saint Vith had ceased to exist.[43]

Unlike Saint Vith, the town of Houffalize was given up without a fight. This small town on the Ourthe river had one main road through it, running north to Liège. Once the Germans punched through the weak U.S. line, Houffalize found itself right in the center of the bulge. With Liège to its north and Bastogne to its south, Houffalize became an important road junction. The Americans had too few troops to hold the town and pulled out on December 19; they would concentrate instead on defending Bastogne. German troops rolled in before dawn on December 20. Though the Germans were engaged in the greatest offensive in the western theater of operations since 1940, they still found the time to arrest and interrogate civilians suspected of resistance activity. Immediately upon their return to town, the Germans ordered the mayor, Joseph Maréchal, to round up all the former resistance members; he refused and, fearing for his own life, fled. But the Germans found documents naming many of the resistance members, who were then arrested, beaten, and murdered. On December 22–23, six suspected resistance members were arrested, interrogated, and shot. On December 24, the Germans killed two more, and on the 26th, three more.[44]

On Christmas day, the killing continued but now it came from the sky. American aircraft of the Ninth Air Force hit Houffalize, trying to destroy German armored units in the town and block road access through the town. But of course civilians paid a high price. The Christmas bombing took two civilian lives; the next day, in another raid, twenty-eight civilians died beneath U.S. bombs. On December 27, eight more civilians were killed. And this continued uninterrupted for almost thirty days. On the 28th, two more died; on the 29th, one; on the 30th, three; on the 31st, two. On each of the first five days of the new year, Allied bombs killed civilians in Houffalize. But it was the raid on January 6 that citizens of Houffalize recall as "atrocious, frightful, horrible, terrible, terrifying." On that day, 119 people were killed in a thirty-minute air raid by U.S. bombers, between 3:25 and 4:00 A.M. The civilian dead ranged in age from an eighty-five-year-old widow, Joséphine Martiny, to a three-year-old boy, Jacques Decker. This was not the last bombing run: on January 8, 9, 10, 12, 19, 20, and 29, more Houffalois died under Allied bombs. But the bulk of the population was by then either dead or in flight. During this month of fighting four members of the Bollet family were killed; five members of the Delme family died, and six of the Dubru family. The entire Hoffman family—father, mother, and four children—was wiped out. Joseph Maréchal, the mayor, returned to his village to find his own family dead beneath the ruins. In all, 192 people died in this small town during the Battle of the Bulge. Twenty-seven of the victims were under the age of fifteen. Of these 192 people, all but eight died at the hands of their liberators.[45]

When Belgian investigators arrived in late January to assess the damage to the town, only 130 people remained of a population of 1,325. Most of them were living, in glacial cold, in the vaulted basement of the rectory. They had nothing: no food, shelter, medicine, clothing. "One cannot say enough," wrote one reporter, "about how these people have suffered." There were not even any cattle or pigs left alive in the town; what livestock the Germans had not pillaged or butchered, the bombs had killed. Hundreds of bodies were unburied, many of them beneath rubble; four shelters with dozens of townspeople in them had been hit on January 6, and those corpses had yet to be uncovered. Although the mayor called for immediate help to recover the

Townspeople of Houffalize, Belgium, return to their homes to inspect the damage done by the fighting there. *U.S. National Archives*

dead, they lay unburied in the ruins for over a month. The aid crews lacked the heavy equipment to pull away the rubble and debris.[46] General Omar Bradley, who had ordered the destruction of the town, wrote later with some regret about it: "Simple, poor, and unpretentious, the village had offended no one. Yet it was destroyed simply because it sat astride an undistinguished road junction."[47] A shockingly honest assessment.

Sometimes, civilians died because Allied air forces were criminally sloppy. Just a few miles to the east of Stavelot, in Malmédy, American aircraft mistakenly bombed both their own soldiers and civilians by accident not just once but three times. On December 23, Malmédy was hit by B-26 Marauder bombers; on the 24th, it was hit by the ill-named B-24 "Liberator" bombers; and on the 25th, another flight of B-26s pounded the town—all mistakenly. In addition to killing 37 American soldiers who were among the heavy presence defending the town, Allied bombers killed 202 civilians: 129 from Malmédy and 73 refugees from other towns. The city was set on fire; the water pumps were either broken by the shelling or frozen and thus useless in containing the blaze. Among the dead civilians were five members of the Anselme family, including two-year-old Jean; five members of the Delhasse family; six members of the Gohimont family; and seven members of the Melchior family. Maria Renier lost her twelve-year-old daughter, Anny, when, on Christmas Eve, a 250-pound bomb from a "Liberator" landed on her house. The girl's body was laid out on a stretcher in the freezing cold, spattered with mud, clothed in a colorful woolen jacket she had made. Her mother recalled "that she loved to knit; she had put it on for Christmas." The town of Malmédy put out a small brochure to commemorate the mistaken Christmas bombing. It concluded, with some restraint: "It was a Christmas unlike any other; in truth, it was a Christmas in hell."[48]

Despite the calamity at Malmédy, civilians were usually safe when their towns were held by American troops. Thus Bastogne, the famous redoubt where the Americans held out against German encirclement, was not heavily bombed by air, making it survivable for civilians who were well sheltered in the caves of the town's stone buildings. To be sure, the city was shelled relentlessly by the German divisions that desperately wanted to take this stubbornly defended town, and residents spent anxious nights in darkness and cold. But according to one report on liberated Bastogne in late January, the health of the 1,200 remaining residents (out of a preinvasion population of 5,000) was good, and only twenty people had been killed in the fighting for the town.[49] The real damage done in the Ardennes came when American troops and aircraft were turned upon towns that had to be retaken from the Germans—a reminder that death always precedes liberation. Just three miles south of Bastogne, the town of Sainlez was seized by the Germans on December 20. It lay directly on the road between Bastogne and Arlon, along which the 4th Armored Division of Patton's Third Army would stage its famous thrust north in relief of Bastogne. On Christmas Eve the town, then in German hands, was leveled by American air bombardment, using phosphorous bombs that set the town ablaze. By the time the Americans retook this village, on December 27, it was a mere smoking pile of rubble. "Only" twenty or so inhabitants were killed. But among these twenty were eight members of the Didier family, whose house took a direct hit: Joseph Didier, forty-six years old; Marie-Angéla, sixteen; Alice, fifteen; Renée, thirteen; Lucile, eleven; Bernadette, nine; Lucien, eight; and Noël, six years old. For a small village like Sainlez, such a loss had an apocalyptic quality to it, a moment of confrontation with the eternal and the unknown. At a memorial service for the victims, a local religious instructor, M. Albert Boeur, spoke with heartrending tenderness about the events of Christmas 1944 in Sainlez. "At the very moment when so many Christians were singing before the crèche in their churches, Joseph Didier, a fervent Christian, departed for eternity with his seven cherubs . . . How difficult it is to penetrate the designs of the Lord! But ladies and gentlemen," he continued, in words that could have been uttered in thousands of villages across Europe,

> let us honor the memory of our dead, victims of the bombing; let us not cry for them in vain but let us pray for them and invoke their names; they are martyrs who will aid us to bear in a Christian manner the hardships we have suffered. They will not have the happiness to celebrate with us the victory that is now at hand; but they will celebrate it in Heaven, more pure and more beautiful. As for us, families cruelly tested—husbands and wives, parents and children, brothers and sisters of our victims, let your tears flow; they are justified. Then recover your courage and recall that your dead ones are still at your side, their eyes— full of glory—gaze into your eyes, full of tears. . . . Dear departed, victims of this catastrophe of December, rest in peace, in eternal peace in close union with the all-powerful God that you served throughout your lives. Goodbye![50]

DURING THE CATASTROPHIC fighting in the winter of 1944–45, Belgians rarely rebuked the American military forces for the damage and destruction they caused. Civilians knew that the Germans were the cause of their afflictions and that the Americans, however clumsily, had come to free the country from the rapacious invaders. To this day, dozens of memorials and tributes to fallen American soldiers dot the Belgian countryside, and are tended reverentially by local groups. This has something to do with the work that the Americans undertook once they returned to these small rural towns in the Ardennes. Consider one small case. In La Roche, a town about ten miles west of Houffalize that was overrun by the Germans in mid-December, repeatedly bombed by the Americans, and finally liberated on January 19, the returning U.S. forces found a town in a state of total collapse. Yet Americans went to work to tackle the health and sanitation problems of the civilians still in the village. Major Edward O'Donnell of Detachment E1G2, Company G, 2nd ECA Regiment, of the First Army's G-5 section, traveled to La Roche to evaluate the recovery work. He found that 50 percent of the buildings had been destroyed; about 200 civilian and 100 German bodies still lay trapped beneath the rubble of the town, unburied and rotting; there was no municipal water or sewage; water was obtained from a stream running through town; and of 1,200 civilians there, 400 had chronic diarrhea. Yet the 24th Cavalry Reconnaissance Squadron was feeding 190 people three meals a day, working with the Belgian Red Cross to assure steady supplies. The Belgian government had also sent a detachment of nurses, trained rescue personnel, an ambulance, and quantities of medical supplies into the town. Two nurses had made house-to-house calls with a DDT sprayer, delousing the inhabitants. About 100 children under ten still in the town were eligible for extra rations of canned milk and bread. American soldiers from the 298th Combat Engineers were busily setting up a water purification and pumping station. And La Roche was no anomaly: this sort of work was going on in dozens of other villages and towns, both during and after the Battle of the Bulge. Having done so much to destroy, Americans proved more than willing to begin the work of repair and recovery.[51]

Yet this picture of hardworking relief efforts must be placed against other, less appealing images left by American and British soldiers, especially in the larger cities. At precisely the same moment as American soldiers and Belgian relief workers were toiling in the rubble of La Roche, General Erskine, the chief of the SHAEF mission to Belgium, received a disturbing appeal from the head of the Belgian High Commission for State Security, Advocate General Walter Ganshof. "It is my duty to acquaint you with the fact that from all parts of the country where the American and British troops have been in action, innumerable complaints are being made by the population on the looting which is going on," Ganshof wrote. "The Belgian population is as you know extremely grateful to the Allied Forces for having been liberated by them. They realize, no doubt, the extremely difficult conditions in which these forces are now fighting. . . . I feel nevertheless that if the troops realized better the appalling distress of the populations in the regions in which fighting has been going on lately, they would undoubtedly avoid some unnecessary looting, destruction and wastage of items vital to the populations." Ganshof said he had received many reports of American units "destroying or wasting great quantities of food in front of local populations. Tins of fats and other ingredients vital to the people are being thrown away half filled, after having been spoiled. . . . In the very distressing state of the population, this creates of course an extremely unfavorable impression."[52]

Unfortunately, as High Commissioner Ganshof knew well, these were not the first such reports, nor were the incidents limited to the battlefield. Back behind the lines, numerous Allied troops had been causing public disturbances, getting drunk and disorderly, robbing, raping, and thieving their way across Brussels, Liège, Namur, Charleroi, Antwerp, and just about every other town where they were stationed. One charge sheet in the archives of the High Commission shows a complaint was lodged against Allied troops in Brussels on almost every day since September 11, 1944, when the first troops had rolled into Belgium. Some of these offenses were predictable and fairly minor: drinking, fighting, breaking furniture and windows in cafés and bars, brawling. But some were serious: armed robbery, theft of watches and rings, wallets and clothing, and of course rape.[53] The frequency of such reports of Allied misbehavior picked up significantly following the winter fighting. One local study suggests that Liège became, after May 1945, "a veritable cauldron of banditry," with soldiers involved in armed holdups, theft of valuables and money from passersby, and frequent public disorders like breaking café windows. The Liège press increasingly used the term "gangsters" in its reporting about U.S. soldiers in the city, while in Brussels itself, women raised constant complaints about the public behavior of American soldiers, who spoke rudely to them, assaulted them, and pursued them relentlessly in hopes of initiating sexual contact.[54]

In the war-ravaged eastern part of the country, Belgians bitterly complained about the quantity and quality of supplies the Americans enjoyed, and compared this abundance to their own destitution. "In many localities damaged by the recent invasion, a chill has set in between the civilian population and the American Army," one report for the High Commission for State Security concluded. The Americans were accused of wasting their own precious food stocks while requisitioning Belgian homes and supplies, and leaving them ruined and broken—a veritable second invasion. "It is not rare to hear it said that during the German occupation, there was not such wanton destruction," according to a report in mid-February. "If the situation is not remedied immediately, the great majority of people will turn away from the allies, who will thereafter enjoy only the favor of the prostitutes."[55] Business owners complained to Belgian government officials that the American Army was recruiting laborers at higher wages than they could match, usually to work in mines whose coal was to be used for military purposes. But the workers too complained of the poor treatment they received at the hands of American military overseers. "They treat us like convicts," said one, while others spoke of being subjected to constant body searches to look for pilfered American goods. Workers, wrote one observer, "have developed a distinctly unfriendly attitude toward our American allies." One of the most persistent rumors passed along by Belgians was that the U.S. Army was stockpiling huge warehouses of luxury goods that were soon to be dumped on the Belgian market, earning windfall profits for the liberators. Despite a number of official investigations into this rumor, no organized plot was uncovered. Yet the widespread black market was awash in ladies' toilet articles, soap, underwear, chocolates, fruits, candies, cigarettes, sewing scissors, and dozens of hard-to-find articles that the Army had shipped to the continent. One official noted that in a warehouse in Morlanwelz he had seen fifty cubic meters of crates filled with nothing but playing cards—a million decks of cards, he calculated. Though the High Commission made a "discreet *démarche*" to SHAEF about these complaints, little was done. The High Commissioner's brother, François Ganshof, who had been recruited to work on fact-finding missions on the Commission's behalf, wrote in despair over the huge increase in anti-American sentiments that was breaking out across the country. "I am more and more worried," he wrote to the prime minister's office, "by the deplorable state of opinion that I have observed."[56]

As important as these criticisms were, the chief area of contention between Belgians and the Allies was sex, and the role the liberators should play in determining the morals and public health of liberated territory. The site on which this debate played out was, quite literally, women's bodies, and the problem on which the debate converged was that old scourge of men in uniform, venereal disease (chiefly syphilis and gonorrhea). "The incidence of VD among allied troops deployed in Belgium has recently reached such disquieting proportions as to merit the issue of a special order on the subject by the Commander in Chief himself," wrote the deputy commander of SHAEF's mission in Belgium in December 1944, and the picture worsened through-

A romantic tryst between liberator and liberated.
U.S. Army

out the year. Figures gathered by the U.S. Army show that by June 1945, roughly 15 percent—about half a million—of all the American soldiers in continental Europe had some form of VD.[57] This, on a continent that already had abnormally high civilian VD rates. The problem had become so serious that it compromised "effective conduct of military operations." But what solution did SHAEF propose to stop their men from getting VD? One obvious answer was to stop soldiers from having sex with prostitutes, and SHAEF declared brothels "out of bounds." Yet SHAEF's public health branch did not stop there. The Civil Affairs public health authorities believed that the real culprit in spreading VD were the prostitutes working their trade by themselves, in alleys, cafés, and taverns "of doubtful character." These women, therefore, must bear the principal burden of ensuring that their bodies were free of VD. The Allied soldier, in this configuration, bore no responsibility, and indeed, the Army had in September 1944 prevailed upon the U.S. Congress to repeal a law that punished soldiers who contracted VD. The War Department argued that the law had no deterrent value and if anything only encouraged a soldier to be silent about his symptoms. Thus, Army policy was premised on the assumption that men would seek sex at all times, in all possible venues, and so the best curb on VD was to close brothels, distribute condoms, institute rigorous inspection of any women suspected to be involved in the sex trade, and encourage immediate and penalty-free treatment for soldiers who might contract VD.[58] SHAEF drew up a draft decree for Belgium concerning prostitution and VD that it presented to the Belgian government for passage into law. Prostitutes, according to the proposed law, must register at the town hall in their neighborhood, present three photographs, obtain a license, provide names of all cafés in which they sought customers, submit to biweekly medical examinations, and, if infected, agree to detention at a clinic for whatever period of time the doctor prescribed. Furthermore, any woman alleged to be a prostitute by an Allied soldier could be forced to undergo a medical examination immediately. Finally, proprietors of cafés and bars where prostitutes regularly worked were liable to heavy fines and penalties.[59]

Despite "very energetic representations" by SHAEF authorities, the Belgian government refused to accept the decree. It was considered far too intrusive. In its place, the government offered an alternative law that placed the burden for curtailing the spread of VD on the infected man, and in particular, on his doctor. The Belgian law focused on the behavior of the "consumer," as it were, declaring that "every person who exhibits the symptoms of venereal disease is required to have himself treated by a doctor of his choice." The doctor was then obliged to report the infection and the date and location when the infection occurred; but he did not have to report the name of the infected man. The inspector of health must "use every discretion" but he could, if necessary, commit the infected man to a hospital. In any case, the expenses would be borne by the patient—a serious disincentive to go to the doctor in the first place. Any man who had sexual relations while knowingly carrying an infection would be subject to imprisonment and fines. The Belgian law failed to discuss the issue of prostitution at all, and placed the burden of curtailing sexually transmitted diseases on men rather than on women who sold sex for money. Why did the Belgian law make no mention of brothels, and indeed, why did Belgians prefer to see soldiers use a *maison tolerée* to appease their sexual appetites? The reason became clear in a series of exchanges, both public and private, during February and March 1945 when Belgian health officials demanded that SHAEF close the Army dancing clubs where soldiers were permitted to entertain female guests. These centers were chaperoned and although plenty of alcohol was available, military police were never far; Belgian girls frequented these halls to meet and socialize with soldiers who could offer them drinks, music, cigarettes, attention, and perhaps some light romance. Yet precisely because these clubs attracted nice middle class girls, Belgian officials saw them as a serious threat to the overall health of the female public. It was assumed that Allied soldiers, having been banned from brothels, would naturally seek sexual contact with the nice girls at the dance clubs. Far better, the Belgian health authorities reasoned, if the brothels remained open so that soldiers could satisfy their desires among the known prostitutes in recognized brothels, which were perfectly legal. If men contracted VD, they could find a doctor to cure them. Brothels, in the mind of the Belgian government, offered a buffer zone between soldiers and good Belgian girls; if men could be diverted into the houses of "doubtful character," the purity of the clean Belgian female body could be preserved.[60]

The Belgian government's approach to the VD problem, as a public health measure, left much to be desired. Allied experience in southern Italy in 1944 had shown that closing brothels, cracking down on clandestine prostitution, and insisting that soldiers with VD be treated not by local doctors but within the Army, where they could be monitored, worked effectively to contain the spread of VD.[61] In Belgium, by contrast, VD rates soared in 1944–45 precisely because soldiers were having sex with many partners in an uncontrolled environment with little regulation of prostitution. But the legal tussle over the issue sheds light on a key theme of liberation: that Belgians saw their liberated territory, its social and moral values, and indeed its young bearers of feminine virtue, as vulnerable to subversion by foreign occupation. Soldiers, one report declared, had brought to Belgium "morals [*moeurs*] to which we are not accustomed." In mid-March 1945, over a dozen mayors around Verviers, a town near Liège with a heavy foreign troop concentration, signed a public appeal, aimed not at the soldiers but at Belgian youth, especially girls. "This spring," it began, "our young people face great dangers. We do not refer to the youths who have rallied to the flag and responded to the call of their country, for whom to die in battle would be a great honor. Rather, [we refer to] the youth that have been seized by a frenzy of pleasure. While so many others suffer on the battlefield or in the deportation camps, these young people have thrown themselves into a sentimental adventure where they risk losing their moral dignity and physical health." The appeal praised the "valiant young boys who have brought us liberty," but asked parents if they did not fear that their "young, impressionistic girls were being manipulated by the prestige of the uniform." The mayors chided in particular the young girls of the area who, they felt, were too eager to consort with Allied soldiers:

> Young ladies, so sure of yourselves, do you not fear that your example will lead others into weakness? . . . Do you not know that the road along which Victory has traveled passed through North Africa, from which these unfortunate diseases have come? . . . Do you know that the [Army] rest camp in our area has attracted women by the hundreds who are the waste of the great cities, and who by avoiding any medical surveillance are spreading these diseases? Do you know that in Verviers, many of your peers, after having strayed just once, have already been obliged to submit to emergency treatments, which are as horrible as they are indispensable? Remember, young girls, the essential mission for the future of our race which you bear: the mission to represent our people proudly before our allies! For one hour of abandon, do not stain your conscience with painful and often hereditary "stigmata" . . . The time of national recovery is at hand. No nation can revive unless it has a youth that is healthy in its body and its soul.[62]

The notion that American soldiers were vectors of "North African" diseases stirred up vigorous and outraged protests from SHAEF officials, who remonstrated with the local mayors.[63] Yet the truth was that VD, along with prostitution, crime, smuggling, violence, and mayhem, closely accompanied the hundreds of thousands of Allied soldiers in Belgium; civilian leaders believed their behavior placed the moral and physical health of the country in jeopardy. It is no accident that the appeal of the mayors explicitly linked the recovery of the nation with the physical health of young girls: these bearers of national virtue would have to be protected, perhaps liberated, from promiscuous, drunken, profligate, demanding liberators.

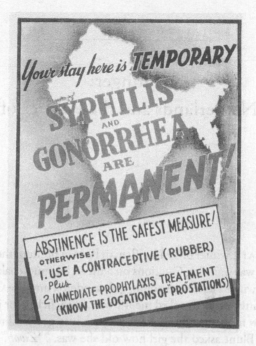

A U.S. Army poster cautioning soldiers about the risks of venereal disease. *U.S. National Archives*

This is quite different from saying that Belgians were ungrateful for their liberation, or that they preferred the Germans to the Americans—a charge that some American soldiers leveled at them. Rather, Belgian complaints remind us how unsettling, violent, and dynamic the entire process of liberation was at the close of World War II. Liberation in Belgium had brought death and destruction, the annihilation of cities, the creation of refugees, the bombing of small rural villages and their occupants; and it had opened the way to a social threat from the weary, sex-starved, and perhaps emotionally scarred Allied soldiers. Given the trauma of war and liberation in Belgium, it is not surprising that the people of this now war-shattered country simply wanted to be left alone. Belgium had been invaded in 1940 by the Germans, in 1944 by the Americans and British, and again in 1944 by the Germans. Thirty thousand Belgian civilians died as a result of these events. The war over, Belgians wished to heal, to recover some sense of national independence and dignity. It is all too easy to understand why a local police commissioner in September 1945 found that in his part of the country, the common phrase on the lips of all the citizens was simply, "O Lord, deliver us from our liberators."[64]

3

Hunger:
The Netherlands and the Politics of Food

IN THE LATE winter of 1944, rifleman Roscoe Blunt of the 84th Infantry Division was warming C-rations on a fire in his mud-soaked campsite in the Dutch town of Heerlen. A young girl wandered into the GI's compound "and then matter-of-factly asked me if I wanted to 'ficken' or just 'kuszen.' It took me a few moments for my brain to click into gear and realize what she was asking." Blunt asked the girl how old she was. " '*Zwolf*,' she whispered passionately."[1]

It was not uncommon in the winter of 1944 to see Dutch children like this twelve-year-old girl fighting over the trash pails where the GIs threw their uneaten rations, or offering sex in exchange for food. And in the spring of 1945, the picture in the Netherlands only worsened. The Allied armies that had dashed through northern France and Belgium in August arrived on Holland's doorstep in early September, but then failed to drive the Germans out of the country. Only a small slice of southern Holland was freed from German control, and the rest of the country, including the main cities of Amsterdam, the Hague, and Rotterdam, remained under occupation until the end of the war. Although the Allied armies periodically launched attacks on the German lines in Holland—the First Canadian Army fought bitterly there—the ugly truth is that the liberation of northwestern Holland was simply not a strategic priority for the Allies. The Anglo-American armies hit the Germans along the Siegfried Line in Belgium and France, and in spring 1945 pushed eastward into Germany proper. This left a large contingent of German soldiers effectively cut off in Holland, though still in command of much of the country. A gruesome sideshow ensued: the doomed German occupiers pursued a policy of vengeance against the citizens of the Netherlands, and deliberately allowed them to starve.

During the late winter and early spring of 1945, when life had revived in liberated Brussels and Paris, northwest Holland was a lifeless zone of darkness and hunger, a pitiful encampment of skeletal children and cadaverous people, surviving on tulip bulbs and beets. The Dutch people's deliverance did not come until the collapse of the Third Reich itself, by which time some 16,000 people had died of starvation in what had been one of the richest, most intensively cultivated countries in Europe. When the Canadian and British troops did finally enter the main cities in early May, they were of course greeted warmly, and many soldiers thought at first glance that the Dutch people seemed to have survived on their meager rations. But that was because the desperately ill were not among the crowds. As Major-General J. G. W. Clark, the head of the SHAEF mission in the Netherlands, put it tartly in a memo to London, "men and women who are slowly dying in their beds of starvation unfortunately cannot walk gaily about the streets waving flags."[2]

THE GERMANS OCCUPIED the country on May 10, 1940; but they never decided precisely what to do with the Dutch. After the conquest of the country, Queen Wilhelmina and the Dutch government removed to London and established a Dutch government-in-exile—one of the many castaway cabinets then crowding into Britain. Despite ongoing surrender talks with the remaining Dutch military authorities, the Germans bombed Rotterdam on May 14, gutting the city center and killing 900 people. There could be no doubt of the brutality the Germans intended to visit upon the Dutch if they did not yield immediately. They did so, and a curtain of suffering was drawn over the country for the next five years. The country presented the Germans with a tricky problem: how to treat a people so racially, linguistically, and culturally similar to the Aryan ideal. Hitler, typically, let his deputies fight the issue out among themselves. The Reichskommissariat Niederlande (Netherlands Reich Commissariat) was headed by Arthur Seyss-Inquart, who was, like Hitler, an Austrian. He had been a central figure in manipulating Austrian affairs to allow for Hitler to seize that country in the 1938 Anschluss and incorporate Austria into the German Reich. Hitler later appointed Seyss-Inquart as deputy governor general in occupied Poland, where he gladly engaged in the ghettoization of Jews. In May 1940, he was sent to run the defeated Netherlands. Seyss-Inquart wished to preserve some degree of autonomy for Holland while squeezing it for every last bit of materiel it could provide to the insatiable German war effort. He approved the delegation of certain powers to the collaborationist Nationaal-Socialistische Beweging der Nederlanden (Dutch National Socialist Movement), headed by the Dutchman Anton Mussert, and which claimed a membership of 50,000 by 1940. Seyss-Inquart would have been content to govern the Netherlands essentially as a colonized fiefdom of the German Reich. By contrast, the SS commander and police chief in Holland, Hanns Albin Rauter, another Austrian Nazi, envisioned a direct form of rule that annexed and incorporated Holland into Germany, removing any vestiges of Dutch identity and independence. The two rivals never came to a common understanding, and in fact worked at cross purposes for much of the war.[3]

As a practical matter, these doctrinal differences at the top had little meaning for the Dutch people, who suffered under an increasingly burdensome and interfering German occupation. Virtually all aspects of life in the country fell under German control. Access to food was controlled through rationing cards; the radio, press, political parties, and labor unions were all given over to collaborationists. The country was ransacked: factories were dismantled and shipped into Germany. Metals, clothing, textiles, bicycles, food and produce, cattle and livestock, all were sucked into the German war machine. Curfews governed civilian freedom of movement; tens of thousands of people were forcibly moved from coastal towns where the Germans erected massive fortifications. Four hundred thousand people were shipped into Germany, where they were compelled to work for the German war effort. And of course the Germans targeted Jews. In June 1942, the Germans began a systematic deportation of Dutch Jews, managing in the end to find and murder 105,000 of the 140,000 Jews in Holland at the start of the war: a higher percentage than any western European country.[4]

A significant number of Dutch people participated in some form of resistance to German rule, though this was rarely militant, armed resistance. The Order Service grouped former army officers together and had the favor of the government in exile; the Council of Resistance directed sabotage and espionage in close cooperation with the British secret service; and a national association for assistance to the many *onderduikers*—those who "dived under," or went into hiding—served as a way station for false documents, transport, and funds. Unfortunately, the Dutch resistance was totally penetrated by German counterintelligence, which was able to stymie all major sabotage activities between 1942 and 1944. Yet a much broader, national resistance did develop in daily life, which manifested itself through a vigorous underground press, an active counterfeiting of ration cards and identity papers, a network of aid to those in hiding, and periodic strikes. These strikes in particular could be a serious nuisance to the occupation authorities and tended to provoke the ire of the Germans. A nationwide strike in February 1941 in response to initial roundups of Jews in Amsterdam led to the execution of seventeen Dutch people. In April 1943, another nationwide strike was called in response to German arrests of former Dutch POWs who had already been released; 150 Dutch people were killed by the Germans in savage reprisals.

By the start of 1944, living conditions in Holland had become nearly intolerable. The Dutch economy had been stripped bare and the only available food were potatoes, mealy bread, and beets. Children were beginning to show signs of malnutrition while diseases like diphtheria and typhus had begun to break out. The Germans flooded large swaths of the country in anticipation of an Allied invasion, and Allied bombing of dykes also devastated thousands of acres, taking still more land out of cultivation. The resistance occasionally carried out successful operations against the occupiers, and badly wounded Hanns Rauter himself in a March 1945 assassination attempt; but the reprisals for such acts took a ghastly toll. The Germans killed 250 Dutch prisoners in response to the attack on Rauter, and constantly shot hostages in reply to Dutch sabotage. Death also came from the skies, inevitably. One report from within occupied Holland in June 1944 said that the people were "becoming increasingly anti-American and anti-British because of the reckless air bombardment."[5] The Netherlands Red Cross begged the British to reconsider their air assaults on cities. A report in April 1944 gave a grim tally of damage and destruction, including the attack on Nijmegen on February 22 that "left one-third of the centre of the town in ruins," killed 500 civilians and injured several hundred. "One school was completely wiped out, and all the children and those in charge of them perished. Several churches and historic buildings were reduced to rubble and ashes," the Red Cross reported. To this, British Foreign Minister Anthony Eden laconically replied, "I fear loss of life and damage to property and cultural monuments are inevitable. It is part of the price of liberation."[6] But liberation seemed a long way off: in May 1944, one source concluded a gloomy report on conditions in Holland with these words: "If the British could see how things are in Holland, they would hurry up. It simply cannot last much longer."[7]

In early September, the Allies were strung out along the Dutch-Belgian border and it seemed a matter of days before the country would be liberated. On September 17, the day that the Allies launched Operation Market Garden, flooding the skies over Nijmegen and Arnhem with paratroopers, liberation appeared at hand. The Dutch government in London ordered a nationwide railway strike on the same day in an effort to snarl German military movements and cut off rail traffic. But the airborne invasion failed to achieve the Rhine crossing that had been hoped for, and only a small patch of southern Holland was in Allied hands. The Allied armies turned their attention eastward, away from Holland and into Germany proper. It would be months before the Allies fought their way northward, across the watery fingers of the Maas, Waal, and Rhine rivers. In retaliation for the Dutch strikes, Seyss-Inquart placed an embargo on all food imports into the German-held areas. This marked the start of the gravest period of the war for the Netherlands.

Even before the war, Holland had relied on imported food to feed its larger cities, and even imported fodder to feed its livestock. The importing of food ceased in 1940, after the German invasion, and the Germans had been busy stripping the country bare since then. Between May 1940 and September 1944, all the produce from 60 percent of Holland's arable land was sent directly to Germany. Shortages of fertilizer, farm machinery, and of course men to work the fields—many had been sent into Germany as labor—left the country unable to produce sufficient food, and teetering on disaster by the fall of 1944. From 1940 on, the Dutch authorities rationed what food was available. The German food embargo now pushed the country over the edge. Potatoes and bread were severely rationed; sugar beets had to be used to make foul-tasting mash that was served at soup kitchens; nasty and unsatisfying alternatives like tulip bulbs could be found on the black market at exorbitant prices. As winter closed in on 3.6 million souls in occupied Holland, it looked as if a gigantic national tragedy was about to unfold.

———

ON SEPTEMBER 28, just a few days after the obvious failure of Market Garden, Dutch Prime Minister Pieter S. Gerbrandy, directing the government-in-exile in London, cabled a desperate appeal to Winston Churchill that set the tone for Anglo-Dutch communications over the next nine months:

> I have the honor to bring to your attention that most alarming tidings have reached Her Majesty and the Netherlands Cabinet regarding the deplorable situation which has arisen in the Netherlands. . . . Many railway strikers and members of the resistance movement have been and are being executed, and the strongest reprisals are being taken against members of their families. Starvation in the big cities—the term is not too strong—is imminent. Destruction of port installations, wharves, factories, power plants, bridges, etc., is being carried out by the Germans on a very extensive scale. I should be most grateful if you would give me an opportunity in the near future of discussing this matter with you.[8]

The British government, which in Allied planning documents had claimed both Belgium and the Netherlands as "British spheres of influence," now faced the serious problem of what to do about the possible death by starvation of millions of people in Holland.[9] Churchill and Gerbandy met at 10 Downing Street on October 5, and it was a difficult meeting indeed. Gerbrandy wanted to relate the details of Germany's scorched-earth strategy in Holland in the face of probable defeat by the Allies. Churchill tried to assuage Gerbrandy with promises that after the war, Germany would be forced to offer restitution, as well as forced labor to rebuild the country; Holland might even annex some parts of Germany, Churchill suggested. But Gerbrandy persisted, and painted an apocalyptic scenario. "The Germans were no longer feeding the Dutch," he said, and instead were looting the country's food supplies. "Leiden was now out of food, and Amsterdam would have no more food by October 24th. In an emergency," Gerbrandy went on, "people could exist for longer than they supposed. He was prepared to say that Western Holland could continue to live somehow until December 1st, but this was the limit, after which the people of Western Holland would die of starvation. Was there a chance of Western Holland being liberated by that date?" If not, Gerbrandy wondered if Churchill would agree to allowing the Swedish government to intervene and negotiate some kind of food transport, through the British bloackade of the continent, into Holland. Churchill was not moved. "Any food admitted to Holland would directly or indirectly nourish the Germans, who were themselves short of food and ammunition," Churchill said. Besides, he thought "that there was a very good chance that western Holland would be liberated before December 1st."[10]

Gerbrandy went away dispirited, but he and his colleagues pressed the British government on multiple fronts. Two days earlier, the Dutch ambassador had met with Sir Alexander Cadogan, the permanent undersecretary for foreign affairs, and told him that the Swedish government was in fact prepared to send some food supplies into Holland provided that both the Germans and the British agreed to ensure safe passage of the relief ships. The minister for economic warfare, Lord Selborne, also received the Dutch ambassador, and was given a detailed report on the food shortages. According to the Dutch government's assessment, stocks of bread grains would run out by the end of October; the occupied territories had but three weeks of potatoes left; there was no milk; and most calamitous, the military operations in the south had disrupted coal shipments into the cities, so that the gas and electric works, as well as bakeries and factories, could not function. Coal stocks would be gone by mid-October, Dutch sources reported. The country was on the verge of total collapse. The only hope was immediate aid through

Sweden, or even food drops by plane into occupied Holland. "There will be a famine after mid-October," the Dutch report concluded.[11]

Unlike Churchill, the British Chiefs of Staff as well as the Foreign Office had no real objection to the proposal to allow the Swedes to assist the Dutch people, provided that the plan in no way interfered with General Eisenhower's military operations. The Chiefs recognized that one Swedish ship could scarcely carry sufficient quantities of materials for 3.5 million people, but it would be a humanitarian mission they could hardly oppose. General

Eisenhower concurred. On October 29, he informed the War Department and the British military authorities that "on the grounds of humanity, relief from neutral sources through International Red Cross . . . should if possible be arranged without delay, if the German government can be persuaded to agree." Eisenhower said he knew that some of the supplies might be pilfered by the Germans "but I accept this risk. Any assistance to the Dutch civil population that can be provided before the liberation will ease the relief problem subsequent to liberation."[12] On November 2, Britain's top military officials, meeting at a conference of the Chiefs of Staff, agreed that allowing a Swedish ship into Amsterdam was acceptable and raised no military objections. Yet they did oppose any airdrops of food directly into Holland because it was not possible to arrange safe conduct for the British aircraft involved, "and there could be no guarantee that the supplies would reach the civil population—in fact the probability is quite the reverse." No less significant, the British and American military authorities rejected any possibility of letting Red Cross ships travel down the Rhine from Switzerland to Holland, which the Dutch had asked for and which the Germans had agreed to. Eisenhower refused outright. He said his war plan called for the bombing of bridges over the Rhine. Moreover, he claimed that "the prompt manner in which the Germans agreed to allow supplies to move on the Rhine is actuated, we believe, by their desire to keep the river open for their own purposes."[13]

The various constraints thrown up by the military planners kept the Swedish relief operation small: in late January, two ships, the *Noreg* and the *Dagmar Bratt*, delivered 3,000 tons of flour, margarine, and cod-liver oil to Delfzyl in northeast Holland. From there, the food was delivered south on barges through the canal network. These initial shiploads created a great boost for the morale of the hungry Dutch. Yet by April, the Swedes had been able to deliver only 20,000 tons of food and supplies: extremely welcome, but not nearly sufficient to avert catastrophe. Prime Minister Gerbrandy had hoped these deliveries would be just the start of an expanded relief convoy system from Sweden. The British Chiefs of Staff, however, did not wish to see a limited relief supply turn into a regular operation. On February 14, the Chiefs of Staff concluded that a relief convoy using the Kiel Canal would become a serious obstacle to military operations: it would force the Allies to restrict mining of the canal and to redirect air bombing. Further, the Chiefs believed the Germans would essentially use the Swedish vessels as minesweepers, sending naval vessels in behind the civilian relief convoys. They therefore objected to any regular relief scheme for occupied Holland.[14]

The issue was not easily dismissed, however. Mounting evidence of the humanitarian crisis inside occupied Holland began to accumulate in London, and the issue became a highly charged one. Queen Wilhelmina herself wrote to Churchill and President Roosevelt in mid-January, imploring that something be done for occupied Holland now, before liberation, in order to avoid "a major catastrophe the like of which has not been seen since the Middle Ages." In early February, Sir Jack Drummond, a professor of bio-chemistry at the University of London who was gathering information in Holland for the British government, sent an alarming report to the Ministry of Food in which he described "a critical situation in west and northwest Holland. Amsterdam, Rotterdam, and the Hague appear to be reduced to practically starvation level and 500 to 800 calories a day. There has been a typhoid epidemic in Amsterdam and diphtheria in Rotterdam." Drummond believed that "if it is not alleviated quickly thousands are likely to die directly or indirectly from starvation. At this level of nutrition the normal human being could not live for more than two or three months." This crisis now had major political ramifications: Could the British government really stand by as thousands dropped dead of starvation? And did the potential deaths of so many people require a rethinking of Allied war strategy, one that would give a higher priority to the liberation of northwest Holland than to the battles in the Rhineland, on Germany's flank? Queen Wilhelmina certainly thought so, and demanded immediate "military action for the purpose of driving the Germans out of Holland."[15]

The problem of how to approach the relief of the starving people of occu-pied Holland became closely tied up with the troubles in the southern, liber-ated portion of the country. There too a severe food shortage had become a serious political issue. The Dutch press had become increasingly critical of the Allied occupiers in January 1945, as mountains of food and supplies flowed to the ravenous armies on the front, while the Dutch people went without. The food issue had become "the burning question" for the Dutch, and "the people in the liberated territory have become more critical than they ever have been before." Prime Minister Gerbrandy told Eisenhower in mid-January that the care and feeding of the liberated Dutch had fallen well short of the required amounts, even though SHAEF refused to delegate the job to the Dutch government itself while the region was still part of a fluid and unstable military front.[16]

In early February, General Bernard Montgomery, whose 21st Army Group was the chief occupying force in Belgium and southern Holland, wrote to Eisenhower to tell him that "the level of subsistence of the Belgian and Dutch civil population is too low and that there are signs of disintegrating morale. There have already been sporadic strikes among Antwerp dockers and coal miners. A strike of railway operatives would be most serious. The present rations for civilians amounts to 1600 calories as compared with some 4500 for military personnel. It is obvious that this cannot be sufficient for labor doing hard physical work. I feel that the seriousness of the position may not be fully realized and would be grateful if you would personally intervene." Monty also complained bitterly to his friends in Whitehall. Writing to Sir P. J. Grigg, secretary of state for war, he said that the food and coal situation in Holland was catastrophically bad and that strikes were breaking out in many sectors. "The plain truth is that Eisenhower is running around the front trying to run the battle and show that he is a great general, and he is neglecting his higher functions; he cannot do both jobs."[17]

Montgomery could be extremely irritating, but in this case his words prompted Eisenhower into action. The Supreme Commander cabled his superior in Washington, General George Marshall, and told him that he was "very much concerned about the food situation in Belgium and liberated Holland." He said the Allied governments simply were not carrying through on their commitments, and that the import program would be 60,000 tons short of what was needed by the end of March. The result "will be increasing unrest, civil disturbances, and disorders in the rear areas of 21st Army Group. . . . Food shortage is at the bottom of all the trouble." Eisenhower's solution, however, was politically sensitive: to feed the Belgians and the freed Dutch, he proposed to raid the stocks that had been built up in Britain for the emergency relief of *northwestern* Holland. These stocks were the central pillar of the British government's plan for relief once Holland was fully liberated, and they had been used as a demonstration of good faith to the Dutch that serious planning for the immediate relief of the Dutch was well in hand. Eisenhower, perhaps knowing that the liberation of occupied Holland was not imminent, decided to use the stockpiles for the immediate needs of liberated territory. But he also appealed to the Combined Chiefs of Staff for an immediate additional shipping program to Britain that would replenish those stocks. "Unless these withdrawals are replaced," he argued, "the whole relief plan for Western Holland is jeopardized." Eisenhower was robbing Peter to pay Paul; the relief of the liberated had to come before the relief of the still-captive Dutch. In order both to supply the shortfall of food and to restock the supplies intended for western Holland, Eisenhower called for the immediate shipment of 109,000 tons of food and supplies into the 21st Army Group area. It was a staggering figure, and presented serious shipping problems, but President Roosevelt lent his support to the plan and urged Churchill to do the same.[18]

In part because of this decisive intervention, the food situation in liberated Holland improved marginally by the end of March 1945. But this did nothing to address the real crisis unfolding north of the Maas, Waal, and Rhine rivers, in occupied Holland. There, the food shortage worsened and became a political and indeed a moral crisis for the Allied high command. The moral dimension was put with extraordinary force by Major-General J. G. W. Clark, the head of the SHAEF mission to the Netherlands. "I feel very strongly," he wrote,

> that far more active steps should be taken here and now to enter the occupied portion of the Netherlands in order to effect some measure of relief to this distressed people. By neglecting to do this, the Allies are running the risk of having at their doorstep a disaster of unparalleled magnitude. If we are really fighting for an ideal and fighting to liberate a people, surely it is time to take some very definitive action in the matter instead of tacitly allowing starvation and death to overcome some 3 million of our nearest neighbors.[19]

Not only the British expressed such concerns. Stanley K. Hornbeck, the American ambassador to the Dutch government-in-exile, sent a remarkably frank letter directly to President Roosevelt. "There is a very real question today of whether many of their people . . . may not in the course of the next six months die of starvation, neglect or abuse." Whatever needs there were in France or Belgium or Italy, Hornbeck claimed, "in western Holland the Dutch are now confronted with conditions of *desperate* need."[20]

In early March, with such telegrams pouring in from Allied diplomats and under relentless pressure from Prime Minister Gerbandy, Winston Churchill began to push harder to find a solution. He set the question to the British army chiefs of staff: should the plan for attacking Germany be altered so that troops and resources could be diverted to northwest Holland, essentially on a humanitarian mission? The Joint Planning Staff of the British War Cabinet met on March 8, 1945. The planners were highly doubtful of the wisdom of any shift in overall strategy. "At present, there are some 80,000 Germans in Holland," they noted. "There is every indication that the enemy intends to turn western Holland, in which the bulk of the civil population is located, into a fortress to be defended to the last." Meanwhile, all engineer, transportation, and troop supplies were already engaged in the fight to the east, trying to get across the Rhine and into Germany. An immediate attack across the Rhine at Arnhem, the Chiefs calculated, would require five divisions, and take a month to mount—that is, too long to be of much use to the starving Dutch. It would also delay the main effort of the Allied attack across the Rhine into Germany. "From a purely military point of view," the planning staff concluded, "it is preferable to concentrate our efforts against the enemy and continue the offensive into Germany, without any specific operation to bring direct relief to Holland." The issue was put to the Chiefs of Staff the next day, and as the diaries of Field Marshal Alan Brooke, the British chief of the Imperial General Staff, show, it was not received sympathetically: "This morning," he wrote of the March 9 meeting, "our main problem at the COS was the Dutch PM's lament to Winston concerning the starvation of the Dutch population and urging a reconsideration of our strategy so as to admit of an early liberation of Holland! . . . However it is pretty clear that our present plans for Monty's crossing of the Rhine cannot be changed. After the crossing of the Rhine again from a military point of view there is no doubt that we should work for the destruction of Germany and not let any clearing up of Holland delay our dispositions." Despite this dismissive attitude, the Chiefs hedged their bets: they decided to ask General Eisenhower to "prepare an appreciation and plan showing requirements of an operation to liberate Holland as soon as practicable after you have secured your Rhine crossing [into Germany]."[21]

Eisenhower, also skeptical, complied. His memorandum shows that, while he was aware of the political and humanitarian arguments for diverting his armies into Holland to save the Dutch people, he opposed any such shift of emphasis away from the attack into Germany. Opening his assessment of the operation, he said he thought there were 200,000 German troops in northern Holland—far more than earlier estimates—and any attack there would be "a major undertaking." The Germans had already flooded large parts of the country, and would continue to break dikes as a defensive measure. That meant the assault into Holland would require a huge engineering effort to build bridges, and engineer companies were "already critically short." Eisenhower pointed out that a large bombing campaign against the Germans in Holland "would inevitably involve very heavy casualties among Dutch civil population." But most troubling of all for Eisenhower was that an operation for attacking into Holland "would probably coincide with the opportunity for breaking out from our Rhine bridgeheads. These breakouts should culminate in a rapid advance to complete the isolation of the Ruhr and possibly a junction with the Russians." That meant that saving Holland would delay victory. Eisenhower's conclusion was unmistakable: "Most rapid means of ensuring liberation and restoration of Holland may well be the rapid completion of our main operations." But Eisenhower, ever sensitive to the political dimension of his war plans, was open to the idea that the Allied air forces might begin to plan for a campaign of airdrops of food supplies over Holland. It would be a major air effort—he thought as many as a thousand heavy bomber sorties a day to deliver sufficient quantities of food to 3.6 million people—but Eisenhower was willing to give it a try. The Joint Planning Staff of the War Cabinet agreed: a plan would be drawn up to see if an air supply operation might save the Dutch from total catastrophe.[22]

The threat posed by the food crisis in occupied Holland was not only humanitarian: there was a political dimension that worried the British. SHAEF's political intelligence office had contacts inside occupied Holland that reported considerable radicalization of the population there. "Their condition is pitiable, they are impoverished and their mental state has been affected," one local source reported. "There is a strong element of Communism among them because they now have nothing and Communism offers them at least a share-out of what remains." The Dutch hatred of the Germans was intense, but the attitude toward the Allies was not especially warm, either. The lack of an Allied plan to help the Dutch under occupation had stoked the fires of resentment, as had the bombing of Dutch towns. The Dutch, this source claimed, felt "abandoned by all and sundry and it is not therefore surprising that confidential information reports a growth of Communism in the areas west of the Ijssel. The Communist party is very active and is forming cells wherever possible. They are pro Russian and have played an active part in the resistance movement . . . They offer something positive to the overwhelming majority of have-nots in western Holland: nationalization of whatever remains after German depredations." The report concluded with an ominous hint of future trouble: "should a man with a really strong personality arise in the western Netherlands and go over to the Communists or present a radical program, the bulk of the people would be with him." As the British leaders eyed the swift Soviet march into Germany, and faced powerful Communist parties in France, Italy, and Belgium, the news that even the level-headed Dutch were now being swept up into a maelstrom of left-wing passions caused considerable anxiety in London.[23]

Thinking along both political and humanitarian lines, Winston Churchill wrote to President Roosevelt on April 10. In a message labeled "Personal and Top Secret," Churchill declared that "the plight of the civil population in occupied Holland is desperate. Between two and three million people are facing starvation. We believe that large numbers are dying daily, and the situation must deteriorate rapidly. I fear we may soon be in the presence of a tragedy." Churchill now wanted "action to bring immediate help." His idea was to deliver a message to the German government, through the Swiss, putting the Germans on notice that they bore the responsibility for feeding the Dutch people in the territory they occupied. As they had failed to do so, the Allies would now offer help. The Germans should allow safe conduct for ships and aircraft that would provide food relief. If they failed to do so, and blocked such efforts, the Germans would "brand themselves as murderers before the world." President Roosevelt, in a brief telegram sent two days before he died, agreed. The Germans would be presented with a simple public statement that the Allies were prepared to deliver aid to the Dutch, through the International Red Cross, the Swedes, and even using their own aircraft to drop in supplies. General Eisenhower now ordered that four million stockpiled rations be prepared for immediate packaging and shipment into occupied Holland by air. Almost seven months had passed since Gerbrandy's first appeal to Churchill. Help, at long last, was on the way.[24]

———

STARVATION KILLS SLOWLY. Thousands of Dutch people during the early spring of 1945 knew this all too well. While the Allied powers dithered, thousands of people in western Holland simply wasted away. The average diet fell to about one thousand calories a day, and for the poor and elderly it often slipped below that. "We got in a week one pound of very bad bread and two pounds of potatoes," recalled Miss Margaret von Lenip, who lived in Heemstede, just west of Haarlem. Writing to an English friend just after the war, she described the privation.

> No butter, no meat, no other things. The whole winter people went walking and cycling to farms to get some potatoes or wheat, so we could make our own bread and use the wheat, cooked in water, for porridge. But we had no milk, no cream, no sugar, no treacle. I cannot say that I liked it but you had to eat it. Except that, we had tulip bulbs and sugar beets. Both were very expensive and really awful, but again you had to eat something. . . . Heaps of people died from the hunger. On the road that goes along our house you could see a long trail of people, coming from the Hague or Rotterdam and walking to what we called the "North," that is the north of the country where there are many big farms. But because everyone did it the farmers could not give very much. . . . Everyone was worn out; many died along the road. The farmers would not give anything for money and therefore the people gave their last shoes, their last coat, just for a little bit of food.

She closed her letter with a plea: "Do not think I exaggerate. When I read what I wrote to you now, I can only say, it was still worse."[25]

Worse, indeed, as one resident of Amsterdam described it: "The city is Oriental. Garbage heaps piled against tree stumps. Starved dogs, warped with hunger, their tails between their legs, pawing at the heaps. Barefooted people, grey-haired people, sitting or lying in doorways; begging children with hunched-up shoulders and gunny-sacks under their arms." Thousands walked north toward the countryside in hopes of scraps that might be bartered. That physical activity took a toll, as Liedewij Hawke vividly recalled. "My father went on hunger trips. I remember one day very clearly, my mother had said, 'When Father comes home, we'll have pancakes,' because if he made it back safely he would have flour, he would have eggs, he would've bartered against supplies that we had, like soap or whatever. He finally did come back, and I remember running along the narrow corridor of the house to the front door and I said, 'Father, we're going to have pancakes!' and he never even said anything to me, he didn't even look at me. He walked past me into the kitchen where he just dropped down into a chair, he was so exhausted." Rations were distributed at central communal kitchens, but were scarcely fit for human consumption. Elly Dull remembered that "we ended up eating sugar beet pulp, which was so nauseating and so sweet I can still taste it. And we ate tulip bulbs. There was no food. There was no school at that time, everything was closed, there was no transportation. Our school became a central kitchen, and every member of the family would get a card and everyday we would go to the central kitchen and every stamp would be one scoop of whatever they were serving, and it was usually sugar beet pulp." Not only food was scarce: so was clothing and fuel. Coal shortages led to a cutoff of electricity and gas supplies, so home heating became impossible. "It was incredibly cold that winter, the moisture just dripped off the inside of the walls. We all went to bed at seven o'clock with everything that we had that we could wear. . . . Our shoes were cut open at the top, the front and the back to allow for growth, because we couldn't get new shoes."[26] The cold froze the canals, making any transport of supplies impossible. Medicine was in short supply, hospitals could not function without heat or light, and public health standards deteriorated. Even clean drinking water was hard to find. Bodies could not be buried for lack of wood for caskets; in January, 235 corpses were piled up in an Amsterdam church, awaiting burial.[27]

The most authoritative survey of the effects of the food crisis in Holland was carried out immediately after the war by Sir Jack Drummond of the British Ministry of Food, in cooperation with the Dutch government. Drummond's research showed that during the early spring of 1945 in occupied Holland, "fall of bodyweight was progressive and rapid. All the characteristic signs of calorie-deficiency appeared: undue fatigue on moderate exercise, feeling cold, mental listlessness, apathy, obsession with thoughts of food, etc." Food rations had dropped to 400 calories a day; some got more, but some got less. By January 1945, "the first cases of hunger edema appeared and were admitted to hospitals. Soon the numbers multiplied. Little relief could be offered these patients. Even in the hospitals there was little food." In fact, the hospital staff was also on rationed food: one slice of bread and tea for break- fast, two potatoes for lunch; a slice of bread, perhaps some watery soup for dinner. Yet on this they worked round the clock. By February, so many people sought admission to hospitals that they had to be turned away. Schools had to be turned into hospital wards for the dying. A strict scale was established: those who had lost 25 percent of their body weight received extra rations of bread and beans. Yet even this could not be sustained. By the springtime, only those who had lost 35 percent of body weight qualified for extra rations, and by April 1945, there simply was no food left at all. It is worth quoting Drum- mond's description of the long-term impact of these shortages:

> In spite of this local organization and effort, conditions became worse.
> People dropped from exhaustion in the streets and many died there.
> Often people were so fatigued that they were unable to return home,
> before curfew; so they hid in barns or elsewhere to sleep, and there
> died. Older people, who lacked the strength to go searching for food,
> stayed at home in bed and died. The worst cases were hidden in the
> homes and being unknown to the physicians could not be treated.
> Famine took its course with all its consequences. Vermin became com-
> mon; there was no soap; frequently there was no water, gas or elec-
> tricity. Many people had skin infections and frequently abscesses and
> phlegmones.

As a result of shortages, diabetics received no insulin; infections could not be treated with sulfa drugs; disinfectants were unavailable and dysentery and typhoid broke out; hospitals, having no fuel, could not easily sterilize instru- ments. Surgery rooms had no water, heat, or light.[28]

The struggle for survival dominated daily life: making a meal out of scraps of inedible foods, avoiding roundups by the Germans, selling valuables on the black market for something to eat. "Nothing was so important as food," recalled Henri van der Zee, who as a ten-year-old in Hilversum managed to survive the Hunger Winter. "I remember getting up in the morning thinking of food; the whole day long we talked food; and I went to bed hungry and dreaming about food." In January, sugar beets became a staple of the official ration. These fibrous, massive roots, used for cattle feed, could be shredded, boiled, mashed, and eaten as a pulpy porridge. Those people who could secure a supply of tulip bulbs boiled them with an onion and powdered seasoning to make a bitter meal. House cats and dogs began to disappear. "Hunger. Hunger. It's getting worse," wrote a tram conductor from Rotterdam in late April. "Now that we're not even getting one slice of bread per day, we're at our wits' end. We stare at each other's hollow eyes all day and every look, every word, every movement betrays it, Hunger! . . . How much longer can we hold out?"[29]

MORE THAN ANY single country, it is Canada that holds pride of place in the Dutch story of liberation. Rightly so: the Canadians performed extraordinary feats in fighting against the Germans in Holland from September 1944 until the very end of the war. Extraordinary because of the difficulties of the terrain—waterlogged and flooded—because of the strength of the well-defended German positions, and because they themselves were not terribly well led and were often poorly equipped and certainly weakly supported by air power. Stubbornly, slowly, with doggedness and resilience, the First Canadian Army ground its way into Holland, inch by sodden inch. They cleared the Scheldt estuary of Germans in October 1944, liberating the southern stretch of Holland south of the Maas river and allowing Antwerp to play its role in landing desperately needed supplies for the Allied armies. This, at a cost of 12,000 casualties. During the cold, wet winter of 1944–45, the Canadians played a mostly static role along the riverbanks of the Maas, but on February 8, the Anglo-Canadian armies launched Operation Veritable, aiming to clear the Germans from the western banks of the Rhine between Nijmegen and Wesel. It took a month of heavy fighting in flooded terrain, and cost the First Canadian Army 15,000 casualties. But it allowed the British and Canadians to cross the Rhine at Rees on March 23. The Canadians then turned left and dashed to the North Sea. They liberated Zutphen and Deventer. Leapfrogging canals and rivers with remarkable speed, they raced up to Groningen and Leeuwarden. By April 15, the maple leaf rather than the swastika flew over the eastern Netherlands, and the Canadians were poised to push westward, to free the captive, starving cities.[30]

The German Reich commissioner in the Netherlands, Arthur Seyss-Inquart, could read a map, and knew he was cut off and doomed. He also knew that by mid-April, the Russians were on the outskirts of Berlin, that the British and American armies were deep inside western and northern Germany, and that the war was unquestionably lost. He therefore sought to save his own skin by negotiating a separate peace, first with the local Dutch authorities, then through them with the Allied powers. On April 15, Prime Minister

Gerbrandy visited Churchill at his official country residence, Chequers. Gerbrandy told Churchill that, three days earlier, Seyss-Inquart had met with the leaders of the Dutch underground; together, they outlined a possible deal to neutralize Holland. Seyss-Inquart would not surrender unconditionally, he said, as long as there was an effective government in Germany; but he would offer a truce. Montgomery's forces, he proposed, should halt their advance into western Holland on the Grebbe Line—a fortified defensive line made up of dikes and strong points running north-south from the Ijsselmeer to the Rhine. In return, Seyss-Inquart would agree not to flood the country as part of a last-ditch defensive strategy; he would allow Red Cross ships and trucks into the country; and he would surrender immediately once the German government had capitulated. If his offer was refused, and the Anglo-Canadian forces wanted to fight for Holland, Seyss-Inquart promised wholesale destruction and flooding and a fight to the last man. Churchill was obviously angered by this freelancing from a devoted Nazi and war criminal, and tartly told Gerbrandy that "it was not for Seyss-Inquart to dictate to us." But the offer could not in good conscience be refused. The war was all but over; further fighting would mean the death of Allied soldiers, Dutch civilians, and more destruction of towns and cities in western Holland. In a letter to his foreign secretary, Anthony Eden, he said he wanted to know the American view of the matter, and indicated his own sympathy for the deal: "We must not be too stiff and proud where the life of a whole nation rests on a murderer's bell-push." It was not an easy decision, because the Allies had been wedded to the "unconditional surrender" doctrine for years. But Churchill recognized the stakes here: "It is a terrible thing to let an ancient nation like the Dutch be blotted out. . . . I would rather be blackmailed in a matter of ceremony than be haughty and see a friendly nation perish."[31]

The Combined Chiefs of Staff agreed with Churchill and decided to leave the matter in Eisenhower's hands to pursue as he thought fit, provided that "the Soviet military authorities are not only kept informed but, if they so desire, have military representatives present at any discussions with the German commander." The Chiefs wanted no complaints from the Russians about their seeking a separate peace. The Chiefs also spelled out the terms of the deal. The Allies would halt military operations in occupied Holland. In return, the Germans would open up the country to immediate food convoys by land, sea, and air; cease any punitive measures against resistance forces; and refrain from any further inundations of Dutch territory. To his great credit, Eisenhower wanted to start the airdrops immediately; he had the supplies ready to supply one million rations by air every twenty-four hours. "For sheer humanitarian reasons, something must be done at once," he cabled to Washington and London. But to protect the Allied fliers who would drop the food, Eisenhower needed Seyss-Inquart's approval of the deal first. Through the Dutch underground, SHAEF contacted the Reich commissioner and asked for a meeting immediately to discuss his proposals for a truce.[32]

On April 28, Allied representatives and German officials met in a schoolhouse in the village of Achterveld, about five miles from Amersfoort and inside Allied lines. The meeting was presided over by Major-General Sir Francis de Guingand, chief of staff of 21st Army Group and Montgomery's representative. The Germans arrived in a convoy escorted by Canadian military vehicles; the German delegates had been blindfolded for the trip through Allied lines. The German delegation was led by Ernst Schwebel, who commanded the province of Zuid-Holland for Seyss-Inquart. De Guingand memorably described him as "a plump, sweating German who possessed the largest red nose I have ever seen, the end of which was like several ripe strawberries sewn together." The brief meeting established designated drop zones for air supply and also set up a meeting between Seyss-Inquart himself and Eisenhower's chief of staff, General Walter Bedell Smith, to be held in two days' time, to discuss more fully the terms of the truce. The next day, a Sunday, the moment millions of Dutch had long awaited came: the air above western Holland filled with Lancaster and B-17 bombers, each stuffed with desperately needed rations. Flying low over the famine-shrouded cities, the Allied aircraft unleashed five hundred tons of supplies on four drop zones, each carefully identified with white crosses and red lights: the Duindigt race course and Ypenburg airfield at the Hague, the Valkenburg airfield near Leiden, and Waalhafen airfield at Rotterdam. No aircraft were lost. The German guns were silent.[33]

The terms of the truce were fully hammered out on April 30, when General Walter Bedell Smith met Seyss-Inquart in the same schoolroom in Achterveld. The commander in chief of the Dutch armed forces, Prince Bernhard of the Netherlands, accompanied General Smith, as did Russian officers, led by General Ivan Susloparov. In an exquisite act of defiance, the prince arrived driving Seyss-Inquart's limousine—the car had been stolen by the Dutch resistance a few weeks earlier and presented to the prince as a trophy. The small village was crowded with staff cars, the German ones flying white flags. In what de Guingand described as an efficient staff college exercise, the Allied and German officers broke into working parties and carefully set out the precise arrangements by which roads, ports, and air lanes would be opened to humanitarian aid convoys immediately. Over the next nine days, airdrops delivered an additional seven thousand tons of food and supplies to the Dutch, while trucks and ships carried in thousands more. Seyss-Inquart, however, would not agree to the capitulation of the German forces in Holland. He claimed that this military decision lay with General Johannes Blaskowitz, commander of the German Twenty-Fifth Army. He did not wish to be remembered by history as a quitter, he said. To this absurd pretension, General Smith tartly replied, "In any case, you are going to be shot." Seyss-Inquart said, "That leaves me cold." Smith seized the opening and cooly responded: "It will." (Smith was not entirely right: rather than face a firing squad, Seyss-Inquart was hanged in October 1946 after being tried as a war criminal at Nuremberg.)[34]

Seyss-Inquart's efforts to stall were undermined by the simultaneous collapse of the Third Reich itself. In Berlin on April 30, with the Russians just yards from his underground bunker beneath the Reich Chancellery, Hitler took his own life, and left the control of the defunct regime in the hands of the commander in chief of the German navy, Grand Admiral Karl Dönitz. There was no longer any hope for the remnants of the German army in Holland. On May 5, in a cold, dark hotel in the shattered town of Wageningen, General Blaskowitz surrendered his 120,000 men to Lieutenant-General Foulkes, commander of the 1st Canadian Corps. The war in Holland was over, just three days before the complete surrender of the German High Command to the Allies.[35]

"FROM THE TIME of the cease fire in Holland until all the troops had moved in, the Dutch people gave welcome," noted the official Canadian account of the 1st Canadian Corps of the final days of the war.

> Roads and streets everywhere were decorated with flags, bunting and flowers. Dutchmen of all ages lined the roads from early morning until late evening shouting and waving as each unit passed. Our jeeps gave cause to the most comment by the people. Everyone wanted to ride in a jeep. To say that the joy of the Dutch people was boundless is not complete. Their expression both in civil festivities and in the willingness to assist was without limit. Our troops, many of whom had traveled from Sicily to over the Ijssel river had never seen such happiness and rejoicing as poured from the hearts and homes in West Holland.[36]

Dozens of personal testimonies, both Canadian and Dutch, bear witness to the remarkable outpouring of sympathy and gratitude toward the liberators.

The Canadians relished it: they passed out the usual gifts of chocolate and cigarettes, were hailed in the streets, were hugged, followed, cheered, and hurrahed for days. "We could do no wrong, they couldn't do enough for us! They were wonderful," recalled Doug Barrie of the Highland Light Infantry. "The Dutch people went absolutely berserk," according to Sydney Frost of Princess Patricia's Canadian Light Infantry. "The Dutch people are supposed to be stolid, calm people; they climbed all over our cars and trucks and kissed and embraced us. We had some great parties, I'll tell you. . . . Many times, I'm asked, 'What was the most important part of your service?' That was it, right there. It all seemed worthwhile, all the wounds and the suffering, suddenly it seemed very much worthwhile." And yet, as in all liberated towns in 1945, heartbreak and loss were never far from the surface. "Liberation came, church bells were ringing, and my mom and I stood on the sidewalk and we held hands and cried," remembered Jack Heidema. "There was no joy. The joy came later on. We had gone through too damn much. Seen too much. And had too much pain and suffering."[37]

Nor did the suffering cease with the liberation. One of the first thorough surveys of the western Netherlands carried out by the G-5 section of SHAEF showed just how serious the food shortages had been in the spring of 1945. A long period of recovery lay ahead. "Hospitals are overcrowded with patients in the preliminary stages of starvation, i.e., suffering from hunger edema," the report said. "Instances of this are 15,000 cases in Amsterdam and 10,000 in Haarlem. It is, however, clear that the number of patients in hospital, large though it is, does not accurately reflect the state of the community. In driving through the poorer quarters of both Amsterdam and Rotterdam it was evident that many of the people in the streets and more especially those visible inside the houses were really in need of a course of hospital treatment to enable them to recover from the effects of a long period of malnutrition." The report concluded that the flow of supplies now arriving "has begun just in time to avert a major disaster."[38]

The *Times* of London sent a reporter to inspect the relief convoys now queuing up to carry food northward. The highway running from Allied lines north to Utrecht "presents an impressive and heartening sight," the correspondent wrote on May 7. "On either side, as far as the eye can see, are stacks of boxes, tins, and sacks of foodstuffs, medical stores and coal, with long columns of Army lorries incessantly bringing more." Dutch men enthusiastically worked alongside the Allies in loading trucks; but they could only labor for fifteen minutes before feeling faint. This writer had not yet reached Amsterdam, but reported dreadful rumors: the city was "a vast concentration camp beyond all imagination." The *Times* editorial page echoed these words

Three Dutch children in battered Arnhem clutch Red Cross parcels after months of privation. The First Canadian Army liberated Arnhem on April 14, 1945.
U.S. National Archives

by declaring that "horrors comparable to those of Belsen and Buchenwald appear to have been enacted."[39]

Fearing an apocalyptic, nightmarish scenario, Allied soldiers and relief workers moved into Amsterdam, Rotterdam, and the Hague with trepidation. What they found was an unsettling and alarming picture of the effects of nine months of deprivation. In Amsterdam, the presence of suffering was everywhere, in the sunken, colorless faces, the pipe-stem legs, the swollen joints of the children. The tree-lined streets had been denuded as residents had descended like leaf-cutter ants and cut down trees for firewood. The railroad ties from beneath the tramways had been dug out and hauled away for the same purpose. Even the homes of deported laborers and Jews had been broken into and systematically dismantled, their floorboards and bookshelves having been used for fuel. A tour by two British officials in mid-May revealed "large numbers of people suffering from extreme starvation who were unable to walk about the streets." In the last stage of the war, the *weekly* ration for Dutch people had fallen to 400 grams of bread—about half a small loaf—and 500 grams of potatoes or beets. A small milk ration was available for children only. Days after the liberation, there were at least 20,000 cases of "extreme starvation" in Utrecht and possibly 50,000 in Amsterdam. The Military Government Branch of the First Canadian Army reported that in western Holland there were 100,000 to 150,000 cases of starvation edema, "with a death rate of 10%," chiefly among people over sixty. The black market, and trips to the countryside for foraging, had kept many people alive; those who suffered most were the poor and elderly who had no such resources. An orphanage and a mental institution whose patients had been limited to the official ration contained "patients on the 'Belsen' level." The situation was "not as catastrophic as feared," but millions of Dutch people were in a desperate state of emaciation and required immediate and effective aid.[40]

It stands as a vivid testament to the commitment of the Allied forces and the international relief societies that aid did come, and in remarkable fashion and with stunning speed. Since January, SHAEF had been working with the Netherlands Military Administration—the provisional Dutch military power in the liberated part of the country—to prepare fifty-one medical feeding teams to be rushed into western Holland, and these teams now leaped into action. Each team included a doctor, six nurses, five social workers, and other staff. They had all received Red Cross training and were well supplied with specially prepared packages of emergency rations. Overall they treated some 279,000 patients in the early summer of 1945, mostly on an outpatient basis. They combed byways, back streets, and slums, searching for the poor and the destitute; they sent sound trucks through the towns, announcing the presence of aid and clinics for the hungry and ill. SHAEF supplied trucks and 189,000 tons of supplies, all of which had been stockpiled in southern Holland since the winter for precisely this purpose. On May 5, the first ships arrived in Rotterdam and many more followed. Relief organizations poured in: the Red Cross, the Friends Relief Service, the Salvation Army, Save the Children, and the Catholic Committee for Relief Abroad, all sent staff, aid, and supplies. Further aid was raised by the Holland Council in Britain through charity operas and clothing drives. Within two weeks, the Allies were able to offer the Dutch people a daily ration of two thousand calories, four times what the Germans had given them. Here was liberation at its best.[41]

The Allied armies achieved a great deal in Holland in the final weeks of the war, and their strenuous efforts to deliver aid upon the liberation of the country no doubt saved thousands of lives. Throughout the summer of 1945, Canadian and British troops labored to clear the country of mines, repair roads, bridges, and dykes, repatriate German POWs, and offload massive imports of food into the country that by August totaled 669,244 tons of food, medical supplies, clothing, vitamin tablets, vehicles, picks, shovels, and of course cigarettes—five million of them. In July, the SHAEF mission handed over control of the country to the Dutch government. Yet for all the cooperation and mutual respect between liberated and liberators, the Dutch could not fully forgive the delay in getting aid into the country in that awful spring of 1945. It had been a deliberate choice by Eisenhower on military grounds, and it naturally left some people wondering if more lives might have been saved by an earlier air supply effort or perhaps a revision of Allied military strategy. This is turn led British and Canadian officials to blame the Dutch for failing to give sufficient credit to their liberators for the immense efforts they had made. "It would improve the reputation of the Netherlands with the many British officers and men who have come into contact with the country in the past months and who are now leaving, if there was rather more public expression of gratitude for the debt which the Netherlands owe to those who have freed them," concluded a detailed British Embassy report in September 1945.[42]

The gratitude would come soon enough. Ever since the end of the war, numerous Dutch communities have erected testimonials of thanks to their

In Utrecht, Dutchmen shoulder welcome boxes of food and supplies shipped in by Allied forces in the days following the German surrender.
U.S. National Archives

liberators, especially the cheerful, underdog Canadians. But in 1945, as the war finally ground to its miserable end, the Dutch still faced the bitter realities of shortages, deprivation, destruction, and of course the memories of missing loved ones, some of whom had dropped dead in the dusty streets simply for lack of food. For Holland, liberation had been a slow, excruciating passage between war and freedom. A fifth of the country was freed in September 1944, but there was little to celebrate. The rest of the Netherlands suffered through nine months of bitter fighting, the destruction and flooding of the once carefully tended Dutch landscape, and the unforgivable cruelty of Germany's deliberate starvation policies. The generally agreed upon figure for deaths due to starvation and related illnesses is 16,000, reached by comparing the mortality rate in the first six months of 1944 against the first six months of 1945. In Amsterdam, 5,336 more people died in the spring of 1945 than had died in the same period the year before. In Rotterdam, the figure was 4,599, and in the Hague, the number was 3,422. The precise cause of death for these tragic individuals cannot be known, since malnutrition opens the door to many other fatal illnesses, weakening the body as well as the spirit. Yet it cannot be denied that these thousands of Dutch civilians died in great misery, just a few miles from Allied lines, in cities whose prosperity, learning, and culture had once expressed the essence of European civilization.[43]

INTO GERMANY

II

Prologue

Armies of Justice

O N THE VERY day that Hitler shot himself in a stifling, dust-choked bunker deep beneath the Reich Chancellery in bombed-out Berlin, Ruth Andreas-Friedrich and a few companions huddled in their own basement sanctuary in the city's ruins. Ruth and her friends were members of an anti-Nazi underground cell, and for years they had lived in fear and anxiety in Berlin, powerless against the massive terror apparatus of the Nazi state, but determined somehow to stake a claim in their own small way for humanity. Their cell was tiny, comprising only a handful of members, and theirs was perhaps more an intellectual resistance than a militant one. On April 30, with Hitler dead upon the floor of his bunker next to the lifeless corpse of his bride, Eva Braun, Ruth could imagine a future not dominated by fanaticism and hatred. Liberation, she believed, was at hand. These thoughts of the future, however, had to be pushed to the back of her mind, for on this day she was preoccupied with survival in a city that had been bombed and shelled into an apocalyptic wreck. Everything was scarce, including shelter, clothing, drinkable water, and especially food. "The streets are deserted," she noted in her diary, and then corrected herself. "There are no more streets. Just torn-up ditches filled with rubble between rows of ruins. What kind of people used to live here," she wondered. "The war has blown them away."

When she and her friends saw, from the slits in the basement windows, a disoriented white ox, "with gentle eyes and heavy horns," stumbling through the streets, lost amid the bricks and craters in the road, they knew what they had to do. Slipping out of their subterranean cavern, they darted out into the street, seized the beast by the horns, and pulled it into a courtyard. There, they slaughtered it, slavering over the thoughts of the lavish meal to come. But they were being watched, as she recalls in her remarkable diaries.

Suddenly, as if the underworld had spit them out, a noisy crowd gathers around the dead ox. They come creeping out of a hundred cellar holes. Women, men, children. Was it the smell of blood that attracted them? They come running with buckets. With tubs and vats. Screaming and gesticulating, they tear pieces of meat from each other's hands. "The liver belongs to me," someone growls. "The tongue is mine! The tongue, the tongue!" Five blood-covered fists angrily pull the tongue out of the ox's throat. . . . I sneak away. Never in my life have I felt so miserable. So that is what the hour of liberation amounts to. Is this the moment we have awaited for twelve years? That we might fight over an ox's liver?[1]

Like Germany, also defeated and dismembered, the white ox lay in a pool of blood, a corpse swarming with scavengers.

IN MID-MARCH 1945, the Anglo-American armies, recovered now from the losses of the Bulge, finally crossed the Rhine, encircled 300,000 German soldiers of Army Group B in the Ruhr pocket, and sped on into the heartland of Germany. By April 12, the Americans had reached the Elbe river, while the horns of this advancing bull sliced outward, one northward toward Hamburg, one to the south, through Bavaria and into Czechoslovakia. They soon encountered the massive armies of the Soviet Union, which since January had been churning up the Germans at a stupendous rate, leaping from the Vistula in Poland to the Oder river in eastern Germany in a matter of weeks; on April 16 the Soviets launched their final assault from the Oder to Berlin, swallowed the capital city, and pressed west to the Elbe, where they shook hands with the Americans on a bridge at Torgau on April 25. Five days later, his country overrun, his army defeated, and his capital city ground to rubble by the powerful Red Army, Adolf Hitler killed himself in his bunker. The men of the Allied armies had put to rest the lunacy of the thousand-year Reich.

What were these men fighting for? Certainly not for the liberation of Germany or of Germans from an oppressive regime. During the war, American leaders sharply distinguished between the peoples who deserved liberation—the French, Belgians, Dutch, Poles, and others who had suffered under German occupation—and the Germans. Whereas the liberation of western European states had involved the restoration of freedom and autonomy to once-oppressed peoples, American officials had in mind a very different fate for Germany. America's war strategy unequivocally sought to destroy Germany, its Nazi regime, and its military-industrial capacity. The Anglo-American bombing campaign, which reached unprecedented intensity in the last nine months of the war, revealed that Americans and Britons accepted massive numbers of civilian deaths as the price of victory. They agreed to wipe out German cities, raze German schools and hospitals and air raid shelters, and set fire to the bodies of the children, patients, and refugees within. They believed that these things had to be done to win the war. Nor would postwar Germany escape punishment. The Allies' planning documents for the postwar occupation were characterized by suspicion, antagonism, and spite toward the brutal Germans. The country would be broken up, dismantled, shorn of its industries, its people made to suffer the hunger, privation, and want that they had so readily inflicted on others. Hitler, Americans believed, had made this the inevitable price Germany would have to pay.

In the waning months of the war, the concept of a "liberated" Germany might have provoked wry mirth from Allied soldiers and war planners, whose single aim had been to reduce Germany to a lifeless wreck. *Time* magazine correspondent William Walton reported in February 1945 that among frontline soldiers penetrating into the Reich, he discerned "a sharp increase in hatred of Germans." Soldiers spoke with "amazing unanimity," and in particular expressed admiration for the Russian approach to the Germans: "'I hope the Russians get to Berlin first,'" many soldiers said. "'They'll know what to do with those Krauts!'" Of the Germans, Captain John Lane of Cascade, Iowa, said "'I know these bastards. They're no good. They're treacherous, no morals, no scruples, no religion, no nothing . . . I don't know what in hell you're going to do about educating their officers. Most of them are just hopeless. My private suggestion is that you just kill them all.'"[2]

As for the Russians, their attitude toward the Germans in these final months of the war had been shaped by four bitter years of unimaginable atrocity and ideologically driven conflict in the east. Citizens of the Soviet Union had endured the enslavement and murder of millions of their countrymen by the German occupation. Once the tide of war had turned against the Germans, and the Red Army began to push them out of the Soviet Union, soldiers encountered every day new evidence of the brutality of the German occupiers. As the Red Army reached East Prussia—that easternmost bastion of German power, cradle of the Teutonic Knights and the setting of Hitler's eastern command headquarters, the Wolfsschanze—Red Army propagandists sharpened their pencils and went to work:

East Prussia—the nest of Prussian Junkers and landowners, the hideout of high-ranking fascist gangsters—hears the rumble of our cannon, the engines of our tanks and self-propelled weapons. It sees the endless flow of our troops. It is the Red Army, the army of justice and revenge marching along its roads, destroying the nests of fascism, the Hitlerite armed machine of extermination, destroying it forever. And toward the glorious regiments comes a flow of people, day and night come the liberated, the people our victorious weapons snatched from the hands of death. . . . These are not simply tired, tormented people. They have been saved for life. They were saved by the Red Army.[3]

This kind of writing, common enough in the pages of the Red Army newspaper *Red Star,* bore little relation to reality. What the Soviets brought to East Prussia, and to the eastern German lands of Pomerania, Brandenburg, and Silesia, was not liberation but a carefully calibrated catastrophe: extreme violence, looting, rape, death, and destruction on a scale as vast as the climactic battles of the war themselves. And before the advance of these vengeful Soviet soldiers flowed a stream of millions of panic-stricken German refugees, bearing not only their children and a few belongings in creaky wooden carts, but also the weight of their consciences, which perhaps whispered to them that they had richly earned this awful fate.

We know that the story did not end there. The Soviet assault into Germany from the east, and the Anglo-American conquest from the west, converged in central Germany at the end of April 1945. Hitler's suicide on April 30 was followed by the surrender of German forces in Berlin to General Vasily Chuikov of the Soviet Red Army on May 2. The German forces in Holland, Denmark, and northwest Germany followed suit on May 4, surrendering to Field Marshal Bernard Montgomery in a somber ceremony on the flat, windy expanse of Lüneburg Heath. On May 7, at SHAEF headquarters in Reims, France, General Eisenhower accepted the unconditional surrender of all German forces; the surrender was signed by General Alfred Jodl, Chief of Staff of the German army, and was effective an hour before midnight on May 8. Stalin, however, demanded that the Germans surrender to Red Army forces in Berlin, and so late at night on May 8, in an old engineering school on the outskirts of Berlin, Field Marshal Wilhelm Keitel, the chief of the Supreme Command of the German Armed Forces, signed the surrender documents before Soviet Marshal Georgi Zhukov.

Germany lay prostrate and inert, and it soon fell to these great powers to resurrect their zones of Germany in their own image: in the west, as a democratic, denazified Germany that could serve as a bulwark against the Soviets; in the east, as a Communist state closely linked to the interests of Moscow. This all lay in the future. Looking back to the records of the Allied powers from 1944 and early 1945, it is hard to find evidence that the Big Three of

Roosevelt, Stalin, and Churchill saw their mission as the "liberation" of Germany. In some future time, perhaps, the German people as a whole might be redeemed, and offered an opportunity to live among civilized nations. But in late 1944 and early 1945, Allied leaders framed their war strategy around a simple principle that released them from any responsibility for human suffering: in starting the war and killing millions of innocent people, they believed, the Germans had turned their backs on civilization. Now civilization was going to turn its back on them.

4

Red Storm in the East:
Survival and Revenge

E ARLY ON MAY 9, 1945, just hours after the German High Command capitulated to a delegation of Soviet generals in Berlin, Russia's war with Germany came to an end. Ilya Ehrenburg, the fiery wartime propagandist for the Red Army newspaper *Red Star,* described in his memoirs the joyous celebrations in Moscow. The city was filled with delirious singing and dancing, fireworks pierced the sky, and spontaneous street demonstrations erupted throughout the night. But Ehrenburg sensed beneath the surface of these celebrations an undercurrent of pain. "There was a great deal of sorrow. Everybody was remembering the dead . . . That evening there could not have been a single table in our country where the people gathered round it were not conscious of an empty place."[1]

This was no exaggeration. One of the incomprehensible facts about the Second World War is the sheer scale of the human losses in the Soviet Union during four years of war with Germany. The latest scholarship reports that somewhere between 23 million and 26 million Soviet citizens died in the war. Of these, 8.66 million were soldiers; the rest, civilians: women, old men, children. A million of these were Jews. The Soviet Union was a large country, with a population of 190 million people. About 14 percent of them died in the war—one person in eight. Millions more endured wounds, hardships, losses of homes, land, dignity.[2]

The scale of Soviet losses, and of the great battles in the east that churned up thousands of square miles of Poland, the Baltic states, Belorussia, Ukraine, the Caucasus, and the Russian heartland, makes the battles of the western front, in Normandy, the Ardennes, and along the Siegfried Line, seem small in comparison. Total U.S. service deaths in World War II, including Army, Navy, and Marines, came to 405,399, including the Pacific Theater, and including nonbattle deaths. This is a huge and frightful number, and for every death there was a family in America that also faced an empty place at the dining table, a closet filled with clothes that would never be worn again. But it bears insisting that total Soviet losses were 65 times greater than American; and that by the time America entered the war in December 1941, two and a half million Soviet soldiers had already been killed. The point here is not to detract in any way from the American sacrifice, but to explain why the Soviet soldiers that pushed into Germany in the spring of 1945 acted with such ferocity and violence toward the German people. Unlike American, British, or Canadian soldiers, the men and women of the Red Army had tasted German occupation on their own homeland. They had fled, with millions of others, from the advancing Germans in the summer of 1941; they had seen the German armored divisions rip into the Russian heartland and flay it open; they had watched in horror as city after city was occupied, looted, savaged by the German invaders; they had seen millions of people enrolled into forced labor for the German war machine; and as the Red Army began to push the Germans back, slowly but remorselessly, across that charred land, they uncovered all the death and destruction that the Germans left behind. For Soviet citizens, the war against Germany was something that it could never be for their western comrades in arms: a war of survival and, in its final months, revenge.[3]

"Our holy war, a war foisted upon us by the aggressor, will become the war of liberation for an enslaved Europe."[4] That is how Ehrenburg, whose patriotic and sulfurous anti-German articles in the Soviet press were read carefully by millions of soldiers and civilians, framed the German-Soviet war on the very day of the German attack of June 22, 1941. But it was not immediately obvious to many citizens of the Soviet Union that the German invasion would bring a worse fate than that already imposed on the country by Josef Stalin. The Soviet Union was barely two decades old; its birth was attended by bloody revolution and civil war; and for most of the time since its founding in 1922, Stalin had waged war on his own people. He imprisoned, starved, shot, or transported to Siberia countless millions of people in an effort to consolidate his power and impose Communist rule. In the Ukraine, Stalin had forced the collectivization of agriculture upon the peasants, and treated resistance to this policy by cutting off grain supplies and waging war on the so-called "kulaks," or "rich" peasants. In 1932–33, 3 million people died of starvation in the Ukraine, the breadbasket of the Soviet Union.[5] In 1939, through the nefarious terms of the Hitler-Stalin pact, the Soviet Union grabbed the independent states in the Baltic—Latvia, Lithuania, and Estonia—as well as a large slice of eastern Poland; these lands were immediately subjected to a ruthless Sovietization. It was an open question, therefore, just what Ehrenburg meant when he spoke of liberation: for whom, and from what?

In a country made up of such diverse nationalities, and held together by a tyrannical dictatorship, it might have been easy for the Germans to stir up local grievances and win anti-Stalin allies along the way. There were initial signs in the Ukraine that many welcomed the chance to get rid of Soviet rule there, and looked to the German soldiers as liberators. Yet, if Stalin had been brutal and dictatorial, the Germans were to prove even worse: they aimed at nothing less than the wholesale enslavement or eradication of the Slavs of the east, and the incorporation of their lands into a German New Order that would serve only the interests of the master race. Whatever ill will many Soviet citizens felt toward Stalin, most of them quickly set their feelings aside in face of the far greater and immediate danger posed by the marauding German invaders. With remarkable speed, the many peoples that made up the Soviet Union converged on a single goal: to push back and defeat the Germans.

Hitler invaded the Soviet Union, after all, for ideological reasons. The prospect of a long-term accommodation with Stalin—and with communism—was impossible to accept. Hitler had long dreamed of the destruction of the Soviet Union and its peoples. He spelled out his goals repeatedly. In *Mein Kampf,* his bloated, rambling 1925 political testament, he wrote that National Socialists desired "to secure for the German people the land and soil to which they are entitled on this earth." This land of course lay in the east, across Germany's borders, in the USSR. No matter: as he put it, "state boundaries are made by man and changed by man." The Soviet Union's fertile lands, once conquered and settled by Germans, would provide the Reich with a new field of colonization. The issue was urgent, not only because Germany needed *lebensraum,* living space, in which to expand, but because Russian Bolshevism represented nothing less than "the attempt undertaken by the Jews in the twentieth century to achieve world domination. . . . Germany is today the next great war aim of Bolshevism." The war in the east, Hitler believed, would settle the question of the domination of Europe and also provide the opportunity for the final destruction of the Jewish-Bolshevik threat. The war against Russia was conceived explicitly as a war of extermination.[6]

The scale and ambition of the German invasion, code-named Barbarossa, are almost impossible to comprehend. Three million German soldiers (joined by half a million troops from Axis-allied Finland and Romania) crashed across a front line that ran nearly a thousand miles, from the Baltic shores in East Prussia down through Poland and along the Romanian border to the Black

Sea. This force of 153 divisions, 3,600 tanks, and 7,000 artillery pieces faced off against an equally large (but far less well-prepared) Soviet force of 2.9 million men drawn up in 140 divisions. Hitler sent one giant army group to the north from East Prussia through the Baltic states toward Leningrad; another army group moved from Warsaw into Belorussia, toward Minsk, Smolensk, and Moscow; and a third massive army group drove southeast, across the Ukraine and into the Caucasus. These swift moving, heavily armored thrusts, carefully coordinated with 2,770 aircraft, aimed to penetrate deeply into Soviet territory, surround and crush the Red Army, and then reach out for the hinterland, occupying finally all of European Russia along a north-south line from Archangel in the Arctic Circle down to the Volga river and the Caspian Sea. This was a continental-sized war of conquest.[7]

The initial weeks of the invasion were a disaster for the Soviet defenders. The Germans had the element of surprise: despite early warnings and a variety of intelligence, the Soviet leadership did not believe—refused to believe—that a German attack was imminent. Worse, the Red Army, despite the large numbers of soldiers in it, was badly equipped, with many soldiers having no weapons and little ammunition. Defensive positions were thin and quickly overrun by the swift-moving panzers; the Soviet air force had nothing but obsolete aircraft with poor radar and radio equipment. Despite a certain fatalistic spirit—soldiers lined up for frontal attacks on the invaders, sometimes on horseback with sabers drawn, only to be mown down by the thousands—the Red Army simply disintegrated amid chaos and panic. Even Stalin, the iron dictator, took to his dacha outside of Moscow, seized by fear and indecision. On July 3, having regained his nerve, he gave a stirring speech that depicted the battle in the starkly racial-nationalist language that became common during the rest of the German-Soviet war: "The enemy is cruel and merciless," he told his countrymen. "He wants to restore the power of the landowner, re-establish Tsarism, and destroy the national culture of the peoples of the Soviet Union . . . and turn them into the slaves of German princes and barons." In response, the Soviet people must be defiant, militant, courageous: "There should be no room in our ranks," he snarled, "for whimperers and cowards, for deserters and panic-mongers. Our people should be fearless in their struggle and should selflessly fight our patriotic war of liberation against the Fascist enslavers."[8]

These bold words did nothing to stop the German onslaught. The Germans surrounded and destroyed whole Russian armies, and took hundreds of thousands of prisoners, many of whom were shot or penned in and left to die. On June 28, the Germans seized Minsk and took 300,000 prisoners; on July 16, Smolensk fell, along with another 300,000 prisoners; in early September the Germans surrounded Leningrad and were poised to swallow the city. The huge numbers of soldiers who were surrendering evidently alarmed Stalin, who on August 16, issued Order No. 270, denouncing the "panic and scandalous cowardice" of some officers and soldiers. The order directed all military personnel to shoot anyone unwilling to fight to the death; the wives of captured officers were henceforth to be imprisoned.[9] But such threats had little initial effect against the encircling panzer divisions. In mid-September, the Germans captured Kiev, and half a million Soviet soldiers surrendered. Millions of people fled the advancing armies, adding huge waves of refugees to the general chaos. Vasily Grossman, one of Ehrenburg's fellow war correspondents for *Red Star*, described the scenes he saw near Orel, three hundred miles south of Moscow:

I thought I'd seen retreat, but I've never seen anything like what I am seeing now, and could never imagine anything of the kind. Exodus! Biblical exodus! Vehicles are moving in eight lanes, there's the violent roaring of dozens of trucks trying simultaneously to tear their wheels out of the mud. Huge herds of sheep and cows are driven through the fields. They are followed by trains of horse-driven carts, there are thousands of wagons covered with colored sackcloth, veneer, tin. In them are refugees from Ukraine. There are also crowds of pedestrians with sacks, bundles, suitcases. This isn't a flood, this isn't a river, it's the slow movement of a flowing ocean, this flow is hundreds of meters wide. Children's heads, fair and dark, are looking out from the improvised tents covering the carts, as well as the biblical beards of Jewish elders, shawls of peasant women, hats of Ukrainian uncles, and the black-haired heads of Jewish girls and women. What silence is in their eyes, what wise sorrow, what sensation of fate, of a universal catastrophe![10]

On October 2, the German army turned its focus toward the seizure of the biggest prize: Moscow. The city was bombed and shelled. Millions of panic-stricken residents fled, piling their belongings and families into wheelbarrows, private cars, buses, taxis, carts, fire engines, or anything with wheels. Official offices set about burning their archives and the air filled with black ash; the government transferred most of its offices five hundred miles eastward to Kuybyshev (Samara), though Stalin stayed behind. (He was obliged to set up an office in the Moscow subway, as the city had failed to prepare for the possibility of German air raids by building adequate shelters).[11] He declared martial law; looters and "panic-mongers" were shot on the spot. Stalin called on Marshal Georgi Zhukov, who had been directing the defense of Leningrad, to organize of the defense of Moscow. Citizens, mostly women and boys, were forced to dig antitank trenches. Soviet reinforcements from the Far East were thrown into the battle. The October weather turned foul and wet, leaving attackers and defenders to struggle in the sticky mud that slowed their movements. A bitter struggle for the capital ensued, with threats of reprisals handed out to Soviet officers who did not stand firm. As ever, the Russians resorted to powerful words to rally their peoples. Ilya Ehrenburg captured the essence of the fight when he wrote, in late October, that "the war is changing its character now, it's becoming as long as life, it's becoming the odyssey of a people. Now everyone understands that it is a question of Russia's fate—whether Russia will exist or not." He boldly concluded: "we will survive."[12] Stalin too roused his people to fury: on November 6, in celebrating the anniversary of the October Revolution, he defied the German claims to superiority: "These people without honor or conscience, these people with the morality of animals, have the effrontery to call for the extermination of the great Russian nation . . . Very well then! If they want a war of extermination," he declared, "they shall have it!"[13] Yet the Germans were a mere ten miles from Moscow, and on November 17, Stalin was forced to give orders for a scorched-earth policy: everything that could be of any value to the invaders must be destroyed. Villages, crops, homes, were now set ablaze by retreating Red Army units.[14]

The Germans failed to seize Moscow, and in the end failed, just, to destroy the Red Army. The Germans had overextended their lines and underestimated Soviet resilience; they spent too much of their resources in gobbling up thousands of square miles of the Ukraine, when they should have concentrated all their efforts on Moscow; they took too many casualties in the drawn-out battles around the big cities, and finally were beginning to run low on ammunition and supplies; the weather, first rainy, then bitterly cold, hampered resupply and logistics, and took the speed and mobility away from the panzer spearheads. In total, Hitler lost 250,000 soldiers killed, 500,000 wounded. Yet perhaps the most important element in the German failure was the amazing ability of the Red Army to recover from the appalling losses between June and December—2.6 million soldiers killed, three million soldiers taken prisoner—and to continue not only to fight but to go on the offensive. Soviet war leaders managed to find more men and get them to the front (ordering death for any man who retreated), and the Soviet war economy continued to produce arms, drawing upon the resources of thousands of plants and factories that had been moved and rebuilt in the east with astonishing rapidity.[15] Now it was the turn of the Germans to be surprised. On December 5, Stalin threw a counterattack of half a million men at the German positions, which pushed the invaders back some two hundred miles. It was not a general rout, but the threat to Moscow had ended, and the war looked set to bog down into a bloody stalemate: just what Hitler could not afford.

The counteroffensive of December and January was decisive in the military history of the war, not only because it blunted the German attack, but because it drew back the curtain on German occupation policy in the east. In the towns and villages that the Germans had occupied, and which had now been liberated by the fighting, the Red Army soldiers came across astonishing atrocities that served to fire up their own sense of outrage and quickened their desire for vengeance. Town after town had been ransacked and set ablaze. Captured partisans had been brutally tortured and publicly hanged. Food stores had been stolen, livestock and horses killed or sent west, the land savaged. Gallows had been erected in every public square. In the town of Klin, which the Red Army liberated in mid-December, a journalist went to inspect the damage the Germans had wrought. Much of the city was shattered, burnt by the retreating soldiers. Yet for this journalist, and presumably for his readers, it was the desecration of a great cultural monument that left the deepest impression. The composer Tchaikovsky had lived here, and his home had been turned into a little museum. The Germans used the house as a toilet, relieving themselves on the floor. They ripped up floorboards for firewood, and threw priceless manuscripts and books on the ground. "They burned music and books, trampled old photographs with dirty boots, pulled portraits down from the walls. . . . Empty cans and cognac bottles littered the room." Excrement stained the floors and walls. "A herd of crazed pigs could not have filthied the house the way the Germans had."[16]

It is telling that, in the midst of unspeakable human carnage and death, a writer for the Red Army newspaper would spend an entire essay on the destruction of single small home that had once belonged to a Russian composer. The writer, Yevgeny Petrov, clearly felt that such behavior perfectly described the heathen, uncultured, and animal qualities of the German invaders: a race of beasts, no more. Indeed, Russian war correspondents frequently deployed a bestial vernacular when describing the enemy. The Germans became, variously, hordes, vultures, mad dogs, cannibals, jackals, wolves (and, when retreating, sheep), snakes, beetles, and grubs. If not animals, they were likened to gangsters, hangmen, degenerates, pygmies, bandits, sadists, and devils. This language came from the period of the Bolshevik Revolution, when it was directed at capitalists and the bourgeoisie; in 1941, these terms seemed apt indeed to describe the predatory Germans. Yet by dehumanizing the Germans, Soviet war writers, who wept over the tattered manuscripts of Tchaikovsky, were themselves laying the ground for a ferocious retribution against the German invaders. Rabid beasts or pestilential locusts deserved only death and extermination. "This is a very grim war," a captain told journalist Alexander Werth. "And you cannot imagine the hatred the Germans have stirred up among our people. We are an easy-going, good-natured people, you know, but I assure you . . . I have never known such hatred before."[17]

Though the battle of Moscow had been won, the situation facing the Soviet Union at the start of 1942 was extremely grave. Millions of soldiers had been killed or taken prisoner, and most of the large cities of the western part of the country were under German occupation, as were the food-producing regions of the Ukraine. The war economy had been badly disrupted by the invasion, and had to be rebuilt from scratch in the distant east, without the great assets of coal, steel, iron, aluminum, and copper that now lay in German hands. Moreover, the Germans had only been bloodied in the great December-January counteroffensives; they were hardly beaten. Along an immense front line, the war settled into a violent, brutal slugging match that still favored the better-armed, better-trained Germans. To the north, Leningrad was surrounded and cut off. The city became a symbol of a martyred people, apparently condemned to suffer a slow, irreversible death. Three million people were trapped there, freezing and hungry; a million of them would die. Along the southern front, the Germans scored huge victories at Kharkov, Sevastopol, Voronezh, Rostov, and Krasnodar. On July 28, 1942, Stalin issued another of his periodic threats to his own people: "Not one step back!" he roared. "If we retreat any further we are digging our own graves and letting our Fatherland go to the dogs. It is therefore time to end the retreat." The means for doing so were typically brutal: soldiers who retreated were to be arrested and enrolled in penal battalions; and military police units were set up behind the lines with orders to fire at any Soviet troops that retreated.[18] Yet by August, the Germans were across the Don river, and pushing toward Stalingrad on the Volga.

There, at long last, the line held. "How the Red Army survived in Stalingrad," writes Richard Overy in his excellent survey of the Russian-German war, "defies military explanation." The city was a dull, flat industrial center spread out twenty miles along the western bank of the Volga. If the Germans took it, they could place a choke hold on the supplies of oil and American lend-lease aid moving into Russia from central Asia and Iran. But of course the symbolic value attracted Hitler even more: the city, once known as Tsaritsyn, had been the setting for heroic defenses against the White Russian armies in the civil war, and none other than Stalin himself had then directed the defense of the city. For this reason, as John Erickson put it, Stalingrad "drew Hitler like a magnet."[19]

The Germans seemed to have all the advantages. On August 23, Stalingrad was hammered by a huge Luftwaffe bombing raid that set the city alight and killed 40,000 citizens. The same day, the German Sixth Army and Fourth Panzer Army, a quarter of a million men altogether, under the command of General Friedrich Paulus, reached the banks of the Volga, thereby surrounding the city. The defenders were pushed back to a narrow slice of the riverbank about twelve miles long and about a mile wide. They had their backs to the Volga, across which supplies could still come, though the pitiful barges that traversed the river were under constant and effective German artillery and air attack. The city, blackened and ruined by the initial bombing attack, became the setting for horrific street-to-street and hand-to-hand fighting. Every conceivable ruse and tactic of urban fighting was used by both sides, from snipers to infiltration to tunneling and mining and nighttime assaults, while artillery and air attacks filled the skies with shrieking missiles. For all of September and October until November 12, the Germans slowly chewed their way, foot by foot, into the city, pouring in men and materiel to try to push the Soviet defenders into the river. Their commitment to take the city at all costs proved their undoing, for on November 19, General Zhukov unleashed a massive encircling attack that had been under preparation since mid-September: a million men, secretly deployed well to the north and south of the city, knifed past and around the German armies laying siege to Stalingrad, and fell on their flanks. In four days, 330,000 German and Romanian soldiers were surrounded in a massive pocket from which they tried and failed to fight their way out. Over the next eight weeks, the Red Army tightened the noose around Paulus's surrounded divisions, and pummeled them to pieces. Hitler refused to allow them to surrender, and instead promoted Paulus to field marshal in the hopes of inspiring greater resistance. But the next day, on January 31, 1943, Paulus's headquarters was overrun, and he was taken prisoner. So too were 90,000 German soldiers. One hundred and fifty thousand Germans died in the losing fight for Stalingrad. But the harvest of death had been far greater for the Soviets. They lost 470,000 killed and 650,000 wounded. Here was an apocalyptic bloodbath.

"NOW EVERYBODY KNEW that victory would come," wrote Alexander Werth. "No one doubted that this was *the* turning point in World War II." Werth, who visited the city in February, soon after the German capitulation, memorably described the scenes he saw there: the trenches filled with debris, burned out tanks and vehicles, bits of clothing containing frozen chunks of bodies; steel girders and tangled barbed wire everywhere, mines, scorched

Soviet soldiers in Stalingrad run along a trench to get into position
before an attack. *U.S. National Archives*

buildings. "But now everything was silent and dead in this fossilized hell, as
though a raving lunatic had suddenly died of heart failure." Amid the rubble
and piles of corpses, small groups of gaunt, dazed, disease-racked Germans
sat about, ignored by their captors, gnawing on the bones of horses. "For a
moment," Werth wrote, "I wished the whole of Germany were there to see
it." Inevitably, this victory was also a time for exultation by the Soviet leadership. Stalin gave himself a promotion to Marshal of the Soviet Union, and
bestowed medals and honors upon Zhukov. Vasily Grossman, the sensitive,
clear-eyed journalist, seemed to reach back to Shakespeare's *Henry V* when he
wrote, in *Red Star*, of the soldiers who fought there, and the half million of
them who died there. "If a quarter century from now the men who led the
62nd Army meet with the commanders of the Stalingrad divisions, this will

be a reunion of brothers. The old men will embrace, wipe away a tear, and begin recalling the great days of Stalingrad. . . . It will be a triumphant, joyous reunion. But it will be full of great sorrow, too, for many will be unable to come, the many who are impossible to forget, for no commander will ever forget the great and bitter exploit of the Russian soldier who defended his homeland with his blood."[20]

With the victory at Stalingrad, the tide seemed to be turning against the Germans in the east; yet it must be recalled that the front line was still 1,500 miles from Berlin. Two and a half years of great battles lay ahead, costing untold numbers of lives, before the Germans were pushed back and out of Soviet territory. And behind that front, in the thousands of square miles under German control, a fearful occupation had been put in place, one whose brutality and sadism profoundly affected the way that Russians would treat the Germans, both soldiers and civilians, as they began their long, slow march westward.

———————————

THE INVASION OF the Soviet Union opened extraordinary new vistas for Adolf Hitler. At last, after two decades of tawdry boasts and beer-hall invective, Hitler possessed both the power and the opportunity to impose his Aryan fantasies upon millions of people in his newly seized eastern territories. His long-cherished goal now seemed within reach: a pacified, Jew-free paradise of farms and factories, governed by a race of Germanic settlers, worked by a race of Slav laborers, linked to Germany by modern rail and road networks. The first steps had already been taken: since the invasion and partition of Poland in September 1939, Hitler had begun the process of cleansing Jews from the areas of Poland to be incorporated into the German Reich and pushing them into a sort of dumping ground in southeastern Poland, called the General Government. Jews had already been rounded up and sent into ghettoes in various cities across Poland, a preliminary stage in their eventual elimination. The acquisition of thousands of square miles of new territory in the Soviet Union, however, along with millions of new subject peoples of dubious racial value, presented Hitler with a new challenge: to advance the German "New Order" deep into the Soviet Union. On July 16, 1941, just a few weeks after the initial stunning success of the German army in Russia, Hitler spoke at length—for five hours, in fact—with his chief lieutenants about the future of Russia and the east: he told them, "we have now to face the task of cutting up the giant cake according to our needs, in order to be able, first, to dominate it, second, to administer it, and third, to exploit it." Any opposition would be crushed, and partisans exterminated. His ambitions were clear: "we shall never withdraw from these areas." Here at last was the *lebensraum* he had sought, the new German imperium for an imperial people. "We have to create a Garden of Eden," he declared.[21]

Yet there was to be no place in this Garden for millions of men and women and children who already inhabited these lands. From the Baltic states in the north, down through Belorussia and the Ukraine in the south, the newly acquired Soviet lands would have to be cleansed of their undesirable peoples, chiefly Jews, but also ardent Communists, intellectuals, partisans, and any other potential sources of resistance to Nazi rule. As historian Christopher Browning has documented, the German forces were prepared. Immediately after the July meeting, Reichsführer-SS Heinrich Himmler, Hitler's principal henchman for racial matters, sprang into action, sending special *Einsatzgruppen* (task forces) made up of SS troops and Order Police into Belorussia, the Baltic, and the Ukraine right on the heels of the advancing armies, with special orders to round up and shoot Jews. "All the Jews must be shot," he told these forces, and indeed mass killings of Jews began in Lithuania two days after the invasion began. In late June and July, Himmler himself toured the killing grounds to inspect the progress of his troops and to egg on the German commanders there to kill off the Jews immediately; in mid-July he delivered a rousing speech to Waffen-SS troops that urged them to see their fight against the Soviets as part of a racial struggle against "animals" and the threat of Judeo-Bolshevism; on July 31, he was in Riga and gave explicit orders to begin shooting Jews. On August 15, he personally witnessed a mass shooting in Minsk. Under Himmler's prodding, the forces of the *Einsatzgruppen* dramatically increased their shooting of Polish and Soviet Jews in the summer of 1941.[22] As historian Martin Gilbert has pointed out, from September 1939 until the invasion of the Soviet Union, around 30,000 Jews had died because of German actions, either through shootings, reprisals, beatings and pogroms, or starvation in the ghettoes of Warsaw and Lodz. After Barbarossa, that figure rose rapidly. Within five months of the German invasion, about half a million Jews in Soviet territory had been killed; by the end of the war, one million Soviet Jews were dead.[23]

The manner of the killing varied, but had not yet achieved the industrial-style gassing of the death camps. Rather, the killing of Jews in Soviet lands was crude, dirty, difficult work, carried out by shooting or other forms of brutality. On June 27, in Bialystok (in Soviet-occupied Poland), German soldiers rampaged through the Jewish quarter, killing Jews in the streets, and herding others to the great synagogue which, once full of people, was set on fire. On June 30, German units entered Lvov (also in Soviet-occupied

Poland), and immediately set about slaughtering Jews. In July, in Minsk, two thousand Jews were rounded up and shot; in Vilna, Jews were rounded up, marched to a great pit at Ponary, outside the city, and shot; five thousand died there over two weeks. And on it went, in every town and city across the battle-scarred lands from which the Red Army had been expelled. In Martin Gilbert's words, "within five weeks of the German invasion of Russia on June 22, the number of Jews killed exceeded the total number killed in the previous eight years of Nazi rule."[24] Despite the growing ruthlessness of the killings of Jews—such as the shooting of 33,771 Jews in a ravine outside Kiev at Babi Yar in late September—the German leaders quickly realized that small killing teams could not possibly act with sufficient speed or efficiency to wipe out all the Jews of Europe. For that, a more systematic approach was called for. In the context of the rapid military victories in Soviet Russia, Hitler's lieutenants put into motion a planning process in late July that would propose "a final solution of the Jewish question" and would lead directly to the erection of centralized killing centers to which Jews from all across Europe would be sent and gassed to death. The road to Auschwitz passed directly through the battlegrounds of Barbarossa.[25]

During these assaults on the Jews, the Germans found many willing partners in Lithuania, Latvia, and the Ukraine, where anti-Semitism had strongly affected daily life long before the war and where Jews were often identified with the much-hated Soviet Communist regime. With the retreat of the Red Army, local police units in these regions, joined by rampaging bands of thugs and bullies, happily, even joyfully, fell upon the Jews. They were determined to settle long-imagined grievances and perhaps eager to show the Germans their own enthusiasm for the new Jew-free order they hoped to establish. In Kovno, Lithuania, one man killed forty-five to fifty Jews by clubbing them to death in public, while onlookers clapped.[26] Boris Kacel, a young boy who lived with his Jewish family in Riga, gives an entirely typical account of the local anti-Semitic violence that attended the arrival of German troops in that city on July 1, 1941:

By that afternoon, the calm and peaceful streets of Riga had become crowded and filled with violence. The Latvians were celebrating independence from Communist repression, flying their large national red, white, and red flags over buildings and waving smaller ones by hand. I saw happy faces everywhere, which I understood, since I, too, was glad to see the fall of the Soviet system. To my surprise, though, I also saw anger and irrational behavior on the streets. The Latvians expressed their hatred of the Jews through physical acts and angry words. They accused the Jews of being Communists and blamed them for all the ills to which they had been subjected during Soviet rule. In my wildest dreams, I could never have imagined the hidden animosity the Latvians had for their Jewish neighbors. . . . The Latvians saw themselves as the messengers of Nazi evil and began to govern the city as if they had received consent from Berlin to do so. . . . Trucks appeared carrying small vigilante groups of ten to fifteen armed Latvians, who wore armbands in their national colors of red, white, and red. These men intended to kidnap Jews off the street and take away their personal belongings. The prisoners were then forcibly loaded onto the trucks, taken to the woods, and killed. It was terrifying to go outside, as one had to be aware of the vigilante groups that drove around the streets. The mobile killing squads, as I called them, were in full command of the city, and nobody challenged their presence or their unconscionable killings. . . . I had lived my entire life there among Latvians, who now considered me their mortal enemy and were prepared to kill me. No one was willing to protect my life.[27]

Similar scenes of local populations anticipating German violence against Jews occurred in most of the major towns and cities in the areas occupied by Germans. In the Ukraine, the Germans formed a local police auxiliary, and gave them a yellow and blue armband; they were encouraged to round up Jews, and torment and kill them, which they did.[28] Because of such local assistance, German killing squads could be effective in conducting roundups, finding Jews in hiding, and in terrorizing Jewish communities. Though many of these occupied peoples shared with their German masters a murderous anti-Semitism, however, Nazi ideology did not accord a place at the table in the Garden of Eden for Slavs of any kind. Indeed, any early enthusiasm for the German "liberation" of Soviet lands from Stalinist rule quickly wore off, as the Germans extended their murderous assaults to all manner of Soviet peoples.

Along with the Jews, the first targets of the German invaders were the Red Army political-ideological officers known as commissars. These officers were the enforcers of ideological discipline and zeal within the army, and as such were among the most rabid Communists. Hitler ordered their liquidation even before the invasion began: the June 6, 1941, "Commissar Order" stated that "the originators of barbaric, Asiatic methods of warfare are the political commissars. So immediate and unhesitatingly severe measures must be undertaken against them. They are therefore, when captured either in battle or offering resistance, as a matter of routine to be dispatched by firearms."[29]

But the killing did not stop with commissars. In early July the *Einsatzgruppen* were given orders to kill all Bolshevik party officials, party activists, people's commissars, "Jews in the service of the Party or the state," and "saboteurs, propagandists, snipers, assassins, agitators, etc."[30] In practice, this was a license to kill anyone who had any official capacity at all, including Red Army officers and soldiers, as well as anyone who expressed opposition to German rule, especially partisans, broadly defined. Red Army prisoners of war, some of whom may have surrendered out of sheer unwillingness to fight for Stalin's regime, were shot to death in huge numbers; perhaps 600,000 were shot outright. Those who were not killed were sent on lengthy death marches westward to camps in which they were housed in shacks, neglected, and allowed to die of starvation and exhaustion. Of the 5.7 million Soviet POWs who fell into German hands during the war, 3.3 million died in captivity. The maltreatment of POWs by the German army became widely known in the Red Army and naturally proved to be a considerable motivation to fight fanatically against the invaders.[31]

Paradoxically, the Nazi state wasted the lives of millions of able-bodied prisoners of war by killing them or allowing them to starve to death at the very time that it desperately needed foreign labor to work in its war industries. The obvious solution was to import labor from the east. From March 1942, under the direction of Hitler's labor minister Fritz Sauckel, millions of people were sucked into Germany by force and set to hard labor. By July 1942, 697,000 *Ostarbeiter*, or eastern workers, had been deported to Germany; a year later, that number had risen to 1.7 million; by June 1944, 2.79 million Soviet citizens had been conscripted for labor in Germany, and 2.1 million of them had come from the Ukraine. Many workers resisted and avoided deportation into Germany, and the military police had to resort to surprise roundups and labor press-gangs. Failure to comply with German demands led to extreme reprisals: the burning of houses and confiscation of property, savage beatings, death. Captured workers were packed onto boxcars without food or water or toilets. Once in Germany, these people toiled under extreme hardship, lived in rude barracks, were fed poorly, and suffered from malnutrition and disease at rates higher than even the forced laborers from western nations. Easterners were forced to wear a badge with the word *OST* on their jackets, indicating their eastern origins and subhuman status. They were worked, literally, to death. Heinrich Himmler approved of the formula, declaring in October 1943 that "whether 10,000 Russian females fall down from exhaustion while digging an anti-tank ditch interests me only in so far as the anti-tank ditch for Germany is finished." These eastern peoples, he sneered, were but "human animals."[32] Daily life in the German-occupied territories became a nightmarish struggle for survival. As the German occupiers ransacked the region, the living standards of the average peasants, already dreadfully low, became even worse. In the Ukraine, German soldiers looked upon the peasants as the lowest form of life, and abused them for the slightest infraction, such as failing to address a German properly, or being late for work. Public whippings and periodic hangings instilled fear in the population. As part of a deliberate policy of depopulation, German authorities denied food supplies for the large cities of the Ukraine; famine broke out in Kiev and Kharkov. The German occupation, which some in the Soviet lands had hoped would liberate them, had in fact condemned millions to suffering and death.[33]

In the summer of 1943, following the defeat of a huge German offensive around the city of Kursk, the Soviet Red Army went on the offensive, pushing back the Germans slowly as far as the river Dniepr by the end of the year. A large portion of the eastern Ukraine was liberated; Kiev was retaken in early November. Ilya Ehrenburg, with his gift for vitriol, captured the sense of deadly resolve that now pervaded the Soviet troops. "We want Germany to drink the bitter cup," he wrote. "Nothing can save Germany from inexorable retribution." The scenes that greeted the liberators were appalling and only fueled their anger. "Our soldiers," wrote Ehrenburg, "see how the Germans introduced feudal labor service for the collective farmers, how they whipped people for insubordination, how they raped, intimidated and infected girls. The invaders will answer for everything." Vasily Grossman, too, described the red-hot temper of the Soviet soldiers: "every soldier, every officer and every general of the Red Army who had seen the Ukraine in blood and fire, who had heard the true story of what had happened in the Ukraine during the two years of German rule, understands to the bottom of their souls that there are only two sacred words left to us. One of them is 'love' and the other one is 'revenge.'"

For Grossman, these words had personal meaning. A Jew who grew up in the Ukrainian town of Berdichev, ninety miles southwest of Kiev, Grossman was staggered to find that the Ukraine's Jews had been wiped out. As he traveled through village and town, he discovered the sheer scale of the slaughter. This killing of an entire people, he wrote, was different from the death of soldiers bearing arms, of which Grossman had seen a great deal. "This was the murder of a great and professional experience, passed from one generation to another in thousands of families of craftsmen and members of the intelligentsia. This was the murder of everyday traditions that grandfathers had passed to their grandchildren, this was the murder of memories, of a mournful song, folk poetry, of life, happy and bitter . . . this was the death of a nation." And it was more even than this: Grossman, speaking to an old neighbor, discovered that in September 1941, his own mother had been among thousands of residents of Berdichev who were rounded up, marched to an airfield outside of town, ordered to stand on the edge of a pit, and shot to death.[34]

IN THE MINDS of President Franklin Roosevelt and Prime Minister Winston Churchill, the phrase "the liberation of Europe" meant something quite concrete: the removal of Nazi oppression from the subject peoples of Europe; the restoration of the freedom and self-government that had obtained before the war began; and the creation of a European order in which peace and democratic rule might flourish. For the western leaders, liberation promised not simply military victory over Germany, but a return to stability, freedom, and national sovereignty in a world of peaceable states.

Josef Stalin, however, did not conceive of liberation in these terms. For Stalin, the chief aim of the war against Germany was, of course, military victory, but once that was secured, Stalin did not desire to return Europe to the *status quo ante bellum*. On the contrary, Stalin saw the political order of pre-1939 Europe, with its multitude of small, independent, and anti-Communist states in the Baltic, in Poland, Czechoslovakia, and the Balkans, as a threat to Soviet security. Poland had long been a thorn in the side of the Russians; the Poles went to war against the nascent Soviet Union in 1920, a war that had ended in humiliation for the Soviets. The Baltic states were fiercely anti-Russian; Hungary, Romania, and Bulgaria had all entered the war on the side of Hitler; and Yugoslavia was a "nest"—one of Stalin's favorite words—of royalists, nationalists, Fascists, and British subterfuge. Through the Hitler-Stalin Pact of 1939, Stalin had gone some way to expanding the Soviet Union's borders westward: he swallowed up the Baltic states and secured for the USSR the eastern half of Poland. These achievements had all been endangered by Hitler's attack of 1941, but now that the tide of war was turning, Stalin envisioned not only recovering the prizes he had seized in 1939, but expanding his control into central Europe through a territorial and political settlement that favored Soviet strategic and ideological interests. He also could begin to think about the total elimination of Germany as a threat to the USSR by carving up the Nazi state into smaller pieces. And he sought to ensure ideological control of the region by establishing powerful Communist parties that would organize a postwar realignment of Eastern Europe with the Soviet Union. Stalin by late 1943 had the power to achieve these aims: he possessed a gigantic army of 5.5 million men under arms in 480 divisions, now well equipped with tanks, air support, artillery, and weapons. These huge armies were now just a hundred miles from the 1941 borders, and would soon be well across them and on into Germany itself. Stalin knew that soon he would be in a position to "liberate" Eastern Europe in a manner that suited his own ideological and strategic interests.[35]

Stalin's powerful position within the anti-German coalition became perfectly clear to the western powers at the first wartime meeting of the Big Three leaders, which took place in late November 1943 in Tehran. President Franklin Roosevelt had been trying for some time to arrange a meeting with the Soviet leader, yet Stalin consistently refused to travel outside his own country. Churchill had been to Moscow, but the Big Three had never met together. With the change in the military fortunes of the Red Army, and especially with his desire to press on his allies the vital need for a second front in Europe against Germany, Stalin finally agreed to leave Moscow to meet his counterparts in Tehran. The narrative of this Big Three meeting cannot be rivaled for sheer drama and intrigue. As the delegations converged on the Iranian capital on November 27, the Soviets announced that they had intelligence of a German plot to assassinate one or all of the Big Three. They therefore urged that Roosevelt and his entourage move into the large Soviet legation instead of remaining some distance away in the American Embassy, and FDR accepted this hastily prepared arrangement. The meetings were held in the British and Soviet compounds, which were next door to each other. Security was tight, with phalanxes of Soviet secret police shoulder to shoulder with a brigade of Anglo-Indian troops—turbaned Sikhs, in fact. The twenty-four-year-old Shah of Iran, Mohammed Reza Pahlavi, who had taken over from his pro-German father only two years earlier, briefly appeared on the scene to greet the three great leaders; he was politely brushed to the side of the proceedings. As the meetings went on, there was ample time for the Big Three to socialize. One evening, FDR mixed iced martinis for Stalin. On November 29, in a solemn ceremony that featured an honor guard of Russian and British soldiers, Churchill presented to Stalin a jewel-encrusted sword, designed by His Majesty King George VI, in thanks for the victory at Stalingrad; Stalin kissed the blade with great reverence. The next evening, Churchill celebrated his sixty-ninth birthday, and was fêted by the world's most powerful men in the dining room of the British legation, whose walls were inlaid with tiny pieces of mirror and whose windows were cloaked in red velvet. And throughout the four days of meetings, amid lavish dinners and rivers of wine, champagne, and vodka, the leaders of the great alliance raised toast after toast to one another, delivering encomiums that ill concealed their mutual rivalry and suspicion.[36]

For all the rich theater of the meeting at Tehran, enormous issues of strategy and the postwar order lay before the men. Each leader had his own objectives, of course. Roosevelt wanted to win Stalin's support for his cherished dream of a postwar international organization called the United Nations, and he also wanted to win Soviet participation in the war against Japan. Churchill wanted to sustain Britain's dominant position in the Mediterranean by hitting Germany through southern Europe, the Balkans, and Turkey. Stalin wanted a second front in France as soon as possible, to help share the heavy burden of fighting the Germans, and he also wanted to feel out the Allies about the future of Eastern Europe and Germany itself. There was a good deal of friction and tension, especially between Churchill and Stalin, who regarded each other as old antagonists going back many years. Roosevelt managed to ply his traditional charm on Stalin, and wrung a few smiles from that pockmarked, sallow face. Indeed, as the four-day meeting progressed, Stalin found he had reason to smile.

From the very first moment of their talks, Stalin made it plain that he thought that the most important task facing the Allies was to open a second front against Germany. Stalin cast serious doubts on the slow, slogging effort of the British and Americans in Italy, which he thought was a sideshow and in any case unlikely to bring about a real threat to Germany. Stalin was impatient with Churchill's lengthy monologues about bringing Turkey into the war, or invading the Balkans and thus creating havoc in southern Europe. Stalin wanted an invasion of France, and a big one, as soon as possible. This plan had in fact already been agreed to in August 1943 at the Quebec Conference, but Stalin suspected that the Allies were dragging their feet. The Allies had not yet set a date, nor even named a commander of the operation. Roosevelt gave Stalin what he wanted, pressing the British to agree that Overlord would occur in May 1944. It was the first of many concessions to Stalin.

On the question of Germany, Stalin was also strident in his views, and went on at some length about the need for a hard peace for the defeated Reich. Their common enemy "must be rendered impotent ever again to plunge the world into war," he said. Stalin floated the idea of breaking Germany into smaller states, and mused about the hopelessly authoritarian character of the German people. Roosevelt, trying to ingratiate himself with the Soviet leader, said he was "100% in agreement" on this approach to the German problem. Churchill, not wishing to appear soft on Germany, generally assented, but said he thought the German people might be reformed and reeducated after the war. This only added to Stalin's suspicions of the British leader, who, Stalin implied, "nursed a secret affection for Germany." At dinner on November 29, these dynamics took a nasty turn, when Stalin,

Josef Stalin, Franklin Roosevelt, and Winston Churchill
pause between meetings at Tehran. *FDR Library*

evidently intending to provoke Churchill, suggested darkly that in his view, the best way to deal with the German army after the war was to take "at least 50,000 and perhaps 100,000 of the German commanding staff" and shoot them. Stalin was evidently making mischief, though he was certainly capable of this kind of brutality. Roosevelt inexcusably tried to add to the fun, suggesting puckishly that the victors should not go to extremes, but limit the number of liquidated officers to 49,000. Churchill failed to see the humor in this, and shot back that he would have nothing to do with the "cold blooded execution of soldiers who had fought for their country," even if they were Germans. He said he would rather "be taken out into the garden here and now and be shot myself than sully my own and my country's honor by such infamy." Churchill stormed out of the room, only to be coaxed back to the table by a smiling Stalin. It was an awkward moment that perfectly revealed the dominating position Stalin now held within the Big Three coalition, and the diminishing role held by Churchill, and Britain.[37]

Finally, the discussions at Tehran foreshadowed the dark fate that awaited Poland. This country, partitioned by Stalin and Hitler in the notorious 1939 pact, and occupied by each of these predatory neighbors, had endured a horrible experience since then. The western part had come under a violent, geno-cidal Nazi occupation, while its eastern half had been "Sovietized": 1,250,000 Poles in this multiethnic region were deported to Siberia, the better to incor-porate these lands into the Ukraine and Belorussia.[38] Germany had overrun all of Poland in 1941, but as the tide of war turned, Stalin could envision the Soviet Union soon returning to Polish soil. In Tehran, Stalin wished to secure recognition of his earlier land grab of Poland's eastern lands as a fait accom-pli, although it had been obtained with Hitler's connivance. Stalin clung to the ethnographic argument that these seized eastern lands were not "Polish," strictly speaking, as the people living there were a mix of ethnicities, includ-ing Ukrainians and Belorussians, and indeed Poles were in the minority. In any case, the line of partition that Hitler and Stalin imposed in 1939 closely resembled the line drawn up in 1920 by British Foreign Secretary Lord Cur-zon, when he was trying to arrange a truce between then-warring Poland and Russia. The Curzon Line seemed logical in 1920; why should Britain object to it now?

Indeed, Britain did not object to it. Winston Churchill believed that he bore great responsibility for the fate of Poland. Britain, after all, had gone to war with Germany in 1939 precisely over the Polish question, after Ger-many had invaded that sad country. The British prime minister had sheltered the Polish government-in-exile in London, and accommodated its leaders: at first, General Wladyslaw Sikorski and, after his death in July 1943, Stanisław Mikołajczyk. Churchill, however, understood the correlation of power all too well: only the Soviet Union could defeat Hitler in the East. If Stalin wanted 75,000 square miles of Polish soil as recompense, he would take it. Thus, Churchill developed a formula in speaking to the London Poles: Brit-ain wanted a strong, independent Poland, but it was not wedded, nor would it fuss over, any particular frontier or border. Poland would be liberated by Soviet arms, and should be happy with whatever it got. The Poles in London argued that they could not accept the Curzon Line as their eastern border, and claimed that the borders of a sovereign state could not be rearranged without the permission of Poland's internationally recognized government. They were, of course, wrong.[39]

During the dinner on the first night of the Tehran conference, Stalin took up the Polish question. Working from the premise that the eastern border question was really already settled, Stalin suggested some compensation for Poland in the west: he said Poland's western border should be revised to reach the Oder river, thus biting off a large chunk of eastern Germany. Churchill seemed to warm to this topic, calculating that such a handsome offer of Ger-man lands might bring the London Poles around to agree to the Curzon Line.

Churchill, knowing full well that the Polish government-in-exile was dead set against losing territory in the east, nonetheless agreed with Stalin about rearranging Poland's borders, and produced three matchsticks, which he laid out on the table to indicate the way they might adjust the national boundaries. He told Stalin that "he would like to see Poland moved westward in the same manner as soldiers at drill execute the drill 'left close.'" And so, with mere matchsticks, the three men shaped the future of millions.[40] During this time, Roosevelt was noncommittal, and the reason became clear on the last afternoon of the conference. Just before convening the plenary session, Roosevelt met briefly with Stalin alone, and told him that "personally he agreed with the views of Marshal Stalin" about the revision of Poland's borders, but that he had to consider the reaction of "six to seven million Americans of Polish extraction," as well as people of Baltic origin, whose votes he did not wish to lose in the elections of 1944. As a consequence, he would not make any public statement about the Polish issue at Tehran. Stalin now had FDR's private assurance that the Polish issue would be settled in a way that favored Soviet interests, whatever the Poles themselves might think.

With this valuable gift in his pocket, Stalin then went into the plenary session, the last of the Tehran meeting. There, Churchill tried weakly to extract at least one concession from Stalin in return for Britain's support for Stalin's land grab of half of Poland: that he treat with the London-based Polish government-in-exile. Yet these exiles, as Churchill knew, were staunchly anti-Soviet and deeply distrusted the Soviet Union; indeed, General Sikorski had led the most successful military offensive against the Bolsheviks in 1920. It was extremely unlikely that Stalin would have anything to do with them. Stalin continued to claim that these Poles in London were Fascists, and that they had publicly slandered the Soviet Union by suggesting that the Soviets had been involved in the murder of 8,000 Polish army officers in the forests of Katyn (a crime Stalin continued to blame on the Germans, though he had in fact personally authorized the slaughter). Stalin—who had already won so much at Tehran, getting a commitment to launch Overlord, getting agreement on a harsh peace for defeated Germany, and getting Allied support for extending Poland's western border to the Oder—knew also that he had Roosevelt's acquiescence in settling Poland's fate as he saw fit. Stalin therefore brushed off any notion that he could work with the London Poles. Instead, he demanded Allied support for the Polish-Russian border that he and Hitler had delineated. Stalin told Churchill that "the Soviet Government adheres to the 1939 line and considers it just and right." When Foreign Minister Anthony Eden noted that "this was the line known as the Ribbentrop-Molotov Line," Stalin shamelessly replied, "Call it what you will. We still consider it just and right." There was some confusion about the precise contours of the border, and a map of Poland was produced. In an imperial flourish, Stalin drew out a stubby red pencil and scratched away at it. He drew in thick red lines the new Soviet-Polish border, one that confirmed the loss of a huge chunk of eastern Poland to the Soviet Union, and also demarcated the division of East Prussia between Poland and Russia, too, with the valuable port city of Königsberg falling into Soviet territory.[41]

Churchill and Roosevelt remained sullen during this exchange, knowing that Stalin had run the table on them. In any case, with his army of millions, he could take by force whatever he could not win at the conference table. Stalin had now the power, and the acquiescence of the Allies, to shape Eastern Europe as he saw fit. For millions of Poles and Germans, Stalin's swift red strokes on the map at Tehran wrote another chapter in the long nightmare of Eastern Europe, as a new round of refugee columns, flight, expulsion, and death loomed. The session at which these matters had been settled had lasted a bit more than two hours.

IN THE SUMMER of 1944, the Red Army unleashed a gigantic offensive against the German forces along the German-Russian front—a line that ran from the Gulf of Finland and Leningrad through Belorussia, western Ukraine, and on down to Odessa on the Black Sea—a length of 1,500 miles. This was the great campaign that would finally break the back of the Wehrmacht and open the way into Poland, Warsaw, and on to Berlin. This massive, multipart assault—Operation Bagration, named for a storied general who had fought Napoleon—revealed how far the Red Army had come since its collapse before the German onslaught exactly three years earlier. The attack was well coordinated between air, artillery, tanks, and infantry; plans had been made to cross the marshy swamps of Belorussia using wooden bridges, logs, and brushwood supplied to each tank; swift thrusts and encirclement—just what the Germans had unleashed in 1941—were now adopted by the Soviets. More astonishing was the sheer size of the operation: despite having lost well over 3 million POWs, the Red Army in 1944 fielded an army of 5,568,000 men and 480 divisions; the Germans, who at this moment were preparing to fend off the expected cross-channel invasion in the West, deployed on the eastern front 4,906,000 soldiers in 236 divisions. In Operation Bagration, the Red Army mustered 1,254,000 men, 2,715 tanks and 1,355 self-propelled guns, 24,000 artillery pieces, 2,306 Katyusha rocket launchers, 70,000 trucks, and over 5,000 aircraft. The Germans were powerful but could not match this sheer numerical superiority along such a long battle line. Although they expected a Soviet offensive, the Germans were fooled by excellent Soviet counterintelligence into thinking the chief thrust would come farther south, or in the far northern Baltic front. The result was a catastrophe for the Germans: a week after Operation Bagration commenced, Soviet troops had surrounded Minsk, the first objective, and ten days later had taken Vilnius and were pouring through a huge gap in the German line into the Baltics. To the south, in a carefully timed delay, Soviet forces launched another major operation on July 13, throwing a million soldiers toward the Polish cities of Lvov and Lublin; by the end of July they had reached the Vistula and were a few miles from Warsaw. In five weeks, the Red Army had cracked open the German line, expelled the Germans from Belorussia, taken 400,000 German prisoners, and completely destroyed thirty German divisions of Army Group Center. Incredibly, the Red Army still had enough resources to commence yet another offensive, this one into Romania against the German Army Group South, which collapsed in two weeks, leaving Romania no choice but to abandon its German ally and switch sides, which it duly did on August 23. Within another month, the Red Army was pushing into Bulgaria, Yugoslavia, and Hungary.[42]

Did these Soviet military victories augur liberation? Ilya Ehrenburg, the Red Army's ardent propagandist, claimed they did. In May 1944, Ehrenburg recalled that fateful Sunday in June 1941 when the Germans had poured into Russia, "marching and signing, whistling and spitting. . . . They shot our children. Their tanks flattened our fields. Their bombs burned our towns. Their Führer howled, 'This is the end of Russia.'" But what had happened to these German soldiers? "Their bones litter our soil. Their contemptible dreams are scattered to the winds." Ehrenburg depicted this reversal of fortune as a great victory not just for Soviet arms but for the cause of humanity. "The campaign of justice has begun," he wrote. "The judges are marching west." Of course, for Ehrenburg, as for millions of his fellow citizens, the verdict had already been returned; all that remained was punishment. "We will draw the fangs from the reptiles. We will break their habit of fighting. The world looks with hope toward the Red Army. It brings freedom."[43]

In order to penetrate into the lair of the German "reptiles," however, the Soviet Red Army had to pass through Poland, and for millions of Poles, what the Red Army brought did not look much like freedom. Instead, the passage of the liberating Soviets through Poland brought violence, repression, and occupation to this already divided, mutilated country. In the wake of the Allied agreements at Tehran, the Polish government-in-exile in London had watched with growing alarm as the Red Army continued to roll westward and across the prewar border of Poland. The London Poles had been pressured relentlessly by Churchill to accept reality: they were going to lose their eastern territories to the Soviet Union, he told them; they must bear up and accept this as the cost of liberation. Churchill told his Polish protégés that half a loaf was better than none; if they refused to accept it, then Stalin would proceed without them, and their entire country might soon be subsumed under Soviet domination. Poland then would be lost forever, "little more than a grievance and a vast echoing cry of pain." Churchill told Polish Prime Minister Stanisław Mikołajczyk that "his heart bled for them but the brutal facts could not be overlooked."[44]

As Churchill himself put it during this same exchange, "no one had ever accused the Poles of lack of courage." Yet they were not only courageous but intransigent. The Polish government-in-exile felt it could not accept the partition of its own country by Soviet fiat because to do so would undermine its legitimacy with the strong Polish resistance movement—the Armia Krajowa, or Home Army. The Home Army was Europe's largest and most powerful resistance movement. It had endured six years of German occupation and now felt itself to be on the cusp of freedom once again. It would not accept a partition of the country without a fight. Prime Minister Mikołajczyk therefore resisted Anglo-Soviet pressure to accept the Curzon Line as Poland's eastern border. Instead, he and his London colleagues, in loose coordination with the Home Army commanders in Warsaw, envisioned a dramatic turnaround in Polish fortunes. They believed that the Polish internal resistance could rise up against the German occupiers just as the Red Army moved in to liberate the country, seize the levers of power and the capital city, and so present the Soviets and the world with a strong, national, and independent Polish government. Only such a bold gamble could forestall the partition of the country that Stalin desired. Of course, Stalin anticipated these manuevers. With the Red Army racing toward Warsaw, on July 21, 1944, Moscow announced the formation of a new Polish Committee of National Liberation: a government-in-waiting made up of Communists who had the backing and support of the Soviet Union. The Red Army planned to transfer nominal control of liberated Polish territory to this body, just as Churchill had prophesied. And there was more: troops of the Soviet secret police—the NKVD—began to hunt down and arrest Polish resistance members in eastern Poland. There could be no question that the Red Army's intention was to seize control of the country and crush the internal Home Army. The London Poles had only one card left to play. Warsaw must liberate itself from the Germans. Only the physical possession of the capital city would give the Poles leverage against Stalin as they faced off in the final struggle over who would control this country's destiny.

The tragic story of the Warsaw Rising turns on a paradox: its chief aim was to forestall the Soviet conquest of the city, yet the rising was crushed because the Soviets failed to do just that. During July, the Red Army had made breathtaking advances against the Germans, and the military commander of the Polish Home Army, General Tadeusz Komorowski (whose underground name was "Bór"), believed it likely that the Soviet troops would be in Warsaw imminently. The military advance of the Soviets would bring about the much-desired defeat of the Germans, yet at the same time, would assuredly bring Soviet and Communist domination. On July 12, General Bór-Komorowski told his Home Army commanders that the Soviets were "dangerous conquerors threatening our cardinal principal, independence."[45] Knowing that his own Home Army soldiers—40,000 at most—were armed with only pistols, homemade explosives, and a few machine guns, and would be unable to defeat the Germans in Warsaw single-handedly, Bór-Komorowski had to gauge the right moment to call an uprising against the Germans in the city. By July 25, it looked as if the Germans were starting to withdraw their administrative machinery from the capital, and on July 31, reports came in that Russian tanks had arrived in the eastern suburb of the city, across the wide Vistula river.[46] The sounds of fighting east of the city could clearly be heard in the capital.[47] Without any information about the state of these Soviet troops, their orders, or about the German intentions in Warsaw, General Bór-Komorowski ordered his underground army to rise up against the Germans and seize control of the city.[48]

On August 1, at 5:00 P.M. precisely, Warsaw erupted in a hail of small-arms fire, as 600 small units of Home Army troops assailed the 20,000 German occupiers at strategic strong-points across the city. German units were dug in behind barricades and gun emplacements, and they suspected an assault was coming. The first day went badly for the resistance. In the historic center of the city, Home Army attacks were repulsed, their losses were high, and none of the principal strong-points were captured. But by fortifying and blockading apartment blocks, streets, and alleys, the resistance managed to carve out three central pockets of territory in the city that they could defend from German assaults. They believed they would only have to wait a few days at most, until the Red Army arrived. And so the front lines in an urban battle of attrition were laid out in the first few days.

Of course, the Germans were infuriated by the uprising, and embarrassed at their own inability to quell it immediately. It was essential for them to hold Warsaw, as it was a vital strong-point in the entire Russian-German front. Hitler had declared it a "fortress city." The commander of the German troops in Warsaw, General Rainer Stahel, called for reinforcements, and by August

4, the Dirlewanger Regiment and the Kaminski Brigade—two notorious units of criminals, thugs, and collaborating former Ukrainian soldiers—had arrived on the scene to "pacify" the civilian population. In the western section of the city, called Wola, these units went from block to block herding citizens into the streets and shooting them to death: 30,000 to 40,000 people were shot to death in this manner on or around August 5. Extensive looting by the Dirlewanger Regiment accompanied these atrocities, as did the mass rape of the female population and the burning of hospitals.[49] At the same time, SS Obergruppenführer Erich von dem Bach assumed command of the rapidly growing German force in the city. Von dem Bach had been hunting down partisan units across Poland and Russia for two years; the Warsaw operation called for his brand of brutality. Aircraft were called in to bomb and strafe Home Army positions; artillery was rained down upon apartment blocks in which Home Army units might be hiding; human shields, formed of terrified civilians, were gathered in front of German tanks as they passed down barricaded alleys. In the contested areas, in which 100,000 people now huddled in cellars, electricity and water were cut off. Food supplies dwindled, and sanitation became impossible. By August 13, von dem Bach had 26,000 soldiers under his command, along with twenty-six tanks, plenty of artillery, and aircraft support. The Germans were severely hampered by fighting amidst urban destruction, huge piles of smoking rubble, narrow streets, and resilient snipers. Thousands of Home Army soldiers managed to survive in this desolation. But their fate was sealed. The rising could not possibly defeat the Germans in a battle for control of the city. Their only hope was to hold out long enough until their liberators—the Red Army—could save them.[50]

Ominously, the Russian advance toward Warsaw, so swift and brutal during the previous five weeks, and upon which the hopes of the rising depended, came to a halt on the same day the rising began. There were serious military reasons for the Soviet delay, as historian John Erickson has shown. The Germans maintained as many as fifteen armored divisions to the east of Warsaw that counterattacked the Red Army in late July and early August, threatening their flank and communication lines. Furthermore, the Vistula river was a major natural obstacle that held back the Russian advance not just at Warsaw but to the north and south of the city. In mid-September, the Soviets took the eastern portion of the city, but could not cross the Vistula.[51] In this context, the actions of the Home Army—which ordered the insurrection in the absence of any coordination with the Soviets or knowledge of their intentions—may have doomed the rising from the start.[52] Yet of course it is impossible to detach this purely military explanation from Stalin's own cynical reasoning and his profound suspicion, indeed loathing, for the nationalist

Poles. During the first two weeks of August, Stalin pretended the uprising was insignificant, a "reckless adventure" for which he bore no responsibility.[53] Furthermore, Stalin refused to give permission to the Anglo-American air forces to use Soviet landing fields from which to stage air relief efforts of the beleaguered Home Army. Stalin told the Allied leaders that the Warsaw Rising had been launched by "a handful of power-seeking criminals" and that far from aiding the Polish cause, the uprising had exposed civilians to danger and slowed the liberation of the city by drawing in enormous German reinforcements.[54] The RAF and U.S. Army Air Forces did launch a relief effort from bases in Italy, but the route was long and hazardous and the parachuted supplies often fell into German hands. Only on September 10 did Stalin relent, ordering airdrops to the Home Army in Warsaw and allowing Allied planes limited access to Soviet airfields. But these drops were too late, and designed chiefly to inoculate Stalin from the claim that he had done nothing to help the Poles. Stalin was content to see Warsaw burn, and to see the Home Army die with it.

The failure of the Red Army to enter Warsaw in August and September condemned the rising to death. For sixty-three days, the Poles held out against enormous odds, but finally succumbed to superior firepower, hunger, thirst, and wounds. On October 2, General Bór-Komorowski capitulated to the Germans. Fifteen thousand Home Army soldiers had been killed, and as many as 200,000 civilians of this sprawling city of over a million had died at the hands of the relentless German bombing and slaughter. Over 200,000 surviving civilians were deported from the city and sent to labor camps or concentration camps. Hitler ordered the city to be razed. Building by building, the Germans proceeded to demolish what remained of Warsaw. By the time of their final withdrawal in January 1945, the Germans had demolished 85 percent of the city. Warsaw had all but ceased to exist.[55]

There is a coda to this achingly sad tale. One week after the capitulation of the Home Army to the Germans—indeed, precisely at the same moment as thousands of Warsaw residents were being expelled from their city and herded into boxcars for a journey to the camps—Winston Churchill flew to Moscow to confer with Stalin about the map of Eastern Europe. For two months, Churchill had fumed and railed against Soviet treachery in Warsaw and the failure to help the heroic Poles. Yet suddenly, all seemed forgiven. "We alighted at Moscow on the afternoon of October 9," wrote Churchill in his memoirs, "and were received very heartily and with full ceremonial by Molotov and many high Russian personages." That very evening, Churchill and Stalin had their infamous "percentages" conversation about southeastern Europe, through which the Red Army was marching steadily and relentlessly.

Churchill suggested a rough division of the spheres of influence, with the Soviet Union holding "ninety percent predominance" in Romania and 75 percent share of Bulgaria; Britain would have "ninety percent of the say in Greece," and the two would "go fifty-fifty" over Yugoslavia and Hungary. Stalin assented. Churchill seemed immediately embarrassed by his own high-handedness, and offered to burn the document on which these percentages were written, though Stalin, more comfortable with such methods, suggested Churchill keep it. Even so, the British prime minister knew, as he wrote later, the percentages "would be considered crude, even callous, if they were exposed to the scrutiny of the Foreign Office and diplomats all over the world."[56]

Yet when it came to tidying up the Polish question, Churchill displayed no such qualms. He had commanded the Polish premier, Mikołajczyk, to appear in Moscow and meet his opposite numbers in the Soviet-sponsored Polish provisional government. He then hectored Mikołajczyk into agreeing to the Curzon Line, and seemed eager to be cured of what he called "the festering sore of Soviet-Polish affairs." In the presence of Stalin, on October 13 in a meeting at the Spiridonovka Palace, Churchill told Mikołajczyk that "the sacrifices made by the Soviet Union in the course of the war against Germany and its efforts toward liberating Poland entitle it, in our opinion, to a Western frontier along the Curzon line." Britain too, he went on, had fought on Poland's behalf and now had the "the right to ask the Poles for a great gesture in the interests of European peace." The next day, Churchill threatened Mikołajczyk: if he did not accept the Curzon Line, Britain would wash its hands of the London Poles. "We shall tell the world how unreasonable you are. . . . Unless you accept the frontier you are out of business forever." When Mikołajczyk continued to refuse to agree to the loss of Poland's eastern territories to the Soviet Union, Churchill shouted, "You are callous people who want to wreck Europe. I shall leave you to your own troubles. . . . You do not care about the future of Europe, you have only your own miserable interests in mind." And finally, with complete exasperation, Churchill erupted: "I feel as if I were in a lunatic asylum." Mikołajczyk refused to accept the fait accompli that had been in place since Tehran. He glumly agreed to take the matter back to his cabinet in London; a month later, unable to persuade his colleagues to agree to the Curzon Line, he resigned. Stalin's Communist proxies now took center stage, prepared to govern under Soviet rule. The London Poles would never regain power in postwar Poland, and the nation's borders emerged from the war precisely as they had been etched into the map at Tehran by Stalin's red crayon.[57]

SOMETIME IN THE early fall of 1944, as Operation Bagration gobbled up territory and pushed the Wehrmacht out of the Soviet Union, the Soviet war correspondent Vasily Grossman jotted down in his notebook the following description of the murder of two German POWs:

> A partisan, a small man, has killed two Germans with a stake. He had pleaded with the guards of the column to give him these Germans. He had convinced himself that they were the ones who had killed his daughter Olya and his sons, his two boys. He broke all their bones, and smashed their skulls, and while he was beating them, he was crying and shouting: "Here you are—for Olya! Here you are—for Kolya!" When they were dead, he propped the bodies up against a tree stump and continued to beat them.

As the Red Army penetrated into Germany proper in January 1945, scenes like this became common. Brutality was meted out to Germans on a vast, epic, inhuman scale. The Soviet soldiers descended onto Germany in a tidal wave of rape, beatings, wanton violence, looting, destruction, murder. Was this officially sanctioned? Some have suggested that this sort of violence was the fault of Ilya Ehrenburg, whose foaming editorials had seemed to give license to such behavior. Certainly, throughout the war, *Red Star* had given voice to a chorus of anti-German diatribes. And Ehrenburg was not beyond whetting the sexual appetites of his Red Army readers. In April 1944 he wrote a piece called "The Grief of a Girl," in which he described the pitiful fate of one Zina Baranova, who had been deported from Russia to work as a serving girl in Heidelberg. A group of young German boys, having a party in the home in which she worked, "forced her to strip, then diced for her." Zina hanged herself afterward. Ehrenburg stoked up the rage of the men who read his newspaper:

> Russian soldier! Hero of Stalingrad, Kursk, Korsun, the Dniester—you hear what the Germans did to Zina, a Russian girl? If you know what love is, if you have a heart, you will never forgive this thing. You will go to Heidelberg, too. You will find her violators. You won't deny yourself the honor of defending a girl's honor. Thousands of girls are languishing in Germany. They may be saved. They must be saved. They are our flowers, our birds, our love. They are awaiting you, soldier of Russia.[58]

It must have been easy for a young soldier, reading this, to conclude that his duty lay not only in avenging the honor of Russian girls, but in violating German girls as retaliation.

Even so, what occurred in eastern Germany in the bitter winter and icy spring of 1945 cannot all be placed on Ehrenburg's shoulders. Soviet commanders urged their men to behave as brutally as possible. In January 1945, as his vast army was about to cross onto German soil, Soviet Marshal Georgi Zhukov exhorted his men to crush the Germans without pity:

> The great hour has tolled! The time has come to deal the enemy a last and decisive blow, and to fulfill the historical task set us by Comrade Stalin: to finish off the fascist animal in his lair and raise the banner of victory over Berlin! The time has come to reckon with the German fascist scoundrels. Great and burning is our hatred! We have not forgotten the pain and suffering done to our people by Hitler's cannibals. We have not forgotten our burnt-out cities and villages. We remember our brothers and sisters, our mothers and fathers, our wives and children tortured to death by Germans. We shall avenge those burned in the devil's ovens, avenge those who suffocated in the gas chambers, avenge the murdered and the martyred. We shall exact a brutal revenge for everything.[59]

With such rhetoric burning in their ears, Soviet soldiers unleashed a campaign of terror in the eastern German lands of Pomerania, Silesia, and East Prussia that was barbaric even by the standards of an already ghastly war. Not only were Germans abused, terrorized, and driven off their land, but they were murdered in large numbers, and women in particular were made into targets of abuse. This violence that the Soviet Union's soldiers now brought to Germany formed a continuum with the violence they had received since 1941, at the hands of the Germans. The war in the east had been predatory and merciless long before the Red Army arrived in Germany. What followed was, quite simply, a matter of vengeance.

On January 12, 1945, Red Army forces launched a massive assault from the Vistula river. One thrust sliced north into East Prussia, the other, starting along a two-hundred-mile front from Warsaw to Krakow, leaped across the Vistula, rolled across western Poland, and smashed its way to the Oder river. By early February, Soviet forces were forty miles from Berlin. East Prussia received the brunt of the Russian ferocity. This easternmost appendage of the old Kingdom of Prussia that had forged German unity in the nineteenth century was a fist of German power and culture, pushed deep into the heart of northeastern Europe. Lithuanians to the north, White Russians to the East, and Poles to the south gave East Prussia its ancient frontier character, and served to forge strong cultural ties among its people based around the land, the monarchy, Prussian militarism, and Lutheranism. There were about two million Germans living in East Prussia at the start of the war. Between January and April 1945, virtually all of them fled.

The Germans of East Prussia had been told to fear the Asiatic hordes for years by German propaganda. It was also rumored among both Germans and Russians that East Prussia was going to be sliced away and given to Poland after the war—in which case, the Germans would have to leave anyway, by choice or by force. But the speed of the Soviet advance placed refugees on the roads just as the Red Army poured through, making for dangerous, and often mortal, encounters between victor and vanquished, and spread panic across the country. Josephine Schleiter of Osterode, East Prussia (now Ostróda, Poland), recalled walking for miles to get away from the battle front, through thick blankets of falling snow with freezing fingers and feet, clutching some bread and milk she had hastily gathered. The roads were choked with refugees, cars, carts, horses, and the flotsam of an entire people fleeing in panic. They were moving northwest, away from the Russian advance, but the troops soon overtook the struggling refugees. Near the village of Preussisch Holland (now Pasłęk, Poland), Soviet tanks fired on the refugees, then rolled into the column of civilians, crushing whole families. For Josephine, these Russian tank troops were terrifying and awesome.

> These were strong and strapping fellows, and gun-women in the full bloom of health were sitting next to the soldiers, all in new uniforms, and with felt boots and fur caps. We stood at the edge of the road looking at the panzers rolling past and at the soldiers. Most of them had primitive faces, round heads and expressions of unbounded joy. They waved at us and shouted out "Hitler kaput!" Some of them jumped off the panzers, when they moved more slowly, and came toward us: "Urr, urr" ["watches, watches"] they shouted hoarsely, and for the first time in my life I heard the Russian language which sounds hoarse and not pleasant to our ears.

What followed was still more unpleasant. The soldiers briskly looted and robbed the refugees, stripping them of watches, valuables, gloves, and clothing. These forlorn wanderers struggled to find shelter in farmhouses or barns along the road, though most of these structures had already attracted a congeries of panic-stricken runaways. Amid scenes of weeping parents looking for lost children, or trembling children searching for lost parents, the Russians looted and robbed, often drinking pilfered alcohol. Josephine, on the road for days, was captured by a carload of Russians, raped, then tossed out onto

the road like a broken rag doll. That night, she found shelter in a stinking cowshed, among a hundred other refugees.

> Terrible hours followed, particularly for the women. From time to time, soldiers came in, also officers, and fetched girls and young women. No shrieking, no begging, nothing helped. With revolvers in their hands, they gripped the women round their wrists and dragged them away. A father who wanted to protect his daughter was brought out into the yard and shot. The girl was all the more the prey of these wild creatures. Toward morning, she came back, terror in her child-like eyes. She had become years older during the night.[60]

A hundred miles to the east, in Eichmedien (now Nakomiady, Poland), a prosperous farmer recalled that the Russians took not only his corn, grain, flour, and peas but also his carpets and radio set. "In the evening," he said, "one could see everywhere the blaze of burning houses, barns and piles of straw, which the Russians had set on fire." This farmer owned a telephone, and this was considered decisive evidence of his being "a great capitalist." He was arrested, put on an open truck, and shipped to Insterburg (now Chernyak-hovsk, Russia), where he was interrogated and released. He walked home, which took him five days across snow and ice, to find his home had been occupied by a troop of Russians who had put his wife into servitude for them. These men ordered her to cook and wash, but they also had seized numerous local women whom they kept for sexual gratification; one of these was preg-nant, another but fourteen years old. Throughout the long nights, the family heard the "lamentations and shrieks" of the captive women echo through their house. This continued for weeks, as soldiers passed through their farm, help-ing themselves to provisions, linens, clothing, food, and of course women. From his locale, "young women and girls were deported every day by the Russians to do forced labor in Russia."[61] One such woman, Gerlinde Winkler of Dörbeck (now Prochnik, Poland), was ejected from her home, confined in a variety of sheds, barracks, and jails, fed a thin diet of foul gruel, and finally trucked to a camp at Insterburg. On March 3, she and fifty other women from Dörbeck were herded onto a cattle car and sent on a twenty-one-day journey to a labor camp in Chelyabinsk, Siberia. After three years of hard labor, Ms. Winkler fell gravely ill; she was not released until June 1948.[62]

Major Lev Kopelev, a political officer in the Red Army who was assigned by his headquarters to ride into East Prussia to search for German Communist networks that could be mobilized against the Nazis, was appalled by what he saw his own soldiers doing. No sooner had he stepped across the border into East Prussia than he saw the villages of Gross-Koslau and Klein-Koslau on fire; the Germans had fled. Kopelev spoke to a group of soldiers.

"What happened here—a clash?"

"What clash? They took off—couldn't catch up with them. Not a single civilian stayed behind."

"You mean they mined the town? Set fire to it?"

"Who—the Germans? No, there weren't any mines. It was our guys who set fire to it."

"Why?"

"Who the hell knows? Just did it, without thinking."

A moustached soldier said with a kind of indolent bitterness: "The word is, this is Germany, so smash, burn, have your revenge. But where do we spend the night afterwards? Where do we put the wounded?"

Another of the men stared at the flames. "All that stuff going to waste. Back home, where I come from, everyone's naked and barefoot these days. And here we are, burning without rhyme or reason."

A few days later, in Neidenburg, Kopelev saw more homes on fire, and the soldiers were dragging bed linen, quilts, oaken chests and tables, grandfather clocks, and other trophies out into the streets. "On a side street, by a garden fence, lay a dead old woman," Kopelev recalled. "Her dress was ripped; a telephone receiver reposed between her scrawny thighs. They had apparently tried to ram it into her vagina." In Allenstein, which had been taken without a fight, thousands of frightened refugees gathered near the train station, many of them recently arrived from Königsberg. "It was a scene of utter confusion," Kopelev recalled. "Train whistles, sporadic shouts, bursts of automatic fire, the tumult of a panicky crowd, a child's cry, a woman's scream, a babble of German speech punctuated by the shouts of our men herding the arrivals out of the station." And then the city was set alight by the Russians, and burned for days. Women were raped constantly, in plain sight. In front of the post office, Kopelev saw a tragic pair, a mother and her thirteen-year-old daughter. "The woman's head is bandaged with a bloodied kerchief. The girl has blonde pigtails, a tear-stained face and blood on her stockings. They walk away hurriedly, ignoring the catcalls of the soldiers on the sidewalk." Kopelev was so ashamed of what he saw that he wrote it up in a report to his superiors. He was immediately arrested and sent to the gulag on the charge of "bourgeois humanism," "pity for the enemy," and "agitation against vengeance and hatred—the sacred hatred of the enemy."[63] Revenge, it seems, had become a duty.

It is no wonder, in light of such fanatical, officially sanctioned brutality, that the Germans of East Prussia fled the advancing Red Army. About 250,000 people trekked from East Prussia westward over land, or rail, toward the Oder and into western Germany. The Russian advance along that same route deterred the bulk of the fleeing civilians. Perhaps 650,000 people walked north to the coast of the large Vistula lagoon, called the Frisches Haff. This lagoon was still frozen in early spring, and hundreds of thousands set out across its cracking ice, toward the narrow coastal barrier strip, the Nehrung. There, hundreds of thousands of weary, frightened refugees gathered along the two-lane road, and amid mud, filth, dead horses, dying travelers, hunger, thirst, and dysentery, they set out on the march toward Danzig. From there, the German navy evacuated many by sea to western Germany or even Denmark. Still others made their way northeast to Pillau (now Baltiysk, Russia), a town on the northern tip of the Haff from which

450,000 people were able to board ferries to take them to Danzig. This was a dangerous means of escape, as Soviet submarines lurked in the Baltic and periodically sank refugee ships: on January 30, the *Wilhelm Gustloff,* sailing out of Gdynia with over 9,000 refugees on board, was sunk by a Russian torpedo. Yet for those who remained, an awful fate awaited. The Russians captured Danzig on March 28. Anna Schwartz recalled that in her air raid cellar in Danzig, Soviet troops arrived amid a stinking haze of "alcohol, sweat and dirty uniforms." After the usual search for watches and valuables, the now-predictable ritual followed: "we heard the shrieks of women, who were being raped by Mongols." Herded out into the street, amid falling shells, burning houses, and plundering troops, Anna was eventually incarcerated with a group of residents, marched to a railhead in Graudenz, about eighty miles away, and then sent into forced labor in Siberia.[64]

For East Prussia, the final reckoning came in Königsberg, the ancient hometown of the Teutonic Knights and a city in which refugees had been seeking shelter for weeks. At the end of January, the city was surrounded by Soviet forces of the 3rd Belorussian Front. Ensnared within were the German Third Panzer Army—130,000 soldiers—and a terrified group of about 150,000 civilians. The thick walls of the ancient city, formed in concentric rings, served to keep out the invaders until April 6, when the Russians launched their final assault, preceded by days of massive air and ground bombardment. Late on April 9, the German commander in the city capitulated, having lost 50,000 casualties. Eighty-five percent of the town was destroyed during this fighting, and tens of thousands of civilians were killed.

Hans Graf von Lehndorff was a surgeon from Insterburg who had fled into Königsberg in January, and worked in a city hospital during the siege. The first days of the Russian arrival in April were worse than anything he had witnessed during the prolonged bombing and shelling of the city. His first glimpse of the invaders was on April 9, when he beheld a group of crouched soldiers "rummaging in a trunk. There was something frightening about the sight. I felt like someone who had gone bear hunting and forgotten his gun." Von Lehndorff, like so many of his countrymen, limned the Russians in bestial terms: bears, hyenas, baboons, or rats. "An attempt by my companion to talk to them had no effect. They reacted with short, growling noises and carried on their work [of looting] methodically. . . . My fountain pen vanished, money and papers flew all over the place. My shoes were too worn for them. They hurried away with a short-legged gait over ruins and through bomb craters to the other blocks and disappeared in the doorways. Their way of moving with a set purpose was bewildering: if the situation demanded it, they used their hands and ran on all fours." A fantastical image of ape-men, on the rampage.

In Lehndorff's hospital, the looting and raping that followed did exceed all imaginings. Soldiers descended on the hospital's storeroom, and thoroughly destroyed its valuable contents. Patients on their cots were searched, prodded, some were raped. The nurses took refuge in the operating room, pretending to be engaged in delicate operations; it did them no good, as they were dragged away to suffer the now-inevitable gang rape. The arrival of Russian officers in the hospital did nothing to stay the savagery: they happily joined in the raping, and dragged shrieking nurses along the corridors. "What is it we are witnessing here?" von Lehndorff asked himself. "Is it not the animal revenging itself on the human? . . . Moreover, this dull, growling speech, from which the world seemed to have withdrawn itself long ago; and these maddened youngsters, fifteen and sixteen-year-olds, flinging themselves like wolves on the women without really knowing what it is all about." When the soldiers discovered a menthol liqueur factory next door to the hospital, events took a turn for the worse. The alcohol stirred the men to new extremes: "Now something like a tide of rats flowed over us, worse than all the plagues of Egypt together." The looting was now joined with wanton murder, while "on all sides, we heard the desperate screams of women: 'Shoot me then! Shoot me!' But the tormentors preferred a wrestling match to any actual use of their guns. Soon, none of the women had any strength left to resist."[65]

Variations on these scenes occurred across eastern Germany in the spring of 1945, triggering a gigantic outflow of Germans. About two million people fled the Red Army from East Prussia; 800,000 fled East Pomerania, 300,000 fled Brandenburg, a staggering three million people fled out of Silesia, over 200,000 fled the city of Danzig, and an additional one million Germans fled from their homes in occupied Poland.[66] Between January and April, an exodus of truly biblical proportions occurred in eastern Germany that saw the mass migration of some seven and a half million people. In due course, as these lands became incorporated into Polish territory by the terms so breezily worked out by the great powers, those Germans who remained behind, perhaps five million people, faced intimidation, beatings, murder, and violence from Polish authorities and citizens. By 1950, there would be few signs left that these lands had ever been the home of twelve million Germans.

The brutality visited upon the Germans was by no means limited to the territory that was already assigned to fall under Polish control. As the Red Army fought its way, with extraordinary exertions, into the capital city of the Third Reich, conquering soldiers continued their barbaric, atavistic behavior. In Berlin, which was encircled by mid-April, Hitler shot himself in his bunker on April 30; aboveground, his people endured the arrival of the conquerors. Ruth Andreas-Friedrich, the Berliner who had hoped that the end of the war might "liberate" Germany from the Nazis, recalled the fear triggered by Russian behavior:

These days have become dangerous to many. Panic prevails in the city. Dismay and terror. Wherever we go, there is pillaging, looting, violence. With unrestrained sexual lust our conqueror's army has flung itself upon the women of Berlin.

We visit Hannelore Thiele, Heike's friend and classmate. She sits huddled on her couch. "One ought to kill oneself," she moans. "This is no way to live." She covers her face with her hands and starts to cry. It is terrible to see her swollen eyes, terrible to look at her disfigured features.

"Was it really that bad?" I ask.

She looks at me pitifully. "Seven," she says. "Seven in a row. Like animals."

Inge Zaun lives in Klein-Machnow. She is eighteen years old and didn't know anything about love. Now she knows everything. Over and over again, sixty times.

"How can you defend yourself?" she says impassively, almost indifferently. "When they pound at the door and fire their guns senselessly. Each night a new one, each night others. The first time when they took me and forced my father to watch, I thought I would die."

. . . "They rape our daughters, they rape our wives," the men lament. "Not just once, but six times, ten times and twenty times." There is no other talk in the city. No other thought either. Suicide is in the air. . . .

"Honor lost, all lost," a bewildered father says and hands a rope to his daughter who has been raped twelve times. Obediently she goes and hangs herself from the nearest window sash.[67]

For Germans, this widespread sexual violence came to serve as a sort of explanatory framework for their story of the Second World War. In West Germany, where millions of refugees finally found shelter and an end to their treks, it became common to argue that these events in the spring of 1945 somehow served to balance out the books: Germans had been cruel, this argument ran, but they had been victims as well. They had been victims of a rampaging Asiatic army and a vile alien ideology. Even Germans who later accepted some degree of responsibility for Hitler's atrocities could point to these travails of the spring of 1945 as if to say, we have paid our debt. Such claims have found little sympathy among Germany's former victims. The atrocities of the Red Army can in no way be used to lessen the burden of guilt shared by all those millions of Germans who had applauded Hitler's rise, spurred on the German conquest of the east, and sneered as millions were sent to the crematoria.[68]

Yet for all the later unseemly debates about victimhood and the moral authority it bestows, the suffering of countless women in eastern Germany in 1945 was real enough. For them, the end of the war brought on a catastrophe so great, so unseemly, that it could only be met with a search for transcendence, withdrawal, or even death. An anonymous diarist in Berlin who wrote one of the most searing, terrible accounts of the abusive Russian treatment of German women had a "strange vision" one morning, while lying on her battered, broken bedstead, in the room where she had been raped the night before. Her vision might stand as an epitaph for the millions of women who fell prey to these violent assaults.

> It was as if I were flat on my bed and seeing myself lying there when a luminous white being rose from my body, a kind of angel, but without wings, that floated high into the air. Even now, as I'm writing this, I can still feel that sense of rising up and floating. Of course, it's just fantasy, a pipe dream, a means of escape—my true self leaving my body behind, my poor, besmirched, abused body. Breaking away and floating off, unblemished, into a white beyond.[69]

5

A Strange, Enemy Country:
America's Germany

G ERMANY WILL NOT be occupied for the purpose of liberation but as a defeated enemy nation." This statement, made in the September 1944 directive on the occupation of Germany to General Eisenhower by the Joint Chiefs of Staff, unambiguously asserted America's intentions. "Your aim is not oppression, but to prevent Germany from ever again becoming a threat to the peace of the world," the directive continued. The occupation authorities must carry themselves like victors: "Your occupation and administration will be just, but firm and distant. You will strongly discourage fraternization between Allied troops and the German officials and population." Above all, Eisenhower was told, he would have supreme power to act in Germany as he saw fit. In a curious turn of phrase that suggests imperial robes, the Joint Chiefs told Eisenhower he was "clothed with supreme legislative, executive and judicial authority in the areas occupied by forces under your command."[1] Rarely if ever had a single American held so much power over so many millions of people as General Eisenhower was granted on the eve of America's entry into Germany.

It had not been easy for American officials to draw up this directive. Before D-Day, President Roosevelt had shown a maddening indifference toward the details of American occupation policy, and generally delegated the problem to his feuding cabinet officers and the lower echelons of the military. He even said, as late as October 1944 when American soldiers were already on German soil, "I dislike making detailed plans for a country which we do not yet occupy."[2] Such prevarication opened the door to the machinations of his headstrong subordinates. Henry Morgenthau, the Treasury secretary, an old friend and neighbor of FDR's from the clubby world of Dutchess County, New York, politics, made the best of the opportunity. Since 1943, Morgenthau, unique among Roosevelt's senior staff, had been pushing the president to adopt a more robust public criticism of Nazi Germany's treatment of European Jews, and he had called, not very successfully, for more aggressive efforts to rescue Jewish refugees. By late summer of 1944, consumed with justifiable anger at Germany's barbaric treatment of European peoples, he became the strongest voice in the cabinet for a severe postwar occupation policy. Evincing little hope that the defeat itself would be sufficient to change the German character, Morgenthau argued that the only way to halt the revival of postwar German aggression was to hobble permanently the German economy. Using his access and old personal ties to the president, Morgenthau in August began a concerted campaign to ensure that the United States publicly committed itself to a severe, punitive policy in Germany that would make impossible any restoration of Germany's military-industrial might. Roosevelt often seemed to be sympathetic to these views: welcoming his old friend back from a European trip, he told Morgenthau that "you either have to castrate the German people or you have got to treat them in such a manner so that they can't just go on reproducing people who want to continue the way they have in the past."[3] Roosevelt even rebuked Secretary of War Henry Stimson when the president got wind of an early draft of the War Department's occupation handbook that was insufficiently harsh on Germany. The Germans, Roosevelt told Stimson, would not be treated like the liberated nations, France, Belgium, and the Netherlands. "It is of the utmost importance that every person in Germany should realize that this time Germany is a defeated nation. I do not want them to starve to death but, as an example, if they need food to keep body and soul together beyond what they have, they should be fed three times a day with soup from Army soup kitchens. That will keep them perfectly healthy, and they will remember that experience all their lives." The president concluded in words that reveal the intensity of his antagonism for Germany at the close of the war: "Too many people here and in England hold the view that the German people as a whole are not responsible for what has taken place—that only a few Nazi leaders are responsible. That unfortunately is not based on fact. The German people as a whole must have it driven home to them that the whole nation has been engaged in a lawless conspiracy against the decencies of modern civilization."[4]

Despite continued stiff resistance from Henry Stimson, who was annoyed at Morgenthau's meddling and opposed his economically suspect ideas, Morgenthau pressed ahead and prepared a detailed plan for the occupation that stressed the deindustrialization of Germany. It was entitled "Program to Prevent Germany from Starting a World War III." Morgenthau knew that he had an unrivaled opportunity to influence the course of American policy toward Germany, for on September 14, he joined President Roosevelt and Prime Minister Winston Churchill in Quebec, where they had convened two days earlier to discuss problems of the postwar world. He brought a copy of his plan with him and pressed it on Roosevelt. The plan called for the complete demilitarization of Germany, and the destruction of industries "which are basic to military strength." It urged a policy of territorial dismemberment, envisioning East Prussia being given to Poland and a smaller chunk of valuable coal mining land in the Saar given to France. In addition, the remaining German state would be subdivided into two separate states: a northern and a southern portion. The Ruhr and the Rhineland and the industrial cities within that region would be "stripped of all presently existing industries," with the bulk of industrial equipment being dismantled and shipped to Allied states as reparations. Once denuded, the area would fall under international trusteeship. Germany would be forced to pay Allied nations heavy reparations, the country's assets would be seized, and some Germans would be enrolled in forced labor brigades in neighboring countries. Schools, universities, and media outlets would be closed until entirely reformed by Allied occupiers. The Allies would create a political structure for the country that took power away from central government and gave it to the states; and they would not take any steps to restore or revive the German economy. Foreign trade would be strictly controlled and large agricultural states would be subdivided. The Allies would arrest and try war criminals and ban martial parades and uniforms. At Quebec, Morgenthau managed to persuade not only Roosevelt but even Churchill to sign off on the plan's basic theses.[5]

In subsequent years, after West Germany became a valued ally of the United States, policy makers and historians alike tended to dismiss the significance of Morgenthau's harsh peace plan, chalking it up to the wartime passions of a Jewish cabinet officer.[6] But Morgenthau's ideas were not unconventional; even Secretary of State Cordell Hull and Henry Stimson, Morgenthau's chief critics, accepted the need for a severe curtailing of Germany's industrial power. American planners, as well as their British and Soviet allies, generally agreed that Germany would be demilitarized, that its borders would be redrawn and the state partitioned, that the Ruhr industries would have to be broken up and placed beyond the control of any future German central government, and that the Germans would have to pay significant reparations. There had been widespread agreement too among the Allies that the political structure of the country was going to be radically decentralized, and that German society would be denazified, meaning that all cultural and political institutions must be wholly restructured. Morgenthau expressed his ideas crudely, perhaps, and went further than his colleagues in calling for the total breakup of German industrial capacity. But in most respects, his ideas were consistent with the general direction of American and Allied policies as they were emerging in late 1944.

This convergence was perfectly evident in the directive to Eisenhower of September 22, known as JCS 1067, which though agreed to by the State, War, and Treasury departments, bore many hallmarks of Morgenthau's influence. That directive ordered Eisenhower to occupy Germany, arrest war criminals, break up all institutions of the Nazi Party, eliminate the officer corps of the army, abrogate Nazi laws, seize Nazi property, close the courts, close schools and universities, eliminate Nazi textbooks, and halt all political activities. Most important, the document ordered Eisenhower to "take no steps looking toward the economic rehabilitation of Germany nor designed to maintain or strengthen the German economy." Finally, German civilians would be given aid only to the extent that was necessary to prevent disease and disorder. "It will be necessary to hold German consumption to a minimum" so the needs of other Europeans could be met first. Taken as a whole, the policy debates and directives that emerged from Washington in the fall of 1944 made one thing perfectly clear: the Germans were going to be punished.[7]

Any notion that Morgenthau's plan was a dead letter is belied by Roosevelt's continued support for harsh treatment of postwar Germany. Even after the plan was leaked to the press, causing the media to label the proposal "Carthaginian," Roosevelt did not back away from a radical restructuring of postwar Germany. Though he conceded to Secretary Stimson that he did not want Germany to be permanently destroyed as an industrial nation as Morgenthau wished, he continued to insist that Germany be so changed by the occupation that it could never wage war again. On October 21, while in the midst of a reelection campaign, FDR told the American public that he was going to make the Germans learn a tough lesson once the war was over. Speaking to the Foreign Policy Association in New York in an address that was broadcast across the country on radio, the president indicated his desire for punishment and his hope for redemption through trial and toil:

> As for Germany, that tragic Nation which has sown the wind and is now reaping the whirlwind—we and our allies are entirely agreed that we shall not bargain with the Nazi conspirators, or leave them a shred of control, open or secret, of the instruments of government. We shall not leave them a single element of military power, or of potential military power. . . . We bring no charge against the German race, as such, for we cannot believe that God has eternally condemned any race of humanity. We know in our own land, in these United States of Amer-

ica, how many good men and women of German ancestry have proved loyal, freedom-loving, and peace-loving citizens. But there is going to be a stern punishment for all those in Germany directly responsible for this agony of mankind. The German people are not going to be enslaved, because the United Nations do not traffic in human slavery. But it will be necessary for them to earn their way back into the fellow-ship of peace-loving and law-abiding Nations.[8]

Even as Roosevelt and his staff prepared for the forthcoming meeting of the Big Three allies to be held at Yalta in the Crimea, the American government remained committed to exacting serious penalties from Germany. While FDR's new secretary of state, Edward Stettinius, Jr., shied away from "a program of sweeping deindustrialization," the State Department continued to call for "economic disarmament," meaning major restrictions on any German industries that might be susceptible to war uses. As for the German people themselves, Stettinius believed, "we should favor, in the initial period, the lowest standards of health, diet and shelter compatible with the prevention of disease and disorder. . . . The needs of the liberated countries should, in any event, receive priority." Even though the State Department called for less industrial destruction than Morgenthau wanted, the president said "he was still in a tough mood and that he is determined to be tough with Germany."[9]

It is not surprising, then, that when Roosevelt met with Stalin and Churchill in the hastily repaired, repainted, deloused Livadia Palace at Yalta, on the Black Sea shore, from February 4 to 11, 1945, the Big Three had no trouble agreeing on a very severe settlement for postwar Germany. Roosevelt brought with him a set of ideas that called for harsh treatment indeed for the defeated German state. And his hatred toward the Germans was stoked by the destruction he witnessed while in the Crimea. On February 3, the President flew from Malta to Saki, eighty miles from Yalta, and then endured a jarring five-hour road journey along rutted roads, through charred war-ravaged countryside, to reach Yalta. "We saw few, if any, trees," wrote the naval officer in charge of the president's daily log, "and many reminders of the recent fighting there—gutted-out buildings, burned out tanks and destroyed German railroad stock that had been abandoned and burned by them in their flight." In the white granite Italianate palace that had served as the summer palace of the czars—and was converted by the Bolsheviks into a sanatorium for tuberculosis patients—the three war leaders discussed the political challenges facing the alliance in the final stages of the war. The agenda was laden with thorny problems, from Poland and its future, to the formation of the

United Nations Organization, the question of German postwar reparations, and the entry of the Soviet Union in the war against Japan. Throughout all these talks, one searches in vain for any indication of leniency or forgiveness toward Germany. Roosevelt struck the opening tone when he said to Marshal Stalin in their first meeting on February 4 "that he had been very much struck by the extent of German destruction in the Crimea and therefore he was more bloodthirsty in regard to the Germans than he had been a year ago, and he hoped that Marshal Stalin would again propose a toast to the execution of 50,000 officers of the German army," as Stalin had done at their meeting in Tehran in November 1943. To this remarkable opening, Stalin replied that "everyone is more bloodthirsty than they had been a year ago." He added that "the Germans were savages and seemed to hate with a sadistic hatred the creative work of human beings." The minutes record simply that "the president agreed with this."[10]

As they had done at Tehran, FDR and Stalin marginalized Churchill and pressed for a punitive German peace. Roosevelt supported Stalin's call for the "dismemberment" of Germany and for significant reparations. "We don't want to kill the people," Roosevelt said casually. "We want Germany to live but not to have a higher standard of living than that of the USSR." This startling suggestion—that urbanized, highly industrial Germany be reduced to the living standards of the peasant-based, agrarian Soviet Union—would have found favor with FDR's old pal Henry Morgenthau. "I envision a Germany that is self-sustaining but not starving," Roosevelt said, if only because starving people might require additional aid from the occupiers.[11] The final conference documents left little doubt about the severe treatment the leaders had in store for Germany. Though they kept their agreement to dismember Germany private, they made their overall ambitions plain. "Nazi Germany is doomed," said the official statement released to the press at the conclusion of the conference:

It is our inflexible purpose to destroy German militarism and Nazism and to ensure that Germany will never again be able to disturb the peace of the world. We are determined to disarm and disband all German armed forces; break up for all time the German General Staff that has repeatedly contrived the resurgence of German militarism; remove or destroy all German military equipment; eliminate or control all German industry that could be used for military production; bring all war criminals to just and swift punishment and exact reparation in kind for the destruction wrought by the Germans; wipe out the Nazi party, Nazi laws, organizations and institutions, remove all

Nazi and militarist influences from public office and from the cultural and economic life of the German people; and take in harmony such other measures in Germany as may be necessary to the future peace and safety of the world. It is not our purpose to destroy the people of Germany, but only when Nazism and Militarism have been extirpated will there be hope for a decent life for Germans, and a place for them in the comity of nations.[12]

Roosevelt had no doubt that this was the right policy to adopt toward Germany. Leaving Livadia Palace by car en route to Sevastopol and the waiting naval vessel U.S.S. *Catoctin*, the president saw the devastation of this port town wrought by the Germans. "The city," observed the president's naval aide, "was virtually leveled to the ground except for the walls of homes and other buildings which the mines, bombs and shells in recent battles left standing like billboards—mute testimony of the horrorful wanton Nazi vengeance. Of the thousands of buildings in the city, the president was told that only six were left in useful condition when the Germans fled."[13]

THE AVERAGE AMERICAN soldier, who knew little about governing and had no desire to remain in Germany after the war, would nonetheless shoulder the burden of imposing the Big Three's harsh peace. To prepare soldiers for the transition from fighting the Germans to ruling them, both the U.S. and British armies drew up short guides to be distributed to the fighting men in the field to define the goals of the occupation and provide a basic code of conduct for the occupiers. These texts reveal the profound hostility and suspicion that U.S. military officials harbored toward German civilians and wished to inculcate in their soldiers. The American *Pocket Guide to Germany*, prepared by the War Department, told U.S. soldiers to remain "Firm, Fair, Aloof and Aware." The thesis of the guide was simple: Germans could not be trusted. "You are in *enemy* country! These people are not our allies or friends," the guide warned. Clearly, military officials worried that the average soldier might put the travails of the war behind him and seek out a rapid accommodation with the vanquished foe. But forgiveness was unacceptable, for Americans were not on "a good will errand." Rather, "the Germans have sinned against the laws of humanity and cannot come back into the civilized fold merely by sticking out their hands and saying 'I'm sorry.'" The guide drew out in fifty pages of text some basic elements of the German national character, which compared unfavorably with American habits of mind. Where Americans were forgiving, democratic, and well schooled since childhood in the rules of fair play, decency, and the concept of the fair fight, Germans shared none of these ideals. Teachers and political leaders taught German children to cheat, bully the weak, snitch on friends, betray family, fight unfairly, and to brutalize and torture their enemies. The mass program of indoctrination pursued by the Third Reich spelled trouble for the occupation. Germans could be expected to go underground, and continue to resist the Americans, or to try to manipulate the occupiers, to lie to them, to seek their pity, to blame others for the war and for the atrocities of the regime. The guide also sought to show that Hitler was no anomaly. In a brief historical survey, replete with terms like "treachery," "henchmen," and "gangsters," the guide placed Hitler squarely in the tradition of aggressive, dictatorial leaders like Wilhelm II and Bismarck. Hitler was but "a cruel new version of an old story" of German aggression and war. The guide assumed that a generally unpolitical, war-weary U.S. soldier would be happier making friends with Germans than hating them, and so reiterated the mission of the occupation: "you will be doing a soldier's job on the soil of the enemy."[14]

The British War Office prepared its own guide, with a somewhat more sophisticated and elegant text. "You are about to meet a strange people in a strange, enemy country," it began. The British guide insisted that the German people bore full responsibility for their present suffering, for they had legally placed Hitler in power, cravenly obeyed him as he consolidated his powers, and failed to throw up any serious resistance to his regime. British officials clearly worried, however, that the defeated Germans, so haggard and unlike the once-feared master race of German propaganda, might prey on the sympathies of the British soldier and try to escape responsibility for the war. The Germans might look like familiar cousins, but these first impressions would be deceptive. They could not be trusted, they would tend to whine and complain, and they would try to take advantage of the good-hearted Tommie. "Many of them will have suffered from overwork, underfeeding and the effects of the air raids and you may be tempted to feel sorry for them." They "will protest with deep sincerity that they are as innocent as a babe in arms." But their "hard luck stories . . . will be hypocritical attempts to win sympathy." Thus, the best solution was for the soldier to avoid contact unless they had to give orders, and then "give them in a firm, military manner. The German civilian is used to it and expects it." The booklet concluded: "Germans must still be regarded as dangerous enemies."[15]

Both guides placed particular emphasis on an aspect of occupation policy that was later to cause a good deal of embarrassment: "There must be no fraternization! This is absolute," barked the American guide. This term referred to informal contacts between soldiers and German civilians. The authors of the guides were all too aware of just how much fraternization there had been between soldiers and civilians in Italy, where brothels had been filled to the rooftops with Allied soldiers from their first days on the continent, and in France and Belgium, where bartering between soldiers and local women for cigarettes, food, and sex was commonplace. In liberated countries, such warm relations between liberator and liberated could hardly be denounced by Allied authorities. But in Germany, the occupation aimed to educate Germans about their moral and political failings, and this required a distant, cold, and firm demeanor. The Allied authorities wanted no repeat in Germany of the recent photographs of Belgian girls dancing on British jeeps, which had been pasted across newspapers in Britain and America. While the American guide merely stated the injunction against interaction with Germans, the British guide faced the issue squarely: keep clear of German women, it suggested. They would make the most of their distraught, helpless circumstances. Their "standards of personal honor, already undermined by the Nazis, will sink still lower" following the defeat of the once-invincible Third Reich. "Numbers of German women will be willing, if they can get the chance, to make themselves cheap for what they can get out of you."

Such stringent rules against fraternizing with the Germans grew out of fears that the defeated Germans would try every tactic, both forceful and manipulative, to undermine the Allied occupation of Germany. By the middle of August 1944, SHAEF had outlined policies on these matters that held in place until the summer of 1945. Drawing for comparative purposes on the allied occupation of the Rhineland in 1918, when German attitudes had ranged from "hatred, through friendliness, to fawning subservience," planners believed that the Germans in 1945 would prove far more troublesome. The Allies' massive air bombardment, the intense ground combat, sustained Nazi indoctrination of civilians, and the total occupation of the country would all make "German hatred . . . far deeper and more universal than in 1918." The German "master Race" ideology was thought to be so widespread that "the Germans will accept defeat only as a temporary phase of a continuing struggle. . . . Plans for an underground continuance of the struggle are believed to exist." As a result, occupying forces could not lower their guard; they must be "prepared for civil disorders, including sniping and assaults on individuals, sabotage, provoked riots, perhaps even organized raids. Hidden arms will undoubtedly be available." Yet more worrisome than underground activities, which could be dealt with through sheer force of arms, military planners worried about ideas: "there is likely to be," their initial document on fraternization argued, "deliberate studied and continuous effort by the

"No, Heinrich, it won't wash."

Illingworth in The London Daily Mail

A blood-soaked hand is extended in friendship. This cartoon suggests that Allied soldiers refused to accept it, though in fact relations between liberators and Germans were quite warm. *The New York Times*

Germans to influence the sympathies and thoughts of the occupying forces, with a view to minimizing the consequences of defeat and preparing the way for a resurgence of German power." Germans would wage a "word-of-mouth propaganda" campaign. "Its methods will include attempts at fraternization by civilians (especially by children, women, and old men); attempts at 'soldier-to-soldier' fraternization; and social, official, and religious contacts." This campaign would make appeals to the occupiers for pity and sympathy while also playing on the shared racial and ideological solidarity of Germanic-Anglo-Saxon peoples against the Slavs. Most common would be the portrayal of Nazism as an "alien idea implanted against the general will in the cultured and unaggressive minds of Germans." For these reasons, Allied authorities insisted on a strict separation of officers and soldiers from the German people, meaning "the avoidance of mingling with Germans upon terms of friendliness, familiarity or intimacy." No billeting among the civilians, no marriages, not even common religious services, no shaking hands, playing of games or sports, accepting gifts, no walking with Germans on the streets, attending dances, and certainly no "discussions and arguments with Germans, especially on politics or the future of Germany." "The Germans," as Eisenhower put it simply, "must be ostracized."[16]

No sooner had Allied soldiers put their toes onto German soil in mid-September 1944 than the ban on fraternization ran into trouble. When units of the VII Corps fought their way through the West Wall into the towns of Rötgen and Stolberg, just south of Aachen, a few timid Germans appeared in the streets to speak to the not-unfriendly Americans. U.S. Army press photographers snapped pictures, and these immediately appeared in newspapers under captions suggesting that the German people had given Americans a warm reception. Eisenhower reacted immediately. "Press reports and those from other sources indicate already a considerable extent of fraternization by US troops with the German Civil population," Ike wrote to General Bradley, commander of the 12th Army Group. "This must be nipped in the bud immediately." Having then received an earful from Washington about these press reports, Eisenhower told his public relations staff that "the President has noted with concern pictures of American troops fraternizing with the German population." There was only one way to handle this matter: censorship. "All pictures of American troops fraternizing with German population, together with any stories playing up fraternization, are to be placed on the censor list."[17]

Between October 1944 and early March 1945, the Allies held merely a tiny sliver of German territory, mostly south of Aachen and, after February, the narrow band of land between the Roer and Rhine rivers. Fighting here was fierce, as it had been during the December-January Battle of the Bulge, and Allied soldiers had no difficulty in finding reasons to hate the Germans. There were incidents of fraternization behind the lines, and accounts from press reporters suggested that American GIs were indeed tempted to act with expressions of kindness toward elderly, homeless, war-weary German civilians, and toward the children who flocked with curiosity around the foreigners. Yet there was a palpable distance between occupier and occupied. Drew Middleton of the *New York Times* reported in October that "American soldiers' initial reaction to Germany and German civilians is a mixture of contempt and indifference and in the case of many front line outfits, hatred. . . . There is very little fraternization of any sort. . . . Their attitude seems to be that of the old Indian fighters, that a dead German is the only good one." Middleton also noted in a later article that the German civilians were adopting precisely the self-defense that Allied planners had most feared, and which had motivated their ban on fraternization in the first place. In a piece called "The Great Alibi in the Making," Middleton depicted Germans as engaged in massive denial for the crimes of the Third Reich. They refused to accept responsibility for Hitler, claimed to have no knowledge of his atrocities, and affected to have been anti-Nazi all along. In the same breath, however, they were happy to acknowledge that at least the Germans had "saved the world from Bolshevism" by fighting so tenaciously against the Russians. Middleton found these explanations an indication of "the moral poverty of the German nation" and suggested that Americans would have to be on their guard against this exculpatory German propaganda.[18] "No one is a Nazi. No one ever was," wrote the caustic American journalist Martha Gellhorn of this exculpatory banter. "It should, we feel, be set to music. Then the Germans could sing this refrain and that would make it even better."[19] Clifton Daniel of the *New York Times* also hinted at the difficulties ahead for the Americans. Writing from Aachen in December, he reported that Germans and Americans "pass on the streets without looking directly at each other. They manifest no hostility but they invite no intimacy." The Germans "accept the authority of the military government," and obey orders. But they were sycophants who "try to ingratiate themselves with their new masters. . . . By their very docility, the Germans help thwart those who advocate rougher treatment of the civilian population." Beneath this outer docility lay a cynical attempt to deny responsibility for the war. "The Germans generally show no consciousness of wrongdoing," Daniel reported. "They seem either surprised or distressed at suggestions that collectively or individually they may be held responsible for Germany's crimes." Judging from early encounters in Aachen, Americans concluded that controlling the Germans would be fairly easy; persuading them to accept responsibility for the crimes of the Third Reich, however, looked like a far taller order.[20]

Poised to enter farther into Germany in spring 1945, SHAEF remained on guard against fraternization. Not only did SHAEF release the *Pocket Guide* to its soldiers, but it also ran radio spots on Armed Forces Radio that tried to boil down the issue in simple terms. These spots, placed at intervals between regular programming, reveal the anxiety of military planners toward the natural inclination of soldiers to make friends with the local German civilians:

Remember—the Germans you see now are just the same people who strutted with pride when Warsaw was bombed; who roared with approval when Rotterdam was flattened; who cheered when London burned. These are the same Germans. Don't fraternize.

After a good clean fight, you can shake hands with your opponent. This hasn't been a good clean fight—not on the German side. You can't shake hands with a Hun. Don't fraternize.

Don't be misled into thinking of Germans, "Oh, well, they're human." So is a murderer, so is a cannibal. The German people have loved war too long. Let them see it doesn't pay. Show them clearly. Don't fraternize.

That frau going to market may look harmless enough. The odds are she walks in a dead woman's shoes, sent from the murder furnaces of Maidenek. Don't forget that in a hurry. Steer clear. Don't fraternize.

Kids are kids—all over the world—except in Hitler's Germany. Sure they're loveable—but ten years ago, the Jerry that got your buddy was loveable too. It's tough to do, but make the kids realize now that war doesn't pay—they may remember when they think about starting the next war! Don't fraternize.

You can't tell a rotten egg by the shell. Don't let looks fool you! When you're tempted to fraternize with the friendly looking German civilian, remember the rotten egg! Don't fraternize.

Soldiers wise don't fraternize![21]

These radio spots sought to sustain the wariness of soldiers about civilians, and also to reinforce Allied policy that all Germans were responsible for Hitler's crimes: that the German public bore collective responsibility, and that they must be collectively punished. But when the Allied soldiers moved into full command of Germany as occupiers, they confronted a nation that looked as if it had already been punished, indeed punished more severely than anyone could have imagined.

———

"IT WAS IN Cologne that I realized what total destruction meant," wrote the poet and author Stephen Spender. He had gone to Germany in July 1945 on an official British government assignment to seek out German intellectuals in the hopes of finding some nonfascist life still flickering amid the ruins of the Reich. Spender knew well what aerial bombing had done to London and other cities in the British Isles. But what he saw in western Germany, where he had once lived and studied, stunned him.

My first impression on passing through was of there being not a single house left. There are plenty of walls but these walls are a thin mask in front of the damp, hollow, stinking emptiness of gutted interiors.

. . . One passes through street after street of houses whose windows look hollow and blackened—like the open mouth of a charred corpse. . . . In England, there are holes, gaps, wounds but the surrounding life of the people themselves has filled them up, creating a scar which will heal. In towns such as Cologne, and those of the Ruhr, something quite different has happened. The external destruction is so great that it cannot be healed and the surrounding life of the rest of the country cannot flow into and resuscitate the city, which is not only battered but also dismembered and cut off from the rest of Germany and from Europe. The ruin of the city is reflected in the internal ruin of its inhabitants who, instead of being lives that can form a scar over the city's wounds, are parasites sucking at a dead carcass, digging among the ruins for hidden food. . . . They resemble rather a tribe of wanderers who have discovered a ruined city in a desert and who are camping there, living in the cellars and hunting amongst the ruins for the booty, relics of a dead civilization. The great city looks like a corpse and smells like one, too.[22]

The destruction Spender saw was also visible in over seventy German cities at war's end. It was the result of the massive Allied bombing campaign against Germany that began in 1940 and increased steadily, slowly, until by the end of 1944 it had become a gigantic force of unequaled power, and for Germans, unequaled terror. The "strategic" bombing of Germany (distinguished from "tactical" bombing in support of soldiers in battle) is a dimension of the war that has generated a long, controversial history. It conjures up a gallery of ghastly images: burnt corpses being gathered up in wagons; shriveled, carbonized bodies stacked ten feet high; blackened churches, shattered homes. The slaughter of half a million German civilians, and the means by which it was delivered, from the sky, thousands of feet above the battlefield, has tarnished the record of the Allied war effort ever since. Randall Jarrell, the American poet who flew in these missions, captured something of the grotesque indifference of bombing with these lines:

> *In bombers named for girls, we burned*
> *The cities we had learned about in school.*
> *. . .*
> *They said "Here are the maps"; We burned the cities.*

Yet during the war, many intelligent people accepted the massive bombing of Germany's cities, and the large numbers of civilian deaths such bombing caused, as essential to defeating Hitler and winning the war. Why?

The blackened cathedral stands sentinel over shattered Cologne.
U.S. National Archives

At first, the British bombed Germany because it was the only way they could do Hitler any harm at all. Having swept the Poles, Dutch, Belgians, French, and British land armies aside in 1939–40 like tin soldiers, the powerful Wehrmacht and its allies commanded all of central and western Europe. From July 10, 1940, until October, Hitler threw his air force at the British, hoping to wrest control of the skies over the English Channel from the Royal Air Force (RAF), and so opening the way to his planned invasion of Britain. The pilots of the RAF managed to hold off the Luftwaffe in the Battle of Britain, and Prime Minister Churchill paid these young men a great tribute in the House of Commons when he said, on August 20, 1940, "Never in the field of human conflict was so much owed by so many to so few." But Churchill, not wishing to appear as if Britain was condemned to remain on the defensive, continued: "we must never forget," he said, "that night after night, month after month, our bomber squadrons travel far into Germany, find their targets in the darkness by the highest navigational skill, aim their attacks, often under the heaviest fire, often with serious loss, with deliberate careful discrimination, and inflict shattering blows upon the whole of the technical and war-making structure of Nazi power." Such bombing, Churchill told

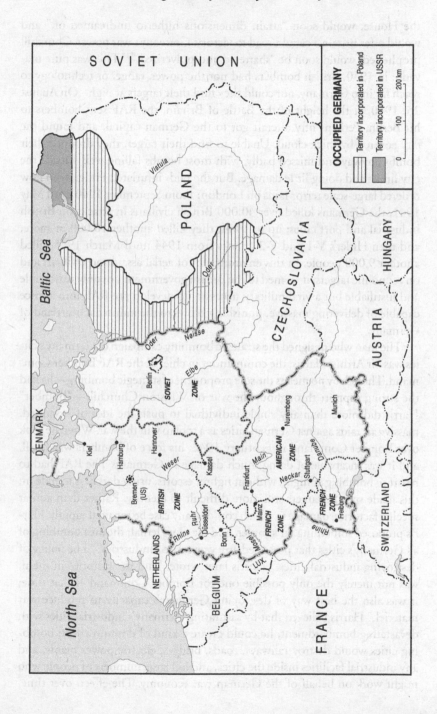

SOVIET UNION

POLAND

CZECHOSLOVAKIA

HUNGARY

AUSTRIA

Baltic Sea

Vistula

Oder

Neisse

Oder

DENMARK

Kiel

Hamburg

Weser

Hannover

Elbe

Berlin

SOVIET
ZONE

Nuremberg

Munich

Danube

North Sea

Bremen
(US)

BRITISH
ZONE

Kassel

Main

AMERICAN
ZONE

NETHERLANDS

Ruhr

Düsseldorf

Rhine

Bonn

LUX.

Mosel

FRENCH
ZONE

Frankfurt

Mainz

FRENCH
ZONE

Neckar

Stuttgart

Freiburg

FRENCH
ZONE

Rhine

SWITZERLAND

BELGIUM

FRANCE

OCCUPIED GERMANY

Territory incorporated in Poland

Territory incorporated in USSR

0   100   200 km

the House, would soon "attain dimensions hitherto undreamed of," and would offer Britain a certain road to victory. Germany's war power, Churchill prophesied, would soon be "shattered and pulverized."²³ This was pure bravado: in 1940, British bombers had not the power, range, or technology to reach far into Germany, nor could they find their targets at night. On August 25, 1940, at the height of the Battle of Britain, the RAF sent bombers to hit Berlin. Perhaps fifty aircraft got to the German capital, and found the city covered by thick cloud. Unable to find their target, they dropped their bombs anyway and missed badly, with most bombs falling well outside the city limits and doing little damage. But the raids infuriated Hitler, who now ordered large-scale terror raids on London. From September 1940 until May 1941, the Germans killed over 40,000 British civilians in attacks on British industrial and port cities; up to 1944, they killed another 10,000 or more; and then Hitler's V-1 and V-2 attacks from 1944 until March 1945 killed another 9,000 people. In this environment of aerial assault on civilians and on economic targets, it seemed to the British government not only reasonable and justifiable but a vital military necessity to develop the RAF into a force capable of delivering massive, punishing blows to the industrial heartland of Germany.

The man who designed the strategic bombing campaign of Germany's cities was Sir Arthur Harris, the commander in chief of the RAF Bomber Command. Though by no means the sole proponent of strategic bombing—he had the strong support throughout the war of Winston Churchill—"Bomber" Harris did more than any single individual to push the idea of sustained, massive air raids against German cities as a tool to win the war. When he took over Bomber Command in February 1942, his force of bombers was small, and it was incapable of doing much damage to Germany. The RAF had to resort to bombing at night, without fighter escorts, using darkness to hide in; this made specific targets still more difficult to identify. Rather than aim at specific factories, damage to which could in any case be repaired rapidly, Harris proposed something far simpler, and far more lethal: the area bombing of all Germany's cities that possessed any war-related industries. "The policy of destroying industrial cities," Harris later wrote, "and the factories in them, was not merely the only possible one for Bomber Command at that time; it was also the best way of destroying Germany's capacity to produce war materiel." Harris believed that by saturating Germany's industrial cities with devastating bombardment, he could create a kind of domino effect: bombing cities would destroy railways, roads, bridges, electric power plants, and any industrial facilities inside the cities, and kill large numbers of people who might work on behalf of the German war economy. The effect, over time, would be to erode the capacity of the German economy to get arms, fuel, and supplies to the front. Harris argued that limiting bombing to factories within a given city could not achieve this sort of knockout blow: *the city as a whole* had to be destroyed.[24]

The U.S. Army Air Forces (USAAF), which reached sufficient strength to play a major role in the bombing campaign only by the end of 1943, never fully accepted Harris's emphasis on area bombing as opposed to precision bombing. The Americans chose to try their hand at daytime attacks on specific targets such as submarine bases, aircraft and ball-bearing factories, and later, oil refineries. At first they faced the same problems the RAF had experienced, and American bombers were shot down in high numbers. But the Americans developed a new tactic: the creation of a fleet of long-range fighter escorts that could accompany the large bombers on their runs across Germany and engage and destroy the Luftwaffe at the same time. The destruction of the Luftwaffe in the air gradually opened the way toward total Allied mastery of the sky, just at the moment when the bombing fleets had grown to massive and threatening size. Although the Americans continued to try to hit precision targets, they also grew increasingly willing to bomb cities in much the same manner as their British counterparts: indiscriminately. In the spring and summer of 1944, the Allied air forces concentrated their efforts on France, in preparation for the Normandy assault. But after the breakthrough across France and Belgium in September 1944, they reverted to hitting targets inside Germany. In the eight months between September 1944 and April 1945, the Eighth U.S. Air Force and the RAF dropped 729,000 tons of bombs on Germany—more than they had achieved in all the previous months of the war combined. In March 1945 alone, the two air forces dropped 133,000 tons of bombs on Germany, the largest total for any month of the war, and about 10 percent of the entire tonnage dropped on Germany during the war.[25]

What were the results of this massive bombing? We have a great deal of information to answer this question, because hard on the heels of the first Allied units into Germany came teams of investigators from the United States Strategic Bombing Survey. This group of over one thousand military and civilian experts undertook to examine the impact of the bombing campaign on both Germany and Japan. In Germany, they gained access to many records from German official ministries, and were able to draw up 212 remarkably detailed reports on the effect of bombing on all aspects of German war industries, transportation, communications, armaments production, as well as civilian morale and civil defense efforts. The summary report, which was released to the public on October 30, 1945, claimed that

Allied aircraft dropped 2.7 million tons of bombs on Germany; destroyed 3.6 million dwellings; and killed at least 305,000 German civilians. (That was a minimum figure, and the number of German dead was surely higher; even the survey's own documents suggested the number of dead was closer to half a million.) Allied bombing wounded 800,000 people and left 7.5 million people homeless. It forced the evacuation of five million people from stricken regions, and deprived twenty million people of utilities for some period of time. The report noted that the huge attacks the RAF and USAAF mounted after June 1944 were especially damaging both to the German economy and to civilian morale. "Allied air power was decisive in the war in Western Europe," the report concluded. Not only did it make the invasion of Europe in 1944 possible, but it "brought the economy which sustained the enemy's armed forces to virtual collapse." The Allied bombing campaign "brought home to the German people the full impact of modern war with all its horror and suffering."[26]

The words "horror and suffering" were appropriate. Although there has long been a debate about the actual *economic* effects of the bombing, there can be little doubt that the *human* effects were appalling. In their efforts to determine precisely how many people the bombing killed, the survey team did extensive research in German medical and civil defense records. These revealed that Allied bombing had killed in a variety of gruesome ways. Civilians were buried beneath rubble, dismembered or mortally wounded by bomb fragments, or burned to death by incendiary bombs filled with napalm or phosphorous. Germany had developed a sophisticated and extensive system of air raid shelters for civilians, and these served to protect many people from death. But in the case of a firestorm, as in Hamburg, or simply extensive incendiary bombing, carbon monoxide poisoning killed thousands of people both inside air raid shelters and even outdoors. In addition to deadly gases, the heat from fire killed civilians in shelters, basements, and brick buildings. Others died from choking on inhaled dust, heart attacks, internal hemorrhages, and skull fractures. In Hamburg, at least 40,000 people died after repeated Allied air strikes on July 24–29 and August 2, 1943, triggered a roaring, cataclysmic fire that contemporaries called a "fire typhoon." Temperatures in the city reached 800 degrees Celsius (1,472 degrees Fahrenheit). German documents revealed that thousands of people had been trapped inside air raid shelters and had been roasted alive; civil defense workers found whole families inside shelters whose bodies were "dry, shrunken, resembling mummies."[27] Similar scenes had played out across Germany between the spring of 1942 and the end of the war; the single most notorious attack came on Dresden, an eastern German city of limited strategic importance. On

February 13 and 14, 1945, Allied aircraft struck the city with high explosives, incendiary bombs, and flares, triggering a firestorm that devastated the city and killed at least 25,000 people, perhaps twice that number.[28]

The first American and British press accounts from the occupied Rhineland reveal that even to those reporters who had covered the war in Europe, the bombed cities of Germany were a ghastly revelation. Cologne, Germany's fourth-largest city and the capital of the Rhineland, fell to the Allies on March 6, with American tanks of the 3rd Armored Division of General Collins's VII Corps driving into the center of the town and right up to the twisted wreck of the Hohenzollern bridge over the still-uncrossable Rhine. Press reports spoke of "the utter destruction" of the city, its "twisted, rusty rails, battered trucks, and deep piles of rubble from which dust and smoke were still rising." This city had been a favorite target of the RAF. Between March 1942 and March 1945, Bomber Command sent no fewer than twenty-two major air strikes against Cologne, dropping about 30,000 tons of bombs on it and destroying over 70 percent of the city. Only Essen and Berlin received a greater tonnage of bombs. At first, the scale of the damage did not seem to perturb Allied commanders. Such destruction had been intended. On March 13, just a few days after the capture of Cologne, General Eisenhower issued a public message of praise to Air Chief Marshal Harris saying that his visit to the Rhineland cities revealed "striking evidence of the effectiveness of the bombing campaigns. . . . City after city has been systematically shattered." Ike acclaimed the "heroic work" of Bomber Command and the U.S. Air Forces.[29]

Such sangfroid proved hard to maintain. General Walter Bedell Smith, Eisenhower's chief of staff, saw Cologne shortly after its capture. "The center of the ancient town was completely flattened," he wrote, "a picture of absolute destruction greater than I had seen anywhere"—this from a man who had seen every American battlefield in the European Theater. *Time* magazine's Sidney Olson wrote that Allied soldiers who had "exulted over 1,000-plane assaults and 3,500-ton bomb loads" could now see for themselves what strategic bombing had achieved. "A mud-stained veteran stared with dazed eyes at the desolation about him, murmuring over and over, 'Ain't it awful! Ain't it awful!'" Olson was struck by the "silence and emptiness" of the city. A few timid cellar-dwelling citizens appeared, shaken and jumpy, deathly afraid of the sound of aircraft. In a remarkable survey of Cologne in late April titled "Dead German Cities," the London *Times* correspondent wrote that "there are simply no words to describe the devastation of Cologne." The future of the city seemed in doubt. "No plan for military government, however foreseeing, can have reckoned with the reality of the fearful retribution that has fallen upon the cities of the Rhineland. . . . The fundamental problems of living, of picking up the slender threads of existence from the mountain of rubble" were sure to stymie Allied military government, for bombing had turned the region into a "wilderness of blasted stone." The correspondent felt it necessary to say, as if bucking up his courage before gazing at the horrors before him, that "we have to remind ourselves that the enemy brought it on himself." But it was hard to see this once-vital, bustling place in ruins, without water, gas, electricity, transportation, even roads or rails. "Cologne, indeed, is a dead city—silent as the grave and full of the grit and dust that swirl from the hillocks of rubble." As for the inhabitants, "it seems a little foolish to talk of the attitude of the people. So far as one could judge, theirs is the numb bewilderment of any people who have survived a cataclysm and are down to the clothes they stand in." Press reporters spoke of the densely packed, factory-filled cities along the Ruhr river as "inert," "lifeless," "spectral and morose," looking like "the bowels of the earth." Ben Hibbs of the *Saturday Evening Post* wrote, "Cologne is finished, I should imagine, literally erased from the map forever."[30]

A view of Cologne taken from the spire of the cathedral.
U.S. National Archives

As Allied armies pushed farther into Germany, similar scenes greeted them. The cities along the Ruhr valley that formed the great industrial powerhouse of Germany had been hit repeatedly. Essen (hit by twenty-eight major RAF attacks between March 1942 and March 1945), Duisburg, Düsseldorf, Dortmund, Wuppertal, Bochum, these towns "burned like torches for a night, smoldered for a day, then lay blackened and dead"—until they were reignited by repeated air strikes.[31] Frankfurt, just a few miles across the Rhine and the city that would soon become the headquarters of the American zone of occupation, was taken by the 5th Division of XII Corps on March 26. It had endured eleven major RAF attacks and received over 23,000 tons of bombs. The London *Times* reporter who arrived four days later described Frankfurt as a "melancholy sample" of Germany's cities. The shopping districts were in ruins, the streets clogged with rubble. In front of one of the cultural shrines of the city, Goethe's birthplace at no. 23 Grosse Hirschgraben, a cardboard sign had been propped up with a handwritten message: "Here was the house where the old great poet Goethe was born." The house was gone, as was the museum next door and indeed the whole street and neighborhood. The Romerberg, the medieval marketplace, was vaporized; the opera house was roofless, and its walls gashed open; the cathedral, scene of the coronation of German emperors, had lost its roof; only the tower remained, a blackened finger pointing skyward. "I have been in Frankfurt before," reported *Time* magazine's Percy Knauth, but "today I found no single landmark I recognized. In these miles and miles of ruins, there is nothing but dullness and apathy, a state that seems like a sleepwalking trance."[32]

Farther down the river Rhine, the city of Mainz, which had endured repeated incendiary raids, looked "like the excavated ruins of an earlier civilization, or like watered-down fragments of children's sand-castles." To the east, Nuremberg fell to the Americans on April 20, Hitler's birthday. It was a heap of cinders and stone. Richard J. H. Johnston of the *New York Times* reported the next day that "there is no more hideous spot in Europe today than Nuremberg, shrine city of the Nazis." Not one building inside the walled old city remained standing. "Like timid ground creatures, a few Germans came up from their shelters, caves and cellars this morning to blink in strong sunlight and stare unbelieving at the awful mess that was their town." The ancient churches, historic homes, and cultural monuments were in pieces. The glorious Church of Saint Sebaldus was reduced to "a clutter of broken stone, bits of broken stained glass, and little chunks of melted lead and statuary." The storied buildings that had made the city a glittering showcase, such as the Gothic city hall, the Haupt Markt, the Frauenkirche, all were in total ruins. Beneath the rubble lay uncounted dead bodies. Johnston concluded gloomily: "Nuremberg is a city of the dead."[33]

Cornelia Stabler Gillam, a young Quaker from Philadelphia who signed up with the USO to play piano concerts in Army canteens across occupied Germany, wrote home to her family in late June and described her first journey from Belgium into Germany along roads lined with shattered tanks, concrete pillboxes, and devastated villages. The destruction of Aachen stunned her. Not a house was left standing, she wrote, and "it makes you tremble inside. People crawling like rats out of the ruined buildings where they live. Sad-faced children trying to play in the streets blocked with stone and plaster. I was afraid several times that I would cry, and I knew it would be misunderstood. I would not be weeping for the Germans but for all the world."[34]

THE AMERICAN ZONE of occupation extended over 41,000 square miles of southern and central Germany, including all of Bavaria and some chunks of Baden-Württemberg and Hessen. This area, the size of Tennessee, included about fifteen million Germans—a number in constant flux, due to the large refugee flows across Germany in 1945. The Americans had 1,622,000 men in Germany on V-E Day, a number that began immediately to decline as troops were either reassigned to the Pacific or sent back home. The U.S. zone included some of the most beautiful landscape of Germany, including the Bavarian Alps where Hitler had built his mountain retreat at Berchtesgaden. Its main cities were small: Munich had a prewar population of 800,000; Frankfurt, Nuremberg, and Stuttgart about half a million each; Mannheim less than 400,000; Karlsruhe 300,000. All had been heavily bombed, but the countryside in Bavaria had not been badly damaged, and the zone contained a few miracles, like the ancient university city of Heidelberg, which emerged from the war wholly unscathed.

With amazing speed, the Army dispatched 269 Military Government detachments across the zone to establish official control and begin the process of registering civilians, rooting out top Nazis, arresting war criminals, and assessing the state of the damage in the zone. In small towns, a Military Government unit could work effectively. But in a city like Frankfurt, the shortage of American staff was readily apparent: nineteen officers and twenty-four men had to look after this shattered city by themselves, carefully avoiding the use of local administration until they had been vetted for Nazi Party connections. A reporter who watched the work of these initial detachments was impressed by the orderliness of it all:

The prostrate body of a city is given artificial respiration. The dead are buried, and the streets are cleared. Wherever possible, the water system is restarted as a first check against epidemics. Reliable Germans must be found to run the show. I say they must be found because every Military Government team in the American zone has from the start been so desperately understaffed that it could not dream of operating without civilian assistance. Luckily, there was no hitch in getting the civilians to collaborate—to everyone's amazement, most Germans did not seem to bear any grudge against the invaders. Besides, the Germans are well trained in obeying orders and putting themselves at the disposal of the authorities, whoever they are.[35]

Whereas SHAEF had prognosticated darkly about pockets of fanatical armed resistance, sabotage, underground terrorist cells, and so on, occupied Germany was extremely quiet in the first months. Advance units reported

German civilians and an American GI read the orders of the U.S. Occupation authorities posted in a German town. This photo was taken on October 20, 1944, when American forces had occupied only a small sliver of German territory around Aachen. *U.S. National Archives*

that the people were "passive," and were in a state of "stunned despondency over their misfortunes." Other than petty looting, and a good deal of theft and sporadic violence by migrating displaced persons and former forced laborers, the country was calm. The only thing that irked occupation officials was the marked tendency of Germans "to disclaim all responsibility for the action of both the *Wehrmacht* and the NSDAP [Nazi Party]. Many, for instance, when told of the horrors of the concentration camps have almost indignantly disclaimed all knowledge of or responsibility for these institutions." Otherwise, the weekly field reports reported little crime committed by Germans, and an "attitude of civilian cooperation and resigned adherence to occupation policy."[36]

American soldiers, by contrast, were not always quiet and cooperative. "The behavior of some of the troops," according to an American officer attached to the Psychological Warfare office of SHAEF, "was nothing to brag about, particularly after they came across cases of cognac and barrels of wine. I am mentioning it only because there is a tendency among the naïve or the malicious to think that only Russians loot and rape. After a battle, soldiers of every country are pretty much the same."[37] The Army's Judge Advocate General was even more direct: "A tremendous increase in the number of rapes occurred when our troops arrived on German soil," concluded the JAG's report, which also noted that 88 percent of the reported rapes of German women by U.S. soldiers occurred in March and April 1945. "We were members of a conquering army, and we came as conquerors," the JAG continued. "The rate of reported rapes sprang skyward." The JAG believed that the sudden increase in rape was partly due to Nazi propaganda, "which had prepared the way by telling the German people that the American troops would rape and pillage and kill. The German population was cowed." This explanation seemed to blame the victim: a cowed woman, it suggested, was a vulnerable target. In fact, the American Army had spent the previous year instructing soldiers to view German people as treacherous enemies, prone to sabotage, deceit, and malice. The fighting of the winter and early spring had been extremely difficult and the Germans had put up a ferocious resistance to the advancing armies, only stoking American hatred. And the discovery of the concentration camps, and the massive publicity they received in April, made soldiers feel that the German people deserved whatever awful fate awaited them. In the words of the JAG, "the situation was ripe for violent sex crimes, and the avalanche came."

In the typical case, one or more armed soldiers entered a German house, either by force or by stratagem (such as a pretense of searching for German soldiers), and engaged in sexual intercourse with one or more of the female occupants. Sometimes the act was accomplished through the application of direct force, at other times by submission resulting from the occupants' fear for their lives. Housebreaking, larceny, the shooting of firearms, and the commission of various violent crimes upon the occupants, were common concomitants of these rapes and an increasing occurrence of acts of sodomy upon the rape victims was noted.

The JAG report claimed that "it was only in a very exceptional case that the German victim vigorously resisted her armed attackers. . . . In the great majority of cases, there was no such resistance. The German victims were apparently thoroughly cowed by the threatened use of the weapons in the hands of members of the conquering army. Their mortal fear was not entirely groundless, as demonstrated in a number of cases in which the Germans who sought to prevent the soldiers from carrying out their designs to commit rape were mercilessly murdered." This lack of resistance became a puzzle for the military court: "if a soldier, armed as he was required by orders to be, enters a German home and engages in sexual intercourse with a German woman, who submits to his lust through fear (fear of his weapons and fear sometimes engendered by Nazi propaganda), giving no outward signs of resistance, is this rape?" Even though German accusers told the courts that "it was best not to resist; otherwise we would be killed," the courts believed that in some cases, a failure to resist might indicate some degree of consent; or at least it could undermine a finding of intent to rape. Generally, however, the Army courts-martial found that the context mattered: armed men, in a country under military occupation, had enormous power as well as enormous responsibility. "A man who enters a strange house, carrying a rifle in one hand, is not justified in believing he has accomplished a seduction on the other hand."[38]

The Judge Advocate General's report referred to the increase in rape cases as an "avalanche," though the actual number of cases it considered—552—seems small when one considers that 1.6 million U.S. soldiers were in Germany at the end of the war. To be sure, as the JAG's report acknowledged, "many more rapes undoubtedly occurred than were reflected in general court-martial records." Rape charges were often settled on the spot by officers; unknown numbers were never reported. This was an embarrassing subject for the Army and it was not one they wanted aired in public. When on March 14, a *Stars and Stripes* reporter filed a story about the widespread prevalence of rape in the Rhineland, it was promptly suppressed by Army censors. That piece noted that "since the records of such assaults come from reports of the Germans themselves to U.S. Military Government officials or other Army authorities, it is probable that the total number of rape cases is considerably higher" than the number that had made it through Army channels.[39] Yet there may be another reason that cases of rape were not as numerous as the overall size of the U.S. military presence might have predicted: U.S. soldiers who wanted sex did not have to resort to the use of force. They could buy sex, cheaply.

From the moment American troops put their boots on German soil, they sought out German women. The fraternization ban that General Eisenhower had imposed in September 1944 never worked. As early as October 1944, the editor in chief of *Stars and Stripes,* Major Arthur Goodfriend, prepared a devastating critique of the policy and passed this up to his superiors. Goodfriend, who was then passing through the Army in the guise of "Private Arthur Goodwin" in a bid for good story material, wrote that American soldiers found it easy, and even enjoyable, to talk to German civilians; if they were to be punished for doing so, the Army would have a massive disciplinary challenge on its hands. In towns outside Aachen, Goodfriend saw American soldiers help German housewives with their chores, play with children, and "through other acts of friendship make living more tolerable through the creation of a friendly atmosphere." In the eyes of the GI, the Germans fared well when compared to the French: said one trooper, "'these people are cleaner and a damn sight friendlier than the frogs. They're our kind of people.'" One commanding officer of a battalion told Goodfriend, "'When I see two or three thousand old and fear-crazed and feeble women and kids with all their belongings and their houses and futures all shot to hell, I can't help but feel pity. . . . We have no qualms about knocking down a city, but we do have pity for the old and weak.'" Soldiers were looking for companionship, a respite in "the agreeable cleanliness and warmth of German farms and homes," and a "sanctuary from the misery and indignity of living and fighting through a winter campaign."[40]

Soldiers were not looking chiefly for the company of elderly farmers. Saul Padover of the Psychological Warfare team put the situation bluntly. "To a man bored and fed up with the company of other men, almost anything in skirts is a stimulant and a relief, and German women were not just skirts. They were undeniably attractive in a wholesome, physical, sexy way. They were what the boys called 'easy' . . . GI and Fräulein were magnet and steel."[41] American troops, now fanning out into the cities and towns of Germany and setting up barracks and camps as part of the occupation administration, found German women willing to exchange sex for food, cigarettes, chocolates, soap, and other luxuries. As the historian Petra Goedde has noted, "the border line between love affairs and prostitution became blurred" in occupied Germany. German girls, who lacked so many goods, "used their bodies as bargaining chips." They resorted to prostitution "to save themselves and their families from starvation" or to gain access to scarce goods and cigarettes.[42] And the GI had an astonishing quantity of goods to offer. The Army provided him with candy, coffee, cigarettes in limitless abundance, soap, towels, writing paper, pens and ink, clothing, and six quarts of liquor a month. In the post exchange (PX), the soldier could buy at reduced price whatever little luxuries he might desire, and in clubs, mess tents, barracks, and snack bars that were erected for his comfort, he could get doughnuts, coffee, ice cream, theater tickets, haircuts, and recreation. With his pockets filled with desirable and scarce goods, the GI found himself able to buy sex with the greatest of ease.[43]

This illicit sex economy threatened to erupt into a major health crisis, as venereal disease rates soared among GIs once they moved into Germany. Medical Corps officials complained that the fraternization ban deterred GIs from getting checkups at prophylactic stations for fear that they would be fined for fraternizing. Eisenhower on June 11 had to issue a special order that made nonsense of his own nonfraternization policy: "the contraction of venereal disease . . . will not be used directly or indirectly as evidence of fraternization." Soldiers who got treatment for VD would be spared the sixty-five-dollar fine that those caught fraternizing had to pay. (How one could contract VD from a German in the absence of fraternization remained unclear.) Another factor helping to spread VD: in summer 1945, the Army suddenly found itself facing a condom shortage—supplies fell from six per man to four per man each month. VD rates skyrocketed. In June 1945, Army VD rates were at the highest they had ever been, with ground forces hitting a record rate of 140 cases per 1,000 men, or 14 percent; by September 1945, the figure reached 190 cases per 1,000 men. The alarmed chief surgeon of the U.S. forces, European Theater, Major General Albert W. Kenner, noted that with two million men in the European Theater, he might have as many as 380,000 VD cases on his hands. In November, American aircraft flew in emergency doses of penicillin for the treatment of gonorrhea among German civilians. VD rates did not subside until the middle of 1946. Clearly, the American soldier liked to fraternize.[44]

On June 2, General Eisenhower made an important gesture. He cabled his superior in Washington, General George Marshall, seeking approval for an easing of the ban on talking to German children. "Everyone must recognize," he wrote, "that the American soldier is not going to be stern and harsh with young children, but on the contrary feels an inner compulsion constantly to make friends with them." General Marshall agreed, and replied that "there is a natural tie between the soldier and small children"; an order revising the ban on fraternization with German children was soon issued.[45] But this only opened the floodgates; a wave of press criticism erupted, as reporters wrote stories depicting "hourly" breaches of the fraternization ban. In the British zone of occupation, it was "common knowledge" that it was being ignored.[46] On June 25, the *New York Times* ran a long piece by Drew Middleton reporting that senior officers in the U.S. Military Government opposed the ban; it was simply unenforceable. "German girls wait on the roads near the woods outside the occupied towns and villages for soldiers who stroll out of town with their pockets stuffed with candy, chewing gum and cigarettes." According to one GI, "'girls throw themselves at you if you give them half a chance.'"[47] On July 14, Eisenhower conceded the fraternization policy was a failure by rescinding restrictions on public conversation with German adults, though GIs had been openly defying the ban for months. In October, all restrictions on fraternization were lifted.

The lifting of the ban merely acknowledged the close and intimate ties that had sprung up between Americans and German women. A *Time* magazine reporter, himself evidently taken by the charms of the Germans, asked a few women in a Bavarian lakeside town their reaction to the news. "Ilse Schmidt, a gorgeous 19-year-old brunette with a figure designed to make men drool," seemed bored by the conversation and asked the reporter for a cigarette. "A 28-year-old blonde, blousy German girl named Helga" who had been sharing a hotel room with an American GI for over a month was pleased that the two did not have to hide their romance anymore. Two other girls leaning out of the window of the hotel, Brigitte Heidenrich and Ingeborg Gassau, both twenty-one, "were giggling like bobby-soxers" when they were publicly propositioned by two GIs. One of the soldiers shouted up, "Hey there Brigitte, how ya doing, baby? How about us coming up? It's not *verboten* anymore!" The door swung open and in he went.[48]

HAD LOVE CONQUERED all? It is tempting, in light of these stories about German-American sexual relations, to depict the first summer of the occupation as suffused in a pink glow of love, lust, and giggling intimacies between youthful girls and brawny GIs. The sweet passions of the heart had triumphed, it seemed, over ideological foulness. The German girls were not only pretty; they were "so neat and clean in their freshly washed and pressed summer dresses, their bobby-socks and their long braids," gushed an enthusiastic reporter. Overall, the American soldier was amazed at how "surprisingly well dressed and healthy" the former enemy was. Germans also worked hard. "In a matter of weeks, cities that had been deathly ruins" were transformed into "neat piles of brick and stone; bombed houses, patched with scraps from neighboring heaps, became habitable hutches." In a short time, "the angers of battle, the horrors of the death camps, were wearing off." The dutiful Germans and the big-hearted Americans seemed inclined to forgive, forget, and move on.[49]

Certainly many Germans initially seemed pleased by the remarkably forgiving attitude the Americans and British demonstrated toward them. The Strategic Bombing Survey conducted 3,711 interviews with civilians in thirty-three western German cities in the summer of 1945. Though their intention was to uncover the impact of wartime bombing on civilians, the first question Germans were asked was, "How is it going with you now under the occupation?" Invariably, the answer was, "good." Germans were enormously relieved by the end of the war and the end of the terrible bombing. They were pleased to find themselves under American or British control rather than Russian. And they were amazed at the leniency with which they were treated. They had been pumped full of horrible propaganda in the final months of the war, dark invocations of rapes, kidnappings, forced labor, extermination that lay in store for a defeated people. The reality was wholly different. "We were delighted that the war had ended," said a fifty-three-year-old housewife from Münster. "I've had enough of raids. I'm scared stiff of them." The occupation, said a twenty-four-year-old house cleaner from Witten, was "going quite well. One has rest finally and one doesn't have to run into the cellar." The foreign troops were "quite friendly." The occupation was "much better than I expected," said a relieved house-wife from Dortmund. "We were told that the most terrible things would happen—rape, looting, robbery—even that our own children would be taken away from us, and we would be systematically starved." But she had no such problems. A forty-year-old lawyer from Munich was distressed at the criminal behavior of DPs (displaced persons), but the Americans had been "very well behaved." A former clerk in the highway office in Munich said he was "satisfied, and delighted the Americans came." A sixty-three-year-old worker in an aluminum factory in Neumünster said that he "really could not complain. If I ever feel anything disagreeable, I only think that the war is over due to those occupation troops, and therefore those terrible air attacks on Neumünster stopped. I greeted the allied troops as libera-tors from those bad bombing attacks." A housewife from Kempten, in the Rhineland, told her interviewers that when the Americans did not kidnap her children and prove to be villains, the women of the town "broke out laughing, and couldn't stop, their fear had been so great. I laughed more in the last few weeks than I have for years." A thirty-eight-year-old housewife from Dortmund who had worked in a factory in the last stages of the war thought "the troops would despise us and that they might even be cruel to us. But they are very friendly and helpful. I can't get accustomed to being treated so well by your men."[50]

A success story? Perhaps. Yet these same interviews also revealed a remarkably ugly side that the somewhat comical *Pocket Guide* had presciently predicted. The Bombing Survey asked each respondent why they thought Germany had lost the war. Many referred to America's better equipment and the use of heavy bombing; others spoke of the large alliance arrayed against an isolated, encircled Germany. A common explanation for Germany's defeat in the war was treachery: "Hitler was surrounded by traitors who deliberately sabotaged his plans," said a thirty-two-year-old secretary from Nuremberg. "Let me tell you one thing," said a twenty-year-old housewife and mother from Hamburg. "You all misunderstand Adolf Hitler. He was really an idealist and wanted the best for Germany." Hitler "was a competent leader and it is not his fault that he didn't win the war." The army "worked against Hitler," who in any case was "a genius."[51] Often, explanations for Germany's defeat centered on the Jews. The persecution of the Jews had harmed the war effort, many concluded. A thirty-eight-year-old housewife from Hamburg, whose husband was in the army, asserted that since Britain and America were controlled by Jews, they went to war against Germany to save them. "Everyone knows that," she said. The Nazi leaders "should not have forced the Jews to leave Germany," said a twenty-six-year-old woman from Darmstadt, with a husband in the army. "They should have taxed them very heavily and let those who wanted to leave go and the rest stay here. Do you think that the Americans, who have always stuck together with the Jews, would have bombed our cities if they had known that there were Jews living there?" Persecuting the Jews had been a "political mistake," mused one twenty-four-year-old student in Munich who had served in an artillery unit in Russia. The Nazis started out fine, but "overdid it." Hitler's government was "good" and "had been doing wonderful things for the German people before the war broke out," said a forty-five-year-old nurse who had served in the German Red Cross in the war. The Jews, "as you know, fought against National Socialism and in time of war that cannot be tolerated." One young woman in Hamburg, a mere eighteen years old, expressed disappointment about losing the war because now "the Jews will come back and they will soak us again, like they did before '33. . . . After Hitler threw the Jews out, order and honesty was in Germany. We will lose that."[52]

The faces of these Berliners as they watch the British 7th Armored Division
march into Berlin reveal a range of emotions: curiosity, defiance, and,
perhaps, relief. July 4, 1945. *U.S. National Archives*

Having pinned the defeat on treachery, the Jews, or simple political
mistakes, many respondents then went on to suggest that the bombing of
German cities, while no doubt a kind of payback for German bombings
of British, Dutch, and Polish cities, had been tantamount to a war crime.
The air raids were "the lowest thing possible . . . Even the SS would never
do that," declared an outraged twenty-year-old woman in Kempten, who
acknowledged that "our leaders were criminals." "Germany suffered much
from bombing," according to a woman from Nuremberg. "The war should
have been ended to spare the people suffering. The people themselves always
wanted peace but were unable to do anything about it." For a woman from
Hamburg who had lived through the bombing of that city, the bombing was
worse than Hitler's atrocities. "It was bad in the concentration camps, but not
as bad as seeing human torches running down the streets. I feel the German
people have suffered enough through the terror attacks to more than make
up for the sins they committed in the concentration camps. The innocent
have to suffer for the crimes of the guilty, but they *have* suffered." A woman
from Bremen sniffed, "I don't think any people had to suffer as much as the
German people. Germany has accomplished miracles."[53]

These average Germans, it seemed, had no desire to accept responsibility for the war or its consequences; were prone to self-pity; found it hard to hate Hitler; viewed the Russians and any Communist as the real enemy; continued to blame Germany's misfortunes on the Jews; and saw themselves as having already paid for their sins by suffering through the Allied bombing. More worrisome, the Germans were not the only ones who expressed some of these views. In September, journalist Tania Long of the *New York Times* penned a scathing article about the effectiveness of German civilians in pressing these opinions on American occupation forces. U.S. soldiers were now quite ready "to spout the enemy propaganda line" that the Germans knew nothing about the concentration camps, or that Germany was forced into war by Hitler against the wishes of a peaceful nation, or about how the Germans and Americans must join hands against the Russians. "The superficial aspects of German life, such as their cleanliness, their higher standard of living and their willingness to work hard, are confused, in the average soldier's mind, with the whole. The basic factors that govern the German people and have made them the world's problem children twice within a generation are forgotten in the face of Germany's modern highways, chrome plumbing, and well-dressed girls."[54]

What to do with such a people, who could be gracious, charming, flirtatious, welcoming, obedient, cooperative, hardworking, and capable of spouting hateful nonsense as if it were Scripture? Officially, the United States was committed to a policy of exacting heavy reparations, dismantling German factories, breaking up large industrial cartels, and controlling every aspect of Germany's own economic life. Americans planned to arrest war criminals, control education, and remove all members of the Nazi Party—there were twelve million of them—from public office and even from positions of leadership in private firms. All this was designed, as the Allied powers said at the Potsdam Conference in July 1945, "to convince the German people that they have suffered a total military defeat and that they cannot escape responsibility for what they have brought on themselves."[55]

In practice these policies, like the fraternization ban, simply could not hold up against the day-to-day pressures of restoration and recovery. How, for example, could the American Military Government find capable, efficient Germans to help run local municipal government and services—as indeed they had to do, given their own rapidly dwindling numbers of Army personnel—while at the same time they were supposed to be arresting and interrogating all Germans who had served in such posts under the Nazis? General Eisenhower's deputy for military government, General Lucius D. Clay, complained to Eisenhower in July that U.S. policy left the average local Military

Government officer in a serious bind, for "all too often it seems that the only men with the qualifications . . . are the career civil servants" who were active in the Nazi Party. Clay needed 300,000 local and municipal employees in the U.S. zone alone; where was he to find so many people without a blemish on their record? The Military Government dutifully prepared a questionnaire, the *Fragenbogen,* that required Germans to lay out in detail all their previous political affiliations. Military Government eventually collected thirteen million of the completed forms. By September 1945, 82,000 former party members were incarcerated in internment camps, ready to be investigated and tried, and an additional 100,000 people had been dismissed from public employment and private enterprise for their previous ties to the Nazi Party.[56]

But everywhere the Military Government turned to look for capable administrators, they found people who had worked in some way for the Nazi regime. General George Patton, now commander of the Third Army Military Government in Bavaria, spoke for many of his subordinate officers when he said it was "silly" to get rid of "the most intelligent people" in Germany; he then caused a furor by telling a reporter that "far too much fuss had been made regarding denazification in Germany." Though Eisenhower immediately forced Patton to retract these unguarded comments, his remarks revealed that U.S. military government officers viewed the denazification process as wasteful and certainly incompatible with restoring order, stability, and security —objectives that Patton said mattered more than "politics." Although Patton was disciplined for speaking his mind on the subject, he was probably right that the large-scale political reorientation of an entire nation was not something soldiers had been trained to accomplish. General Clay himself soon realized that the problem of denazification would be a prolonged and painful one, involving thousands of investigations, and it was a problem he felt his administration could not handle. In mid-1946, he handed the whole thing over to the Germans themselves. The results were predictable: of the 3.2 million people the German authorities investigated, only 1,284 were convicted as "major offenders." Another 100,000 people were found to have been "offenders" or "lesser offenders." The punishments were laughable: about 8,000 people received brief jail sentences; others were fined. The Germans were quick to sweep the Nazi past under the rug, and the U.S. Military Government supplied the broom.[57]

America's growing leniency appeared in its approach to the German economy, too. Despite the severity of the language of Potsdam, the Information Control Division of the U.S. occupation used its English-language newspaper, *News of Germany,* to trumpet the Americans' achievements in restarting the German economy. In July, headlines blared "Six Rail Lines

Resume Operations," and "I.G. Farben Factories to Produce Medical Supplies"; in August came news that "33 Trains Arrive, Depart Now Daily from Frankfurt," while "Bavaria's Rapid 3-Months Progress" disproved the prognostications of the Nazis that the American occupation would unduly punish the Germans. The town of Pforzheim, which had been totally obliterated by Allied bombing, was "Rebuilding in the Pattern of Freedom," the paper reported. "Wurzburg, 85% Ruined, Rebuilds"; "Osnabrück Plans Modern City"; "Auto Manufacture Starts Here Soon"; "5 Trucking Firms Operating in Anspach"; "First Steel Plant in US Zone Starts Peace Production"; "More Railroad Lines Restored to Service," and so on. These were the sorts of indices that American information officers clearly liked to report—far more encouraging than charts indicating the number of former Nazis languishing behind bars. It even seemed worthwhile reporting the good news that I. G. Farben, which had manufactured the Zyklon-B pellets used to exterminate millions of Jews, was now helping the occupation by making DDT to keep lice-borne typhus at bay: "Farben-Made DDT Powder Fights Typhus."[58]

In a message to the German people on August 6, General Eisenhower enumerated a long list of successes that the Americans had achieved in their zone: in addition to crushing Nazism, the Americans had begun to transfer political authority to the German people, started reopening schools, courts, newspapers, and even allowed unions and political parties to form. Not all the indices, however, were encouraging. Eisenhower acknowledged that "the coming months will be a time of trial. They will inevitably be hard. All signs point to shortages of food, fuel, housing and transport." Most alarming, "coal will not be available for heating houses this winter. In the next few months you must cut and gather enough wood in the forests to take care of your essential needs." But Eisenhower told his German subjects that "you can redeem yourselves . . . through your own efforts. It lies in your power to build a healthy, democratic life in Germany and to rejoin the family of nations."[59] And the Germans would not be facing these challenges alone. It is indicative of the shift in Allied opinion about the Germans that military leaders in the British and American zones approached the challenge of feeding the people with great zeal. General Clay, Eisenhower's deputy, wrote later that he "was certain that we could not arouse political interest for a democratic government in a hungry, apathetic population." General Bernard Montgomery even dubbed the food effort "the Battle of Winter," perhaps to evoke the successes of previous great campaigns like the Battle of Britain, the Battle of Stalingrad, and the Battle of Berlin. Success in those great military campaigns required killing large numbers of Germans; success in the Battle of Winter meant feeding them instead.

The U.S. Military Government reprinted this *St. Louis Star-Times* cartoon in its German-language newspaper, *Die Neue Zeitung*, showing the German people setting out on the climb up from destruction toward the civilized United Nations. *Die Neue Zeitung*

The British zone of occupation faced perhaps the most serious food crisis. This zone contained the Ruhr valley, Europe's largest concentration of heavy industry; but its great coal and steel producing cities had always imported food from eastern Germany. With the Soviets now rapidly denuding their zone, and with transport in any case wrecked, there was no food to be had from the east. Hamburg and Hannover had some modest stocks of food but these were quickly exhausted. The British and Americans had agreed that their own stocks, accumulated in the last stages of the war, would be enough to assure a diet in their zones of 1,550 calories a day, mostly made up of bread, potatoes, and oatmeal. There were few vegetables to be had, no fruits, little fats. This ration could not sustain people for long, and it certainly was inadequate to feed the heavy laborers whose work was needed in the coal mines. The only thing to do was import food into Germany from Britain and the United States—a major turnaround from SHAEF plans that had envisioned Germany living off of its own supplies. In the summer of 1945, the British zone imported about 70,000 tons of wheat per month, and also distributed 50,000 tons of potatoes imported from Britain as well as surplus

Army ration packs. But these were only stopgaps. Without fertilizers, coal, transport, and manual labor, there was no hope of getting self-sustaining agriculture up and running. By the fall, the British zone was forced to cut back its official daily ration to just over 1,000 calories: virtually a starvation diet. In November, Field Marshal Montgomery called the food situation "more critical than at any one time since we entered Germany." A detailed survey by the *Times* concluded that "Germans are going to have a miserable time this winter—not so bad as those they brought upon allied peoples, but still bad, precarious, lean."[60]

The conditions in the American zone were equally bad. Historically, the area under American occupation had imported 25 percent of its food and had never been able to sustain itself. General Clay thought he could supply the Germans in his zone with 1,500 calories a day, but only with significant imports from America. Military Government set up community kitchens which served over four million meals a month. One survey in late August con-

Children in Berlin scavenge for food in trash pails and cooking pots near a U.S. military mess tent. *U.S. National Archives*

cluded that 60 percent of the Germans were living on a diet that would lead to disease and malnutrition. By October, random weighing of German civilians revealed a falloff in body weight of 13–15 percent in adult men and women. Children, pregnant women, and the elderly suffered most. Their diets lacked sufficient protein and vitamins, and cases of rickets were common among infants. In December, the U.S. government announced that it had approved private relief agencies in America to begin collecting food and clothing for shipment into Germany. Six months after the bombs stopped falling on Germany, Americans were packaging up bundles of supplies for humanitarian relief.[61] This irony was not lost on Military Government administrators. In one of their weekly information bulletins, an unsigned article mused on the problem of Germany's food shortages. "We can say they should have thought of that before they started the war, and then let them starve as best they may. That might be alright if we were not trying to maintain law and order in the country and convince people that democracy is the best way to live. It is difficult to govern, much less persuade to your views a hungry people." And so Military Government buckled down to work, urgently trying to restore coal production, repair transportation, find fertilizer and farm machinery, and secure additional imports from overseas to keep the German people alive.[62]

German observers understood the significance of the shift in their fortunes, and in Anglo-American policy. The *Stuttgarter Zeitung*, one of the earliest postwar publications to appear in Germany under U.S. license, profoundly approved of the efforts that the Allies were making on behalf of the German people. "If we consider what unbelievable sacrifices Hitler's war has demanded from the allies," the paper wrote in an obsequious editorial, "how the strengths of nations were taxed to the utmost, it fills us with immense gratitude, and the sense that humanity still has a place in this world, when we hear that the allied occupation governments have adopted the German cause as their own." The Germans could see that the "new struggle" at hand was one of recovery and stability in Germany, and that Americans and Germans would fight it side by side. The American-produced German-language press echoed this newfound sense of solidarity. "The allies have created the essential conditions for the long and difficult—yet hopeful—process of German reconstruction," said a *Heute* magazine editorial, "by assuming most of the responsibility for the preservation of public order and public life in Germany." This opened the way for Germans to do their part in the work of recovery, and the results had been positive. "Water and electricity are up and running. Thanks to the support of the military governments, railroads are partially repaired. . . . Trams are running in cities. . . . Moreover, the occupying powers have begun to import food from overseas to regions that suffer most from a lack of food—regardless of the principle that Germany has to feed itself as much as possible." The United States could not have been more open about its aims: to feed, clothe, house, and nurture the German people.[63]

Americans had arrived in Germany as conquerors and occupiers. In September 1944, U.S. military directives insisted that "Germany will not be occupied for the purpose of liberation but as a defeated enemy nation." Within weeks of the end of the war in May 1945, this policy changed. Americans went to great lengths to help Germans, to repair the damage Allied aircraft had caused, and to build the foundation for German recovery, just as the Allied armies had done in France, Belgium, and the Netherlands. This required a willful forgetting of the intensity of American hatred for the Germans just a few months earlier; it required an almost schizophrenic ability to separate the occupier's duties of denazification and reeducation from the liberator's role of giving comfort and aid. Americans, uncomfortable with a punitive occupation of Germany, chose to transform themselves into liberators of their former enemy. In doing so, they had a great deal of help from the German people themselves. After all, both Germans and Americans had a common interest in laying claim to liberation. Americans did not wish to occupy if they could liberate instead, while the Germans gladly embraced the notion that they had been liberated from Hitler and his "alien" ideology, Nazism. Germans were quite happy to get on with the tasks of recovery, side by side with these wealthy, generous, earnest, sometimes messy and provincial but protective Americans. Liberation arrived late in western Germany; but it arrived all the same, accompanied by a gratifying forgetfulness.

MOVING BODIES

III

Prologue

"They Have Suffered Unbearably"

I T IS A tribute to the breadth of vision of Allied leaders that they conceived of the liberation of Europe as a complex process involving at least three dimensions: a military dimension—the defeat of Germany's armed forces; a political dimension—the restoration of political freedom to those countries under German occupation; and a social dimension—the caring for Europe's war-stricken civilians. Historians of World War II, and especially its final months, have given pride of place in their writing to the military achievements of the Allied armies, and some scholars have explored the political challenges of restoring sovereignty to Europe's liberated states. But the social aspect of liberation, which loomed so large in the minds of wartime planners, has largely been ignored by the war's chroniclers. This omission is odd, because the humanitarian aspect of the liberation forms one of the most impressive legacies of the period 1944–45, and stands as a testament to the basic decency of the Allied cause. Americans and Britons did not wish merely to destroy; they also wished to repair and to heal. They had already given so much to defeat Hitler, yet they also took on the additional burden of humanitarian relief, mobilizing in an unprecedented fashion to send to Europe nurses, doctors, relief workers, and an avalanche of food, medical supplies, clothing, and goods that could provide Europeans with the means to sustain themselves in the aftermath of total war.

Of course, such efforts to help liberated civilians served a military purpose. In December 1944, with the Allied armies gathering for the final assault into Germany, Dean Acheson, the razor-sharp, influential assistant secretary of state, set out in a brief memorandum for Harry Hopkins, President Roosevelt's special assistant, his views on the importance of caring for liberated peoples of Europe. "The war," Acheson wrote, "can be lost in the liberated countries. It cannot be won without success in the liberated countries." By this, he meant that as the great armies of liberation passed through Europe on their way into Germany, they would have to do more than destroy the German armies. They would have to offer food, medicine, shelter, and most important, the opportunity for work and a promise of a better future. Liberated peoples, Acheson believed, "are the most combustible material in the world. They are fighting people. They are violent and restless. They have suffered unbearably." To ignore them now, to fail to meet their needs, to leave their nations in shambles without attending to their economic and social concerns, would invite "agitation and unrest," which would lead to "arbitrary and absolutist controls. Then follows the overthrow of governments, with rival aspirants for the succession from the right and the left." This was a dire portrait of liberated peoples, facing scarcity, frustration, and hunger, falling into civil war. As Acheson wrote, this very scenario was unfolding in Greece and Yugoslavia; such scenes might multiply across the continent, drawing the great powers into further conflict. In such a scenario, the great campaigns of liberation would have been for nought.

"To win the war requires that we win the battle of the liberated countries," concluded Acheson. But how was this to be done? Fortunately for the Allied cause, a new institution had been created in late 1943 to address precisely this matter. The United Nations Relief and Rehabilitation Administration (UNRRA), funded almost exclusively by the United States and Britain, set out to organize a gigantic global relief effort of a kind never before attempted, one that would dwarf the private relief efforts of the First World War. At a time of scarcity in food and medicine, and a period of severe shortages of shipping that could carry such materials across the ocean to the theaters of war, UNRRA sought to mobilize the world's supplies on behalf of liberated Europe. It was a huge challenge, one that came close to failure and never entirely fulfilled its leaders' expectations. Nonetheless, UNRRA served as a beacon for thousands of citizens from around the world who volunteered to work for UNRRA in the field, trying to restart the most basic elements of life in a broken continent. For the millions of people who benefited from its work, UNRRA offered relief as well as that rarest of commodities in 1945, hope for a humane future.[1]

Soup kitchens and medical aid stations, DDT dustings and registration cards, stinking straw mattresses on dirt floors, borrowed clothes, ill-fitting shoes, flea bites, lice, filth, coughing, and foul-smelling people: these were the daily realities for millions of people in Europe at war's end, but none suffered these indignities as much as the eight million displaced persons that the war unleashed. These were the men and women whom the German war machine had sucked into the infernal industries of the Reich; they came from

Russia, Poland, France, Italy, and a dozen other countries that the Germans had ransacked for forced labor. The great majority of them wanted nothing more than to go home, and as the Third Reich collapsed, millions of them flowed out onto the roads of central Europe, trekking homeward along byways already choked with military vehicles, soldiers, and endless refugee columns. UNRRA worked hard to make this passage between war and home a tolerable one. But UNRRA could not answer every call. There were far more needy souls than could easily be cared for by international organizations. Allied armies, faced with such a huge flood of people, proved somewhat less interested in caring for displaced peoples than they were in sorting them out and getting them shipped back whence they came. And so it all began again: great clattering boxcars full of ashen, gray, exhausted people set out across Europe, threading their way across the burned earth, bearing their woeful cargo home.

6

Freedom from Want:
UNRRA and the Relief Effort
to Save Europe

O N MAY 20, 1945, twelve days after the official end of the war in
Europe, the last German garrison in Greece surrendered. The Germans turned over control of this outpost—on the Greek island of Milos, in
the Cyclades—to a small British and Greek force of soldiers. For four years
this island and its 6,500 inhabitants had been ruled by Germans. The occupiers had built a nearly impregnable system of fortifications there, ringed by
over ten thousand mines. They constructed an underground hospital, laid in
large stockpiles of food and medicines, and were prepared to fend off whatever landing force was sent against them. But the people aboard the landing
craft that came to the island on this day in May were not bent on destruction.
Instead, the ships that knifed through the blue-green Mediterranean waters
toward Milos carried tons of clothing and medical supplies, and among the
soldiers stood a team of physicians, health, welfare, and sanitation experts, all
wearing a uniform not yet familiar in these parts: a drab gray ensemble with
a strange new shoulder patch bearing the letters UNRRA. The German soldiers, once taken into custody as POWs, inquired about this acronym. They
were told that these letters stood for the United Nations Relief and Rehabilitation Administration, an international humanitarian agency representing
forty-four Allied nations that had taken up the challenge of feeding and healing the victims of war in Europe. One of the soldiers said, "you must mean 44
states of America"; no, he was told, there were in fact forty-four nations ready
to offer help to the millions of victims of Germany's predatory war.[1]

Founded in November 1943, a year and a half before the United Nations
itself saw the light of day, UNRRA (pronounced *un*-ruh) was more than just

another wartime bureaucracy. It was designed not for war but for peace, and it aimed to organize the world's goods and foodstuffs, which were in desperately short supply, on behalf of the liberated peoples of Europe (and China, though we shall leave UNRRA's Asian dimension aside here). UNRRA evolved into a massive purchasing agency, a global shipping network, and a sophisticated medical emergency operation that, by 1945, was serving in over a dozen European nations with a staff of 10,000 trained employees. UNRRA also supervised nearly 125 international private relief organizations, which throughout the war raised money and goods for the relief of Europe. Where there had been starvation, disease, and scarcity, UNRRA aimed to provide shelter, food, supplies—and hope. Allied leaders believed UNRRA could help win the peace and transform victory on the battlefield into an enduring liberation.

This work was not easy, and UNRRA provides a superb case study of the difficulties facing the liberators in the aftermath of war. UNRRA's founders bickered over who would pay for it, and who would benefit from its largesse. No one was ever quite clear over the relationship between this new organization and the powerful armies that held the field. Some American political figures questioned the wisdom of spending money on assisting people such as the Poles, Ukrainians, and Yugoslavs who seemed increasingly pro-Soviet and ideologically hostile to the West. On the ground level, UNRRA suffered from a good deal of reckless amateurism, poor planning, and just plain naïveté. Its well-meaning but overmatched staff sometimes seemed like playground matrons trying to keep order in a nasty world of knife fights and street brawls. The new agency hired thousands of people from across the world, among whom inevitably figured a variety of do-gooders, zealots, proselytizers, church folk, amateur doctors, adventure seekers, retired majors from the British colonies, New Dealers, wheeler-dealers, and other people who perhaps just wanted a piece of the "good war." UNRRA also fell afoul of the Allied armies, which saw it as meddling, and a threat to their control of the European occupations. Even the voluntary relief groups it was supposed to supervise felt UNRRA curtailed their independence, and placed obstacles in the way of their own work. Contemporaries often stressed UNRRA's shortcomings and the flaws of its personnel, and historians have tended to follow suit.[2]

Yet the records left by many who received its aid show that UNRRA succeeded on the human scale. The agency shipped about $4 billion of food, medicine, and agricultural and industrial equipment to Europe and Asia, and did so at a time of world shortages and enormous transportation and shipping difficulties. Just as important was the compassion and decency that most

UNRRA workers demonstrated under difficult circumstances. Grouped into teams of about a dozen workers and sent out into the field, UNRRA staff were often the first nonviolent foreigners many Europeans encountered after the war. After a few weeks of rudimentary training in centers in the United States (at College Park, Maryland) or in France (chiefly at Granville, in Normandy), relief teams were sent into the field to start the hard work of creating order: by registering displaced persons (DPs), setting up clinics, restarting import offices, assessing public health needs, and calling back to the central headquarters with detailed accounts of what they found and what further help was needed. It required courage and a great deal of ingenuity and commitment for UNRRA staff to make a difference in wartime conditions, but their work did register on the lives of Europeans, especially on the DPs, who were Europe's most vulnerable. These men and women were paid poorly; they were amateurs; they sometimes earned the scorn of local officials and even the refugees they were supposed to serve. For those Europeans who desperately yearned for some simple, humane gesture to show that peace had really come, UNRRA's simple gifts—a new suit of clothes, or a medical examination, an inoculation, shelter and a meal—provided a link to a new world, one in which violence and cruelty and murder gave way to dignity and freedom.

The idea for UNRRA emerged first from exchanges between British and American officials in early 1942 about how to provide relief for the devastated areas of Europe once the war ended. Sir Frederick Leith-Ross, the British government's chief economic adviser, stressed in February 1942 that "unless steps can be taken rapidly to ensure at least minimum supplies to the necessitous areas, a process of social disintegration may set in which will create further dangerous strains. . . . It appears essential that arrangements should not be left for settlement until an Armistice has been concluded." After the Allied landings in North Africa in October 1942, and the smashing Soviet victory at Stalingrad in early 1943, the Allied nations began to see the need for an international humanitarian agency that could bring initial relief to newly liberated peoples. By March 1943, the great powers had sketched a draft for UNRRA, and in November 1943, representatives of forty-four nations convened in Atlantic City, New Jersey, to sign the new agency's charter.[3]

But no one seemed to know just what UNNRA was supposed to do. President Franklin Roosevelt told the U.S. Congress that UNRRA would restore health and vigor to newly liberated Europeans so they could get back in the fight against Hitler. The brutal German and Japanese occupations, he said, had created "a generation of half-men—undernourished, crushed in body and spirit, without strength or incentive to hope—ready, in fact, to be enslaved and used as beasts of burden." If the Allied armies could heal these people and deploy them in the war against Germany and Japan, "the length of the war may be materially shortened. . . . Aid to the liberated peoples during the war is thus a matter of military necessity as well as of humanity."[4] Dean Acheson, then assistant secretary of state for economic affairs, depicted UNRRA as more than a wartime measure: it was an instrument for winning the peace, something Americans had plainly failed to do after the last world war. "It is just as important to be prepared for the emergency that will come when the fighting is over as it is to be prepared for the victorious drives that will end in Berlin and Tokyo," he told a radio audience in December 1943. "It would be a hollow victory indeed that brought with it famine and disease in large parts of the world, and economic chaos that would inevitably engulf us all." One of Acheson's colleagues in the State Department, Francis B. Sayre, was still more effusive. Speaking to the University Club of Boston, Sayre claimed that "never before had the peoples of the West and the East, the North and the South, met together to pool their resources and to organize themselves upon an international scale to help bind up the wounds of war, to assist in feeding the hungry, and to help care for the sick." UNRRA, he said, was "a new enterprise, based fundamentally on human brotherhood."[5] Herbert H. Lehman, the governor of New York and the man Roosevelt tapped to lead the new agency, also embraced the idea that UNRRA was not merely in the soup-kitchen business. Echoing Roosevelt's 1941 "Four Freedoms" speech, Lehman told a dinner audience in New York in June 1943 "that freedom from want is a basic component of any enduring peace." He continued: "The cry of nations and their peoples for assistance in the first hours of liberation will present democracy with a supreme test. The fate of attempts by all the United Nations to banish global wars may well be determined by the success of their first joint action in relief and rehabilitation."[6]

The early stages of UNRRA's work quickly gave the lie to most of this inflated rhetoric. In November 1943, when UNRRA was established, Hitler and his allies still controlled most of continental Europe; not until the middle of 1944, with Anglo-American forces moving up the Italian peninsula, and into France, could UNRRA hope to swing into action. As director, Herbert Lehman spent most of 1944 fighting bureaucratic battles in Washington and London rather than helping refugees. The American and British armies desired to keep their lock on all available resources, especially food, shipping, transport, and talented personnel: precisely the things UNRRA needed if it was going to be effective. General Eisenhower signed an agreement with Lehman on November 25, 1944, stating that the military recognized UNRRA's role in health, welfare, and displaced persons in Belgium, France, Luxembourg, Netherlands, Norway, and in former enemy territories. Yet Eisenhower proved reluctant to provide supplies, trucks, and transport to the proposed teams of UNRRA staff that were to go into the field. Not until March 1945 did UNRRA finally secure a training center in France: a rundown hotel on the Normandy coast in Granville. When SHAEF authorities did ask UNRRA to send relief teams into Germany in the early spring of 1945, UNRRA did not yet have the supplies and personnel it needed, and repeatedly asked the Army for more, causing some exasperation in SHAEF headquarters.[7] Lehman's colleagues in Foggy Bottom were little help: "there was a good deal of jealousy within the State Department," Lehman later recalled, "which felt that a new man in a new bureau or division would limit their authority and opportunities for managing operations. . . . Everyone in Washington was fighting for power." Lehman never resolved the problem of resources while the war was still going on; the armed forces simply would not provide a relief organization with supplies or shipping until their work was done.[8]

Two additional problems faced UNRRA from the start: who would receive aid, and who would pay for it? For all the expectations of a global mission of healing and assistance, UNRRA's charter stipulated that the agency was to give aid on quite a restrictive basis only to those states that had been invaded by the Axis powers and that, at the end of the war, did not have sufficient means to pay for goods and supplies on the world market. This limited UNRRA's scope, since France, Belgium, Luxembourg, Norway, and the Netherlands all technically had the national resources to pay for imports, while Germany and Italy, as enemy states, were not supposed to be receiving UNRRA handouts. In fact, this formula proved much too narrow, and Italy and Germany would soon become a major part of UNRRA operations. Furthermore, UNRRA took responsibility for caring for displaced persons across Europe. But at the outset, UNRRA was restricted to a narrow band of countries in southeastern Europe: Greece, Yugoslavia, and Albania. By the spring of 1945, UNRRA began to expand its efforts into liberated Eastern Europe, including Poland, Czechoslovakia, Belorussia, and Ukraine. UNRRA's postwar work in former enemy states, Germany, Italy, Austria, and Hungary, was limited to the health and welfare of refugees, destitute and displaced persons, and a feeding program for children and young mothers. Thus, UNRRA was explicitly not designed to be the major institution for rebuilding Europe. For countries that had been invaded and needed help, it offered immediate relief in the form of food and clothing; medical supplies and public health services; and some rehabilitation supplies such as farm equipment, seeds and fertilizers, machinery and spare parts, loading and docking equipment, and vehicles—the materials needed to get Europe's agricultural and industrial production back into gear.

Recipients of UNRRA Commodity Aid
(thousands U.S. $)

Albania	26,250.9
Austria	135,513.2
Byelorussian SSR	60,820.0
China	517,846.7
Czechoslovakia	261,337.4
Dodecanese Islands	3,900.4
Ethiopia	884.9
Finland	2,441.2
Greece	347,162.0
Hungary	4,386.5
Italy	418,222.1
Korea	943.9
Philippines	9,880.2
Poland	477,927.0
San Marino	30.0
Ukrainian SSR	188,199.3
Yugoslavia	415,642.0

Source: Woodbridge, *UNRRA*, III: 428–29.

As for who would pay for all this bounty, there was little mystery here: the only nation in the world that had the capacity to pay for such a program was the United States, just as it had bankrolled much of the Allied war effort. The budget was structured to make it appear that this was a genuinely global undertaking: a formula was devised in which member states whose countries were not invaded would contribute a sum equivalent to 1 percent of their annual income to the relief agency. In practice, of course, this meant the United States, Britain, and Canada paid for almost all of the $3.9 billion of resources UNRRA provided, with the United States covering about 73 percent of the total bill and the United Kingdom about 16 percent. Canada, Australia, Brazil, South Africa, India, and New Zealand made up most of the balance, though by the time UNRRA closed down in 1947, all its members had contributed something to its operations.[9]

UNNRA'S LEADERS WERE capable, seasoned veterans, virtually all men. Its three directors were Lehman; his successor Fiorello La Guardia, former mayor of New York City; and Major General Lowell W. Rooks, former assistant chief of staff of the G-3 section of the United States Forces European Theater (USFET). Lehman and La Guardia were steeped in New York City and state politics, and had close ties to Washington. Rooks, a veteran of administrative affairs during the occupation of Europe, knew the issues UNRRA faced well. The staffing of senior positions was always a problem because so many of the "good men" that Lehman needed were already claimed by other wartime duties. It was a constant complaint in the early days of the agency that they simply could not find capable people. Eventually, they did find such men: men such as the Australian naval officer Commander Robert Jackson served as senior deputy director general for two and a half years and became the operational chief of the agency; Roy F. Hendrickson, who had worked for the Combined Food Board during the war and in the War Food Administration in Washington, headed up the Bureau of Supply; a somewhat cagey Russian named Michail Menshikov was named head of the Bureau of Areas, and was obviously in close contact with Moscow about UNRRA policies; Francis B. Sayre, a former assistant secretary of state, high commissioner to the Philippines, and senior adviser to the the State Department's Office of Foreign Relief and Rehabilitation Operations (OFRRO), served as diplomatic adviser; and Fred K. Hoehler, who had worked for OFRRO in North Africa, held the job of director of the Displaced Persons Division. In addition to Washington-based staff, UNRRA had a European Regional Office, based in London, headed by Lieutenant-General Sir Humphrey Gale, who had been the chief administrative officer for SHAEF. In short, these were experienced, war-tested men who knew how to operate inside large bureaucracies.

Whatever the talents of its senior staff, UNRRA would be judged by the capabilities and resourcefulness of its people on the ground, thousands of people from various walks of life who volunteered to serve as the front-line troops of the world relief organization. The staff of the agency was divided into three classes: Class I were those hired for international employment, and might be posted anywhere. By December 1945, UNRRA had hired nearly 10,000 such people; 31 percent were Americans, 34 percent were British, 10 percent were French. Of the Class I staff, 2,500 worked in Washington or London in administrative jobs, and the rest were in the field—4,000 working in displaced persons operations, mostly in Germany, and the rest scattered across the globe. In Europe, Greece, Italy, and Yugoslavia had the largest UNRRA personnel contingent. Class II staff were local employees, hired for service in their own countries, and their local skills and knowledge were essential. Almost 2,000 Greeks worked for UNRRA by December 1945, as did over 2,500 Italians, and 300 Yugoslavs. Class III personnel were volunteers attached to private voluntary relief organizations, supervised but not salaried by UNRRA.[10]

Many of these volunteers were women. Despite the dangerous conditions in which UNRRA staff worked, humanitarian relief was still considered the preserve of women, at least at the point of delivery. By mid-1946, 42 percent of UNRRA's employees were women, and that number increased to 45 percent by the end of 1946. At that time, over 1,800 women were working for UNRRA's DP operations inside Germany, staffing camps and health centers; 242 were then in Greece and 181 were in Italy. Francesca Wilson, a Briton and an early UNRRA employee, had served in wartime relief during the First World War. Her motives for joining are plain enough from her memoir, written just after her return from service in Europe: she believed she could help others, and that her labor in Europe was part of a continental project to restore European civilization. She dedicated her book to the Liberal historian-journalists J. L. Hammond and Barbara Hammond, and it speaks in the tone of socialist egalitarianism that the Hammonds, and many others in progressive circles, would have recognized. Sent into Germany to work on the repatriation of displaced persons, she "felt exhilarated by being with so many Europeans who had worked to be free—and were now not only free but with something exciting to do ahead: to liberate their own and others' countries deportees from enemy territory." Yet she seemed to have contempt for the other Britons she encountered in UNRRA: "Most of the British recruits were retired Army officers. They had been retired because of age or health, and some looked death's-heads." Wilson herself was a formidable figure: no-nonsense, disciplined, hardworking, rail-thin, tight-lipped and zealous in carrying out her duty, which she saw quite plainly as restoring humanity and order to a world that had been destroyed not just by the Nazis but by all armed, violent men.

All the staff passed through the training center at Granville, in Normandy, France, en route to being posted to villages, towns, and DP camps across Europe. But Wilson scorned what she saw as an old-school, imperial type of British officer that seemed prevalent in UNRRA ranks: "Sitting in the lounge of the bar of the Hotel Normandie, one heard many nostalgic stories about the Regiment, the Northwest Frontier, and Poona, and one wondered how they would get on with Polish and Russian 'natives' in Germany." UNRRA, Wilson claimed, "was suffering at this time, more than it did later on, from its misfits. Relief work, even when it is unpaid, does not attract only the charitable—it has special charms for adventurers, tired of the sameness and restricted opportunities of life at home. . . . Their presence in UNRRA in the early days, even though their proportion to the whole was not large, did harm to its mission and made the military skeptical of its efficiency and chary of calling in its aid."[11] Yet perhaps it was not just the adventurers in UNRRA's ranks that made the Army uneasy about this new agency. Wilson herself had a short fuse around military men and was not afraid to let her feelings show. "I hate the army," she found herself shouting at an American lieutenant after he had ordered a large band of DPs moved without notice. "Why don't you go and fight someone? Why do you meddle with civilians, with peaceable human beings? They are counters to you—you think you can move mothers and babies and sick people as you move companies and batteries in the war. Why don't you stick to something you understand?" A revealing comment: while the Army saw UNRRA as meddlesome and naïve, UNRRA staff often saw the Army as a behemoth, ruthless, insensitive to human needs.

Mrs. Rhoda Dawson Bickerdike, a Briton, joined UNRRA without having any experience in relief work, yet still marveled at its amateur quality. The training facilities at Granville in Normandy were terribly shabby; her accommodations were located in an old school building, where "the lavatory accommodation is on the Chinese pattern, a hole with stands for the feet, except for 2 or 3 WCs with proper doors which are either nailed up or used by the men. Even the French people complain." (The latter comment reveals the frequently expressed contempt of Britons for French standards of cleanliness.) The food at the training center was poor and one had to wait for over an hour in line at each meal. Meanwhile, their training consisted of classroom lectures. "The presiding genius [at Granville] is an odd little personality called Arnold Forster, artist, international figure, linguist, a friend of [former League of Nations high commissioner for refugees Fridtjof] Nansen who has worked at Geneva a good deal, from Oxford and Chelsea, Paris, Budapest, Oslo, and all the rest. . . . He lectured us in two languages from morning to night. . . . In the intervals between standing in queues at meals, complaining about the lavatories, trying to soothe the indignant newcomers by telling them how much worse it was when we arrived, we sat at Forster's feet and absorbed details of the work before us." Most of this training proved totally useless in the DP camps of central Europe; but as a period of initiation, it served to set out the terms of UNRRA's mission in the language of humanitarian, progressive one-worldism that UNRRA workers shared. And like Francesca Wilson, Mrs. Bickerdike developed a good deal of cynicism toward her naïve American colleagues. One of the first people she met in France was an American doctor: "like all Americans, he is deeply grieved and disappointed that all his good actions do not at once produce in Europe an affectionate response. He does not understand that to be American is not enough; that to be beneficent is not enough; that above all to be efficient in an inefficient country is not a way to be popular." And inevitably, the sheer weight of American wealth struck her as simply too much of a good thing. She even complained about eating American rations while on the road in Germany: "Two days' lunch on the perfect US Emergency pack containing cheese, biscuit, fudge, chocolate, chewing gum, cigarettes, matches, and tinned rice pudding and peaches and orangeade powder and I could scream. I eat it but I could scream: it's too perfect, too luxurious, too rich and far too sweet. I long to see a plain quiet Englishman and some plain English chocolate."[12]

Other UNRRA employees were motivated by a strong personal and spiritual imperative to help. Isabel Needham, a young American nurse and a Quaker, wrote a short letter while in Italy that started "Why did I join UNRRA? The simplest answer is because I knew that if I weren't here, I'd want to be." She was drawn to UNRRA for two reasons: "First, I believe in any undertaking, large or small, which offers help where help is needed. Secondly, I am a pacifist, deeply convinced not only of the value but of the imperative need of international cooperation in constructive directions." Ms. Needham's profile was typical for many UNRRA staff. Born in 1914, she earned a degree at Skidmore College and went into nursing and social work. In 1938, she joined a summer program called the Student Peace Service in Pennsylvania, and became a Quaker. The following year, she was invited by the American Friends Service Committee to direct a camp in southern France for Spanish refugee children who were fleeing the civil war. She was the perfect kind of recruit for UNRRA, which she joined in 1944: experienced, tested, and deeply committed to human welfare. She started out in the Yugoslav DP camps outside of Cairo, and then was transferred to southern Italy while awaiting a posting in Yugoslavia. It was hard work, and like so many other relief workers in postwar Europe, she found deep spiritual satisfaction in it. She expressed this commitment in the following words: "In quiet moments, my spirit reaches up, outside of me, beyond me, with a prayer felt rather than spoken: That I may use those gifts I have to do my best in the work that is ahead; that I may be patient and courageous in times of apparent failure; that I may be sensitive to need, and understanding toward all; and that even the humblest service be done in God's name."[13]

Sometimes this sort of spiritual quest could become a burden for UNRRA, which after all faced many ugly, pedestrian chores that required shortcuts, compromise, and the occasional bending of the rules. A nursing student from the University of New Mexico, Marie Pope Wallis, signed up for UNRRA work in 1945. She was a devoted Christian Scientist, and found herself quite unprepared for the work that lay ahead in Europe. She arrived in London in July 1945, and spent six weeks in casual UNRRA training; her diary suggests her days were filled chiefly with visits to the theater. In late August she was shipped to Normandy and the UNRRA training center at Granville, where she bunked on cots with other recruits, three to a room. Not until early September was she sent forward into Belgium and then Germany through devastated countryside and cityscape. The Germans she found "sullen and hostile," and the atmosphere—women could not be unaccompanied on the streets—fearful. In Hamburg, she found a Christian Scientist reading room and was able to express her thoughts to her diary: "I get so fed up with corruption, confusion, and irresponsibility that I think I'd like to give up and go home, then I remember that I am here where I can let my light shine out in this raging chaos. 'Thy Will be Done.'" Her first duties in Hamburg were to register and sort out 134 orphans from Riga, forgotten in the hold of a ship in the Baltic and found by the British army. But within a few weeks, the "persistent evil suggestions of graft, inefficiency, dishonesty, intolerance, drinking, etc.," brought her very low. By late September she decided that she wasn't cut out for the work of "cleaning or mopping up European tag-ends." She found UNRRA full of "ill-prepared and unscrupulous people" who were faced with sorting out "the dregs" of Europe's displaced. "Good personnel are being wasted and the poor ones are feathering their nests with black-market profits. . . . What a mad, artificial business!" On the first of October, she resigned from UNRRA.[14]

UNRRA was not perfect. It was indeed beset by inefficiency, bad planning, shortages, and frequently dubious personnel. Yet these faults must not be overstated. Placed in context, UNRRA's work in delivering aid, food, and medicine and in repairing the bridges between shattered Europe and the rest of the world was a vital stage on the path toward recovery. Its successes were modest but in certain locations—especially in southeastern Europe—UNRRA helped transform the end of the war into a genuine liberation, helping to bring about FDR's "freedom from want." UNRRA worked best where it arrived early, had a large staff, and received support from the local government. This was the case in Greece, Italy, and Yugoslavia, the scene of a number of enduring triumphs.

UNNRA'S HUMANITARIAN CAMPAIGN to rescue Europe's war victims commenced in a most unpromising location: a series of fly-blown refugee camps near Suez, Egypt. Here, on April 3, 1944, UNRRA's Balkan Mission, still based in Cairo, took over command of a few bedraggled camps that the British had set up to shelter Greeks, Yugoslavs, and assorted other refugees from the German and Italian invasions of southeastern Europe. In this "city of the sands," UNRRA relief workers helped look after some 50,000 refugees, relying mainly on goods and supplies donated by the Cairo Council of Voluntary Societies, there being too few military stores to go around. The plan was that as soon as the military situation allowed, these refugees would be repatriated and UNRRA staff would be transferred to the Balkans. In the meantime, however, zealous young relief workers sat around in Cairo doing very little, as the camps had long since settled into a routine and were run by the refugees themselves. One young American wrote home that she was "ashamed to have nothing to report," and had "got pretty discouraged with the seeming inefficiency of the headquarters at Cairo."[15] Perhaps most galling to UNRRA staff was that their aid was not always welcome. In the Tolumbat camp, outside of Cairo, over 2,000 Yugoslavs had been encamped for almost three years; all but 154 of these were women, and they ran the camp committee. The camp operated smoothly, though in the eyes of UNRRA workers, the camp leaders were too rigid politically and allowed the 1,200 children far too little play time, contributing to their aggressive behavior. Yet when UNRRA workers proposed educational initiatives, sports, games, or concerts, they often were met with "open expressions of resentment." "Advice tends to be regarded as criticism," complained one relief worker.[16] This was a foreshadowing of things to come: UNRRA staff across Europe would soon find that refugees, especially when gathered in national groupings, tended to guard their autonomy jealously and to view relief workers as interfering do-gooders with insufficient respect for the struggles and sacrifices their peoples had made in the war.

On April 7, 1945, a steamer pulled out of Port Said bound for the island of Chios, carrying on board five hundred Greek refugees, mostly women, children, and old men, some of whom had been living in camps for three years. This was the first wave of repatriations that eventually carried thousands of Greeks out of Middle East camps toward home. UNRRA had prepared these refugees with an astonishing bounty of supplies: each returning refugee received four blankets, a mattress, ten days' dry rations, one month's medical supplies, and outfits of clothing. Each family was given utensils and cooking equipment, and the ship carried a repatriation team to guide the group back to their island. "As the ship stood ready to pull out," one observer recalled, "colorful refugees lined the decks waving, cheering, lustily singing Greek patriotic songs, calling excited farewells to friends who will follow

The El Shatt camp in the desert outside of Cairo housed thousands of Yugoslav refugees, and was the first major relief operation undertaken by UNRRA.
U.S. National Archives

later."[17] This was a promising beginning, but these relief workers, after the relative calm and order of the Egyptian camps, were not entirely prepared for what awaited them.

"Greece—where malnutrition among children is normal, where 85% of the country is malarious [*sic*] and where economic prostration has followed war and enemy occupations—is the testing ground today of UNRRA, the United Nations' giant program to abolish want and restore economic stability to a battle-ravaged world." That is how the Associated Press bureau chief William B. King set the stage in his April 13, 1945, cable from Athens, raising the stakes for UNRRA to very high levels. King was right: in the early spring of 1945, Greece would be UNRRA's first and perhaps hardest test. The conditions in liberated Greece that confronted UNRRA were shocking and demoralizing. The country, poor before the war, had been ravaged by the German occupation. The German-Italian invasion in April 1941 disrupted trade and shipping into the country, and German soldiers systematically plundered the country. Within months of the invasion, Greece faced a famine that by 1943 left about 250,000 people dead from starvation.[18] Nearly 1,700 villages had been burned and left uninhabited. Malaria, tuberculosis, typhus, and venereal disease as well as effects of long-term malnutrition were widespread. The country had been dependent upon imports for 30 percent of its food; yet during the war, domestic production of food fell by half, and now the required seeds, fertilizers, pesticides, and draft animals were unavailable. Greece once again faced imminent famine conditions. The war caused massive disruption to Greece's infrastructure. The port at Piraeus, which handled 60 percent of the country's prewar imports, was badly damaged. Three-quarters of the country's once-proud merchant fleet was gone. Coastal transport, so vital in a maritime nation, had been wrecked. Greece's 1,660 miles of railway lines and 7,700 miles of roads were almost entirely in ruins, the result both of deliberate German scorched-earth policy and of resistance attacks; over 1,000 bridges too had been blown up. The nation's finances were in a shambles and the country had no hope of paying for vital imports or even getting them to the people once they arrived. As a nation-state, Greece had virtually ceased to function.[19]

UNRRA opened its Athens-based mission on October 23, 1944, ten days after the withdrawal of the German forces and the entry of British troops into the capital. But in December, UNRRA found itself caught up in a crisis that would shape the future of Greece for years to come, and in important ways would undermine the very mission of UNRRA itself. The powerful Communist resistance forces, called the National People's Liberation Army (ELAS), which had done so much to help defeat German rule in Greece, fell into conflict with the government-in-exile, which had been sheltered under British protection in Cairo. King George II and his prime minister George Papandreou had strong British support; after all, Winston Churchill's "percentages" agreement with Stalin had given Churchill reason to think that Britain could expect to have its way in Greece without Communist interference. The Soviets did in fact stay out of Greek affairs, but the powerful, armed, and battle-tested Communist resistance fought openly with the royalist and British-backed forces for control of the country. In December, fighting broke out in Athens and the British called in reinforcements from Italy to take control of the capital. Churchill was adamant that Britain retain control of Greece. He ordered the commander of British troops there, General Ronald Scobie, "to fire at any armed male in Athens who assails the British authority or Greek authority with which we are working. . . . Do not hesitate to act as if you were in a conquered city." The British fought for six weeks to regain control of the city from ELAS, and in February the British, the Greek government, and ELAS forces agreed to an uneasy truce. Still, Churchill's decision to use force against one of the biggest and most effective anti-German resistance forces in Europe earned him sharp condemnation in much of the world press.[20] This brief period of fighting in Athens placed UNRRA personnel in a war zone, and they were repeatedly fired upon by both sides while trying to deliver goods to hospitals and schools, despite waving Red Cross signals and white flags.[21] In mid-December, UNRRA recalled all its personnel in Greece back to Cairo, and returned only after the British had restored order in a now devastated capital city. Despite this civil strife, UNRRA managed to deliver to Greece 200,000 tons of food and 1,250 tons of clothing, including 34,000 blankets, between October 1944 and March 1945.[22]

Because of the gravity of the looming humanitarian crisis, the Greek government was willing to accept a very large UNRRA role in the country, one that went well beyond the delivery of relief. UNRRA's Greek Mission grew into something approaching a parallel government. UNRRA staff helped govern the country, writing laws, planning import programs, running and staffing the ports, operating hospitals and clinics, and deploying truck fleets and medical teams across the country. By October 1945, more than 289 UNRRA staff, mostly Britons and Americans, were serving in Greece, assisted by 1,059 local employees and 300 personnel from voluntary relief societies. They had achieved deliveries of food totaling 100,000 tons per month, had managed to import 4,500 trucks and 2,253 tractors, and more than 5,000 draft animals. UNRRA helped reopen two key rail lines, one from Salonika to Istanbul, the other Athens to Patras, thus opening up the interior of the country; it sent 65,000 children to summer camp, started an emergency feeding program for infants and pregnant mothers, and deployed eight DDT-spraying airplanes across the country. By the fall, although the country was still in peril, UNRRA's efforts had started to make headway.[23]

Yet from the ground-level view, the picture was still deeply depressing. Isabel Hunter, a British observer on an UNRRA team, made a tour in April and May 1945 of northeastern Greece, which had endured a brutal Bulgarian occupation. Starting in Salonika, she visited an overcrowded and under-staffed hospital, then went to see the Jewish cemetery, where the tombs had been ripped out of the ground by the Germans and used for tiling and road paving. In Sérrai and Drama, towns to the east of Salonika, she heard detailed descriptions of Bulgarian despoliations and atrocities, including a case in which Bulgarian soldiers played football with the head of one of their Greek victims. "We were inclined to doubt the authenticity of such a statement," she wrote in her report, "but when we were shown a snapshot of Bulgarian officers sitting with two heads placed in the foreground we were disgusted and convinced." North of Drama, on the road to Kato

Nevrokopion, they saw deserted villages with doors and windows gone, now occupied by rail-thin, frightened refugees. Amid this squalor, Hunter was heartened to see ships offloading goods in the harbor of Kaválla, and truckloads of rations and milk delivered to outlying villages. As yet, there had been no Greek government presence in the area at all: what relief there was had come from UNRRA and British military supplies. In Patras, the coastal city in western Greece, the American Nancy Hayward, along with three other UNRRA workers, set up a clothing distribution program for the whole Patras region, which included over 750,000 people. They were hopelessly overworked, and not until a ten-person British team from the YWCA arrived in their own trucks did the burden ease a bit. Yet the lack of supplies caused constant frustration. The luxurious packages given to the returning refugees from Cairo were a thing of the past: now everything was running short, especially clothing, shoes, and food.[24]

To outside observers, UNRRA appeared to be failing in Greece. The *New York Times* ran a story in late May headlined "UNRRA in Greece Draws Criticism," which said that to date, the agency had "accomplished little apparent good" and had "fallen far short of hopes." The chief defense given by the Greek Mission director, Buell Maben, was that the demand was great, and that Greece itself faced terrific road and transport difficulties. Furthermore, the absence of a stable Greek government meant that aid, once delivered by UNRRA to ports, was often not delivered promptly, and Greek officials were selling much of the foodstuffs at high prices rather than distributing it freely.[25] Herbert Lehman, UNRRA's director, seems to have felt some of this criticism was justified. In July he traveled to Europe for a series of field trips and meetings, and arrived in Greece on the 16th to inspect the UNRRA mission. In Salonika, he found the usual troubles: poor hospital facilities, overcrowding, refugees clothed in rags. One hospital for orphans was, he wrote in his diary, "extremely distressing." It was housed in a former Jewish hospital, and now had no trained nurses. "The little ones, all under a year, were a wretched lot. Most of their legs were no larger than my thumb and their color was terrible and the mortality was staggering. One baby died right in front of me." Back in Athens, he told the mission staff that while he understood the difficulties they faced, there was criticism back in the United States, and any inefficiency in the field would only fuel the flames. Tractors sitting on quay-sides, warehouses with clothing in them, foods not being delivered: such things were unacceptable, and he urged the staff to make the best of the supplies they had.[26]

The results of UNRRA's work in Greece were mixed. The official history naturally makes significant claims: that despite the "lethargy, inefficiency, and

UNRRA aircraft at the Elefsis airfield near Athens prepare to spray swamps with mosquito-killing DDT pesticide in an effort to suppress malaria. *UNRRA*

corruption" of the Greek government, "the Greek people and the nation were quite literally kept alive by the contribution of UNRRA supplies and by the hard, practical work of hundreds of UNRRA employees without whom the supplies would never have reached the Greek people."[27] By the end of 1945, the organization had shipped 5,000 tons of clothing, shoes, and blankets into the country, opened welfare centers in every province, distributed over 1,000 tons of raw wool to families with looms to weave their own textiles, shipped in over $3 million of medical supplies, and were delivering 8,000 vials of penicillin each month. The list of the goods offloaded each month from UNRRA ships reveals that UNRRA was doing more than merely providing a hot meal: it was repairing the basic fabric of life for millions whom the war had left destitute. By the start of 1946, UNRRA had shipped to Greece 14,000 cases of matches, 2.8 million razor blades, 6,500 pounds of candles, 96,000 rolls of toilet paper, 324,000 tubes of calcium hydrochlorite for water purification, along with hundreds of thousands of household items such as cooking utensils, cutlery, soup bowls, lamps, bathtubs, tents, tables, garden hoses, shovels, tea towels, soap, brooms, mops, and even corkscrews. Far more important than such household items was the monthly total of

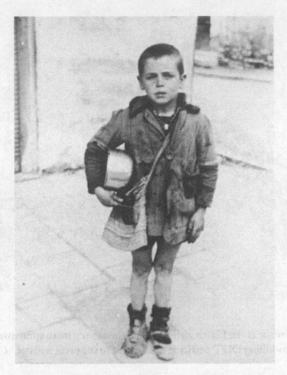

A malnourished Greek boy in Patras clutches an empty tin dish while
waiting for the UNRRA-supplied school lunch to begin. *UNRRA*

grain UNRRA brought into Greece: 77,000 tons per month, about half the
daily ration of every person in the country. Yet there was no getting around
the massive work that still lay ahead. The Germans had wrecked the country
and it would take years to recover. Food stocks, transport, water and sewage
systems, medical facilities—all had completely collapsed and even UNRRA's
work made only modest progress against such a massive crisis. UNRRA
workers often felt the Greeks themselves were simply helpless, too corrupt or
simply too ignorant to pull themselves out of their misery. One medical officer claimed that the reason typhus and fly-borne diseases were rampant was
that "the Greek people have a profound disrespect for the infectious nature
of fecal matter," and left rather a lot of it piled in heaps around their homes.
UNRRA's labors could not heal Greece, nor steer it away from another cataclysm: by late 1945, tormented Greece was heading into four years of civil
war that would further delay the nation's recovery. The deputy chief of the
Greek Mission summed up UNNRA's work at the end of 1945 with a tone

of resignation. "I hope the more fortunate peoples of the United Nations," he told a press conference wearily, "will understand how deep-rooted and desperate are the needs of the Greek people and how limited must be the assistance which UNRRA can provide."[28]

"THE ITALIANS ALL seemed to be dirty, ragged, dejected and without hope." This was a fairly typical assessment of Italy and its inhabitants made by Anglo-American relief workers and military personnel in early 1945. In this case, the writer was Anne Dacie, a Briton who, under Red Cross auspices, had spent ten weeks in Naples, and in the displaced persons camps at Bari, on Italy's Adriatic coast. "The streets [of Naples] were crowded with homeless people who walked around to get warm," Dacie went on. "Many of them were living in dirty shelters which the military were making efforts to clean. . . . The great concern of the military authorities was venereal disease, which is going to be one of the problems of Europe."[29] For Anglo-American relief workers, there was a tendency to explain this state of affairs as indicative of a general and predictable Italian turpitude. Yet this was simply the face of war, visible now through the dust and wretchedness of systemic poverty and neglect.

Of course, there are various explanations for Italy's sad state of affairs in 1945. The Anglo-American military occupation of southern Italy began with the landings in Sicily in July 1943. In early September, the Allies jumped across to the mainland and within a few weeks controlled the "foot" of Italy; by November 1943, the Allies had made it just north of Naples. There, however, their progress slowed, and it would take another year and a half to free the rest of Italy from German control. The "hot rake of war"—in Churchill's memorable phrase—clawed Italy to bits in 1944 and early 1945. The parts of the country that were liberated first, from Sicily and Sardinia up through Naples, were historically Italy's poorest. Even before the war, Naples was notorious for its disease, public health crises, malaria, unemployment, crime, high child mortality, prostitution, and venereal disease. By the time the Allies got there, the city was a total shambles and the people in a state of extreme filth and dejection. While the recovery and relief efforts slowly got under way in southern Italy, the northern part of the country, where Italy's larger, industrial cities lay, was under German occupation. Italy was only partly liberated, and wholly occupied, by these contending armies.[30]

As a former enemy country, Italy was not supposed to receive any UNRRA aid at all. But Italy's circumstances—it switched sides and joined the Allies in September 1943—meant that in some sense Italy was UNRRA's responsibility. The Americans and British asked UNRRA to deliver a minimum of $50 million in emergency food and medicine for Italy's children and pregnant mothers. Despite the huge transportation problems, with roads, ports, and rail lines either in use by the military or out of commission, UNRRA managed to sustain over one million mothers and children with this initial food aid.[31] Italy's place in the international system shifted after the summer of 1945. The Big Three, though deadlocked about what to do with occupied Germany, agreed to work out a peace treaty with Italy and at Potsdam acknowledged the importance of Italy's switch to the Allied cause in 1943. UNRRA's council swiftly took advantage of this improvement in Italy's position and announced a change of its own policy in August 1945: Italy was to receive aid on the same terms as any other liberated Allied state. This marked the significant expansion of UNRRA's program in Italy, and indeed by the end of the UNRRA experience in 1947, Italy had become UNRRA's second largest recipient of aid, receiving $418 million in food, clothing, textiles, medical supplies, and industrial and agricultural equipment. Italy's UNRRA staff expanded to over 4,000 individuals, and UNRRA actually became the principal import agency for Italy until spring 1947, when it turned over this role to the Italian government.

Yet if UNRRA aid began to flow in earnest in 1946, for most of 1945 the country was in a wretched state, with food production well below prewar levels, industrial activity at a halt, and disease, malnutrition, and homelessness ubiquitous. An UNRRA survey of April 1945 painted a woeful picture indeed. A third of Italy's roads, it said, were unusable; 13,000 bridges were destroyed or damaged; 80 percent of the railroads' carrying capacity was gone; the merchant marine was a wreck; 90 percent of the country's trucks and 70 percent of the buses were inoperable. This crisis of transportation was "one of the main causes of the paralysis of the country." It also contributed to a collapse of food distribution. "Food riots continue throughout the country," the report continued. The Anglo-American occupying authority, called the Allied Commission, set the bread ration at 200 grams in late 1943 and failed to raise it for all of 1944. By December 1944, the food situation was "critical, and much worse than under the Germans." The falloff in food production and transport contributed to a sharp rise in mortality rates, especially among the very old, and in a general lowering of resistance to illness: in June 1944, "one in five people in Rome had tuberculosis." To make matters worse, the Allies—not the Germans or Mussolini—were by mid-1944 blamed for the shortages. The report concluded, "The fall of Fascism, the Armistice, and the declaration of war on Germany led the people to believe that the

Allies were really their friends, and this belief was fostered by Allied propaganda which contained many promises. When these promises were not carried out, it is easy to understand how disappointed the people became within a few weeks after their liberation."

The Allies made some things worse when trying to do good. The black market, which the Allied occupation initially tried to suppress, had been a fairly regular source of food supplies in Italy's large cities. The occupation, by instituting regular roadblocks around the cities, and fixing prices for key goods such as bread, effectively shut off black market supplies; but it failed to replace them with sufficient goods. This led to even more acute shortages and soaring prices, as farmers and black marketers now simply withheld goods altogether. In Naples, according to the April survey, "in a few weeks' time the food conditions of the population greatly deteriorated," and the Allies got the blame. The same happened in Rome, and "a great outcry was raised to lift the prohibitive regulations and remove the road blocks." The Allied authorities evidently concluded that the black market was better than no market and allowed goods to trickle into the city for illegal sale. As a result of "the Black Market sprang to a new life."[32]

Medical supplies were even scarcer than food. Dr. Mario Volterra, a pathologist from the University of Cagliari in Sardinia, surveyed a few large hospitals in Rome in late 1944 and reported his findings in a letter to the UNRRA mission. It makes sobering reading. In Rome, he wrote, conditions in hospitals have taken "a step backwards of nearly a century." Basic supplies for disinfecting equipment, for example, were lacking, as were drugs of all kinds. Patients were limited to two meals a day; the lack of bedding and linens "is a common disaster." At the San Giovanni hospital—"the worst hospital in Rome"—a surgeon invited Volterra into the operating room. The place was infested with ants. "They come in droves from the walls," he noticed, "from the gray cracks in the floor. They try to climb the cold legs of the table and get into the bandages." The surgeon shrugged his shoulders: "'Men are dying; it is so easy to let them die. But it isn't easy to kill these darn ants.'" There were no sterile bandages, no operating gloves, insufficient anesthesia. The patient on which the surgeon was operating began to scream. Then the generator cut out, and the rooms went dark.[33]

In May 1945, the Unitarian Service Committee (USC), based in Boston, secured UNRRA's approval to launch a long-term nutritional study in Italy, focusing on selected cities and towns in southern Italy. Their work was conducted throughout 1945 and 1946, and the results reveal the awful toll that the war, coming on top of widespread poverty, had taken, especially upon children. Dr. Frank Gollan of the U.S. Public Health Service, and a pediatri-

Beneath an UNRRA poster promising aid, a mother and child
huddle together in a cave in Naples. *UNRRA*

cian by training, served on the USC's team in Italy, and delivered a sobering
summary of the mission's findings. After examining over 24,000 people, the
survey found that tuberculosis was widespread, that malaria had staged a
comeback due to the flooding of once-drained swamplands, and that "the
low standard of sanitation and cleanliness in the population of Naples due to
unsanitary latrines or their complete absence and the lack of soap and warm
water" had contributed to rampant diarrhea and intestinal parasites among
much of the population of that city. Ten percent of the children in Naples
had dysentery, which made the absorption of nutrients difficult. The food
shortages made recovery even harder, as "the daily hunting for food requires
again a great amount of energy," and so the very young, the elderly, and the ill
were often left behind in the competition to find food. The results of a survey
of two hundred children in a Naples foundling home make the point: they
all suffered from malnutrition, vitamin deficiency, rickets, stunted growth,
and deformities of the legs. Dr. Gollan and the USC team, after spending a

year in Italy, knew that what they were witnessing was not just the result of a food shortage, but of a collapse of the entire social fabric in Italy. "The breakdown of public health measures, sanitation and medical service, the lack of transportation, cold in wintertime and dehydration in summer, crowded and unsanitary living quarters due to the destruction of homes and the shift of populations, the constant infections and infestations of the people due to polluted water and milk, the ignorance of the population concerning matters of sanitation and cleanliness," all of these factors turned daily life in southern Italy during the war and its aftermath into a desperate struggle for survival.[34]

Like every European country at the war's end, Italy also had its share of displaced persons. Hundreds of thousands of internally displaced Italians were settled fairly rapidly, but in 1945, UNRRA faced the prospect of caring

Displaced Persons in UNRRA Camps in Italy, as of February 1946[35]

Camp Location	Number of Residents
Santa Maria di Bagni	2403
Santa Maria di Leuce	1937
Tricase	738
Genoa	297
Milan	630
Turin	1167
Bologna	235
Cremona	721
Forli Hospital	96
Reggio-Emilia I	1272
Reggio-Emilia II	503
Modena	808
Riccione	414
Senigallia	467
Fermo	2064
Servigliano	1288
Jesi-Fano	1156
Bari	600
Asersa	1142
Cinecittà	1520
Total	**19,458**

for 20,000 non-Italian refugees, some trying to get home, others afraid of returning home. From the earliest days of the Anglo-American landings in southern Italy, DPs had sought shelter in liberated southern Italy while awaiting the end of the war. They congregated in small camps set up by the Allied forces that were turned over to UNRRA in the fall of 1945. The conditions in these camps were difficult, though not as bad as those UNRRA would later encounter in Germany. Most camps had one to two thousand or fewer residents, which made them easier to run.

Who were these people? Many were the typical residents of Europe's DP camps: Polish Jews, men, women, and children who did not wish to return home and were trying to make their way out of central Europe, down into Italy, and on to Palestine. But the makeup of any one camp varied over time: in early 1945, there were large numbers of Yugoslavs and Greeks in Italy who were able to return to their countries by mid-1945. By the end of the year, it was more likely that the camp inmates would be Eastern Europeans and Jews. The national origins of the 4,700 people in four camps in the Lecce region are indicative: 56 percent were Poles, 14 percent were Romanian, and the rest came from a dozen different European states.[36]

Naturally, the conditions in which they lived were difficult. The health problems so prevalent in Italy were magnified inside DP camps, as UNRRA's early reports revealed. Anne Dacie, who worked with the British Red Cross in the Bari camp, claimed to be the first woman aid worker inside the camp, arriving in January 1945. She went to work to help bathe, disinfect, and clothe the women and girls, mostly people from the Balkans. Their conditions were often so bad that their hair had to be shaved and their clothes burned. Dacie said that "all the refugees needed shoes and clothing, razors, combs, brushes and toothbrushes in order to gain some sense of self respect and well-being"—yet many of these things were in short supply until the UNRRA program got under way in mid-1945. Dacie and her fellow Red Cross workers had to scrounge up outfits for the refugees from cast-off army surplus; rubber tires were converted into makeshift sandals for the shoeless. Prostitution was rife, as was general promiscuity among inmates. Relief workers were too busy to care, this being part of the normal course of war and something everyone was thoroughly used to by 1945. Dacie seemed to think "a little promiscuity, though undesirable, denoted a gradual return to the feelings of life, and finally of balance"; and at the weekly dances held in the camp, women camp residents dressed up as well as they could. "Others outside the camp might have thought them dowdy, but to us who knew them as they had been, they seemed charming." This became a constant theme in the world of the DP camp: both inmates and camp staff were eager to reestablish even the most elementary kinds of normal social interactions: a nice dress and a dance, after six years of hell, was a kind of liberation.[37]

WHERE GREECE AND Italy depressed UNRRA workers with their vast needs and defeated people, Yugoslavia lifted their spirits. "The inhabitants are all clean, proud, self-respecting and friendly," wrote acting director of the Yugoslav mission, Alan Hall, upon arriving in the country, "and a welcome change from southern Italy." The head of the public relations office concurred: "the first general impressions of this place are wonderful, especially compared to the general feeling of depression and lack of initiative that one senses among the Italians." Yugoslavs were full of "energy and enthusiasm," and the streets were filled with youthful partisan boys and girls, singing and dancing. "Everyone here is amazed at the fine work the Jugoslavs [*sic*] are doing."[38] With UNRRA and Yugoslavia, it was love at first sight. Such first impressions, in a country that had passed through four years of bitter occupation and civil war, are curious. What did these UNRRA observers see in this ravaged country that impressed them so? What did they not see?

From the moment of the German invasion in the spring of 1941, Yugoslav society had splintered. The Yugoslav government, under the monarch King Peter, rallied elements of the army and the Serb elite, but the king fled to London in June; a proroyalist resistance movement headed by Colonel (later General) Draža Mihailović established links to the British government. The Germans, meanwhile, established a collaborationist regime in a much-expanded Croatia under the Fascist and Croatian nationalist Ante Pavelić, who now saw an opportunity to wage ethnic war against the long-hated, domineering, and Orthodox Serbs. The Croatian nationalist Ustaše movement began in May 1941 a long-term campaign of terror and extermination against the Serbs. Mihailović's Chetnik forces, instead of fighting these Fascists and their German patrons, seemed content instead to play a waiting game, withdrawing to the hills of southern Serbia. The British, on whom Mihailović was dependent for supplies, began by 1943 to lean toward the more effective resistance movement led by Josip Broz, or Tito, a Communist revolutionary who eschewed ethnic warfare and preferred killing Germans. Precisely because of the challenge they presented to Mihailović's control of the anti-Fascist movement, Tito's partisans were targeted by the Chetniks. The partisans fought back, so Yugoslavia, in addition to facing a German occupation, was also engaged in a three-way civil war between the Fascist Ustaše, the royalist-Serb Chetniks, and the Communist partisans. The result was horrifyingly predictable: of the 1.2 million Yugoslavs who died in the Second World War, most were killed by their fellow countrymen.[39]

By late 1943, when British aid and support turned decisively toward the partisans, it became clear that the future of Yugoslavia lay in Tito's hands. A devoted Communist, a charismatic and vain, handsome, sometimes preening leader, Tito also showed enormous political acumen in outmaneuvering Mihailović for British favor, and then in ensuring that—unlike in Greece, where the Communists had been pushed into the hills—his movement would dominate the postwar government. In June 1944, through British brokerage, representatives of Tito and King Peter worked out an agreement for a postwar power-sharing government, but there were few illusions that any real sharing would occur. In the fall of 1944, the Soviet Red Army swept through eastern and northern Yugoslavia to liberate Belgrade, leaving Tito in full command of the political stage. The coalition government that took shape in March 1945 was only nominally multiparty; Tito controlled the levers of power, the secret police, and a powerful force of battle-tested rebels.

Yugoslavia in 1945 faced an economic and social crisis. Reports gathered chiefly by British military authorities revealed the predictable carnage. In Dalmatia, the beautiful coastal region that had been occupied by the Italians after April 1941 and by the Croatian Fascists after September 1943, 600,000 civilian inhabitants faced a severe shortage of food, housing, and clothing; heavy fighting had killed off much of the livestock and spoiled grain supplies. In the Banat region, north of Serbia and bordering Romania and Hungary, the Germans had ruled with the willing aid of a large minority of ethnic Germans, who had ruthlessly persecuted the Serbs. By the fall of 1944, the tables had turned, and these *Volksdeutsche*—perhaps 200,000 of them—were now slated for destruction. Most were expelled from their land and many were shipped in convoys to labor camps in the Soviet Union. The result was a denuded territory of empty farms. Bosnia, much of which had suffered under Croatian Fascist rule, faced an epidemic of disease: "hardly a village in eastern Bosnia has not been struck by typhus," concluded one report, and the lack of soap and clean clothes compounded the problem. In Montenegro, which had been under nominal Italian control but in fact was a partisan stronghold, disease and food shortages were beginning to take their toll. There had been "no medical attention in these areas for nearly four years," according to one assessment. "Rickets, tuberculosis, typhus, ringworm, and impetigo are prevalent. There is no attempt at sanitation anywhere, and lice, fleas, and rats are ever present." Only Belgrade had escaped catastrophic damage, in part because the German occupation had enforced a kind of calm there. The population was anxious about Tito's troops, and wild rumors circulated about mass arrests and purges; but the food supply was adequate, though expensive due to unregulated prices. "The avenues are untidy," wrote one observer, "with unswept leaves, and the streets are littered with bins of uncollected garbage, until quite recently often liberally intermixed with deceased Germans."[40]

The war's end did not bring peace to Yugoslavia. On V-E Day, as Europe celebrated the defeat of Nazi Germany and the arrival of peace, Yugoslavia was still deep in a season of war. Milovan Djilas, one of Tito's closest political friends and allies in the partisan movement, and a man whose two brothers and pregnant sister were murdered by the Chetniks, recalled that "we leaders greeted the unconditional surrender of Germany—Victory Day—in bitter loneliness. It was a joy not meant for us. . . . We were still waging war on a grand scale." Chetniks, Ustaše, collaborators—those who had taken up arms against the partisans—were now marked for liquidation. "The killings were sheer frenzy," Djilas admitted. Perhaps 20,000–30,000 were tracked down and killed; the violence continued right down to the end of the year. Why so much bitterness? Djilas explained: "side by side with the invader they [Ustaše and Chetniks] had waged war for many years against the children of their own people; they had run to new masters; they had burned, tortured, slaughtered; . . . they took no prisoners." And so the wartime enemies were hunted down and wiped out. Djilas said that he and his fellow partisan leaders embraced this policy of retribution "with bitter conviction."[41]

Did the UNRRA teams that arrived in the spring of 1945 overlook this violent endgame of a civil war in a country that apparently was not yet ready to stop killing? Perhaps. Or maybe they liked what they saw—not, to be sure, the purges and murders but the zeal of the fiery partisans. There was something in the Yugoslavs that outsiders wished to identify with: their revolutionary enthusiasm, the virtue of a righteous cause, their membership in a warrior race that had sustained itself and its people on ideas of patriotism, justice, and liberation. These categories and typologies, useful in explaining the success of the rugged partisan against the tyrannical German, were core ideals of the Allied cause as it had been rehearsed by Roosevelt and Churchill. Yugoslavs needed little more than a helping hand, it seemed, to aid their fierce experiment in democracy. It was not that UNRRA observers failed to see the violence of the war and its aftermath: rather, they saw in it a political commitment that filled them with a fearful admiration.

The reputation, so carefully promoted by the BBC during 1944, of the Yugoslavs as proud warriors who had rid their country of the Germans, prepared foreign relief officials to find heroes on every hand. When in April 1945 the first convoy of Yugoslav refugees boarded trucks at the El Shatt camp near Cairo, en route to the coast and a ship that would take them home to Split, UNRRA's public relations bureau invested the scene with a certain grandeur: these 1,300 Yugoslav refugees were "returning with proud, happy hearts, determined to help build a new and democratic Jugoslavia." These were, according to one observer, "not refugees in the ordinary sense of the word; they are people going home to do a job" of rebuilding their land. On the docks, as the refugees embarked, they filed to the ships "with the precision of soldiers." The American commander of UNRRA's Middle East office, Dr. H. van Zile Hyde, depicted this refugee repatriation as a veritable victory march: "As the first Jugoslavs leave us today, we see men, women and children returning to the land they cherish with determination to add their strength to work in their nation, whose name holds forever a high and honored place among the foes of evil and destruction. These people are returning as victors over hardship."[42] Such discipline made UNRRA look good, at a time when UNRRA needed successes. "It will be almost impossible for UNRRA to fail in Jugoslavia," public relations director Sydney Morrell wrote. "If any people were ready and able to help themselves it is this one. . . . These people have a bottomless capacity for perseverance."[43]

For Irving "Jack" Fasteau, an American who had worked during the war for the Social Security Board and was now part of the Military Liaison that served as a link between the Army and UNRRA, the country's revolution was part of its appeal. "From what I've seen," he wrote to colleagues back in Washington, "it is a broad movement, supported by the large majority of the people; it is a shifting of power from a small well-to-do group to another portion of the population that although small in number appears to have been thrown up by the rigors of the last few years, who have demonstrated leadership qualities under a period of great stress and privation, and who seem thereby to have gained the confidence of large masses of the peasants." Fasteau adopted a philosophical view about the cost of this upheaval: "As you know, revolution, social and economic changes, wherever and whenever they take place are not pleasant. Not everyone is satisfied. . . . We know that the conditions of war limit the development and application of civil liberties." Fasteau was naturally stunned by the devastation the war wrought. "Community graves, with as many as 80 bodies, who had been shot or tortured. . . . Whole villages without a house standing. Miles of devastation." Yet again, the "strenuous efforts" of the people stood out. There were no draft animals for planting; no matter: "It is not uncommon to see an entire family pulling a plow." Improvisation: "I saw a tractor that was being built from odd parts of cars and planes, both German and American." In local hospitals and welfare centers, people "do so much with so little. . . . Beds are made from whatever wood there can be found or scrounged. Tin cans are used as utensils, wooden spoons are carved by hand from pieces of scrap lumber. The homes are very clean, everything in them is clean." Above all, the population is "almost painfully hospitable, giving freely of what little they have."[44] Here was just what UNRRA needed: a determined people, capable and rugged, fueled by ideals of patriotism and egalitarianism.

As a result, Yugoslavs featured prominently in UNRRA's public relations effort. The Yugoslav peasant was transformed into a heroic everyman in one radio script, written by UNRRA: he was a man who "had stoically resisted countless acts of God and man in the shape of barbaric invasion, droughts, and human and animal epidemics." The ruthless German occupation threatened to end his way of life but "the unhesitating sacrifice of the Jugoslav peasant"—who plowed his own fields when animals were lacking and carried buckets of water across the parched, rocky mountain-scape—defied even Hitler's designs. Yugoslavia "had been occupied but never conquered," exclaimed one UNRRA field-worker on a BBC broadcast. "We of UNRRA felt privileged to work with such a people."[45]

UNRRA WAS NOT the only agency deployed in the broken landscape of Europe in 1945 to deliver hope and healing. Alongside and technically under UNRRA, some 125 private charitable organizations stood ready to deliver supplies, money, and staff workers wherever they could be best used. These voluntary organizations, most of which dated back to the start of the war and in some cases back to the First World War, presented both an opportunity and a headache for UNRRA. Voluntary agencies wished to guard their independence to some extent, for they had raised money and contributions from their own constituencies, often on behalf of particular groups within Europe. UNRRA had to guard against the duplication of efforts and wastage of scarce space aboard ships bound for Europe from American ports. Nor did UNRRA need the administrative hassles of registering, and supervising, the staff of these agencies, most of whom wished to be sent into Germany and Eastern Europe, where the need was evidently greatest. Over time, however, UNRRA worked out basic structures for these agencies that allowed them to play a role in delivering aid to Europe. UNRRA was wise to do so, for the American public was far more closely tied to these church-based or national, grassroots organizations than to the vague acronym "UNRRA." In finding a role for voluntary relief organizations, UNRRA helped sustain the American public's commitment to continued sacrifice on behalf of European civilians.[46]

In the United States, the American public began to raise funds for European war relief from the very opening of the war in 1939, chiefly along lines of ethnic identity. Polish-Americans raised millions in 1939 and 1940 as their homeland fell under German and Soviet occupation; British War Relief raised $4 million in 1940 and $8 million in 1941 on behalf of the British civilians suffering under the German blitz; Greek-Americans contributed $4.3 million in 1941 alone for war relief in Greece. And on it went: Americans set up committees to raise funds for Albanians, Armenians, Czechs, Danes, Lithuanians, Dutch, Norwegians, Russians, Yugoslavs, and dozens of other nationalities inside Europe. Such was the profusion of fund-raising appeals that the U.S. government—which wished to encourage broad-based voluntary contributions to war relief—was forced to create supervisory machinery to avoid oversaturation of national appeals and the inevitable rivalry of different ethnic groups competing for scarce dollars. For example, in 1940, over seventy separate organizations were busy soliciting money for British war relief. In July 1942, President Roosevelt established the President's War Relief Control Board, and assigned it the duty to regularize and oversee war relief appeals in the United States as well as the disbursement of monies raised. It was authorized to streamline fund-raising chiefly by consolidating voluntary organizations; the British War Relief Society, for example, grouped together dozens of smaller operations. The board also initiated the National War Fund, which conducted an annual nationwide campaign on behalf of war relief that raised some $321 million and used it to support the USO, the War Prisoners Aid, and twenty-seven other relief agencies. The board also urged private charities to step up their own coordination so as to avoid duplication in the field. Some did so and formed the American Council of Voluntary Agencies for Foreign Service (ACVAFS) in 1943, which gradually expanded to include most of the major private agencies operating in Europe.[47]

The end of the war opened a new chapter for these relief groups, for it meant that they could expand their efforts from raising money in the United States to sending skilled relief personnel along with the aid their funds had purchased. Hundreds of American relief workers representing dozens of organizations traveled to Europe in 1945, mostly to Germany, to join other equally committed European relief agencies in the field. By mid-1946, over 1,100 personnel from voluntary agencies, European and American, were at work side by side in Germany, and many others were scattered across the European landscape.

Disbursements by Select U.S. Voluntary Agencies for Foreign War Relief in 1945

British War Relief Society	$1,400,606
American Relief for France	3,333,369
Greek War Relief	1,203,553
American Relief for Italy	3,039,619
American Relief for Holland	1,863,411
United Palestine Appeal	14,358,196
American Relief for Poland	1,824,806
American Society for Russian Relief	4,311,171
American Friends Service Committee	1,661,843
American Jewish Joint Distribution Committee	17,589,005
YMCA	4,571,353
Unitarian Service Committee	600,561
National Catholic Welfare Conference	5,125,117

Source: Voluntary War Relief during World War II: A Report to the President, by Joseph
Davies, Charles P. Taft, and Charles Warren (Washington D.C., March 1946).

Predictably, these agencies viewed the creation of UNRRA with trepidation. UNRRA was the designated international agency for supplying aid in the liberated areas, and the voluntary groups faced a new level of bureaucracy before they could make their own mark in Europe. UNRRA controlled the supplies these smaller groups would need, and of course UNRRA had gobbled up what vehicles were left over from military surplus. Voluntary agencies could not enter Germany without approval and specific orders from UNRRA, and once there, they were technically under UNRRA supervision and could be assigned anywhere. By the end of September 1945, twelve agencies had signed agreements with UNRRA; that number expanded to thirty-six by the fall of 1946, heavily focused on work with displaced persons in Germany. UNRRA guarded its options by insisting that volunteers would not be assigned to work with their own choice of national group, nor at their choice of camp. The important exception to this was the Jewish relief agencies: after a great deal of prodding and pressure, the American Jewish community secured special dispensation to work with Jewish DPs and the American Jewish Joint Distribution Committee (AJJDC) was designated as the coordinating agency for other Jewish relief organizations. This agreement served UNRRA's interests, as well as the Jewish DPs', since until September 1945, the Allied armies gave Jews no special rights or status as a persecuted people; they were simply lumped by nationality with other DPs. When it

Voluntary Agency Personnel with UNRRA in Germany as of August 31, 1946

American Jewish Joint Distribution Committee	177
YMCA/YWCA	127
American Polish War Relief	45
Refugee Relief Committee	25
Polish Red Cross	187
Jewish Agency for Palestine	89
World ORT Union	12
World Student Relief	1
Vaad Hahatzala	8
Netherlands Red Cross	13
National Catholic Welfare Conference	35
Jewish Committee for Relief Abroad	88
Belgian Red Cross	1
Italian Red Cross	7
Hebrew Immigrant Aid Society	33
Friends Relief Service	2
Don Suisse	11
British Red Cross and COBSRA*	250
French Red Cross	4
Czech Red Cross	6
Comité Catholique de Secours	35

*Council of British Societies for Relief Abroad was a British umbrella organization that included over a dozen leading British humanitarian organizations.

Source: UNRRA Archives, PAG-4/1.3.1.1.1, box 21.

became clear in late summer that German, Polish, Baltic, and Hungarian Jews refused to be housed with their often anti-Semitic conationals, leaders of the international Jewish community demanded, and won, the significant reform of UNRRA and SHAEF's policy toward Jewish DPs. With this important exception, however, UNRRA deterred relief groups from focusing on specific religious or national groups, and sought instead to deploy voluntary agencies in regions where their skills and labor would be most useful.[48]

Despite such minor rivalries with UNRRA, the extensive work of private humanitarian agencies in postwar Europe shows plainly that Americans at the war's end were just as ready to work hard, give money and time, and make personal sacrifices on behalf of European recovery as they had been to fight and destroy Hitler's regime. Indeed, one could suggest that they were even more zealous in this final stage of the war: Americans understood that what was at stake in 1945 was precisely the fulfillment of all the great efforts that soldiers had made on the battlefield. Were Americans to fail to administer to a brutalized Europe now, the pain and bitterness of the war would be for naught. Americans understood this instinctively—that here in Europe something awful had happened and now must be set right.

HISTORIANS, AS WELL as many contemporaries, considered UNRRA something of a failure when it finally closed down in 1947, to be broken up and succeeded by various UN agencies.[49] It is hard to accept this verdict. UNRRA managed to deliver to Europe, as well as Asia, almost $4 billion of goods, food, medicine, and industrial and agricultural machinery at a time of global shortages, worldwide transport difficulties, and political chaos. The 25 million long tons of goods that UNRRA delivered was three times the amount the United States gave after World War I. Millions of people benefited from UNRRA's work. True, it did not create the sort of sustained institutional machinery that the Marshall Plan later did. It had not sought to do so. Herbert Lehman in December 1943 had explicitly stated that the agency should be "measured by the speed with which it is able to liquidate itself; the sooner it becomes unnecessary, the greater will have been its accomplishments."[50] Even so, the London-based *Economist* magazine lamented the planned demise of UNRRA, for in an increasingly divided world, it was a genuinely international enterprise, "the only organization or activity still bridging the gulf between East and West."[51] Perhaps for that very reason, it could not long survive. The United States government felt that for all the money it had thrown at Europe in 1945–46, it had not gained much traction in restarting the giant economic engine of the continent. Nor did Americans like having to share decision making in an agency funded largely with dollars. When Dean Acheson's colleague in the State Department, Will Clayton, was sketching out plans in 1947 for what would become the Marshall Plan, he specifically said "we must avoid getting into another UNRRA. The United States must run this show."[52]

So perhaps UNRRA fell short as a vehicle for American foreign economic interests. Yet as Francis B. Sayre said, this organization was "a new enterprise, based fundamentally on human brotherhood."[53] And brotherhood is what it supplied. UNRRA brought the human touch back to Europe in 1945. The men and women who worked in DP camps, staffed transport and distribution centers, drove trucks, and handed out medical supplies and food—these people offered the simple and longed-for gift of decency and charity to Europeans in desperate need. The remarks made by a thirteen-year-old French girl, Yvette Rubin, might stand as a kind of epitaph for the UNRRA experience. Yvette, deported to Germany in 1942, was imprisoned for almost three years, during which time she witnessed the brutal murder of her mother. Returned to Paris in the spring of 1945, she sat one day in her father's apartment in Paris, describing at length the horrors through which she had passed to her uncle, Jean Newman, a staff employee of UNRRA. After her painful monologue, she looked more closely at her uncle's uniform. "Then suddenly, excited and with shining eyes, she jumped off her chair," recalled Newman. "'*Tonton*, you are not a soldier. You are UNRRA. I know them. I was with them for more than two weeks after I was liberated by the British armies. They are wonderful. They have saved my life. They saved me from typhus, which I was still sick with. They fed me and gave me this dress I am now wearing.'" This girl, prematurely aged, her eyes staring out of gray sockets, her limbs as fragile as dried stalks, looked happily at her uncle and said, "'so you are UNRRA. I am so glad. I love them so much. They were the first people to be nice to me.'"⁵⁴

7

"A Tidal Wave of Nomad Peoples":
Europe's Displaced Persons

I N THE SPRING of 1945, as the Allied armies bore into the heart of the Third Reich, millions of captive people inside Germany—prisoners of war, political prisoners, and forced laborers—slipped out of their work camps, prisons, factories, farms, barracks, and shelters and began searching for a path homeward. This sudden flood of civilians rushing along the roads and rails features as one of the largest and swiftest mass migrations in history, described by one awed observer as "a tidal wave of nomad peoples."[1] The Allied military authorities had devised elaborate logistical schemes to channel, register, shelter, and repatriate these millions of people, yet little prepared them for the scale of the problem. Nor were they fully prepared to deal with the acute social and human consequences of such catastrophic displacement.

Over the years, scholars have produced various estimates of the numbers of displaced persons in Germany at war's end. Though the precise numbers can never fully be known, the historian Ulrich Herbert, among others, has given us a detailed accounting of the foreign labor force based on German records. These show that as of August 1944, 5.7 million foreign civilians were toiling in Germany, one-third of whom were women. In addition, the Germans compelled some 1.9 million POWs to work. This labor force was a valuable asset, making up 26 percent of the total German workforce. Foreigners worked in all sectors of the economy, from agriculture to mining, metallurgy, chemicals, construction, and transport. The bulk of the laborers came from the east: 2.7 million Soviets, 1.6 million Poles, half a million Yugoslavs, and 280,000 Czechoslovaks. Yet the Germans had enlisted 1.3 million French workers, half of them POWs, in German war industries, while 500,000 Belgians and a similar number of Dutch had also been pressed into servitude during the war. More than half a million Italians, mostly POWs taken by the Germans after Italy's switch to the Allied side in October 1943, also languished in work camps.[2] Herbert's total figure of 7.6 million forced workers in Germany would appear to be a minimum; other contemporary sources suggest the number was closer to 8.6 million. If we add to this the numbers of prisoners of war who were not laborers, and other political prisoners of the Nazis, it is clear that about 11 million people inside Germany were set free by the collapse of the Third Reich.[3]

Technically, the Allied armies differentiated between civilians and RAMPs—"recovered Allied military personnel"—who were to be turned over directly to military liaison officers from their own respective nations. In practice, of course, it was often hard to sustain the distinction, since captured members of the French, Polish, Soviet, and other armies had long since been compelled to work in camps on behalf of the German war effort. Nonetheless, the U.S. Army stood by these definitions: refugees were "civilians *not* outside the national boundaries of their country, who desire to return to their homes"—that is, internally displaced due to war operations; this category was broad enough to include the fleeing and expelled Germans from the east who were now choking roads and railway stations across Germany. The DPs, by contrast, were defined as "civilians outside the national boundaries of their country by reason of war" who wished to be repatriated. Those who did not wish to return to their homelands—and there were many—were deemed "stateless," and this was a category used to indicate chiefly Jews but also those Poles whose hometowns were, after the crude surgery of Yalta, now part of the Soviet Union.[4]

The Anglo-American military authorities saw the DP problem chiefly as one of security and order: millions of angry foreign workers rampaging through a prostrate Germany could engage Allied soldiers in massive policing efforts, something that would take away valuable resources from the war effort. DPs might also present a large public health problem: planners assumed that DPs would be ill with contagious diseases, certainly hungry, possibly deranged. In addition to these practical objectives, the Army and UNRRA assumed that these millions of DPs had been so traumatized by their harsh experience in the war that they might well have lost the basic social habits that bind societies together. The Army believed that, after years of mistreatment at the hands of the Germans, the DPs might have been warped and twisted, becoming a potentially harmful mass of people. If not properly healed and recivilized, they might act like some malignant agent released into a vulnerable European body politic. They had to be cleaned, repaired, morally as well as physically disinfected, before they could be reintroduced into society. Without an aggressive policy toward DPs, the whole liberation project might be placed in jeopardy.

Given such profound suspicions, it is perhaps not surprising that the liberators did not develop a warm and tender relationship with DPs. Although the United States military and UNRRA had given the DP problem a good deal of thought, most of their planning focused on transportation, shelter, feeding, and registration: the bureaucratic control of humans that the U.S. Army, by 1945, was very good at. Less thought, it seems, went into the human element. Army officers in the field readily acknowledged this important shortcoming. "Implicit in the planning for care and control of DPs," one report from the field concluded,

> was the assumption that the individuals would be tractable, grateful, and powerless, after their domination from two to five years as the objects of German slave policies. They were none of these things. Their intractability took the form of what was referred to repeatedly by officers in contact with them as "Liberation Complex." This involved revenge, hunger, and exultation, which three qualities combined to make DPs, when newly liberated, a problem as to behavior and conduct, as well as for care, feeding, disinfection, registration and repatriation.[5]

Dealing with the liberated, it turned out, would not be easy.

The Army and UNRRA officials were not wholly unprepared for the "Liberation Complex." In August 1944, the European Regional Office of UNRRA formed an Inter-Allied Psychological Study Group, and charged it to investigate the likely state of mind of the newly freed DPs. The committee that authored the study comprised Dutch, British, Czech, and American members, including Edward A. Shils, a University of Chicago scholar on loan from the Office of Strategic Services who, in the postwar years, became a world-renowned sociologist. Their June 1945 report, "Psychological Problems of Displaced Persons," reveals much about the place DPs occupied in the minds of their liberators. Basing their report on evidence gathered by former POWs and forced workers, as well as almost a year of experience in southern Europe and in France, the authors argued that the multiple traumas DPs had experienced—deportation, enslavement, forced labor, humiliation, servitude, extreme violence, loss of family ties—tended to reduce a normally functioning adult to the level of an intemperate, irrational child. "People who have been displaced from their social background . . . tend to return at least in part to the dependent attitudes of childhood," the report claimed. DPs developed "a deep, unreasonable sense of having been cast out of society, hence of being suspect and unloved by their own community." This created in them a powerful conflict "between the primitive need for affection on the one hand and on the other hand the dread of further rejection by a world which has already shown hostility."

In explaining the downright nastiness DPs often showed toward their liberators, the report noted that "allied to the sense of unworthiness and increased lawless aggressiveness there are other common reactions, of which perhaps the most obvious are bitterness and touchiness. Once this state of mind is established, nothing that is done even by helpful people is regarded as genuine or sincere." The constant theme here was the DPs' reversion to infancy: "such peoples' demands become insatiable, like a greedy baby's. . . . It will be found out that, coupled with their gratitude and welcome, there will be a curious undercurrent of hostility and suspicion which may surprise us unless we realize that we are dealing with 'hurt children' whose world has let them down." DPs had fallen back "to earlier, more primitive and, for example, infantile habits." They "do not restrain themselves anymore; the brakes have been taken off." Their symptoms included "increased restlessness," lack of intellectual interests, no attachment to community, "complete apathy," and "loss of initiative." Most troubling, "a great and sullen suspicion has arisen towards all authority. No one is trusted any longer."

If the DPs had become children, the occupation authorities felt obliged to play the role of parents. In sexual matters especially, the report expressed the opinion that European DPs would have to be reschooled. "Young girls and women have been forced into prostitution by the usurper, led behind the fronts and debased into mechanical lust-gratification machines. Young men have been dragged to Germany and forced to impregnate German women. They have all been forced into a world where there can be no feeling of affection or responsibility towards the object of erotic interest. They were humiliated, robbed of their ideals as well as becoming physically diseased." The stakes were enormously high, UNRRA believed. These millions of sexually debased and depraved peoples presented a moral and social threat to the stabilization of the continent. In responding to this human crisis, the report called for "patience." Occupation officials should "arrange for the development of sincere human relations which contain elements of genuine affection and tenderness. This must be done against a serious internal barrier in the women concerned; but if and when this can be overcome, recovery is likely to happen to an extent and to a degree which may well be surprising. . . . Assisted by our knowledge of what has been inflicted upon these people, we must try to see them as human beings, as personalities, who react to the events of life in varied ways."[6]

If UNRRA adopted the language of rehabilitation when considering DPs, the U.S. Army was more blunt. Its guide for handling DPs simply stressed that "speedy repatriation remains the chief objective." Those who could not be repatriated immediately would have to be kept in assembly centers, which meant improvised collection points and often camps—sometimes the very same camps that had been used by the Germans. The DPs would likely be "difficult to control; they may have little initiative; their desire to take revenge may result in looting and general lawlessness." Such problems could be minimized, the Army believed, if DPs were kept in national groups, and if they were allowed to select leaders to speak for them. In addition, families should be kept together and DPs should be allowed to carry personal possessions. The Army envisioned a team of three officers, eight enlisted personnel, and one UNRRA staff member as a sufficient team to supervise a DP camp of 3,000 people; it was expected that UNRRA teams would take control as soon as possible. The chief goal of the assembly centers, then, was not to house but to process DPs. The Army guidelines included a "Flow Chart" illustrated in a manner reminiscent of plumbing, in which a series of pipes carried DPs along six stages. These included arrival and the receipt of a DP card; assignment of accommodations; registration and division into categories; verification of nationality (here DPs might be siphoned off via various tubes to prisoner of war camps if they were determined to be ex-enemy nationals). In the fifth stage, DPs were gathered in a holding tank "awaiting disposal," during which time they might be employed by the camp administration in useful work; and then the final stage, "disposal," which meant repatriation or transfer to a more permanent camp. The document left the impression that DPs were human refuse in need of waste treatment.[7]

These planning documents reveal the presence of a basic conflict among occupation officials. On the one hand, they understood that DPs were traumatized human beings who needed care, treatment, and a great deal of empathy; on the other, the authorities viewed DPs with deep anxiety and concern, saw in them a threat to order, and desired that they be efficiently cleaned and then transported out of Germany as soon as possible. The tension between these two modes of handling DPs was never resolved.

Between March and June 1945, SHAEF began to implement its plans for the DPs, but the scale of the crisis stunned and overwhelmed military planners. In March, as the Allied armies pushed onto German soil, they encountered only small groups of foreign workers west of the Rhine, for the Germans had relocated most of the war industries toward the interior of the country. After crossing the Rhine in late March, the liberators began to see many more. On March 16, SHAEF counted 58,000 DPs under its control;

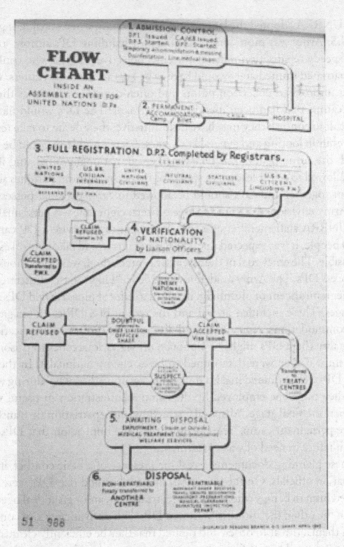

A U.S. Army "flow chart" for processing DPs, from arrival to "disposal."
U.S. National Archives

by March 31, that number swelled to 350,000; by April 14 the numbers held by SHAEF reached 1,072,000. Two days after the German surrender, SHAEF reported that it held three and a half million DPs, of whom almost a million were Russians. For a period of about twelve weeks, SHAEF tried with little success to impose order on this swift-running tide of people. SHAEF's DP Branch in mid-April conceded that "the handling of displaced persons may almost be described as chaotic."[8] Part of the problem in handling DPs was the speed of the Allied advance into Germany after early March; in the fluid conditions of combat, field commanders were frequently out of touch with headquarters for some time, and in any case they did not wish to use their troops to look after DPs in the midst of combat operations. Another problem was what SHAEF called "self-repatriation." Hundreds of thousands of Western European DPs disregarded SHAEF's stand-fast instructions and took to the road on their own accord. These marches homeward were frequently conducted in a "joyous atmosphere of holiday-making," according to one account, and while there was looting, military observers noted that "much of the looting attributed to foreigners is actually being carried on by the Germans themselves. In the destroyed areas of every city one sees German men and women carrying marketing bags filled with loot from the remains of other people's homes or shops." Even so, Germans constantly complained to occupation soldiers about the rapacious looting of DPs.[9]

The military planners had anticipated that there would be a time lag between liberation and repatriation efforts; they were wrong. Homeward treks were uncontrolled and massive, in part because the relief personnel that were supposed to conduct DP operations were completely absent. UNRRA had almost no staff or equipment in Germany yet, and in any case the destruction in Germany meant that there were insufficient holding facilities to pen in the DPs. All the army groups in Germany had called for more personnel. "Repeated instances are encountered," noted SHAEF's DP Branch, "where a few persons are running large camps with 10,000 or more displaced persons. For example, when the camp at Wiesbaden was visited on April 11, a lieutenant and a sergeant were dealing with 12,000 persons."[10] Marguerite Higgins of the *New York Herald Tribune* vividly described the scene in Frankfurt a week after the Allies had moved into and beyond the city. "The displaced person situation in large cities such as Frankfurt and Heidelberg has been in a state of near-chaos for the past week," she wrote, "and military government officials themselves will admit that facilities for caring for the freed Russians, Polish, French and other slave laborers are so inadequate as to produce extremely grave and often tragic results." Military officials, despite "valiant" efforts, had been overwhelmed: in Frankfurt, twenty-one military government officers tried to care for 40,000 DPs, and not a single Russian or French liaison officer was present to assist. "Crowds of laborers . . . , not knowing that camps were being set up for them, did the natural thing and set out post-haste for France." In an airplane factory outside of Frankfurt, 3,000 laborers awaited some direction from military officials; none arrived. Nor were there any officials available who could speak any of the dozen European languages spoken by the DPs. Had they been informed, they would have been disheartened, for usually the camps in which DPs were supposed to be housed were the same ones the Germans had used. "It is sometimes quite a job," Higgins laconically observed, "to persuade the laborers who check in at the main receiving center in the town to return to their former quarters." Not surprisingly, many tried to get home on their own, by whatever means possible.[11]

Despite these impressions of widespread chaos, SHAEF did manage to organize the mass movement of almost six million people out of its control area of Germany, Austria, and Czechoslovakia. The overall rapidity of this repatriation process is stunning, as the chart below reveals. In the months of May and June, 80,000 people each day were being struck off the rolls of DPs, and by early fall, one of the largest and fastest migrations in European history was nearly over.

Repatriation of Displaced Persons Completed by September 30, 1945

Country of Origin	Total Repatriated	Number from SHAEF-Controlled Germany, Austria, Czechoslovakia
France	1,536,300	1,200,000
Belgium	298,132	239,000
Netherlands	326,300	274,500
Denmark	21,000	21,000
Norway	65,000	7,000
Italy	851,000	608,000
Soviet Union	5,218,000	2,034,000
Poland	1,593,335	910,000
Czechoslovakia	367,128	138,000
Yugoslavia	443,269	229,000
Greece	81,100	14,000
Hungary	303,000	235,000
Totals	**11,103,564**	**5,909,500**

Source: Malcolm Proudfoot, *European Refugees, 1939–52: A Study in Forced Population Movement* (London: Faber & Faber, 1957), chapter 8; NARA, RG84, Office of the U.S. Political Adviser to Germany, box 34.

The three largest national groups of DPs, as this chart shows, were Russians, French, and Poles; together, these accounted for three-quarters of all DPs. Yet each of these national groups had starkly varying experiences as they faced the problem of returning home. Behind the numbers there lie countless stories of disoriented, hungry, exhausted people, most of whom yearned for home, some of whom looked with anxiety on the prospect of returning home, and some of whom did not wish to go home at all.

———————————

PRIMO LEVI, THAT keen-eyed observer of human nature, was among the huge multitude of DPs flowing out from Germany. Liberated from Auschwitz in January 1945, he had been borne along in unknown directions on intermittent trains across Poland and western Ukraine for months, in search of a way home. His destination, he hoped, was Odessa, the Black Sea port that had served as an embarkation point for POWs and DPs being repatriated to the west by ship; but getting there proved an enormous challenge and for Levi consumed many months. His wandering allowed him to observe firsthand the great Babel of humanity that the war had dumped out onto the lands of Eastern Europe. In one hastily erected way station, "there were men, but also a good number of women and children. There were Catholics, Jews, Orthodox Christians and Muslims; there were people with white and with yellow skins and Negroes in American uniform; Germans, Poles, French, Greeks, Dutch, Italians, and others; and in addition, Germans pretending to be Austrians, Austrians declaring themselves Swiss, Russians stating that they were Italians, a woman dressed as a man and finally, conspicuous in the midst of this ragged crowd, a Magyar general in full uniform, as quarrelsome, motley and stupid as a cock." Amidst this anthill of assorted peoples, there was a multitude of tragedies. Levi noted, for example, "trainloads of Ukrainian women returning from Germany." These were women who, during the German occupation of their country, had been shipped to work in the Reich. "Women aged sixteen to forty, hundreds of thousands of them, had left the devastated fields, the closed schools and bombarded factories for the invader's bread. . . . In Germany, they had found bread, barbed wire, hard work, German order, servitude and shame." Now they were being sent home. But "victorious Russia had no forgiveness for them." They were grouped into open cattle cars, and they were frightened: "their closed and bitter faces, their evasive eyes displayed a disturbing, animal-like humiliation and resignation."[12]

These women that Levi so poignantly described could have been found on board hundreds of eastbound trains in the summer of 1945. The Soviet Union was calling its people back: and many went, against their will, to an uncertain but darkly imagined fate. In truth, the western Allied powers, Britain, France, and the United States, did everything in their power to speed this vast repatriation of Soviet citizens from central and western Europe, knowing full well that for many of the men and women caught in the German web of wartime labor and imprisonment, a return home to Stalin's Russia might well be a death sentence.

The Allied governments had struggled with the question of Soviet DPs ever since their armies had landed in France. In the summer of 1944, American and British units in Normandy reported that among the German prisoners they were taking appeared a significant number of Russians, serving in German uniform; and there were also large numbers of Soviet laborers, shipped to France to build defensive fortifications. In July 1944, the British Foreign Office asked the Soviet government how it would like to have these men "disposed of." The Soviet government replied that it wanted these Soviet nationals repatriated immediately. The problem presented a moral quandary: as Foreign Minister Anthony Eden put it, "if we do as the Soviet government want and return all these prisoners to the Soviet Union, whether they are willing to return to the Soviet Union or no, we shall be sending some of them to their death." But Eden was not unduly troubled. These were men who had served a foreign master and in fact were traitors of a kind; the British government had "no legal or moral right to dictate to any allied government what steps they should or should not take in dealing with their own nationals" and perhaps most decisive from the British point of view, any delay in returning Soviet nationals could imperil British efforts to secure the speedy release and humane treatment of British prisoners liberated by the Red Army in eastern Germany. Eden called on the cabinet to approve the Soviet request: all citizens of the Soviet Union must be returned immediately, regardless of what lay in store for them.[13]

Yet in the chaotic conditions of newly liberated France, it proved rather easy for Soviet nationals to evade the authorities; many went on the lam, to be tracked by intrepid Soviet liaison officers, raking through towns and villages to distribute leaflets that promised good treatment, such as this one:

> Comrades! The hour of your liberation is near.
>
> Everyone knows that through lies, abduction and terrorism you have been forced to put on the German uniform, to fire on your brothers and your friends. Do not believe the flagrant lies put out by the enemies of the USSR that your Soviet Fatherland has forgotten you, and has abandoned you and no longer considers you as being one of its citizens. . . . Even though Soviet citizens, under the yoke and terrorism of Germany have acted against the interests of the USSR, they will not be considered as responsible if they return to our country and honestly fulfill their duty.[14]

These appeals did not work. By January 1945, SHAEF had 21,000 such Russians on their hands, which General Eisenhower characterized as "a serious problem"; in March the number had risen to 78,000 and the Allies were not even on German soil yet, where the bulk of the Soviet POWs were being held. The French certainly did not want these wayward Russians remaining in their country. In January 1945, alarmed reports from the hills of south-central France told tales of Russian DPs "roving about, stealing food," even shooting at farmers and burning farmhouses. Many "were armed with pistols, carbines and rifles." In March, the French foreign minister, Georges Bidault, prevailed upon the British for help in getting these men home. He felt they could no longer be lodged in safety in France, which had no supplies to feed them; and any delay in getting them home only delayed the repatriation of Frenchmen in Soviet custody. In short, the Russian DPs were, for the Allies, the most undesirable of guests.[15]

This helps to explain why, at the Yalta meeting in the Crimea in February 1945, the British and American governments were ready to accede to Soviet demands that all Soviet nationals in Allied hands—whether POWs, laborers, refugees, men or women, willing or unwilling—be returned to Soviet hands immediately. The matter hinged on the need to get American and British prisoners freed by the Russians back home safely. Article One of the agreement laid out these reciprocal terms clearly: "All Soviet citizens," the agreement said, "liberated by the forces operating under United States command and all United States subjects liberated by the forces operating under Soviet command will, without delay after their liberation, be separated from enemy prisoners of war and will be maintained separately from them in camps or points of concentration until they have been handed over to the Soviet or United States authorities." Soviet and American representatives were to have "the right of immediate access into the camps," and in the meantime all such personnel were to be treated well, fed and clothed, and looked after. It seemed an agreement filled with advantages for the Soviets, for it was known that as many as five million Soviets might be inside Germany, while only 75,000 American POWs were thought to be in German hands. Nonetheless, in the interest of getting these men home, the Americans willingly made the deal; an identical agreement was signed between the USSR and Britain. There followed detailed instructions to U.S. commanders in the field on how to treat, identify, and repatriate any Soviet nationals uncovered in Germany.[16]

Of the two million men and women who were now collected and shipped back to Russia by British and American forces, some surely wanted to go home. Their consciences were clear: perhaps they had been taken prisoner by the Germans after strenuous fighting, or perhaps they had been compelled to work for the Germans under severe duress. Surely they would find some forgiveness and compassion upon their return home. Yet in Stalin's devious mind, any person who had given himself up on the battlefield or, worse, volunteered to serve under German command, was a traitor and possibly a spy. These people, upon their return to the Soviet Union, were uniformly imprisoned, interrogated, and often sent to the gulag, that notorious nation-wide system of labor camps. One resident of the Soviet prisons—a former artillery officer who was himself arrested in February 1945 while fighting the Germans, for the offense of criticizing Stalin in a private letter to a friend—has described the arrival of these forlorn Soviet repatriates in unforgettable terms: "That spring of 1945 was, in our prisons, predominantly the spring of the Russian prisoners of war. They passed through the prisons of the Soviet Union in vast dense gray shoals, like ocean herring." In the eyes of this pris-oner, Aleksandr Solzhenitsyn, Russia had betrayed these ill-fated repatriates three times: once "through ineptitude"—poorly preparing for war; second, when they were left to rot in German camps, with no provisions sent in, like those enjoyed by prisoners of other allied nations; and third, by coaxing them back home, "with such phrases as The Motherland has forgiven you! The Motherland calls you!'" and then snatching them up "the moment they reached the frontiers." Solzhenitsyn described their predicament with bitter irony: "For not wanting to die from a German bullet, the prisoner had to die from a Soviet bullet for having been a prisoner of war! Some get theirs from the enemy; we get it from our own! . . . In general, this war revealed to us that the worst thing in the world to be was to be a Russian."[17]

It was no better to be a Cossack. This tribe, a perennial enemy of the Bol-sheviks—it had fought for the Tsar in the Russian civil war—had provided tens of thousands of its warriors to the German army. During the German occupation, Cossacks aided the occupiers in hunting down Soviet partisans in the rear areas and ruthlessly killing them. The Cossacks fought Stalin and his regime—a legitimate enough enterprise—but had done so at the side of the Nazi invaders. In the waning days of the war, Cossack units surrendered to British forces in Austria, hoping perhaps for some lenience, given their openly expressed desire not to be repatriated. Their appeals fell on deaf ears. Between May 28 and June 7, 1945, in the border town of Lienz, Austria, the British army gathered about 23,800 men, women, and children belonging to Cossack and Caucasian tribes. Their morale was "surprisingly high," the official British army report said. Perhaps their spirits were high because their fate was as yet unknown to them: "it was considered essential that the fact that they were to be sent to the USSR should be kept from them as long as possible." First, the British troops disarmed them. Then they called the 1,600 officers to a bogus conference, arrested them, and placed them in a prison camp in nearby Spittal. There, the officers spent the night, now aware of their fate. Two officers committed suicide by hanging themselves on the lavatory chains. The next morning, on May 29, trucks were produced to deliver the men to the waiting Russians. The Cossack officers resisted, and a platoon of British soldiers was sent in to drag the men out of their barracks and into the trucks. "The difficulties were considerable," according to the army report, "as they all sat on the ground with linked arms and legs." The British soldiers resorted to force: "rifle butts, pick helves and the points of bayonets were freely used." In due course, the officers were loaded onto the trucks. Two more officers committed suicide during the truck ride to Judenburg, where they were handed over to the Russians.

While this sinister transport was under way, the remaining lower ranks, along with their families, were told that they too were to be handed over to the Russians. The opposition to this plan was intense. From the windows of their barracks, Cossacks hung signs saying "We will die or starve rather than return to the USSR." Over the course of the next few days, Cossacks tried either to escape into the surrounding countryside, where they were tracked down by the British soldiers, or resisted as best they could the British soldiers who loaded them onto trains. More rifle butts and beatings were required to entrain the thousands of doomed Cossacks. "It was not until a platoon had advanced with fixed bayonets and administered some further blows that any movement started. This movement was continued only by the further persuasion of the bayonets and the firing of automatic weapons into the gaps between the groups of Cossacks." Three people, including one boy, were killed. But gradually, the armed force of the British soldiers prevailed. By June 7, the British they had turned over 22,934 Cossacks to the Russians.

There remained only the awkward question of what to do with the 4,000 horses that the Cossacks left behind. Three hundred of them, too ill to be of any use, were shot. Some were given away to local farmers. Many were eaten on the spot by ravenous local citizens. But about 2,000 of these beasts simply wandered away into the Austrian hills, riderless and alone.[18]

"HE EATS A mutton chop. Then he gnaws the bone, eyes lowered, concentrating on not missing a morsel of meat. Then he takes a second chop. Then a third. Without looking up." The eater was Robert Antelme, recently returned home to Paris after a year in German concentration camps. His wife, the writer Marguerite Duras, anxiously observed this silent eating from a distance. Her husband, once large, powerful, and dynamic, had been reduced to a skeletal figure of eighty pounds. "His legs look like crutches inside his trousers," she wrote in her mournful memoir of the war years. "When the sun shines, you can see through his hands."[19]

At first, he could not eat anything at all, so devastated was his digestion from prolonged starvation. On his first day home, he saw a cherry clafoutis in the kitchen and asked to have some. He could not; it was too rich for him. At this, "a great silent pain spread over his face because he was still being refused food, because it was still as it had been in the concentration camp. And, as in the camp, he accepted it in silence. He didn't see that we were weeping."

Upon his return, Antelme fell ill with a high fever, and he was carefully nursed back to a semblance of health. A spoonful of gruel seven times a day at first, no more. For seventeen days, he lay feverish, half conscious, lying on pillows to protect his fleshless bones. At long last, he ate some solid food. But then, his hunger grew, and became insatiable. "It took on terrifying proportions," Duras recalled. "We put the dishes in front of him and left him and he ate. Methodically, as if performing a duty, he was doing what he had to do to live. He ate. It was an occupation that took up all his time. He would wait for food for hours. He would swallow without knowing what he was eating. Then we'd take the food away and he'd wait for it to come again. He has gone, and hunger has taken his place."[20]

Five years earlier, in 1940, Robert Antelme had been serving in the French army; after the defeat, he was demobilized and got a job in police headquarters in Paris as a civil servant. He also quietly established links to the Resistance and provided aid, shelter, papers, and contacts to downed pilots, foreigners, and others trying to escape wartime France. He soon secured a post as private secretary to Vichy's minister of the interior, Pierre Pucheu. By mid-1943, Antelme became increasingly involved in Resistance activities, using his position to gain access to documents that he passed to the Resistance. He and Duras had a close friendship with François Mitterrand, an ambitious young man who had briefly been a prisoner of war after the fall of France, and then after the armistice worked on POW matters for the Vichy government before turning to the Resistance in January 1943. Mitterrand worked out of Duras's Paris apartment, which became the hub of a small but influential Resistance network. In the spring of 1944, Mitterrand founded an underground cell called the Mouvement National des Prisonniers de Guerre et Deportés (National Movement of Prisoners of War and Deportees), in which Antelme was involved. But the group was betrayed, and although Mitterrand narrowly escaped a number of attempts to arrest him, Antelme did not. He was arrested on June 1, 1944—just five days before the D-Day invasion. He was sent to Drancy, the French transit camp, and then deported to Germany. He spent ten months in a labor camp in Gandersheim, before being transported to Dachau in late April. When the Americans liberated the camp, Antelme was near death.[21]

Yet his Resistance connections now saved his life. Marguerite Duras and Mitterrand kept a careful eye out for reports from the liberated camps for any word of Antelme. On April 24, Duras had word that Antelme was still alive, and in Dachau. Mitterrand, who by this time had risen up the ranks of the Resistance and become a major player in liberated France, was appointed to a commission sent into Germany to inspect the liberated camps. On April 30, he found Antelme in Dachau, but the American soldiers in command of the camp refused Mitterrand's request to take Antelme home with him to France; they had standing orders to allow no one out, for fear of spreading typhus and other diseases that were rampant in the camp. So Mitterrand flew back to Paris, and detailed two friends to go back to Germany for Antelme. Outfitted with phony papers, gasoline rations, and a few French officers' uniforms, these two men drove through the war-wracked countryside until they reached Dachau, where they secreted Antelme out of the camp and drove him back to Paris. One of the friends called ahead to warn Marguerite Duras of Antelme's condition: "it's more terrible than everything we've imagined."[22]

Antelme's story—of a painful return, in which the joy of survival is suppressed by the memory of the recent past and the sheer effort of recovery—was only one of millions playing out across France in the spring and summer of 1945, as the prisoners of war and deportees began to make their difficult way home. In the early months of 1945, there were almost two million French people inside Germany—the second largest national group, after the Russians, of displaced persons in the Reich. Of these, 1.2 million were POWs who had been taken upon France's defeat in 1940. But there were also about 700,000 forced laborers who had been sent to Germany during the war to work in war-related industries—some of them voluntarily. And there were 200,000 people deported to Germany for Resistance activities, for criminal activity, or because they were Jewish. Almost 76,000 Jews did not return, having been killed in German camps.[23]

As early as November 1943, the Gaullist government in exile, then in Algiers, had started planning for the repatriation of prisoners and deportees; the task of running the new Ministry for Prisoners, Deportees and Refugees was assigned to Henri Frenay, a former prisoner (he had escaped from a POW camp in 1940) and the founder of the influential Resistance network

Combat. With Allied forces pushing into Germany by early 1945, Frenay sprang into action. The government established reception centers for the anticipated returnees along the French border with Belgium, Luxembourg, and Germany and in the port cities of Marseilles, Bordeaux, and Cherbourg. The largest of these camps were located in Paris itself, as well as in Marseilles (where prisoners and deportees liberated by the Soviets were shipped, via Odessa), and along the northeastern border with Germany at Mulhouse, Longuyon, Strasbourg, and along the Belgian border at Lille and Maubeuge. French nationals began to flood into France well before the end of the hostilities. Frenay remembers that in the first week of March, with Allied troops just barely crossing into Germany, an aide burst into his office to announce breathlessly that "last night the Longuyon center received the first group of displaced persons!" By the end of that month, 36,300 nationals had returned; by the end of April, the number stood at 265,474. On June 3, 1945, France welcomed home its one millionth returnee—a tall, blond POW named Jules Caron, who was received with huge acclamation and driven home to his village in southeastern France in a limousine. By September another half a million had arrived. They returned by the tens of thousands each day in May and June, choking the roads and rails. Some walked, often with fellow prisoners, waving flags and singing songs. Some were flown into Paris on lumbering U.S. transport aircraft. But most came back the same way they had left: on trains, stuffed into crowded boxcars.[24]

If ever there was a time for joyful reunions, surely the return home after liberation from Hitler's camps would be it. And indeed there were rapturous reunions between long-separated loved ones, between fathers and children, husbands and wives, sons and parents, sisters and brothers. France for a brief moment was awash in the explosive and heartbreaking sweetness of *le Retour*—the return. Yet this homecoming proved more complex than anyone might have anticipated. For amidst the happiness was also longing, sadness, frustration, anger, alienation, and a host of complex, contradictory emotions that welled up in many of those who survived captivity. Many prisoners of war and deportees who have left us their reminiscences of this time speak of awkward silences, repressed anger, and unbearable tension. The country to which they had come home was no longer the France of their imagination and longing, but a country that had suffered through years of war and occupation, a country devastated by fighting, a country without wealth or self-confidence. And the prisoners and deportees themselves had been transformed by their long captivity. Even for those who returned home to find their family and friends safe and sound, the most difficult task was simply returning to normal.[25]

Returning French prisoners of war, for example, faced particularly awkward questions. These 1.2 million men, taken prisoner after their embarrassing defeat in May–June 1940, were on some level failures—they had failed to fend off the invading Germans, failed then to die fighting, failed at the very least to escape from prison during their long ordeal. The POWs were also tarnished, through no fault of their own, by the associations between them and the Vichy regime. As part of a cynical effort to lend legitimacy to his government, the Vichy government's aged, collaborationist leader Marshal Henri-Philippe Pétain in 1940 had decided to make the protection of the POWs his personal concern. His government made it clear to the German authorities that Vichy, not the Red Cross, would take responsibility for these men, provide them with food packages, reading materials, letters from home, and so on. Pétain asked all Frenchmen to identify themselves with the suffering of the prisoners, to make sacrifices on their behalf, and to devote themselves, through Vichy's agency, to their eventual release and restoration to the nation. To this end, Pétain's government promoted a much-maligned scheme to exchange three civilian French workers for the release of one POW. This was the much-dreaded *relève,* or "relief" scheme that was so unpopular that it led many young Frenchmen to flee into the forests in search of Resistance organizations to join. Yet for Pétain, it was meant to remind French people that they were paying a stiff price for the moral and political failings of prewar France and the defeat of 1940, and that only through hard work and shared sacrifice could the prisoners, and France itself, be redeemed. The plan was a disaster. Only 90,000 of the 1.8 million prisoners taken in 1940 were released through the *relève,* but it made the prisoners appear complicit in Vichy's policy of collaboration with Nazi Germany.[26]

For the moment, these difficulties were forgotten, and the return of the POWs became the great national event of the year. The liberation of Paris had come and gone nine months earlier, yet millions of families still anxiously awaited the promise of reunion with long-separated loved ones. For the politicians, of course, the prospect of a new constituency of over a million grateful returnees meant that their return would be given special attention. Henri Frenay, the director of the repatriation effort, and François Mitterrand, the man delegated to handle veterans affairs, worked to transform the return of the prisoners into a grand national fête, an acclamation of their suffering but also their sacrifice. They were to be held up as courageous men whose struggle was no less valorous than the men of the Resistance who fought the Germans inside France. That explained the trappings that greeted them in the train stations: the flags, the posters, the military bands. It also explains why the French government, despite the pressing priorities of reconstruction, spent large sums on the returning men. About 20 percent of the state's budget in the year 1945 was devoted to spending on the returning prisoners. By law, each prisoner was to receive a thousand francs upon arrival, and another thousand upon demobilization. Depending on his rank, he was to receive some of his back wages, and a month of paid vacation. He was also eligible for state aid in clothing, food, medical treatment, and job placement. A nation with few heroes, France now looked to the prisoners of war to fill out the roll of honor.[27]

It did not all go quite so smoothly, however. Despite the apparent largesse of the state, most POWs felt their reception, while warm, left much to be desired. They felt the financial rewards to be laughable—a few thousands francs in exchange for five years' imprisonment. One suit of clothes cost about ten thousand francs, so the money was soon exhausted. Nor could the POWs hope to buy anything on the thriving and expensive black market, the only source of many foods and luxuries. Despite Frenay's best efforts, the prisoners were simply too numerous for all of them to be adequately clothed, fed, and housed, in a country itself still suffering from wartime privations. They were obliged to wait in lengthy lines, fill out paperwork, and face the delays of an inefficient bureaucracy. What is more, it was obvious to the men that despite the government propaganda, the real heroes of the moment were the men of the Resistance, especially the Gaullists who had declared their loyalty to the General and fought at his side since 1940. They were the men who had entered into government; no place had been reserved in the political life of the nation for the prisoners themselves.[28]

Predictably, the French Communist Party was willing to make use of the prisoners' grievances, and staged a series of protest marches and public denunciations of Frenay and the entire repatriation effort. For days on end, some prisoners stood beneath Frenay's windows in his ministry, shouting "Food! Clothing! Shoes! Down with the black market! Out with Frenay!" On June 2, twenty thousand former prisoners marched from the place Maubert to the Arc de Triomphe in Paris demanding better treatment from the government. Communist papers around the country blared out headlines denouncing the repatriation effort and the lack of basic supplies offered to the returning men.[29] Frenay in his memoir was probably right to blame this on the machinations of the Communists, who sought to embarrass him politically. "The walls of Paris and the provinces," he wrote, "were plastered with posters denouncing me. All over France meetings were organized to indoctrinate our exiles as they arrived home and to escalate their demands for clothing (of which I disposed of only a very small store), bonuses, and discharge pay." But the grievances were real. In the eyes of the prisoners, the promises of a great national welcoming on which these men had nourished themselves during the long years of captivity had not been kept.[30]

Far more awkward than the return of the POWs was the return of the racial and political deportees—that is, Jews and *résistants* who had spent time not in POW camps, with the advantages of official status, packages from home, government oversight, and the comradeship of other POWs, but in the death camps. Their return could not be transformed into an exercise of patriotic unity and celebration. For these deportees were victims not only of the Germans but of their French compatriots as well. Vichy turned 76,000 Jews over to the Germans, and deployed a ruthless French-staffed police force to hunt down, arrest, torture, and shoot members of the Resistance. The return of the survivors could only be a painful reminder of France's shameful wartime policy of collaboration. The Gaullist provisional government hoped that their return could be incorporated into the general homecoming of the POWs themselves, thus averting much discussion of the particular tragedy of the deportees; de Gaulle, eager to bind up the fractured country, had little desire to encourage national introspection and debate about the recent past. Yet by papering over the fate of the deportees, the government failed adequately to prepare the public for their return. By the spring of 1945, detailed reports had begun to reach France of the full scale and nature of the camps, but even so, these reports coincided with other major news events, such as the death of Roosevelt, the suicide of Hitler, the fall of Berlin, and the collapse of Germany itself in early May. The images that are so widely known nowadays of emaciated prisoners and piles of bodies had not yet been widely disseminated. The great majority of the French public simply had no idea what the Jews and the resisters had experienced, nor was the public eager to know more.[31]

This explains the almost comic incongruity between the condition of the returning prisoners and the atmosphere they encountered upon their arrival in France. The transit centers where deportees were processed were designed as if the returnees simply needed a rustic retreat and a comfy chair after a long vigorous walk in the countryside. The center at Mulhouse, for example, boasted buildings decorated with "paintings of French home life; the exterior of the area is surrounded with beds of colorful flowers. Music is continually broadcast through a loudspeaker and a motion picture theater is in operation. There are also comfortable lounges and recreation rooms where newspapers, magazines, games, etc., are available for amusement. . . . A large bar for liquid refreshments and sandwiches is open at all times."[32] In the Paris train stations, well-meaning officials had laid on bunting and flags, brass bands, sandwich tables and drinks, and set up painted tableaux depicting liberty, freedom, family, and so on, designed to celebrate the return of "les Absents." Stirring and repeated renditions of "La Marseillaise" greeted each arriving trainload. The assumption was, as one government official, Olga Wormser-Migot, later acknowledged, "that after the formalities, [the deportees] would return to their homes and resume normal life." Instead, "the preparations for repatriation and welcome of the deported were not, could not be, adequate for the dimension of the tragedy that the liberation of the camps had revealed."[33] The veteran *New Yorker* reporter, Janet Flanner, witness to the arrival in Paris of a trainload of deported women on April 14, brilliantly captured the essence of this awkward gap between expectation and reality:

> These three hundred women, who came in exchange for German women held in France, were from the prison camp of Ravensbrück, in the marshes midway between Berlin and Stettin. They arrived at the Gare de Lyon at eleven in the morning and were met by a nearly speechless crowd ready with welcoming bouquets of lilacs and other spring flowers, and by General de Gaulle, who wept. . . . There was a general, anguished babble of search, of finding or not finding. There was almost no joy; the emotion went beyond that, to something nearer pain. So much suffering lay behind this homecoming, and it showed in the women's faces and bodies. . . . One woman, six years ago renowned in Paris for her elegance, had become a bent, dazed, shabby old woman. When her smartly attired brother, who met her, said, like an automaton, "Where is your luggage?," she silently handed him what looked like a dirty black sweater fastened with safety pins around whatever small belongings were rolled inside. In a way, the women all looked alike: their faces were gray-green, with reddish-brown circles around their eyes, which seemed to see, but not to take in. They were dressed like scarecrows, in what had been given them at the camp, clothes taken from the dead of all nationalities. As the lilacs fell from inert hands, the flowers made a purple carpet on the platform and the perfume of the trampled flowers mixed with the stench of illness and dirt.[34]

From the train stations in Paris, deportees—if they were not met by family members—were sent to the Hôtel Lutétia, a grand hotel in central Paris that became the setting for some of the most bitter memories of the return. Located on the boulevard Raspail and formerly used as offices for the German military occupiers, Lutétia was commandeered by Frenay's ministry for processing deportees. Here the new arrivals were again told to fill out documents, then given a meal, a thousand francs, a bed (often of straw) for the night if they needed it, a cursory medical examination, and sent on their way. The halls of the first floor had been set up with large lighted panels, of the kind used for billboards on the sidewalks of the boulevards. These had been hauled indoors where they now held hundreds of photographs of missing men, women, and children, placed there by anguished family members searching for lost loved ones.

The whole atmosphere at the Hôtel Lutétia left a lasting impression on the returnees, and this first moment of arrival back in France stands out in almost all the narratives of the return. Jacqueline Fleury, who had served in the Resistance along with her parents, had been arrested and imprisoned in Ravensbrück. Her first taste of liberated France came at the transit center in Nancy, where she found the doting female volunteer workers irksome. "I was very shocked. We had come from another planet, and among those who received us were these simpering painted ladies, who seemed to us in poor taste." She was transferred to Paris at the end of May, and sent to the Hôtel Lutétia: "There, we submitted again to more interrogations. And once again we were shocked by the ambiance of these decked-out ladies. To be sure, it had been almost a year since France was liberated. We were the ones coming home late. But for us it was hard: these people could not comprehend what we had endured. There was a divide between us."[35]

The officials at Lutétia were overwhelmed, and carried out their work with a certain officiousness that clearly struck the returnees as insensitive. Papers had to be filled out, exams submitted to. Esther S., a survivor of Birkenau and a death march to Belsen, couldn't bear the peremptory tone of the nurses at Lutétia. She was "in rags," she recalled, "without a hair on my head." But when ordered to go to the hospital for recovery, she refused, saying "I am not a dog; I am no longer in Auschwitz." She needed the medical attention, of course, but resisted being told what to do.[36]

Lutétia was also a setting for exchanging news about loved ones. In the halls of the hotel, anxious relatives scavenged for any word of their family members. The new arrivals were besieged, with photographs pressed into their faces—had they seen this one, or that one? Did they have any news? Louise Alcan, a survivor of Drancy and Auschwitz, recalled that as she got off the bus at Lutétia, "we were assaulted by dozens of people holding photographs, some large, some small. They were photos of men, women, children, of families on vacation, of married couples. These people stretched their hands to us, their faces in agony, their eyes brimming. Look, they said, have you seen him? Did you perhaps know him? He was strong. He seemed young for his age. Where did you come from? Where were you? Auschwitz-Birkenau? Then the silence set in. It became heavier and heavier, as if these photographs were tombstones." Sometimes the returnees did have news to report. Max L. sadly recalled his duties as messenger for one family. Amid the crowds at Lutétia, "a family named Kimmel arrived and asked me if I had seen their relative. I knew him very well. He did not have the will to live and he threw himself against the barbed wire—he killed himself."[37]

Of course, many of the returnees themselves also received heartbreaking news. Amanda S., a survivor of Ravensbrück and Mauthausen, encountered a schoolmate who reported to her that while she had been in Germany, her father too had been arrested and deported. "There was no trace of him left." Liliane Lévy-Osbert, returning to Paris from Auschwitz, was not met by anyone at the train station or at Lutétia. She made her way to the apartment where she had lived with her family. "I arrived at the rue de la Tour d'Auvergne," she recalled. "My heart was pounding. In a few moments, I would finally know. . . . I went up, then came down again. No one. I crossed the street and went into the baker's. She recognized me. I asked the question. The blow came, brutal, tragic, irreversible. Almost casually, naively, she said, 'But the Germans took them.' I was alone." Her sister and parents had not survived the camps.[38]

For many returnees, arrival in Paris meant readapting and even relearning social codes and behavior that had been stripped away in the camps. Jacqueline Fleury recalled that she and her mother—they had both survived Ravensbrück together—were given a metro ticket by the officials at Lutétia and sent home, since they had an address in the Paris suburb of Versailles. They were told, " 'All right, ladies, please go back to your home.' We took the metro to Saint-Lazare, and then the train. I can see us now, tired, exhausted. As we had the habit of living on the ground, and I was very tired, the curb alongside the gutter looked very appealing to me [as a place to rest]. I said, 'Wait, Mama, I want to sit for a moment.' And I can still hear her reply: 'But my child, we are in Versailles; you cannot do that.'"[39]

Returnees could also be met with a certain degree of suspicion, for the authorities feared that Germans or their Eastern European collaborators might well try to sneak into France, to escape justice back in their own countries. Isidore R., liberated from Belsen by the British, managed to steal a British soldier's uniform in order to flee Belsen and get back to France as quick as he could. He made his way to Lille, where he went to the town hall to get aid and something to eat. But a Frenchman in a British uniform struck the authorities as odd, and they questioned him suspiciously. "I showed them my

— *Vous savez, jeune homme nous avons terriblement souffert des restrictions, nous aussi !*

"You know, my dear boy, we too suffered terribly from the restrictions!" June 13, 1945. *La Marseillaise*

number [the tattoo on his arm] but they said that would be easy to replicate. I was arrested by the police! They locked me up in a cell." He spent three days in the cell, until being released. "I was not happy. They gave me a package, 1,000 francs, and told me which train to take. They had treated me like a criminal."[40]

For others, the problem of the return was the lack of interest or sympathy shown by their compatriots for what they had endured. Charles B., a survivor of Auschwitz, a death march to Dachau, and five months of hospitalization after his liberation, went to visit his aunt one day after the war. She nattered on about her own wartime travails, saying "My dear Charles, if only you knew how hungry we were here!" "When I heard that, I didn't say anything. That was the end of my efforts to talk about it." Alexandre Kohn, an Auschwitz survivor who had returned to France via Odessa and Marseilles, said that "when we got back, we started to tell about everything that had happened to us. But there was a general indifference." And also some disbelief. Mary-Rose Mathis-Izikowitz was released from Ravensbrück on the initiative of the Swedish Red Cross on April 23, 1945. She recuperated in Sweden until early July, when she was flown back to France. She had been well looked after by the Swedes, and was nicely dressed and not as feeble as many returning deportees. And thus eyebrows were raised. "People said, 'Well, well, who are these nice ladies coming back?' No one believed we had been in a camp."[41] Charlotte Delbo, a member of the Resistance who had survived Auschwitz, captured the awful paradox of the return in a few lines of a poem:

> *You don't believe what we say*
> *Because*
> *If what we say were true*
> *We wouldn't be here to say it.*[42]

Throughout the many testimonies of return, these themes reappear. The returnees were treated with officiousness, or as suspects; they were met with some degree of scorn, as if life in wartime France had been harder than survival in a German camp; their stories were brushed off as incredible, exaggerated, and in any case inappropriate now that the war was over and the time of restoration had begun. "This return was so different from what we had dreamed of," said another survivor. "We were starved for tenderness, for human warmth. We were thirsty for pure air, for freedom, for a France that was more beautiful, glorious, washed of its shame—we had paid dearly—but all we got was a sandwich and a glass of wine flavored with a few drops of pity."[43] A curtain was drawn over the war years; the fewer war stories, the better. They were urged to start life over again. But as one of Charlotte Delbo's fellow camp survivors put it, "To start life over again, what an expression. . . . If there is a thing you can't do over again, a thing you can't start over again, it is your life."[44]

"WE BEGAN BY being lost in the middle of a German forest on a night in late July, 1945." That frank assessment by Kathryn Hulme, a forty-four-year-old American who worked as the deputy director of a large DP camp in Bavaria, might stand as an apt summary of the early days of UNRRA's DP operations. Hulme, in her stunning memoir of her two years working in the Wildflecken Camp, captured the essence of the UNRRA project with that vignette: a small multinational group, UNRRA Team 302, made up of willing but unprepared volunteers, stuck on a road in a wheezing army surplus truck in southern Germany, lost, completely unsure of what lay ahead. They had received orders on July 21 to proceed into Germany from their training center in France, and were assigned the job of supervising a camp for displaced Poles. They thought there might be two thousand camp residents under their charge. When at last they arrived at their new destination, they were thunderstruck: Wildflecken was no small temporary settlement of nomads. It was a former secret SS training facility in the Rhön mountains of Bavaria, forty-three miles north of Wurzburg. Its eighty-seven well-built stone buildings spread out in a vast fan, and contained a dozen kitchens, five hospital wards, and a bakery capable of producing nine tons of bread each day. The perimeter of the camp measured seven miles. Within it, 15,000 Poles had already gathered, and more were on the way. "Wildflecken means 'wild spot,'" Hulme wrote home to her family. "A perfect description for this end-of-the-world place." It was to be her home for more than two years.[45]

In the late summer of 1945, after the Russians and Western Europeans had been repatriated, there remained in Germany about 810,000 Poles, anxious enough about conditions in their homeland to resist immediate repatriation. The Army referred to them as the "hardcore" DPs. They believed that staying in the relative security of a DP camp was a far better alternative than returning home to a Communist-run Poland whose borders had been so extensively rearranged as to place thousands of square miles of their country inside the Soviet Union. Rather than jump on board a boxcar heading east, they hunkered down in camps across Germany, facing an uncertain fate and worsening relations with the armies that had freed them. The largest of these Polish DP camps was Wildflecken. It was chosen by the Army as a DP center because it was large and had a railhead just a mile from the camp—a station with the capacity to handle two hundred rail cars and the thousands of SS troops that had been in training at the camp. Yet it had always been intended as a transit camp, a place where Poles could get a delousing and a meal before being reloaded onto boxcars and shipped home. Hulme's small team of UNRRA officials, then, faced two challenges: how to care for the largest single assembly of Polish DPs in Germany, and how to persuade them to go home.[46]

The team's director was French: Georges Masset, an experienced international businessman, well-spoken in English and German, and a man who had spent the war years in the French Resistance. Hulme fondly recalled that he was "as full of emotions as a Paris taxicab driver and not ashamed of a single one." He received praise both from his own staff and from G-5 inspectors—a rare achievement. One report called him "eminently qualified," a man who "understands the things which must be done. His team works in complete harmony and agreement." Hulme, the deputy director, was something of a peculiarity: from 1943 to 1945, she worked as a welder at Kaiser Shipbuilding in Richmond, California; before that she ran a travel agency and did a good deal of travel writing; she knew German and French very well, and the daily language of the team was French. The team's supply officer was a forty-six-year-old Belgian named Rouwens, who before the war had been an accountant. The welfare officer, whose job was to provide educational, cultural, and constructive amusements, was a twenty-three-year-old French woman, Germaine Jourde. About a dozen other staff members filled out the ranks.

The UNRRA team worked closely with the DPs' own elected representatives, who had formed a vigorously political camp committee. Its president, Zygmunt Rusinek, had been a deputy in the prewar Polish parliament and an economist. (The UNRRA team nicknamed him "Tak Tak Schön," because when he was pleased, he nodded his head and said the Polish words for "yes, yes," and the German for "fine.") Nine Polish military officers were stationed in the camp as liaison officers, assigned to interact with and offer help to the DPs, but they seemed bored by the assignment and the DPs viewed them with deep suspicion. The overall command of the camp was held by a series of obviously fed-up and frustrated American officers from the 79th Infantry Division of the Third Army; two dozen U.S. Army soldiers, living outside the camp, were detailed for security. A large number of Polish DPs were enrolled into a police force, though as they were unarmed their enforcement powers were limited. Camp inmates were not fenced in, but twenty-five guardhouses surrounded Wildflecken and DPs were required to have a pass to leave the camp. As of early September, 14,353 souls inhabited the camp—really a small city, complete with births, deaths, marriages, prostitutes, a black market, and elections. Virtually everyone in the camp was Polish, and 1,428 of them were under twelve years old.[47]

Kathryn Hulme readily acknowledged that whatever rudimentary training this small UNRRA team had received left them hopelessly unprepared for the realities of running a camp of this size, inhabited by people who had faced such extraordinary hardship. In Wildflecken, Hulme wrote, the UNRRA team learned "what it really meant to be displaced, to have been removed abruptly and totally from your homeland, not by the hand of God but by a human conqueror in one deliberate scoop that had swept up the grannies, the babies and the cripples as well as the young and able, since slavery has no selectivity and every body that breathed was deemed fit for labor until it stopped breathing." Day after day, more DPs arrived at the rail station. These people, six years earlier, had started their long tormented journey on just the same kinds of boxcars when they were shipped into Germany to toil on behalf of the Nazi war machine. With the war finally over, they were again herded into unheated, overcrowded cars under armed guard. Hulme got her first look at the massive scale of the human crisis just days after her arrival at the camp, when a trainload arrived carrying almost four thousand DPs. She and her small team stood on the station platform, agape:

> The cars slid slowly by us, each car door decorated with wilted boughs which framed a still life of haggard faces shawled, bonneted, turbaned, or simply wrapped around with shreds of old blanket wool, each car door framing the same tight-packed composition varied slightly here by the addition of an infant at the breast, there by a crying child slung clear to ride on a man's shoulders, or at intervals by a graybeard or granny to whom chair space had been allowed in the precious footage of the open door. I stared at the composite face of human misery, unsmiling, stoic and blue with cold.

She learned from the exhausted American GI who had commanded the train that they had been in the rail cars for five days, and had run out of food a day earlier. The travelers—including pregnant mothers, babies in filthy five-day-old diapers, and fainting elderly—poured out of the cars, bewildered, drained, ashen. Not enough trucks were available to transport them; hundreds just curled up on the ground at the train station, built fires from railroad ties, and slept.[48]

In tackling this and many subsequent challenges, the UNRRA team frequently fell afoul of the U.S. Army. These two institutions simply did not understand each other: one had been successful at defeating the German army but was still feeling its way from wartime operations to the tasks of civilian governance. The UNRRA team, by contrast, was strong on people skills—they had empathy in abundance—but often had little conception of the logistical difficulties inherent in the occupation of Germany and railed against the Army for failing to provide sufficient supplies to the DP camp. When Hulme needed trucks and truck drivers to haul four hundred DPs from the rail junction to the camp late one rainy night, an American lieutenant in charge of a truck detail simply refused to rouse his men, saying in a southern drawl that "his men were 'tahred.'" That was that—the Poles spent another night on the ground, in the rain. "This is the first time in my life I have been ashamed of the American Army and I'm so god-damned ashamed I could sink into the ground as I stand here," Hulme shouted at the bored lieutenant.[49] It was a typical encounter. Director Masset bombarded the UNRRA district director, J. H. Whiting, with twice-weekly requests for supplies: he needed trucks to haul firewood; his five hospitals had only one UNRRA doctor; the camp had no DDT powder for delousing; clothing for women and children was nonexistent; and his skeletal staff had trouble supervising the four hundred DPs the camp employed in sewing, warehousing, driving, cooking, cleaning, and so on. The Army rarely complied with such demands but found time to send officers to the camp to conduct lightning inspections. After one such inspection on September 13, a Third Army entourage, led by one Brigadier General Williams, left orders that the camp be militarized so as to enforce improved sanitation: armed guards must enforce cleanliness, a new prison must be erected for incarceration of slovenly and recalcitrant DPs, the Polish camp committee must be disbanded, examinations of every DP for venereal disease were to be undertaken (although there was only one UNRRA doctor), and forcible repatriation of Polish DPs must commence. As one sympathetic Army major whispered to Kathryn Hulme, "they're beginning to forget already that these are the little guys we fought the war for."[50]

Masset sent off an anguished telegram to UNRRA headquarters declaring that this militarization of the camp would shatter morale; "we see the ideal of UNRRA mashed under an army boot." Masset, with the help of a new Army camp commander, managed to soften much of these orders. But similar inspections continued. Masset noted that as of late November, Wildflecken had been inspected twenty-seven times in sixty-six days by Army officials. Every shortcoming was examined under a microscope, while sufficient supplies to improve the conditions were rarely forthcoming. In late November, Colonel R. J. Wallace of G-5 (Third Army) in Munich arrived for an unannounced inspection, and after searching for two hours found one of thirteen kitchens to be untidy, with sawdust on the ground, a discovery that led him to abuse a Polish kitchen worker who spoke no English. Director Masset, perhaps reaching a breaking point, wrote a stinging, furious rebuttal to UNRRA regional headquarters. The shortcomings of the camp, he wrote, were the result of UNRRA and the Army's failure to provide sufficient clothing, cleaning supplies, food, fuel, transport, and supplies to a huge encampment, while the immense labor of the UNRRA staff went unappreciated. "Alone," he wrote of his co-workers, "these few isolated ones, deprived of leaves, deprived of mail and with no replies to their official appeals, with no moral or material aid, managed somehow to maintain an organization" whose only shortcoming was a slightly messy kitchen. "You could certainly never realize how much has been corrected, created, ameliorated and innovated in this camp since our arrival."[51]

The inspections slowed only in December, with the arrival of fifteen feet of snow that effectively cut off the camp from the outside world. Life in the camp changed in winter. Kathryn Hulme recalled that in the barracks, "the Poles were settling in for their winter in Slavic style. They nailed windows to stay shut until spring, bound babies like papooses in endless unhealthy yards of woolen swaddling clothes, and swung ever burdened clotheslines in the crowded interiors to produce, as our medical people say sadly, the proper incubating steam for swift transmission of respiratory diseases." Each blockhouse was subdivided into rooms, in which families had been thrust pell-mell and in which they had arranged a kind of village order. Rooms were usually partitioned into cubicles by means of trunks, possessions, and Army blankets strung along a line. These "khaki labyrinths" were "the last ramparts of privacy to which the DPs clung, preferring to shiver with one less blanket on their straw filled sacks rather than to dress, comb their hair, feed the baby or make a new one with ten to twenty pairs of eyes watching every move." The rooms smelled the same: "a synthesis of drying diapers, smoked fish, cabbage brews and wood smoke from wet pine. It was not an unpleasant smell once you got used to it. For us it became the identifying odor of homeless humanity."[52]

Christmas 1945 in Wildflecken brought new surprises. The DPs arranged a week of dances and merriment, enhanced by Christmas parcels of Red Cross luxuries that the UNRRA team arranged into packages for each camp resident. Everyone got the same share of long-unavailable treats: chocolate, cigarettes, tea, coffee, sugar, biscuits, raisins, and liver paste. The value and rarity of these luxuries cannot be overstated. "It is hard to believe that some shiny little tins of meat paste and sardines could almost start a riot in the camp," wrote Hulme to her family, "that bags of Lipton's tea and tins of Varrington House coffee and bars of vitaminized chocolate could drive men almost insane with desire. But this is so. This is as much a part of the destruction of Europe as are those gaunt ruins of Frankfurt. Only this is the ruin of the human soul. It is a thousand times more painful to see."[53] And yet, with exquisite cruelty, just two days after the delivery of these treasured Red Cross Christmas packages, the Third Army sprang Operation Tally Ho on the camp: a secret raid to crack down on black market smuggling. At 6:45 A.M. on December 27, hundreds of U.S. soldiers surrounded, then penetrated, the camp, checking papers, opening lockers and storerooms, upended bedding and chests, only to find the hundreds of Red Cross packages, which they began to confiscate. Hulme, in command while Masset was in Paris enjoying his own Christmas revels, spent hours persuading the Army captain in charge of the wholly legal provenance of this booty. Truthfully, there was a good deal of smuggling and black market dealing emanating from the camp. Even Hulme admitted she "could buy anything" in the camp's black market, "except my mother, and sometimes I was not even sure she would not turn up!"[54] These Poles, after all, had lived via black market exchange for years in camps in Germany, and this was nothing new. A fairly active exchange developed: Germans offered clothing, farm produce, and liquor for Lucky Strikes, sugar, and coffee, courtesy of the Red Cross. Yet the Poles were not entirely prepared to play fair with their old adversaries. The DPs set up a carefully choreographed scam, whereby a German who had just filled his rucksack with illicit goods from a deal with a Pole in the camp would be arrested by the Polish DP police on his way out of the camp, only to have his recently acquired delicacies confiscated.[55]

Despite the comical element to this anecdote, exchanges between military authorities and political leaders in London and Washington show that at the most senior level, the criminal dimension of the Polish DP problem caused serious anxiety and frustration. In early August, after a series of reprisals, thefts, and brigandage by DPs in Germany, General Montgomery, commander of the British zone of occupation, wrote to Prime Minister Clement Attlee and the Foreign Office to declare his opinion that the behavior of DPs was "most serious. Looting, rape and murder by organized bands prevails in spite of every attempt made to restrain. In the interest of military security and orderly government I am determined that these outrages stop. I have accordingly instructed my Corps district commanders to take drastic measures including shooting at sight offenders caught in the act. Persons involved are mainly Poles and to lesser extent Russians." The Foreign Office replied that DPs had to be treated humanely and not treated like criminals, to which Monty replied, "The Prime Minister has not been given a true picture regarding the DP situation in the British Zone. . . . We are confronted by terrorism, murder, rape [and] robbery by well organized and armed bands." The victims of such crimes by DPs—the details of which are obscure—were of course Germans, a people toward which military authorities still maintained considerable animus. General Eisenhower's own order of September 20 stated clearly that DPs were to be treated humanely, that their needs must be met before those of the German public, and that any restraints placed upon them, such as guards at camps, were strictly there for protection. "Everything should be done," he ordered his commanders in the field, "to encourage displaced persons to understand that they have been freed from tyranny and that the supervision exercised over them is merely necessary for their own protection and well-being and to facilitate essential maintenance."[56]

Yet as the occupation policy toward Germans softened, so did the military attitude toward DPs harden. In December, the British Control Commission in Germany argued for a firmer hand with DPs. "Up to now, the policy of His Majesty's Government is that Poles who are unwilling for political reasons to repatriate should not be repatriated. . . . The time has now come when this policy should be revised. The presence of a large number of Poles who refuse to go home and choose to be housed and fed in idleness in this country amongst a hungry German population may lead to disorders and certainly consumes a lot of food which should be used . . . to feed the Germans." In late November, Eisenhower's successor as head of the U.S. forces in Europe, General Joseph T. McNarney, delivered new, harsher orders to the commanders of the 3rd and 7th Armies:

> Serious disorders by displaced persons, particularly Poles, require immediate change in theater policy. You will immediately place the necessary guards at such camps as may in your opinion require being guarded, instituting such pass system for the camp occupants as you deem proper. . . . Meanwhile, report to this HQ name and location of those camps where you have decided to reinstitute the use of US guards. The arming of German police to assist at once in reducing depredations by displaced persons will be expedited by you in order that roving bands known to exist among DPs may be brought under control promptly.[57]

In this environment of increasing tension and hostility toward DPs, UNRRA had to work creatively to prod its reluctant charges to go home, though for many in the camp, there was no Poland to return to: their ancient villages now lay in the Soviet Ukraine or Belorussia. Hulme recalled DPs staring at a large map of Poland tacked up in the camp: "You could tell from their faces which ones came from east of the river Bug. Some of the women wept quietly while the men stared in disbelief, too keen for comment, uttering only the names of home towns in a lost litany of sorrowful sounds: Lwow . . . Rovno . . . Stanislav. . . ." Thousands of repatriated Poles actually began to return to Germany in late fall 1945, bearing dismal accounts of conditions in Poland and finding DP camps a more attractive alternative. One man who had returned from Poland told an UNRRA official that "there is no food, accomodation, coal and, what is worse, no work. . . . The Russians have taken all the machinery out of the factories and farms and sent it back to Russia." The word circulated throughout the camps that there was no future in Poland.

By October 1946, increasingly desperate to unburden itself of the Polish DPs, UNRRA offered them an extraordinary incentive to leave: the promise of sixty days of rations per person upon their arrival in Poland if they went home. At Wildflecken, a gleaming, artfully arranged display of what this much food looked like was set out on tables in the central camp canteen: ninety-four pounds of "flour, dried peas, rolled oats, salt, evaporated milk, canned fish and a small mountain of lard." A family of four could take with them 376 pounds of this abundance. As a result of this largesse, the transports began filling up again. "Gradually," Hulme wrote wistfully, "we forgot the secret shame we had felt when we had first stood beside the free food displays and had watched our DPs stare at the terrible fascination of the bait, thrashing, twisting and turning before they took the hook."[58] Over the next few months, the camp authorities persuaded most of the Poles to board transit trains that would take them back to Poland. A few DPs managed, through family connections or sheer persistence, to enter the United States or other Western countries. But a small number of DPs remained behind, embracing the temporary security of Wildflecken, and turning the place into something like home. For six more years, the camp stayed open, a quiet shelter in the Bavarian hills for the forgotten refuse of war.

TO LIVE AGAIN
AS A PEOPLE

IV

Prologue

"We Felt Ourselves Lost"

THEY WERE FOUR young soldiers on horseback who advanced along the road that marked the limits of the camp, cautiously holding their sten-guns. When they reached the barbed wire, they stopped to look, exchanging a few timid words, and throwing strangely embarrassed glances at the sprawling bodies, at the battered huts and at us few still alive."

The date was January 27, 1945. The soldiers were Russians, part of advance units of the 100th Infantry Division of the 106th Corps, 60th Army, 1st Ukrainian Front. Standing that icy morning by the gates of the Buna-Monowitz camp of the Auschwitz complex, Primo Levi and his companion, Charles, silently observed the Russians as they advanced. Levi, an Italian chemist, briefly a partisan, and a Jew, had survived eleven months in Auschwitz. This was his first sighting of soldiers who did not mean him harm. These Russians were "four messengers of peace, with rough and boyish faces beneath their heavy fur hats." Levi also observed in them something that he had never seen in his German tormentors: a sense of shame. It was, Levi remembered, "the shame that the just man experiences at another man's crime; the feeling of guilt that such a crime should exist." The young horsemen evinced no satisfaction at being present at the liberation of Hitler's worst death camp. "They did not greet us, nor did they smile; they seemed oppressed not only by compassion but by a confused restraint, which sealed their lips and bound their eyes to the funereal scene." In short, the soldiers stared, in disgust and bewilderment. Levi and his companion stared back.

What emotions did these liberated Jews feel? Levi tells us:

For us even the hour of liberty rang out grave and muffled, and filled our souls with joy and yet with a painful sense of pudency, so that we should have liked to wash our consciences and our memories clean from the foulness that lay upon them; and also with anguish, because we felt that this should never happen, that now nothing could ever happen good and pure enough to rub out our past, and that the scars of the outrage would stay with us forever. . . . Face to face with liberty, we felt ourselves lost, emptied, atrophied, unfit for our part.

Ill, emaciated, disoriented by a year of malnourishment and trauma, Levi and his few skeletal companions were free: but freedom presented its own burden. Levi now had to face the complex task of finding a way home across occupied, war-blackened Eastern Europe; and the still more difficult task of explaining to his family, and the world, what exactly had happened to him in the depraved Nazi concentration camp system. The trial ahead proved arduous; Levi did not make it back to Italy for another ten months, unable to find a means of transport home, unable to find shelter, friends, or security. "Liberty," he tell us, "the improbable, impossible liberty, so far removed from Auschwitz that we had only dared to hope for it in our dreams, had come; but it had not taken us to the Promised Land. It was around us, but in the form of a pitiless, deserted plain. More trials, more toil, more hunger, more cold, more fears awaited us."[1]

It is uncomfortable to think that at the very moment when the Allied cause seemed most just, when the good war really fulfilled its promise—the moment when Hitler's camps finally were torn open and their inmates freed—that Jewish survivors of Hitler's atrocities found little joy in the proceedings. Their physical deterioration, the looming presence of death everywhere in the camps, the absence of lost loved ones—all these complex emotions left survivors at a loss, confused, benumbed. The dominant impression of the moment of liberation that one takes from the accounts of survivors is one of immense sorrow mixed with shame, anger, and humiliation. Liberation brought freedom, but freedom weighed heavily on the survivors. For now began the mourning, the tallying up of losses, and the search for an answer to that great unanswerable question that hangs over these events: why did this happen?

The moment of liberation was no easier for the soldiers doing the liberating. The young men who stumbled across Hitler's camps in the spring of 1945 were on the whole oblivious to Hitler's genocidal war on the Jews. During the war, the death camps remained largely invisible to the American public, and even when U.S. government officials came to know in 1942 significant details about Hitler's war on Europe's Jews, they did not use this information to galvanize public opinion or to refine America's war aims. Because U.S. soldiers had not been told what to expect when they arrived at the camps, they also had not been told how to react or what to say about what they saw. The words they spoke, and the first reactions of the press corps that entered the camps alongside the soldiers, reveal much about what liberation looked like as it unfolded: an awkward, painful moment, a hideous encounter with a kind of war even battle-hardened soldiers could not have imagined.

These two groups of people—Jewish survivors and Allied liberators—found themselves locked in a tense standoff in the months immediately following the war. Liberated Jews, mostly from Poland, refused to return to their blood-soaked homeland, for their families, homes, synagogues, and towns had been eradicated, and the Communist-controlled regime in postwar Poland offered them little solace or encouragement. Jews nourished the hope that they could travel to British-controlled Palestine, to join the fledgling Jewish settlement there and begin a new life. But the British government closed this avenue of escape even to the few surviving Jews of the Holocaust, fearful that additional Jewish immigration to Palestine would further inflame the region, and weaken Britain's colonial hold on the territory. And so Jews waited, settling against their will in rough-hewn huts and disused barracks, mostly in the American zone of Germany, beseeching their liberators for aid, help, and attention. The British and American governments provided little more than temporary shelter and barely adequate sustenance. In the months and years after May 1945, thousands of Jews continued to live in camps in the heart of the country that had caused them such torment, bearing their sorrows and looking anxiously into a future they could not divine. For these men and women and children, caught in limbo between slavery and freedom, liberation had come, and gone.

8

A Host of Corpses:
Liberating Hitler's Camps

AUSCHWITZ WAS THE German name for Oświęcim, a town about thirty miles west of Krakow, in southern Poland—an area annexed to the Reich after the German invasion of Poland in September 1939. It was conveniently located on the main rail lines coming from Germany, Poland, and western and southern Europe. Built on the site of a former Austro-Hungarian artillery barracks, it grew into a vast complex of three concentration camps and thirty-six subcamps. Auschwitz I was opened in June 1940, chiefly to hold Polish political prisoners. Auschwitz II, or Birkenau, began construction in October 1941. It was initially intended to house POWs but by the spring of 1942 was designated chiefly as a killing center, with gas chambers built for this purpose. It also housed the women's camp. Auschwitz III, or Buna-Monowitz, supplied forced labor to nearby I. G. Farben, the factory where the Germans were attempting to develop synthetic oil and rubber. It was here that Primo Levi had been incarcerated and forced to work in the chemical section of the camp. The Auschwitz complex covered some twenty-five square miles, and was the largest of Hitler's extermination camps.

Other extermination camps—Chelmno, Sobibór, Belzec, Treblinka, and Majdanek—were used for killing mainly Polish Jews; Auschwitz received transports of Jews from all across Europe. Jews from Upper Silesia began to arrive in February 1942, followed by the first transports of Jews from France and Slovakia in March. Trains from Holland began to arrive in July, trains from Belgium and Yugoslavia brought Jews in August 1942, and transports from Czechoslovakia, Germany, Greece, Italy, Latvia, and Austria delivered victims between December 1942 and November 1943. In August 1944, the last significant community of Jews left in Poland—those in the Łódź ghetto—were sent to Auschwitz and liquidated. The final large transports into the camp, from May to early July 1944, carried some 430,000 Hungarian Jews. Most of them were exterminated upon their arrival. At a minimum, 1.1 million people were killed at Auschwitz; 960,000 of them were Jews.[1]

Auschwitz was not the first of Hitler's camps to be liberated. As the Soviet Army moved farther into territory once held by the Germans, increasing evidence of the scale and nature of the Nazi barbarity became available to the Allied public. On July 24, 1944, the Red Army took the Polish city of Lublin, and discovered a massive death camp—Majdanek—two miles from the city center. This camp had been the setting for the gassing, shooting, and incineration of at least 59,000 Jews (though some estimates are much higher).[2] The SS had evacuated the camp and the prisoners before the Soviet troops arrived, but in haste they left most of the evidence of their work intact. The Soviets allowed war correspondents of the Allied armies to come and gape at the gas chambers and crematoria, and soon newspapers around the world carried photographs and descriptions of the gruesome scene. Correspondents viewed vast storehouses, filled with clothing, luggage, piles of razors, scissors, pencils, notebooks, and, in one cavernous room, 850,000 pairs of shoes. In another storeroom, toys: "marbles, jigsaw puzzles, teddy bears, pink celluloid dolls, and an American-made Mickey Mouse," according to a *Newsweek* reporter. Nearby, an enormous pile of bones and ash lay next to the neatly tended vegetable gardens. The Russian officer in charge captured the essence of the scene by declaring: "This is German food production. Kill people; fertilize cabbages."[3]

Hitler was infuriated by the sloppy work of the camp's SS officers in failing to destroy the evidence of genocide at Majdanek, and as a consequence Reichsführer-SS Heinrich Himmler—chief of the SS and architect of the Final Solution—began to plan for the gradual evacuation of the many camps and prisoners still under German control.[4] Weak and ill prisoners were to be killed, while others capable of labor were to be transferred into the Reich, where they might continue to toil in German war industries. At Auschwitz, the gradual dismantling of the massive camp complex commenced. Camp officials began to burn documents, and prisoners were assigned the horrific duty of digging up bodies previously buried in mass graves and incinerating the remains so as to hide the evidence of the camp's activities. Transfers of prisoners picked up pace in the summer, and between August and December 1944, some 65,000 prisoners were sent westward, most to Buchenwald, Dachau, and Ravensbrück. In November, Himmler halted the gassing of prisoners at Auschwitz, and work details began to drill holes in the concrete foundations of the gas chambers in preparation for their demolition.[5]

As of January 17, 1945, when the last roll call was held, there were still about 67,000 prisoners in the entire Auschwitz complex, including Birkenau, Monowitz, and the various nearby subcamps.[6] These men and women formed a cross-section of tormented Europe: among their number were Gypsies, Russian POWs, German political prisoners, French, Poles, Yugoslavs, Dutch, Belgians, Czechs, Slovaks, Hungarians, Italians, Greeks, and Croatians. Most, but by no means all, were Jews. Over the course of January 17–21, about 56,000 of these long-suffering people were formed into groups and marched out of the camp—human convoys destined for other camps farther inside the Third Reich. After the prisoners' hurried departure, SS soldiers blew up the crematoria and gas chambers, set fire to storehouses of goods stolen from the captives, and attempted to destroy any remaining documents concerning the operations of the camp. Aerial bombardment of the factories at Buna-Monowitz furthered the destruction of the camp. (Allied bombing of the rubber and oil plants at Buna had increased in the previous months, but no air strikes ever targeted the crematoria or gas chambers.) By the time units of the Red Army entered Birkenau on January 27, much of the camp was in ruins. Only 7,600 prisoners—those too ill to walk—remained in the entire complex when the Soviet troops arrived.

On January 18, when the Germans evacuated the camp, one of two possible fates lay before the prisoners: to march westward, or to stay behind. The general view of the prisoners at the time was that evacuation was the better choice. Those who were too ill to walk, it was assumed, would be shot, or if not shot, simply forgotten and left to starve. Those who marched out of the camp were fearful, but they were leaving Auschwitz, and that at least offered some slight reason for hope. In fact, those that stayed behind—if they did not succumb to hunger or disease—proved to be the lucky ones. After ten days of lonely isolation, they were liberated by the advancing Russian army. Primo Levi found himself among this group. Yet his was an atypical story. The less well-known but far more common experience for the Jews of Auschwitz who survived into 1945 was a horror-filled, exhausting series of convoys—the aptly named death marches—that took them into the heart of war-stricken Germany. For thousands of Auschwitz inmates, and for hundreds of thousands of camp prisoners across central Europe, these marches ended in an agonizing death.

Primo Levi stayed behind in Auschwitz on January 18 and survived the war. He was, he insists, lucky, as he had been throughout his year in the camp. After all, he survived. "There was no general rule" to surviving, he maintained, "except entering the camp in good health and knowing German. Barring this, luck dominated." And what luck: Levi arrived in Auschwitz on February 26, 1944, in a transport of 650 Jewish men, women, and children deported from the Fossoli camp, near Modena in northern Italy. Of this group, 95 men and 29 women were assigned numbers, and life. The rest—526 people—were immediately killed in the gas chambers. And when he returned to Italy in late 1945, he was accompanied by only three fellow deportees from that convoy. Levi's luck came in various forms: he was deported to Auschwitz only in 1944, when the chances of survival for skilled laborers had become somewhat better due to the demands of the German war machine for certain goods produced at Buna-Monowitz. He also had help from others at critical moments, particularly one Lorenzo, a Catholic mason from Italy who had been drafted by the Germans in 1942 for labor at the Buna complex. Lorenzo, living in a workers' barracks outside the camp, was able to smuggle to Primo small portions of extra food. And he got sick only once, but—as he put it—"at the right moment." On January 11, 1945, Levi came down with scarlet fever and was sent to the infectious ward of the infirmary, which allowed him access to a bunk—"really quite clean"—and doses of sulpha drugs. When the Germans evacuated the camp on January 18, Levi—weak, exhausted, and feverish—stayed in his bunk. Levi thus avoided a death march that would in all likelihood have killed him.[7]

For ten days after the departure of the German guards, the camp was in limbo. A few thousand prisoners clung to life, and hope, during this strange interregnum. Marcel W. was one of them. A Frenchman of Polish origin and a Jew, Marcel had been arrested by the Vichy police during the infamous Vel d'Hiv roundup in Paris in July 1942.[8] He was sent to Birkenau, along with his father and brother, neither of whom survived the war. His skills as a watchmaker and a mason allowed him to secure much-valued assignments to various work kommandos and the support of other French prisoners kept him alive at critical moments, for example, when he contracted tuberculosis in March 1943. Transferred in July 1943 to an arms factory in Silesia, he was returned to Buna-Monowitz in November 1944. He recalled that by January 1945, one could hear the sound of advancing Soviet artillery, and this prompted a mixture of hope and anxiety among the prisoners: what would happen to us, they wondered, when the war turned against the Germans? For Marcel, as for Primo Levi, a providential illness intervened. Sometime around January 11, Marcel suffered a serious foot injury. He reluctantly went to the infirmary, his foot swollen and pus-filled. There, his toenail was removed and the pus flushed out, and he was assigned a berth in the surgery to recover. Thus, on January 18, the day of the evacuation, he was in his sickbed. It brought little comfort: "We were afraid of staying," he remembered. "We expected to be killed."

Marcel vividly recalled that during the night of January 18, a massive aerial bombardment of the camp occurred, which he thought ironic since the only people left in the camp were ill prisoners. The camp was badly damaged, and the barracks near his were set on fire. His hut was unscathed, however, and the morning of January 19—the day of his twenty-first birthday—he felt that "his life was his again." He was among a lucky few, however. Of the 800 patients in the infirmary, he estimated that 500 died within the next ten days. There was, after all, no food distribution, water, or electricity. Only those well enough to forage could hope to survive. Moreover, a vast column of German soldiers, tanks, trucks, and artillery—the German army in full retreat—passed by the camp, leaving the sick men deeply uneasy about their fate. Periodically, shells struck the camp, as the Germans and Russians engaged in running battles. Worse, various SS and SD (security service) soldiers intermittently appeared at the camp to carry out further murders of the remaining Jews. On January 20, a camp guard, SS Corporal Perschel, reappeared and ordered the shooting of some two hundred women in the women's camp in Birkenau. On January 22, another unit of SD soldiers returned to Birkenau and murdered five Russian POWs who were alleged to possess hidden weapons. They also shot prisoners on the camp grounds. And on January 25, another unit of SD soldiers carried out random shootings in Birkenau. The Germans killed as many as three hundred camp prisoners in these final days.[9] Only on January 27, when the first Russians arrived, did Marcel feel any sense of relief. "We had put together a few little red flags, as we were afraid." The first Red Army officer Marcel encountered, he recalled, "was a Jew from Kiev."[10]

During this strange ten-day passage between slavery and freedom, Primo Levi and his ill, emaciated companions in his block also managed to stay alive. With the camp virtually empty, they could roam the grounds at will. They scoured the camp for useful objects—a truck battery, some turnips, even a few down quilts looted from the hurriedly evacuated barracks of the SS guards. These men worked together, showed great ingenuity, but also a necessary ruthlessness, for there were many ill and dying patients in the infirmary, lying in pools of filth and excrement, shivering in the cold, who begged for help, imploring Primo and his friends for soup, food, water, anything. They could do nothing for them, and many of them died.

There was no question of leaving the camp. The gates were open and the barbed wire breached in various places, but the cold, their illnesses, and total uncertainty of where to go kept them in the camp, amid piles of frozen corpses and burned-out barracks. Levi recalled that many prisoners "fell ill with pneumonia and diarrhea; those who were unable to move themselves, or lacked the energy to do so, lay lethargic in their bunks, benumbed by the cold, and nobody realized when they died." Levi and his small band of diseased bunkmates clung to life. Only one of the eleven men in their room died: Sómogyi, a fifty-year-old Hungarian chemist. On the night of January 26, after days of torment, he dropped out of his bunk onto the concrete floor, dead from typhus and scarlet fever. Levi and his comrades awoke the next day, ate breakfast, emptied the latrine bucket, and then—only then—carted the body outside. While they were tipping the dead man's body into a pit—in this "world of death and phantoms"—the Russian horsemen (significantly, four horsemen) arrived. On this day, January 27, 1945, Primo started on yet another journey—of almost a year in duration—toward home.[11]

MOST OF THE prisoners in Auschwitz on January 18, 1945, were not so fortunate as Levi and the others in his company. In a final act of wanton cruelty and insanity, the Germans forced the great majority of the surviving inmates—about 56,000 people—out of the camp and transported them, on foot and on rail, toward other camps farther west. Although little scholarly work has been conducted on these "death marches," the experience forms a central part of most testimonies given by survivors. For some, the death march was an altogether new level of pain and terror—"worse than all the camp years," said one survivor.[12] All across Poland, Germany, Austria, and Czechoslovakia in the early months of 1945, hundreds of such murderous convoys crawled along the roadways, choking them with the dead and dying. These marches started on a large scale with the evacuation of Auschwitz in January and continued right up until the very day of the German surrender. Soon after Auschwitz was emptied, the 47,000 inmates from the Stutthof camp were similarly evacuated. Then in early February, the large camp of Gross-Rosen—where many Auschwitz prisoners had been sent—was emptied; its 40,000 prisoners were pushed ever westward. As the Russians drove into Germany from the East, and the U.S., British, and other Allied forces penetrated deeper into Germany from the west, the entire camp system was thrown into chaos: perhaps 750,000 camp prisoners were vomited out onto the muddy, battle-scarred roads of central Europe, and herded toward the center of Germany. As many as 250,000 of them died.[13]

January 18, when this hellish trek began, was a day of "great confusion throughout the camp," recalled Filip Müller, a survivor of three years in Auschwitz. "Early in the morning, columns of smoke could be seen rising in all parts of the camp. Quite obviously the SS men were destroying card indexes and other documents." As the sounds of Russian artillery came closer, "the prisoners were seized by alarm and euphoria at one and the same time." Formed up into enormous columns, the prisoners set out at midnight. "The snow crunched under our feet, a cold wind blew into our faces. We talked about nothing but where they were taking us and what they intended to do with us."[14]

The evacuation inevitably brought new torments to the prisoners. The SS guards who oversaw the marching columns beat and frequently killed marchers, especially those who could not keep up with the merciless pace. Eli Wiesel, a skeletal fifteen-year-old boy who had survived seven months in Auschwitz alongside his father, remembered being forced to run the entire way to a rail junction at Gleiwitz—a distance of some thirty miles—without any pause. They were given no food, no water—they ate the snow off the shoulders of the men in front of them—and those who stumbled were shot dead where they lay.[15] "As we formed into a ragged column," remembered Sara Nomberg-Przytyk of her transport of women from Birkenau, "SS men escorted us with dogs on each side." Amidst the freezing wind could be heard, every few minutes, the crack of shots as the guards killed another woman. "The bodies were thrown onto the side of the road. We walked through a valley of death formed by the bodies of the prisoners." Within a few hours, her "skin was completely peeled from my feet. I could feel the blood swishing around inside my boots."[16] And for those who straggled, instant execution. "A few steps ahead of me," wrote Marco Nahon of his convoy, "I see a prisoner collapse by the roadside, completely exhausted. His face is livid. It is easy to see that he cannot walk another step. An SS guard who has seen him approaches and stands before him. Very quietly, he takes his rifle from his shoulder strap, places the barrel a few inches from the poor devil's head, and shoots."[17]

Once at the railhead in Gleiwitz, some prisoners were packed onto open train cars; others remained on foot for countless miles of further marching in the bitter January cold. They went to various destinations: Gross-Rosen, then on to Buchenwald, Dachau, or Mauthausen. Riding on the trains, in the bitter cold, was little better than marching on foot, especially because no food of any kind was provided. "When we came into Czechoslovakia," recalled a Frenchman, Marcel Stourdze, "the locals threw us bread. That was it; otherwise, nothing to eat." Henry B. recalled that extreme measures were required to survive. "It's not nice to say, but you had to urinate on your feet to keep the gangrene out of your wounds; or if you couldn't do it you got someone else to do it." Fred B., who marched from Auschwitz to Gleiwitz and was then shipped in a cattle car to Gross-Rosen, recalled that by the time of his arrival in Buchenwald he had endured seven straight days on the train convoy without food. He survived on snow. "After seven days in these cattle cars," he recalled of his physical deterioration, "you couldn't recognize your own body. It wasn't your own body." Henry F., who had been at the Auschwitz subcamp Blechhammer, estimated that of the 4,000 who marched out of his camp in mid-January, only 1,500 made it to Gross-Rosen. The rest were shot or died along the way. Of the 56,000 men and women forced out of the Auschwitz camp complex between January 17 and 21, some 15,000 would be dead by the end of the war.[18]

Why were these prisoners marched across central Europe in these miserable columns, under such extreme duress? Who gave the orders to evacuate the camps, and where were the prisoners supposed to be going? And to what end? After all, if the chief objective of the German leadership had been to fulfill Hitler's final wishes and liquidate every remaining Jew in their custody, this could have been carried out in the camps themselves. Why require them to march across Poland and Germany, often aimlessly, toward other camps that were already being emptied, or toward railheads that were desperately needed for military purposes? And if the idea was to secret the Jews away from the sight of the advancing Allies, why leave so many corpses along the roads on which the Allies were sure to pass in a matter of days? None of these questions lends itself to easy answers.

The evidence, though patchy, suggests that in the last months of the war, the central control and ruthless efficiency that had characterized the operation of the massive camp system and the murder of many millions of people had begun to break down. In the fall of 1944, SS chief Heinrich Himmler began to plan for the dismantling of the concentration camps. Yet his concern with the needs of the war industries led him away from a policy of immediate extermination of the remaining prisoners. Healthy prisoners were to be shipped into the Reich to serve as a labor force; the ill and the sick, presumably, would be killed. The earliest evidence for such a plan of general evacuation dates from July 21, 1944, though it does not come from Himmler. The head of the security police for occupied Poland (the General Government, as it was called by the Germans) ordered that prisons be evacuated, their inmates shipped to other concentration camps or, if necessary, killed to prevent their being liberated. The orders also specified that corpses be disposed of by incineration, thus revealing the concern of the retreating Germans to cover up the scale of their crimes.[19] Not until late December 1944, with the Red Army rapidly advancing through Poland, were precise evacuation plans issued. The instructions from the gauleiter of Upper Silesia, Fritz Bracht, issued on December 21, 1944, make it clear that the prisoners from Auschwitz were to be transported and redeployed to other labor camps. The evacuation was to be carried out via forced marches, because it was expected that the rail lines and rolling stock would be taken up by military needs. The prisoners would go on foot, and any sign of disruption or resistance was to be put down immediately "with the utmost severity." Here was a free license to shoot prisoners.[20] In mid-January 1945, Himmler gave the order to evacuate all the eastern camps, demanding that "no healthy prisoners remain in any of the camps." The former commandant of Auschwitz acknowledged that "this was the death sentence for thousands of prisoners."[21] Over the next four months, convoys choked the roads, leaving the dead and dying scattered in the ditches of rural Germany. Only with superhuman effort did these marchers survive, after walking mile upon mile along frozen roads, in ill-fitting clothes, under a hail of blows and abuse from sadistic guards. Even then, survival was no certainty, for once they were herded into camps such as Dachau, Buchenwald, and Belsen, they faced a constant risk of death from typhus, dysentery, or starvation. It is no wonder, then, that when the first Allied soldiers arrived at the gates of these camps in early April 1945, the scenes they encountered shocked them more than anything they had yet seen in a war filled with death and destruction.

───────────────

AMERICA'S ENCOUNTER WITH the camps began at Ohrdruf, a small labor camp about thirty miles west of Weimar. This was a subcamp of Buchenwald, and though Ohrdruf was small in size, it offered vivid evidence of German atrocities: fetid barracks, torture rooms, piles of burnt bodies. It was not the first camp American soldiers had entered—that was Natzweiler, in German-occupied Alsasce—but Ohrdruf has particular importance because General Dwight Eisenhower visited it on April 12, along with Generals George Patton and Omar Bradley. There were almost no survivors there, as the camp had been emptied a few days earlier and the SS guards shot the last remaining laborers. In the yard of the camp, Ike and his generals observed a twisted mass of smoldering, charred bones. Patton explained later that the guards had built "a sort of mammoth griddle of 60 cm. railway tracks laid on a brick foundation. The bodies were piled on this and they attempted to burn them. The attempt was a bad failure. Actually, one could not help but think of some gigantic cannibalistic barbecue. In the pit itself were arms and legs and portions of bodies sticking out of the green water which partially filled it." Patton, a man who had seen just about every kind of battlefield horror, dashed behind a shed and vomited.[22]

Generals Eisenhower, Bradley, and Patton inspect the remains of victims murdered at Ohrdruf, a sub-camp of Buchenwald. The camp was liberated on April 4 by units of the U.S. 4th Armored Division and 89th Infantry Division. The photo was taken on April 12, 1945. *U.S. Holocaust Memorial Museum*

It was only the start. About sixty miles to the north, on April 11, American soldiers entered the camp complex at Nordhausen, which housed prisoners working in the subterranean V-1 and V-2 rocket factories. Three thousand corpses lay in disordered heaps on the camp grounds, with a few hundred survivors aimlessly wandering among them. Immediately, U.S. Army officers enrolled local townspeople in burial brigades, and over the course of the next few days, under the stern watch of American soldiers, German civilians dug a series of long narrow trenches on a hill overlooking the camp. Then they carted the corpses to the burial site and laid them in these shallow mass graves.[23]

These grisly scenes, however, could not prepare the men for what awaited at Buchenwald, just a few miles north of Weimar. Ohrdruf and Nordhausen had been small camps, with only a few survivors to liberate. Buchenwald, by contrast, had been one of the largest in the camp system. Buchenwald had been opened in 1937 as a prison chiefly for political opponents of the Nazi regime, but during the war it became a depository for prisoners who were then

Some of the thousands of prisoners in Dachau upon its liberation wave through barbed wire. *U.S. National Archives*

farmed out as labor to local arms manufacturers. Over 238,000 people passed through its gates, and 56,000 of them died there. In the early days of 1945, the Germans transported many prisoners into Buchenwald from the eastern camps; 24,000 prisoners arrived in January 1945 alone, and many of these were near death because of the conditions they had encountered on the death marches. In keeping with the general plan of evacuating the camps before the Allies arrived, Buchenwald's commandant initiated the partial clearing of the camp on April 4, and in the week before the Americans arrived, 24,500 prisoners were marched out of the camp, and many died during this last transport. Even so, upon their arrival at Buchenwald on April 11, American troops found a massive camp filled with 21,000 emaciated, diseased, and exhausted prisoners, about 4,000 of them Jews. The camp also held 700 children.[24] Just a few days later, farther to the north, British troops entered Bergen-Belsen, where they found an astonishing 60,000 prisoners in a state of total chaos and depravity. And two weeks after that, the Americans reached Dachau, just ten miles from Munich, in Bavaria. They found 35,000 prisoners, amid scenes of unspeakable carnage, including a train of forty boxcars filled with a shipment of evacuated prisoners—all 2,000 of them dead.[25]

During late April and early May, reports of what the Allies had uncovered in these camps began to appear in news reports; the first impressions of reporters, as well as soldiers who witnessed these days of liberation, have also been widely published. It is worth studying these initial reports about the camps, both for what they say and for what they do not.[26] The first striking feature of these reports to a contemporary reader is the absence of any discussion of Jewish victimization. In part, this is explained by the evidence uncovered in these initial encounters: Nordhausen was a slave labor camp, and its inmates had been members of many national groups; Dachau had a long history as a prison for political opponents of the Nazi regime, as well as criminals, homosexuals, and other "undesirables"; while Buchenwald, upon liberation, was teeming with a multitude of nationalities and POWs. At the moment of liberation, the Jewish presence in these western camps—with the significant exception of Belsen, where most of the survivors were Jews—was fairly small, and so there was no immediate recognition that what the soldiers had uncovered was part of Hitler's campaign to exterminate all of Europe's Jews. On April 30, *Time* magazine published a detailed, three-page report on "a series of concentration camps for political prisoners from most of the nations the Nazis had conquered, including the German nation." Jews are not mentioned once. When a delegation of U.S. congressmen, hastily gathered at Eisenhower's urging, came to visit Buchenwald, Nordhausen, and Dachau, they too seemed entirely unaware of the role the concentration camp system had played in the Jewish catastrophe. Their final sixteen-page report said that these three camps held "slave laborers and political prisoners" and "were typical of all the concentration camps in the Third Reich." The camps' main purpose, according to the congressmen, was to incarcerate and work to death "civilians who were opposed to, or who were suspected of being opposed to, the Hitler regime." As of yet, the story of Jewish persecution and genocide had little or no place in the emerging reports about the camps.[27]

But there is another dimension of these accounts that requires scrutiny. The standard narrative of liberation suggests that at the moment of freedom, a bond was established between the Allied troops and the grateful and overjoyed prisoners they freed. Indeed, the emotional power of the liberation story depends upon the forging of this bond, and the sense of mutual obligation and respect that it engendered. Yet to hear the witnesses tell it, no such bond existed at the moment of liberation of the camps. Rather, for the Allied soldiers and reporters, the overwhelming sentiment was one of physical repulsion and disgust. In these early reports, it is not the closeness but the distance between the liberated and the liberators that stands out.

It is remarkable how, in the first accounts of the camps by Western journalists, names of individual prisoners, their countries of origin, and their personal experiences are totally absent. Rather, reporters and soldiers described an undifferentiated mass of human refuse. Margaret Bourke-White, the renowned *Life* magazine photographer, said of her tour of the camps that "using the camera was almost a relief; it interposed a slight barrier between myself and the white horror in front of me." The corpses in Buchenwald, notoriously, were described as being "stacked like cordwood"—or as Percy Knauth of *Time* put it, "stacked more or less the way I stack my firewood back home, not too carefully." But even the living were reduced to inanimate, nonhuman objects of pity and almost contempt. Knauth went on: "they stink like nothing else on earth and many . . . have lost the power of coherent speech." Marcus Smith, a medical officer attached to the Seventh Army, also had trouble seeing anything but a mass of ill and dying specimens: "Starvation diminishes physical differences," he noted, "and thus the emaciated inmates look alike: faces without expression, eyes lifeless and sunken, cheekbones prominent, lips cracked, hair (when present) unkempt, skin ashen. Their legs are often swollen; this interferes with knee bending. Starved people find walking difficult or impossible. They shuffle along, seem to droop; their breathing is labored. . . . Their reflexes are sluggish, they lack mental and physical stamina, they seem to be mentally dull, exhausted, and depressed." General Patton thought the prisoners "looked like feebly animated mummies and seemed to be of the same level of intelligence." Al Newman of *Newsweek* referred to the survivors as "miserable wrecks" and "creatures—you could not by any stretch of the imagination call them human beings." The first U.S. Army report on Buchenwald declared the survivors to be "unpleasant to look on. It is easy to adopt the Nazi theory that they are subhuman, for many have in fact been deprived of their humanity." These men and women and children were "gibbering idiots" or "ape-like living skeletons" lying in "piles of filthy straw fouled by their own excrement. Only a handful could stand on their rickety, pipestem legs." Said one American private of the survivors at Gunskirchen Lager in Austria, "they seemed to have no hair, big eyes, big sockets in the eyes, bony arms reaching out for food, just hard to describe. The only similarity to human beings is, they were standing."[28]

Edward R. Murrow, the renowned CBS broadcaster, reported from Buchenwald three days after its liberation. He clearly was not ready for what he encountered. "There surged around me an evil-smelling horde. Men and boys reached out to touch me; they were in rags and the remnants of uniform. Death had already marked many of them, but they were smiling with their eyes." Inside one of the barracks, Murrow said, he found 1,200 men. "The stink was beyond all description," he said. "As I walked down to the end of the barracks, there was applause from the men too weak to get out of bed. It sounded like the hand-clapping of babies." Percy Knauth considered these broken forms in the camps quite inhuman. "You cannot adequately describe starved men; they just look awful and unnatural. Their skin is stretched with incredible tightness over their bones, as if it would burst at a touch, revealing emptiness. The rounded parts, the curving and the flat places, the swelling muscles that men usually have—all these are missing. They walk or creep or lie around and seem about as animate as the barracks and fence posts and stones on Buchenwald's bare, hard-packed earth." If they saw the smallest morsel of food, "they struggled for it blindly, as a baby struggles instinctively to fill its empty stomach at its mother's breast." A fellow reporter for *Time*, Sidney Olson, vividly recalled his discomfort when the prisoners got too close to him: "They began to kiss us, and there is nothing you can do when a lot of hysterical, unshaven, lice-bitten, half-drunk, typhus-infected men want to kiss you. Nothing at all. You cannot hit them, and besides they all kiss you at the same time. It is no good trying to explain that you are only a correspondent."[29]

One British member of Parliament who toured Buchenwald was aware that she and her colleagues were unable to consider these pitiful survivors as human. "One realized," she recalled, "that though one had looked at them with pity and dismay, one was still failing to appreciate them as living humanity with feelings and reactions similar to one's own. That was the most appalling and shocking thing." And she went on to prove her own point, by saying that, although there were many naked and half-dressed men on the camp grounds, a woman felt "no more embarrassment in Buchenwald than there would be in passing a heap of dying rabbits, so little did these people give the impression of being ordinary human beings." For Harold Denny, the *New York Times* correspondent who reported on liberated Buchenwald, "there was hardly a man of those hundreds who could be restored to humanity now. Easy death was the most life could now offer them."[30]

If anything could exceed the vileness of Buchenwald, it was Bergen-Belsen. Liberated by British troops on April 15, just four days after the Americans had arrived at Buchenwald, Bergen-Belsen was in a state of anarchy and horror—indeed, British press reports referred to it as the "horror camp." Belsen had at one point been considered a "good" camp—that is, it was not an extermination or work camp, but a prison for prominent prisoners who might have some future use as bargaining chips with other countries. In the last months of the war, however, Belsen—because of its location in north-central Germany, near Hannover—was chosen as one of the final roundup destinations for the prisoners trekking in from the eastern camps. Thus, while in December 1944 there were just over 15,000 prisoners in the camp, during the spring of 1945 thousands more arrived, most in a terrible state of decrepitude. By April 15, there were 60,000 people imprisoned here, yet the structure of the camp had fallen apart, so there was no food distribution and even the rudimentary medical services of the camp had ceased to function. The mortality rate was staggering: 7,000 prisoners died in February, 18,000 in March, and 9,000 in just the first two weeks of April. There were no facilities for burial, and most of the corpses were simply piled up randomly around the camp. No water, no sanitation, dysentery and typhus rampant, the ground littered with the dead and dying: a scene of total depravity.[31]

The comments of the young British men and women who first encountered this camp reveal the same sense of pity and disgust as do those of the Americans at Buchenwald and Ohrdruf. They naturally had no previous experience of this sort of human degradation, nor did they really know what to make of these ghastly-looking prisoners. Lieutenant Derek Sington, part of an intelligence unit and the first British officer to enter liberated Belsen, recalled the camp smelled like "a monkey-house" and described the prisoners as a "strange simian throng." Their "shaven heads and their obscene striped

An exhausted and emaciated prisoner near death in liberated Belsen.
Imperial War Museum

penitentiary suits" were "dehumanizing"; these "almost lost men" could manage only a few halfhearted cheers for the arriving British soldiers; even then, the survivors looked liked "prancing zebras."[32] Lieutenant-Colonel J. A. D. Johnston of the Royal Army Medical Corps (RAMC) described the prisoners as "a dense mass of emaciated, apathetic scarecrows." The prisoners had been reduced to a less than human state: "I heard a scrabbling on the floor," recalled Alan MacAuslan, a young medical student volunteer. "I looked down in the half light, and saw a woman crouching at my feet. She had black matted hair, well-populated, and her ribs stood out as though there were nothing between them. . . . She was defecating, but she was so weak that she could not lift her buttocks from the floor, and as she had diarrhea, the yellow liquid stools bubbled up over her thighs. Her feet were white and podgy from famine edema, and she had scabies. As she crouched, she scratched her genital parts, which were scabetic too." Two or three prisoners shared each bunk in the barracks, and they were all stricken with dysentery: "urine and feces dribbled through the wooden boards of the top two bunks on to the lowest one, and as this was the least comfortable, all the dying and weaker patients could be found there." As for the dead, another medical student said, "there were thousands and thousands of dead bodies and you couldn't really relate to them as people, you couldn't really consider them to be your aunt or your mother or your brother or your father because there were just too many and they were being bulldozed into graves." Indeed, the British estimated that 10,000 bodies lay unburied in the camp upon their arrival, and perhaps 13,000 more died in the weeks following the camp's liberation.[33]

It was not uncommon, then, for liberators to see the liberated as nonhuman, as lost souls, like shades from the underworld. Leslie Hardman, a Jewish chaplain in the British Second Army, reached Belsen in the first days of its liberation. "I shall always remember the first person I met," he wrote in his memoir. "It was a girl, and I thought she was a negress. Her face was dark brown, and afterwards I realized that this was because her skin was in the process of healing, after being burnt. When she saw me, she made as though to throw her arms around me; but with the instinct of self-preservation, I jumped back. Instantly I felt ashamed; but she understood, and stood away from me." Hardman, entering the camp, joined two young British soldiers who were carrying heavy bags of potatoes for the prisoners.

Almost as though they had emerged from the retreating shadows of dark corners, a number of wraithlike creatures came tottering towards us. As they drew closer they made frantic efforts to quicken their feeble pace. Their skeleton arms and legs made jerky, grotesque movements as they forced themselves forward. Their bodies, from their heads to their feet, looked like matchsticks. The two young Tommies, entering camp for the first time, must have thought they had walked into a supernatural world; all the gruesome and frightening tales they had heard as children—and, not so many years since, they had been children—rose up to greet them; the grisly spectacle which confronted them was too much. They dropped their heavy sacks and fled.

The prisoners then "fell upon the sacks and their contents almost like locusts descending upon a field of corn. With queer, inarticulate cries, in voices which were thinner and more reedy than those of children, they fell upon the ground, upon the sacks, upon one another . . . to gain for themselves a precious, priceless potato."[34] Derek Sington was no doubt right in saying that "words like 'liberation,' 'tomorrow,' 'wait,' had lost all meaning for them. They were consumed by the famine which was burning them up, possessed only by the wild urge to eat and survive."[35]

In Belsen, as in Buchenwald, accounts of the liberation drew upon a common vernacular that limned survivors as locusts, skeletons, the living dead—the stuff of ghoulish fairy tales. Liberators rarely perceived the camp survivors as human beings. Instead, survivors appeared as apes, mummies, idiots, babies, cordwood, scarecrows, and dying rabbits: a veritable thesaurus of diminished humanity. For some of the liberators, survivors evoked not only disgust but hatred. "All I felt was horror, disgust, and I am ashamed to admit it, hate," wrote Captain R. Barber of the RAMC of the men in the Sandbostel camp. "Hate against the prisoners themselves for looking as they did, for living as they did, for existing at all. It was quite unreasonable, but there it was, and it gave us one possible explanation of why the SS had done these things. Once having reduced their prisoners to such a state the only emotions the guards could feel were loathing, disgust and hate."[36]

It was no wonder, then, that few of the liberators wanted to linger in these camps. At Dachau, units of the 42nd and 45th Infantry divisions liberated 32,000 prisoners. But the Americans were so shocked by the camps that there was no pride or evident satisfaction in the task. Nor was there much personal empathy or contact between liberator and prisoner. As one American soldier put it, "I for one was very happy to get out of there after three days. For me, it was wracking, and it was one of the happiest days of my life when they told me that, 'OK, you're going back, you're going away.' Because I don't know how much more I could have taken of that camp."[37] We can hardly fault him for wanting to flee the corpse-littered scene after three days; but it bears recalling that some people spent as long as ten years at Dachau.

FOR MOST OF the soldiers, the camps were something one passed through on the way toward some other military objective. But what does this moment of liberation look like if we adopt the perspective of those who were liberated? Of course, for the camp inmates, liberation meant an end to Nazi brutality. Liberation offered the prospect, however distant, of a return to families and to freedom. But such thoughts were for the most part overwhelmed by profound grief and anguish. The trauma of the camps was too great, their present focus on survival too single-minded for these prisoners to think much about the future. The prisoners also interposed a certain distance from their liberators. Yes, there was some cheering and embracing and heartfelt gratitude expressed toward the Allied soldiers. There was also a deep sense of unease, almost dread, that many articulate survivors have described as being their primary sensation. In part it was shame; in part it was an awareness of the sense of loss; and in part it was fear: fear that no one would ever believe the story they had to tell.

Robert Antelme, a Frenchman arrested in June 1944 for Resistance activities, survived his incarceration in a labor camp but almost died on the eve of liberation. He might well have been one of those apelike creatures the Allies saw haunting Dachau in the days after the camp's liberation. Antelme, after almost a year of hard labor, survived a ten-day death march from his camp at Gandersheim to Bitterfeld; then, on April 14, he was put into a boxcar and sent to Dachau: he did not get out for thirteen days. On the floor of the boxcar, exhausted, dying, and dead men lay in a heap. "There wasn't room enough to straighten out our legs. . . . Intertwined legs would knot and then come violently unknotted, in the dark; nobody wanted to have legs on top of his. It was a free-for-all of legs." One morning, Antelme awoke, itching madly. "Pick off your lice," a mate ordered. He took off his shirt.

> Long black strings of lice run down the cloth. I squash whole bunches of lice at once. I don't have to search, the shirt's full of them. . . . They're brown and gray and white and full of the blood they've pumped out of me. These lice can kill you. My arms haven't the strength to squash them anymore. . . . I put the shirt back on and take off my pants and underpants; the underpants are black in the crotch. It's impossible to kill them all. . . . They're all around my genitals, hanging on my pubic hair. I pull them off. I provide their nest and their happiness; I am theirs.

His Dachau imprisonment lasted a mercifully short two days. And then on April 29, a quiet, almost invisible liberation. Ill, emaciated, pestiferous, Antelme was lying on a hard wooden bunk that he shared with a cadaverous old man. "'They're here,'" a voice called. "I sit up. A round helmet moves along the walkway, outside the window. . . . Leaning on my elbow, I watch the helmets going by on the walkway. Putting all my strength into it, I bang at the old man's feet. 'We're free! Look, will you! Look!'" His bunkmate slowly turned his aged head to peer out the window, but "the helmets have all gone by. Too late. He falls back. I fall back too. I wasn't able to sing, I wasn't able to jump down right away, to run towards the soldiers. The old man and I are almost alone on our tier. The vision of round helmets had glided over my eyes. He hadn't seen a thing. The Liberation has passed by."

Antelme downplays what should have been the central moment of his narrative of captivity. For he tells us that liberation brought no clarity, no sense of immediate relief. Freedom carried with it a growing anxiety that these young American soldiers, so helpful and courteous, just might not believe what these inmates had seen. Some of his fellow prisoners try to explain to an American what has happened here, what has happened to all of them. "The soldier listens at first, but then the guys go on and on, they talk and they talk, and pretty soon the soldier isn't listening anymore." The inmates now come to terms with that awful burden that all survivors acknowledge they must carry, the possession of a terrible truth that can never be fully revealed, or as Antelme put it, "a kind of infinite, untransmittable knowledge."[38]

For those at Belsen, there was little question of celebration upon being liberated. The camp grounds were strewn with ten thousand dead bodies and the living were all near death. Hanna Lévy-Hass, a Yugoslav partisan and Jew, recalled that the prisoners in Belsen had no hot water after January 1945, that the whole camp was rife with lice and vermin. Dysentery was widespread, and the entire camp was awash in excrement. These prisoners knew that the Allies were nearby, but for Lévy-Hass, "this air of uncertainty" about the future was "a form of mental torture." Just a month before Belsen's liberation, she wrote in her secret diary that "there is no point in knowing when the Allies will arrive, though it seems certain they are only a few dozen kilometers away. For the present, our closest and most loyal ally is death. And if we do begin to count the days again, then it is not with an eye to the moment of our liberation, but in order to see how long the one or the other of us can still survive. There is a kind of medical curiosity in us, a strange obsession." Liberation, while welcome, also made the survivors confront their own state of degradation. Fela Lichtheim, a Pole who was forced to work for more than three years in various Silesian textile factories, survived a death march from

Gross-Rosen to Belsen in January 1945. For her, the months in Belsen, from January to April, were the worst of the war. Above all, the lice tormented her. "I didn't have any more strength to remove the lice from me. They crawled over me like ants." But even her words, recorded in the summer of 1946, seemed inadequate to plumb the depths of her misery. "One cannot describe it in words," she said, "because words hurt too much." This young woman of twenty-one said she "looked like a seventy-year-old woman. I was unable to move. I was all run down, emaciated, unwashed for weeks, without undressing. In that one dress and coat I was lying on the floor. I wanted some water for a drink, but I couldn't get it. I had diarrhea for two months, and then I had typhus." What did freedom mean in these conditions?[39]

The liberated prisoners at Belsen generally described the British as kind and warm, though many of the young women hated having their heads shaved, which the British insisted on to control lice. Sora M., a French Jew of Polish origin, recalled that Belsen in the last days of the war was "a lot worse than Auschwitz." There was no food: "we ate grass, anything. Corpses littered the ground." In a paradoxical reversal, Sora said she was surprised at the vulnerability of the young British soldiers who helped her: "they were embarrassed to see us naked, and turned their heads and blushed when they put DDT on us." Fernande H. remembered that by the time the British arrived the inmates looked like "larvae," and "we were dying like flies." She too was ashamed of having her head shaved—"I cried." The dose of DDT powder that the soldiers sprayed onto every prisoner "burned, as we were covered with scabs." Yet the English were "charming, adorable, very sweet." The moment of liberation was "wonderful," yet she was so weak she could not walk and so she had only "a subdued celebration." Dr. Hadassah Rosensaft, a Polish Jew whose medical training had helped get her assigned to a team of doctors, first in Auschwitz and then in Belsen, recalled that despite the arrival of the British, conditions were very slow to improve after liberation. "Within the following eight weeks, 13,944 more died." It is hardly surprising, then, that "for the greatest part of the liberated Jews of Bergen-Belsen, there was no ecstasy, no joy at our liberation. We had lost our families, our homes. We had no place to go to, nobody to hug. Nobody was waiting for us anywhere. We had been liberated from death and the fear of death, but not from the fear of life."[40]

The experience of liberation also depended upon who was doing the liberating, and in what context. Not everyone was freed from a camp. Nadine Heftler, a Frenchwoman who had spent time in Birkenau and Ravensbrück, was liberated while on a death march. She saw the star on an approaching American tank, and ever since, "the American flag has always been the flag of my heart." For Charles Baron, a French Jew who had been held in Birkenau and Dachau but managed to escape during a transport, the arrival of the Americans in the village in which he was hiding was a miraculous moment. "We jumped on them, hung on their necks, I started to blubber, and I cried and cried. They looked so sad, and they patted me on the shoulder saying 'Don't cry, Frenchy, don't cry.' They made the villagers gives us omelets and threatened reprisals if anything happened to us. And then they continued on their way." But the Americans could be abrupt as well. Ida Grinspan, lying half dead on a bunk in Ravensbrück, was stunned to see a few Americans appear in the infirmary on the 2nd of May. They smiled, handed out chewing gum, and departed without a word. Nathan Rozenblum saw the Americans arrive in the camp at Ebensee on May 6 and declare "You are free!" He wondered, "free of what? Of dying of hunger?" Then the tanks left, and abandoned him in the camp. They didn't return for three days.[41]

Camp inmates feared the Russians above all. While there are accounts of Russian generosity, there was also a higher likelihood of mistreatment at the hands of Russians than from the American soldiers, judging by the testimony of survivors. Yvette Levy, a Frenchwoman deported to Auschwitz in July 1944, was later transported to Weisskirchen, in the industrial region of eastern Moravia near Ostrava, where she toiled in a munitions plant. She was liberated by the Russians on May 9 or 10. By the time the Russians arrived, the SS guards had fled. She had great trouble with the Russians. "We tried to tell them we were hungry but we couldn't understand them and they had nothing to give us. We went to the town, but others had already beaten us to it and the houses were stripped bare." After scavenging in the countryside, she and her companions returned to the camp, and found the Russians now installed in the prisoners' barracks. "They were boorish men. Savages. There were rapes. As no one came to our aid, we fled." But according to Yvette, the British troops she encountered were no better. "The Tommies behaved just as bad as the Russians. A man in uniform loses all his dignity. The English soldiers said they would give us food only if we slept with them. We all had dysentery, we were sick, dirty . . . and here was the welcome we got! I don't know what these men thought of us—they must have taken us for wild animals." Yvette Bernard-Farnoux, freed from a camp near Prague called Litoměřice, evinced horror at the Mongolians in Soviet uniform. She and her bunkmates painted, in large white letters, the Russian word for "TYPHUS" on their barracks to deter the Mongolians from coming into their camp. They "were a frightening sight: brutes, standing on their tanks, lashing their horses. . . . They fired their guns everywhere, it was maddening." When the "real" Russians arrived, two or three days later, they were very well behaved. "They gave us great slaps on the back, offered us enormous slabs of lard, and invited us to drink the health of General de Gaulle and Guy de Maupassant."[42]

Clearly, there was no one typical liberation story. Thousands of prisoners were freed from Hitler's camps in the spring of 1945, but many others were liberated while on the death marches, and still others took matters into their own hands by escaping the marches, and hiding in woods, on vacant farms, or in sheds and barns. Some simply walked out of their camps after the guards had fled, and had to go in search of Allied soldiers. And those behind Soviet lines, such as those in Auschwitz, were freed from German captivity but not yet returned to safety. For all this variety, however, one theme unifies the many varying accounts of liberation: profound sorrow. The young Americans and Britons who entered the camps in the spring of 1945 were shocked and appalled by the scenes that greeted them, but perhaps could take some degree of satisfaction in their achievement. Upon first encountering the smoldering corpses at the small labor camp at Ohrdruf, General Eisenhower declared "we are told that the American soldier does not know what he is fighting for. Now, at least, he will know what he is fighting against."[43] Ike was right: for the soldiers, liberation of the camps lent a moral clarity to the war. In dozens of war memoirs by U.S. soldiers, the discovery of the camps is said to have answered the question of what the war was all about. But for the surviving Jews, liberation brought not answers but questions. Why had these horrors happened? Who was responsible, and what must now be done? Liberation was not an endpoint but a prologue to a long discourse about how to plumb the meaning of these events, and how to bear witness to them. Here then lies a fundamental divergence in the meaning of liberation: while Americans have sought to use the atrocities to underscore the essential benevolence of their war, survivors have found nothing redeeming in their experiences. "I live in Auschwitz every day today," said one survivor forty years later. "I am not liberated yet." Liberation could not bring a release from the terrible burdens of experience, after all. Perhaps it had come too late. Surely this is the meaning of Elie Wiesel's remarks to a group of World War II veterans about his own liberation from Buchenwald:

April 11, 1945. Buchenwald. The terrifying silence terminated by abrupt yelling. The first American soldiers, their faces ashen. Their eyes. I shall never forget their eyes. Your eyes. You looked and you looked. You could not move your gaze away from us. It was as though you sought to alter reality with your eyes. They reflected astonishment, bewilderment, endless pain and anger. Yes, anger above all. Rarely have

I seen such anger, such rage contained, mute, yet ready to burst with frustration, humiliation, utter helplessness. Then, I remember, you broke down, you wept. You wept and wept uncontrollably, unashamedly. You were our children then, for we—the 12-year-old, the 16-year-old boys in Buchenwald and Theresienstadt and Mauthausen—knew so much more than you about life and death, man and his endeavors, God and His silence. You wept. We could not. We had no more tears left. We had nothing left. In a way we were dead, and knew it.[44]

9

Americans and Jews in Occupied Germany

T HE ENCOUNTER BETWEEN Jewish Holocaust survivors and the Allied armies in the summer and fall of 1945 presents one of the most surprising, puzzling, and troubling episodes in the history of Europe's liberation. It is a shocking and uncomfortable fact: the Jews who emerged from Hitler's camps in the spring of 1945 were not truly free on the morrow of their liberation. The destruction of Hitler's regime made it possible for surviving Jews to contemplate a life after the Holocaust. But it did not bring that life into being. Long before dreams of revival and renewal could be fulfilled, Jews experienced many new travails, long delays, and most appalling, many more months and even years of life in crude wooden huts and barracks, eating at soup kitchens and wearing borrowed clothes, awaiting a future they could only distantly glimpse.

Yet theirs is not only a story of disillusionment, of delays in returning to them their freedom. It is also a story of recovery of that freedom by the Jews themselves who, in the face of crushing odds, slowly carved out a kind of life in the heart of defeated Germany. Caught in limbo, between the nightmare of the camps and the distant prospect of emigration to Palestine, thousands of Jews gathered in DP camps in Germany. In barracks used by the Nazis as Hitler Youth training camps, or officers' quarters, or military bases, Holocaust survivors waited—and while they waited, they organized, agitated, and strategized. During the summer of 1945, when the heated brickwork of the crematoria still smoldered, occupied Germany became a safe haven for Jews, so much so that Jews from Poland and southeastern Europe began to flee—illegally—westward, seeking shelter and respite from rampant anti-Semitism. In the American zone, camps near Munich at Landsberg, Föhrenwald, Feldafing, and Deggendorf, and at Zeilsheim near Frankfurt, evolved into Jewish settlements, hardscrabble encampments where prayers could be heard each

Sabbath, where kosher kitchens served hot rations, where Jews published newspapers and organized elections, taught Hebrew, studied Scripture, and where Yiddish folk songs could be heard on the evening air.

The Allied armies had almost nothing to do with this Jewish revival, at least in its earliest months. Throughout the summer, the British and American occupiers were focused chiefly on the massive problem of repatriation, and coping with the strains this dramatic outflow of forced laborers and POWs placed on transportation, roads, and the security of the occupied areas. Jewish survivors were not a priority for the liberating armies; it was assumed that Jews, like other DPs, would make their way home, after perhaps a brief period of recovery in makeshift medical facilities or camps. It is abundantly clear that the American and British military authorities were totally unprepared to deal with the particular issues presented not only by Jewish destruction but by Jewish survival. The liberation of Jews from concentration camps was done piecemeal and pell-mell. No serious preparation for the care and treatment of Jews had been arranged. The British and American armies were under orders to classify and house all DPs, regardless of religion, by their national origin. This was considered enlightened policy, for had it not been the Nazis who segregated people on the basis of religious faith? Rather, the Allies sought simply to enable DPs to go home.

Such bucolic notions were meaningless for Jews in occupied Germany. Most Jews in the DP camps in 1945 had national origins in countries that had openly embraced the ideology of anti-Semitism or where hatred of Jews was part of the fabric of daily life: Poland chiefly, but also Hungary, Romania, Lithuania, Czechoslovakia, and indeed, Germany itself. Though anxious to connect with loved ones in their hometowns and villages, most Jews had few illusions about resuming their prewar lives. They had seen their families uprooted, persecuted, and destroyed. Their villages, as many testified after the war, were now nothing more than cemeteries, full of ghosts and awful memories. For these Holocaust survivors, their only hope lay in their faith, their only comfort came from being among those who believed as they did, who shared common religious rites, and above all, who hoped soon to embark for the promised land of a Jewish national home in Palestine. It is no indictment of the stalwart Anglo-American liberators to say that all this baffled them. They did not know what the Jews had experienced, nor did they now know what the surviving Jews wanted. The scene was set for a painful dialogue of the deaf: between a brisk, businesslike military occupation that sought to sort out the DP problem quickly, and a small but resilient, resourceful Jewish remnant that interposed itself between the Allies and any tidy end to the war.

AS THE FLOOD of DPs began to recede—almost six million people had left Germany by the start of September—a few thousand Jews remained behind, spread out in vulnerable groups like tidal pools on a muddy beach. The formation of what Jewish survivors would soon begin to call *She'erit Hapleitah*—the surviving remnant—started in the waning days of the war, and gained momentum in June and July.[1] The precise numbers of Jewish Holocaust survivors in Germany at the end of the war can only be estimated. Contemporary sources suggest not less than 50,000 and not more than 70,000 Jews remained in Germany by the late summer of 1945. Roughly 45,000 of these were in the American zone of occupation, and 15,000 or so were located in the British zone. A small number resided in camps in the French zone. Perhaps 15,000 Jews had been accounted for in Austria. The precise number of Jews was in flux in any case, as some Jews were repatriated and others, fleeing the lethal anti-Semitism that still stalked Jews in postwar Poland, sought the relative security of the occupied zones of Germany and Austria. This exodus of the few remaining Eastern European Jews swelled the numbers in the DP camps, so that by the end of 1946, there were perhaps 130,000 Jewish DPs in the American zone alone, with much smaller numbers in the British zone, and in Austria. By that time, the international community had been well-informed of the particular plight of Europe's surviving Jews. In those first few weeks and months after liberation, however, the surviving Jews in Germany were largely left to themselves.[2]

In the American zone, which included Bavaria, small pockets of Jews began to stir in the spring of 1945. At a Benedictine monastery outside of Munich, for example, one of the founding episodes of Jewish revival took place. In the confusion of the last days of the war, when the Germans were still transporting Jews out of the reach of advancing Allied armies, a trainload of Jews from Dachau en route to the Austrian border was strafed by American aircraft, and disabled. The German guards having fled, a small band of Lithuanian Jews, survivors of the Kovno ghetto, sought out medical attention for those injured by the strafing. Dr. Zalman Grinberg, a thirty-three-year-old physician from Kovno, strode into the nearby town of Schwabhausen and demanded from the burgermeister immediate aid, on the grounds that the American Army would soon be arriving with orders to lock up any German mayor who failed to assist the wounded. Remarkably, the bluff worked, and the wounded Jews were transported to the monastery of Saint Ottilien, a picturesque, tranquil retreat that had been serving as a German military hospital during the war. As soon as the American troops arrived, Grinberg was able to secure Saint Ottilien as a Jewish hospital and within days, some 400 Jews from Dachau and nearby camps were receiving medical attention there. Three weeks later, on May 27, a gathering of 800 Jewish survivors met at Saint Ottilien. Dr. Grinberg presided over a somber ceremony marked by speeches, *Kaddish*, or Prayer for the Dead, and a musical concert performed by survivors of the Kovno ghetto orchestra. These were the first stirrings of a communal Jewish life in postwar Germany. By late August, the Jewish hospital at Saint Ottilien, staffed by seven Jewish DP physicians, fourteen German

The Catholic monastery at Saint Ottilien was used as a Jewish hospital and displaced persons camp from April 1945 until November 1948.
U.S. Holocaust Memorial Museum

doctors, and 120 nurses, had emerged as the central medical facility for critically ill Jews in Bavaria.[3]

Similar scenes played out in other collection points for surviving Jews. When the American military authorities emptied Dachau of its prisoners, they transferred many of the Jews to a complex of military barracks in the town of Landsberg (in whose town jail an imprisoned Adolf Hitler had written *Mein Kampf* in 1924) and to a Hitler Youth school at Feldafing, on the shores of Lake Starnberg. Though not yet restricted to Jews, these two camps now had large Jewish populations, and attracted Jews located in other Bavarian DP centers. At Deggendorf, a small community of 700 German Jews, all survivors of Theresienstadt camp, found shelter, though only after a harrowing journey by military truck to Prague and into Germany during which road accidents claimed a number of lives and left the survivors holed up in a disused army barracks in Winzer, forgotten by the military authorities. In an act of shocking insensitivity, American authorities initially housed these Jews alongside a thousand Yugoslav DPs and a group of notoriously anti-Semitic Hungarian *Volksdeutsche*—many of whom had been voluntary laborers in the Reich; only later were they separated. And in addition to Jews in camps, perhaps 6,000 Jews were living outside the DP centers in towns and villages in the Munich area. Freed from the dehumanizing experience of camp life, these Jews were nonetheless vulnerable, because they had no special access to the rations given to DPs nor could they gain access to rudimentary medical care.[4]

It is remarkable to observe how quickly this disparate, unfortunate community of survivors gathered strength and built the foundations of an effective political organization. On the first of July, a group of forty-one Jewish leaders met at Feldafing and elected a Central Committee of Liberated Jews in Bavaria. They named Dr. Zalman Grinberg chairman of its executive committee. Three weeks later, on July 25, the Central Committee organized a conference at the Saint Ottilien monastery; ninety-four representatives from forty-six DP centers across Germany and Austria attended. Although this conference received no official recognition from the Allied armies of occupation, a representative of the Jewish Agency for Palestine was present.[5] The accomplishment of these men cannot be overstated: without resources or official recognition, still housed in dire conditions in DP camps, still bearing up under the intense strain of their own personal losses in the war years, these Jewish leaders had managed to lay the foundations for an organization that would press Jewish interests with the Allied armies and with the public in the United States, Britain, and around the world. They could not possibly know just how much of a struggle lay ahead.

Much of this early organization can be credited to the extraordinary activities of First Lieutenant Abraham J. Klausner, a thirty-year-old Reform rabbi from Memphis, Tennessee, who had been serving in the 116th Evacuation Hospital Unit of the Seventh Army at the end of the war. He arrived at Dachau in May, and during the course of his duties, which involved presiding over funeral services at mass burial sites, he visited the nearby DP camps that the Army had hastily established. He was shocked to find Jewish survivors still in camps, without resources, contact with the outside world, or a helping hand inside the U.S. military establishment. One of Klausner's first actions was to draw up a list of as many Jewish survivors as he could find in all the DP camps, and then distribute this list as widely as possible, in order to make reunions between dispersed family members possible. Klausner, who appears to have maintained only a tenuous connection to his official Army unit, gave his heart to the plight of the surviving Jews, and used his status to press the military authorities to attend to their needs.[6] It was Klausner who organized the first transports of Jewish survivors from Dachau to nearby camps at Feldafing and Landsberg, thus establishing their reputation as Jewish camps—in direct contradiction to official U.S. military policy. In mid-June, Klausner also secured a headquarters for Grinberg's Central Committee in the partly ruined Deutsches Museum in Munich—the storied museum of science and technology, founded in 1906 as a showcase of German scientific achievement and later used by the Nazis for, among other things, the grotesque 1937 exhibition on "The Wandering Jew." Badly damaged by American bombing in 1944, the building housed UNRRA headquarters and became a hub of activity for DPs in southern Germany. (DPs founded the "UNRRA University" at the museum, which was a continuing education program for transient peoples; by October 1945, 1,267 students of twenty-nine nationalities were enrolled in courses there). In recognition of his efforts,

Lieutenant Abraham J. Klausner was the first Jewish chaplain to enter the Dachau concentration camp after its liberation. In June 1945, Klausner compiled the first list of Jewish survivors. He was instrumental in establishing services for survivors and bringing their problems to the attention of the American Jewish community and the U.S. government. *U.S. Holocaust Memorial Museum*

the Central Committee invited Klausner to serve on its executive committee as its honorary president.[7]

Yet Klausner's methods were not to everyone's liking. In particular, Klausner crossed swords with the American Jewish Joint Distribution Committee—the international humanitarian organization set up in New York by Felix M. Warburg at the start of the First World War to aid Jews in distress. The Joint, as it was universally known, had hoped since the last months of the war that it would be allowed to send its representatives into liberated areas and organize relief and medical aid for Jews. But the U.S. military was extremely reluctant to give civilians access to the DP camps. Thus the Joint did not get its representatives into the camps until August, and even then was slow to produce results. This would change quickly: by 1946 the Joint was a major player in providing millions of dollars' worth of goods, food, clothing, and educational materials to Jewish DP camps. But in that critical summer of the liberation, leaders of the Central Committee of Liberated Jews felt abandoned by the American Jewish community.

Klausner used his position as something of a public figure in occupied Bavaria to give voice to the rage of the Jews over the perceived failure of the Joint to provide them aid and assistance. In a memo he prepared in June for general distribution to American Jewish leaders, he attempted to survey the conditions in which 14,000 Jews in Bavaria lived: some were still in camps behind barbed wire and under curfew; almost all lacked basic supplies for hygienic living conditions, including plumbing or clean water; their food generally consisted of bread, coffee, bean soup, and tinned meat. Klausner meant for his words to bite: "Liberated, but not free—that is the paradox of the Jew," he wrote. "In the concentration camp his whole being was consumed with the hope of salvation. That hope was his life, for that he was willing to suffer. Saved, his hope evanesces, for no new source of hope has been given him. Suffering continues to be his badge." He continued: "the greater percentage of the liberated are still imprisoned in the striped uniform forced upon them by the oppressor. UNRRA, supposedly the organization to assist in this matter, has thus done nothing." In the seven weeks since liberation, "missions and representatives of varying hues have trekked through the misery of the liberated, offering verbal balm for their wounds. . . . The Jew has been constantly asking, most times with tears, 'where are our representatives? . . . Can they not send word to sustain us in this bitter hour? A word of reassurance?'"[8]

Whenever he addressed American soldiers in his capacity as a spiritual leader, Klausner ferociously criticized the Joint, and instructed servicemen to write home and ask their families to put pressure on the American Jewish community. In the Joint archives, one finds numerous letters, passed on to the Joint from the anxious parents of GIs who had heard Klausner's stem-winding orations. "Dear Florence," began one GI's letter home.

> I just returned from services where we had a Jewish chaplain to speak to us. He gave us the most astounding and horrifying story I've ever heard and spoke for over an hour. He is the head of a small organization here in Bavaria to help the Jewish displaced persons here. He told us stories of what was and is still being done with the Jews in Germany, Poland, and these other countries. The people at home think that when the Americans came in, all the Jews were liberated and everything was just fine from that moment on, but this is anything but the truth. . . . He asked us to write home about these things and see to it that this information is disseminated to as many people as you can possibly tell it to.[9]

Sergeant Edward Mayer of Chicago wrote home to his congregation's rabbi to say that he too had met Klausner and toured Saint Ottilien hospital. Klausner, Mayer reported, had to "scrounge enough odds and ends from captured enemy stores to keep the patients alive. . . . Since these people have been liberated, some three months ago, not one single bit of help has come, nothing from the International Red Cross, nothing from UNRRA, and what hurts worst of all, nothing from the 'great' Joint Distribution Committee." Staff Sergeant L. P. Brewster of the 2nd Armored Division wrote home in agony to his parents: "Why haven't the Jews in the USA helped? Where is the fellowship spirit toward a human being?" And Chaplain Klausner himself wrote to his teachers, friends, and associates in the United States, underscoring the failure of the American Jewish community to act with haste.[10]

Not surprisingly, the leaders of the Joint found Klausner exasperating. They dutifully replied to these various letters with careful explanations for the delays in getting aid to surviving Jews. But in their eyes, Klausner had become a menace. A telegram from the Joint's headquarters in New York to the office in Paris stated that "critical letters from chaplains particularly Klausner doing great damage fundraising efforts throughout country. . . . Many communities and prominent leaders aroused but in direction withholding support campaign rather than providing for increasing activities which essential to help meet some of the dire needs referred to by chaplains."[11]

And indeed, much of Klausner's criticism of the Joint was misdirected. The Joint, explained Executive Vice Chairman Joseph Hyman in a letter to one of many inquiries he received, was constrained by the military. "Several months before the war ended," he wrote, the JDC negotiated with SHAEF in Germany to secure admission. After repeated exertion and pressure the JDC finally reached an understanding in June that when the Army commanders in the field called up the JDC, i.e., actually invited the JDC field teams, the JDC would be permitted to come in under the auspices of the UNRRA. The UNRRA itself gained admission in early July. They also had to wait for Army invitation. We made the most insistent demands of Army Corps commanders to come in and we began toward the end of July, after heartbreaking delays on the part of the Army to send in a few teams. We gained admission through pleading and negotiating, all of which we did in the most patient, thorough and persistent way, both in Washington and Europe.

Implicitly deflecting the criticism of Klausner, Hyman wrote that "the GIs and the Jewish chaplains, because they were in the US military uniform, naturally were able to enter those camps long before the JDC could be permitted. . . . The JDC is a civilian agency which can go into the camps only under Army control."[12] Hyman had every reason to feel aggrieved by Klausner's criticisms. Yet from inside the camps of liberated Germany, where Jewish suffering was so pronounced and so ubiquitous, it was hard to accept these excuses. Klausner demonstrated his disdain for the Joint when its first representative arrived at the Deutsches Museum in mid-August, empty-handed. Klausner told his assistant to steal the gasoline out of the visitor's truck. "I told him, 'Just record it as the first contribution that the American Joint Distribution Committee is making to the liberated of Germany.'"[13]

FROM INSIDE THE DP camps, it appeared that the plight of the surviving Jews was being callously disregarded by the American occupation authorities. In fact, however, the American government was not entirely complacent about their fate. In early June, in response to the urgings of Jewish advocacy organizations, Secretary of the Treasury Henry Morgenthau persuaded the U.S. Department of State and President Harry Truman of the need for a high-level investigation of the problem, and on June 22, the president named Earl G. Harrison, the dean of the University of Pennsylvania Law School and a former commissioner of immigration and naturalization, to lead a fact-finding mission to Europe. Perhaps it was predictable that in response to a desperate plea for food, shoes, and medicine, Washington would send a blue-ribbon panel. But in the long run, the Harrison mission had a dramatic impact on the shape of America's policy toward the Jews in Europe and indeed toward the broader question of a future home for the Jewish people in Palestine.

During the month of July, Harrison toured DP camps in the U.S. occupation zone, was briefed by Army and UNRRA officials, and met with the Central Committee of Liberated Jews and with Rabbi Klausner in Dachau. Harrison was accompanied by a small team of experts that included Dr. Joseph Schwartz, the director of the JDC office in Paris and the leading Jewish relief official in Europe. Schwartz played a key role in Harrison's mission because he visited Poland, Hungary, Romania, and Czechoslovakia as well as the German DP camps, and wrote a lengthy memo of his own that Harrison drew on for his final report to President Truman. In all the meetings and interviews Harrison held, two themes predominated: first, that if Jews must remain in camps, they wished to be housed in separate, Jewish-only facilities; and second, that the surviving Jews wished overwhelmingly to go to Palestine and desired American intervention with the British government to make this possible. Toward the end of July, Harrison cabled a preliminary report to Morgenthau, confirming that the worst reports on the living conditions of Jewish survivors were true. Although his official report did not reach Washington until late August, General George Marshall, Army chief of staff, and Henry Stimson, secretary of war, knew this was a humanitarian crisis as well as a political bombshell, and raised the issue of Jewish DPs with General Eisenhower. Marshall's August 3 cable to Eisenhower demanded "immediate improvement in billeting" and "separate camps for Jews" along the lines of the Feldafing camp. Stimson, on August 10, also conveyed to Eisenhower his grave concern and his desire "that everything be done to improve the present situation," and that Harrison's claims about American Army mishandling of the Jewish DP question be immediately examined. Eisenhower, who had been dutifully carrying out SHAEF policy of separating Jews by nationality, began to change course, and in response to Marshall's and Stimson's messages agreed to the appointment of a special adviser on Jewish affairs. Eisenhower also consented to the creation of separate Jewish-only camps.[14]

Even though Eisenhower was already altering SHAEF policy toward Jewish DPs, the Harrison report, when it was finally submitted to Truman on August 24, dealt a shattering blow to the reputation of the occupation army, and clearly wounded Eisenhower personally. It was a powerful and explosive indictment of Allied policy toward the Jewish survivors; and it was released to the press with a searing cover letter from the president to Eisenhower that pointed to evident mismanagement and delay on the part of SHAEF. Truman lectured the general that the stakes were enormously high, for the

Germans must know that Americans abhor the Nazi policies of "hatred and persecution." The president wrote that "we have no better opportunity to demonstrate this than by the manner in which we ourselves actually treat the survivors." Truman asked Eisenhower "to report to me as soon as possible the steps you have been able to take to clean up the conditions mentioned in the report."

The report itself painted a horrific picture, one totally at variance with the broad public view that European Jews, having been liberated by Allied forces, were now safe and secure. On the contrary, wrote Harrison, Jews "have been liberated more in a military sense than actually; . . . they feel that they, who were in so many ways the first and worst victims of Nazism, are being neglected by their liberators." Three months after V-E Day, Harrison went on, Jewish DPs "are living under guard behind barbed-wire fences, in camps of several descriptions (built by the Germans for slave-laborers and Jews), including some of the most notorious of the concentration camps, amidst crowded, frequently unsanitary and generally grim conditions, in complete idleness, with no opportunity, except surreptitiously, to communicate with the outside world." Death continued to stalk the weakened and ill survivors; for lack of clothing, they were obliged to wear their prison garb; food was scarce and unpalatable; barracks in the camps were unfit for winter use; and in their despair they "frequently ask what 'liberation' means." Neither UNRRA nor the Allied military authorities, Harrison argued, had grappled effectively with the issue, and they had actually impeded the entrance of voluntary organizations such as the JDC into the camps. In a final and deliberately provocative flourish, Harrison wrote that "as matters now stand, we appear to be treating the Jews as the Nazis treated them except that we do not exterminate them. They are in concentration camps in large numbers under our military guard instead of SS troops. One is led to wonder whether the German people, seeing this, are not supposing that we are following or at least condoning Nazi policy."[15]

Harrison's colleague during his mission, Joseph Schwartz of the JDC, prepared a memorandum for Harrison that was slightly more temperate but equally condemnatory. Schwartz thought the Army had done a "remarkable job of repatriation," but had become part of the problem with respect to Jewish DPs. "The concept of statelessness," he wrote in his August 19 memo for Harrison, "is a very difficult one for the army to grasp." A refugee without a state or a homeland was, in the eyes of the military, a burden, possibly dangerous, and perhaps even a person unworthy of liberty. This helps explains why, in the Third Army area especially, "every camp is still surrounded by barbed wire and armed guards are placed at the entrances." Predictably, "the internees feel that they are still prisoners three months after their liberation." This feeling was reinforced by the awful food, the overcrowded conditions, the lack of medical supplies, inadequate toilet and washing facilities, and poor clothing. Schwartz was shocked to find some camp dwellers still in their striped prison uniforms, three months after their liberation. The DPs were idle, as there were no jobs or vocational training, so their morale was very low. And the DPs uniformly expressed the view that the German citizens in villages and towns nearby were being treated better than they by the American Army. Schwartz agreed, claiming that the Army was reluctant to requisition supplies from local Germans. "Very often the military detachments look upon the civilian German population as 'their' people, and upon the DPs as intruders who are a nuisance." Naturally, the Jewish DPs were impatient and growing angry. What they wanted above all was to be allowed to get away from this land of sorrows and emigrate to Palestine.[16]

Harrison's report, which drew heavily on Schwartz's memo, recommended for the short term that stateless DPs be housed in German homes and apartment complexes, even if this required the evacuation of local German populations; and if this could not be done, at the very least Jews should be allowed to establish and administer Jewish-only camps, in order to provide them with a sense of community and autonomy inside a nation they viewed as both hostile and foreign. The SHAEF authorities were already putting into practice this recommendation; but it was Harrison's broader recommendation that occasioned much political comment, and exacerbated a bitter quarrel between the United States and Britain. "For some of the European Jews," Harrison concluded, "there is no acceptable or even decent solution for their future other than Palestine." Harrison voiced his support for the request of the Jewish Agency for Palestine that one hundred thousand Jewish emigrants from Europe be allowed to go to Palestine immediately. Politics aside, "the civilized world owes it to this handful of survivors to provide them with a home where they can again settle down and begin to live as human beings."[17]

General Eisenhower did not dither in responding to the Harrison report, and to an equally dismal portrait of camp life painted by his chief adviser on Jewish affairs, Major Judah Nadich. He wired Truman that he was "very much concerned" by the president's August 31 letter, and that he was "starting a personal tour of inspection of Jewish Displaced Persons installations." He reassured the president that "in the US Zone in Germany *no* possible effort is being spared to give these people every consideration toward better living conditions, better morale, and a visible goal."[18] On September 17, Eisenhower—accompanied by a recalcitrant General Patton—made his first tour of a Jewish DP camp: the generals visited Feldafing to attend the services for Yom Kippur, the holiest day of the Jewish year. Three days later, Eisenhower issued an order to all his subordinate commanders that conditions for DPs must be drastically improved, that the goods they required must be requisitioned from the German people, that in offering employment the occupation forces should always favor DPs over Germans, that food must be improved and stockpiled for winter, and that all camp policing should be done by DPs themselves, without arms. Eisenhower wanted to hear no more about American MPs keeping Jews behind barbed wire, as was common in the Third Army area of Bavaria.[19] Finally, in response to Harrison's report, the administration appointed a special adviser on Jewish affairs, Judge Simon Rifkind of New York, who was to work as a conduit between Eisenhower and the Jewish leaders in the camps.

By early October, Eisenhower felt confident enough to deliver a detailed report to the president on his activities since the Harrison report. "I can assure you," he wrote, "that the most unsatisfactory conditions reported by Mr. Harrison no longer exist." He laid out what had been accomplished, described improvements in food, clothing, and shelter, and assured the president that the American Army was working to protect and secure Jewish survivors. Yet Eisenhower also could not resist challenging Harrison's report. He believed the report was misleading and unfair, not least because it failed to place the Jewish problem in the broader context of the massive war damage Europe had sustained, the acute shortages of housing and supplies, the huge waves of displaced and repatriated peoples, and the sheer logistical challenge of transforming the Army from a combat organization to a humanitarian relief operation. Harrison, Ike suggested, had looked at the Jewish DP problem through a straw, and failed to see the larger picture. Worse, the general felt Harrison had shortchanged the enormous efforts already made on behalf of Jews by the American Army. His report, Eisenhower concluded, "gives little regard to the problems faced, the real success attained in saving the lives of thousands of Jewish and other concentration camp victims and repatriating those who could and wished to be repatriated, and the progress made in two months to bring these unfortunates who remained under our jurisdiction from the depths of physical degeneration to a condition of health and essential comfort."[20] In Philadelphia, Earl Harrison issued a terse reply to the press: "General Eisenhower refers to improved conditions in the camps. What we need is more action in getting the people out of the camps and less talk about improving conditions within the camps."[21]

But did the well-meaning Eisenhower really deliver "health and essential comfort" to the Jewish DPs? For all of Eisenhower's alacrity in responding to directives from Washington, conditions in DP camps did not improve quickly, and the interactions between Army officials and Jewish DPs grew worse as the summer passed into fall. Why was this so? The evidence suggests that, rather than create a sense of shared solidarity, the great challenge of restoring and reviving Jewish life in the DP camps served to divide Jews from their protectors and liberators.

Approximate Numbers of Jewish DPs in Bavaria as of October 1945[22]

Munich	2,500
Landsberg	5,500
Feldafing	4,000
Föhrenwald	2,500
Saint Ottilien hospital	700
Gauting hospital	500
Deggendorf	1,000
Villages and towns	8,500
Total	**25,200**

After an initial outburst of activity upon the publication of Harrison's report, relief workers and military officials became inured to the complaints of Jewish DPs and grew increasingly to view the Jews as difficult, obstreperous, annoying, and insatiable. Earl Harrison had been right that Army commanders were not particularly eager to carry out Eisenhower's orders with respect to DPs, as they tended to see DPs as obstacles to their mission of pacifying German civilians. Inside the camps, Army officers and UNRRA officials complained bitterly about what they considered the willful, stubborn, even hostile attitude on the part of the Jewish camp residents. Zorach Warhaftig, secretary of the Polish Jewish Restitution Committee and an adviser to the Institute on Jewish Affairs in New York, made a detailed assessment of the camps in October and November, and was stunned by "the tendency to blame camp inmates and make all kinds of insinuations against them." Relief workers, Army officials, and correspondents "all are eager to claim that the Jewish camp inmates are broken mentally and morally." Worse, "the guilt of the Germans has been forgotten" by U.S. Army officials and "the Jewish DPs are looked upon as intruders."[23] Warhaftig suspected anti-Semitism and anti-Zionism motivated such calumnies. Yet similar assessments could be found even among the most stalwart allies of the Jewish DPs. "They have lived and been treated as animals, and much of the animal is in them now," wrote Oscar Mintzer, a legal adviser working for the JDC, in early November.

"Many of them are dirty, even filthy. Their moral standards are shot to hell. They connive, and finagle, and contrive—all the time. They lie and cheat and steal. They had to do this under the Nazis to remain alive, and our crazy red tape and regulations, particularly Army and UNRRA, are making them continue this in order to remain alive."[24] This was a common perception by American officials and soldiers: that the Jews were almost beyond recovery, and in any case ungrateful for the efforts made on their behalf.

It is clear that Jews did complain most bitterly about their circumstances. They viewed their continued incarceration in DP camps as an outrage, a mockery of the promises of liberation that had opened up such hopeful vistas in May 1945. The visible failure of the Army, UNRRA, and the Joint Distribution Committee to bring about immediate improvement in their lives struck them as an unforgivable failure. In November, food rations were actually cut in many DP camps; as the weather grew colder and the need for winter clothes, firewood, and adequate housing grew, DPs began to despair about spending yet another winter in a camp in Germany. Quite naturally, their complaints took on a new edge and sharpness. Warhaftig sensed among the displaced Jews in the fall of 1945 "a terrible disappointment . . . a bitterness, nervousness and depression, because of the unclear prospects for their future."[25] Yet at the heart of Jewish anxieties lay not just concern about housing and clothing. There was also something in the worldview of the Jewish DP that placed a distinct barrier between him and those who were prepared to offer help and succor. For example, Koppel Pinson, who spent a year in Germany as educational director for the Joint, observed that the Jewish DP

> is preoccupied almost to the point of morbidity with his past. . . . He is always ready to recount in minutest detail the events of his past or the past of his relatives. In their entertainments and in the education of their youth there is the constant preoccupation with their experiences under the Nazis—gruesome recapitulation of concentration camp incidents combined with vows of undying loyalty to these memories and hopes for vengeance. It is especially depressing to see young boys and girls of 8–12 years of age, whose rehabilitation to normal childhood should emphasize obliteration of these memories, participate in and be encouraged to share in such demonstrations.[26]

Here is one clue to the yawning chasm that had opened up between Jewish survivors and the community of relief workers: the Jews were beginning to construct a narrative of their fate in which history, memory, commemoration, and retelling of the persecution they endured would accompany and condition their recovery. There was to be no "new" life, but a conscious carrying of the recent past into the future. This insistence on placing the catastrophe at the center of Jewish identity did not mesh with the American idea of liberation and its insistence on a clean break with the past. And it consciously placed the community of UNNRA personnel and relief workers at a distance: as Pinson noticed, "the relief workers from the USA and from England . . . no matter how hard they worked, no matter how efficient they were, no matter how much thanks and deference was given to them officially, none the less remained outsiders. A wide gulf separated them from the DPs. Most of them knew no Hebrew, but a smattering of Yiddish, had no background of Jewish culture, had no understanding of the civilization and way of life of East European Jews, and hence could never find a common intellectual or emotional basis with the DPs."[27]

The DP camps, then, became a site of conflict between two sets of priorities: the American Army offered shelter and aid to stateless Jews but in return demanded order and compliance, and expected the Jews, now liberated, to act like "civilized" people again. The Jews, of course, wanted security and safety, too, as well as tolerable lodgings; but above all they wanted freedom—the freedom to organize political activities, to publish appeals to world Jewry, and to agitate on behalf of that elusive goal, emigration to Palestine.

THESE CONFLICTING TRENDS were all patently visible in Landsberg, the largest Jewish DP camp in the American zone, where in September 1945, a twenty-seven-year-old major named Irving Heymont took over command. The Lansdberg DP camp was located in Landsberg am Lech, about thirty-five miles from Munich; as Major Heymont described it in his diary, it contained about 6,000 people, and 5,000 of them were Jews; by October, as repatriation continued, the non-Jews left and virtually all the remaining residents were Jews. The inhabitants lived in former Wehrmacht army barracks, originally built to house cavalry units in the First World War. The camp comprised large brick buildings and a series of seventeen requisitioned houses and apartment blocks adjacent to the camps. The camp was under the command of the Army but staffed by a poorly prepared UNRRA team; as the JDC noted, the UNRRA personnel only arrived at Landsberg in mid-August, and no one on the team was Jewish; only two members of the ten-member team spoke German or Polish, and so they had no way to communicate with the inhabitants. An UNRRA inspection report noted that the JDC officers were far more connected to camp residents and tended to marginalize the UNRRA staff—

the "dual machinery" had developed "into a competition" for status within the camp.[28] Major Heymont's arrival marked the start of a new period for the camp. His leadership brought stability and continuity, as well as a significant improvement in living conditions, and Landsberg soon grew to become the largest all-Jewish camp in the American zone of occupation. Yet, as Heymont explained in his diary, the challenge of running a DP camp was filled with difficulties and setbacks.

Place of Birth of Jewish Residents of Landsberg, October 1945[29]

Poland	3,740
Hungary	283
Romania	162
Lithuania	141
Germany	129
Czechoslovakia	106
Greece	58
Other or unspecified	357

Major Heymont's initial assessment was that the camp residents were "demoralized beyond hope of rehabilitation." Upon his arrival in mid-September, the Landsberg camp was in a terrible state. "The DPs sleep in bunks of rough, unfinished lumber that are often double and even triple decked. Mattresses are straw filled sacks. Bedding consists of shoddy gray Wehrmacht blankets or US Army blankets." It was also surrounded by a fence of barbed wire. "The outside perimeter is patrolled by soldiers from the battalion. A soldier and a member of the camp police are stationed at the entrance gate. . . . I saw large numbers of DPs lolling along the fence and watching the Germans walking freely along the opposite street." Food supply was disorganized, with no central mess. Each family used a hot plate for cooking. Wall lockers were stuffed with clothing and personal supplies. "The number of idle people is surprising. Many of the beds were occupied by people either dozing or just lying there listlessly. One could sense an air of res-ignation." Heymont was appalled at the lack of basic sanitation. "The toilets beg description. About half the bowls were inoperative but full of excrement. Toilet seats, while not entirely lacking, were smeared with excrement or wet with urine. No toilet paper was in sight. . . . In the washrooms, most of the sinks were out of order." The kitchens were filthy. "I asked one cook, who was kneading dough, to extend his hands. His fingernails were encrusted with dirt, and his hands looked as if he had been greasing a wheel bearing."[30]

Heymont was well aware of the Jewish demands for self-government, and sympathetic to their plight. The Jewish leaders "keep after me hammer and tongs to permit complete self-management of the camp. The word they use over and over is autonomy. . . . They naturally resent being treated as wards of foreign benevolence rather than full free citizens. After their sacrifices and sufferings, they undoubtedly find it galling to be objects of charity. . . . They must surely find it rankling to have their private lives regulated and subjected to constant inspection while the Germans lead a relatively free life. I am sure they still feel like prisoners."[31] Yet Heymont remained reluctant to grant the Jews greater freedoms. A camp population that exhibited such poor hygiene, such disorganization, such uncivilized behavior, surely could not administer itself, he reasoned. He periodically hectored his camp inmates in astonishingly condescending tones: "Now is the time to relearn the habits of work and industry," he told them in a speech in late September. "Now is the time to relearn how to be self-respecting civilized persons. No man can ask you to forget what you and your families have been through. However, you can't live in the shadow of the past forever. . . . This is the time for relearning habits of work and smiling, to live again as a proud people, unashamed and unafraid before the world. You have only to prove that you are capable of handling it."

And when the Jews failed to live up to these expectations, Heymont expressed deep distress. In early October, the new corps commander, General Horace McBride, visited Landsberg to inspect the progress made since Harrison's report. For Heymont, this was "a day I would rather forget. . . . The camp was dirty and filthy. It was almost as bad as when we took over. . . . The living areas and latrines were horrible. . . . We had all worked so hard trying to help the people—and they even fail to keep just their own living areas and latrines tolerably clean. Even after concentration camp life, it is not too much to expect people to flush toilets that are in working order. Is it too demanding to ask that they use the urinals in the latrines and not the floors? . . . I feel so discouraged because I thought we had made some progress."[32] Heymont also professed to be shocked by the absence of personal modesty among the prisoners. "The morals of these people are amazing," he wrote with dismay. "Concentration camp life seems to have completely destroyed the normal inhibitions as we know them. Here, men and women mix and sleep in the same room in a manner that would be considered scandalous back home. . . . Many couples live together without the sanction of wedding rites. This practice is accepted in a very matter of fact fashion." Heymont's diary, like the accounts by soldiers who had helped liberate the concentration camps, reveals the tension between a genuine desire to provide comfort to those in his care, and a profound revulsion at the apparent unwillingness of these survivors to demonstrate the obedience, loyalty, and self-respect of a people that aimed at collective autonomy and indeed statehood.[33]

Heymont, as camp commander, worried incessantly about the little things: cleanliness, order, the black market, and so on. Leo Srole, who served in Landsberg throughout 1946 as the welfare director of the UNRRA team installed in the camp, took a longer view and attempted to explain some of the behavior of Jewish DPs that so irked Heymont. Srole was a prominent American sociologist who took a leave of absence from his academic post at Hobart College to work in the DP camps. After five months in Landsberg, he prepared a report on the psychological outlook of the Jewish DPs at Landsberg, and expanded the report for publication in *Commentary* magazine. Srole believed that the Jews in Landsberg were suffering from what he called an "anxiety state" similar to combat fatigue or shell shock. They exhibited excessive perspiration, disturbed sleep, impaired memory, impatience, irritability, depression, and "regression to a more childlike personality." Srole readily acknowledged that these troubled Jews had accomplished a great deal while at Landsberg. They demonstrated an "almost obsessive will to live normally again, to reclaim their full rights as free men." Srole believed that their frequent intractability derived in large part from their lack of freedom and dignity in the camps. Srole reported that one Jewish DP had told him that the food he was given in the camp was "the bitter bread of charity" and asked, "When will I be able to buy my own bread and say to myself, 'I am a man again like all men. I am free—I earn my own bread!'" Jewish DPs, Srole concluded, lived under "a heavy weight of anxieties and strains." Their dependent status embarrassed them; the evidence of German recovery and even of comfort infuriated them; and the closed doors of Palestine drove them to bouts of despair and anguish over the prospect of a prolonged period of sequestration in the camps. Even the strongest of souls would be worn down by such travails; yet these were survivors of a massive onslaught against their faith, their villages, their families, themselves. The superstructure of normality these Jews attempted to build stood on the shifting, shallow soil of personal loss, grief, and despair.[34]

This inner emotional turmoil makes the modest achievements within Landsberg so much the greater. It is important to stress just how much effort the Landsberg committee expended on creating institutions of a communal life. They established a profusion of schools in Landsberg—a kindergarten, an elementary school, a technical high school, an adult education program for camp residents, and a yeshiva for fifty students preparing for the rabbinate—and this despite the overwhelming difficulties of securing reading materials and textbooks, paper, pencils, and chalkboards. Cultural activities, including a theater and library, even a café, and the successful weekly newspaper, *Landsberger Lager-Cajtung*, with a circulation of 15,000, demonstrated the determination of the resident Jews to live dignified and full lives while awaiting the longed-for emigration to Palestine. Under Jacob Oleiski and the innovative programs of the World ORT Union, Landsberg benefited from an extensive program of job training in practical skills that would not only serve the needs of the camp but also prepare Jews for a trade when, at long last, they should be allowed to settle in Palestine.[35]

But perhaps most astonishing to outside visitors was the alacrity with which the Jews in Landsberg embraced politics. This was not yet party politics—Jewish leaders had developed a tacit consensus that party divisions, which had so profoundly divided Jews in prewar Eastern Europe, would be set aside under the common banner of unity of Zionism, and this unity held intact through the first postwar year. Rather, politics meant organization, and the assertion of Jewish autonomy over camp life. Landsberg already had a visible and competent temporary committee, chaired by Samuel Gringauz and staffed by David Trager, Jacob Oleiski, and Moses Segalson, all Lithuanian Jews who had passed through the Kovno ghetto and Dachau, as well as Dr. Abrasha Blumovicz, a Pole and former partisan. They constantly pressed Major Heymont for greater independence from Army regulations and oversight, demands Heymont was reluctant to grant. In an address to the camp residents in the large Sport Hall on September 26, Major Heymont asserted that the Jews "must develop in yourselves the kind of self-discipline that will eventually lead you to complete autonomy. . . . You want autonomy and you will have it. But you must prove that you are capable of exercising it."[36] Of course, Heymont's notions of discipline meant cleanliness, an end to black market activities, and scrupulous attention to the orders laid down by the occupying army. Jewish leaders in the camp, however, focused on political activity, and the development of their own vision of self-help, reliance, and rehabilitation. The elections for an official Camp Committee, held on October 21, were preceded by active politicking, complete with election slogans, banners, leaflets, posters, and campaigning by the candidates. Even if this election served only as a referendum on the temporary committee, all of whose members were reelected, the very fact that Jews held a vote in the heart of Germany a mere five months after the war stood as a clear assertion of Jewish claims to political activism and autonomy.

The greatest boost in morale for the Landsberg camp residents coincided with the elections: on October 21, David Ben-Gurion, chairman of the Jewish Agency Executive in Palestine and leader of the Zionist movement, visited

Landsberg. Ben-Gurion was in Germany to make a tour of Jewish DP camps and to meet with Generals Eisenhower and Walter Bedell Smith about the Jewish refugee problem. He saw the camp at Zeilsheim, near Frankfurt, and then traveled on to Munich—a city indelibly linked to the rise of the Nazi party—where he met members of the Central Committee of Liberated Jews. After inspecting the hospital at Saint Ottilien, Ben-Gurion was driven to Landsberg. Arriving at about 3:00 P.M., he was greeted by over 5,000 camp residents lined up in rows along the main road toward the Sport Hall. As the camp newspaper described the event, the large audience in the hall listened attentively to this messenger from "the land of prophets and pioneers." Ben-Gurion delivered the welcome message that the Jewish community now in Palestine was strong, politically and economically mature, and "resolved to struggle so that the future of Eretz Israel and the Jewish people will no longer be dependent upon the will of foreign powers." Ben-Gurion afterward met with Major Heymont as well as the leaders of the Camp Committee. He elaborated more fully on the positive trends in Palestine for the Jews, stating that there was a desperate need for labor and skilled workers and that it would be easy to absorb a large number of immigrants, once the British resistance was overcome. On this topic, Ben-Gurion was subdued, making plain his doubts about the Labour government and especially the permanent civil service in the British administration. But he urged his listeners to continue their efforts: the survivors, he said, must "gather and concentrate all lively remaining energies in order to transform the downfall of European Jewry into a redemption of the entire Jewish people."[37] The message he sought to convey was plain: that the Jewish DPs were not merely victims who needed help, but a political force, capable of shaping the future of Israel. "You must not regard yourselves subjectively but from the standpoint of the Jewish nation. . . . You, the direct emissaries of the suffering of our people, are the driving force. You must be strong."[38]

Ben-Gurion's speech rallied the hopes and spirits of the camp residents. Privately, however, Ben-Gurion was somewhat more guarded about the role of the DPs in the Zionist project. To Major Heymont, he expressed his sympathy about the difficult challenges of restoring these Jews to dignity, saying it would take time to change the psychology of the surviving Jews and to get them to take more pride in their conditions. "In Palestine we too have comparable problems," he said. "A voyage on a boat does not transform people." Indeed, for Ben-Gurion, these DPs served a more useful purpose in the camps than outside of them. While in Frankfurt, he confided to Zorach Warhaftig his view that "the concentration of Jewish DPs in Germany, especially in the American Zone of occupation, creates a difficult and pressing problem for the United States and this may be used by us in the fight for

Abraham Klausner (left), Major Irving Heymont (center), and the chairman of
the Jewish Agency for Palestine David Ben-Gurion in the Landsberg DP camp
during Ben-Gurion's visit in October 1945. *U.S. Holocaust Memorial Museum*

the opening of the gates of Palestine."[39] Even the painful captivity of the
survivors had its uses.

Ben-Gurion's visit was probably the high point of optimism and morale
in the Jewish DP camps. His appearance had given a face and a name to the
project of building Israel, and made it seem as if Palestine was an attain-
able goal for the surviving Jews. Yet with November came dispiriting news
from London: the British government, despite pressure from Washington,
refused to allow an increased number of Jews to emigrate to Palestine. At
the same time, increasing numbers of Jews were arriving in the American
zone of Germany, fleeing from anti-Semitism in Eastern Europe, and filling
up already crowded camps with a new wave of DPs. In Landsberg, the new
arrivals forced camp authorities to reopen formerly condemned wooden
barracks. An inspection of Landsberg by Major General Arthur A. White,
71st Infantry Division, in late December described the sanitation situation
there as "deplorably bad—human excreta spotted the entire area surrounding the four wooden barracks, housing 300, of which most were children.
. . . In shower rooms, the inmates defecated on the floor. . . . Garbage is
still inadequately handled, being spilled and thrown about the grounds.
Kitchen floors are littered with cans and waste food." In general, camp

residents showed "disregard for camp rules and regulations."[40] Army officers evinced little sympathy for the Jewish DPs. The overcrowding in the camps, one colonel told the Landsberg camp leaders, was "brought on by their own people coming into the area voluntarily and often illegally"— not, that is, by continued persecution of Jews. The colonel told camp leaders that the Germans could not be forced to give up their homes "because the Jews were here only temporarily and two wrongs don't make a right, etc. . . . I told them that they must help rehabilitate themselves."[41] One officer from the Third Army surgeon's office, downcast by the sanitation problems in Landsberg, chalked it up to the "liberation complex" that so many military officials used to describe DP behavior: "They have been liberated, have freedom, and with it apparently expect freedom from restriction or regulation. . . . They should be made to realize that certain regulation of individuals and modification of so-called private rights is necessary for the welfare and proper sanitation of groups of individuals living together in a common society." The memo concluded, with no evident sense of irony, that the "need for regulatory control" in the camps "must be instilled even, if necessary for the common good, by coercive or disciplinary action."[42] Yet again, American military officials failed to see the larger context: the Army wanted order, tidiness, and rules. Jews in camps, half a year after the end of the war, could not accept continued regulation, continued hardship, waiting, privation, delay, and incarceration with equanimity. All the goodwill in the world could not reconcile these positions.

As conditions in the camps deteriorated, and as U.S. Army officers continued to berate camp leaders for their failures in running clean, orderly, and happy installations, camp leaders' spirits sank. Dr. Zalman Grinberg, the chairman of the Central Committee of Liberated Jews in Bavaria, gave voice to his distress when meeting in Munich with representatives of American Jewish organizations in mid-November. After making due acknowledgment of the gift of survival that American soldiers had given Jews in April 1945, he did not hide his disappointment. "We had hoped that the time after liberation would be quite different," he said. The American military was slow to address the crisis of surviving Jews, American relief organizations were dispersed and ill equipped; the Central Committee had to fight to win recognition as the representative body for Jews in Bavaria; General Eisenhower's directives ordering significant improvements in camp conditions, he said, were not followed and Jews still lived in squalid conditions. In such an environment, Jews struggled. "The average Jew in the camps," Grinberg said, "is depressed. The reasons for that are: the bitter yesterday, the bad today, and the hopeless tomorrow. . . . That is how things are six months after the liberation."[43]

BETWEEN THE FALL of 1945 and the spring of the following year, the overall picture of the Jewish DPs worsened due to a sudden influx of Jewish refugees, mainly from Poland, but also from the Soviet Union, Hungary, and Slovakia. This new population presented a serious challenge not only to the military and relief organizations that were charged with dealing with them, but also to the Jewish DP community, whose minimal resources would be stretched beyond the breaking point. Placed alongside the deeply dispiriting British refusal to allow increased immigration to Palestine, the surge in the camp populations toward the end of 1945 worsened the morale of Jewish camp residents and exacerbated tensions between the military and the Jews. As winter settled over Europe, there were more Jews in camps in Germany than there had been in April 1945, when the Allied armies first arrived to rip down the barbed-wire fences.

Who were these newcomers, and why did they seek to gain entry into Germany? Historian Yehuda Bauer has devoted careful attention to this movement of Eastern European Jews. In the two years after the war, perhaps 250,000 Jews traveled westward, into Austria, Germany, and Italy. Most were Poles, and they came because their homeland had become uninhabitable, its anti-Semitism in no way diminished by the defeat of the Nazi regime. On the contrary, the political turmoil inside Poland at the end of the war, as right-wing nationalists fought the Soviet-backed Communists for control of Poland, placed the Jews in an especially vulnerable position, and resulted in their renewed persecution and dispossession. Even Poles who had returned to Poland from Soviet Russia or indeed from Germany itself at war's end now felt obliged to take to the roads again. Many took advantage of the secret network of Jewish operatives known as the Brichah to secure false papers, arrange convoys, and deliver them to the relative safety of occupied Germany, Austria, or Italy, with the distant hope that they might from there travel to Palestine. The British army cut off the routes via Austria into Italy by September, however, thus channeling the flow of refugees into occupied Germany. In the fall of 1945, these underground caravans carried over 30,000 Jews out of Poland and their numbers continued to rise in 1946. According to Bauer, this was good news to Jewish leaders in Palestine, especially Ben-Gurion, who saw the Brichah effort as serving both a humanitarian and a political purpose; Jews were being moved to safety, but they were also being used to place more pressure on the Allied occupation authorities.

The military and UNRRA officials who oversaw the DP camps, already struggling with the problems of housing, feeding, and providing for the Jewish remnant, met this new influx with hostility and befuddlement. With the Harrison report still fresh in the public eye, and President Truman and General Eisenhower's commands to improve the conditions of Jewish DPs, officials on the ground knew that they could not forcibly turn away these new arrivals. Even so, Army officials complained that these new refugees were not, strictly speaking, displaced persons but "infiltrees" with all the criminal connotations that word implied; they asserted that because many of them had survived the war in Soviet-occupied Poland or in the USSR itself, they had not been persecuted by Nazis, but were instead opportunists seeking to flee westward simply to find a better life under the shelter of the U.S. Army. And the Allied authorities were dimly aware of the secret organization at work moving Jews westward, a fact they resented and that certainly contributed to the icy reception the Jews received in Germany and Austria. Under duress, the American Army agreed to let them into their zone in occupied Germany, swelling the numbers of Jewish DPs and complicating an already difficult problem in liberated Germany.[44]

Although Yehuda Bauer has calculated that almost 10,000 Jews were spirited out of Poland by the Brichah in August, and another 6,475 in September, it was not until October that relief officials began to perceive this new influx as the start of a new pattern of migration and resettlement. Joseph Levine of the Joint Distribution Committee, stationed in Schwandorf, northeast of Munich and fairly close to the Czech border, wrote to Moses Leavitt, executive vice chairman of the JDC in New York, to fill him in on broad outlines of the new influx of Jews. Levine noted that "everyone reports murder and pillage by the Poles and that all the Jews want to get out of Poland." Levine's sources had told him, for example, that some Jews had attempted to return to Łódź after the war, only to find that the Polish police were terrorizing Jews and expelling them from the city. The same, Levine heard, was true in Radom and Lublin. Polish Jews had thus started to flee, some to Romania, some to Austria and Italy, and if possible across Czechoslovakia into southern Germany. Levine also reported that many of the Jews were coming from Russia as well. "How large a number will arrive from Poland here and elsewhere in the American zone I don't know. I do know that the problem here is going to be a difficult one." Eli Rock, the senior field representative of the JDC in the Third Army area, also reported in October that "in the last six weeks, on the heels of the growing anti-Semitic outbreaks in Poland, a steady flow of Polish Jews to Czechoslovakia [and] to Bavaria has taken place." Because their movements were illegal and furtive, they usually arrived in Bavaria in a bad way, short of food, clothing, and blankets, and in need of medical attention. "Of a recent large group," Rock said, "it was found that 40% were tubercular and 90% had scabies." Rock noted that the Army did not consider them "legally DPs" and so was loath to care for them. They were now in dread of the prospect of being forcibly sent back to Poland. Rock was right to insist to his JDC superiors that these new refugees must first have their status as legitimate persecutees clarified so the Army and UNRRA bureaucracy would treat them properly. In November, Jacob Trobe, the head of the JDC operation in Germany, wrote to the Army's chief liaison for Jewish affairs, Judge Simon Rifkind, that as of mid-November the rate of new arrivals was increasing and that the Army's unwillingness aggressively to requisition German homes would leave thousands of Jews without shelter in the coming weeks.[45]

The midlevel Army commanders who faced the additional logistical burdens of the new arrivals were initially skeptical and indeed hostile. A memorandum for the War Department, prepared after a meeting held in Berlin on November 19 between Army, JDC, and UNRRA officials, makes the exasperation of the military plain. The memo stated that "Jews were seeping into Berlin at average rate of 200 daily," and "ninety percent of them are Polish or Baltic. Most appear to have been victims of Nazi persecution or profess to be victims of Polish persecution." But the memo also insisted that "nearly all admit to leaving their homes voluntarily [underscored in original] now, several months after cessation of hostilities, and set Berlin as their objective because from this point westward they assume aid will be given." Lieutenant Colonel Harry Messec, representing the Office of Military Government for Germany at the meeting, declared that "the whole problem gave every indication of an organized and directed movement despite an attempt to make it appear otherwise." Messec was right, of course, as these Jews had certainly passed into Germany with the aid of the Brichah. Messec clearly felt the Army was being manipulated and lied to. "It is believed here," his memo concluded, "that these people are not being displaced by any internal policy of the Polish government or organized persecution and that all movements are recent individual decisions, and therefore that the United States Government has no moral responsibility toward such persons." Yet Messec knew this could be an explosive issue. "It appears," he wrote in a cover letter to the memo, "that insufficient specific guidance has been given this office in the matter, and that the problem is of such magnitude and implications that advice on a governmental level is desirable." The Army, quite clearly, was at a loss.[46]

Part of the problem lay in getting a clear picture of what was going on. The fluidity of the overall situation must be stressed: there was very sketchy information about the new arrivals, and often the reports that were available were contradictory. The number of Jewish "infiltrees" was infinitesimal compared to the massive flows of ethnic Germans who were being expelled from Poland, Hungary, and Czechoslovakia at just the same time. There was also an important change in the military occupation structure: in November, General Eisenhower returned to the United States. His position as commander of U.S. forces in the European Theater and of the occupation forces in Germany was taken over by General Joseph T. McNarney. Eisenhower, through the Harrison report, had become personally invested in the Jewish DP problem and had made sincere efforts to improve their lot; McNarney had little background or awareness of the issue, and was reluctant to make it one of his priorities. Through the late fall, commanders on the ground had no clear directives from Washington or from the occupation authorities about how to handle the new Jewish refugees. Without clear guidance, a gentleman's agreement took hold between Jews and the Army: Jews from Poland and the east would be let into the U.S. zone and treated humanely, but they would have to manage within the existing camp system, as no major new effort on their behalf would be made.

The result, predictably enough, was that existing DP centers quickly became overcrowded. According to a JDC report, the conditions in Landsberg had shown "marked deterioration" after October; "overcrowding is serious, sanitation is deplorable; clothing supplies are extremely short." At Föhrenwald, "the situation has deteriorated to such an extent that problems there are of a graver character today than in any other camp in the American zone." The housing shortage at Zeilsheim was also acute and the military refused to requisition any more German homes; camp residents were packed into damp barracks, sleeping on concrete floors, while facing an extreme shortage of coal.[47] Yet these conditions, bad as they were, did not unduly alarm American military authorities. In early December, Leo Srole, the educator and UNRRA official in Landsberg, announced his resignation and sent a strongly worded protest to Judge Rifkind and, via Abraham Klausner, to the newspapers, about the overcrowded conditions and lack of comforts in Landsberg. Immediately, General Walter Bedell Smith conducted a tour of inspection and declared the camp adequately supplied. This report was given added credibility by the presence of Judge Rifkind, who soon cabled to the World Jewish Congress headquarters in New York that hyperbolic assertions of epidemics, starvation, and misery inside the DP camps were "irresponsible stories." Conditions were not perfect, he readily acknowledged, but in his estimation the Army was making a great effort on behalf of the Jewish camp residents, while providing minimal shelter and aid to newcomers.[48]

If the camps continued to provide for a rudimentary level of existence, the infiltrees nonetheless antagonized Army and UNRRA officials. Numerous observers were struck by officials' steadfast refusal to undertake major requisitions of housing, in part because to do so would displace Germans and so create a new aggrieved population of homeless, and partly because there remained deep skepticism about the motives of the newly arriving Jews. U.S. military officers cast doubt on the claims of persecution. Messec made a tour of three assembly centers in Berlin on December 19, and after interviewing dozens of recently arrived residents, concluded that "the stories of persecution [by Poles] do not stand up under interrogation." Instead, Messec claimed that "as a group, they are congenital psychopathic liars" and dismissed them with contempt: the "real cause" of the migration of Jews out of Poland was simply that they did not wish to engage in "the hard work to reestablish a war wracked nation."[49]

This was a view apparently shared by British commanders, who encountered Jewish refugees in the British zone of Austria. As early as October 2, Lieutenant-Colonel O'Dwyer, deputy director of the Displaced Persons division in the Allied Commission for Austria, declared that the arrival of Jews at the Austrian DP camps in Graz, Trofaiach, and Judenburg was the result of "a highly organized racket." The new arrivals, he said, were "well clothed, well shod, full of money, and prosperous looking; they are fat, greasy, and arrogant. Their story is that they have been in concentration camps in Poland and elsewhere. This may be so, but if so, they must have been very comfortable camps. . . . They are obstructive, undisciplined, and thoroughly uncooperative." A month later, Major General W. H. Stratton, chief of staff in the British headquarters in Austria, also reported to London his conclusion that Jewish movements were the result of "an organized move into the British zone by refugee Jews, directed by Jewish agencies." These newcomers stood out because "they arrive generally better fed and clothed, have more money, move more freely and are less well-behaved" than other DPs. And again, a few weeks later, British headquarters in Austria complained that the Jewish refugees "have been difficult to handle since their arrival and have openly avowed their intention of making a nuisance of themselves until they are allowed to proceed to Palestine."[50] Given that these views were fairly widespread among the British commanders on the ground in Europe, it was perhaps not surprising that another senior British general, Sir Frederick Morgan, the head of UNRRA's DP branch in Germany, should have aired similar sentiments. Following a press conference in early January, Morgan casually told reporters that he suspected that Jews were being aided by a secret Jewish organization, and that new arrivals were "well dressed, well fed, rosy-cheeked, and with their pockets bulging with money." These Jews "all have the same monoto-nous story about pogroms," but their stories were unsupported by fact.[51] This seemed to be a widespread view, despite growing evidence of atrocities in Poland against Jews. Not until the especially bloody murder of forty-one Jews in the town of Kielce on July 4, 1946, would the doubters finally be silenced.

With that pogrom, the exodus out of Poland gained still greater momen-tum: in the summer of 1946, according to Bauer, over 90,000 Jews from Eastern Europe made their way westward, there to join a fragile, tenta-tive population of camp-dwelling Jews, suspended between liberation and freedom. It is a sordid truth: for thousands of Jews in Europe, the promise brought by the Allied armies in April had turned sour by the end of 1945. For most of them, this awkward limbo would endure until 1948, when at long last the final leg of their journey ended on the shores of an independent Israel. For Jews, then, the war's end was no end at all but an intermediate stage on a longer path toward survival and regeneration. Their long wait appears in retrospect an unconscionable delay, another tragedy in a landscape already crowded with tragedies. Even so, this Jewish passage through postwar Europe contains within its complexity and messiness something of the mirac-ulous. Here, among blackened bricks and bleached bones, small bands of Jews faced their future with grim determination; and alongside them stood, often uneasily, American soldiers who had defeated the Nazi regime, and now provided shelter and protection for its victims. There is ample evidence to show that many Army officials were slow to realize the scope of the Jew-ish catastrophe, and reluctant to take up the cause of these survivors. Yet as Judge Simon Rifkind stated in an address to an audience of American Jews in April 1946, "were it not for the [American] Army, there would not be any Jews in Central Europe today to constitute a Jewish problem. The survival of the remnant of Israel is the result of the courage and devotion of American soldiers of all creeds and colors." Rifkind was right to salute the efforts of the U.S. Army, which had done so much to secure Jewish liberation. Yet it fell to the Jews alone to transform this liberation into freedom, and here is where the real heroism lay. After a decade of genocide and persecution, Jews in Europe remained focused on renewal and regeneration, and they did so, as Judge Rifkind put it, "as a brigade of free men, united by common memories and fired by a common aspiration to live again as a people."[52]

10

Belsen and the British

A T THE CLOSE of the Second World War, the surviving Jews in Europe believed that the suffering they had endured at the hands of the Third Reich now entitled them to a state of their own: a home that would be built in Palestine. The Jews of Europe had tried integration; they had even tried segregation; and still they had been persecuted and slaughtered. Surely now, in the wake of the Holocaust, the world would make every effort to hasten the Jews on their passage to Palestine, where they might pursue the lives and hopes that Europe had so cruelly denied them.

The British government did not see things the same way. Britain in 1945 controlled Palestine under a two-decade-old League of Nations mandate, making Palestine a colony at one remove. Yet for Britain, it was also a piece of an informal empire, a wide sphere of influence that stretched the length of the Mediterranean Sea, from Gibraltar through Greece to the Near East and down to Cairo and Suez. Palestine was an important foothold in a strategically vital part of the world through which the routes to India ran, and whence came Britain's oil supplies. Britain had long held to a policy of limiting Jewish immigration into Palestine and had done so throughout the 1930s, claiming that the interests of the region would be served by maintaining an Arab majority there. Jewish immigration, this argument ran, could only upset this balance, cause civil strife, and require a more muscular British police role there. In 1945, a weakened and financially insecure Britain did not have the resources to police its empire in this manner, making it all the more imperative that Jews not be allowed to go to Palestine in large numbers. To defend this indefensible position, the British frequently resorted to a convenient formulation. Jews, British officials stated repeatedly, did not constitute a separate people or "race." Indeed, to assert their difference was only to play into the hands of the anti-Semites who had persecuted Jews all these years. Jews had suffered, but so had others; they deserved only the same treatment and rights as other DPs in liberated Europe. Unlike, say, Poles or Czechs, this argument went, the Jews did not constitute a distinct "nation," and they certainly could make no special claim to a Jewish state that rested solely upon their persecution at the hands of the Nazis. The positions staked out by the British government and the Jewish survivors were diametrically opposed. The stage was set for a violent clash, and it occurred in Germany, in a highly charged setting: the camp of Bergen-Belsen.[1]

In the American zone of occupation in Germany, the Jewish DPs were spread out in a dozen main camps and many smaller groupings. In the British zone, however, most Jewish DPs congregated in one place: the DP camp that was built on the ruins of Bergen-Belsen. This concentration camp occupied a central place in the British popular mind. On April 15, Belsen was liberated by British soldiers of the 21st Army Group. Grotesque images of this sprawling camp complex, in which were imprisoned 60,000 people, saturated the British press in the months of April and May. At the moment of its liberation, the camp was in a state of indescribable filth and desolation. More than 10,000 bodies were strewn about the grounds. In the British vernacular about World War II, "Belsen" became the standard term to refer to the evils of the concentration camp system and the depravity of the men who had designed it.[2]

As the spring yielded to summer and fall, however, the reality of Belsen changed. The bodies were buried. The army evacuated the pestilential huts of the camp and burned them; on May 21, a solemn ceremony was held as the last hut was torched. A giant portrait of Hitler was placed atop the structure, and the flames soon rendered it into ashes. The camp inmates, most of whom were ill and emaciated, were transferred to other parts of the camp with more substantial barracks that had been used by the German soldiers and by the panzer training facility nearby. By midsummer, the British forces had set up an efficient and well-supplied hospital to serve the camp, and named it after the deputy director of the medical service of the Second Army, Brigadier Llewelyn Glyn Hughes, who led the relief effort in the camp just after its liberation. Belsen became a displaced persons camp, and the British authorities renamed it Camp Hohne, after a nearby village. But for its Jewish inhabitants—and Jews made up about two-thirds of the residents of this DP camp—it was always Belsen.

In the months following liberation, the Belsen DP camp became the site of an acute political struggle between Jews and the British authorities in occupied Germany. For the British, relief work inside liberated Belsen possessed a certain nobility. Army officers and relief workers often conceived of Belsen as a stage on which a certain kind of British decency and justice was on display.

As the British occupation forces described it, their mission at Belsen was to heal these victims of the Nazis so that they could return to their lives inside a liberated, and tolerant, Europe. In addition to feeding, clothing, and sheltering over ten thousand desperately needy Jews, the British initiated a vigorous war crimes trial of Belsen's former commandant, Josef Kramer, and over forty guards who had turned the camp into such a hellhole. In the British mind, Belsen was a case study of liberation and the restoration of order.

The Jews of Belsen saw the camp in a very different light. They devoted single-minded focus to an objective that Britain steadfastly opposed: their release from the blood-soaked soil of Europe and the pursuit of a new life in a Jewish state in Palestine. For these survivors, there could be no question of remaining in Europe, or indeed of returning to a now-lost prewar Jewish life. In this line of reasoning, Belsen served not as a place of healing and recovery so much as a staging point for the battle ahead—a battle directed principally against Britain. As part of this struggle, Jewish camp residents, often through intermediaries in London and New York, strategically deployed an image of an unfree Belsen—a place where illness and hunger still stalked Jews, where barbed wire confined Jewish freedom, where British guards had taken over the persecution once practiced by Germans. Leaders in the camps knew that such explosive images could undermine the British defenses that still enclosed Palestine. Belsen, then, was no mere way station for the ill and the homeless; it was a tinderbox of competing hopes and aspirations, a dangerous mixture of anger, pride, and determination.

The conditions that the British soldiers encountered as they entered Belsen on April 15 were carefully, meticulously documented by the British medical personnel who arrived in the camp in late April.[3] An investigation carried out by Lieutenant-Colonel F. M. Lipscombe of the Royal Army Medical Corps reported that camp inmates had been subsisting since January on a daily diet of 300 grams of rye bread, watery soup, and a root vegetable called mangold wurzel, a cousin of the beet and normally used as cattle feed. As in all concentration camps, "what each individual actually received depended mainly on his ability to obtain it"—that is, the weak and feeble went without. "The great majority of the internees had received no food or water for some five days before the camp was uncovered." The inmates suffered from scabies, dysentery, sepsis of sores and wounds, typhus, tuberculosis, and the debilitating effects of prolonged malnourishment. The psychiatric scars were also visible. According to Lipscombe, "the loss of moral standards and sense of responsibility for the welfare of others was widespread," and the normal human "fear of death and cruelty was blunted by repeated exposure—this especially noticeable in children."[4]

Military reports that account for the conditions inside Belsen adopted a somewhat callous, even contemptuous tone, reflecting the fact that the army found the prisoners difficult, awkward, and repellent. Their very survival raised the suspicions of the officers, as is evident from one summary report.

The internees were from every strata of society, of every race and nationality in Europe and in all stages of mental, moral and physical degeneration. From the highest type of intellectual and member of the *Maquis* [underground resistance] to the lowest habitual criminals, homosexuals and murderers. Those who survived at the time of our arrival did so for one or more of three reasons: 1) recent arrival 2) the holding of some position on the staff of the camp under the Germans and 3) through being above the average unscrupulous cunning evaders of the rules. Then it is to be remembered that their sanitary habits had had to be perforce of the most animal. . . . It was very difficult to find internees with both the physical capacity and the moral fibre to perform even a light days work or undertake responsibility with any degree of reliability.[5]

A medical officer, after examining the worst of the patients in the field hospital, painted an unspeakable picture: All of the "seriously ill were incontinent of feces and their beds were continually soiled, as there were insufficient orderlies to change them and in any case many of them had no sheets but simply lay on covered palliasses. Almost every patient when first seen had diarrhea, although this varied from 2–3 loose stools a day to an almost continuous production of watery stools. In the latter, a movement of the bowels invariably followed after taking anything by mouth, so that the patient was afraid to eat or drink." The bodies of the patients were grotesque: "The eyes were sunken and the cheek bones jutted out. These extreme changes made all the patients look alike so that it became quite difficult to distinguish one from another. This difficulty was accentuated by the fact that all patients had had the bulk of their hair shaved off. The skin of their arms legs and anterior-abdominal wall was often very rough, dry and scaly. There were large bed sores on the buttocks and the lower part of the back. The ribs stuck out. . . . The average weight of 18 males who were strong enough to stand upright on scales was 44 kilos [97 pounds]. 11 females averaged 35.3 kilos [78 pounds]."[6] At the moment of liberation, according to one estimate, the death rate in the camp was running at about 300–400 people per day. The British medical teams took pride in reporting that by May 15—one month after the liberation of the camp—the death rate had fallen to 88 per day.[7]

The challenge of restoring order and basic hygiene to this appalling place proved difficult. The camp had no food, the meager water supply was contaminated—bodies were floating in the concrete water tanks—the camp was littered with corpses, and there were no medical supplies. Of the 60,000 in the camp upon liberation, nearly 14,000 died within days. While some 17,000 able-bodied prisoners were repatriated quickly, after receiving a dose of DDT and perhaps a rudimentary bath, the British army still faced the task of providing shelter and medical aid to some 29,000 camp inmates, half of whom were desperately ill. Although precise records were not kept, it appears that after further repatriation of inmates and various transfers both in and out of the camp, by June the camp contained about 18,000 people, 12,000 of whom were Polish, Hungarian, and Romanian Jews.[8]

The British army moved quickly. The Eighth Army delivered a convoy of food and water within a day or so of the camp's liberation. Just down the road from Belsen, the Germans had built a large panzer training school, complete with ninety concrete barracks, recreation and medical facilities, and well-stocked supply depots. As the British soldiers began to transfer Belsen inmates there, they found in the storerooms tons of canned foods and supplies, locked away, untouched. These were gradually distributed, though many prisoners could not yet eat solid food. A bakery and a dairy nearby were mobilized on behalf of the camp—actions the Germans had notably failed to undertake—and the requisitioning of food from the nearby villages also commenced. Within two days of the camp's liberation, a British medical unit arrived on the scene; by April 18, typhus patients were transferred to an improvised quarantine area among the former German military barracks. The full-scale evacuation of the camp to the panzer school and other nearby barracks began on April 24. This was a massive project, as the chief nurse in the camp, Muriel Knox Doherty, described in her letters home during this period. All inmates, she wrote, "were taken to a large building, all their clothing removed and burned and their bodies cleansed of the gross filth and deloused. A colossal undertaking, dusting some 30–40,000 people with DDT powder!" A cleansing station—termed the "human laundry"—was set up to wash patients. Here, "British Tommies supervised German nurses and attendants, who were obliged to cleanse, wash and dust these poor naked and ill creatures, cut their hair and wrap them in three fresh blankets."[9] Within a matter of weeks, the former recreational facilities of the German soldiers were transformed into a makeshift hospital sufficient for 14,000 patients—and this at a time when the war had not yet terminated, and supplies were short across Germany and Europe.

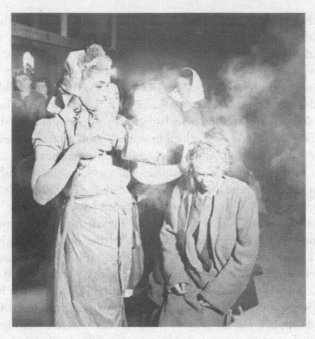

A nurse in Belsen sprays a freshly washed and clothed camp resident
with DDT powder to kill typhus-bearing lice. *Imperial War Museum*

Conditions in the new camp remained awful, however. As Doherty
recalled, there were not nearly enough doctors or supplies to handle such a
flood of patients; many died, or lay in stinking cots amid patients with typhus
and dysentery. Even in the new medical facilities, "nursing conditions were
primitive and over-crowded. There were insufficient bed-pans, practically no
sputum mugs, and drugs were in hopelessly short supply in the early days.
. . . Thousands of patients were in the advanced stages of tuberculosis and it
was impossible at first to separate them from the typhus cases; others were
still dehydrated and exhausted." Among the beds that crammed every room
and lined every corridor, "an army of flies had taken possession; they were
everywhere in millions, thriving on the food hoarded by the prisoners. They
occupied the wards and swarmed over everything. There were no mosquito
nets and the weak were unable to protect their faces."[10]

In all, it took almost a month to empty Belsen and transfer the former
prisoners to better facilities in the panzer school barracks, and in the meantime, many prisoners remained in Belsen amidst the filth in which the Germans had imprisoned them. Yet the British soldiers and doctors and nurses

worked tirelessly in wretched conditions to save lives. They did so, by the thousands. And the survivors of Belsen knew that what had been accomplished there was worth protecting. In late May, the British authorities tried to transfer a thousand Polish Jews to another DP camp located in a former SS camp at Lingen, near the Dutch border. As the Jewish chaplain Leslie Hardman told it, "they were taken in army trucks, traveled over bad roads, and arrived at Lingen after dark. . . . On arrival they did not want to leave the trucks, and implored to be taken back. The authorities had not sufficient notice of their coming and, although a meal was hastily prepared, it was difficult to distribute the food. People stumbled about in the darkness and there was great confusion. The chaplain who went with them reported that everything was below the standard of life already reached in liberated Belsen. The accommodation consisted of wooden huts, many rooms of which were unfit for habitation, since there were holes in the sides and roofs; there was no electricity, and the sanitation arrangements were inadequate." A Quaker relief worker in Lingen confirmed that the camp lacked "paper, pencils, furniture, bedding, clothing," and faced "gross overcrowding." Newcomers, including the 1,117 Jews from Belsen, were expected to provide their own utensils and bedding. The Reverend I. Richards reported to the *Jewish Chronicle* that the transport to Lingen of Belsen Jews was a fiasco, and that "everything is so far below the standard of the past few weeks at Belsen that many did not wish to leave the trucks and implored to be sent back." Within a few days, many of these survivors began to flee Lingen on their own, gradually making their way back to the camp at Belsen. Here is a vivid example of the paradoxical world of 1945: in late May, Jews seeking safety, security, and a minimal standard of living and medical care wished to get *into* the camp at Bergen-Belsen.[11]

———

NOT ONLY DID the British seek to restore the bodies of the freed Belsen survivors, they also believed it was their duty to restore their "character." This posed an awkward challenge. Derek Sington, the intelligence officer who spent most of May and June in Belsen, felt it was imperative that the camp authorities make the inhabitants "feel, think, behave, and react as people in a normal moral society. For in the inferno they had come out of, corruption, superior physical strength, cunning, evasion, plunder and illegal action had been the only means of survival. . . . Who can be astonished that these thousands of human beings who emerged from these years of terror were amoral and unsocial?" Consequently, "British troops were faced with a problem of mental and moral reconditioning."[12] Indeed, the leading Jewish newspaper in London, the weekly *Jewish Chronicle*, agreed: "no people," its editorial page wrote, "who have lived through such an ordeal can possibly be normal. . . . Their sickness is no less real because it is of the mind."[13] But as a practical matter, how was such "moral reconditioning" to be undertaken? And who would guide it, along what lines?

For Sington and other British camp authorities, rehabilitation meant recivilization: "There remained the task," he wrote, "of re-accustoming 15,000 people to enjoyment in work, of teaching many of them to trust and respect authority rather than defy and outwit it, of persuading them to regard regulations and rules as benevolent and not diabolical." To do so, efforts were made to create some sense of culture: a reading room was arranged and two hundred volumes were made available, including incongruous works such as "Macaulay's *Essays* and the novels of Galsworthy, Oscar Wilde, Alphonse Daudet and Warwick Deeping." There were, however, no Polish or Hungarian books, and as most DPs at Belsen could not read English, "the library was not used a great deal."[14] More successful was the staging of cabarets, featuring Polish dances, a choir of Russian girls singing partisan songs, a Yugoslav women's choir ("tough and Amazonian in blue slacks and white pullovers"), and violin and piano concertos, staged under a great tent in the panzer training school grounds. The first of these debuted on May 24, a mere six weeks after the liberation of Belsen. A Quaker relief volunteer, Hugh Jenkins, recalled that after that evening's concert, a dance was held, and the camp residents danced under the lighted tents for hours. A "bonny lass" reminded him that a month earlier, he had given her aspirin in a first aid post just days after the camp's liberation. Jenkins danced with a Romanian girl who had sung in the performance. "I never thought I'd know how to dance, sing, and be happy again," she told him. Small comfort, perhaps, but evenings such as these, with their ability to suspend the unpleasant realities of camp life, became a constant feature in Belsen.[15]

In the Belsen hospital, which was run by UNRRA welfare staff, patients were urged to undertake needlework, sculpture, and crafts of all sorts; in October, their work was put on display in UNRRA's London headquarters. Ms. Erica Fischova-Gachova, the hospital's chief welfare officer, explained the project in these terms: "a large percentage of the former slave laborers and war victims were not merely diseased skin and bones physically, but were like animals in temperament and action. Our welfare policy, however, called for treating them from the first as if they still had the dignity, health, and mental balance of cultivated people. . . . I try to act with each one of them just as I would with English aristocracy or with the President or First Lady of the United States." Ms. Fischova, herself a Czech Jew whose family was murdered in the gas chambers, believed that working with their hands would give Belsen patients a chance to show their creative powers while also restoring to them a sense of self-worth and dignity.[16]

But for the Jews of Belsen, politics mattered more than the kind of cultural and intellectual self-improvement that seemed to preoccupy the British authorities. Within days of the liberation, Josef Rosensaft, a thirty-four-year-old Polish survivor of Auschwitz and a former left-wing Zionist organizer, headed up the formation of a leadership committee of Jewish DPs in Belsen; this remained provisional until September, when the Central Committee of Liberated Jews in the British Zone was founded. (Rosensaft remained its chairman until 1950).[17] Rosensaft operated in an atmosphere of conflict and rivalry with the British military authorities in the camp. No sooner had the provisional committee been formed than it made demands upon the British authorities: unrestricted emigration of Jews to Palestine; prompt improvement of living conditions, including improved cultural, educational, and vocational services; recognition of the committee as the legitimate representative of the Jews in the British zone; and the creation of Jewish-only camps. Grateful though they were for the humanitarian aid the British had delivered, Jewish leaders knew their priority lay in breaking this dependence upon the British and in redressing the balance of power within the camps. The committee leaders in Belsen wanted to be self-governing, and wanted British authorities and regulations kept to a minimum. The committee supported the publication of what was really at first an underground Yiddish newspaper, *Unzer Sztyme* (Our Voice), which the British authorities did not officially recognize until May 1947. Rosensaft used "devious" and "illegal" means, according to one Joint official, to help subvert British control of the camp, especially in registering Jewish camp residents, operating an unofficial tracing service, and running a mail service that circumvented the military.[18] In further defiance of British regulations, on September 25–27, the committee hosted a meeting in Belsen of Jewish leaders from across the British zone; 210 delegates, including representatives of international Jewish aid organizations, convened and uniformly called for the prompt opening of Palestine to Jewish emigration.[19] Certainly, any effort by camp authorities to encourage Jews to "respect authority rather than defy and outwit it," as Sington had hoped, appeared hopelessly naïve.[20]

With such unequivocal Jewish demands, there could be little prospect of any easy Anglo-Jewish cooperation in the camp once the crisis of the liberation period had passed. The degree of antagonism between Jews and the British increased steadily as the summer changed into fall. The reason for this lies in the intransigence of the British government with respect to

Palestine. Repeatedly pressed by Jewish survivors to allow the creation of Jewish-only camps, and Jewish self-government in the British zone, the British army refused, fully aware that to relent would only make it easier for Jews to organize and exert greater pressure for emigration to Palestine. British officials opposed Jewish emigration to Palestine and the creation of a national Jewish state because it complicated their colonial and strategic position in the Near East. Therefore, Britain refused to sanction the creation of any Jewish political institutions in Germany. The language that was used to state this policy is striking in its frank defiance of Jewish aspirations. When Leonard Cohen of the Jewish Committee for Relief Abroad in London sent an urgent letter to the British military government in early July asking that Jews be allowed to congregate in Jewish camps in order to find solace, community, and fraternity, his request was dismissed in the following peremptory tone by Major-General B. V. Britten of the British military government in Germany: "segregation would result in a large body of Jews of many nationalities who would probably refuse repatriation and constitute a continuous embarrassment. It is considered that the policy should continue to be to emphasize a Jew's political nationality rather than his race and religious persuasion. Preferential treatment of Jews would be unfair to the many non-Jews who have suffered on account of their clandestine and other activities in the Allied cause. It would also cause irritation and anti-Jewish feeling on the part of the non-Jewish DPs which might well have far reaching results and give rise to persecution at a later date. . . . The cruelties and hardships to which the Jews in Germany have been subjected are appreciated but the Jews have not been the only sufferers and a balanced view is necessary."[21] General Britten's attitude was consistent with a widely shared view at the time within British official circles that Jews deserved nothing less but nothing more than other Europeans who also were struggling to rebuild their lives after the war. At the very least, this comment reveals a striking ignorance of what Europe's Jews had experienced in the preceding twelve years, and how those experiences might condition Jewish demands.

General Britten was not alone in his sentiments. The British official records are permeated with this tone of irritation, annoyance, and downright hostility to the idea of treating Jews at all differently from any other group of displaced or distressed persons. The idea that Jewish DPs ought to have a special Jewish chaplain serve as a liaison to the Allied armies was considered by General A. V. Anderson in the War Office "to involve the creation of special preferential treatment for the benefit of a particular religious sect," and therefore unacceptable.[22] When General Eisenhower announced, in the wake of Earl Harrison's visit, that Jews in the American zones would now be housed together in Jewish-only camps, the Foreign Office denounced the policy in these terms: "We are strongly against the idea, sedulously fostered by many Jewish organizations, that Jewry enjoys a supranational status, and it would indeed be disastrous for the Jews themselves if they were accorded special treatment on this basis in comparison with the people of the country where they live."[23] Major-General G. W. R. Templer, the army's chief of staff in the British zone of occupation, believed that "segregation of Jews as a special race . . . would be in accordance with the theory propounded by the Nazis and all other organizations which have persecuted Jews in the past."[24] The cabinet agreed with this view, and the Foreign Office conveyed its displeasure to the United States government: "To accept the policy advocated by Harrison is to imply in effect that there is no future in Europe for persons of Jewish race. This is surely a counsel of despair. . . . Indeed it would go far by implication to admit that Nazis were right in holding that there was no place for Jews in Europe."[25] The British seemed eager to take the moral high road, arguing that segregation of Jews in camps was a policy against which the Allies had fought and one that should not now be practiced in occupied Germany. But at the heart of the British policy lay a profound and shocking denial of the realities and the scope of the Jewish catastrophe that had just unfolded in Europe. The British opposed both a Jewish homeland in Palestine and Jewish camps in Germany. The future for Jews, it seemed, could be secured only if Jews ceased to be Jews, and simply melted away into the landscape of postwar Europe.

An example of this official self-satisfaction is evident in an exchange of letters between the Marchioness of Reading, head of the British section of the World Jewish Congress, and British military officials. Lady Reading wrote to Field Marshal Montgomery in late September, beseeching him for help in improving conditions for Jews still in Germany. "I feel sure," she implored, "you cannot be cognizant of the conditions that still exist in the camps today," such as "lack of bedding, overcrowding, insufficient diet, an atmosphere of imprisonment, total lack of occupation, breeding a spirit of despair among the captives who hoped for so much from their liberation." She concluded: "I find it difficult to write with restraint when I think of these things, for I can so vividly imagine all the hopes that were focused on the liberation during the hell these people passed through: of their intense desire to leave the scene of their anguish forever, to walk out into the world free men and women."[26]

Lady Reading received a detailed reply and memorandum from General Templer, thanking her for her letter but refuting entirely its contents. "In no case are camps quite as bad as your letter might lead one to believe." Admittedly, the army had focused initially on repatriation, "possibly at the expense of the welfare of DPs who could not be repatriated," in other words, Jews. Yet since the summer, housing, food, clothing, and quality of life in the DP camps had all improved, he asserted. Postal links between camps had been set up, a tracing service begun, educational facilities put in place; DPs were even getting a weekly ration of cigarettes "greater than that of British troops." An attached memorandum sent to Lady Reading underscored these broad points, insisting, among other things, that Jews were not living in Belsen, which had been burned, but in a new camp called Hohne; that levies had been made upon German citizens to provide blankets, food, and clothing for DPs; that DPs were now accommodated in "German barracks . . . or in wooden huts properly waterproofed and with heating arrangements." Above all, DPs in the British zone were assured of 2,000 calories per day in food-stuffs. As to claims of an atmosphere of imprisonment, the memo stated that the barbed wire that encircled camps was "purely to prevent any German civilians wandering around the camp." The real problems that camp authori-ties faced were due to the inclination of DPs to sell their clothes, cigarettes and rations to Germans on the black market, and to the unwillingness of Jewish camp residents "to work and help themselves." In short, the Brit-ish occupation authorities had persuaded themselves that Jews, like all other DPs, were being treated fairly, and what troubles did arise were largely due to their own impatience and frustration.[27]

Lady Reading's anxious letter was but one in a chorus of voices in Brit-ain and the United States that raised pointed and embarrassing questions about the British government's handling of the DP problem, and by the fall of 1945 it became increasingly difficult for British officials to dispel such criticism. Whereas the Americans after Harrison's visit had embraced the idea of Jewish-only DP camps in their zone, the British occupation authori-ties resisted it, and Jewish leaders kept up a barrage of criticism that soon turned into a bitter standoff. The *Jewish Chronicle* kept up a steady drumbeat about the fate of Jewish DPs. Belsen featured prominently in its pages in May and June, as reporters, Jewish chaplains, and relief workers toured the camp. Reports stressed the grave humanitarian crisis, the deplorable conditions, and the need for concerted Jewish action in Britain to provide food, medicines, and supplies to the camp. The early editorials stressed common cause with the military authorities—"the Allied authorities in charge of this problem are doing their best, and may be sure of the widest gratitude in return," said the *Chronicle* editorial page on June 1. But by mid-June, the newspaper began to run sharply worded pieces about the administrative malfeasance in the camps. "Sufferers Still Suffer," "Jewish Victims of Official Bungling," "Jewish Survivors' Hopelessness," blared headlines on June 15. On July 13, an editorial titled "They Are Being Allowed to Die!" excoriated the Allied policy in the DP camps and focused on what was becoming an obvious, and powerful, argument: "is it reasonable to forbid them [the Jewish DPs] access to that soil to which alone they turn their wistful eyes in their distress, their only possible home, their own home, the Jewish National Home? . . . It is not to be believed that this appeal will be callously rejected."[28] On July 15, the Board of Deputies of British Jews issued an appeal to the great powers, then meeting at Potsdam, to open Palestine to Jewish immigration in order to address the "desperate position" of the stateless Jews. The World Jewish Congress followed suit, and released a report on July 20 decrying the "callous and shameful neglect by Allied Military Control authorities," and cited the wretched state of Belsen in particular. This led to an investigation by British military authorities with the predictable outcome that the British army absolved itself of the charges.

The calls for linking the DP crisis to the Palestine question only increased. The World Zionist Conference, meeting in London on August 1, featured Dr. Chaim Weizmann's plea to the Labour government to open Palestine to Jewish survivors. Is it possible, Weizmann asked, that after the catastrophe of the Nazi genocide, the world would now "read over the gates of Palestine 'No Jews need apply'?" In late September, the International League for the Rights of Man added its voice to these calls for emigration of Jews in camps to Palestine; the same week, leaders of the American Jewish Committee, which had not been pro-Zionist, met with President Truman and urged him to pressure Britain to open up Palestine as a humanitarian measure to ease the crisis of the camps. The argument for doing so had become irresistible by late September, and was deftly summarized by Lady Reading herself in a letter to the London *Times:* the Jewish survivors had nourished the hope for twelve years that one day they would make it to Palestine. "What dreadful lack of imagination condemns them to exist amid the daily remembrances of past brutalities while holding out no prospect for the future?" She summarized sharply: "The Nazis broke their bodies. The United Nations are breaking their spirit."[29]

It was just at this moment when the Harrison report was released to the public, triggering President Truman's rebuke of Eisenhower for the condition of the DP camps in the American zone and leading to a sharp shift in American policy. Harrison's report also gave Truman the moral advantage to press Britain for a similar change of policy on Jewish DPs. Naturally, President Truman was sensitive to the domestic political implications of the Jewish DP crisis, but he was also genuinely aggrieved by the problem and now brought sustained pressure on the British government to ease immigration restrictions for Jews who wished to go to Palestine. Truman in fact had already sent his views to Prime Minister Attlee in late August, asking Attlee to consider revising upward the numbers of Jews allowed to emigrate to Palestine—set at 1,500 per month—as set out in the 1939 White Paper on Palestine that still formed the basis of British policy. Attlee simply refused, replying that 100,000 Jewish immigrants in Palestine would vastly complicate Britain's position in the Middle East and India by inflaming Muslim opinion. But the public campaign in the press had reached into the U.S. Congress, and a debate on October 2 in the Senate revealed an emerging consensus there that Britain's immigration policy was wrong and must be changed. Senator Edwin C. Johnson of Colorado charged that Britain has "made the Jew a political football," a comment that no doubt the British government would have had trouble swallowing. Not to be outdone, Senator James E. Murray of Montana declared British rule in Palestine to be "a black chapter in English history," and full of "evasion and duplicity." Robert Taft of Ohio, a perennial rival of Truman's, also called for the prompt transfer of 100,000 Jews "who survived the horrible persecution and tortures of the Nazis."[30]

Ernest Bevin, the embattled British foreign secretary, proposed to deflect American criticism by creating a joint Anglo-American committee to investigate the entire Jewish DP problem as it related to Palestine policy, thereby buying time and engaging the Americans in finding a solution to the problem. The Americans agreed. But Bevin's announcement of the new committee did nothing to ease the barrage of criticism the government faced. Indeed, Bevin sadly mishandled the announcement, burying it inside a House of Commons statement that also reiterated the policy of the government to abide by the terms of the 1939 White Paper. Bevin reiterated the government's "dual obligation" to Jews and Arabs, and in any case declared that immigration by Europe's Jews to Palestine would not solve the problems that European Jewry now faced. What Jews in Palestine and in Europe had been hoping for—a new departure, and a revision of immigration quotas—had not materialized. Instead, there was to be a committee to investigate a problem that had been in full-blown crisis for over six months. Bevin, while speaking to reporters after his Commons speech, said that the great problem with the Balfour Declaration, which in 1917 had promised the Jews a national home in Palestine, was that it had been "unilateral" and had "not taken account of the Arabs." They had "their fears of Zionism" which must be taken into account, Bevin said. He hoped "the Jews in Europe shall not overemphasize their racial position. . . . If the Jews with all their sufferings want to get too much at the head of the queue, you have the danger of another anti-Semitic reaction through it all."[31]

The reaction to Bevin's House of Commons speech among Jews was furious. In Palestine, on November 14, Jews went on a twelve-hour strike; a crowd set fire to British government buildings in Tel Aviv and clashed with military police, resulting in seven deaths and twenty-seven wounded. The British 6th Airborne Division turned Tel Aviv into "an armed camp."[32] In London, the Board of Deputies of British Jews denounced Bevin's speech, as did Chaim Weizmann, the president of the Jewish Agency, who was in Atlantic City, New Jersey, to address the convention of the Zionist Organization of America. Some members of the House of Commons dismissed Bevin's idea for a committee, and called the immigration quota of 1,500 Jews per month "a meager contribution towards the desperate need of the people still living in concentration camp conditions in Germany." Barnett Janner, a member of Bevin's party, said "the White Paper ought to be swept aside and the gates of Palestine opened at once."[33] The reactions among the DPs in Germany was especially anguished. In the British zone, a number of scuffles with British military police took place, including one incident in Hannover (just a few miles from the Belsen camp). There, four hundred Polish Jews from the DP camp at Vinnhorst staged a protest of British policy, and waved banners reading, in English, "We want the gates of Palestine opened," and "We demand a Jewish country." A military policeman, one Corporal Cooper, ordered the banners taken down, resulting in a clash and a thrashing of Corporal Cooper by the protestors. Ten arrests were subsequently made. (In December, eight protestors were convicted of promoting an unauthorized gathering and resisting British police forces.)[34] In the American zone, Jews were equally outraged and announced a twenty-four-hour hunger strike. In Landsberg, Samuel Gringauz, in the *Landsberger Lager-Cajtung*, wrote that Bevin's decision "not to open the gates of Eretz Israel for the survivors is one of the greatest betrayals that a democratic and socialist body has ever committed." In a scathing editorial, Gringauz called Bevin's message "a fivefold betrayal." It was a betrayal of the sacrifices made by the thousands of Jews who fought under arms alongside the Allies in the war; a betrayal of the Balfour Declaration; a betrayal of the historical reality of the Nazi war on the Jews; a betrayal of the moral purpose of the war against Nazism and brutality; and a betrayal of the socialist ideals of the Labour Party. The break between Britain and the Jewish DPs appeared complete.[35]

What did Bevin achieve by his delaying tactics and his prevarication? Underground Jewish organizations in Palestine now opened up a sustained campaign of violence against the British presence there that would lead to increased deaths of British soldiers. Bevin's Anglo-American Committee of Inquiry backfired: once it got under way, its members became increasingly convinced of the need to relent and allow Jewish immigration to Palestine, if only to relieve the horrible conditions they found in DP camps. The committee's final report, to Bevin's everlasting fury, called for the immediate immigration of 100,000 Jews from DP camps to Palestine.[36] Truman left Bevin hanging by indicating that he still supported prompt immigration to Palestine, whatever the committee might conclude. And in a remarkable coincidence, the *New York Times* ran a critical story on November 20, just a week after Bevin's speech, that quoted unnamed UNRRA officials and the leader of the Belsen Jewish committee, Josef Rosensaft, to the effect that conditions in Belsen were "appalling." There was no heat, inadequate clothing, and shortages of medicine; worse, Rosensaft said, the British censored the camp newspaper and prohibited any expressions in favor of emigration to Palestine. The British ambassador in Washington, Lord Halifax, saw this as a deliberate effort to embarrass the British government, and asked London "for some clear public statement . . . on what we are attempting to do to improve conditions for Jews in the camps in Europe."[37] Halifax also had secured a copy of an especially damning report sent (via telegram) by Joint chairman Edward Warburg to Truman's adviser, White House counsel Sam Rosenman. While praising the job done by Judge Rifkind in the U.S. zone, Warburg leveled a serious charge at the British. "Seven months after Liberation, conditions British zone most alarming. . . . No winter clothes, no desperately needed shoes, no coal or wood, inadequate housing . . . threat of epidemic alarmingly real. Corrective action still lacking. Urge consideration highest levels." The response of the British army to these allegations—which were real enough—typified the general attitude of the military authorities to the Jews at the close of 1945. "This is the last straw," seethed the British Control Commission in its reply to headquarters. "Jews seem to be using Belsen as a focal point for world agitation to emigrate to Palestine." One solution, recommended here, was simply to transport all the Jews out of the Belsen camp and break them up into smaller groups, thus squelching such agitation. "If we move Jews from Belsen they will not be able to use the magic word 'Belsen' in connection with this propaganda."[38]

The Jews had indeed become "a continuous embarrassment" for the British: the entire encounter with Jews in liberated Germany cast a harsh light on an ill-conceived, illogical, and self-defeating policy of curtailing Jewish emigration while incarcerating Jews in German camps. How far from the heady days of April, when those young, startled Tommies at the gates of Belsen had brought with them liberation and the promise of a new beginning.

THIS SAD TALE of deteriorating relations between the British and the Jews, starting from a high point in April and running down to the low of Bevin's November speech, has long obscured one significant achievement of the British occupation authorities. Just when the British government was coming in for heavy criticism both from Jews inside DP camps and from around the world for its policy on Palestine, the British army opened up a two-month-long war crimes trial of the Belsen commander, Josef Kramer, and his subordinates.[39] The "Belsen trial," as it became known—though in fact it included crimes committed at both Auschwitz and Belsen by Kramer and the others—ended in the hanging of Kramer and ten other defendants. It charted important new legal ground, being the first war crimes trial in occupied Germany, and it was carried out with thoroughness and careful attention to judicial norms. More than this, the trial was obliged to carry a heavy burden, for it was set up as a kind of noble project, a showcase of the rule of law, the restoration of order, and the fulfillment of the promise of liberation. The trial might offer a counterargument to those Jews clamoring for "special treatment." British law, the trial declared, could serve out justice fairly, with evenhandedness and moderation, and so provide a kind of benchmark for other nations aspiring to civilization. As we shall see, in the highly charged

Josef Kramer, styled the "Beast of Belsen" in the British press, shown in a mug shot while awaiting trial. He was hanged in December 1945.
Imperial War Museum

atmosphere of the time, the trial failed to meet these high expectations. What accounts for the failure?

Since the liberation of the camp, the British public had clamored for swift justice for Josef Kramer, Belsen's commandant, who was caricatured in the British press as the "Beast of Belsen." His evident disdain for the dying prisoners who surrounded him, his effort to deny any knowledge or responsibility for the camp and its state of desolation upon its liberation, had outraged British soldiers and the public, and he was generally portrayed by the press as a sullen, dull, brutal criminal. Kramer was described in the *London Illustrated News* as "a typical German brute—a sadistical, heavy-featured Nazi. He was quite unashamed."[40] News reports just after the camp's liberation recounted that "Britons, revolted by the daily disclosures from the newly liberated torture camps, were bitterly tired of the niceties and legalities surrounding the treatment of Kramer and other brutal Nazi jailers. In a flood of letters to newspapers and in the comment that ran through all discussion of German atrocities the British people made it clear this week their feeling that they wanted swifter justice for war criminals." "How will you kill Kremer [*sic*]?" was the cry of liberated inmates, according to the *New York Times*.[41] One Londoner concurred: "I wish the Russians had got in there and started hanging them."[42] Raymond Phillips, a barrister and the editor of the trial's official published transcript, concurred, writing in 1949 that "to many it seemed superfluous that there should be a trial at all, and the popular cry was for a summary identification and execution of the offenders." This view was never completely dispelled from the proceedings, and indeed, for many, the trial itself, with its emphasis on protecting the rights of the accused, seemed "an insult to those who had died at Belsen, and to those who had died to liberate it."[43]

The British authorities, however, were determined to follow the practices being laid out by the U.N. War Crimes Tribunal, and it was not until early June that a clear division of labor had been established: while "arch criminals" would stand trial under the International Military Tribunal being established at Nuremberg, "ordinary war criminals" in the custody of Allied military authorities could be dealt with by military courts. Kramer and his subordinates fell into the ordinary category, and so faced a court made up exclusively of five British military officers. Although the British government wanted to move speedily, it also wished to establish a process that would do credit to British legal traditions, so as to make the contrast with the Nazi regime all the more clear. The army painstakingly gathered evidence, produced witnesses, provided the accused with defense counsel, allowed the defense to answer the charges against them, and treated the prisoners with a degree of respect and dignity that they had no moral right to expect. Just five months after the liberation of Belsen, the trial of forty-five war criminals began, and it was concluded in fifty-four days. By contrast, the Nuremberg trials—against twenty-two defendants—lasted almost a year. Raymond Phillips ended his analysis of the Belsen trial by praising the government's refusal "to be stampeded into the wild justice of revenge and, at the end of a war, in bringing to the trial of its enemies . . . a cool, calm, dispassionate and unhurried determination."[44]

If the British had hoped to impress world opinion by this demonstration of evenhanded justice, however, they failed miserably. Wartime allies, especially the Russians but also the French, criticized the trial proceedings as unnecessarily attentive to the rights of the defendants. The Soviets saw this as evidence of the West's unwillingness to eradicate fascism.[45] More surprising, Jewish organizations and Jewish survivors paid the trial little heed. Partly this had to do with coincidence: the trial reached its critical stage just as Bevin's November speech on Palestine so inflamed Jews around the world. But there is also another factor—the absence of Jews at the heart of the Belsen trial. British prosecutors, though diligent in ferreting out details of the criminality of the Belsen guards, refused to place Jewish victimization in the forefront of their case. For the British military and civil administration, the Jewish wartime experience was not unique, or even qualitatively different from that of other victims of Nazi oppression. The Belsen defendants, in the charge laid out by the British military court, were not on trial for crimes against Jews, nor indeed for genocide, but for mistreating and abusing *Allied nationals*. This latter was a broad category and one that certainly included Jews from Allied nations like Poland and the Soviet Union. But the fact that Jews as a distinct people, with a destiny now marked by unique tragedy, did not occupy a central place in the trial only underscored Britain's failure to address the realities of the Nazi genocidal war on Europe's Jews.

Jewish victimization did not frame the Belsen trial, and for some scholars this absence has been enough to condemn the proceedings as seriously flawed.[46] Yet suffering there was aplenty in the exposition set out by the prosecution, and it is worth noting the detailed record that the prosecution amassed in drawing a portrait of life inside Belsen and Auschwitz. Indeed, the British undertook the investigative work with enormous zeal. Almost immediately upon entering the camp, British soldiers diligently set out to gather evidence that would help convict Belsen's camp commandant, Josef Kramer, and officers, guards, and *kapos* who were arrested in Belsen upon its liberation. (The *kapos* were notoriously brutal prisoners who, in exchange for some privileges, collaborated with the camp authorities in policing the camp.)

Given the enormous press coverage of the ghastly conditions uncovered in Belsen, the army felt it imperative to begin judicial proceedings against those responsible without delay. On April 27, just two weeks after Belsen's liberation, the 21st Army Group sent to Belsen a team of war crimes investigators consisting of two majors, a captain, and a few noncommissioned translators. This small team was supplemented by about fifteen personnel in mid-May. Thus, some two dozen investigators were allotted to a camp of nearly 60,000 potential witnesses.

The difficulties of gathering evidence in the circumstances of a newly liberated concentration camp were extreme, and throughout the trial, the defense cast serious doubts upon the methodology of the war crimes investigators. The largest body of evidence presented at trial were affidavits gathered by these investigators. The war crimes team simply walked through the camp grounds with a stack of photographs of guards and *kapos,* and asked witnesses to come forward to make statements about them. These statements were taken down and sworn by the deponents. The accused were seldom if ever present when the statements were sworn, and by the time the Belsen trial opened, in September, the great majority of witnesses had either been repatriated or disappeared. In short, few witnesses were produced in court, and the prosecution had to rely on what amounted to hearsay. Such a proceeding would not have been accepted in an ordinary courtroom. This did not unduly concern the military court, however, which briskly dismissed requests by the defense to throw out such questionable documentation.[47]

The trial therefore opened on September 17, 1945—Yom Kippur, as it turned out, and the very day that General Eisenhower was visiting the Feldafing DP camp. The defendants were sixteen male members of the SS, including Josef Kramer, commandant of Belsen; Dr. Fritz Klein, camp doctor in Belsen; and Franz Hoessler, commandant of Camp 2 at Belsen. Also accused were sixteen female SS guards, including Irma Grese, who commanded a compound, and Elisabeth Volkenrath, who acted as a camp overseer. Grese, who while working in Belsen had sported two long blond braids, high leather boots, and a short whip, became an irresistible target of the more lurid press accounts of the trial. In addition, twelve former *kapos* were also accused of mistreating their fellow prisoners. (The case against three other defendants was dropped.) The prosecution team was composed of four officers of the legal staff of the British army of occupation, led by Colonel T. M. Backhouse; the accused had a larger defense counsel made up of eleven British regimental officers and one Polish officer, all of whom had legal training.[48] In all, forty-four accused were arrayed in rows in a specially built dock in a gymnasium on the outskirts of Lüneburg, a small city about forty miles northeast of Belsen.

While seated in the courtroom, each defendant wore a number pinned to his or her shirtfront.

Expectations in some quarters were high. Alex Easterman, the political secretary of the British Section of the World Jewish Congress, was in attendance as an official observer, and after the opening day sent WJC headquarters in New York a perhaps hyperbolic telegram that depicted the trial as a "significantly dramatic moment in the story of civilization," as these "beasts in human form" would be "brought to justice to answer for their crimes." The trial, Easterman claimed, was recognition "that the crimes by Nazi Germany against Jews of Europe bear their own distinctive significance in character, in purpose, and in extent." Easterman relayed his sincere disappointment that the British military had not placed the "colossal crime against Jews" at the center of the indictment, but once the prosecutor began to detail the crimes of the accused, Easterman's hopes were raised that the trial would give sufficient publicity to this "drama of perfidy."[49] The *Jewish Chronicle* was also pleased with the first day of the trial: "it is fully expected," the paper reported, "that even in its limited form, this, the first war crimes trial, will be a powerful indictment of Fascism, Nazism, and anti-Semitism." The *Times* described the testimony in the opening days as "worthy of Dante" and a "nightmare."[50]

After such a buildup, the trial itself came as a disappointment. The charges were twofold: first, that the accused had, in violation of the laws and usages of war, mistreated Allied nationals in Bergen-Belsen; and, second, that some of the accused had done the same in Auschwitz. This double charge stemmed from the fact that twelve of the accused, including Kramer, Klein, Hoessler, Grese, and Volkenrath, had all worked in Auschwitz before being transferred to Belsen. As Colonel Backhouse, the lead prosecutor, made clear in his opening statement, "we are not, of course, concerned in this trial with atrocities by Germans against Germans." This distinction was vital in placing the case on the plane of international law: this was no mere internal German police matter but a question of violating previously accepted laws of war, namely, the Hague and Geneva conventions (of 1907 and 1929 respectively, to which Germany was a signatory), which governed the care and protection of prisoners of war and civilians. The Allied nationals were mistreated by the Germans, Colonel Backhouse stated, "because of their religion, or their nationality, or their refusal to work for the enemy, or merely because they were prisoners of war." Jews as a group were only occasionally singled out by the prosecution as having any particular status as victims of the Nazis. Backhouse declared that the defendants had shown "a complete disregard for the sanctity of human life and for human suffering," and that the conditions in Auschwitz and Belsen were "caused by deliberate starvation and ill-treatment, with the malicious knowledge that they must cause death." In light of the later Nuremberg trials, in which prosecutors had a difficult time showing specific acts of war crimes on the part of each individual, it is instructive that at the Belsen trial the prosecution could show "personal acts of active and deliberate cruelty and, in many cases, murder."[51]

Backhouse spent much of his opening statement dealing with the conditions in Belsen that the liberating troops had encountered on April 15—"its abominable smell, the filth and squalor of the whole place which stank to high heaven." Backhouse also zeroed in on Josef Kramer, who from December 1944 had been in command of Belsen, and was "primarily responsible for everything that happened in that camp." But Kramer had a long and horrifying personal history that predated Belsen. Kramer had spent his entire career in camps. Born in 1906 in Munich, Kramer had volunteered for the SS in 1932 and was immediately sent for duty in a concentration camp, and within this ghastly secret world he remained for the next thirteen years, moving from Dachau in 1936 to Sachsenhausen in 1937, to Mauthausen in 1939, and to Auschwitz in May 1940, where he served briefly as adjutant to camp commandant Obersturmführer Rudolf Höess. In April 1941 he was named commandant of the camp at Natzweiler, where he remained until May 1944. He was then reassigned to Auschwitz, and took charge of the camp complex of Birkenau; in December 1944, just as the death marches were getting under way, Kramer was sent to Belsen to take command of that camp—a target destination for many of the death marches. Kramer was therefore present at—and at times in command of—some of the worst charnel houses of the Second World War.[52]

Colonel Backhouse also highlighted a number of the individuals in the dock alongside Kramer. Dr. Fritz Klein, a Romanian by birth, had joined the Waffen-SS in 1943, and while in Auschwitz conducted selections of Jews for the gas chamber. Franz Hoessler, a member of the SS since 1933, had served at Auschwitz and also at the notorious Dora camp. The prosecutors, along with the press, laid particular emphasis on the cruelties perpetrated by some of the female defendants. Juana Bormann, Elisabeth Volkenrath, and Herta Ehlert had all allegedly enjoyed beating prisoners, depriving them of food and clothing, and setting dogs on them. But twenty-one-year-old Irma Grese, who with her custom-made whips and calf-high boots fit perfectly the caricature of a sadistic dominatrix, occupied a particularly prominent role in the demonology of the Belsen trial. Grese had served as a camp guard at Ravensbrück from July 1942 to March 1943; then was at Auschwitz until January 1945, when it was evacuated; she was then sent to Ravensbrück again and finally Belsen for the last month of its existence.[53] Throughout the trial, the press commented on the "defiant, contemptuous look that marred her undeniable good looks." The WJC's representative, Alex Easterman, reported that "the attention of all in court has been riveted on her" and commented on her "savage beauty—she has the cruelest eyes and tightly drawn mouth ever seen in woman." At Auschwitz and Belsen, Backhouse said, Grese was known as "the worst woman in the camp." Raymond Phillips in his account of the trial seemed unable to comprehend how so "striking" a young woman "with her youth, her blond hair, broad forehead, firmly modeled nose, and blue defiant eyes" could have carried out such atrocities.[54]

During the first eighteen days of the trial, the prosecution laid out their case using witnesses and previously gathered depositions. There were a few star witnesses, such as Brigadier Llewelyn Glyn Hughes, who gave precise and detailed descriptions of the medical crisis in the camp upon its liberation, as did Captain Derek Sington. Sington, who had been among the very first British soldiers in the camp, told the court that when he encountered Kramer, the commandant was wholly unmoved by the death around him, and merely "sat back in his arm-chair, tilted his hat back, and was generally confident. He expressed no emotion about the camp." Sington said that Kramer described the prisoners of Belsen as "habitual criminals, felons and homosexuals."[55] In addition to watching a film made by the British army that showed the state of the camp in April, the court also toured the camp grounds. There was moving testimony from a number of Jewish survivors; the courtroom was electrified by the testimony of Dr. Ada Bimko (who later married Josef Rosensaft), a Polish doctor who had survived both Auschwitz and Belsen. On September 20, she recounted—with tears running down her face—how her father, mother, brother, two sisters, husband, and six-year-old son were among the dead of Auschwitz. Given the chance to identify her tormentors, she walked slowly along the dock, pointing out fifteen of the defendants by name, and said she had seen Kramer and Grese both participate in beatings and selections in Auschwitz.[56] Two dozen other witnesses gave similar testimony alleging Kramer and the others to have participated in beatings, deliberate starvation, selections, and murder.

The defense strategy was predictable. First, they questioned the charges, bringing in a professor of international law from London University, one Colonel H. A. Smith. He argued that concentration camps in Germany had existed before the war and were legal under German law; therefore what went on in them could not be considered a war crime. He also suggested that many of those who were killed or mistreated in these camps were not, strictly speaking, Allied nationals, because once parts of Poland and various other swaths of Europe had been annexed to the Reich, the citizens there fell under

German law, and the competence of the court did not reach into internal German affairs. Finally, Colonel Smith pointed out that all the defendants were acting under superior orders. These points carried little weight with the court, and indeed the prosecution dismissed the first two as "nonsense" and asserted that superior orders alone was no defense for acts of inhuman cruelty. Thus, the defense was obliged to pick apart the various allegations piece by piece, looking for factual inaccuracies in the affidavits, of which there were many, and trying to raise reasonable doubts about the charges. It was a difficult task, especially in the case of Josef Kramer. Major T. C. M. Winwood, who had the unenviable task of defending Kramer, made a rather ham-fisted effort. He asserted that at Auschwitz, it was Hoess, not Kramer, who gave orders; Kramer was merely a supernumerary "confined to the administration of people inside" the camp—he had no involvement with gas chambers. Yes, there may have been beatings, Winwood said, but "the Court should take into account the many difficulties there were and the scarcity of personnel to cope with them." After all, he said, "the language of a concentration camp is blows." At Belsen, Winwood contended, Kramer encountered a tragic situation not of his own making, and no evidence had been produced to show that he pursued a deliberate plan to starve and mistreat prisoners. The mess at Belsen was laid at the doorstep of Kramer's superiors in Berlin, Richard Glücks and Oswald Pohl, for it was they who ordered the transports of ill prisoners to Belsen in the first place. And after all, Belsen was simply "an example of what was happening to Germany as a whole country—order changing into disorder, disorder into chaos." In short, Kramer bore no personal responsibility for the circumstances either at Auschwitz or Belsen. Much the same defense was used for other defendants, although in the cases of alleged specific acts of cruelty, the defense tried to raise doubts about the use of uncorroborated affidavits.[57]

The prosecution had something of an easier time of it. No one disputed that the accused were present in Auschwitz and Belsen, or that they played a role in the administration of the camps. Kramer himself did not deny his membership in the SS, or his career history in the camp system. Naturally, many of the accused disputed specific allegations of brutality or murder. Kramer said he never beat anyone or mistreated anyone; he also denied that there was a gas chamber at Auschwitz, or that there were mass executions or beatings. The only people who died in Auschwitz, Kramer said, did so from natural causes. Kramer acknowledged that prisoners at Belsen were dying in large numbers, but was unable to show that he did anything to ameliorate the conditions.[58] Others, like Klein and Grese, were unrepentant. Klein admitted his role in the selections at Auschwitz and acknowledged that he thereby condemned thousands to death. Grese too admitted using her specially made whip on prisoners at Auschwitz. At Belsen, she said, "although I carried a whip and beat people at Auschwitz, for some reason I never did it at Belsen. I always used my hands at Belsen." Colonel Backhouse tried to avoid the question of precisely who did what to whom; instead, he asserted that the accused knew that the camps were wrong and contrary to every law and custom of war. In his closing summary, he went carefully over the details of what happened in Auschwitz: the transports, beatings, shavings, tattooing, forced labor, starvation, selections, gassings, crematoria. He asserted that Belsen, though it had no gas chambers, was an extension of the same horrors and indifference toward life as was evident in Auschwitz. The accused, he said, took part in this world of brutality and murder, and so "participated in a conspiracy to ill-treat the persons who were under their care." However small their part, they must be found guilty if they played any role at all in contributing to this machinery of death.

Backhouse could certainly have done more to frame the trial around the determination of the Third Reich to destroy Europe's Jews. In his emphasis on Allied nationals, he seemed unnecessarily constrained by the need to link German actions to violations of specific laws concerning treatment of POWs and civilians. Yet it would be wrong to suggest that Backhouse ignored the Jewish catastrophe altogether. He stressed that "in Auschwitz alone, literally millions of people were gassed for no other reason than that they were Jews." In his closing argument, he made a point of emphasizing that, while he as a prosecutor had to be concerned "with minor matters" about "whether this person did this or that," he urged jurors to consider the larger picture: those on trial had knowingly participated in "an attempt to destroy the whole Jewish race." Using language quite unusual in official British parlance, he stated that "the martyrdom of the Jews . . . was a war crime which has never been equaled."[59] What appears to have most angered contemporary Jewish observers was not chiefly the absence of Jewish victimization at the trial, but rather the callous manner in which the defense was obliged to make its case. When Major Winwood said that the concentration camps contained merely "the dregs of the ghettoes of Central Europe," his statement was denounced by the Board of Deputies of British Jews as "besmirching the memory of millions of men, women, and children who died amid unspeakable horrors or were murdered for no fault but that they were Jews." (Remarkably, Winwood apologized to the court during his closing arguments for making offensive statements; he had been merely the "mouthpiece of the accused," he said.) Major Cranfield, the defense counsel appointed to Irma Grese, also came in for sharp criticism because he made the argument that his client could not be aware that her actions were wrong because concentration camps were common in Europe during the war; and Cranfield went on to draw parallels between the Nazi genocide and the forced deportations from Poland of ethnic Germans then being undertaken by Britain and its allies, and of the use of chain gangs of prisoners in the United States. These were the laws in place in Germany, Cranfield argued, and it was normal that they would be obeyed by the defendants. These sorts of lawyerly pirouettes were labeled "cowardly slander against the dead" and eroded support among Jewish observers for the whole trial.[60]

On November 16, 1945, the court adjourned; a mere six hours later, it reassembled and delivered the verdicts. Thirty of the forty-four defendants were declared guilty on one or both counts of mistreating Allied nationals at Auschwitz and Belsen. The degree of their personal responsibility was indicated by the varying sentences they received. Eleven defendants—Kramer, Klein, Hoessler, Grese, Bormann, Volkenrath, and five others were sentenced to death, and were hanged on December 12, 1945. Nineteen others received sentences ranging from life in prison to a mere one year of jail time. Kramer evidently went to his death feeling much aggrieved. As he wrote to his wife while in prison, "all the time I am asking myself why this misfortune came over me. How have I deserved this? What have I done that one has to treat me like a criminal? That so many people died in Belsen—I could not alter that anymore. It is all fate and maybe I shall even be punished for that. My father used to say sometimes I was not lucky. Today I believe it only too well."[61]

The press reports of the verdicts reflected a sort of weariness with the whole thing. The London *Times* concluded that the trial revealed "an almost exaggerated desire to accord fair play to the accused," but took some pride that in the end British justice had triumphed over mere vengeance. By late November, many Jews had lost interest in the trial. Bevin's speech on Palestine had seized the headlines, and Jewish fury toward the British had reached a boiling point. And survivors themselves expressed reservations about the very idea of a trial. Hadassah Rosensaft, who had testified at the trial (as Dr. Ada Bimko), "was glad the trial was over," and later refused to testify at the Nuremberg trials or at the trial of Adolf Eichmann in 1961. "I just couldn't take part in any more 'fair play' for the Nazis. At that point in my life, I couldn't understand why someone caught *in flagrante* committing the most brutal acts of murder and torture could possibly be found innocent, or why he would be entitled to what was considered a 'fair trial.'"[62] As if reflecting the same sentiment, the *Jewish Chronicle* devoted only a single paragraph of an inside page to the conviction of Kramer and the others. His death by hanging was allotted one sentence.[63]

For the Jews of Belsen, like the Jewish DPs elsewhere in occupied Germany, liberation did not arrive in 1945. The year that had begun with such tragedy in the death marches of the east had of course seen the soaring joys of the arrival of Allied armies in the camps in Western Europe; it had seen the extreme kindness and devotion of humanitarian interventions by soldiers and civilians alike in the care and treatment provided to Jewish survivors, and certainly 1945 had brought about an end to that awful era in which Jewish lives across Europe could be snuffed out by the merest whim of a German officer or functionary. The year closed out with a sober, careful judicial proceeding against the Belsen guards that completely repudiated and defied the Nazi worldview. Yet this vexed year of 1945 had not marked in any sense an endpoint or a coda to Jewish travails. To the Jews of Europe, 1945 was only one stop in a passage away from the daily struggle for survival and toward a new struggle to build a future. The later months of 1945 brought profound disappointment, bitter recrimination against the liberating armies, confusion and frustration over the question of emigration, and repeated denials of what seemed to be the true meaning of liberation: the freedom to live and to settle in one's homeland, free of fear, of hunger, of persecution. The triumph of Allied arms in 1945 did not fulfill these long-cherished hopes of European Jewry. Such rewards lay in the distant future, across a long stretch of anxious years and the roiling backwash of war.

Conclusion:
The Missing Liberation

IT HAS LONG been a habit in the United States to narrate the history of the liberation of Europe in a heroic register, stressing the selfless sacrifice of ordinary soldiers as well as the talented generalship of American military leaders. The story is usually told in three acts. It opens with the daring cross-channel invasion of France in June 1944, the stalwart fighting from the beachheads, and the bold breakout and pursuit of August; in this initial stage, the world dares to hope that the war might be over by Christmas. In act two, the Allied forces are briefly thrown back on their heels by a still lethal German war machine; a chastened alliance girds itself for the bitter struggles of the winter of 1944. In act three, dogged soldiering and the preponderance of American power finally break the German defenses; with spring comes the dash into central Germany and, at the end, the total victory of May 8, 1945. It is a story that places Americans and their military achievements at center stage.

By contrast, this book has drawn upon the testimony of many ordinary people, civilians as well as soldiers, to offer an alternative way of looking at the events of 1944–45. These voices have spoken of the indeterminate nature of liberation, its paradoxical joys and miseries, and the heavy toll that liberation and its aftermath took upon the liberated peoples themselves. For them, the liberation was truly a time of limbo, a time without structure or form, a time of uncertainty, fear, and loss. The untold joy of seeing the war come to an end was diluted by the almost unbearable sufferings that so many had endured. No one has described these contradictory emotions more clearly than Primo Levi, who in October 1945 finally made it home to Turin, Italy. Arrested and deported in December 1943, Levi spent thirteen months in Auschwitz, then another ten months trying to get home. This return journey, along miles of railways, in countless boxcars, carried him through Poland, the Ukraine, Belorussia, Romania, Hungary, Germany, Austria, and finally into Italy. On the last leg of his trip, through the Brenner pass between Austria and Italy, Levi traveled with two companions, the only survivors of his original cohort of 650 Italians sent to the Nazi camps. "We knew," he wrote about this homeward journey, "that on the thresholds of our homes, for good or ill, a trial awaited us, and we anticipated it with fear." On October 19, Levi arrived in Turin. He brought the war home with him. "No one was expecting me. I was swollen, bearded and in rags, and had difficulty in making myself recognized. I found my friends full of life, the warmth of secure meals, the solidity of daily work, the liberating joy of recounting my story. . . . But only after many months did I lose the habit of walking with my glance fixed to the ground, as if searching for something to eat."[1]

Levi was not alone in finding his liberation a time of trial. As we have seen, thousands of French and Belgians paid for their liberation with their lives, and many Dutch people dropped dead in the streets in the last weeks of the war while Allied war planners dithered over sending airborne food drops behind enemy lines. We have seen that living with the liberators presented its own difficulties; American, British, and Canadian soldiers could be both cruel and kind in equal measure to the civilians they freed from Hitler's grasp. For millions of Europeans, liberation came in the form of displacement. Long after the guns fell silent, forced laborers, prisoners of German camps, as well as ethnic Germans from Eastern European lands, tramped the roads of liberated Europe, victims of renewed hostility, stalked at every turn by hatred, hunger, and illness. Meanwhile, liberated Europeans watched, bemused, as the German people, who perpetrated unspeakable crimes for over a decade, wallowed in self-pity and condemned the violent bombing that had devastated their citadel-cities. And the Jews of Europe—those few who managed to escape Germany's genocidal war—found little freedom on the morrow of their liberation. Many survivors remained in camps for months and even years, safe from extermination to be sure, but compelled to dwell inside temporary shelters in the land of their tormentors, far from a home they could as yet only dimly imagine.

These are the grim realities of liberation. Why have they gone missing from the historical record of World War II and postwar European history? Americans and Europeans share the blame for sanitizing the history of liberation. In the United States immediately after the war, political leaders and the public took justified pride in having defeated Hitler and restored sovereignty to Europe. Americans came to see great nobility in their war against Nazi Germany. There was no place in the national story for awkward questions about civilian deaths, or mass bombing of cities, or looting and sexual assault by occupying troops, or a too-swift reconciliation with unashamed Germans, or Jews still living in camps in Germany. The liberation of Europe had been a great crusade, in General Eisenhower's words. And so it was. Yet its tragedies and paradoxes proved too dangerous to find a secure place in postwar American thinking about the war. By 1946, Americans began to mobilize for a new global contest, a battle of ideologies with Soviet Russia, and they had little inclination to dig deeply into some of the darker dimensions of the recent victories over Nazi Germany and imperial Japan. For half a century, therefore, the American public has been fed a steady diet of triumphalist narratives in which great generals and visionary politicians placed the burden of freedom onto the willing shoulders of the anonymous American GI, who carried out his duties with determination and honor. In the early cold war, Americans needed a story about World War II that stressed the essential purity of the fight, the decency of American men at arms, and the inevitability of victory. These themes, made secure through decades of cinematic treatments as well as popular historical accounts, have resulted in a kind of American myopia that only sees a select portion of the war, while the broader view has become fuzzy and indistinct. This book has offered a new perspective for American readers, one that brings into focus the European experience of liberation. It has shown that for every triumph at arms, for every act of heroism on the battlefield, there was also a home set alight, a child without food, a woman cowering in an unheated barn amid filth and squalor. This is the human face of war and liberation in Europe.

Europeans too have done their share of cleansing the history of their own liberation, though not out of nostalgic reverence for the "good war." Rather, Europeans did not wish to emphasize that they owed their freedom to others. The embarrassing truth is that few of the European resistance movements had been able to inflict much damage on the occupying Germans; only the Yugoslavs and perhaps the Greeks had done much to free their own soil. Yet in the immediate aftermath of liberation, European states needed to restore their own legitimacy, and this required founding new national myths. In the first postwar decade in Western Europe, the sordid history of wartime collaboration, the participation in Germany's New Order, the military weakness of underground resistance movements, all this was deliberately obscured. With it went the brutality of the liberation itself. Instead, a new set of ideas took root. These stressed widespread, popular resistance to Germany, the solidarity of Allied nations in war, a large role for resistance movements in the liberation, and the triumphant restoration of order and democracy. The needs of the moment called for simplicity. At a time of fragile national unity, with contending political parties vying for power, in a climate of simmering hatred between former collaborators and their victims, any emphasis on the personal, human losses of the war, or on the violence that the liberators had visited upon Europe, could find no traction. Whereas local communities ravaged by war had emphasized their own martyrdom at the hands of the liberators, the image that the national governments wished to project in 1945 was of unity and a stalwart common effort of reconstruction. "Retroussons nos manches," blared posters pasted up by the new French government: "Let us roll up our sleeves." Beneath this slogan, a brawny, smiling laborer grasped his tools and strode forward. The message was clear: victims make poor heroes.

The nations liberated by Soviet arms had no choice in the matter of public memory. Their national memories were prepared for them in Moscow. The party line was straightforward: the Red Army liberated Eastern Europe from fascism and offered a new antifascist, Communist order to the peoples of the liberated eastern states. Local peoples were depicted as victims of Germany's rapacious imperialism, which they had been, but other elements of the war in the east were excised from public memory: the Hitler-Stalin pact of 1939 that had divided Poland between Germany and the USSR; the massive local collaboration in Eastern Europe and indeed inside the USSR itself with the German occupiers; the Soviet Union's open war against noncommunist local resistance movements in eastern and southern Europe; and of course the atrocities committed by Red Army "liberators" as they swept through eastern Germany. In the new postwar Communist mythology, all war crimes were committed by Fascists, all Eastern Europeans had opposed German occupation, all had wished for and welcomed liberation by the Soviet Union. Remarkably, this nonsense was deployed even in East Germany, where it was used to suggest that Nazism had been imposed by a capitalist, elitist clique upon the socialist workers of Germany. For obvious political reasons, then, there was to be no room in the Communist bloc for a discussion about the paradoxes and brutality of the liberation era. Liberation instead was depicted as the first act in a new era of freedom and renewal.

Not all Europeans shied away from discussing their own suffering. Postwar West Germany readily adopted an exculpatory identity of victimhood. The reasons are easy to divine. In the last stages of the war, the German people, who had mercilessly persecuted others, came to experience themselves the genuine horrors of war. The extensive bombing of Germany, the heavy fighting across the country, the Soviet onslaught in East Prussia and the uprooting of millions of eastern Germans as well as *Volksdeutsche* from Eastern Europe, all contributed by the end of the war to an atmosphere of chaos and suffering. But context is all, and Germans in 1945 proved unwilling to accept the relationship between cause and effect. Instead, the people of western Germany who fell under U.S. or British occupation used their evident suffering as a shield against further punishment. Germans also sensibly deployed their own anticommunism as a bridge to the Allies, knowing full well that this shared ideological fixation would serve to bind victor and vanquished. The results worked better than anyone could have predicted. Even before the war was officially over, Allied occupation in the western part of Germany had softened, soldiers were making friends with Germans, and the occupiers committed themselves to shelter, feed, and clothe the once-despised enemy. In the German case, the defeat opened the way to pity and self-pity, and laid the foundations for a paternalistic relationship between the United States and West Germany that has survived for half a century.

Nor did the war crimes trials, held with considerable fanfare across Europe soon after the conclusion of hostilities, help matters much. Despite the genuine and earnest efforts of military and civil authorities, postwar trials tended to serve the interests of the prosecutors, not the plaintiffs. As we have seen in the case of the Belsen trial, Jews who had survived Auschwitz or Belsen cared little about Josef Kramer's fate; they felt their suffering could not be made good by the conviction and hanging of one man. Yet the British authorities used the Belsen trial as a stage on which to exhibit British "fair play" and the rule of law: the trial was about their own eagerness to denounce Nazism, establish the moral righteousness of the war, and then put the war away. The same dynamic defined the postwar purge trials in France and Italy. There, the new postwar democratic states put on display a small number of leading malefactors, condemned them in most cases to light punishment for injuring the interests of the state, and quickly shut down the proceedings. The brief outbursts of anger in 1944 and 1945 that had led to drumhead justice and considerable bloodletting in France and Italy were suppressed. In the end, only a very few Fascist or Vichy leaders were punished; the rest were encouraged to slip quietly into obscurity.

In Germany, war crimes trials briefly played a visible and important role in illuminating and condemning the actions of the Third Reich. Opened in November 1945 and presided over by the four major Allied powers—the United States, Britain, the USSR, and France—the International Military Tribunal held in Nuremberg charged twenty-two defendants with a variety of hateful acts, from criminal conspiracy to crimes against humanity. The Allied prosecutors presented millions of pages of detailed evidence and eyewitness testimony to make their case that the German leaders bore personal responsibility for atrocious crimes, including the genocide of the Jews. Eleven of the accused, including Hermann Göring, Joachim von Ribbentrop, Wilhelm Keitel, Ernst Kaltenbrunner, Alfred Rosenberg, Hans Frank, and Arthur Seyss-Inquart, were condemned to a death they richly deserved. Twelve additional trials, focusing on other institutions inside the Third Reich, from industry to banking, the courts, the foreign ministry, and the military, all unearthed mountains of documentation and left no doubt about the facts of Germany's culpability for war crimes. Finally, further trials of camp commanders and guards, like the one held at Belsen, led to further convictions. These proceedings, which continued until 1949, burnished the reputation of the occupiers and made them feel that they had delivered a stern verdict on Nazism. Yet Nuremberg and the associated trials also closed the books on the war. The defendants in these trials were saddled with the crimes of all Nazis, all Fascists, even all the collaborationists and opportunists across Europe who had in some way aided and abetted the German wartime imperium. The number of those punished was tiny: in the end, only 5,025 persons were convicted of war crimes or crimes against humanity by the three Western occupying powers. The trials, in rendering verdicts on this handful of big fish, released millions of small fry from culpability, who swam away on the warm currents of anonymity and forgetting.[2]

Instead of guilt, German people preferred to stress their own suffering and the troubled fate they now faced—their nation shattered, occupied, and divided, their people hungry and worn. The new Federal Republic of Germany embraced the task of reconstruction with a certain manic zeal, as if to clean up the wartime rubble might also lead to a rapid healing of the diseased German soul. The Americans lent a hand, scaling back the once-bold denazification efforts and economic dismantling of Germany in favor of restoration and forgiveness. By the start of 1946, American policy openly embraced the task of restoring to "liberated" western Germany its freedom and its sovereignty once some semblance of democratic rule could be established. In this environment of reconciliation and the shared geopolitical aim of German recovery, there was no room to discuss the tragedies of the war itself, and certainly no desire to return to the bloodied fields of Normandy, or the shattered ravines of the Ardennes, or the hunger-ravaged streets of Amsterdam and the Hague, or the blackened fields of East Prussia, and ask for a detailed accounting of why liberation had taken so many civilian lives and left such a devastating legacy of destruction. The war years were allowed to slip away into the past, willfully forgotten.

And so the postwar era closed off inquiry instead of raising questions. After so much bloodshed and violence, Europeans and Americans welcomed a period of collective amnesia about the realities of war. Fortunately for posterity, the scholarship on the Second World War, and especially on the ways that we remember the war years, is burgeoning. More than half a century later, we now have the evidence, and perhaps the critical distance, to develop a richer, more complex history of the "good war" that incorporates both its glories and its misfortunes. The liberation of Europe will always inspire us, for it contains a multitude of heroic and noble acts, and was at its core an honorable struggle to emancipate millions of people from a vile and barbaric regime. But this book has suggested that when considering the history of Europe's liberation, we not lose sight of the human costs that this epic contest exacted upon defenseless peoples and ordinary lives. There is surely room enough in our histories of World War II for introspection, for humility, and for an abiding awareness of the dreadful ugliness of war.

Acknowledgments

PRIMARY SOURCES RELATING to the Second World War are abundant, indeed, overwhelming. In examining government records, memoirs, private letters, newspapers, and thousands upon thousands of stunning photographs, I felt myself extraordinarily fortunate to have such archival riches to work with. At times, though, the scope of the sources was so intimidating that I thought back to Lytton Strachey's depiction of the historian as a small person adrift on a wide sea: "he will row out over that great ocean of material, and lower down into it, here and there, a little bucket, which will bring up to the light of day some characteristic specimen, from those far depths, to be examined with a careful curiosity." That has been my approach in these pages. In this endeavor, though, I have been guided by more than ocean currents. Many colleagues, friends, students, archivists, and librarians kept me on course, giving me prompt feedback and answering queries with great good humor and sincerity. This book would never have been possible without them, and I want to offer them a personal word of thanks.

My very first research trip related to this book was to the Fortunoff Video Archive in Sterling Library, Yale University, where Joanne Rudoff guided me through the invaluable testimonies of witnesses and survivors of Hitler's war on the Jews. These materials had a profound impact on the way I conceptualized the book. I am grateful to the Fortunoff Archive for permission to quote from these sources. The collections in the U.S. National Archives at College Park, Maryland, are so huge that no one could begin to work there without guidance from the excellent staff of archivists; I received welcome advice early on from Amy Schmidt of the military records branch, as well as from the attentive staff in the research room. The staff at the United Nations archives in New York helpfully made available the UNRRA records, which are a gold mine of insights into wartime and postwar European life. Mikhail Mitsel at the American Jewish Joint Distribution Committee in New York kindly helped me with the JDC papers. Frances O'Donnell, Curator of Archives and Manuscripts at the Andover-Harvard Theological Library at the Harvard Divinity School, guided me through the Unitarian Service Committee records. Andrea Williamson-Hughes of Save the Children forwarded to me a number of useful documents about Save the Children's relief work in Europe. The staff of the American Friends Service Committee in Philadelphia was forthcoming with materials relating to AFSC's work in postwar Europe. Natalia Sciarini of the Beinecke Library, Yale University, facilitated my work in the Kathryn Hulme Papers. Susan Watson at the American Red Cross archives in Lorton, Virginia, provided useful materials. I owe a special thanks to Richard Sommers and his staff at the U.S. Army Military History Institute in Carlisle, Pennsylvania; its collection of first-person accounts, memoirs, letters, and divisional histories is invaluable for historians. Temple University's library staff never once complained about the innumerable interlibrary loan requests I have made over the past three years, and David Murray in particular has been a great stalwart of historical scholarship at Temple.

In Belgium, I was warmly welcomed by Dr. Dirk Martin and Dr. Chantal Kesteloot of the extraordinary and still rather secret Centre d'Etudes et de Documentation Guerre et Sociétés Contemporaines in Brussels. This institution served as my home during a Fulbright grant in Belgium, and while I was there, Dr. Martin shared with me his deep knowledge of the archives and of Belgium's wartime history. I am also grateful to the incomparable Margaret Nicholson of the Commission for Educational Exchange in Brussels. Maggie has been introducing Americans to Belgium for many years, and she is perhaps that country's most passionate advocate.

In Caen, France, at the Archives Départementales du Calvados, I was made welcome by the director, M. Louis Le Roc'h Morgère and his helpful staff, who produced all sorts of archival treasures relating to the D-Day landings and the tragic destruction of Caen.

In Britain, I worked at the Public Record Office at Kew, now grandly renamed the National Archives. Americans are constantly amazed at the courtesy and unfailing assistance by the staff there; the PRO, as I still call it, is one of the wonders of the world, at least for the historian. The staff at the Imperial War Museum in London helped me seek out permission from the copyright holders of material deposited at the Museum so that I could publish quotations from a variety of documents and diaries. Though in some cases the Museum had lost contact with the families of those who had deposited papers there, I did receive many kind responses to my requests, sometimes in very touching personal letters. I should like to thank in particular Mrs. Elsie M. Astley, Mrs. M. Caines, Jayne and Barry Greenwood, Mary Herbert, Keith and Jane McDougall, Brenda Morris, Mr. Les Roker, and Diana and Peter White.

In Rome, I had particular assistance from Lorenzo Costa, who helped me navigate the Archivio Centrale dello Stato during a rushed three-day sprint through the records relating to postwar trials. I also want to thank Aldo Patania, of Temple University's Rome campus, and the Dean of Temple–Rome, Kim Strommen, whose good humor and warm welcome made my trip to Rome unforgettable.

I have at various times imposed upon some exceptionally intelligent, skilled historians for advice and counsel. Daniel Cohen, Mark Lawrence, Fred Logevall, Len Smith, and Jeremi Suri offered comments, criticisms, and encouragement. I benefited from my colleague Greg Urwin's careful reading of some early draft pages, which saved me from a few gaffes. My brother-in-law Jeremy Varon deserves special mention: he constantly challenged my ideas with a fierce intelligence that forced me to articulate and defend my theses. I have profited immensely from exchanges and arguments with him. My dear friends and *anciens combattants,* Paul Kennedy, John Gaddis, and Ann Carter-Drier of Yale University, were once again supportive, amiable, and always hospitable whenever I appeared on their doorsteps.

My literary agent, Susan Rabiner, played an invaluable role throughout the project, especially at the start, as I mulled over various ways to approach this subject. She gave me frank, direct, and wise advice that helped me enormously in shaping this book. She then found the book a home at Free Press, where I have been awed by the smart, incisive editing skills of Bruce Nichols—with whom I started the book—and Martin Beiser, who did the lion's share of the final editing. These two are the best in the business, and I count my lucky stars that I had the chance to work with them.

This has been a Temple book from the very start, and it is to my friends at Temple that I owe most. In 2004, an extraordinary person named Susan Herbst, then the Dean of the College of Liberal Arts, hired me to come to Temple, and I am eternally grateful to her for her confidence in me and her unflagging friendship. In the Temple history department, three young historians of great promise became friends and trusted confidants during the writing of this book. Kristin Grueser helped me work through mountains of relevant periodicals; Holger Löwendorf combed a number of useful German sources; and David Zierler offered detailed readings of early drafts. To work with students of their caliber is a privilege.

At Temple, I found the things that academics yearn for: smart, hardworking, and fun colleagues who are also dear friends. Richard and Marion Immerman have been warm and welcoming neighbors, as well as wise counselors, since the day Liz and I moved in across the street. Vlad Zubok's charm and wisdom are incomparable. Beth Bailey read many of these pages and gave me superb advice and gentle cautions, while David Farber's energy, abundant good humor, and intellectual rigor have motivated and inspired me. Drew Isenberg and Petra Goedde have opened their home with inexhaustible generosity, and over countless dinners, with our various offspring reenacting the Normandy invasion in their basement, I have learned much from these two about scholarship and friendship.

As ever, David and Lee Hitchcock cheered me on during these past few years; they are models for me of how to live a life in which ideas matter. To Liz, Ben, and Emma, who tolerated my long absences from home and my vacant looks at the dinner table as I rewrote sentences in my head, I can only apologize, thank them, and offer this book with all my heart as a token of my love.

Notes

Preface: A Cemetery in Luxembourg

1. John Babcock, *Taught to Kill* (Dulles, Va.: Potomac Books, 2005), 54.

PART I: LIBERATION IN THE WEST
Prologue: D-Day

1. These casualty numbers have been gathered by the D-Day Museum in Portsmouth, England, and can be seen at http://www.ddaymuseum.co.uk/.
2. Dwight D. Eisenhower, *Crusade in Europe* (Garden City, N.J.: Doubleday, 1948), 263.
3. Eisenhower, *Crusade in Europe*, 270.

1: "Too Wonderfully Beautiful"

1. Ernie Pyle, *Brave Men* (New York: Henry Holt, 1944), 256–57.
2. The excellent if dry official histories are Gordon A. Harrison, *Cross-Channel Attack* (Washington, D.C.: Office of the Chief of Military History, 1951); Martin Blumenson, *Breakout and Pursuit* (Washington, D.C.: Office of the Chief of Military History, 1961). The relevant British volume is L. F. Ellis, *Victory in the West*, vol. 1, *The Battle of Normandy* (London: HMSO, 1962). Journalists with superb access to the leading officials have contributed excellent histories of the landings and subsequent fighting. Chester Wilmot's *The Struggle for Europe* (New York: Harper, 1952) offers a robust defense of General Montgomery from any criticism, yet remains a superb history of the war's final year. John Keegan's *Six Armies in Normandy* (London: Cape, 1980) and Max Hastings's *Overlord* (New York: Simon & Schuster, 1984) integrate sophisticated analyses of military operations with eyewitness testimony gathered from soldiers' diaries and memoirs, and have deservedly won wide readerships.
3. Ronald J. Drez, *Voices of D-Day: The Story of the Allied Invasion, As Told By Those Who Were There* (Baton Rouge: Louisiana State University Press, 1994). Other such cut-and-paste collections, which offer snippets from interviews, letters, and diaries without much analysis or context, include Jonathan Bastable, *Voices from D-Day* (Newton Abbot, U.K.: David & Charles, 2004); John C. McManus, *The Americans at D-Day: The American Experience at the Normandy Invasion* (New York: Forge, 2004); Robin Neillands, *D-Day: Voices from Normandy* (Cold Spring Harbor, N.Y.: Cold Spring Press, 2004); David Stafford, *Ten Days to D-Day: Citizens and Soldiers on the Eve of the Invasion* (New York: Little, Brown, 2004).
4. Jean-Claude Valla, *La France sous les bombes américaines, 1942–1945* (Paris: Librarie Nationale, 2001), 11. Similar figures are given in Eddy Florentin, *Quand les alliés bombardaient la France, 1940–1945* (Paris: Perrin, 1997).
5. Examples of local and firsthand accounts are Edouard Tribouillard, *Caen après la*

bataille: la survie dans les ruines (Rennes: Ouest-France, 1993); Hélène Dufau, *Le tragique été Normand* (The tragic Norman summer) (Paris: La Nouvelle France, 1946); Maurice Lantier, *Saint-Lô au bûcher* (Saint-Lô on the pyre) (Saint-Lô: Société d'archéologie et d'histoire de la Manche, 1969); Joseph Poirier, *Le martyre de Caen* (Le Mans, 1945); Philippe Huet, *Les rescapés du Jour-J: les civils dans l'enfer* (The survivors of D-Day: Civilians in hell) (Paris: Albin Michel, 2004 ed.); J.-P. Lafontaine, *Mémoire de ma ville: Condé-sur-Noireau, ville martyre* (n.d.). In the rich two-volume collection of firsthand testimonies gathered and published by René Herval in 1947, the testimonials about the experiences of specific war-scarred towns bear revealing titles: "The Terrors of a Small Village," "Exodus from Saint-Lô," "Valognes Devastated," "The Agony of Granville," "The Double Agony of Vire," "The Suffering of Argentan," and, simply, "Falaise is No More." René Herval, *Bataille de Normandie: Récits de Témoins*, 2 vols. (Paris: Editions de Notre Temps, 1947). An early take on the liberation in Normandy, more a survey of data than an interpretation, is Marcel Baudot, *Libération de la Normandie* (Paris: Hachette, 1974). New, more analytical scholarship on the liberation can be found in H. R. Kedward and Nancy Wood, eds., *The Liberation of France: Image and Event* (Berg: Oxford, 1995); Henri Amouroux, *Joies et Douleurs du Peuple Libéré: La Grande Histoire des Français sous l'Occupation* (Paris: Laffont, 1988); Olivier Wieviorka, *Histoire du débarquement en Normandie: Des origines à la liberation de Paris, 1944–45* (Paris: Editions du Seuil, 2007); and the excellent study by Hilary Footitt, *War and Liberation in France: Living with the Liberators* (New York: Palgrave Macmillan, 2004).

6. Imperial War Museum [hereafter IWM] 99/16/1, Corporal L. F. Roker, 1st Battalion, Highland Light Infantry; IWM 99/16/1, Ivor Astley, 236 Antitank Battery, 59th Antitank Regiment, 43rd Wessex Infantry Division, *Tank Alert* (Elms Court, U.K.: Arthur Stockwell, 1999); IWM 99/61/1, Combat Diary of Major Edward McCosh Elliot, 2nd Battalion, Glasgow Highlanders; and IWM 03/28/1, Major Maurice Herbert Cooke, officer commanding B Company, 8th Battalion, Royal Scots. For similar views expressed by American GIs in Normandy and France in general, see Peter Schrijvers, *The Crash of Ruin: American Combat Soldiers in Europe in World War II* (New York: New York University Press, 1998), 124–31.

7. A. J. Liebling, *Mollie and Other War Pieces* (New York: Ballantine, 1964), 213.

8. Public Record Office [hereafter PRO], WO 219/3727, "Preliminary Report on Recce of British Beachhead," Lt. Col. D. R. Ellias, June 9–12, 1944.

9. Stephen Ambrose makes the same assumption: Normans had "quite accommodated themselves to the German occupation," he claimed; there was "no food shortage," and local wine cellars were brimming. Ambrose was unfamiliar, apparently, with French sources about life in wartime Normandy. Ambrose, *Citizen Soldiers: The U.S. Army from the Normandy Beaches to the Bulge to the Surrender of Germany* (New York: Simon & Schuster, 1998), 50–51.

10. Jean Quellien, *Opinions et comportements politiques dans le Calvados sous l'occupation allemande (1940–1944)* (Caen: Université de Caen Basse-Normandie, 2001), 13, 390. The following paragraphs draw heavily from this outstanding local study. Professor Quellien has devoted over two decades to the analysis of Calvados under occupation, and the results of his research have been published in dozens of books and articles.

11. Quellien, *Opinions et comportements*, 264–72.

12. Quellien, *Opinions et comportements*, 338–47.

13. Archives départementales du Calvados [hereafter ADC], M 12127, Prefect Michel Cacaud, March 4, 1944; and report of May 6, 1944, on the impact of defensive preparations on the economy.

14. Quellien, *Opinions et comportements*, 389–417.

15. ADC, M 12127, report of May 6, 1944; Bernard Garnier and Jean Quellien, *Les victimes civiles du Calvados dans la bataille de Normandie* (Caen: Université de Caen, 1995), 21–28.

16. Estimates of civilian deaths in Normandy have varied over the years, but recent research has settled on the following figures: Calvados, 8,140; Orne, 2,200; Manche, 3,800; Eure and Seine-Maritime, 5,750. See Christophe Prime, "Les bombardements du Jour J et de

la bataille de Normandie," in Bernard Garnier et al., *Les populations civiles face au débarquement et à la bataille de Normandie* (Caen: Université de Caen, 2005), 31–47, and Garnier and Quellien, *Les victimes civiles,* 13–20.

17. Martin Middlebrook and Chris Everitt, *The Bomber Command War Diaries* (London: Viking, 1985), 523.

18. Garnier and Quellien, *Les victimes civiles,* 35; Wesley Frank Craven and James Lee Cate, *The Army Air Forces in World War II,* vol. 3, *Europe: From Argument to V-E Day* (Chicago: University of Chicago Press, 1951), 190.

19. In addition to primary sources and memoirs available in the ADC, there are extensive published materials relating to the fate of Caen in the battle of Normandy, mostly gathered by the staff of the departmental archives of Calvados and of the University of Caen. These texts faithfully reproduce dozens of personal testimonies. See the four-part series published by the archives, *L'Été 1944: Les normands dans la bataille* (Caen: Conseil général du Calvados, 1997–2000); and *Cahiers de mémoire: Vivre et survivre pendant la Bataille de Normandie* (Caen: Conseil général du Calvados, 1994). There is also bountiful primary source documentation online at www.debarquement.com.

20. Hastings, *Overlord,* 111–22.

21. Craven and Cate, *Army Air Forces,* 198.

22. Testimony of Bernard Goupil, in Michel Boivin, Gérard Bourdin, and Jean Quellien, *Villes normandes sous les bombes, juin 1944* (Caen: Presses universitaires de Caen, 1994), 87–102.

23. Poirier, *Le martyre de Caen.*

24. Hastings, *Overlord,* 129–51.

25. IWM 94/10/1, Mrs. Collette Day, typescript memoir.

26. *Cahiers des mémoire,* testimony of Mlle. Cécile Dabosville, 151–56. They were finally transported by the Canadians to Creully. For details, see the two-part report by P. Faudet in *Liberté de Normandie,* July 24 and August 5–6, 1945, "La verité sur les caverns de Fleury-sur-Orne."

27. Hastings, *Overlord,* 222.

28. Middlebrook and Everitt, *Bomber Command War Diaries,* 539.

29. IWM 87/35/1, D. Cooper; IWM 90/20/1, Captain W. G. Caines, 4th Battalion, Dorsetshire Regiment, 43rd Wessex Infantry; IWM 90/6/1, J. Y. White, Gunner, Royal Artillery.

30. PRO, WO 219/3727, "Reconnaissance Report on Caen," Capt. E. G. de Pury, June 12, 1944.

31. ADC, I J 16/7, Journal des Bénédictines de Caen, juin-septembre 1944, Abbaye Notre-Dame de Bon-Sauveur.

32. IWM 87/35/1, D. Cooper.

33. IWM 91/13/1, Major A. J. Forrest, 335 Battery, 107 Regiment, Royal Artillery.

34. IWM 95/19/1, Sgt. R. T. Greenwood, 9th Battalion, Royal Tank Regiment.

35. ADC, 20 W 5, inventory of damage.

36. IWM 87/44/1, K. W. Morris, 4th Armoured Brigade.

37. IWM 90/20/1, Capt. W. G. Caines, 4th Battalion, Dorsetshire Regiment, 43rd Wessex Infantry Division.

38. IWM 78/68/1, Lt. William A. Greene.

39. IWM 98/16/1, A. G. Herbert, 4th Battalion, Somerset Light Infantry.

40. IWM 87/44/1, K. W. Morris, 4th Armoured Brigade.

41. IWM 91/13/1, Major A. J. Forrest, 335 Battery, 107 Regiment, Royal Artillery.

42. Roscoe C. Blunt, *Foot Soldier: A Combat Infantryman's War in Europe* (Cambridge, Mass.: Da Capo Press, 2002), 41.

43. IWM 87/44/1, K. W. Morris, 4th Armoured Brigade; IWM 95/19/1, Sgt. R. T. Greenwood, 9th Battalion, Royal Tank Regiment.

44. David Kenyon Webster, *Parachute Infantry: An American Paratrooper's Memoir of D-Day and the Fall of the Third Reich* (New York: Random House, 2002), 48.

45. IWM 78/35/1, Madame A. de Vigneral. Even the official history acknowledges widespread looting by soldiers. In Ouistreham, the 207th Civil Affairs Detachment noted on June 12: "Looting by troops pretty general. British prestige has fallen here today." F. S. V. Donnison, *Civil Affairs and Military Government: Northwest Europe, 1944–1946* (London: HMSO, 1961), 74.

46. IWM 91/13/1, Major A. J. Forrest, 335 Battery, 107 Regiment, Royal Artillery.

47. IWM, 98/16/1 A. G. Herbert, 4th Battalion, Somerset Light Infantry; IWM P 182 Major G. Ritchie; IWM 99/61/1 Edward McCosh Elliot, 2nd Battalion, Glasgow Highlanders.

48. PRO, WO 219/3728, Civil Affairs report, August 30, 1944.

49. ADC, *Liberté de Normandie,* September 24–25, 1944, R.-N. Sauvage, "La grande pitié de la basse-normandie monumentale."

50. Donnison, *Civil Affairs and Military Government: Northwest Europe,* 101.

51. "Civil Affairs Agreement—France," in Donnison, *Civil Affairs and Military Government: Northwest Europe,* 472–76. Also see PRO, WO 219/3727, "Report on Recce of Second Army area," June 19, 1944, on appointment of Coulet and brief visit of de Gaulle to Bayeux on June 14. François Coulet (1906–84) was an early adherent to de Gaulle's London-based Free French movement, and had been named as de Gaulle's delegate in liberated Corsica in September 1943—the first French territory outside of Africa to be liberated. Since November 1943 he had been preparing for the takeover of political control in France. Although determined to assert France's sovereignty, he proved an able go-between with the Allied armies in liberation France; he went on to a long postwar career as a diplomat. See François Coulet, *Vertu des temps difficiles* (Paris: Plon, 1967).

52. "Report of Service with 82nd Airborne," June 15, 1944, in Coles and Weinberg, *Soldiers Become Governors,* 723.

53. Historical Division Interviews with Major James H. Litton, surgeon, and Major Harry Tousley, 298th General Hospital, July 23 and July 29, 1944, NARA, RG 498, European Theater of Operations, Historical Division, Administrative File, Cherbourg Notes, box 115.

54. Report on CA Detachment A1A1, Cherbourg, Lt. Col. Frank O. Howley commanding, in Coles and Weinberg, *Soldiers Become Governors,* 730–38. The French authorities in Calvados endorsed this positive appraisal of the Allied role, and singled out the 209 CA detachment in Caen for its "admirable sensitivity" and support in reviving the distraught city. ADC, 21 W 16, Prefecture du Calvados, Section Militaire de Liaison, January 31, 1945. For a more detailed look at Cherbourg in this period, see Footitt, *War and Liberation,* 66–94.

55. Report on CA Detachment A1A1, Cherbourg, Lt. Col. Frank O. Howley commanding, in Coles and Weinberg, *Soldiers Become Governors,* 732.

56. On "les tondues," or the sheared women, see Alain Brossat, *Les Tondues: un carnaval moche* (Paris: Manya, 1992); for estimate of numbers of shearings, see the pioneering study by Fabrice Virgili, *Shorn Women: Gender and Punishment in Liberation France* (Oxford, U.K.: Berg, 2002), 52.

57. Ulysses Lee, *The Employment of Negro Troops* (Washington, D.C.: Office of the Chief of Military History, 1966), 633; Roland G. Ruppenthal, *Logistical Support of the Armies,* vol. 2, *September 1944–May 1945* (Washington, D.C.: Office of the Chief of Military History, 1959), 134–48. The Red Ball Express ran from August until November; it was joined by the White Ball route from Le Havre and Rouen to forward areas, and the Red Lion route from Bayeux to Brussels. Edna Greene Medford, " 'Keep 'em Rolling': African American Participation in the Red Ball Express," *Negro History Bulletin,* December 1993.

58. ADC, 21 W 15/2, le Commissaire de Police, Trouville-sur-Mer, à M. le Prefet du Calvados, December 16, 1944; ADC, 21 W 16, Report of Chef d'Escadron Coulin, Gendarmerie Nationale, January 16, 1945; ADC, 21 W 16, Commissioner of Police in Vire to the Prefect of Calvados, February 3, 1945; passage on Mézidon cited in Françoise Dutour, *The Liberation of Calvados* (Caen: Calvados County Council, 1994), 138; ADC, 21 W 16, Report of Chef d'Escadron Coulin, Gendarmerie Nationale, Commandant la Compagnie

du Calvados, March 19, 1945; ADC, 9 W 45, le Prefet du Calvados au Commissaire regional de la République à Rouen, March 24, 1945.

59. ADC, 21 W 17, le Commissaire Central à M. le Prefet du Calvados, April 20, 1945; 21 W 17, le Commissaire Central à M. le Prefet du Calvados, June 19, 1945.

60. In August 1944, there were 1.9 million soldiers in the entire ETO; 154,000 were black. Ruppenthal, *Logistical Support,* 288; Lee, *Negro Troops,* 623. Although many more U.S. soldiers would arrive in Europe before the end of the war, black troops never exceeded 10 percent of the total, and the huge majority were assigned to service or rear areas.

61. U.S. Army, *History Branch Office of the Judge Advocate General, 18 July 1942–1 November 1945,* vol. 1, 241.

62. U.S. Army, History Branch Office, Vol 1, 10–12; 235.

63. Details of the cases can be followed in U.S. Army, *Holdings and Opinions, Board of Review,* Branch Office of the Judge Advocate General, European Theater of Operations, vols. 1–34. In particular, the following cases reflect upon the racially charged nature of the American presence in France—and the racially charged quality of American military justice: ETO 3141, *U.S. v. Whitfield;* ETO 370, *U.S. v. Sanders et al.;* ETO 3933, *U.S. v. Ferguson and Rorie;* ETO 4172, *U.S. v. Freeman Davis et al.;* ETO 4444, *U.S. v. Hudson et al.;* ETO 5584, *U.S. v. Yancy;* ETO 7702, *U.S. v. Shropshire;* ETO 8166, *U.S. v. Williams;* ETO 8450, *U.S. v. Garries et al.;* ETO 8451, *U.S. v. Skipper.*

64. U.S. Army, History Branch Office, Vol 1, 337–38.

65. *Holdings and Opinions, Board of Review,* vol. 11, ETO 3933, *U.S. v. Ferguson and Rorie,* 129–41; "Historical Report of the Provost Marshall," December 31, 1944, selection, in NARA, RG 498, European Theater of Operations, Historical Division, Administrative File, Cherbourg Notes, box 115.

66. ADC, *Liberté de Normandie,* August 31, 1944, "Les rations alimentaires de Septembre"; August 5, 1944, "La vente du pain et des biscuits"; ADC, 9 W 45, le Prefet du Calvados au Commissaire regional de la République à Rouen, December 9, 1944; and *Liberté de Normandie,* February 18–19, 1945; ADC, 21 W 15/2, Sous-prefecture de Bayeux, "Rapport bi-mensuel," December 20, 1944; ADC, *Liberté de Normandie,* July 28, 1944, "Tribunal Correctionnel"; 9 W 45, le Prefet du Calvados au Commissaire regional de la République à Rouen, November 23, 1944, and January 24, 1945; on prostitution and venereal disease, PRO, WO 219/3728, "The Army and VD Control in France."

67. ADC, *Liberté de Normandie,* September 6, 1944.

68. ADC, *Liberté de Normandie,* October 10, 1944; ADC, 9 W 45, le Prefet du Calvados au Commissaire regional de la République à Rouen, December 9, 1944; ADC, 21 W 6, Le directeur départemental du service des refugiés et sinistrés à M. le Préfet du Calvados, January 26, 1945. This document gives the figure 125,000 as the number of *sinistrés* [war victims] in the department.

69. Adam Sage, "Museum to D-Day Fails to Mention the War," *Times* (London), January 27, 2006.

2: Blood on the Snow

1. IWM, 95/19/1, Richard Trevor Greenwood, 9th Battalion, Royal Tank Regiment; IWM, 99/61/1, Major Edward Elliot, 2nd Battalion, Glasgow Highlanders; IWM, 03/28/1, Major Maurice Herbert Cooke, B Company, 8th Battalion, Royal Scots.

2. Captain Lord Carrington of the Guards Armoured Division, cited in Max Hastings, *Armageddon: The Battle for Germany, 1944–45* (New York: Knopf, 2004), 7; Peter Schrijvers, *The Crash of Ruin: American Combat Soldiers in World War II* (New York: New York University Press, 1998), 132.

3. On labor numbers, see Centre d'Études et de Documentation Guerre et Sociétés contemporaines [hereafter CEGES], Brussels, Haut Commissariat à la Sécurité de l'État, AA 1311, no. 114, summary by London-based Belgian government, March 13, 1944; for quotation about slavery, see CEGES, AA1311, no. 459, "L'opinion publique en Belgique après 44 mois d'occupation," February 1, 1944; on Jews, Etienne Verhoeyen, *La Belgique occupée: De*

l'an 40 à la liberation (Brussels: De Boeck, 1994), 573–79, and Werner Warmbrunn, *The German Occupation of Belgium, 1940–1944* (New York: Peter Lang, 1993), 169–71.

4. The details of these events and many others like them were gathered by Belgian officials immediately following the German retreat, and relied upon sworn testimony of numerous witnesses. They were gathered by the Commission des Crimes de Guerre of the Belgian government, and the reports are conserved in CEGES, AA 120, VII, 1 and 1bis.

5. PRO, FO 371/38896, Francis Aveling, chargé d'affaires, telegram to London, September 9, 1944; for ambassador's description of Pierlot, PRO, FO 371/48974, Sir H. Knatchbull-Hugessen to Anthony Eden, January 22, 1945; F. S. V. Donnison, *Civil Affairs and Military Government: Northwest Europe, 1944–1946* (London: HMSO, 1961), 115–17.

6. PRO, FO 371/38899, SHAEF Fortnightly Report, period ending November 28, 1944; FO 371/48974, SHAEF Weekly Summary by Gen. Erskine, period ending December 12, 1944; see also FO 371/38899, observations by Charles Peake, "Personal and Confidential," sent to Frank Roberts of the Foreign Office, December 8, 1944.

7. PRO, FO 371/38896, Major D. Morton, "Conditions in France and Belgium," Report to the War Cabinet, October 3, 1944; and PRO, FO 371/48974, "Survey of the General Situation in Belgium," report by Mr. Nand Geersens, Flemish Programme Organizer, of Radio Belgie and the BBC, December 20, 1944.

8. PRO, FO 371/38896, Francis Aveling, chargé d'affaires, to Anthony Eden, September 28, 1944.

9. PRO, FO 371/38896, "Order of the Day," October 2, 1944, General Dwight Eisenhower, "To the Officers and Men in all Belgian Resistance Organizations."

10. PRO, FO 371/48974, Sir H. Knatchbull-Hugessen to Anthony Eden, January 22, 1945; Harry L. Coles and Albert K. Weinberg, *Civil Affairs: Soldiers Become Governors* (Washington, D.C.: Office of the Chief of Military History, 1964), 805–9.

11. Pierre Sulbout, *Les troupes américaines à Liège (septembre 1944–décembre 1945): De l'enthousiasme aux réalités* (Ph.D. dissertation, Université de Liège, 1989), 39, 53, 69–70; and see report by J. S. Patterson of UNRRA, January 9, 1945, which claims that 543 people in Liège were killed in V-rocket attacks between November 20 and December 30, 1944. NARA, RG 331, Allied Operational and Occupation Headquarters, World War II, SHAEF, G-5 Division, Entry 47, box 31.

12. PRO, FO 371/38898, SHAEF Weekly Summary, Gen. Erskine, period ending October 31, 1944; and PRO, WO 205/835, "Effect of V-1s and V-2s on the Morale of the Antwerp Population," reports of November 6 and 16, 1944.

13. Koen Palinckx, *Antwerpen onder de V-bommen, 1944–45* (Antwerp: Pandora, 2004), 80–84. Palinckx provides a chart (135), showing that Antwerp took 5,960 hits from V-1s and V-2s.

14. PRO, FO 371/48974, Nand Geersens report; PRO, FO 371/38897, and 48974, Erskine weekly summaries of October 25 and December 12, 1944.

15. Omar Bradley, *A Soldier's Story* (New York: Henry Holt, 1951), 407. Eisenhower gives the number of fifty-four allied divisions on the continent by October 1, 1944, with six more in England. *Crusade in Europe* (Garden City, N.Y.: Doubleday, 1948), 322.

16. For the logistics headaches, see Russell Weigley, *Eisenhower's Lieutenants* (Bloomington: Indiana University Press, 1981), 268–83.

17. Bradley, *A Soldier's Story,* 416–25. The recriminations over the Antwerp episode may be followed in James L. Moulton, *Battle for Antwerp: The Liberation of the City and the Opening of the Scheldt, 1944* (London: I. Allan, 1978).

18. The relevant official U.S. histories are Charles B. MacDonald, *The Siegfried Line Campaign* (Washington, D.C.: Office of the Chief of Military History, 1963); Hugh M. Cole, *The Lorraine Campaign* (Washington, D.C.: Office of the Chief of Military History, 1950). Weigley has appraised this period of the war with a critical eye on American performance; for a more positive view, see Peter Mansoor, *The GI Offensive in Europe: The Triumph of American Infantry Divisions, 1941–1945* (Lawrence: University Press of Kansas, 1999).

19. Roland G. Ruppenthal, *Logistical Support of the Armies,* vol. 2, *September 1944–May 1945* (Washington, D.C.: Center of Military History, 1995), 317.

20. Bradley, *A Soldier's Story,* 444.

21. Danny S. Parker, *Battle of the Bulge: Hitler's Ardennes Offensive, 1944–1945* (Cambridge, Mass.: Da Capo, 2004), 334–35. For narrative power and technical detail, the best account of this tumultuous monthlong battle remains Charles B. MacDonald, *A Time for Trumpets: The Untold Story of the Battle of the Bulge* (New York: Bantam, 1985).

22. Martha Gellhorn, "The Battle of the Bulge," January 1945, reprinted in *The Face of War* (New York: Atlantic Monthly Press, 1988), 152; Charles B. MacDonald, *Company Commander* (1947; rept. Short Hills, N.J.: Burford Books, 1999), ix. On the brutalization of war in the east, see Omer Bartov, *Hitler's Army: Soldiers, Nazis, and War in the Third Reich* (New York: Oxford University Press, 1992).

23. MacDonald, *Company Commander,* 5; Donald Burgett, *Seven Roads to Hell: A Screaming Eagle at Bastogne* (New York: Dell, 1999), 9; Spencer F. Wurst and Gayle Wurst, *Descending From the Clouds* (Havertown, Penn.: Casemate, 2004), 228; John Babcock, *Taught to Kill* (Dulles, Va.: Potomac Books, 2005), 54. On attitudes toward the war, see Samuel A. Stouffer et al., *The American Soldier,* vol. 1, *Adjustment During Army Life* (Princeton: Princeton University Press, 1949), 433.

24. Marvin D. Kays, "Weather Effects during the Battle of the Bulge," August 1982, prepared for U.S. Army Atmospheric Sciences Laboratory, USAMHI, Kaplan Papers, box 2.

25. George Neill, *Infantry Soldier: Holding the Line at the Battle of the Bulge* (Norman: University of Oklahoma Press, 2000), 80, 85, 91, 95–97; George Wilson, *If You Survive* (New York: Random House, 1987), 205.

26. Roscoe C. Blunt, Jr., *Foot Soldier: A Combat Infantryman's War in Europe* (Cambridge, Mass.: Da Capo, 2002), 122–23; Babcock, *Taught to Kill,* 59.

27. Burgett, *Seven Roads,* 1; MacDonald, *Company Commander,* 60; Neill, *Infantry Soldier,* 112–13; Blunt, *Foot Soldier,* 117; Wilson, *If You Survive,* 206.

28. John Dollard, *Fear in Battle* (Washington, D.C.: Institute of Human Relations, Yale University and *The Infantry Journal,* 1944; rept. Westport, Conn.: Greenwood Press, 1977), 4; Samuel A. Stouffer et al., *American Soldier,* vol. 2, 201–23; Burgett, *Seven Roads to Hell,* 51; MacDonald, *Company Commander,* 45; Burgett, *Seven Roads,* 240.

29. MacDonald, *Company Commander,* 14, 30.

30. Burgett, *Seven Roads,* 243; Blunt, *Foot Soldier,* 86; Babcock, *Taught to Kill,* 86; Blunt, *Foot Soldier,* 81.

31. Burgett, *Seven Roads,* 9, 19; Babcock, *Taught to Kill,* 54, 67, 138–39.

32. Neill, *Infantry Soldier,* 129, 228.

33. Burgett, *Seven Roads,* 163.

34. Blunt, *Foot Soldier,* 138, 145; Neill, *Infantry Soldier,* 145, 247; David Kenyon Webster, *Parachute Infantry* (New York: Dell, 2002), 57; MacDonald, *Company Commander,* 126, 157.

35. Babcock, *Taught to Kill,* 43; Blunt, *Foot Soldier,* 138.

36. The precise numbers of civilian casualties are difficult to pin down. The excellent National Museum of Military History at Diekirch, Luxembourg, under the direction of M. Roland Gaul, has concluded that 3,800 people were killed or wounded in Belgium and Luxembourg during the battle.

37. Laurent Lombard, *Stavelot, cité héroique et martyre,* selection in USAMHI, Kaplan papers, box 1.

38. Hugh M. Cole, *The Ardennes: Battle of the Bulge* (Washington, D.C.: Office of the Chief of Military History, 1965), 262–63.

39. The precise number of Americans killed, and their precise location when they were killed, has been the subject of dispute for many years. For a reliable account, see MacDonald, *Time for Trumpets,* 213–23; and Cole, *The Ardennes,* 260–64. The Malmédy massacre was the subject of a special congressional investigation: *Hearings Before a Subcommittee of the Committee on Armed Services, United States Senate, 81st Cong., 1st session* (Washington, D.C.:

U.S. Congress, 1949). Also see James Weingartner, *Crossroads of Death: The Story of the Malmédy Massacre and Trial* (Berkeley: University of California Press, 1979).

40. The evidence presented here comes from the detailed investigation carried out by the Belgian Commission des Crimes de Guerre, published as *Les Crimes de Guerre commis pendant la contre-offensive de von Rundstedt dans les Ardennes, décembre 1944–janvier 1945, Stavelot* (Liège: Georges Thone, 1945). See also CEGES AA 1311, no. 710, report by mayor, Arnold Godin, "Ville de Stavelot," January 8, 1945.

41. The slaughter of civilians in Bande is detailed in reports for the Commission des Crimes de Guerre, CEGES AA 120/VII/1 bis. The shootings were allegedly in retribution for the attacks carried out by the resistance in the town against the retreating Germans in September 1944. For further detail on these and other atrocities, see Mathieu Longue, *Massacres en Ardennes: Hiver, 1944–45* (Brussels: Editions Racine, 2006), 67–83, 178–83; and Joss Heintz, *In the Perimeter of Bastogne December 1944–January 1945* (Omnia: Ostend, 1965).

42. Cole, *The Ardennes*, 393–422. It is worth quoting the conclusion of Hugh Cole on the military value of the stout defense at Saint Vith: "The losses sustained by the defenders of St. Vith must be measured against their accomplishments. They had met an entire German corps flushed with easy victory and halted it in its tracks. They had firmly choked one of the main enemy lines of communication and forced days of delay on the westward movement of troops, guns, tanks, and supplies belonging to two German armies. They had given the XVIII Airborne Corps badly needed time to gather for a coordinated and effective defense. Finally, these units had carried out a successful withdrawal under the most difficult conditions and would return again to the battle" (Cole, 422).

43. Mme. Meurer in Rivet and Sevenans, eds., *La Bataille des Ardennes*, 27–29; CEGES, AA 1311, no. 758, "Situation à St. Vith," two reports of February 3 and 5, 1945. See also Schrijvers, *Unknown Dead*, 87–92 and 167–87.

44. Alfred Dubru, *L'offensive von Rundstedt à Houffalize* (Houffalize: Editions Haut-Pays, 1993), 49–50.

45. CEGES, "Houffalize: son martyre," pamphlet self-published by town of Houffalize. Dubru also provides a detailed list of the victims, *L'offensive*, 99–110.

46. CEGES, AA1311, no. 715, "Houffalize, 19 Janvier 1945"; AA 1311, no. 758, two reports titled "Situation à Houffalize," January 31 and February 12, 1945. For an account by one reporter, see "Houffalize, vision dantésque," *Les Nouvelles*, February 7, 1945, news clipping in CEGES, AA 1311, no. 758.

47. Bradley, *A Soldier's Story*, 492.

48. *1944: Un Noël en enfer: Des Malmédiens racontent* (Malmédy: Royal Syndicat d'Initiative et de Tourisme, 1994).

49. CEGES, AA 1311, no. 1009, "Extrait Rapport Gendarmerie," January 23, 1945, and letter to the Auditor General, dated December 30, 1944, AA1311, no. 713.

50. L. Didier-Robert, *La Mémoire de Sainlez: L'offensive von Rundstedt vécue au village* (Bastogne: Cercle d'histoire de Bastogne, n.d.).

51. Report by Major Edward O'Donnell, January 29, 1945, "Report on Public Health Conditions in La Roche, Belgium," NARA, RG 331, Allied Operations and Occupation Headquarters, SHAEF G-5 Division, Box 47. For similar assessments that stressed the scale of the physical destruction, see Lt. Anspach report on La Roche of January 22, 1945, CEGES, AA 1311, no. 704, and report of January 14, 1945, by Office of Military Auditor, CEGES, AA 1311, no. 714. First Army Civil Affairs activities in Liège, Verviers, and the Eupen-Malmédy area provided medical supplies, food, sanitation, transportation of wounded, shelter for refugees, and repairs to water mains. Medical Department, United States Army, *Preventive Medicine in World War II*, vol. 8, *Civil Affairs/Military Government Public Health Activities* (Washington, D.C., 1976), 451–52.

52. Ganshof to Erskine, January 25, 1945, CEGES, AA 1311, no. 528.

53. CEGES, AA 1311, no. 528.

54. Sulbout, "Les troupes américaines a Liège," 120–21; CEGES, AA 1311, no. 526, "Rapport de la Sûreté de l'État: Opinion publique," March 5, 1945.

55. CEGES, "Rapport de la Sûreté de l'Etat en date du 10–17 February 1945," AA1311, no. 526; and report on "Esprit public," February 2, 1945, from Charleroi, AA1311, no. 528.

56. These quotations come from a number of regional reports gathered in the files of the High Commission for State Security, compiled by Commissioner Walter Ganshof and his staff, and dated March 9, 11, 16, 17, 18, and 23, 1945. CEGES, AA 1311, no. 526.

57. Medical Department, United States Army, *Preventive Medicine in World War II*, vol. 5, *Communicable Diseases* (Washington, D.C., 1960), "Incidence Rates for Venereal Diseases, all forms, in the US Army," 257.

58. *Preventive Medicine*, vol. 5, 143–46.

59. PRO, WO 219/3734 and WO 219/3735A, Historical Survey, 21st Army Group, Civil Affairs/Military Government Branch, December 1944; WO 219/3736A, Historical Survey, 21st Army Group, Civil Affairs/Military Government Branch, January–March 1945.

60. PRO, WO 219/3737, SHAEF G-5 Public Health Branch, February 6, 1945.

61. *Preventive Medicine in World War II*, vol. 8, report by Major John A. Lewis, December 7, 1945, 332–33.

62. CEGES, AA 1311, no. 759, "Appel à la population," printed in *La Presse verviétoise*, March 17, 1945.

63. CEGES, AA 1311, no. 761, "Prostitution—maladies vénériennes," March 23, 1945.

64. CEGES, AA 1311, no. 526, Report from the police chief of Visé (just north of Liège), September 1, 1945. The tally of civilian deaths was broken down by SHAEF as follows: 13,000 killed due to Allied bombing in 1943–45; 10,000 killed due to V-1 and V-2 bombing (which is likely an overestimate); 7,000 killed in the fighting in 1940 and in the Ardennes. In addition, 6,400 Belgian soldiers died in 1940, and 1,264 died in captivity. SHAEF Intelligence Summary, June 6, 1945, CEGES AA 1311, no. 919.

3: Hunger

1. Roscoe C. Blunt, *Foot Soldier: A Combat Infantryman's War in Europe* (Cambridge, Mass.: Da Capo Press, 2002), 56.

2. SHAEF Fortnightly Report no. 16, May 15, 1945, PRO, WO 202/838.

3. Gerhard Hirschfeld, *Nazi Rule and Dutch Collaboration: The Netherlands under German Occupation, 1940–45*, trans. by Louise Wilmot (Oxford, U.K.: Berg, 1988), 12–27. Seyss-Inquart was hanged in October 1946, after being convicted of war crimes at the Nuremberg tribunal.

4. Werner Warmbrunn, *The Dutch under German Occupation, 1940–1945* (Stanford, Calif.: Stanford University Press, 1963), 5–17, 21–34, 61–82. On the figures for Jewish deportations, see Lucy Dawidowicz, *The War against the Jews, 1933–1945* (New York: Holt, Rinehart, Winston, 1975), 366–68.

5. Two reports from within occupied Holland: PRO, FO 371/39329, May 20, 1944, from Ridley Prentice to Political Intelligence Department; quotation from PRO, FO 371/39330, June 5, 1944, from Press Reading Room, Stockholm, to Political Intelligence Department, London.

6. PRO, FO 371/39329, Max Huber, International Committee of the Red Cross, to Field Marshal Sir Philip Chetwode, Chairman of the Executive Committee of the British Red Cross, April 14, 1944; Anthony Eden to Sir Philip Chetwode, June 12, 1944.

7. PRO, FO 371/39329, May 20, 1944, from Ridley Prentice to Political Intelligence Department, quoting source inside Holland.

8. PRO, FO 371/39330, Gerbrandy, personal letter, to Churchill, September 28, 1944.

9. PRO, WO 219/2286, September 3, 1944, Memorandum by Lt. Gen. Frederick Morgan, "Proposed War Establishments of SHAEF Missions to the Netherlands and Belgium."

10. PRO, AIR 8/823, "Interview between the Prime Minister and Dr. Gerbrandy, Prime Minister of the Netherlands," October 5, 1944, minutes by Major D. Morton. The Dutch

Embassy in Washington had made much the same appeal to the United States Department of State, on October 3. See Secretary of State Hull to Ambassador Winant, October 7, 1944, in *Foreign Relations of the United States* [hereafter *FRUS*] 1944, II: 285–87.

11. PRO, WO 8/823: Foreign Office to Secretary, Chiefs of Staff Committee, October 5, 1944; Ministry of Economic Warfare to Foreign Office, October 2, 1944; Dutch government Memorandum on Food Conditions in Netherlands, September 29, 1944.

12. PRO, AIR 8/823, Eisenhower to AGWAR, October 29, 1944.

13. PRO, AIR 8/823, Chiefs of Staff Alan Brooke, Charles Portal, Andrew Cunningham, War Cabinet, Chiefs of Staff Committee, November 2, 1944; Eisenhower to U.K. Base for British Chiefs of Staff, November 6, 1944.

14. PRO, WO 106/4419, "Relief Supplies for Holland," February 11, 1945; "Supplies for the Civilian Population in Holland," February 22, 1945. On the impact of the Swedish supplies, see Henri A. van der Zee, *The Hunger Winter: Occupied Holland, 1944–45* (Lincoln: University of Nebraska Press, 1982), 176–78.

15. PRO, FO 371/49032, Summary of Drummond Report, February 3, 1945; Attlee to Churchill, February 5, 1945; Queen Wilhelmina to Churchill and Roosevelt, January 15, 1945, in Harry L. Coles and Albert K. Weinberg, *Civil Affairs: Soldiers Become Governors* (Washington, D.C.: Office of the Chief of Military History, 1964), 828–29.

16. PRO, FO 371/49403, Memorandum from Netherlands Government to Ambassador Neville Bland, January 1, 1945; FO 371/49404, Reports in *Vrij Nederland,* summarized in Neville Bland to Anthony Eden, January 5, 1945, and January 18, 1945; PRO, FO 371/49404, SHAEF Mission Fortnightly Report for period ending January 15, 1945. For an earlier exchange of letters between Gerbrandy and Eisenhower on food supplies, see Coles and Weinberg, *Civil Affairs,* 827–28.

17. PRO, WO 32/16168, Montgomery to Eisenhower, cipher message, February 3, 1945; Montgomery to Grigg, February 11, 1945.

18. PRO, FO 371/49032, Eisenhower, "Personal to General Marshall for Combined Chiefs of Staff," February 14, 1945; Eisenhower to CCS, February 25, 1945; Roosevelt to Churchill, March 1, 1945; Churchill to Roosevelt, March 2, 1945; Roosevelt to Churchill, March 11, 1945.

19. PRO, WO 202/838, Fortnightly Report no. 11, period ending February 28, 1945.

20. PRO, WO 321/16168, Richard Law, Foreign Office, to P. J. Grigg, War Office, February 16, 1945, *FRUS* 1945; V: 5–8, Hornbeck to Roosevelt, February 21, 1945.

21. PRO, WO 106/4419, War Cabinet, Joint Planning Staff, "Relief for Occupied Holland," March 8, 1945; memorandum for meeting to be held on March 9, "Relief for Occupied Holland;" summary of meeting, March 9, 1945; Field Marshall Lord Alanbrooke, *War Diaries, 1939–1945,* edited by Alex Danchev and Daniel Todman (Berkeley: University of California Press, 2001), 670; telegram from Chiefs of Staff to General Eisenhower, March 14, 1945; Winston Churchill, *Triumph and Tragedy,* vol. 6 (Boston: Houghton Mifflin, 1953), 410.

22. PRO, AIR 20/5005, Eisenhower to War Department, Combined Chiefs of Staff and British Chiefs of Staff, March 27, 1945; PRO, WO 106/4420, War Cabinet, Joint Planning Staff, "Plans for the Liberation of Holland," April 6, 1945.

23. PRO, WO 202/838, SHAEF Mission, Political Intelligence Report no. 8, March 31, 1945.

24. PRO, AIR 8/823, "Prime Minister to President Roosevelt, Personal and Top Secret," April 10, 1945; *FRUS* 1945, V: 20, Roosevelt to Churchill, April 10, 1945; WO 106/4420, Eisenhower to War Office, April 15, 1945.

25. Imperial War Museum, 94/51/1 Miss Margaret von Lenip, December 25, 1945.

26. Liedewij Hawke and Elly Dull in Lance Goddard, ed., *Canada and the Liberation of the Netherlands* (Toronto: Goddard Press, 2005), 140–42; Margaretha Vasalis, diary excerpt, in Max Nord, ed., *Thank You, Canada* (Amsterdam: N.V. De Arbeiderspers, 1967), 125.

27. David Kaufman, ed., *A Liberation Album: Canadians in the Netherlands, 1944–45* (Toronto: McGraw-Hill, 1980), 50–55.

28. G. C. E. Burger, J. C. Drummond, and H. R. Stanstead, eds., *Malnutrition and Starvation in Western Netherlands, September 1944–July 1945* (The Hague: General State Printing Office, 1948), 20–24.

29. Henri van der Zee, *Hunger Winter,* 148–50; Tram conductor, thirty-nine years old, Rotterdam, diary entry of April 22, 1945, published in the collection *Dagboek Fragmenten, 1940–1945* (Amsterdam: Rijksinstituut voor Oorlogsdocumentatie, 1954), 599–600. For additional details from this tragic collection, see pages 448, 452–53, 557–60, 563–64, and 606.

30. The most comprehensive account is C. P. Stacey, *Official History, Canadian Army in the Second World War,* vol. 3, *The Victory Campaign, 1944–45* (Ottawa: The Queen's Printer, 1960). A more recent and nuanced account is Terry Copp, *Cinderella Army: The Canadians in Northwest Europe, 1944–45* (Toronto: University of Toronto Press, 2006). Overall Canadian casualties between June 6, 1944, and the end of the war were 44,339. Of these, 11,336 were killed. Stacey, *Victory Campaign,* 611. Copp provides a chart of Canadian losses in northwest Europe, week by week, in *Cinderella Army,* 302–3.

31. PRO, FO 106/4420, Prime Minister to Mr. Eden, in Washington, April 16, 1945; and transcript of Seyss-Inquart discussions with Dutch, April 12, 1945.

32. PRO, WO 106/4420, Secretary of War and Combined Chiefs of Staff to Eisenhower, April 23, 1945; Eisenhower to Chiefs of Staff, April 23, 1945; Eisenhower to War Office, April 24; Eisenhower to Combined Chiefs of Staff and British Chiefs of Staff, April 27 and April 29.

33. PRO, WO 106/4420, British Chiefs of Staff meeting minutes, April 30, 1945; EXFOR REAR Q to SHAEF G-4, May [3?] 1945; AIR 8/823, Air Staff SHAEF to Bomber Command and Air Ministry, Whitehall, April 28, 1945; Francis de Guingand, *Operation Victory* (New York: Charles Scribner's Sons, 1947), 445–47.

34. The details of the Achterveld meeting come from a Canadian report on the conference, PRO, WO 205/1073, "Col. Sellors' Report, 1st Canadian Corps, Intelligence Summary no. 290, May 6, 1945, Achterveld Conference," which contains General Smith's *bon mot* to Seyss-Inquart; and de Guingand, *Operation Victory,* 450–53.

35. For an excellent eyewitness account of the surrender, see "Freedom for Holland; Surrender by Blaskowitz," *Times* (London), May 7, 1945.

36. PRO, WO 205/1074, "Brief Historical Outline of the Occupation of N.W. Holland by 1st Canadian Corps," undated.

37. Lance Goddard, ed., *Canada and the Liberation of the Netherlands* (Toronto: Goddard Press, 2005), 212–14. See also Max Nord, ed., *Thank You, Canada.*

38. PRO, WO 32/11704, SHAEF G-5 Branch, "Report on Tour of NW Holland, May 10–15, 1945," prepared by Brigadier L. F. Field, Deputy Chief, Economics Branch.

39. "Relief for Holland," *Times,* May 7, 1945.

40. "Food in Germany for 60 Days; People's Health Good," *Times,* May 23, 1945. "I think they were rather inclined to exaggerate the conditions of starvation," sniffed Francis de Guingand in his memoir, and blamed Gerbrandy for his "propaganda" effort. *Operation Victory,* 438; PRO, WO 202/838, SHAEF Mission, Fortnightly Report No. 16, period ending May 15, 1945; WO 32/11704, reports by M. B. Knowles and Anthony Lousada of the Ministries of Food and Production respectively, filed on May 19 and 22, 1945; Military Government Branch, Main HQ, First Canadian Army, Weekly Report no. 27, period May 13–19, 1945, NARA, RG 331, SHAEF G-5, Entry 47, box 27.

41. Burger, Drummond, and Stanstead, *Malnutrition and Starvation,* 28–43; 48–57; Netherlands District, Weekly Progress Report no. 1, May 20, 1945, "Progress of Relief and Rehabilitation in the Provinces of North and South Holland and Utrecht," NARA, RG 331, SHAEF G-5, Entry 47, box 27.

42. PRO, FO 371/49406, Memo by Sir Paul Grey, first secretary of the British Embassy in the Hague, sent to Foreign Minister Ernest Bevin by Sir Neville Bland, September 25, 1945.

43. M. J. L. Dols and D. J. A. M. van Arcken, "Food Supply and Nutrition in the Netherlands during and Immediately after World War II," *Milbank Memorial Fund Quarterly* 24, 4 (Oct. 1946), 352. C. Banning's analysis suggests that 10,000 people died of malnutrition, at a minimum. "Food Shortage and Public Health," special issue on "The Netherlands during the German Occupation," *Annals of the American Academy of Political and Social Science* 245 (May 1946), 93–110.

PART II: INTO GERMANY

Prologue: Armies of Justice

1. Ruth Andreas-Friedrich, *Battleground Berlin: Diaries, 1945–48,* trans. by Anna Boerresen (New York: Paragon House, 1990), 6, 9.

2. William Walton, "G.I. Wisdom," *Time,* February 5, 1945; Ralph G. Martin, "What Kind of Peace? The Soldier's Viewpoint," *New York Times,* March 11, 1945.

3. Nikolai Tikhonov, "Liberation Army," February 16, 1945, in S. Krasilshchik, *World War II Dispatches from the Soviet Front,* trans. by Nina Bouis (New York: Sphinx Press, 1985), 322–23.

4: Red Storm in the East

1. Ilya Ehrenburg, *The War: 1941–1945* (vol. 5 of *Men, Years—Life*), trans. by Tatiana Shebunina (New York: World Publishing Company, 1964), 188.

2. For a discussion of the problems in determining the number of Soviet war dead, see John Erickson, "Red Army Battlefield Performance, 1941–45: The System and the Soldier," in Paul Addison and Angus Calder, eds., *Time to Kill: The Soldier's Experience of War in the West, 1939–1945* (London: Pimlico, 1997), 233–48.

3. For U.S. war casualties, see Congressional Research Service, "American War and Military Operations Casualties: Lists and Statistics," June 2007, available at http://www.fas.org/sgp/crs/natsec/RL32492.pdf.

4. Ilya Ehrenburg, "On the First Day," June 22, 1941, in S. Krasilshchik, ed., *World War II Dispatches from the Soviet Front* (New York: Sphinx, 1985), 5–7. Alexander Werth, a Russian-born journalist for the *Sunday Times* of London, and a man who spent almost the entire war in Russia, recalled the importance of "Ehrenburg's articles in *Pravda* and *Red Star*—brilliant and eloquent diatribes against the Germans, which were very popular in the Army." *Russia at War, 1941–1945* (New York: E. P. Dutton, 1964), 274.

5. Karel C. Berkhoff, *Harvest of Despair: Life and Death in Ukraine under Nazi Rule* (Cambridge, Mass.: Harvard University Press, 2004), 7–8.

6. On Hitler's war aims in Russia, see Jürgen Förster, "Hitler Turns East: German War Policy in 1940 and 1941," in Bernd Wegner, *From Peace to War: Germany, Soviet Russia and the World, 1939–1941* (Oxford, U.K.: Berghahn Books, 1997), 115–33; Military directive of December 18, 1940, in J. Noakes and G. Pridham, eds., *Nazism 1919–1945,* vol. 3, *Foreign Policy, War and Racial Extermination: A Documentary Reader* (Exeter, U.K.: University of Exeter Press, 1988), 809. For the origins of Barbarosa, see Horst Boog et al., eds., *Germany and the Second World War,* vol. 4, *The Attack on the Soviet Union* (Oxford, U.K.: Clarendon Press, 1998). Adolf Hitler, *Mein Kampf,* trans. by Ralph Manheim (Boston: Houghton Mifflin, 1971), 652–53, 662; Förster, "Hitler Turns East," 131; and Förster's chapter, "Operation Barbarossa as a War of Conquest and Annihilation," in Boog, *Germany and the Second World War,* vol. 4, 481–90. The evidence for the link between a war against Russia and a final solution to the Jewish "problem" is overwhelming, and powerfully presented in Ian Kershaw, *Hitler,* vol. 2, *Nemesis* (New York: Norton, 2000), chapter 8.

7. Earl F. Ziemke and Magna E. Bauer, *Moscow to Stalingrad: Decision in the East* (Washington, D.C.: Center of Military History, 1987), 3–15.

8. Stalin quoted in Werth, *Russia at War,* 163.

9. Marius Broekmeyer, *Stalin, the Russians, and Their War,* trans. by Rosalind Buck (Madison: University of Wisconsin Press, 2004), 54; and Joachim Hoffman, "The Conduct of the War through Soviet Eyes," in Boog, *Germany and the Second World War,* vol. 4, 848.

10. Antony Beevor and Luba Vinogradova, eds., *A Writer at War: Vasily Grossman with the Red Army, 1941–1945* (New York: Pantheon, 2005), 48.

11. Simon Sebag Montefiore, *Stalin: The Court of the Red Tsar* (New York: Knopf, 2004), 399.

12. Ilya Ehrenburg, "We'll Survive," October 28, 1941, *World War II Dispatches,* 29–32.

13. Werth, *Russia at War,* 246.

14. Broekmeyer, *Stalin, the Russians and Their War,* 56, 59.

15. This point is particularly stressed by Richard Overy, *Why the Allies Won* (New York: Norton, 1995), 180–82; and *Russia's War,* 118. In the second half of 1941, despite the invasion and its huge disruptions, the USSR produced significantly more armaments than it had done in the first six months of 1941. Soviet factories churned out 4,470 tanks, 8,000 aircraft, 55,500 artillery pieces, 1.5 million rifles, and 40 million shells in the second half of the year, and the numbers soared in 1942, when they produced 24,445 tanks and 21,000 aircraft. Joachim Hoffman, "The Conduct of the War," 856.

16. Yevgeny Petrov, "In Klin," December 16, 1941, *World War II Dispatches,* 44–48.

17. Werth, *Russia at War,* 194.

18. Broekmeyer, *Stalin, the Russians, and Their War,* 94–95; Overy, *Russia's War,* 158–60; Erickson, *The Road to Stalingrad,* 371.

19. Overy, *Russia's War,* 175; Erickson, *Road to Stalingrad,* 364.

20. Werth, *Russia at War,* 560–62; Grossman, "Military Council," December 29, 1942, *World War II Dispatches,* 157–58. For a superbly detailed account of the battle at Stalingrad, see Antony Beevor, *Stalingrad* (New York: Penguin, 1999).

21. Noakes and Pridham, eds., *Nazism,* 898–99. For Hitler's musings about the destruction of the Soviet peoples and the creation of a German paradise in the east, see Kershaw, *Hitler,* 2, 400–4. An excellent overall survey of Hitler's aims for his conquered territories is Norman Rich, *Hitler's War Aims: The Establishment of the New Order* (New York: Norton, 1974).

22. Christopher Browning, "The Nazi Decision to Commit Mass Murder, Three Interpretations—The Euphoria of Victory and the Final Solution, summer-fall 1941," *German Studies Review* 17, no. 3 (Oct. 1994), 473–81; and *The Origins of the Final Solution: The Evolution of Nazi Jewish Policy, September 1939–1942* (Lincoln: University of Nebraska Press, 2004), 309–14; Richard Breitman, *The Architect of Genocide: Himmler and the Final Solution* (Hanover, N.H.: Brandeis University Press, 1991), 167–97, provides details on Himmler's activities in the summer of 1941.

23. Martin Gilbert, *The Holocaust: A History of the Jews of Europe during the Second World War* (New York: Henry Holt, 1985), 154.

24. Gilbert, *The Holocaust,* 175. The numbers of killings are from Gilbert, 154–75.

25. Browning, *The Origins of the Final Solution,* 315.

26. Kershaw, *Hitler,* 2, 464.

27. Boris Kacel, *From Hell to Redemption: A Memoir of the Holocaust* (Niwot: University Press of Colorado, 1998), 5–6.

28. Berkhoff, *Harvest of Despair,* 42.

29. http://www.ns-archiv.de/krieg/1941/kommissarbefehl.php.

30. Order of July 2, 1941, from Reinhard Heydrich to *Einsatzgruppen* leaders, Noakes and Pridham, eds., *Nazism,* 1091.

31. The numbers of POW deaths is debated; for a survey, see Theo J. Schulte, *The German Army and Nazi Policies in Occupied Russia* (Oxford, U.K.: Berg, 1989), 180–210; and the work of Christian Streit, *Keine Kameraden: Die Wehrmacht und die sowjetischen Kriegsgefangenen 1941–1945* (Stuttgart: Deutsche Verlags-Anstalt, 1978). Werth provides horrific details: *Russia at War,* 703–9.

32. Alexander Dallin, *German Rule in Russia, 1941–1945: A Study of Occupation Policies,* 2nd ed. (Boulder, Colo.: Westview Press, 1981), 428–53; Timothy P. Mulligan, *The Politics of Illusion and Empire: German Occupation Policy in the Soviet Union, 1942–1943* (Westport, Conn.: Praeger, 1988), 111–16; Himmler, October 4, 1943, to SS leaders in Posen, in Noakes and Pridham, *Nazism,* 919–20.

33. Berkhoff, *Harvest of Despair,* 131–36, 164–86; Bohdan Krawchenko, "Soviet Ukraine under Nazi Occupation, 1941–44," in Yury Boshyk, *Ukraine during World War II* (Edmonton: Canadian Library of Ukrainian Studies, 1986), 15–37.

34. Ehrenburg, *We Will Not Forget* (Washington, D.C.: Soviet Embassy, June 1944), articles titled "Two Years," June 1943, and "Beginning of the End," September 1943; Grossman in Beevor and Vinogradova, eds., *A Writer at War,* 252–60.

35. For an excellent exploration of Stalin's thinking, see Constantine Pleshakov and Vlad Zubok, *Inside the Kremlin's Cold War: From Stalin to Khrushchev* (Cambridge, Mass.: Harvard University Press, 1996), especially 1–77. For the size of the Red Army at this point, see John Erickson, *The Road to Berlin* (London: Weidenfeld & Nicolson, 1983), 146.

36. There are a number of detailed studies of the conference, but the most lucid and well written comes from the pen, not surprisingly, of Churchill himself: *The Second World War,* vol. 5, *Closing the Ring* (Boston: Houghton Mifflin, 1951), 342–407. The official record, comprised mostly of notes taken by Charles Bohlen of the State Department, who served as the American translator, is published in *Foreign Relations of the United States: The Conferences at Cairo and Tehran, 1943* (Washington, D.C.: Department of State, 1961). See also Charles Bohlen, *Witness to History, 1929–1969* (New York: Norton, 1973), 134–54. For a full-blown study, see Keith Eubank, *Summit at Tehran* (New York: William Morrow, 1985).

37. Churchill, *Second World War,* vol. 5, 374; *FRUS, Teheran,* 553–54.

38. Jan T. Gross, "Sovietization of Poland's Eastern Territories," in Bernd Wegner, ed., *From Peace to War,* 63–78. Gross considers Soviet actions in Poland in the two years before Barbarossa to have been "far more injurious than those of the Nazis," 78.

39. Churchill made his views plain to the London Poles as early as July 1943, when he told President Władysław Raczkiewicz that despite Britain's strong support for Poland, he "had never wanted, and was still unwilling, to assume any obligation in the matter of Polish frontiers. Frontiers were not a 'taboo' and could be changed, perhaps by exchange of populations." "Note on a Conversation between President Raczkiewicz and Mr. Churchill," July 26, 1943, in *Documents on Polish-Soviet Relations, 1939–1945,* vol. 2 (London: Heinemann, 1967), 25–28. For further details on the British-Polish relations in this period, see Jan M. Ciechanowski, *The Warsaw Rising of 1944* (London: Cambridge University Press, 1974), especially chapter 1.

40. *FRUS, Teheran,* 509–12.

41. A copy of the map with Stalin's red pencil marks is in *FRUS, Teheran,* 601.

42. For Soviet military figures, John Erickson, *The Road to Berlin: Stalin's War with Germany,* vol. 2 (London: Weidenfeld & Nicolson, 1983), 146, 214, 228; narrative in Overy, *Russia's War,* 241–50.

43. Ehrenburg, "The Roads to Berlin," in *We Will Not Forget,* 56. The Red Army did not bring freedom to the Crimea and Caucasus. There, where some of the independent, non-Russian peoples had initially welcomed the Nazi invasion as putting an end to the extreme cruelty of Soviet rule, and where some had agreed to fight alongside the Germans against the Red Army, Stalin swiftly settled scores. In 1943 and 1944, the Chechens, Ingush, Karachay, Meskhets from Georgia, Balkars, Kalmyks from the lower Volga, and Kurds—a hodgepodge of ancient ethnicities that had never felt beholden to Russia's centralizing autocrats, whether Tsarist or Communist—were rounded up and deported to Kazakhstan, Kyrgyzstan, or Siberia. Their crime was simply that they had survived the German occupation, and therefore might be suspected of collaboration or sympathy toward the foreign occupation. Using tactics similar to those of the German invaders, Soviet security police (NKVD) entered towns across the Caucasus, used force and threats of death to compel local inhabitants to appear in town squares or at railheads, pushed people by the hundreds onto U.S. supplied lend-

lease trucks or boxcars, nailed the doors shut, and sent them east. The Tatars of the Crimea, accused of collaboration with the German occupiers, were similarly treated: in May 1944, almost 200,000 were deported to Central Asia. A total of 1.5 million people were deported in this manner in 1943–44; a large percentage died during the deportation. At a time when the Soviet Union was still fighting a war of survival against a powerful foreign enemy, Stalin devoted time and scarce resources to wage war on his own countrymen. One and a half million people met this fate in late 1943 and early 1944. P. M. Polian, *Against Their Will: The History and Geography of Forced Migrations in the USSR* (New York: Central European University Press, 2004), 140–57; and tables, 330–32.

44. "Note on the conversation between Mr. Mikołajczyk and Mr. Churchill," February 16, 1944, in *Documents on Polish-Soviet Relations,* 180–87.

45. "Order of the Commander of the Home Army to the Districts of the latter relating to the attitude of the USSR towards the struggle of underground Poland against Germany," July 12, 1944, in *Documents on Polish-Soviet Relations,* 284–85.

46. Norman Davies, *Rising '44: The Battle for Warsaw* (New York: Viking, 2003), 232.

47. Wlodzimierz Borodziej, *The Warsaw Uprising of 1944,* trans. by Barbara Harshav (Madison: University of Wisconsin Press, 2006), 70–71.

48. Ciechanowski, *The Warsaw Rising of 1944,* 212–42.

49. The astonishing brutality of these hoodlums is detailed in Joanna K. M. Hanson, *The Civilian Population and the Warsaw Uprising of 1944* (London: Cambridge University Press, 1982), 87–92.

50. Borodziej, *The Warsaw Uprising of 1944,* 74–99.

51. Erickson, *The Road to Berlin,* 247–90.

52. Ciechanowski, *The Warsaw Rising of 1944,* 312–15.

53. Edward J. Rozek, *Allied Wartime Diplomacy: A Pattern in Poland* (New York: Wiley & Sons, 1958), 248; Stalin to Mikołajczyk, August 16, 1944, *Documents on Polish-Soviet Relations,* 346–47.

54. Stalin to Churchill and Roosevelt, August 22, 1944, *Documents on Polish-Soviet Relations,* 356.

55. Borodziej, *The Warsaw Uprising of 1944,* 130.

56. Churchill, *The Second World War,* vol. 6, 226–28, 231.

57. Churchill, *The Second World War,* vol. 6, 237; Proceedings of the Moscow Conference, October 13, discussion between Churchill, Stalin, and Mikołajczyk; minutes of two conversations between Mikołajczyk and Churchill, October 14, *Documents on Polish-Soviet Relations,* 405–24.

58. Ehrenburg, "The Grief of a Girl," April 1944, *We Will Not Forget.*

59. Cited in Alfred-Maurice de Zayas, *A Terrible Revenge: The Ethnic Cleansing of the East Germans, 1944–1950* (New York: St. Martin's Press, 1993), 45.

60. Theodor Schieder et al., eds., *The Expulsion of the German Population from the Territories East of the Oder-Neisse Line* (Bonn: Federal Ministry for Expellees, Refugees and War Victims, 1959), 129–33. The documents in this translated collection were drawn from a much larger collection of German documents gathered by the West German authorities in the 1950s. The effort to demonstrate the degree to which Germans had suffered Soviet (and Polish) abuse during the expulsions from Eastern Europe clearly served the purpose of equating German suffering with the suffering of other Europeans. As such, these documents were part of a broader project to relativize German atrocities committed during the war and so must be used with some care. Whatever the motives of the editors, however, the veracity of the eyewitness testimony they gathered has never been called into question. For an illuminating discussion of this documentary material, see Robert G. Moeller, *War Stories: The Search for a Usable Past in the Federal Republic of Germany* (Berkeley: University of California Press, 2001), 51–87. A pioneering study that brought the extent of Soviet rapes to light is Norman Naimark, *The Russians in Germany: A History of the Soviet Zone of Occupation, 1945–1949* (Cambridge, Mass.: Harvard University Press, 1995), 69–140. For a thoughtful discussion about the problems of writing the history of this sexual violence in occupied Germany, see

Atina Grossman, "A Question of Silence: The Rape of German Women by Occupation Soldiers," *October 72* (Spring 1995), 42–63.

61. *The Expulsion of the German Population,* Testimony of A.B. of Eichmedien, Sensburg, East Prussia, 207–18.

62. *The Expulsion of the German Population,* Testimony of Gerlinde Winkler of Dörbeck, Prussia, 162–65.

63. Lev Kopelev, *No Jail for Thought,* trans. by Anthony Austin (London: Penguin Books, 1979), 60–61, 63, 71, 81, 30.

64. For figures, see *The Expulsion of the German Population,* 27–33. The sinking of the *Wilhelm Gustloff* inspired a controversial novel about German war memory by former Danzig resident and Waffen-SS member Günter Grass called *Crabwalk* (New York: Harcourt, 2002). For an arresting depiction of the flight across the Haff and the Nehrung, see testimony of Lore Ehrich, of Sensburg, East Prussia, and testimony of M.M. of Lyck, *The Expulsion of the German Population,* 133–43; on the fall of Danzig, *The Expulsion of the German Population,* Testimony of Anna Schwartz of Schönberg, West Prussia, 178–89.

65. Hans Graf von Lehndorff, *Token of a Covenant: Diary of an East Prussian Surgeon,* trans. by Elizabeth Mayer (Chicago: Regnery, 1964), 68–83. For von Lehndorff, who came from an aristocratic East Prussian family that was loosely affiliated with the July 1944 plot against Hitler, these awful days were just the beginning of a long period of arrest, imprisonment, forced marches, flight, and hiding across a broken, burnt landscape. He eventually made his way to the west, and to a life in Bonn. He died in 1987. His diary was a bestseller in West Germany in 1961 and 1962. Moeller, *War Stories,* 64, 84.

66. *The Expulsion of the German Population,* 62.

67. Andreas-Friedrich, *Battleground Berlin: Diaries, 1945–1948,* trans. by Anna Boerresen (New York: Paragon, 1990), 16–17.

68. The question of how to integrate the Russian conquest of eastern Germany, and the suffering it caused, into a broader history of Germany during the Third Reich has long been a controversial subject for German historians, and indeed lay at the center of a long-running debate in German intellectual circles that has been termed the *Historikerstreit,* or "historian's quarrel." See Richard Evans, *In Hitler's Shadow* (New York: Pantheon, 1989).

69. Anonymous, *A Woman in Berlin: Eight Weeks in the Conquered City,* translated by Philip Boehm (New York: Henry Holt, 2005), 61.

5: A Strange, Enemy Country

1. "Directive to Supreme Commander, Allied Expeditionary Force, Regarding the Military Government of Germany in the Period Immediately Following the Cessation of Organized Resistance," September 22, 1945, *Foreign Relations of the United States* [hereafter *FRUS*]: *The Conferences at Malta and Yalta, 1945* (Washington, D.C.: Department of State, 1955). In relaying similar orders to his deputies in the field, Eisenhower restated the phrase even more precisely: "Germany will always be treated as a defeated country and not as a liberated one." SHAEF Chief of Staff to Headquarters, 21st Army Group, 12th Army Group, 6th Army Group, November 9, 1944, NARA RG 84, Office of U.S. Political Adviser to Germany, box 34.

2. Cordell Hull, *The Memoirs of Cordell Hull* (New York: Macmillan, 1948), 1621. This was in a memo to Hull on October 20, 1944.

3. Michael Beschloss, *The Conquerors: Roosevelt, Truman, and the Destruction of Hitler's Germany, 1941–1945* (New York: Simon and Schuster, 2002), 85–86.

4. August 26, 1944, memorandum from Roosevelt to Stimson, in *Morgenthau Diary (Germany),* vol. 1 (Washington, D.C.: Senate Judiciary Committee, 1967), 445.

5. Summary of Morgenthau Plan, in Henry Morgenthau, Jr., *Germany Is Our Problem* (New York: Harper & Brothers, 1945), frontispiece. For a detailed account of the origins and fate of the Morgenthau plan, see Beschloss, *The Conquerors,* and for the details of the Quebec

meetings especially, see 113–35. For the Churchill-Roosevelt agreement, see *Morgenthau Diary*, 620–21.

6. The American official history of the postwar occupation of Germany saw the Morgenthau plan as full of "black retribution," and suggested that Morgenthau's ideas were discredited early on: Earl Ziemke, *The US Army in the Occupation of Germany, 1944–1946* (Washington, D.C.: Center of Military History, 1975), 103. The Senate Judiciary Committee, investigating the nefarious pro-Soviet activities of Morgenthau's aide Harry Dexter White, believed the plan was in fact a Soviet-inspired plot to drive the German people into the arms of the Russians by destroying western Germany. See Anthony Kubek's introduction to the Senate Judiciary Committee's edition of *Morgenthau Diary*, 1–81.

7. In his memorandum to the president that sought to offer an alternative to Morgenthau, Secretary of State Hull had no trouble calling for demilitarization, denazification, and such economic dismantling and removals as would "eliminate permanently German economic domination of Europe." To these ends, he called for factories to be destroyed and wanted to "eliminate [German] self-sufficiency by imposing reforms that would make Germany dependent upon world markets." Hull also sought controls over foreign trade and key industries, and the redistribution of wealth of large landowners and industrialists. No one could have claimed Hull wanted a "soft" peace. Hull, *Memoirs*, 1618–19; *FRUS, Malta and Yalta*, Hull to Roosevelt, September 29, 1944, 156–58. For JCS 1067, September 22, 1944, *FRUS, Malta and Yalta*, 143–54.

8. Radio Address at a Dinner of the Foreign Policy Association, New York, N.Y., October 21, 1944, http://www.presidency.ucsb.edu/ws/index.php?pid=16456.

9. Memorandum for the President, November 10, 1944; and Memorandum of Conversation, November 15, 1944, *FRUS, Malta and Yalta*, 170–71.

10. *FRUS, Malta and Yalta*, "President's Log at Yalta," 550; Roosevelt-Stalin Meeting, February 4, 1945, 571.

11. *FRUS, Malta and Yalta*, Second Plenary Meeting, February 5, Bohlen minutes, 614, and Matthews minutes, 632.

12. Report of the Crimea Conference, February 12, 1945, *FRUS, Malta and Yalta*, 970–71.

13. The President's Log at Yalta, *FRUS, Malta and Yalta*, 560.

14. *Pocket Guide to Germany* (Army Information Branch, United States Army, 1944).

15. *Germany: The British Soldier's Pocketbook*, facsimile of the 1944 pocket guide (Kew: British National Archives, 2006).

16. "Conduct of Allied Troops and German Characteristics in Defeat," from SHAEF G-1 Division, August 18, 1944, NARA, RG 331, SHAEF Headquarters, Entry 2, box 113. This memorandum was adopted as official policy by Eisenhower on September 12, 1944, and appeared in almost identical form as Chapter XIV, "Policy on Relations between Allied occupying forces and inhabitants of Germany," in the *Handbook Governing Policy and Procedure for the Military Occupation of Germany*, April 1945, NARA RG 331, Entry 2, box 116. Eisenhower comment in letter from Major General J. F. M. Whiteley, D/A C of S, G-3, to A C of S, G-1, "Operation Talisman," September 9, 1944, NARA, RG 331, Entry 6, box 12.

17. Eisenhower to Bradley, September 17, 1944, NARA, RG 331, SHAEF Headquarters, Entry 2, box 113; Chief of Staff Gen. Walter Bedell Smith, signed by Eisenhower, to Allen, NARA RG 331, SHAEF Headquarters, Entry 6, box 12.

18. Drew Middleton, "Into Germany with the First Army," *New York Times Magazine*, October 8, 1944, and "The Great German Alibi in the Making," *New York Times Magazine*, November 5, 1944.

19. "Das Deutsches Volk," April 1945, in Martha Gellhorn, *The Face of War* (New York: Atlantic Monthly Press, 1988), 162.

20. Clifton Daniel, "If You Should Meet a German," *New York Times Magazine*, December 10, 1944; see also Ziemke, *US Army in the Occupation*, 138–39.

21. SHAEF G-1, "Non-Fraternization Spot Announcements," March 29, 1945, NARA RG 331, Entry 6, box 12.

22. Stephen Spender, *European Witness* (New York: Reynal & Hitchcock, 1946), 14–15.

23. Winston Churchill in the House of Commons, August 20, 1940, reprinted in Winston S. Churchill, ed., *Never Give In! The Best of Winston Churchill's Speeches* (New York: Hyperion, 2003), 245.

24. Arthur Harris, *Bomber Offensive* (New York: Macmillan, 1947), 88. Harris showed no remorse in his memoir. He believed that the results of the bombing campaign fully justified his wartime strategy, arguing that the bombing campaign made a decisive contribution to the Allied victory by significantly eroding the German economy, communications, transportation, coal, oil and steel production, as well as the morale of the citizens and soldiers. He believed the bombing of Germany helped to shorten the war, and so saved the lives of Allied soldiers, and he claimed that bombing was no more morally despicable than any number of acts of war that target civilians: siege warfare or naval blockades, for example, which kill through economic strangulation. For a recent indictment of Harris's view and a summary of the moral case against bombing, see A. C. Grayling, *Among the Dead Cities: The History and Moral Legacy of the WWII Bombing of Civilians in Germany and Japan* (New York: Walker & Co., 2006).

25. The RAF and USAAF dropped 1.2 million tons of bombs on Germany during the war. The RAF dropped 955,044 tons, and the Eighth U.S. Air Force dropped 332,904. "Strategic Air Offensive," in I. C. B. Dear, ed., *Oxford Companion to World War II* (New York: Oxford University Press, 1995), table on 1070–71.

26. Summary Report, September 30, 1945, as reprinted in David MacIsaac, *United States Strategic Bombing Survey*, vol. 1 (New York: Garland, 1976), 1–18.

27. United States Strategic Bombing Survey, "The Effect of Bombing on Health and Medical Care in Germany," January 1947.

28. The Dresden attack, though only one of numerous air attacks that killed tens of thousands, has generated particular controversy because of the intensity of the firestorm, the large numbers of casualties, and the lack of significant military value of the target. Yet the debate rages. For an excellent overview of the debate, see Paul Addison and Jeremy A. Crang, eds., *Firestorm: The Bombing of Dresden, 1945* (Chicago: Ivan Dee, 2006).

29. "Civilians in Cologne," *Times*, March 7, 1945; "Effectiveness of RAF Bombing," *Times*, March 13, 1945.

30. Walter Bedell Smith, *Eisenhower's Six Great Decisions* (New York: Longman, Green & Co., 1956), 138; Sidney Olson, "Mission Accomplished," *Time*, March 19, 1945; "Dead German Cities," *Times*, April 20, 1945; "Today in the Ruhr," *Times*, April 28, 1945; Ben Hibbs, "Journey to a Shattered World," *Saturday Evening Post*, June 9, 1945.

31. *Time*, "Vanishing Points," April 2, 1945.

32. "Frankfurt in Ruins," *Times*, March 31, 1945; Percy Knauth in "Letter from the Editor," *Time*, April 9, 1945.

33. "The Battered Face of Germany," *Life*, June 4, 1945; Richard J. H. Johnston, "Nazi Shrine City Now Hideous Spot," *New York Times*, April 22, 1945.

34. Cornelia Stabler Gillam, letter dated June 20, 1945, to her family, American Friends Service Committee records, Philadelphia, Foreign Service/1945/Germany, box 2.

35. Ernest O. Hauser, "Tame Germans are Headaches, Too," *Saturday Evening Post*, June 2, 1945.

36. NARA, RG 331, SHAEF G-5 Division, Entry 47, box 29, Weekly Field Reports for weeks ending April 14, April 21, May 5, May 26, June 30, 1945; and RG 338, Records of U.S. Army Commands, Headquarters Third U.S. Army, Assistant Chief of Staff, G-2, box 6, weekly intelligence reports for weeks ending July 25, August 1, 1945.

37. Saul K. Padover, *Experiment in Germany: The Story of an American Intelligence Officer* (New York: Duell, Sloan & Pearce, 1946), 297.

38. U.S. Army, Judge Advocate General, European Theater of Operations, *History Branch Office of the JAG with the United States Forces European Theater, 18 July 1942–1 November 1945*, vol. 1 (1946), 242–49. For further discussion, see John Willoughby, "The Sexual

Behavior of American GIs during the Early Years of the Occupation of Germany," *Journal of Military History* 62, 1 (January 1998), 155–74.

39. Text of censored article, March 14, 1945, in NARA RG 331, Entry 6, box 12.

40. Memorandum titled "Fraternization between Germans and American officers and men," Major Arthur Goodfriend, no date but written in late fall 1944, NARA RG 331, Entry 6, box 12. This memo is also discussed in Ziemke, *The US Army in the Occupation of Germany,* 142–43; and in Petra Goedde, *GIs and Germans: Culture, Gender and Foreign Relations, 1945–1949* (New Haven, Conn.: Yale University Press, 2003), 58–59.

41. Padover, *Experiment in Germany,* 263.

42. Goedde, *GIs and Germans,* 91; Harold Zink, *The United States in Germany, 1944–1955* (Princeton, N.J.: D. van Nostrand Co. 1957), 132–40.

43. Franklin M. Davis, *Come as a Conqueror: The United States Army's Occupation of Germany, 1945–1949* (New York: Macmillan, 1967), 138–39; Oliver J. Frederiksen, *The American Military Occupation of Germany, 1945–1953* (Historical Division, U.S. Army, Europe, 1953), 115–17.

44. "US Fraternization Rule Faces a Show-Down," *Herald Tribune,* May 15, 1945; for figures, Medical Department, U.S. Army, *Preventive Medicine in World War II,* vol. 5, *Communicable Diseases* (Washington, D.C.: Department of the Army, 1960), 250–66; 324–29; "Fly Penicillin from US to Germany," *News of Germany,* November 17, 1945.

45. Eisenhower to Marshall, June 2, 1945, and Marshall to Eisenhower, June 4, 1945, NARA RG 331, Entry 6, box 12.

46. *Sunday Express,* "The order is broken every hour," June 3, 1945; "British Troops Flout Rule," *New York Times,* June 5, 1945.

47. Drew Middleton, "Officers Oppose Fraternizing Ban," *New York Times,* June 25, 1945; Percy Knauth, "Fraternization," *Life,* July 2, 1945; "German Girls," *Life,* July 23, 1945.

48. Joe Weston, "Ban Lifted," *Time,* July 30, 1945.

49. "It's Got to Work," *Time,* June 25, 1945.

50. USSBS, NARA RG 243, 64b, interview numbers 62442, 62400, 62339, 62148, 62149, 62146, 62135, 62046, 61850.

51. USSBS, NARA RG 243, 64b, interview numbers 62032, 62011, 62007.

52. USSBS, NARA RG 243, 64b, interview numbers 61989, 62147, 62136, 62007. The interview with the twenty-six-year-old from Darmstadt was unnumbered.

53. USSBS, NARA RG 243, 64b, interview numbers 62143, 62032, 61945, 62893.

54. Tania Long, "Pro-German Attitude Grows as US Troops Fraternize," *New York Times,* September 29, 1945. *Newsweek* thought fraternization had opened the GI to appeals from Germans: "Do the Fräuleins Change Our Joe?" *Newsweek,* December 24, 1945. A critical assessment of American tolerance for the Germans was offered by a recently returned veteran, Robert Engler, "The Individual Soldier and the Occupation," *Annals of the American Academy of Political and Social Science* 267 (Jan. 1950), 77–86.

55. "Report on the Tripartite Conference of Berlin (Potsdam), July 17–August 2, 1945," in *Documents of Germany under Occupation, 1945–1954,* ed. Beate Ruhm von Oppen (London: Oxford University Press, 1955), 40–50.

56. Lucius D. Clay, *Decision in Germany* (Garden City, N.Y.: Doubleday, 1950), 67; Zink, *United States in Germany,* 157–60.

57. Ziemke, *The US Army in the Occupation of Germany,* 446. The Patton affair was reported by Raymond Daniell in the *New York Times:* "Nazis Still Hold Key Jobs in Reich," Sept. 20, 1945; "Denazification Hit by US Officers," Sept. 21, 1945; "Patton Belittles Denazification," Sept. 23, 1945; "Patton Alters Stand on Nazis," Sept. 26, 1945; for detailed critiques of the denazification program, see William E. Griffith, "Denazification in the United States Zone of Germany," *Annals of the American Academy of Political and Social Science* 267 (Jan. 1950), 68–76; Joseph F. Napoli, a former military government official, "Denazification from an American Viewpoint," *Annals of the American Academy of Political and Social Science,* 264 (Jul. 1949), 115–23; John H. Herz, "The Fiasco of Denazification in Germany," *Political Science Quarterly* 63, 4 (Dec. 1948), 569–94.

58. *News of Germany,* July 19, August 2, August 21, August 30, September 11, September 13, November 17, December 13, 1945.

59. Eisenhower speech of August 6, 1945, in Military Government, *Weekly Information Bulletin* no. 3, August 11, 1945, G-5 Division, U.S. Forces, European Theater.

60. F. S. V. Donnison, *Civil Affairs and Military Government, Northwest Europe, 1944–46* (London: HMSO, 1961), 328–39; "Montgomery on Future of Germany," *Times,* November 11, 1945; "Organizing against the Rigors of Winter," *Times,* November 26, 1945.

61. Graham A. Cosmas and Albert E. Cowdrey, *Medical Service in the European Theater of Operations* (Washington, D.C.: Center of Military History, 1992), 587–88.

62. Military Government, *Weekly Information Bulletin* no. 5, August 25, 1945, G-5 Division, U.S. Forces, European Theater.

63. *Stuttgarter Zeitung,* November 14, 1945; and the U.S. Military Government German-language magazine, *Heute,* number 3 [not dated; probably September 1945].

PART III: MOVING BODIES
Prologue: "They Have Suffered Unbearably"

1. Dean Acheson to Harry Hopkins, December 26, 1944, *Foreign Relations of the United States, 1945,* 2: 1059–61.

6: Freedom from Want

1. Telegram from UNRRA Athens to UNRRA London and New York, May 22, 1945, relaying AP and Reuters stories about Milos, in UNRRA Archives, United Nations, New York, PAG-4/1.3.1.1.1, box 29.

2. For contemporary criticisms, see "Is UNRRA Doing Its Job?," a radio interview with Herbert H. Lehman printed in Department of State, *Bulletin* 13, October 21, 1945, 629–36. Early accounts include Philipp Weintraub, "UNRRA: An Experiment in International Welfare Planning," *Journal of Politics* 7 (Feb. 1945): 1–24; T. A. Sumberg, "The Financial Experience of UNRRA," *American Journal of International Law* 39 (Oct. 1945), 698–712; Grace Fox, "The Origins of UNRRA," *Political Science Quarterly* 64 (Dec. 1950), 561–84; R. H. Johnson, "International Politics and the Structure of International Organization: The Case of UNRRA," *World Politics* 3 (July 1951), 520–38; no monograph has been devoted to it. The official history is reasonably complete but is a heavily bureaucratic rendering of UNRRA's structure and activities. George Woodbridge, *UNRRA: The History of the United Nations Relief and Rehabilitation Administration,* 3 vols. (New York: Columbia University Press, 1950). UNRRA has received short shrift from historians, despite its rich archival materials held in the United Nations archives. Cold War historians see it as a failed effort of international cooperation; economic historians typically dismiss it as a curtain-raiser for the more substantial relief efforts of the Marshall Plan; and for military historians, UNRRA is depicted as a strange, meddlesome, amateurish operation totally out of its depth. Even its principal architect, Dean Acheson, disowned it in his memoirs. Dean Acheson, *Present at the Creation: My Years at the State Department* (New York: Norton, 1969), 64–80.

3. For early discussions on UNRRA, see Matthews to Secretary of State, February 26, 1942, *Foreign Relations of the United States, 1942,* 1: 92–98; Hull to Winant, May 7, 1942, ibid., 103–5; Memorandum of Conversation by Hull, August 22, 1942, ibid., 132–33; Draft Agreement for UNRRA, March 23, 1943, ibid., 890–95.

4. FDR cited by Cordell Hull, U.S. Secretary of State, to Sol Bloom, Chairman of the House Foreign Affairs Committee, December 7, 1943, Department of State, *Bulletin,* December 11, 1943, 416; and Franklin Roosevelt message to Congress, November 15, 1943, in Department of State, *Bulletin,* November 20, 1943, 372–73.

5. Dean Acheson, radio broadcast of December 18, 1943, and Francis B. Sayre, Special Assistant to the Secretary of State, speech of December 14, 1943, both in Department of State, *Bulletin,* December 18, 1943, 421–29.

6. Herbert H. Lehman, "Relief and Rehabilitation," *Foreign Policy Reports* 19, no. 9, July 15, 1943, 102–5. The text was delivered to the Foreign Policy Association of New York on June 17, 1943.

7. Hugh Jackson to Gen. W. B. Smith, March 31, 1945; "Implementation of UNRRA/ Military Displaced Persons Program," April 9, 1945; Smith to Jackson, April 11, 1945, NARA RG 333, Allied Operational and Occupation Headquarters, SHAEF G-5, Secretariat, Numeric File, box 51.

8. Lehman in Alan Nevins, *Herbert H. Lehman and His Era* (New York: Charles Scribner's Sons, 1963), 226.

9. Vera Micheles Dean, "UNRRA: A Step Towards Reconstruction," *Foreign Policy Reports* 19, 20, January 1, 1944, 266–70; Woodbridge, *UNRRA* III, Appendix Ten, 499–500.

10. Woodbridge, *UNRRA* III, Appendix Ten, 411–21.

11. Francesca M. Wilson, *Aftermath: France, Germany, Austria, Yugoslavia, 1945 and 1946* (London: Penguin, 1947), 10, 23, 79, 131.

12. Diary, Rhoda Dawson [Mrs. R. N. Bickerdike], IWM 95/26/1.

13. Isabel Needham, Regional Nursing Consultant, February 20, 1945, UNRRA, PAG-4/1.3.0.3.1, box 42; Newsletter of the Lake Erie Yearly Meeting, vol. 42, issue 2, Winter 2005, "Memorial Minute For Isabel Needham Bliss."

14. Diary, Marie Pope Wallis Papers, Collection No. 1975-053, box no. 3, serial No. 8582, folder 22, New Mexico State Records Center and Archives, Santa Fe, New Mexico. For equally critical views of UNRRA see the memoir by Marvin Klemme, *The Inside Story of UNRRA: An Experience in Internationalism* (New York: Lifetime Editions, 1949), which is intemperate and hostile to the agency. A more subtle account that pokes fun at the pretensions of American relief workers is Edmund Wilson's short story, "Through the Abruzzi with Mattie and Harriet," in *Europe without Baedeker: Sketches Among the Ruins of Italy, Greece and England* (Garden City, N.Y.: Doubleday, 1947).

15. Nancy Hayward, UNRAA Greece, Region C, May 28, 1945, UNRRA, PAG-4/1.3.1.1.1, box 31.

16. Gwen Chesters, "Observations of the Functioning of the Camp Committee," Tolumbat Refugee Camp, Egypt, February 13, 1945, UNRRA, PAG-4/1.3.0.3.1, box 39.

17. "In the Wake of the Armies," May 1945, UNRRA, PAG-4/1.3.0.3.1, box 18.

18. Mark Mazower, *Inside Hitler's Greece: The Experience of Occupation, 1941–1944* (New Haven, Conn.: Yale University Press, 1993), 26–41.

19. "Magnitude and Urgency of the Need in Greece for UNRRA Supplies," letter from Roy Hendrickson, UNRRA Deputy Director General, to Will Clayton, Assistant Secretary of State, October 6, 1945, UNRRA, PAG-4/1.3.0.3.1, box 18; and "Data for the State Department," October 31, 1945, UNRRA, PAG-4/1.3.0.3.1, box 18.

20. Winston Churchill, *The Second World War*, vol. 6, *Triumph and Tragedy* (Boston: Houghton Mifflin, 1953), 289.

21. UNRRA press release, December 16, 1944, UNRRA, PAG-4/1.3.0.3.1, box 18; Report of Christopher Janus, December 23, 1944, UNRRA, PAG-4/1.3.1.1.1, box 31.

22. "Relief and Rehabilitation Activities in Greece, February 3–March 2, 1945," B. D. Rankin, Senior Economic Analyst, American Embassy Athens, March 8, 1945, UNRRA, PAG-4/1.3.0.3.1, box 18.

23. Quarterly Report for July, August, and September, dated October 9, 1945, UNRRA, PAG-4/1.3.0.3.1, box 18; and Woodbridge, *UNRRA* II, 97–107.

24. Isabel Hunter report on trip to Greece, April 27–May 9, 1945; Hayward letter, May 28, 1945, in UNRRA, PAG-4/1.3.1.1.1, box 31.

25. *New York Times*, May 28, 1945.

26. Herbert Lehman diary, C47-42.1, UNRRA Personal and General; Italy, Greece, and Yugoslavia Diary, July 5–August 20, 1945, Lehman Papers, Columbia University.

27. Woodbridge, ed., *UNRRA* II, 137.

28. Statement by Brigadier Stayner, Deputy Chief, Greek Mission, January 5, 1946,

UNRRA, PAG-4/1.3.1.1.1, box 29; and for details on supplies to Greece, statement received December 31, 1945, from UNRRA Mission Office, Athens, box 29, and memo from Hunt to Preston Kelly, April 18, 1946, box 30; and comment about fecal matter in October 15, 1945, Sanitation Section report, UNRRA, PAG-4/3.0.12.2.3, box 1.

29. Anne Dacie, "Refugee Work in a Camp for Displaced Persons in Ex-Enemy Territory," January 18, 1945, UNRRA, PAG-4/1.3.1.1.1, box 32.

30. C. R. S. Harris, *Allied Military Administration of Italy, 1943–45* (London: HMSO, 1957); and for a superb anecdotal account of Naples in 1944, Norman Lewis, *Naples '44* (New York: Pantheon, 1978).

31. Woodbridge, ed., *UNRRA* II, 265.

32. "Economic Conditions in Liberated Italy," April 5, 1945, written by W. Zbijewski, compiled from various field reports, UNRRA, PAG-4/1.3.0.4.1, box 8.

33. Dr. Mario Volterra, letter, transmitted by George Xanthaky, Chief, Southern European Division, Bureau of Areas, UNRRA, to Edward E. Hunt, Chief, Italian Division, Foreign Economic Administration, November 1, 1944, UNRRA, PAG-4/1.3.0.4.1, box 10.

34. Details of the Unitarian Service Committee's Italian Medical Nutrition Mission can be found in the USC archives, Harvard-Andover Theological Library, bMS 16103, box 1. Dr. Gollan's report was delivered to the American Academy for the Advancement of Science on December 28, 1946, in Boston. USC archives, bMS 16103, box 69.

35. Figures compiled from monthly summary, February 1946; and weekly summary, April 25, 1946, UNRRA, PAG-4/3.0.14.3.1.1, box 2.

36. "Lecce Camp Group, Breakdown of Nationality," UNRRA, PAG-4/3.0.14.3.1.1, box 2.

37. Anne Dacie, "Refugee Work in a Camp for Displaced Persons in Ex-Enemy Territory," January 18, 1945, UNRRA, PAG-4/1.3.1.1.1, box 32.

38. Alan Hall letter to Joel Gordon in Washington, May 4, 1945, UNRRA, PAG-4/1.3.0.3.1, box 40; Sydney Morrell, director of public relations in Yugoslavia Mission, letter to Morse Salisbury and Leonard Ingram, from Dubrovnik, March 25, 1945, in UNRRA, PAG-4/1.3.0.3.1, box 41.

39. The British-Yugoslav tangle during the war has been the subject of numerous postmortems, including many of the key British players. See F. W. D Deakin, *The Embattled Mountain* (New York: Oxford University Press, 1971); and Phyllis Auty and Richard Clogg, eds., *British Policy Towards Wartime Resistance in Yugoslavia and Greece* (London: Macmillan, 1975), which has essays by key wartime British officials.

40. These accounts were written by Military Liaison officers and some are digests of reports from the field. Major R. G. Edholm, to Sydney Morrell, February 1945 (no day given); report on "Montenegro: Economic Conditions," October 8, 1944; report on the Banat, January 21, 1945; report on Bosnia, March 1945 (not dated); and report on "Belgrade Today," November 24, 1944. All in UNRRA, PAG-4/3.0.23.0, box 44.

41. Milovan Djilas, *Wartime*, trans. by Michael B. Petrovich (New York: Harcourt, Brace, Jovanovich, 1977), 443–49.

42. Telegram, April 14, 1945, to Washington and London from Yugoslav office, UNRRA, PAG-4/1.3.0.3.1, box 39.

43. Morrell letter, March 15, 1945, UNRRA, PAG-4/1.3.0.3.1, box 41.

44. Irving J. Fasteau, letter of April 1, 1945, to Miss Jane Hoey, Social Security Board, UNRRA, PAG-4/1.3.0.3.1, box 42.

45. Broadcast texts, April 1946, UNRRA, PAG-4/3.0.23.0, box 51.

46. UNRRA nonetheless made great efforts to publicize its work, and explain how and why American aid was needed in Europe. For one of many examples see Fred K. Hoehler, "What is UNRRA Doing?" *Survey*, April 1945.

47. *Voluntary War Relief during World War II: A Report to the President,* by Joseph Davies, Charles P. Taft, and Charles Warren (Washington D.C., March 1946); and Harold J. Seymour, *Design for Giving: The Story of the National War Fund, 1943–1947* (New York: Harper, 1947), 70–71, for tally of disbursements of National War Fund.

48. The shape of the UNRRA–voluntary agencies agreements can be gleaned from documents in UNRRA, PAG-4/1.3.1.1.1, box 21.

49. For example, see the critical coverage in *New Republic,* March 25 and April 1, 1946; *Nation,* November 23 and 30, 1945, and March 23, 1946; *Time,* April 8, 1946.

50. Quoted in Dean, "UNRRA," 270.

51. *Economist,* August 24, 1946.

52. Acheson, *Present at the Creation,* 231.

53. Francis B. Sayre, Special Assistant to the Secretary of State, speech of December 14, 1943, in Department of State, *Bulletin,* December 18, 1943, 423–29.

54. Jean Newman, in UNRRA status report, May 27–June 2, 1945, filed by J. A. Edminson, Senior UNRRA Officer, SHAEF, in NARA RG 331, Allied Operational and Occupation Headquarters, SHAEF G-5, box 52.

7: "A Tidal Wave of Nomad Peoples"

1. PRO, FO 945/559, September 18, 1945.

2. Ulrich Herbert, *Hitler's Foreign Workers: Enforced Foreign Labor in Germany under the Third Reich* (London: Cambridge University Press, 1997), 298.

3. Malcolm J. Proudfoot, *European Refugees, 1939–1952: A Study in Forced Population Movement* (Evanston, Ill.: Northwestern University Press, 1956), 80, 158–59. Lt. Col. Proudfoot (U.S. Army) served in Germany in the Combined Displaced Persons Executive and accumulated much of the material for his study in the field in 1945. It remains the most comprehensive account of the DP problem. Proudfoot's charts claim that the Soviets repatriated 6.8 million people from their own zone of occupied Germany and from Poland, including 5.2 million of their own nationals, as well as 700,000 Poles, 295,000 French, 210,000 Czechs, 160,000 Yugoslavs, and hundreds of thousands of others they uncovered in the east. This would put the total number of DPs in Europe at over 13 million. These figures, however, are extremely difficult to verify. The chapter focuses on DPs repatriated by SHAEF and UNRRA out of territory under occupation by western authorities.

4. SHAEF Field Handbook, August 26, 1944, cited in Henry L. Coles and Albert K. Weinberg, *United States Army in World War II: Civil Affairs—Soldiers become Governors* (Washington D.C.: Office of the Chief of Military History, 1964), 848.

5. U.S. Forces, European Theater, Study No. 35: "DPs, Refugees, and Recovered Allied Military Personnel," (1945), cited in Coles and Weinberg, *United States Army in World War II: Civil Affairs,* 858.

6. UNRRA, PAG-4/1.3.0.3.1, box 11, "Psychological Problems of Displaced Persons," June 1945, prepared by European Regional Office of UNRRA, Inter-Allied Psychological Study Group.

7. Memo on "Guide to the Care of Displaced Persons," May 18, 1945, Flow Chart drawn up in April 1945. NARA, RG 331, Allied Operational and Occupation Headquarters, SHAEF G-5, Secretariat, Numeric File, box 56.

8. SHAEF, G-5, DP Branch, Report no. 30, April 30, 1945, NARA, RG 331, Allied Operational and Occupation Headquarters, SHAEF G-5, Secretariat, Numeric File, box 57.

9. Excerpt of G-5 Weekly Journal of Information, in Murphy to State Department, May 22, 1945, NARA, RG 84, Foreign Service Posts, U.S. Political Adviser to Germany (POLAD), box 34.

10. SHAEF, G-5, DP Branch, Report no. 30, April 30, 1945, NARA, RG 331, Allied Operational and Occupation Headquarters, SHAEF G-5, Secretariat, Numeric File, box 57.

11. Marguerite Higgins, *New York Herald Tribune,* April 7, 1945, in NARA, RG 84, Foreign Service Posts, POLAD, box 34.

12. Primo Levi, *The Reawakening,* trans. by Stuart Woolf (New York: Simon & Schuster, 1965), 120–21, 126.

13. PRO, CAB 66, 54, "Soviet Prisoners of War," September 3, 1945, including exchange of notes between Britain and Soviet Union, July 20, 1944, and August 23, 1944.

14. PRO, WO 219/2295, flyer signed by Lt. Col. Novikov, Soviet repatriation officer in Paris, November 11, 1944.

15. PRO, WO 219/2295, Headquarters, Southern Zone of Communication, to SHAEF headquarters, January 11, 1945; reports came from Bourg-Lastic in the Puy-de-Dôme; PRO, CAB 119/95, Eisenhower to Combined Chiefs of Staff, January 12, 1945; Eisenhower to Washington, March 28, 1945; Bidault to British Ambassador in France, March 5, 1945.

16. PRO, WO 219/2295, treaty cabled in telegram from General John Deane to Washington, February 11, 1945. For additional insight into the making of this deal, see John R. Deane, *The Strange Alliance: The Story of Our Efforts at Wartime Co-operation with Russia* (New York: Viking, 1947), 182–201; PRO, WO 219/2295, Eisenhower to Commanding General, April 8, 1945.

17. Aleksandr Solzhenitsyn, *The GULAG Archipelago, 1918–1956: An Experiment in Literary Investigation*, trans. by Thomas P. Whitney (New York: Harper & Row, 1973), 237, 240, 243, 256.

18. PRO, WO 204/10449, "Evacuation of Cossack and Caucasian Forces from 36 Inf Bde Area, May–June 1945," July 3, 1945, with accompanying testimony and statements by British officers. Nikolai Tolstoy has written two tendentious books on the subject of the Cossacks and their fate. *The Secret Betrayal* (New York: Charles Scribner's Sons, 1977); and *The Minister and the Massacres* (London: Century Hutchinson, 1986), which claims that Harold Macmillan, then serving as Political Adviser to the Allied Commander-in-Chief, conspired within the British government to surrender various endangered Soviet peoples to the Red Army at the end of the war.

19. Marguerite Duras, *The War: A Memoir*, trans. by Barbara Bray (New York: Pantheon Books, 1986), 61. The original title of Duras's book was *La Douleur*, or "Pain"—a far more appropriate title for this melancholy, distressing book.

20. Duras, *The War*, 55–61.

21. Laure Adler, *Marguerite Duras: A Life*, trans. by Anne-Marie Glasheen (Chicago: University of Chicago Press, 1998), 101–27.

22. Adler, *Marguerite Duras*, 141–44.

23. Henri Frenay, "Réponse aux rapports de Mme. Olga Wormser et de M. Boudot," in Comité d'Histoire de la Deuxième Guerre Mondiale, *La Libération de la France* (Paris: CNRS, 1976), 739–744. For numbers of Jews killed, see Michael R. Marrus and Robert O. Paxton, *Vichy France and the Jews* (Stanford, Calif.: Stanford University Press, 1981), 343.

24. Henri Frenay, *The Night Will End*, trans. by Dan Hofstadter (New York: McGraw-Hill, 1976), 390; for numbers of returnees, Malcolm J. Proudfoot, *European Refugees, 1939–52: A Study in Forced Population Movement* (London: Faber & Faber, 1957), 193.

25. For a fascinating study of the impact of captivity on French society, see Sarah Fishman, *We Will Wait: Wives of French Prisoners of War, 1940–1945* (New Haven, Conn.: Yale University Press, 1991), which is broader than the title suggests. A nuanced discussion of the reception of deportees in the provinces is given by Megan Koreman, "A Hero's Homecoming: The Return of the Deportees to France, 1945," *Journal of Contemporary History* 32 (1), 1997, 9–22.

26. Pieter Lagrou, *The Legacy of Nazi Occupation: Patriotic Memory and National Recovery in Western Europe, 1945–1965* (Cambridge, U.K.: Cambridge University Press, 2000), 106–28; Yves Durand, *La captivité: Histoire des prisonniers de guerre français, 1939–1945* (Paris: FNCPG, 1980), 324.

27. Christophe Lewin, *Le retour des prisonniers de guerre français* (Paris: Sorbonne, 1986), 82–83.

28. For a sensitive summary of the grievances of the returning prisoners, see Robert Gauthier's editorial in *Le Monde*, "Manifestations de prisonniers," June 7, 1945. On the difficulties of returning to family life, see Fishman, *We Will Wait*, 150–67.

29. The Communist paper in Marseilles, *La Marseillaise,* vigorously denounced the handling of the returning prisoners in that port city. See issues of May 16, May 20, May 23, and June 1, 1945.

30. Frenay, *Night Will End,* 399, 410–11. Frenay, years later, refused to accept any blame for the shortages and inefficiencies of the repatriation. Indeed, he was proud of his record. See his comments in his "Réponse," in *La Libération de la France.*

31. François Cochet, *Les exclus de la victoire: Histoire des prisonniers de guerre, déportés, et STO, 1945–1985* (Paris: Kronos, 1992), 234–35; Henry Rousso, *The Vichy Syndrome: History and Memory in France since 1944,* trans. by Arthur Goldhammer (Cambridge, Mass.: Harvard University Press, 1991), 25–26.

32. Proudfoot, *European Refugees,* 197–98.

33. Olga Wormser-Migot, "Le rapatriement des déportés," in *Comité d'histoire de la deuxième guerre mondiale, La Libération de la France,* 726. For a detailed study of the comments in the French press on the return of deportees, see "Revue de Presse," in Marie-Anne Matard-Bonucci and Edouard Lynch, eds., *La Libération des camps et Le Retour des déportés: L'Histoire en souffrance* (Paris: Editions Complexe, 1995), 177–99.

34. Janet Flanner, *The New Yorker,* April 28, 1945, in *Reporting World War II,* part 2, *American Journalism, 1944–1946* (New York: Library of America, 1995), pp. 689–93.

35. Jacqueline Fleury, in Matard-Bonucci and Lynch, eds., *La Libération des camps,* 136.

36. Esther S. (HVT-2827), Fortunoff Video Archive, Yale University Library.

37. Louise Alcan, in *Le Grand Livre des Témoins,* compiled by the Fédération Nationale des Déportés et Internés Résistants et Patriotes (Paris: Ramsay, 1995), 305; Max L. (HVT-3221), Fortunoff Video Archive, Yale University Library.

38. Amanda S. (HVT-3469), Fortunoff Video Archive, Yale University Library; Liliane Lévy-Osbert, *Grand Livre des Témoins,* 305.

39. Jacqueline Fleury, in Matard-Bonucci and Lynch, eds., *La Libération des camps,* 136.

40. Isidore R. (HVT-3452), Fortunoff Video Archive, Yale University Library.

41. Charles B. (HVT-2100), Fortunoff Video Archive, Yale University Library; Alexandre Kohn, in Matard-Bonucci and Lynch, eds., *La Libération des camps,* 133; and Mary-Rose Mathis-Izikowitz, in ibid., 133. See also Daniel Regen's testimony in *Grand Livres des Témoins,* 308.

42. Charlotte Delbo, *Auschwitz and After* (New Haven: Yale University Press, 1995), 276.

43. Anne-Marie Soucelier, quoted in Matard-Bonucci and Lynch, eds., *La Libération des camps,* 148.

44. Françoise, in Delbo, *Auschwitz and After,* 348.

45. Kathryn Hulme, *The Wild Place* (Boston: Little, Brown, 1953). The notes, documents, and letters from which Hulme drew when writing the memoir are kept at the Beinecke Library, Yale University, YCAL MSS 22, especially box 5. Quotation from box 5, folder 92.

46. Proudfoot, *European Refugees,* 281; and for estimates of Polish DPs in SHAEF area, Tedder to London, July 3, 1945, NARA, RG 331, Allied Operations and Occupation Headquarters, SHAEF G-5, box 49.

47. Descriptions drawn from Army G-5 Inspection Report, Capt H. E. McDonald, Displaced Persons Branch, September 5–6, 1945, in UNRRA, S-0436-0008; Team 302 orders, July 21, 1945, UNRRA, S-0436-0008; inspection by Andrew Truelson, UNRRA Field Supervisor, September 19, 1945, UNRRA, S-0436-0008; Hulme, *The Wild Place,* 3, 5.

48. Hulme, *The Wild Place,* 28; Hulme Papers, Beinecke Library, box 5, folder 92.

49. Hulme Papers, Beinecke Library, box 5, folder 92.

50. Hulme, *The Wild Place,* 12.

51. Masset to J. H. Whiting, District Director, UNRRA Eastern Military District, Third Army HQ, September 13, 1945, and October 11, 1945; Col. R. J. Wallace, "Inspection of DP Camp Wildflecken," October 22, 1945; Masset to A. C. Dunn, Regional Supervisor, UNRRA, November 22, 1945, and December 14, 1945, UNRRA, S-0436-0008.

52. Hulme, *The Wild Place*, 90–92.

53. Hulme Papers, Beinecke Library, box 5, folder 92.

54. Hulme Papers, Beinecke Library, box 5, folder 92.

55. Hulme, *The Wild Place*, 110–20, 126.

56. Eisenhower order, September 20, 1945, NARA, RG 260 Records of U.S. Occupation Headquarters, WWII, U.S. Group Control Council (USGCC), Adjutant General, General Correspondence, 1944–45, 383.6–383.8, box 25.

57. Montgomery cables to Foreign Office and War Office, August 6 and 17, 1945, and Foreign Office to Montgomery, August 14, 1945, PRO, FO 945/595; British Control Commission memo, December 4, 1945, PRO, FO 1032/821; USFET Commander to Commanders, Third and Seventh Armies, November 24, 1945, NARA, RG 260 Records of the U.S. Occupation Headquarters, WWII, Office of Military Government for Germany (OMGUS), Records of the Executive Office, Office of the Adjutant General, General Correspondence, box 91.

58. Hulme, *The Wild Place*, 47, 151–52; statement by H. Brining, Acting Director, UNRRA Team 16/72, Düsseldorf, November 17, 1945, UNRRA, S-0408-0009; Proudfoot, *European Refugees*, 282–84.

PART IV: TO LIVE AGAIN AS A PEOPLE

Prologue: "We Felt Ourselves Lost"

1. Primo Levi, *The Reawakening*, trans. by Stuart Woolf (New York: Simon & Schuster, 1995), 15, 16, 18, 40.

8: A Host of Corpses

1. For general information on the camp and its history, see "Auschwitz," in *The Oxford Companion to World War II* (New York: Oxford University Press, 1995), 78; Martin Gilbert, *The Holocaust: A History of the Jews of Europe during the Second World War* (New York: Henry Holt, 1985), 121, 239, 286, 291, 309, 470, 581, 771–78; Leni Yahil, *The Holocaust: The Fate of European Jewry, 1932–1945* (New York: Oxford University Press, 1990), 527–30. The morbid science of calculating the numbers of dead has been the subject of some debate. See for the figures given here Franciszek Piper, "The numbers of victims at KL Auschwitz," in *Auschwitz: Nazi Death Camp* (Oświęcim: Auschwitz-Birkenau State Museum, 1996), 182–95.

2. "Majdanek Victims Enumerated," http://www.auschwitz-muzeum.oswiecim.pl/new/index.php?tryb=news_big&language=EN&id=879.

3. "Merchants of Murder: Lublin slaughter," *Newsweek*, September 11, 1944, 64–67; Richard Lauterbach, "Murder, Inc.," *Time*, September 11, 1944, 36. For similar reports: "Lublin Funeral," *Life*, August 28, 1944, 34; "Vernichtungslager," *Time*, August 21, 1944, 36–38; "Sunday in Poland," *Life*, September 18, 1944, 17–18. Alexander Werth provided a remarkable account of his visit to the recently liberated camp in *Russia at War* (New York: Dutton, 1964), 890–99.

4. Gilbert, *The Holocaust*, 711.

5. Andrzej Strzelecki, *The Evacuation, Dismantling, and Liberation of KL Auschwitz*, trans. by Witold Zbirohowski-Koscia (Oświęcim: Auschwitz-Birkenau State Museum, 2001), tables XVI and XVII, 309–21; and Andrzej Strzelecki, "Evacuation, Liquidation and Liberation of the Camp," in *Auschwitz: Nazi Death Camp*, 269–89.

6. Danuta Czech, *Auschwitz Chronicle, 1939–1945* (New York: Henry Holt, 1990), 782–84.

7. Primo Levi, *Survival in Auschwitz: The Nazi Assault on Humanity*, trans. by Stuart Woolf (New York: Collier, 1993), 151, 180. This was originally titled *Se questo e un uomo* (If This Is a Man), and published in Italy in 1947.

8. The Vélodrome d'Hiver, an outdoor sporting arena in the 15th *arrondissement* of Paris, was used to corral 13,152 French and foreign-born Jews on July 16 and 17, 1942. Among them were over 4,000 children; 12,884 of these individuals were deported.

9. Czech, *Auschwitz Chronicle,* 793, 794, 798, 800; and Strzelecki, *The Evacuation, Dismantling, and Liberation of KL Auschwitz,* 211.

10. Marcel W., T-2165, Fortunoff Video Archive, Yale University Library. Another prisoner, Bart S., felt he was too weak to survive the evacuation, and managed to avoid the last roundup by hiding in a pile of bodies. Bart S., T-438, Fortunoff Video Archive, Yale University Library.

11. Levi, *Survival in Auschwitz,* 169, 171–72.

12. Henry B., HVT-689, Fortunoff Video Archive, Yale University Library.

13. "Death Marches," in Israel Gutman, ed., *Encyclopedia of the Holocaust* (New York: Macmillan, 1990), 348–54. There is also a short introduction to the topic by Yehuda Bauer, "The Death Marches, January–May 1945," in Michael Marrus, ed., *The Nazi Holocaust* (Westport, Conn.: Meckler, 1989), 491–511.

14. Filip Müller, *Eyewitness Auschwitz: Three Years in the Gas Chambers,* trans. by Susanne Flatauer (New York: Stein & Day, 1979), 165–66.

15. Elie Wiesel, *Night,* trans. by Stella Rodway (New York: Bantam Books, 1982), 81–98. Wiesel was transported to Buchenwald. His father, with whom he had endured Auschwitz, died from exhaustion upon arriving at Buchenwald.

16. Sara Nomberg-Przytyk, *Auschwitz: True Tales from a Grotesque Land,* trans. by Roslyn Hirsch (Chapel Hill: University of North Carolina Press, 1985), 128–29.

17. Marco Nahon, *Birkenau: The Camp of Death,* trans. by Jacqueline Havaux Bowers (Tuscaloosa: University of Alabama Press, 1989), 112–14.

18. Marcel Stourdze, in Marie-Anne Matard-Bonucci and Edouard Lynch, eds., *La Libération des camps et le Retour des déportés: L'Histoire en souffrance* (Paris: Editions Complexe, 1995), 48–49; Henry B. (HVT-689), Fred B. (HVT-1497), Henry F. (HVT-1332), Fortunoff Video Archive, Yale University Library.

19. Document 053-L, *Trial of the Major War Criminals before the International Military Tribunal,* vol. 37, *Documents in Evidence,* 486–88.

20. The orders from Fritz Bracht, dated December 21, 1944, have been reproduced in full in Strzelecki, *The Evacuation, Dismantling, and Liberation of KL Auschwitz,* 275–85. This order to kill any prisoners who tried to escape or who lagged behind the column was emphasized in the orders given by Auschwitz commandant SS-Stürmbannführer Richard Baer. Ibid., 135–36.

21. The evidence for Himmler's order of January is vague, but it is referred to by the former commandant of Auschwitz, Rudolf Höss, who at this time was the chief of the department of inspectors of the concentration camp system: *Death Dealer: The Memoirs of the SS Kommandant at Auschwitz,* ed. by Steven Paskuly, trans. by Andrew Pollinger (New York: Prometheus Books, 1992), 175, 290.

22. George S. Patton, Jr., *War As I Knew It* (Boston: Houghton Mifflin, 1947), 293–94; and on Patton's nausea, Robert H. Abzug, *Inside the Vicious Heart: Americans and the Liberation of Nazi Concentration Camps* (New York: Oxford University Press, 1985), 27.

23. Earl F. Ziemke, *The US Army in the Occupation of Germany, 1944–46* (Washington, D.C.: Center of Military History, 1975), 231–35.

24. *The Buchenwald Report,* ed. by, David A. Hackett (Boulder, Colo.: Westview Press, 1995), 96–104, 113–15. This report, made up of reports, documents, and testimonies, was compiled by U.S. Army officers in the Psychological Warfare Division soon after the liberation of the camp.

25. For a detailed account of the Dachau camp at and after the liberation see Harold Marcuse, *Legacies of Dachau: The Uses and Abuses of a Concentration Camp, 1933–2001* (Cambridge, U.K.: Cambridge University Press, 2001).

26. For a careful and thoughtful discussion of the role of journalists during the liberation of the camps, see Barbie Zelizer, *Remembering to Forget: Holocaust Memory through the Camera's Eye* (Chicago: University of Chicago Press, 1998).

27. *Time,* April 30, 1945; and "Report of a Special Congressional Committee to the Congress of the United States," Document 159-L, *Trial of the Major War Criminals,* vol. 37, *Documents in Evidence,* 605–26. The congressmen visited these sites between April 24 and May 2. Nor would Jews specifically be discussed in any of the articles cited below. For a discussion of this point, see Peter Novick, *The Holocaust in American Life* (Boston: Houghton Mifflin, 1999), 21–29, 63–66.

28. Margaret Bourke-White, *"Dear Fatherland, Rest Quietly"* (New York: Simon & Schuster, 1946), 73; *Time,* April 30, 1945; Marcus J. Smith, *Dachau: The Harrowing of Hell* (Albany: State University of New York Press, 1995), 105; Patton, *War As I Knew It,* 300; Al Newman, *Newsweek,* April 23, 1945; *Buchenwald Report,* 7; *Newsweek,* April 30, 1945; Abzug, *Inside the Vicious Heart,* 132; PFC Ralph Talanian, 71st Infantry Division, in Yaffa Eliach and Brana Gurewitsch, eds., *The Liberators: Eyewitness Accounts of the Liberation of Concentration Camps,* vol. 1 (Brooklyn: Center for Holocaust Studies, 1981), 48.

29. Edward R. Murrow, CBS Radio broadcast, April 15, 1945, from Buchenwald, in *Reporting World War II,* part 2, *American Journalism, 1944–1946* (New York: Library of America, 1995), 682–83; Percy Knauth, *Germany in Defeat* (New York: Knopf, 1946), 41–43; Sidney Olson, *Time,* May 7, 1945.

30. Mrs. Mavis Tate, M.P., "More on Buchenwald," *Spectator,* May 4, 1945; Harold Denny, "News of the Week in Review," *New York Times,* April 22, 1945.

31. For a detailed account of Belsen and its history, see Alexandra-Eileen Wenck, *Zwischen Menschenhandel und Endlösung: Das Konzentrationslager Bergen-Belsen* (Paderborn, Germany: Schöningh, 2000); and a shorter account is Eberhard Kolb, *Bergen-Belsen: From "Detention Camp" to Concentration Camp, 1943–1945* (Göttingen, Germany: Vandenhoeck & Ruprecht, 1986).

32. Derek Sington, *Belsen Uncovered* (London: Duckworth, 1946), 16–17.

33. Testimony of Lt.-Col. J. A. D. Johnston, Alan MacAuslan, and John Dixey, in *The Relief of Belsen, April 1945: Eyewitness Accounts* (London: Imperial War Museum, 1991), 10, 14, 16, 20.

34. Leslie H. Hardman, with Cecily Goodman, *The Survivors: The Story of the Belsen Remnant* (London: Vallentine, Mitchell, 1958), 2, 14.

35. Sington, *Belsen Uncovered,* 23.

36. IWM 93/11/1, papers of Capt. R. Barber, Royal Army Medical Corps, "Report on Liberation of Sandbostel Concentration Camp."

37. M.B., of the 63rd Infantry Division, in *Liberators,* 39. The 63rd I.D. entered Germany in February 1945, and on April 29–30, liberated several subcamps attached to the Kaufering camp, which was part of the Dachau network of camps.

38. Robert Antelme, *The Human Race,* trans. by Jeffrey Haight and Annie Mahler (Marlboro, Vt: Marlboro Press, 1992), 289. Originally published in 1957 in Paris as *L'espèce humaine.*

39. Hanna Lévy-Hass, *Inside Belsen,* trans. by Ronald Taylor (Brighton, U.K.: Harvester Press, 1982), 52–53, 67; Interview with Fela Lichtheim, in David P. Boder, *I Did Not Interview the Dead* (Urbana: University of Illinois Press, 1949), 154–59.

40. Sora M. (HVT-2826), Fortunoff Video Archive, Yale University Library, and her testimony in Karine Habif, ed., *Le jour d'après: Douze témoins de la libération des camps* (Paris: Editions Patrick Banon, 1995), where her name is given as Sarah Montard; Fernande H. (HVT-2667), Fortunoff Video Archive, Yale University Library; Rosensaft in *The Liberation of the Nazi Concentration Camps, 1945: Eyewitness Accounts of the Liberators,* ed. by Brewster Chamberlin and Marcia Feldman (Washington, D.C.: U.S. Holocaust Memorial Council, 1987), 152–54.

41. Habif, ed., *Le jour d'après,* 75, 92, 103, 117.

42. Habif, ed., *Le jour d'après,* 171–2; Matard-Bonucci and Lynch, eds., *La Libération des camps,* 54–55.

43. Abzug, *Inside the Vicious Heart*, 30.

44. Siggi Wilzig and Elie Wiesel, in *The Liberation of the Nazi Concentration Camps*, 158, 14.

9: Americans and Jews in Occupied Germany

1. Yehuda Bauer and one of his students, Ze'ev Mankowitz, have written the outstanding works on the subject of the *She'erit Hapleitah*. See especially Bauer, *Flight and Rescue: Brichah* (New York: Random House, 1970), and *Out of the Ashes: The Impact of American Jews on Post-Holocaust European Jewry* (Oxford, U.K.: Pergamon, 1989); and Mankowitz, *Life Between Memory and Hope: The Survivors of the Holocaust in Occupied Germany* (Cambridge, U.K.: Cambridge University Press, 2002). Leonard Dinnerstein's work also remains an essential introduction: see *America and the Survivors of the Holocaust* (New York: Columbia University Press, 1982).

2. For contemporary estimates, see "Jews in the Camps in Germany and Austria," a memo for the World Jewish Congress written by Zorach Warhaftig, November 27, 1945, published in Abraham J. Peck, ed., *Archives of the Holocaust*, vol. 9, *American Jewish Archives, The Papers of the World Jewish Congress, 1945–1950* (New York: Garland, 1990), 110–38, which provides a detailed chart. The AJJDC also placed the number of Jews in Germany in the fall of 1945 at about 55,000. See "Summary of Recent Reports from JDC Representatives in Germany," December 18, 1945, AJJDC Archives, Germany, Displaced Persons, #321. Koppel Pinson, a senior AJJDC official in Germany in 1945–46, also gives 60,000 as a rough figure of Jews in Germany at the end of the war. Pinson, "Jewish Life in Liberated Germany," *Jewish Social Studies* 9, 2 (April 1947), 101–26. For numbers of Jewish refugees from Poland and the east who arrived in Germany in late 1945 and 1946, see Bauer, *Out of the Ashes*, 88, 126–27.

3. Judah Nadich, *Eisenhower and the Jews* (New York: Twayne, 1953), 84–87; Mankowitz, *Life Between Memory and Hope*, 30–31; Bauer, *Flight and Rescue*, 59.

4. For a survey of the predicament of the Jews in the summer and fall, see "Report of the AJJDC Staff Conference of the Eastern Military District, 3rd Army, Held at Passing near Munich, October 21, 1945," AJJDC Archives, Germany, DPs, #321.

5. Bauer, *Flight and Rescue*, 70–73; Mankowitz, *Life Between Memory and Hope*, 49–51.

6. Judah Nadich, who as special adviser to Eisenhower on Jewish affairs, was Klausner's nominal superior, describes his irregular status. He was "completely on his own" and "a man without a unit, an officer without a formal military assignment." But such was the fluid and chaotic situation in the DP camps that Klausner could operate freely in them throughout the summer without any serious intervention by Army authorities. Nadich, *Eisenhower and the Jews*, 72–77.

7. Bauer, *Flight and Rescue*, 59–62. On the UNRRA University, see UNRRA Archives, S-0436-0031, reports from UNRRA Team 108, August 18, September 11, and October 15, 1945.

8. "A Detailed Report on the Liberated Jew as He Now Suffers His Period of Liberation under the Discipline of the Armed Forces of the United States," by Abraham J. Klausner, Jewish Chaplain, U.S. Army, written on June 24, 1945, in Dachau. AJJDC Archives, Germany, DPs, #322.

9. Unsigned letter, dated August 26, 1945, enclosed in a letter from Joseph Leonard of Allentown, Pennsylvania, to Isidor Coons of the JDC, September 6, 1945, AJJDC Archives, Germany, DPs, #329.

10. Sgt. Edward Mayer to Dr. George Fox, Rabbi, South Shore Temple, Chicago, August 3, 1945; letter from Sgt. L. P. Brewster to his parents, July 6, 1945; Klausner letter to Dr. S. Atlas of Hebrew Union College in Cincinnati, Ohio, August 28, 1945, in AJJDC Archives, Germany, DPs, #329. Klausner himself has offered his own account of his motives and actions in this period. See his interview for the documentary by Wentworth Films, *Liberation/DP*, transcript in possession of U.S. Holocaust Memorial Museum Library.

11. Outgoing cable, New York to Paris, September 28, 1945, AJJDC, DPs, General, #1025. These worries proved unfounded. The Joint was able to raise significant sums in 1946 and 1947, and spent correspondingly more each successive year on Jewish DPs in Europe. Bauer, *Out of the Ashes*, xviii.

12. Dr. Joseph Hyman, September 25, 1945, AJJDC Archives, Germany, DPs, #329. Much of the same text was used repeatedly in letters to other inquiries.

13. Interview for documentary *Voices of the Shoah: Remembrances of the Holocaust*, by David Notowitz, vol. 3 (Notowitz Productions, 2001).

14. Stimson to Eisenhower, August 7, 1945, and Eisenhower to Secretary of War, August 14, 1945, in NARA, RG 84, Foreign Service Posts, Office of Political Adviser to Germany, Classified General Correspondence, box 34; other documents cited in Nadich, *Eisenhower and the Jews*, 34–35; and Arieh J. Kochavi, *Post-Holocaust Politics: Britain, the United States, and Jewish Refugees, 1945–1948* (Chapel Hill: University of North Carolina Press, 2001), 89–90.

15. Full text of Truman's letter to Eisenhower and Harrison's report in Department of State, *Bulletin*, September 30, 1945.

16. Report by Joseph Schwartz, August 19, 1945, AJJDC Archives, Displaced Persons, General, #1025.

17. Harrison report, U.S. State Department, *Bulletin* 13 (September 30, 1945).

18. Eisenhower to Truman, September 14, 1945, in NARA, RG 84, Foreign Service Posts, Office of Political Adviser to Germany, Classified General Correspondence, box 34.

19. Eisenhower's order is in NARA, RG 260, Records of U.S. Occupation Headquarters, WWII, U.S. Group Control Council, Adjutant General, General Correspondence, 1944–45, box 25; and reproduced in Nadich, *Eisenhower and the Jews*, 130–32. Nadich gave his own account in his "Report on Conditions in Assembly Centers for Jewish Displaced Persons," September 16, 1945, in AJJDC Archives, Germany, DPs, #322. And see telegram from JDC Paris to New York on the visit, which was "enthusiastically received by the internees." AJJDC Archives, September 20, 1945, Displaced Persons, General, #1025.

20. "Final Report by General Eisenhower on Jewish Displaced Persons in Germany," cover sheet dated November 5, 1945, report written on October 8, 1945, in NARA, RG 84, Foreign Service Posts, Office of Political Adviser to Germany, Classified General Correspondence, box 34.

21. Reported in the *Jewish Chronicle*, October 26, 1945.

22. Report of Staff Conference, October 21, 1945, AJJDC Archives, Germany, DPs, #321.

23. Warhaftig, November 27, 1945, in Peck, ed., *Archives of the Holocaust*, 129, 134.

24. Oscar A. Mintzer, *In Defense of the Survivors: The Letters of Oscar A. Mintzer, AJDC Legal Advisor, Germany, 1945–46* (Berkeley, Calif.: Judah L. Magnes Museum, 1999), 47.

25. Warhaftig, November 27, 1945, in Peck, ed., *Archives of the Holocaust*, 130.

26. Pinson, "Jewish Life in Liberated Germany," 108–9.

27. Pinson, "Jewish Life in Liberated Germany," 118.

28. Report on Camp Landsberg, October 1945, AJJDC Archives, Germany, DPs, #321; Report by R. G. Mastrude, Acting Regional Supervisor, XX Corps Regional Office, October 13, 1945, Inspection of Team 311, Landsberg, UNRRA Archives, S-0436-0042.

29. Report on Camp Landsberg, October 1945, AJJDC Archives, Germany, DPs, #321.

30. *Among the Survivors of the Holocaust, 1945: The Landsberg DP Camp Letters of Major Irving Heymont, United States Army* (Cincinnati: American Jewish Archives, 1982), entry for September 20, 1945.

31. *Among the Survivors*, entries for September 20, 22, 25.

32. *Among the Survivors*, entries for September 28 and October 2.

33. *Among the Survivors*, entries for October 8, 10. Francesca Wilson, an English UNRRA official who was assigned to Feldafing, expressed the same mixture of sympathy and scorn for the Jewish DPs as Heymont had done at Landsberg. "As for the inmates of the camp," she

wrote in her 1947 memoir, "at first it was hard to look on them without repulsion. . . . By years of brutal treatment, by the murder of relatives, by the constant fear of death, all that was human had been taken away from them." As with so many Allied personnel, Wilson saw these bewildered, vulnerable Jews as something less than human, or at least less than adult. A group of Jews from Salonika, for example, she described as filthy and destructive. "How long would their return to infantilism last, I wondered. . . . I was reminded of some of our evacuee children who, with their families gone and every known tie severed, had, by smashing and soiling and burning and stealing everything revenged themselves on a society which had hounded them into the hideous void of the countryside and made them feel outcasts." Francesca M. Wilson, *Aftermath: France, Germany, Austria, Yugoslavia, 1945 and 1946* (London: Penguin, 1947), 41, 49–50.

34. Leo Srole, "Why the DPs Can't Wait," *Commentary,* vol. 3 (January 1947). An earlier version of his essay was prepared as a report for the Anglo-American Commission for Palestine in August 1946. AJJDC Archives, Germany, DPs, #324.

35. Helen Matouskova, Field Supervisor, UNRRA District Headquarters, to S. B. Zieman, District Director, District 5, February 4, 1946, UNRRA Archives, S-0436-0042.

36. Heymont speech quoted in Leo W. Schwarz, *The Redeemers: A Saga of the Years 1945–1952* (New York: Farrar, Straus & Young, 1953), 66.

37. *Landsberger Lager-Cajtung,* October 28, 1945, "Ben-Gurion in Landsberg: A lebediker grus fun E.-J."

38. Schwarz, 51. Schwarz's account of Ben-Gurion's conversations differs considerably from that reported in the *Landsberger Lager-Cajtung.*

39. Heymont, *Among the Survivors,* entry for October 22; and Warhaftig, November 27, 1945, in Peck, ed., *Archives of the Holocaust,* 132.

40. Major General Arthur A. White, Report on Landsberg Camp, December 22–23, 1945, UNRRA Archives, S-0436-0042.

41. Report of Colonel C. A. Nelson, to Brigadier General Walter J. Muller, December 10, 1945, UNRRA Archives, S-0436-0042.

42. Lt. Col. Charles Agar, Third Army Surgeon's Office, to Lt. Col. Pollock, Acting Army Surgeon, Third U.S. Army, "Landsberg DP Camp," December 28, 1945, UNRRA Archives, S-0436-0042.

43. Meeting of the Central Committee of Liberated Jews in Bavaria, November 15, 1945, AJJDC Archives, Germany, DPs, #321.

44. Zorach Warhaftig, "Jews in the Camps," memo in *Archives of the Holocaust;* Bauer, *Brichah,* 75–96; and for numbers see p. 119. Bauer argued that Ben-Gurion transformed what had been Brichah's mission of saving Jews into an act of political pressure: *Brichah,* 96.

45. Joseph Levine to Moses Leavitt, October 24, 1945, AJJDC Archives, Germany, DPs, #321; Eli Rock report, October 25, 1945, part of documents prepared for report on the Jewish Community of Bavaria, AJJDC Archives, Germany, DPs, #321; Trobe to Rifkind, AJJDC Archives, DPs, General, #1024.

46. Cable to War Department, no date; and cover memo by Major G. L. C. Scott and Lt. Col. Harry S. Messec, November 23, 1945, NARA, RG 84, Foreign Service Posts, Office of U.S. Political Adviser to Germany–Berlin, Classified General Correspondence, 1945, box 34.

47. Summary of recent reports from JDC representatives in Germany, December 18, 1945, AJJDC Archives, Germany, DPs, #321.

48. On the Srole affair, see Mankowitz, *Life Between Memory and Hope,* 109–10; Bauer, *Out of the Ashes,* 88–89; Rifkind cable to World Jewish Congress, December 18, 1945, and Rifkind letter, December 7, 1945, to Lech Kubowitzki, in *Archives of the Holocaust,* 153–56. The Bedell Smith visit and Smith's account of his visit to Landsberg are detailed in two UNRRA memoranda, in UNRRA, PAG-4/1.3.1.1.1, box 27, telegrams of December 7 and 9, 1945. Smith said of the camp's Jewish leaders, "in all of my service I have never found such complete ineffectiveness along lines of Administration of large group of people concentrated in one area."

49. Lt. Col. Messec memo to General Mickelsen, NARA, RG 84, Foreign Service Posts, Office of U.S. Political Adviser to Germany–Berlin, Classified General Correspondence, 1945, box 34. For criticism of the failure to seize sufficient housing, see Oscar Mintzer's letters, *In Defense of the Survivors,* 63–66.

50. PRO, FO1020/2409, October 2, 1945; November 6, 1945; and November 25, 1945.

51. PRO, FO1020/2409, *Morning News* clipping, January 4, 1946; *New York Times,* January 3, 1946.

52. Judge Simon Rifkind, address to the American Jewish Conference, April 2, 1946, NARA, RG 407, Administrative Services Division, Operations Branch, Foreign Occupied Area Reports, 1945–54, Germany, box 1005.

10: Belsen and the British

1. A good survey of the Anglo-American tangle over postwar Jewish policy is Arieh J. Kochavi, *Post-Holocaust Politics: Britain, the United States, and Jewish Refugees, 1945–1948* (Chapel Hill: University of North Carolina Press, 2001). A groundbreaking study that devotes particular attention to Belsen is Angelika Königseder and Julianne Wetzel, *Waiting for Hope: Jewish Displaced Persons in Post World War II Germany,* trans. by John A. Broadwin (Evanston, Il.: Northwestern University Press, 2001). Less analytical is Hagit Lavsky, *New Beginnings: Holocaust Survivors in Bergen-Belsen and the British Zone in Germany, 1945–50* (Detroit: Wayne State University Press, 2002). Leonard Dinnerstein is especially critical of British policy in *America and the Survivors of the Holocaust* (New York: Columbia University Press, 1982), following in the footsteps of I. F. Stone's scathing 1946 account, *Underground to Palestine* (rept. New York: Pantheon, 1978).

2. For an excellent survey of the range of official and public reactions to the liberation of Belsen, see Joanne Reilly, *Belsen: The Liberation of a Concentration Camp* (Routledge: London, 1998); and for thoughtful comment on Belsen in the British public mind, see Tony Kushner, "Approaching Belsen: An Introduction," in Jo Reilly et al., eds., *Belsen in History and Memory* (London: Frank Cass, 1997), 3–33. Reilly's work can be supplemented by Ben Shepard, *After Daybreak: The Liberation of Bergen-Belsen, 1945* (New York: Schocken Books, 2005).

3. The most complete account of the camp's liberation and the relief effort is Reilly, *Belsen: The Liberation of a Concentration Camp,* especially 22–42. See also Eberhard Kolb, *Bergen-Belsen: From "Detention" Camp to Concentration Camp, 1943–1945* (Göttingen, Germany: Vandenhoeck & Ruprecht, 1986), 46–49.

4. PRO, WO 222/201, Accounts given to Royal Society of Medicine, June 4, 1945, comments made by Lt.-Col. F. M. Lipscombe, Royal Army Medical Corps.

5. PRO, WO 219/3944A, "What the Army did at Belsen Concentration Camp," undated.

6. PRO, WO 222/208, Starvation in Belsen Camp: Report by Captain P. L. Mollison, RAMC, May 1945.

7. PRO, WO 219/3944A, "What the Army did at Belsen Concentration Camp," undated.

8. Lavsky, *New Beginnings,* 58–59. The numbers fluctuated a good deal. By November 1945, the camp contained about 16,000 DPs, of whom 11,000 were Jews; the numbers of Jews dropped slightly to 9,000 by the start of 1946, but increased during 1946, as Polish Jews fled pogroms in Poland. By August 1946, the number of Jews in Belsen again reached 11,000. Thomas Rahe, "Social Life in the Jewish DP Camp at Bergen-Belsen," in Erik Somers and René Kok, eds., *Jewish DPs in Camp Bergen-Belsen, 1945–1950: The Unique Photo Album of Zippy Orlin* (Seattle: University of Washington Press, 2004), 71.

9. Muriel Knox Doherty, *Letters from Belsen, 1945: An Australian Nurse's Experiences with the Survivors of War,* ed. by Judith Cornell and R. Lynette Russell (St. Leonards, Australia: Allen & Unwin, 2000), 53–54.

10. Doherty, *Letters from Belsen*, 72.

11. Leslie H. Hardman, with Cecily Goodman, *The Survivors: The Story of the Belsen Remnant* (London: Vallentine, Mitchell, 1958), 88–89; Report by Jane Leverson, on DP Centre No. 267 (Lingen), June 6, 1945, in American Friends Service Committee Archives, Foreign Service/1945/Germany, Box 1; *Jewish Chronicle*, June 15, 1945.

12. Derek Sington, *Belsen Uncovered* (London: Duckworth, 1946), 151–52.

13. *Jewish Chronicle*, November 23, 1945.

14. Sington, *Belsen Uncovered*, 160–61.

15. Sington, *Belsen Uncovered*, 161–66; Hugh Jenkins, typescript of diary, American Friends Service Committee Archives, Foreign Service/1945/Germany, box 1, folder 2, entry dated May 24.

16. UNRRA, PAG-4/1.3.1.1.1, box 27, Bryan in London to Salisbury, October 31, 1945.

17. For a moving portrait of this extraordinary man, see the account in his wife's memoir, Hadassah Rosensaft, *Yesterday: My Story* (Washington, D.C.: U.S. Holocaust Memorial Museum, 2004), 61–66.

18. Maurice Eigen, senior JDC official in Belsen, September 9, 1945, memo to JDC in New York, in AJJDC Archives, Germany, DP Camps, #325. Eigen also noted that the existence of non-Jewish Poles in the Belsen DP camp was a "burning problem," especially for the Joint, because it raised the issue of whether supplies intended for Jews should be shared with non-Jews. As long as Belsen was not made a Jewish-only camp, the Joint representative in Belsen found himself in an awkward position.

19. Königseder and Wetzel, *Waiting for Hope*, 170–90; Lavsky, *New Beginnings*, 70–77. The British, naturally, placed an observer at the conference, and he duly reported to the Foreign Office what he had seen. Major C.C.K. Rickford said the conference had consisted of the usual appeals for entry into Palestine, demands for an improvement of living conditions, and frustration at "being regarded as second-rate human beings." "Report of First Jewish DP Congress, Bergen-Belsen, September 25–27," PRO, FO 371/51125.

20. For a useful summary of the work of the Belsen leadership, see "The Central Committee of Liberated Jews in the British Zone, Germany: 1945–1947," a brief handbook prepared in Belsen by the Committee, Archives of the U.S. Holocaust Memorial Museum. This document described the goal of the committee as "the final liberation of the Jews saved in the British Zone" (7).

21. PRO, FO 1032/815, Leonard Cohen memorandum, July 3, 1945, on "The Problem of Jewish DPs in Germany," and Maj.-Gen. Britten's response, July 27, 1945.

22. PRO, FO 1049/195, Anderson to Brigadier B. V. Britten, July 21, 1945.

23. PRO, FO 1049/195, George Rendel, Foreign Office, to Sir William Strang, August 24, 1945.

24. PRO, FO 371/51123, Templer memorandum, September 6, 1945.

25. PRO, FO 371/51124, Foreign Office to Lord Halifax, British Ambassador in Washington, October 5, 1945.

26. PRO, FO 1032/815, Lady Reading to Field Marshal Montgomery, September 20, 1945.

27. PRO, FO 1032/815, Major General G. W. R. Templer, Office of the Deputy Military Governor and Chief of Staff, Main Headquarters, Control Commission for Germany, British Element, Lübbecke, October 26, 1945.

28. *Jewish Chronicle*, July 13, 1945; headlines from June 15, 1945.

29. *Times* (London), July 16 and 21, 1945, August 2, 1945; *New York Times*, July 21, 1945, August 10, 1945, September 29, 1945, September 30, 1945. Lady Reading's letter is in *Times* (London), August 30, 1945.

30. *New York Times*, October 3, 1945.

31. Anglo-American relations can be followed in Kochavi, *Post-Holocaust Politics*, 98–106. Kochavi cites Bevin's "head of the queue" comment but this was not included in the *Times* account of the press conference, *Times* (London), November 14, 1945. Bevin's Com-

mons statement is in *Parliamentary Debates* (Hansard), Fifth Series, volume 415, House of Commons, 1927–31, and *New York Times,* November 14, 1945.

32. *Times* (London), November 15, 1945; *New York Times,* November 18, 1945.

33. Col. Marcus Lipton and Barnett Janner, quoted in *Jewish Chronicle,* November 16, 1945.

34. Maj. Edward Jacobs, "Report on the Jewish Incident at Hanover on Friday November 16, 1945," November 20, 1945; and Berlin HQ to War Office, December 31, 1945, PRO FO 1032/815.

35. Samuel Gringauz, "Finfachike begide," *Landsberger Lager-Cajtung,* November 22, 1945.

36. For accounts of the Anglo-American Commission on Palestine by two members, one British and one American, see Richard Crossman, *Palestine Mission: A Personal Record* (London: Hamish Hamilton, 1947), and Bartley Crum, *Behind the Silken Curtain* (New York: Simon & Schuster, 1947). Crossman's is especially revealing, for he shows that he himself shared Bevin's view that the Jews in the DP camps, like the Jews in Palestine, had no legitimate right to statehood simply by virtue of their faith. Crossman changed his mind after visiting the DP camps. "The abstract arguments about Zionism and the Jewish state seemed curiously remote after this experience of human degradation." *Palestine Mission,* 84.

37. *New York Times,* November 20, 1945.

38. Halifax to London, November 23, 1945, PRO, FO 945/596; for full copy of text, see Warburg to Leavitt at JDC, New York, November 15, 1945, JDC Archives, Germany, #321; Control Commission to Berlin, December 5, 1945, PRO, FO 1049/195.

39. The timing was coincidental. The international military tribunal at Nuremberg opened in November, as did the trial of the Dachau concentration camp staff. Dachau being in the American zone, the accused were tried by an American military court. For a detailed examination, see Harold Marcuse, *Legacies of Dachau: The Uses and Abuses of a Concentration Camp, 1933–2001* (Cambridge: U.K. Cambridge University Press, 2001), 67–71.

40. *London Illustrated News,* four-page supplement, April 28, 1945.

41. *New York Times,* April 22, 1945.

42. *New York Times,* April 29, 1945.

43. Raymond Phillips, ed., *Trial of Josef Kramer and Forty-Four Others* (Willam Hodge: London, 1949), xxiv. Captain Phillips served at the trial as one of the defense counsel, and later had a career as a barrister and judge.

44. Phillips, ed., *Trial of Josef Kramer,* xlv. Also see reporting on establishment of war crimes machinery in the *Times* (London), June 15 and June 18, 1945.

45. PRO, CAB 121/422, Roberts (in Moscow), to Cabinet, October 4 and 5, 1945, and November 5, 1945; "Moscow Sees 'Softness' to Nazis in US Zone and at Belsen Trial," *New York Times,* November 4, 1945. The Soviets pointed to their own record with pride: that same week, they sentenced the former Hungarian premier László Bárdossy to death after just three sittings of the court in Budapest. For the French view, see PRO, WO 311/198, Patrick Dean to War Office, December 21, 1945.

46. Donald Bloxham, *Genocide on Trial: War Crimes Trials and the Formation of Holocaust History and Memory* (New York: Oxford University Press, 2001), 97–101, 180.

47. PRO, WO 309/424, "Interim Report," dated June 22, 1945, on war crimes investigations by Lt.-Col. L. J. Genn and Major S. G. Champion; and Phillips, ed., *Trial of Josef Kramer,* xxxiv–xxxv. Many of the affidavits are collected in PRO, WO 235/24; WO 309/17, WO 309/33, WO 309/55, WO 309/56, WO 309/73, and WO 309/1553.

48. One of the members of the defense was Captain Airey Neave, a decorated officer who had been wounded in 1940; imprisoned by the Germans in "escape-proof" Colditz prison, he nonetheless escaped. After the Belsen trial, Neave became a member of the British prosecution team at Nuremberg. Following his successful career as an MP, Neave was appointed secretary of state for Northern Ireland by Margaret Thatcher, and was killed by an Irish Republican Army car bomb in 1979.

49. Alex Easterman to World Jewish Congress, September 17, 1945, in Abraham J. Peck, ed., *Archives of the Holocaust,* vol. 9, *American Jewish Archives: Papers of the World Jewish Congress, 1945–1950* (New York: Garland, 1990), 76–79.

50. *Jewish Chronicle,* September 21, 1945; *Times* (London), September 21, 1945.

51. Opening speech for the prosecution by Col. T. M. Backhouse, in Phillips, ed., *Trial of Josef Kramer,* 15–17.

52. Kramer deposition, "Statement of Josef Kramer," May 22, 1945, part of the testimony taken by the War Crimes Team, PRO, WO 235/24.

53. Deposition of Irma Grese, June 14, 1945, PRO, WO 235/24.

54. Phillips, ed., *Trial of Josef Kramer,* 25–29; xlii; *New York Times* comment on Grese, September 20, 1945; Easterman telegram, September 17, 1945. The *New York Times* on April 25 had paid special attention to the presence of female guards at Belsen, reporting witness accounts that German women guards had "enjoyed" participating in certain tortures such as beatings and the use of dogs to terrorize prisoners.

55. Phillips, ed., *Trial of Josef Kramer,* 47, 49.

56. For press coverage of Dr. Bimko's testimony, see *New York Times,* September 22 and 23, 1945; *Daily Express,* September 22, 1945; *News of the World,* September 23, 1945; *Jewish Chronicle,* September 28, 1945.

57. Phillips, ed., *Trial of Josef Kramer,* 512–18.

58. Kramer deposition, PRO, WO 235/24.

59. Phillips, ed., *Trial of Josef Kramer,* 596, 599.

60. *Times* (London), October 17, 1945; *Jewish Chronicle,* October 12, 19, 26, 1945; for Winwood's apology, *New York Times,* November 9, 1945.

61. Letter to his wife Rosine Kramer, July 8, 1945, PRO, WO 309/17.

62. Rosensaft, *Yesterday,* 91.

63. *Times* (London), November 19, 1945; *Jewish Chronicle,* November 23 and December 21, 1945.

Conclusion: The Missing Liberation

1. Primo Levi, *Reawakening* (New York: Simon & Schuster, 1965), 206–7.

2. Jeffrey Herf, *Divided Memory: The Nazi Past in the Two Germanys* (Cambridge, Mass.: Harvard University Press, 1997), 206.

Bibliography

Archival Sources

The following list of archival sources lists the country, city, archive, and principal collections that were consulted in the research for this book. The collections are italicized. The footnotes contain more detailed references to specific documents.

BELGIUM

Brussels

Centre d'Études et de Documentation Guerre et Sociétés Contemporaines / Studie- en Documentatiecentrum Oorlog en Hedendaagse Maatschappij

Commission des crimes de guerre [AA120]
François-L. Ganshof papers: Rapports, septembre–décembre 1944 [AA707]
Haut Commissariat à la Securité de l'État / Hoog Commissariaat voor 'S Rijks Veiligheid [AA1311]
RTBF-Mons: Jours de Guerre: television documentary source collections [AA1593]
RTBF-Namur: Collection concernant l'offensive des Ardennes rassemblée par la RTBF-Namur [AA1207–1208]

FRANCE

Caen

Archives Départementales du Calvados

Série M: Administration générale [police, santé, agriculture, commerce, et industrie]
Série W: Archives publiques postérieurs à 1940 [9W, 20W, 21W]
Série 1J: Journaux et mémoires de Calvadosiens sur la Deuxième guerre mondiale
Série 13 T: Collection de presse

ITALY

Rome

Archivio Centrale dello Stato

Presidenza del Consiglio dei Ministri (PCM)
Alto Commissariato per le Sanzioni contro il Fascismo [Titolo I, Busta 1, 2, 3, 11, 12, 39, 41, 49]

UNITED KINGDOM

Kew

National Archives (formerly Public Record Office [PRO])

Air Ministry [AIR]
Cabinet papers [CAB]
Foreign Office papers [FO]
War Office papers [WO]

London

Imperial War Museum

Private papers and documents

86/3/1	Byford, P. F.
86/47/1	Perry, J. G.
87/35/1	Cooper, D.
87/44/1	Morris, K. W.
88/19/1	Lane, A. J.
PP/MCR/328	Tilly, Lieutenant Colonel G. DSO TD
90/6/1	White, J. Y.
90/20/1	Caines, Captain W. G.
90/25/1	Vernon, Major D. R.
91/21/1	Jupp, Captain M. E.
91/13/1	Forrest, Major A. J.
92/22/1	Wild, Mrs. S. P.
92/10/1	Tateson, T.
93/11/1	Barer, Captain R. MC
93/24/1	Smith, Miss D. E.
90/6/1	Gardiner, A. S.
91/8/1	Cross, Captain C. T.
93/29/1	Wilkes, A. A.
95/19/1	Greenwood, R. T.
95/26/1	Bickerdike, Mrs. R. N.
95/2/1	Samuels, S. A. W.
95/33/1	Sweet, Captain H. O.
84/27/3	Whittington, Miss J. CBE
83/18/1	Miller, G. C.
83/52/1	Jones, D.
94/34/1	Crawford, Colonel M. DSO
78/68/1	Greene, Lieutenant W. A.
98/16/1	Herbert, A. G.
98/3/1	Longley, A. J.
99/16/1	Roker, L. F.
98/35/1	Helm, Captain W. H.
99/16/1	Astley, I. D.
03/28/1	Beck, Captain S.
99/61/1	Elliott, Major E. M.
99/63/1	Barker, Major J.
99/85/1	Blackman, W. A.
99/85/1	Gore, T. A.
99/67/1	Elliott, Major D. S. MC
01/13/1	Skinner, Reverend L. F. TD

London, *cont.*

> *Private papers and documents,* cont.

> | PP/MCR/292 | Whittaker, Major N. MBE |
> |---|---|
> | P182 | Ritchie, Major G. M. C. |
> | 03/28/1 | Lawrence, F. H. |
> | 03/28/1 | Cooke, Major M. H. MC |
> | 02/58/1 | Humphries, Reverend J. H. |
> | 02/35/1 | Clift, H. E. |
> | 04/16/1 | Haydon, N. M. |
> | 05/27/1 | Wheway, Major H. F. MC |
> | 94/51/1 | von Lenip, M. Miss |
> | 94/10/1 | Day, Mrs. C. |
> | 78/35/1 | de Vigneral, Madame A. |

UNITED STATES

Cambridge, Massachusetts

> Harvard-Andover Theological Library, Harvard University

> > *Unitarian Service Committee papers*

Carlisle, Pennsylvania

> Carlisle Barracks, U.S. Army Military History Institute

> > *Battle of the Bulge Historical Foundation Collection*

> > *Private Papers*

> > > Delaval, Maurice
> > > Doerr, Robert F., Jr.
> > > Hansen, Chester B.
> > > Kaplan, Richard
> > > McBride, Richard L.
> > > McSherry, Frank J.
> > > Peterson, Margaret
> > > Seale, Robert E.

> > *World War II Veterans Survey Collection*

> > > 101st Airborne
> > > 4th Infantry
> > > 28th Infantry
> > > 99th Infantry
> > > 106th Infantry

Lorton, Virginia

> Hazel Braugh Record Center and Archives

> > *American Red Cross papers*

New Haven, Connecticut

> Sterling Library, Yale University

> > *Fortunoff Video Archive*

Beinecke Library, Yale University
  Kathryn Hulme Papers

New York
American Jewish Joint Distribution Committee
Columbia University
  Herbert Lehman Papers
United Nations
  United Nations Relief and Rehabilitation Administration Records

Philadelphia
American Friends Service Committee papers
  Papers from Germany and Overseas, 1945
Balch Institute, Historical Society of Pennsylvania
  Polish War Relief documents

Santa Fe, New Mexico
State Records Center and Archives
  Marie Pope Wallis Papers

Washington, D.C.
National Archives and Records Administration, College Park, Maryland
  RG 84 Foreign Service Posts; Office of the Political Adviser to Germany, Berlin; Classi-
    fied General Correspondence, 1945–49
  RG 200 Records of the American National Red Cross
  RG 208 AA, Photographs of the Allies and Axis, 1942–45
  RG 243 Records of the United States Strategic Bombing Survey
  RG 260 U.S. Occupation Headquarters, World War II, U.S. Group Control Council
  RG 331 Allied Operational and Occupation Headquarters, World War II, Supreme
    Headquarters, Allied Expeditionary Forces (SHAEF), General Staff, G-5 Division,
    Displaced Persons Branch
  RG 338 Record of U.S. Army Commands
  RG 407 The Adjutant General's Office Records, Administrative Services Division,
    Operations Branch, Foreign (Occupied) Areas Reports, 1945–54, Special, Germany
    (U.S. Zone)
  RG 498 Records of Headquarters, European Theater of Operations, U.S. Army,
    1942–45

United States Holocaust Memorial Museum
  Earl Harrison papers
  Abraham Klausner, Oral History transcript
  Hadassah Rosensaft Collection
  Liberation 1945 oral history collection
  Malcolm Vendig Papers
  YIVO Archives (Microfilm)
    Displaced Persons Camps and Centers in Germany
    Jewish Displaced Persons Periodicals

Press

Dos Fraje Wort (Feldafing Camp paper, U.S. zone of occupation)
Frankfurter Rundschau
Heute
Jewish Chronicle (London)
Landsberger Lager-Cajtung (Landsberg DP Camp paper)
Libération de Normandie (Caen)
Life
London Illustrated News
Manchester Guardian
La Marseillaise
Le Monde (Paris)
Morning News (London)
New York Times
News of the World (London)
Newsweek
News of Germany
Palestine Post (Jerusalem)
Süddeutsche Zeitung
Stuttgarter Zeitung
Spectator (London)
Time
Times (London)
Unzer Sztyme (British zone of occupation)
The World's Children (published by Save the Children U.K.)
Yank

Published Primary Sources

American National Red Cross. *Annual Reports, 1944–45 and 1945–46.* Washington, D.C., 1945 and 1946.

Buchbender, Ortwin, and Reinhold Sterz, eds. *Das andere Gesicht des Krieges: Deutsche Feldpostbriefe, 1939–1945.* Munich: Verlag C. H. Beck, 1983.

General Sikorski Historical Institute. *Documents of Polish-Soviet Relations, 1939–1945.* Vol. 2, *1943–1945.* London: Heinemann, 1967.

Hirschfeld, Gerhard, and Irina Renz, eds. *Vormittags die ersten Amerikaner: Stimmen und Bilder vom Kriegsende 1945.* Stuttgart: Klett-Cotta, 2005.

Józef Piłsudski Institute of America. *Poland in the British Parliament, 1939–1945.* Vol. 3, *Summer 1944–Summer 1945.* Ed. by Wacław Jędrzejewicz. New York: Waldon Press, 1962.

Krasilshchik, S., ed. *World War II Dispatches from the Soviet Front.* Trans. by Nina Bouis. New York: Sphinx Press, 1985.

Noakes, J., and G. Pridham. *Nazism, 1919–1945.* Vol. 3, *Foreign Policy, War and Racial Extermination.* Exeter U.K.: University of Exeter Press, 1988.

Peck, Abraham J., ed. *Archives of the Holocaust.* Vol. 9, *American Jewish Archives, The Papers of the World Jewish Congress, 1945–1950.* New York. Garland, 1990.

Phillips, Raymond, ed. *Trial of Josef Kramer and Forty-Four Others (The Belsen Trial).* London: William Hodge & Co., 1949.

Royal Institute of International Affairs. *Documents on Germany under Occupation, 1945–1954,* ed. by Beate Ruhm von Oppen. London: Oxford University Press, 1955.

Schieder, Theodor. *The Expulsion of the German Population from the Territories East of the Oder-Neisse Line.* Bonn: Federal Ministry for Expellees, Refugees and War Victims, no date, circa 1955.

Strangmeier, Heinrich, and Elisabeth Kraut, eds. *Aus den letzten Kriegswochen 1945: Eine Dokumentation.* Hilden, Germany: Verlag Peters, 1976.

United Nations Relief and Rehabilitation Administration. *The Story of UNRRA.* Washington, D.C.: Office of Public Information, UNRRA, February 1949.

United Nations War Crimes Commission. *Law Reports of the Trials of War Criminals: The Belsen Trial.* First published by HMSO, London, 1947. Reprinted, New York: Howard Fertig, 1983.

United States. Office of the U.S. High Commissioner for Germany. *Information Bulletin,* 1945.

United States Army. *History Branch Office of the Judge Advocate General, European Theater of Operations, 18 July 1942–1 November 1945,* vols. 1–2.

United States Army. *Holdings and Opinions, Board of Review, Branch Office of the Judge Advocate General, European Theater of Operations.* vols. 1–34. Washington, D.C., 1943–46.

United States Department of State. *The Conferences at Malta and Yalta, 1945.* Washington, D.C., 1955.

———. *The Conferences at Cairo and Tehran, 1943.* Washington, D.C. 1961.

———. *Foreign Relations of the United States.* Washington, D.C.: U.S. Government Printing Office.

United States Senate. Committee on the Judiciary. *Morgenthau Diary (Germany).* Washington, D.C., 1967.

United States Strategic Bombing Survey. Edited by David MacIsaac. 10 vols. New York: Garland Publishing, 1976.

War Relief Control Board. *Voluntary War Relief during World War II: A Report to the President by the President's War Relief Control Board.* Washington D.C., March 1946.

Official Histories

Army, Department of. *Russian Combat Methods in World War II.* Washington, D.C., November 1950.

Cole, Hugh M. *The Ardennes: Battle of the Bulge.* United States Army in World War II. Washington, D.C.: Office of the Chief of Military History, 1965.

Coles, Harry L., and Albert K. Weinberg. *Civil Affairs: Soldiers Become Governors.* United States Army in World War II. Washington D.C.: Office of the Chief of Military History, 1964.

Cosmas, Graham A., and Albert E. Cowdrey. *The Medical Department: Medical Service in the European Theater of Operations.* United States Army in World War II. Washington, D.C.: Center of Military History, 1992.

Craven, Wesley Frank, and James Lea Cate. *The Army Air Forces in World War II.* Vols. 1–7. Chicago: University of Chicago Press, 1951–.

Donnison, F. S. V. *Civil Affairs and Military Government: North-West Europe, 1944–1946.* History of the Second World War, United Kingdom Military Series. London: Her Majesty's Stationery Office, 1961.

———. *Civil Affairs and Military Government: Central Organization and Planning.* History of the Second World War, United Kingdom Military Series. London: Her Majesty's Stationery Office, 1966.

Lee, Ulysses. *The Employment of Negro Troops.* United States Army in World War II. Washington, D.C.: Office of the Chief of Military History, 1966.

MacDonald, Charles B. *The Siegfried Line Campaign.* United States Army in World War II. Washington, D.C.: Office of the Chief of Military History, 1963.
———. *The Last Offensive.* United States Army in World War II. Washington, D.C.: Office of the Chief of Military History, 1973.
Pogue, Forrest C. *The Supreme Command.* United States Army in World War II. Washington, D.C.: Center of Military History, 1954.
Ruppenthal, Roland G. *Logistical Support of the Armies.* Vol. 2, *September 1944–May 1945.* United States Army in World War II. Washington, D.C.: Office of the Chief of Military History, 1959.
Stacey, C. P. *Official History of the Canadian Army in the Second World War.* Vol. 3, *The Victory Campaign.* Ottawa: The Queen's Printer, 1960.
Webster, Sir Charles, and Noble Frankland. *The Strategic Air Offensive Against Germany, 1939–1945.* Vols. 1–4. London: Her Majesty's Stationery Office, 1961.
Woodbridge, George. *UNRRA: The History of the United Nations Relief and Rehabilitation Administration.* Vols. 1–3. New York: Columbia University Press, 1950.
Ziemke, Earl F. *Stalingrad to Berlin: The German Defeat in the East.* Washington, D.C.: Center of Military History, 1968.
———. *The US Army in the Occupation of Germany, 1944–1946.* Washington, D.C.: Center of Military History, 1975.
Ziemke, Earl F., and Magna E. Bauer. *Moscow to Stalingrad: Decision in the East.* Washington, D.C.: Center of Military History, 1987.

Microfilm Collections

Conditions and Politics in Occupied Western Europe, 1940–45: Papers from the British Foreign Office (Brighton, U.K.: Harvester Press, 1981–85), 183 reels.
Papers of the War Refugee Board (Bethesda, Md.: Lexis-Nexis, 2002), 29 reels.
Western Aid and the Global Economy, Series 1: The Save the Children Fund Archive, London (London: Primary Source Microfilms, 2002), 60 reels.

Published Memoir and Autobiography

Alanbrooke, Field Marshal Lord. *War Diaries, 1939–1945.* Ed. by Alex Danchev. Berkeley: University of California Press, 2001.
Annan, Noel. *Changing Enemies.* New York: Norton, 1996.
Anonymous. *A Woman in Berlin: Eight Weeks in the Conquered City.* New York: Metropolitan Books, 2005.
Babcock, John B. *Taught to Kill: An American Boy's War From the Ardennes to Berlin.* Washington, D.C.: Potomac Books, 2005.
Beevor, Antony, and Luba Vinogradova, eds. *A Writer at War: Vasily Grossman with the Red Army, 1941–1945.* New York: Pantheon Books, 2005.
Blunt, Roscoe C., Jr. *Foot Soldier: A Combat Infantryman's War in Europe.* Cambridge, Mass.: Da Capo, 2001.
Bohlen, Charles E. *Witness to History, 1929–1969.* New York: Norton, 1973.
Bowen, Robert. *Fighting with the Screaming Eagles: With the 101st Airborne from Normandy to Bastogne.* Mechanicsburg, Penn.: Stackpole, 2001.
Bradley, Omar N. *A Soldier's Story.* New York: Henry Holt, 1951.
Brinton, Crane. "Letters from Liberated France." *French Historical Studies* 2, nos. 1 and 2 (Spring and Autumn, 1961), 1–27, 133–56.
Burgett, Donald R. *Beyond the Rhine: A Screaming Eagle in Germany.* New York: Dell, 2001.

————. *Seven Roads to Hell: A Screaming Eagle at Bastogne.* New York: Dell, 1999.

Cawthon, Charles R. *Other Clay: A Remembrance of the World War II Infantry.* Lincoln: University of Nebraska Press, 2004.

Churchill, Winston. *The Second World War.* 6 vols. Boston: Houghton Mifflin, 1948–53.

Ciechanowski, Jan. *Defeat in Victory.* Garden City, N.Y.: Doubleday, 1947.

Clay, Lucius D. *Decision in Germany.* Garden City, N.Y.: Doubleday, 1950.

Crossman, Richard. *Palestine Mission: A Personal Record.* London: Hamish Hamilton, 1947.

Crum, Bartley C. *Behind the Silken Curtain: A Personal Account of Anglo-American Diplomacy in Palestine and the Middle East.* New York: Simon & Schuster, 1947.

Deane, John R. *The Strange Alliance: The Story of Our Efforts at Wartime Cooperation with Russia.* New York: Viking, 1947.

De Guingand, Major-General Sir Francis W. *Operation Victory.* New York: Scribner's, 1947.

Djilas, Milovan. *Wartime.* New York: Harcourt Brace Jovanovich, 1977.

Doherty, Muriel Knox. *Letters from Belsen, 1945: An Australian Nurse's Experiences with the Survivors of War.* St. Leonards, Australia: Allen & Unwin, 2000.

Dunkelman, Ben. *Dual Allegiance.* New York: Crown, 1976.

Eden, Anthony. *The Memoirs of Anthony Eden, Earl of Avon: The Reckoning.* Boston: Houghton Mifflin, 1965.

Ehrenburg, Ilya. *The War: 1941–1945.* Cleveland: World Publishing, 1964.

————. *We Will Not Forget.* Washington, D.C.: Embassy of the USSR, June 1944.

Ehrenburg, Ilya, and Vasily Grossman. *The Black Book.* Trans. by John Glad and James S. Levine. New York: Holocaust Library, 1981.

Eisenhower, Dwight D. *Crusade in Europe.* Garden City, N.Y.: Doubleday, 1948.

Ellsworth, Ted. *Yank: A Memoir of a World War II Soldier.* New York: Thunder's Mouth Press, 2006.

Fox, Paula. *The Coldest Winter: A Stringer in Liberated Europe.* New York: Picador, 2006.

Friedrich, Ruth-Andreas. *Battleground Berlin: Diaries, 1944–1948.* New York: Paragon, 1990.

Gavin, James M. *On to Berlin: Battles of an Airborne Commander, 1943–46.* New York: Viking, 1978.

Gellhorn, Martha. *The Face of War.* New York: Atlantic Monthly Press, 1988.

Goebbels, Joseph. *Final Entries, 1945: The Diaries of Joseph Goebbels.* Ed. by Hugh Trevor Roper. Trans. by Richard Barry. New York: Putnam, 1978.

Greindl, Countess René. *Christmas 1944 at Isle-la-Hesse (Bastogne).* Self-published, 1965.

Hahn, Lili. *White Flags of Surrender.* New York: Robert Luce, 1974.

Hardman, Leslie H. *The Survivors: The Story of the Belsen Remnant.* With Cecily Goodman. London: Vallentine, Mitchell, 1958.

Harriman, W. Averell, and Elie Abel. *Special Envoy to Churchill and Stalin, 1941–1946.* New York: Random House, 1975.

Harris, Sir Arthur. *Bomber Offensive.* New York: Macmillan, 1947.

Hull, Cordell. *The Memoirs of Cordell Hull.* New York: Macmillan, 1948.

Hulme, Kathryn. *The Wild Place.* Boston: Little, Brown, 1953.

Kayser, Jacques. *Un journaliste sur le front de Normandie.* Paris: Arléa, 1991.

Kingseed, Cole C., ed. *From Omaha Beach to Dawson's Ridge: The Combat Journal of Captain Joe Dawson.* Annapolis, Md.: Naval Institute Press, 2005.

Klemme, Marvin. *The Inside Story of UNRRA: An Experience in Internationalism.* New York: Lifetime Editions, 1949.

Kovály, Heda Margolius. *Under a Cruel Star: A Life in Prague, 1941–1968.* New York: Holmes & Meier, 1986.

Lane, Arthur Bliss. *I Saw Poland Betrayed.* New York: Bobbs-Merrill, 1948.

Lehndorff, Hans Graf von. *Token of a Covenant: Diary of an East Prussian Surgeon, 1945–47.* Trans. by Elizabeth Mayer. Chicago: Henry Regnery, 1964.

Leinbaugh, Harold P., and John D. Campbell. *The Men of Company K: The Autobiography of a World War II Rifle Company.* New York: William Morrow, 1985.

Lewis, Norman. *Naples '44.* New York: Pantheon Books, 1978.

Levi, Primo. *The Reawakening.* Trans. by Stuart Woolf. New York: Simon & Schuster, 1965.

———. *Survival in Auschwitz.* Trans. by Stuart Woolf. New York: Collier Books, 1993.

Lévy-Hass, Hanna. *Inside Belsen.* London: Harvester Press, 1982.

MacDonald, Charles B. *Company Commander.* Short Hills, N.J.: Burford Books, 1999.

Márai, Sándor. *Memoir of Hungary, 1944–48.* Budapest: Corvina Press, 1996.

McNeill, Margaret. *By the Rivers of Babylon: A Story of Relief Work among the Displaced Persons of Europe.* London: Bannisdale Press, 1950.

Meerloo, A. M. *Total War and the Human Mind: A Psychologist's Experiences in Occupied Holland.* New York: International University Press, 1945.

Morgenthau, Henry, Jr. *Germany Is Our Problem.* New York: Harper Brothers, 1945.

Mowat, Farley. *And No Birds Sang.* Boston: Little, Brown, 1979.

Neill, George W. *Infantry Soldier: Holding the Line at the Battle of the Bulge.* Norman: University of Oklahoma Press, 2000.

Nichols, David, ed. *Ernie's War: The Best of Ernie Pyle's World War II Dispatches.* New York: Random House, 1986.

Obermayer, Herman J. *Soldiering for Freedom: A GI's Account of World War II.* College Station: Texas A&M University Press, 2005.

Reese, Willy Peter. *A Stranger to Myself: Russia, 1941–44.* New York: Farrar, Straus & Giroux, 2005.

Rumpf, Hans. *The Bombing of Germany.* Trans. by Edward Fitzgerald. New York: Holt, Rinehart & Winston, 1962.

Samuel, Wolfgang. *German Boy: A Child in War.* New York: Broadway Books, 2000.

Schogt, Henry G. *The Curtain: Witness and Memory in Wartime Holland.* Waterloo, Ontario: Wilfrid Laurier Press, 2003.

Skrjabina, Elena. *After Leningrad: From the Caucasus to the Rhine.* Trans. by Norman Luxenburg. Carbondale: Southern Illinois University Press, 1978.

Stimson, Henry L., and McGeorge Bundy. *On Active Service in Peace and War.* London: Hutchinson, 1947.

Vida, George. *From Doom to Dawn: A Jewish Chaplain's Story of Displaced Persons.* New York: Jonathan David, 1967.

Webster, David Kenyon. *Parachute Infantry: An American Paratrooper's Memoir of D-Day and the Fall of the Third Reich.* New York: Delta, 2002.

Wilhelmina, Queen of the Netherlands. *Lonely but not Alone.* Trans. by John Peereboom. New York: McGraw-Hill, 1960.

Wilmot, Laurence F. *Through the Line: Memoirs of an Infantry Chaplain.* Waterloo, Ontario: Wilfrid Laurier University Press, 2003.

Wilson, George. *If You Survive: From Normandy to the Battle of the Bulge to the End of World War II.* New York: Presidio, 1987.

Wurst, Spencer F., and Gayle Wurst. *Descending from the Clouds: A Memoir of Combat in the 505 Parachute Infantry Regiment, 82nd Airborne Division.* Havertown, Penn.: Casemate, 2004.

Yeide, Harry. *The Longest Battle: From Aachen to the Roer and Across (September 1944–February 1945).* St. Paul, Minn.: Zenith Press, 2005.

Secondary Works

Addison, Paul, and Angus Calder, eds. *Time to Kill: The Soldier's Experience of War in the West, 1939–1945*. London: Pimlico, 1997.

Addison, Paul, and Jeremy Crang, eds. *Firestorm: The Bombing of Dresden 1945*. Chicago: Ivan Dee, 2006.

Auty, Phyllis, and Richard Clogg, eds. *British Policy Towards Wartime Resistance in Yugoslavia and Greece*. London: Macmillan, 1975.

Bailey, Beth, and David Farber. *The First Strange Place: The Alchemy of Race and Sex in World War II Hawaii*. New York: Free Press, 1992.

Banning, C. "Food Shortage and Public Health, First Half of 1945." Special issue: "The Netherlands during the German Occupation." *Annals of the American Academy of Political and Social Science* 245 (May 1946), 93–110.

Barker, Elisabeth. *British Policy in Southeast Europe in the Second World War.* London: Macmillan, 1976.

Bartov, Omer. *Hitler's Army: Soldiers, Nazis, and War in the Third Reich*. New York: Oxford University Press, 1992.

Baudot, Marcel. *Libération de la Normandie*. Paris: Hachette, 1974.

Bauer, Yehuda. *Flight and Rescue: Brichah*. New York: Random House, 1970.

——. "The Initial Organization of the Holocaust Survivors in Bavaria." *Yad Vashem Studies on the European Jewish Catastrophe and Resistance,* vol. 8. Ed. by Livia Rothkirchen. Jerusalem: Yad Vashem (1970), 127–57.

——. *Out of the Ashes: The Impact of American Jews on Post-Holocaust European Jewry.* New York: Pergamon, 1989.

Beaudufe, Christophe. *L'été 1944: Le sacrifice des Normands*. Paris: Perrin, 1994.

Beck, Earl R. *Under the Bombs: The German Home Front, 1942–1945*. Lexington: University Press of Kentucky, 1986.

Berkhoff, Karel C. *Harvest of Despair: Life and Death in Ukraine under Nazi Rule*. Cambridge, Mass.: Harvard University Press, 2004.

Beschloss, Michael. *The Conquerors: Roosevelt, Truman, and the Destruction of Hitler's Germany, 1941–1945*. New York: Simon & Schuster, 2002.

Biddle, Tami Davis. *Rhetoric and Reality in Air Warfare: The Evolution of British and American Ideas about Strategic Bombing, 1914–1945*. Princeton, N.J.: Princeton University Press, 2002.

Boivin, Michel. *La Manche, 1940–44: La guerre, l'occupation, la libération*. Caen: Editions Ouest-France, 1994.

Borgwardt, Elizabeth. *A New Deal for the World: America's Vision for Human Rights*. Cambridge, Mass.: Harvard University Press, 2005.

Borodziej, Włodzimierz. *The Warsaw Uprising of 1944*. Trans. by Barbara Harshav. Madison: University of Wisconsin Press, 2006.

Borowiec, Andrew. *Destroy Warsaw! Hitler's Punishment, Stalin's Revenge*. Westport, Conn.: Praeger, 2001.

Boshyk, Yury, ed. *Ukraine during World War II: History and its Aftermath*. Edmonton, Alberta: Canadian Institute of Ukrainian Studies, 1986.

Breitman, Richard. *The Architect of Genocide: Himmler and the Final Solution*. Hanover, N.H.: Brandeis University Press, 1991.

Breunis, J. "The Food Supply." Special issue: "The Netherlands during the German Occupation." *Annals of the American Academy of Political and Social Science* 245 (May 1946), 87–92.

Broekmeyer, Marius. *Stalin, the Russians, and Their War, 1941–1945*. Trans. by Rosalind Buck. Madison: University of Wisconsin Press, 2004.

Browning, Christopher. *The Origins of the Final Solution: The Evolution of Nazi Jewish Policy, September 1939–March 1942.* Lincoln: University of Nebraska Press, 2004.

Burger, G. C. E., J. C. Drummond, and H. R. Stanstead, eds. *Malnutrition and Starvation in Western Netherlands, September 1944–July 1945.* The Hague: General State Printing Office, 1948.

Calvocoressi, Peter, Guy Wint, and John Pritchard. *The Penguin History of the Second World War.* London: Penguin, 1989.

Chickering, Roger, et al., eds. *A World at Total War: Global Conflict and the Politics of Destruction, 1937–1945.* Washington, D.C.: Cambridge University Press and the German Historical Institute, 2005.

Ciechanowski, Jan M. *The Warsaw Rising of 1944.* London: Cambridge University Press, 1974.

Copp, Terry. *Cinderella Army: The Canadians in Northwest Europe, 1944–45.* Toronto: University of Toronto Press, 2006.

Dallin, Alexander. *German Rule in Russia, 1941–45.* Boulder, Colo.: Westview Press, 1981.

Davies, Norman. *Rising '44: The Battle for Warsaw.* New York: Viking, 2003.

Dean, Martin. *Collaboration in the Holocaust: Crimes of the Local Police in Belorussia and Ukraine, 1941–44.* New York: St. Martin's, 1999.

Dean, Vera Micheles. "UNRRA—A Step Toward Reconstruction." *Foreign Policy Reports* 19, 20 (January 1, 1944), 266–70.

De Jong, Louis. *The Netherlands and Nazi Germany.* Cambridge, Mass.: Harvard University Press, 1990.

Diamond, Hanna. *Women and the Second World War in France, 1938–1948: Choices and Constraints.* Essex, U.K.: Longman, 1999.

Didier-Robert, L. *La Mémoire de Sainlez: L'offensive von Rundstedt vécue au village.* Bastogne, France: Cercle d'Histoire de Bastogne, n.d.

DiFiglia, Ghanda. *Roots and Visions: The First Fifty Years of the Unitarian Universalist Service Committee.* Boston: UUSC, 1990.

Dinnerstein, Leonard. *America and the Survivors of the Holocaust.* New York: Columbia University Press, 1982.

Dobroszycki, Lucjan. "Restoring Jewish Life in Postwar Poland." *Soviet Jewish Affairs* 3, no. 2 (1973), 58–72.

Douglas, W. A. B., and Brereton Greenhous. *Out of the Shadows: Canada in the Second World War.* New York: Oxford University Press, 1977.

Dubru, Alfred. *L'Offensive von Rundstedt à Houffalize.* Houffalize, Belgium: Editions Haut-Pays, 1993.

Duffy, Christopher. *Red Storm on the Reich: The Soviet March on Germany, 1945.* New York: Atheneum, 1991.

Dutour, Françoise. *Le Calvados: 1945–1947.* Caen, France: Conseil générale du Calvados, 1995.

———. *The Liberation of Calvados.* Trans. by Michel and Michele Morin. Caen, France: Calvados County Council, 1994.

Erickson, John. *The Road to Berlin.* London: Weidenfeld & Nicolson, 1983.

———. *The Road to Stalingrad.* New York: Harper & Row, 1975.

Eubank, Keith. *Summit at Teheran.* New York: William Morrow, 1985.

Florentin, Eddy. *Quand les alliés bombardaient la France.* Paris: Perris, 1997.

Footitt, Hilary. *War and Liberation in France: Living with the Liberators.* New York: Palgrave Macmillan, 2004.

Frank, Gerold. "The Tragedy of the DPs." *New Republic,* April 1, 1946, 436–38.

Friedrich, Jörg. *The Fire: The Bombing of Germany, 1940–1945.* Trans. by Allison Brown. New York: Columbia University Press, 2006.

Gay, Ruth. *Safe Among the Germans: Liberated Jews after World War II.* New Haven, Conn.: Yale University Press, 2002.

Gershon, Karen. *Postscript: A Collective Account of the Lives of Jews in West Germany since the Second World War.* London: Victor Gollancz, 1969.

Gilbert, Martin. *The Holocaust: A History of the Jews of Europe during the Second World War.* New York: Henry Holt, 1985.

Goddard, Lance. *Canada and the Liberation of the Netherlands, May 1945.* Toronto: Dundurn Press, 2005.

Götz, Aly. *Final Solution: Nazi Population Policy and the Murder of the European Jews.* Trans. by Belinda Cooper and Allison Brown. London: Arnold, 1999.

Grall, Jeanne. *Les années difficiles: l'Opinion publique dans le Calvados (1940–1944).* Condé-sur-Noireau, France: Éditions Charles Corlet, 1981.

——. *Caen sous l'occupation.* Rennes, France: Ouest France, 1980.

Grayling, A. C. *Among the Dead Cities: The History and Moral Legacy of the WWII Bombing of Civilians in Germany and Japan.* New York: Walker & Co., 2006.

Grossman, Atina. "Victims, Villains, and Survivors: Gendered Perceptions and Self-Perceptions of Jewish Displaced Persons in Occupied Postwar Germany." *Journal of the History of Sexuality* 11, nos. 1–2 (January/April 2002), 291–318.

Hanson, Joanna K. M. *The Civilian Population and the Warsaw Uprising of 1944.* London: Cambridge University Press, 1982.

Harris, C. R. S. *Allied Military Administration of Italy, 1943–1945.* London: HMSO, 1957.

Hart, Nicky. "Famine, Maternal Nutrition and Infant Mortality: A Re-examination of the Dutch Hunger Winter." *Population Studies* 47, 1 (March 1993), 27–46.

Hastings, Max. *Armageddon: The Battle for Germany, 1944–1945.* New York: Knopf, 2004.

——. *Bomber Command.* New York: Dial Press, 1979.

——. *Overlord: D-Day and the Battle for Normandy.* New York: Random House, 1984.

Heintz, Joss. *In the Perimeter of Bastogne: December 1944–January 1945.* Ostend: Omnia, 1965.

Herbert, Ulrich. *A History of Foreign Labor in Germany, 1880–1980.* Trans. by William Templer. Ann Arbor: University of Michigan Press, 1990.

——. *Hitler's Foreign Workers: Enforced Foreign Labor in Germany under the Third Reich.* Trans. by William Templer. London: Cambridge University Press, 1997.

Herf, Jeffrey. *Divided Memory: The Nazi Past in the Two Germanys.* Cambridge, Mass.: Harvard University Press, 1997.

Hirschfeld, Gerhard. *Nazi Rule and Dutch Collaboration: The Netherlands under German Occupation, 1940–45.* New York: Berg, 1988.

Huyse, Luc, and Steven Dhondt. *La répression des collaborations, 1942–1952.* Brussels: Kritak, 1991.

Hyman, Abraham S. *The Undefeated.* Jerusalem: Gefen Books, 1993.

Jackson, Julian. *France: The Dark Years, 1940–1944.* Oxford, U.K.: Oxford University Press, 2001.

Kassimeris, George, ed. *The Barbarization of Warfare.* New York: New York University Press, 2006.

Keegan, John. *Six Armies in Normandy.* New York: Penguin, 1994.

Kershaw, Ian. *Hitler, 1936–1945: Nemesis.* New York: Norton, 2000.

Keshen, Jeffrey A. *Saints, Sinners, and Soldiers: Canada's Second World War.* Vancouver: UBC Press, 2004.

King, Benjamin, and Timothy Kutta. *Impact: The History of Germany's V-Weapons in World War II.* Rockville Centre, N.Y.: Sarpedon, 1998.

Kitchen, Martin. *British Policy towards the Soviet Union during the Second World War.* London: Macmillan, 1986.

Knell, Hermann. *To Destroy a City: Strategic Bombing and Its Human Consequences in World War II.* Cambridge, Mass.: Da Capo, 2003.

Knight, Amy. *Beria: Stalin's First Lieutenant.* Princeton, N.J.: Princeton University Press, 1993.

Kochavi, Arieh J. *Post-Holocaust Politics: Britain, the United States, and Jewish Refugees, 1945–1948.* Chapel Hill: University of North Carolina Press, 2001.

Kolb, Eberhard. *Bergen-Belsen: From Detention Camp to Concentration Camp, 1943–1945.* Göttingen, Germany: Vandenhoeck & Ruprecht, 1985.

Königseder, Angelika, and Julianne Wetzel. *Waiting for Hope: Jewish Displaced Persons in Post World War II Germany.* Trans. by John A. Broadwin. Evanston, Ill.: Northwestern University Press, 2001.

Lavsky, Hagit. *New Beginnings: Holocaust Survivors in Bergen-Belsen and the British Zone in Germany, 1945–1950.* Detroit: Wayne State University Press, 2002.

Lilly, J. Robert. *La Face cachée des GIs.* Paris: Payot, 2003.

Longmate, Norman. *The Bombers: The RAF Offensive against Germany, 1939–1945.* London: Hutchinson, 1983.

Longue, Matthieu. *Massacres en Ardenne: Hiver, 1944–45.* Brussels: Éditions Racine, 2006.

Maas, Walter B. *The Netherlands at War: 1940–45.* London: Abelard-Schuman, 1970.

MacDonald, Charles. *A Time for Trumpets: The Untold Story of the Battle of the Bulge.* New York: Morrow, 1984.

Mankowitz, Zeev. *Life Between Memory and Hope: The Survivors of the Holocaust in Occupied Germany.* Cambridge, U.K.: Cambridge University Press, 2002.

Marcuse, Harold. *Legacies of Dachau: The Uses and Abuses of a Concentration Camp, 1933–2001.* Cambridge, U.K.: Cambridge University Press, 2001.

Mazower, Mark. *Inside Hitler's Greece: The Experience of Occupation, 1941–1944.* New Haven, Conn.: Yale University Press, 1993.

McKee, Alexander. *Caen: Anvil of Victory.* London: Souvenir Press, 1964.

Meacham, Jon. *Franklin and Winston.* New York: Random House, 2003.

Megargee, Geoffrey P. *War of Annihilation: Combat and Genocide on the Eastern Front, 1941.* New York: Rowman & Littlefield, 2006.

Merridale, Catherine. *Ivan's War: Life and Death in the Red Army, 1939–1945.* New York: Metropolitan Books, 2006.

Messenger, Charles. *Bomber Harris and the Strategic Bombing Offensive, 1939–1945.* London: Arms & Armour Press, 1984.

Mintzer, Oscar A. *In Defense of the Survivors: The Letters of Oscar A. Mintzer, AJDC Legal Advisor, Germany, 1945–46.* Berkeley, Calif.: Judah L. Magnes Museum, 1999.

Moeller, Robert G. *War Stories: The Search for a Usable Past in the Federal Republic of Germany.* Berkeley: University of California Press, 2003.

Montefiore, Simon Sebag. *Stalin: The Court of the Red Tsar.* New York: Knopf, 2004.

Mulligan, Timothy Patrick. *The Politics of Illusion: German Occupation Policy in the Soviet Union, 1942–43.* Westport, Conn.: Praeger, 1988.

Nadich, Judah. *Eisenhower and the Jews.* New York: Twayne, 1953.

Naimark, Norman M. *The Russians in Germany: A History of the Soviet Zone of Occupation, 1945–1949.* (Cambridge, Mass.: Harvard University Press, 1995).

Neillands, Robin. *The Bomber War: The Allied Air Offensive Against Nazi Germany.* New York: Overlook Press, 2001.

Nevins, Allan. *Herbert H. Lehman and His Era.* New York: Charles Scribner's Sons, 1963.

Oliver, Beryl. *The British Red Cross in Action.* London: Faber & Faber, 1966.

Overy, Richard. *Russia's War.* New York: Penguin, 1997.

———. *Why the Allies Won.* New York: Norton, 1995.

Palinckx, Koen. *Antwerpen onder de V-Bommen, 1944–45.* Antwerp: Pandora, 2004.

Peterson, Edward N. *The Many Faces of Defeat: The German People's Experience in 1945.* New York: Peter Land, 1990.

Pinson, Koppel S. "Jewish Life in Liberated Germany." *Jewish Social Studies* 9, no. 2 (April 1947), 101–26.

Pipet, Albert. *Le Calvados, 1944: La bataille de la libération.* Caen, France: Ouest-France, 1994.

Polian, M. P. *Against Their Will: The History and Geography of Forced Migrations in the USSR.* New York: Central European University, 2004.

Posthumus, J. H. "Order and Disorder." Special issue: "The Netherlands during the German Occupation." *Annals of the American Academy of Political and Social Science* 245 (May 1946), 1–8.

Proudfoot, Malcolm J. *European Refugees, 1939–1952: A Study in Forced Population Movement.* Evanston, Ill.: Northwestern University Press, 1956.

Quellien, Jean. *La Normandie au coeur de la guerre.* Rennes, France: Editions Ouest-France, 1992.

———. *Opinions et comportements politiques dans le Calvados sous l'occupation allemande (1940–1944).* Caen, France: Presses universitaires de Caen, 2001.

Quellien, Jean, Michel Boivin, and Gérard Bourdin. *Villes normandes sous les bombes (juin 1944).* Caen, France: Presses universitaires de Caen, 1994.

Quellien, Jean, and Bernard Gernier. *Les Victimes civiles du Calvados dans la bataille de Normandie.* Caen: Mémorial pour la Paix, 1995.

Quellien, Jean, et al. *Les Populations Civiles face au débarquement et la bataille de Normandie.* Caen: Université de Caen, 2005.

Reese, Roger R. *The Soviet Military Experience.* London: Routledge, 2000.

Reilly, Joanne. *Belsen: The Liberation of a Concentration Camp.* London: Routledge, 1998.

Reilly, Joanne, et al., eds. *Belsen in History and Memory.* London: Frank Cass, 1995.

Rich, Norman. *Hitler's War Aims.* Vol. 2, *The Establishment of the New Order.* New York: Norton, 1974.

Richards, Denis. *The Hardest Victory: RAF Bomber Command in the Second World War.* New York: Norton, 1995.

Rivet, Luc, and Yves Sevenans. *La Bataille des Ardennes: Les civils dans la guerre.* Brussels: Didier Hatier, 1985.

Ross, Graham. *The Foreign Office and the Kremlin: British Documents on Anglo-Soviet Relations, 1941–45.* London: Cambridge University Press, 1984.

Rozek, Edward J. *Allied Wartime Diplomacy: A Pattern in Poland.* New York: Wiley & Sons, 1958.

Sainsbury, Keith. *The Turning Point.* New York: Oxford University Press, 1985.

Schechtman, Joseph B. *European Population Transfers, 1939–1945.* New York: Oxford University Press, 1946.

Schrijvers, Peter. *The Crash of Ruin: American Combat Soldiers in Europe during World War II.* New York: New York University Press, 1998.

———. *The Unknown Dead: Civilians in the Battle of the Bulge.* Lexington: University Press of Kentucky, 2005.

Schulte, Theo J. *The German Army and Nazi Policies in Occupied Russia.* Oxford, U.K.: Berg, 1989.

Schwartz, Leo W. *The Redeemers: A Saga of the Years 1945–1952.* New York: Farrar, Straus & Young, 1953.

Sherwood, Robert E. *Roosevelt and Hopkins: An Intimate History.* New York: Harper, 1948.

Sington, Derek. *Belsen Uncovered.* London: Duckworth, 1946.

Somers, Erik, and René Kok. *Jewish Displaced Persons in Camp Bergen-Belsen: The Unique Photo Album of Zippy Orlin.* Seattle: University of Washington Press, 2004.

Stein, Zena, et al. *Famine and Human Development: The Dutch Hunger Winter of 1944–45.* New York: Oxford University Press, 1975.

Struye, Paul, and Guillaume Jacquemyns. *La Belgique sous l'Occupation allemande (1940–1944).* Brussels: Editions Complexe, 2002.

Sulbout, Pierre. *Les troupes américaines à Liège (septembre 1944–décembre 1945): De l'enthousiasme aux réalités.* Liège: Université de Liège, 1989.

Taylor, Frederick. *Dresden.* New York: HarperCollins, 2004.

Thurston, Robert W., and Bernd Bonwetsch, eds. *The People's War: Responses to World War II in the Soviet Union.* Urbana, Ill.: University of Chicago Press, 2000.

Tolstoy, Nikolai. *The Minister and the Massacres.* London: Century Hutchinson, 1986.

——. *The Secret Betrayal.* New York: Charles Scribner's Sons, 1977.

Trew, Simon. *Britain, Mihailović and the Chetniks, 1941–42.* London: Macmillan, 1998.

Valla, Jean-Claude. *La France sous les bombes, 1942–1945.* Paris: Librarie nationale, 2001.

Verhoeyen, Etienne. *La Belgique Occupée: De l'an 40 à la Libération.* Brussels: De Boeck, 1994.

Virgili, Fabrice. *Shorn Women: Gender and Punishment in Liberation France.* Trans. by John Flower. Oxford: Berg, 2002.

Volkogonov, Dmitri. *Stalin: Triumph and Tragedy.* Trans. by Harold Shukman. New York: Grove Weidenfeld, 1991.

Warhaftig, Zorach. *Uprooted: Jewish Refugees and Displaced Persons after Liberation.* New York: Institute of Jewish Affairs, November 1946.

Warmbrunn, Werner. *The Dutch Under German Occupation, 1940–45.* Stanford, Calif.: Stanford University Press, 1963.

——. *The German Occupation of Belgium, 1940–1944.* New York: Peter Lang, 1993.

Webster, Ronald. "American Relief and Jews in Germany, 1945–1960: Diverging Perspectives." *Leo Baeck Institute Yearbook* 37 (1970), 293–321.

Wegner, Bernd, ed. *From Peace to War: Germany, Soviet Russia, and the World, 1939–1941.* Providence, R.I.: Berghahn Books, 1997.

Werth, Alexander. *Russia at War, 1941–1945.* New York: Dutton, 1964.

Wieviorka, Olivier. *Histoire du débarquement en Normandie: Des origines à la liberation de Paris, 1941–44.* Paris: Éditions du Seuil, 2007.

Willoughby, John. "The Sexual Behavior of American GIs during the Early Years of the Occupation of Germany." *Journal of Military History* 62, 1 (January 1998), 155–74.

Woodhouse, C. M. *The Struggle for Greece, 1941–1949.* Chicago: Ivan Dee, 2003.

Wyman, Mark. *DPs: Europe's Displaced Persons.* Philadelphia: Balch Institute Press, 1989.

Zubok, Vlad, and Constantine Pleshakov. *Inside the Kremlin's Cold War: From Stalin to Khrushchev.* Cambridge, Mass.: Harvard University Press, 1996.

Index

Aachen, Germany, 63, 67, 69, 72, 181, 192, 193
Acheson, Dean, 211-12, 218, 247
Achterveld, Netherlands, 116
African-American soldiers, 50-55
Air war. *See* Bombing
Albania, 219
Alcan, Louise, 269
Alibert, Joseph, 83
Allenstein, East Prussia, 165
Allied Commission (Italy), 234
Alsace, 72, 295
Ambléve river and valley, 81-83, 85
American Council of Voluntary Agencies for Foreign Service (ACVAFS), 244
American Friends Service Committee, 224, 245
American Jewish Committee, 351
American Jewish Joint Distribution Committee (AJJDC), 245, 246, 316-20, 324, 325, 334, 335
American Military Cemetery, Hamm, Luxembourg, 1-2
American Polish War Relief, 246
American Relief for France, 245
American Relief for Holland, 245
American Relief for Italy, 245
American Relief for Poland, 245
American Society for Russian Relief, 245
Amersfoort, Netherlands, 116
Amsterdam, Netherlands, 98, 103, 105, 106, 111-12, 118-20, 122
Anderson, A. V., 348
André, Achille, 84
Andreas-Friedrich, Ruth, 125-26, 168
Anhée, Belgium, 63
Annevoie, Belgium, 63
Anselme family, 88
Anspach, Germany, 204

Antelme, Robert, 261-63, 304-5
Antwerp, Belgium, 15, 61, 64, 65, 67-69, 72, 73, 91, 114
Archangel, 134
Ardennes, Belgium, 1, 2, 63, 64, 73, 74, 78, 81, 131
Argentan, France, 28, 38, 44
Arlon, Belgium, 89
Armed Forces Radio, 181-82
Armée Secrète (Belgium), 66
Armia Krajowa (Poland), 155-58
Arnhem, Netherlands, 72, 101, 108, 119
Arthur, Jean, 68
Astley, Ivor, 22
Athens, Greece, 228-30
Atlantic Wall, 25, 26
Atrocities. *See also* Jews
    in Belgium, 62-64, 82-85
    in Greece, 229
    in Lithuania, 143-144
    in Netherlands, 100-101
    in Poland, 142-43, 152, 157, 338
    in Soviet Union, 137, 141-143
    in Ukraine, 144-147
Attlee, Clement, 278, 352
Aunay-sur-Odon, France, 28, 38
Auschwitz concentration camp, 143, 269-72, 360
    liberation of, 283, 289-92, 308
    war crimes trial, 355, 357, 359, 361-64, 371
Australia, 220
Austria, 99, 219, 256, 260-61, 311, 333, 334, 337
Avranches, France, 15, 28

B-17 bombers, 116
B-24 Liberator bombers, 88, 89
B-26 Marauder bombers, 88
Babcock, John, 6, 76, 79
Babi Yar massacre, 143

Backhouse, T. M., 358-60, 363
Baden-Württemberg, 192
Balfour Declaration of 1917, 352, 353
Baltiysk, Russia, 165
Bande, Belgium, 85
Baranova, Zina, 160
Barber, R., 303
Bari, Italy, 233, 238
Baron, Charles, 307
Barrie, Doug, 118
Bastogne, Belgium, 73, 75, 86, 89
Bauer, Yehuda, 333, 334, 338
Baugnez, Belgium, 82, 84
Bavaria, 126, 192, 203, 204, 272-77,
    279-80, 312-16, 322, 334
Bavarian Alps, 192
Bayeux, France, 12, 35, 45, 55
BBC (British Broadcasting Corporation),
    27, 66, 68, 241, 243
Belgium, 3, 5, 15, 42, 60-73, 80-97
    Allied advance into, 60-61, 69-71
    Antwerp, 15, 61, 64, 65, 67-69, 72, 73,
        91, 114
    atrocities in, 62-64, 82-85
    Battle of the Bulge, 64, 73-74, 76,
        81-91
    black market in, 92-93
    bombing of, 60-61, 68, 85, 87-90, 97
    Brussels, 15, 60-62, 64-65, 67, 91, 92
    coal production in, 65
    collaborators in, 66, 68
    communists in, 66, 67, 110
    food shortages in, 65-67
    fraternization in, 178
    Germany and, 62-63, 73, 81-85
    Jews in, 61
    logistics problems in, 69-70, 72
    looting by Allies in, 91-92
    Malmédy massacre, 82-83
    political uprising in, 66-67
    refugees in, 81, 86, 97
    relief efforts in, 90-91
    resistance in, 62-63, 66-67, 87
    V-weapon attacks on, 68
    venereal disease and prostitution in,
        93-97
    welcome to Allies in, 3, 60-62
Belgrade, Yugoslavia, 240-41
Belorussia, 4, 131, 134, 142, 151, 153,
    154, 219
Belsen concentration camp. See Ber-
    gen-Belsen concentration camp
Belzec concentration camp, 287
Ben-Gurion, David, 329-31, 333

Berchtesgaden, Germany, 64, 192
Berdichev, Ukraine, 146-47
Bergen-Belsen concentration camp, 270,
    295, 297
    liberation of, 300-303, 305-6, 340-47,
        354-58, 361
    war crimes trial, 37, 355-65
Berlin, Germany, 11, 69, 117, 126-28,
    167-68, 186, 189, 201, 267, 335,
    337
Bernard-Farnoux, Yvette, 307
Bernhard, Prince of the Netherlands, 116
Bernières, France, 28
Beusart, Vicar, 63
Bevin, Ernest, 352-55, 357, 364
Bialystok, Poland, 142
Bickerdike, Rhoda Dawson, 223-24
Bidault, Georges, 259
Bimko, Ada (Hadassah Rosensaft), 306,
    361, 364
Birkenau concentration camp, 287,
    289-91, 293, 306, 360
Bismarck, Otto von, 177
Bitterfeld, Germany, 304
Black market
    in Belgium, 92-93
    in camps, 277-78, 329, 350
    in France, 26, 266
    in Italy, 235
    in Netherlands, 102, 113, 120
Black Sea, 133-34, 153, 257
Blaskowitz, Johannes, 117
Blechhammer concentration camp, 294
Blumovicz, Abrasha, 329
Blunt, Rocky, 76, 77, 79, 80, 98
Blunt, Roscoe, 40
Board of Deputies of British Jews, 351,
    353, 363
Bochum, Germany, 191
Boeur, Albert, 89-90
Bollet family, 87
Bolshevism, 133, 181
Bombing
    of Belgium, 60-61, 68, 85, 87-90, 97
    of Britain, 68, 186
    of France, 3, 14, 15, 20, 21, 27-29,
        31-39
    of Germany, 126-27, 182-92, 199-201,
        368, 370
    of Netherlands, 99, 101, 109, 110
Bór-Komorowski, Tadeusz, 156, 158
Bordeaux, France, 264
Bormann, Juana, 360, 364
Bosnia, 240

Bouillon, Belgium, 63
Boulogne-sur-Mer, France, 69
Bourguebus Ridge, 35
Bourke-White, Margaret, 299
Boys' Crusade, The (Fussell), 74
Bracht, Fritz, 294
Bradley, Omar, 12, 69, 72, 88, 180, 295-96
Brandenburg, 128, 167
Braun, Eva, 125
Brazil, 220
Bremen, Germany, 201
Brest, France, 69
Breuil-en-Bessin, France, 51
Brewster, L. P., 317
Brichah, the, 333-35
Bricquebec, France, 54
Britain
    Battle of, 184, 186
    Bergen-Belsen and, 340-47, 354-65
    bombing of, 68, 186
    liberation of concentration camps, 297, 300-303, 305-8
    Normandy and, 1, 12, 14, 28, 29, 31, 33-37
    Palestine question and, 285, 319, 330, 331, 333, 339-41, 347-49, 351-54
    Royal Air Force (RAF), 28, 29, 33, 35, 60, 85, 184, 186-89, 191
    zone of occupation, 205-6
British Chiefs of Staff, 104, 105, 109
British Eighth Army, 343
British VIII Corps, 35
British I Corps, 33
British Second Army, 12, 33, 35
British 6th Airborne Division, 12, 353
British 7th Armored Division, 201
British 21st Army Group, 12, 106, 107, 116, 340, 358
British War Office, 177-78
British War Relief Society, 244, 245
Britten, B. V., 348
Brooke, Alan, 109
Browning, Christopher, 142
Brussels, Belgium, 15, 60-62, 64-65, 67, 91, 92
Buchenwald concentration camp, 288, 293, 295
    liberation of, 296-300, 308-9
Bulgaria, 147, 154, 159, 229
Bulge, Battle of the, 64, 73-74, 76, 81-91, 180
Büllingen, Belgium, 82

Buna-Monowitz concentration camp, 283, 287, 289, 290
Burgett, Donald, 77-80
Burnotte family, 83

Cadogan, Sir Alexander, 103
Caen, France, 12, 14, 15, 20, 29-37, 40, 44, 52, 55-59
Caines, W. G., 34, 39
Cairo Council of Voluntary Societies, 226
Calais, France, 69
Calvados, France, 12, 23-28, 41, 44, 50-52, 55-57
Camp Hohne. *See* Bergen-Belsen concentration camp
Canada, 12, 14, 29, 34-35, 41, 98, 114, 117-21, 220
Caron, Jules, 264
Caspian Sea, 134
Casualties, 12-15, 20, 21, 27-29, 31-38, 58, 68, 72-74, 78-79, 86-89, 99, 101, 114, 131-32, 136, 138, 139, 166, 183, 188-89
Catholic Committee for Relief Abroad, 120
Caucasus, 131, 134
Cemeteries, museums and memorials, 1-2, 58-59
Central Committee of Liberated Jews in Bavaria, 314-16, 319, 330, 332
Central Committee of Liberated Jews in the British Zone, 347
Chambois, France, 39
Charleroi, Belgium, 91
Charles, Prince of Belgium, 65
Chelmno concentration camp, 287
Cherbourg, France, 31, 45-49, 264
Chernakhovsk, Russia, 164
Chetniks, 239, 241
Chios island, 226
Chuikov, Vasily, 128
Churchill, Winston, 129, 147, 233, 241
    on Battle of Britain, 184
    bombing of Germany and, 184, 186
    German occupation policy and, 172
    Greece and, 228-29
    Netherlands and, 102-3, 106-11, 115
    "percentages" conversation with Stalin, 158-59
    Polish question and, 151-52, 155, 158-59
    at Tehran Conference, 148-53
    at Yalta Conference, 174-75
Civil Affairs (G-5), 44-46, 90, 118

Clark, J. G. W., 99, 108
Clay, Lucius D., 202-4, 206
Clayton, Will, 247
Coal production
    in Belgium, 65
    in Germany, 204, 207
    in Netherlands, 103, 107, 112
    in Soviet Union, 138
Cohen, Leonard, 348
Cold war, 369
Collaborators, 369, 370
    Belgian, 66, 68
    Dutch, 100
    French, 23, 25, 48-49, 267
College Park, Maryland, 217
Colleville-sur-Mer, France, 58, 59
Collier's magazine, 74
Collins, J. Lawton, 14, 189
Cologne, Germany, 182-84, 189-90
Colombelles, France, 28
Colombières, France, 41
Combat, 263-64
Comité Catholique de Secours, 246
Commentary magazine, 328
Commissars, Red Army, 144-45
Communists
    in Belgium, 66, 67, 110
    in France, 110, 266
    in Greece, 228-29
    in Italy, 110
    in Netherlands, 110
    in Yugoslavia, 239-41
Concentration camps, 5, 194, 201, 202,
    267
    Auschwitz. See Auschwitz concentra-
        tion camp
    Belsen. See Bergen-Belsen concentra-
        tion camp
    Belzec, 287
    Birkenau, 287, 289-91, 293, 306, 360
    Blechhammer, 294
    Buchenwald. See Buchenwald concen-
        tration camp
    Buna-Monowitz, 283, 287, 289, 290
    Chelmno, 287
    Dachau. See Dachau concentration
        camp
    Dora, 360
    Gross-Rosen, 292-94, 306
    Gunskirchen Lager, 299
    liberation of, 283-85, 287-309, 311,
        340-47, 354-58, 361
    Majdanek, 287, 288
    Mauthausen, 270, 293, 309, 360

Natzweiler, 295, 360
Nordhausen, 296
Ohrdruf, 295-96, 308
Sachsenhausen, 360
Sandbostel, 303
Sobibór, 287
Stutthof, 292
Theresienstadt, 309, 314
Treblinka, 287
Condé-sur-Noireau, France, 28
Cooke, M. H., 22
Cooke, Maurice, 60
Cooper, Corporal, 353
Cooper, Gary, 68
Correspondents, 19-21, 74, 137, 189-92,
    198, 288, 298-300
Cossacks, 260-61
Cotentin peninsula, 12, 14, 31, 45
Coulet, François, 47
Council of British Societies for Relief
    Abroad (COBSRA)
Council of Resistance (Netherlands), 100
Courseulles, France, 28
Courtrai (Kortrijk), Belgium, 60
Coutances, France, 28
Cranfield, Major, 363-64
Crimea, 174, 175
Croatia, 239
Croix de Feu, 23
Curzon, Lord, 151
Curzon Line, 151, 155, 159
Cyclades, 215
Czechoslovakia, 4, 126, 147, 219, 256,
    311, 319, 334, 336

D-Day landings (Operation Overlord),
    3, 7, 11-14, 19, 21, 27-29, 36, 74,
    149, 152
Dachau concentration camp, 263, 271,
    288, 293, 295, 312, 360
    liberation of, 297, 303-5, 313-15
Dacie, Anne, 233, 238
Dalmatia, Yugoslavia, 240
Daniel, Clifton, 181
Danzig, Poland, 165-67
Darmstadt, Germany, 200
Dautry, Raoul, 57
De Gaulle, Charles, 45, 49, 57, 64,
    266-68
De Guingand, Sir Francis, 116
Death marches, 289, 292-95, 297, 305-8,
    360, 365
Decker, Jacques, 87
Deggendorf, Germany, 310, 313-14, 323

Delbo, Charlotte, 272
Delfzyl, Netherlands, 105
Delhasse family, 88-89
Delme family, 87
Dempsey, Sir Miles, 12
Denmark, 128, 165
Denny, Harold, 300
Deutsches Museum, Munich, 315, 318
Deventer, Netherlands, 114
Didier family, 89-90
Die Neue Zeitung, 205
Dinant, Belgium, 63
Diptheria, 101, 106
Diseases, 76-77, 101, 106, 113, 227, 228,
    232-34, 236, 240, 263, 301, 302,
    307, 341, 343
Displaced persons (DPs), 212, 217, 219,
    222, 249-80, 368
  Eisenhower and, 259, 278, 319-22,
    323, 330, 332, 333, 336, 348-49,
    351, 358
  French, 256, 262-72
  German, 245, 249-50, 251, 255
  Italian, 237-38
  Jews as, 238, 245-46, 310-38, 340-54
  mental states of, 251-52, 328, 330,
    332, 333, 341-42, 345-46, 349
  number of, 249, 254-56, 259, 263,
    264
  Polish, 256, 272-80
  processing of, 253-54
  Russian, 254, 257-61
  self-repatriation, 255, 256
Dives-sur-Mer, France, 28
Djilas, Milovan, 241
Dniepr river, 146
Doherty, Muriel Knox, 343, 344
Don river, 138
Don Suisse, 246
Dönitz, Karl, 117
Dora concentration camp, 360
Dörbeck, East Prussia, 164
Dortmund, Germany, 191, 199, 200
Drama, Greece, 229
Drancy, France, 263, 269
Dresden, Germany, 188-89
Drummond, Sir Jack, 106, 112-13
Dubru family, 87
Duisburg, Germany, 191
Dull, Elly, 112
Dunkerque, France, 69
Duras, Marguerite, 262, 263
Düsseldorf, Germany, 191
Dutch. See Netherlands

Dutch National Socialist Movement,
    99-100
Dysentery, 77, 113, 236, 301, 302, 305,
    307, 341, 343

East Germany, 370, 372
East Prussia, 127, 133, 134, 153, 161-67,
    172, 370
Easterman, Alex, 359, 361
Economist magazine, 247
Eden, Anthony, 101, 115, 152, 258
Ehlert, Herta, 360
Ehrenburg, Ilya, 131-33, 136, 146, 154,
    160, 161
Eichmann, Adolf, 364
Eichmedien, East Prussia, 163
Einsatzgruppen, 142, 145
Eisenhower, Dwight D., 45, 53, 64, 67,
    69, 72, 73, 369
  on bombing of Germany, 189
  D-Day and, 12, 14, 36
  displaced persons and, 259, 278,
    319-22, 323, 330, 332, 333, 336,
    348-49, 351, 358
  German occupation and, 170, 173,
    179, 180, 196-98, 202-4
  German surrender and, 128
  Netherlands and, 104-7, 109-11,
    115-16, 121
  postwar memoir by, 5
  returns to U.S., 336
  UNRRA and, 218-19
  visit to Ohrdruf concentration camp,
    295-96, 308
El Shatt refugee camp, Egypt, 227,
    241-42
Elbe river, 126
Elliott, Edward, 22, 43, 60
Erickson, John, 138, 157
Erskine, George W. E. J., 64, 67, 68, 91
Essen, Germany, 189, 191
Estonia, 132
Eure, France, 28
Évrecy, France, 28

Failon, Belgium, 63
Falaise, France, 15, 20, 28, 36, 38-39, 44
Fasteau, Irving "Jack," 242-43
Fear, 20, 77-78
Feldafing, Germany, 310, 313-15, 319,
    321-22, 323, 358
Féraille, Jeanne, 63
Finland, 133
First Canadian Army, 98, 114, 119, 120

Fischova-Gachova, Erica, 346-47
Flanner, Janet, 268
Fleury, France, 32-33
Fleury, Jacqueline, 269, 270
Föhrenwald, Germany, 310, 323, 336
Food shortages
    in Belgium, 65-67
    displaced persons and, 316, 320, 322,
        324, 341, 343
    in France, 26, 33, 55
    in Germany, 204-8
    in Greece, 227-28
    in Italy, 234-37
    in Netherlands, 98, 99, 101-22, 368
    in Soviet Union, 138, 146
    starvation deaths, 99, 106, 110-13,
        120, 122, 132
    in Yugoslavia, 240
Foreign labor force, in Germany, 25-27,
        61, 65, 100, 102, 132, 145, 249-50,
        257, 258, 263
Forrest, A. J., 41-42
Forster, Arnold, 223
Fossoli camp, Italy, 290
Foulkes, Lieutenant-General, 117
Four Freedoms (Roosevelt), 7, 75, 218
Fragenbogen questionnaire, 203
France, 5
    atrocities in, 53-55
    black market in, 266
    bombing of, 3, 14, 15, 20, 21, 27-29,
        31-39
    collaborators in, 23, 25, 48-49, 267
    communists in, 110, 266
    D-Day landings (Operation Over-
        lord), 3, 7, 11-14, 19, 21, 27-29, 36,
        74, 149, 152
    displaced persons in, 256, 262-72
    fraternization in, 178
    Gaullist government-in-exile, 263
    Germany and, 12-15, 23, 25-29, 31,
        32, 34, 35, 38-39
    Jews in, 263, 267
    labor for Germany from, 25-27
    Normandy, 1-3, 6-7, 11-15, 19-23,
        27-60, 69, 131
    North African soldiers, 50, 52, 54
    Paris, 15, 42-43, 267-70, 290
    prostitution in, 55-56
    resistance in, 25, 27, 28, 48, 59,
        262-67, 269
    Vichy government, 23, 25, 26, 46, 262,
        265, 267, 371

    welcome to Allies in, 19, 22-23, 40,
        41, 43
Frank, Hans, 372
Frankfurt, Germany, 191, 192, 204, 255,
    310, 330
Fraternization
    in Germany, 177-82, 196-98, 202
    in Italy, 178
Free French, 45
Frenay, Henri, 263-66, 269
French 2nd Armored Division, 42
Friends Relief Service, 120, 246
Frisches Haff lagoon, 165
Front de l'Indépendence (Belgium), 66,
    67
Frost, Sydney, 118
Fussell, Paul, 74

Gale, Sir Humphrey, 221
Gandersheim, Germany, 263, 304
Ganshof, François, 93
Ganshof, Walter, 91
Gassau, Ingeborg, 198
Gauting hospital, Germany, 323
Geersens, Nand, 68-69
Gelhorn, Martha, 74, 181
General Government (Poland), 141, 294
Geneva convention of 1929, 359
Gengoux, José, 83
George II, King of Greece, 228
George VI, King of England, 148
Georgin, M., 83
Gerbrandy, Pieter S., 102-3, 105, 106,
    108, 109, 111, 115
German Army Group B, 126
German Army Group Center, 154
German Army Group South, 154
German Dirlewanger Regiment, 157
German 18th Volksgrenadier Division,
    85
German Fifteenth Army, 72
German Fourth Panzer Army, 139
German Hitlerjugend Division, 63
German Kaminski Brigade, 157
German Kampfgruppe Peiper, 81-85
German Panzer Lehr Division, 14, 29
German Prinz Eugen Division, 63
German Sixth Army, 139
German 62nd Volksgrenadier Division,
    85, 140
German Third Panzer Army, 166
German 12th SS Panzer Division, 14, 29
German Twenty-Fifth Army, 117

German 21st Panzer Division, 14, 29
Germany. *See also* Concentration camps
  Allied occupation of, 4, 127, 170-82,
    185, 192-207, 310-38, 371
  Belgium and, 62-63, 73, 81-85
  bombing of, 126-27, 182-92, 199-201,
    368, 370
  coal production in, 204, 207
  denial of responsibility in, 180-82,
    194, 200-202
  displaced persons in, 245, 249-50, 251,
    255
  feelings about Hitler, 200, 202
  food shortages in, 204-8
  foreign labor force in, 61, 65, 100, 102,
    132, 145, 249-50, 257, 258, 263
  humanitarian relief in, 219, 221, 222,
    225, 238
  Netherlands and, 98-102
  Normandy and, 1-2, 12-15, 23, 25-29,
    31, 32, 34, 35, 38-39
  Poland and, 99, 141, 150, 151
  refugees in, 128, 162-63, 165-67, 192
  resistance in, 125
  Soviet Union and, 4, 11, 126-28,
    131-38, 141-46, 153-54, 160-68,
    260
  venereal disease and prostitution in,
    197
Ghlin, Belgium, 62
Gilbert, Martin, 142, 143
Gillam, Cornelia Stabler, 192
Gleiwitz, Poland, 293
Glücks, Richard, 362
Godinne, Belgium, 63
Goedde, Petra, 196-97
Goethe, Johann Wolfgang von, 191
Gohimont family, 89
Gold beach, 12, 23
Gollan, Frank, 235-37
Goodfriend, Arthur, 196
Göring, Hermann, 372
Goupil, Bernard, 29-30
Governments-in-exile
  Dutch, 99, 101-3, 106, 108
  French, 263
  Greek, 228
  Polish, 151-52, 154-55, 159
Granville, France, 217, 219, 222, 223, 225
Graz, Austria, 337
"Great Alibi in the Making, The" (Mid-
    dleton), 180-81
Grebbe Line, 115

Greece, 212, 215, 219
  atrocities in, 229
  civil war in, 232
  Communists in, 228-29
  food shortages in, 227-28
  German occupation of, 227
  government-in-exile, 228
  humanitarian relief in, 215, 219,
    221-22, 225, 227-33
  resistance in, 228-29, 369
  venereal disease in, 228
Greek-Americans, 244
Greek War Relief, 245
Greenwood, Richard, 38, 41, 60
Grégoire, Regine, 84
Grese, Irma, 358-64
Grigg, Sir P. J., 107
Grinberg, Zalman, 312-15, 332
Gringauz, Samuel, 329, 353
Grinspan, Ida, 307
Groningen, Netherlands, 114
Gross-Koslau, East Prussia, 164
Gross-Rosen concentration camp,
    292-94, 306
Grossman, Vasily, 135, 140-41, 146-47,
    160
Guêprei, France, 38
Gulag, 260
Gulf of Finland, 153
Gunskirchen Lager concentration camp,
    299

Haarlem, Netherlands, 118
Hague, Netherlands, 98, 106, 116, 119,
    122
Hague convention of 1907, 359
Halifax, Lord, 354
Hall, Alan, 239
Hamburg, Germany, 126, 188, 200, 201,
    205, 225
Hamm, Luxembourg, 1-2
Hammond, Barbara, 222
Hammond, J. L., 222
Hannover, Germany, 205, 300, 353
Hardman, Leslie, 302-3, 345
Harris, Sir Arthur, 186-87
Harrison, Earl G., 318-23, 348-51
Hastings, Max, 31, 33
Hawke, Liedewij, 112
Hayward, Nancy, 230
Hebrew Immigrant Aid Society, 246
Heftler, Nadine, 306-7
Heidelberg, Germany, 192, 255

Heidema, Jack, 118
Heidenreich, Brigitte, 198
Hendrickson, Roy F., 221
Henry V (Shakespeare), 140
Herbert, A. G., 39-40, 43
Herbert, Ulrich, 249, 250
Hessen, 192
Heute magazine, 207
Heymont, Irving, 325-31
Hibbs, Ben, 190
Higgins, Marguerite, 255, 256
Himmler, Heinrich, 142, 145, 288, 294, 295
Hitler, Adolf, 4, 15, 23, 64, 68, 73, 99, 127, 144, 156, 177, 191, 340
    air war and, 68, 184, 186
    concentration camps and, 284, 288
    German feelings about, 180, 182, 200, 202
    invasion of Soviet Union and, 133, 134, 136-39, 141-42, 147
    Mein Kampf by, 133, 313
    suicide of, 117, 125, 126, 128, 168, 267
    Warsaw Rising and, 158
Hitler-Stalin Pact of 1939, 132, 147, 150, 151, 370
Hodges, Courtney, 73, 83
Hoehler, Fred K., 221
Höess, Rudolf, 360, 362
Hoessler, Franz, 358-60, 364
Hoffman family, 87
Holland (see Netherlands)
Holland Council, 120
Holocaust. See Concentration camps
Home Army (Poland), 155-58
Honsfeld, Belgium, 82
Hopkins, Harry, 211
Hornbeck, Stanley K., 108
Hôtel Lutétia, Paris, 268-70
Houffalize, Belgium, 85-88
Houlgate, France, 28
Hubrecht, Elze, 63
Hughes, Llewelyn Glyn, 340, 361
Hull, Cordell, 172
Hulme, Kathryn, 272-77, 280
Humanitarian relief. See United Nations Relief and Rehabilitation Administration (UNRRA)
Hun, Belgium, 63
Hungary, 4, 147, 154, 159, 219, 240, 311, 319, 336
Hunter, Isabel, 229-30
Hürtgen Forest, Belgium, 72, 73
Hyman, Joseph, 317-18

I. G. Farben, 204, 287
Ijsselmeer river, 115
India, 220
Institute on Jewish Affairs, New York, 323
Inter-Allied Psychological Study Group, 251
International League for the Rights of Man, 351
International Military Tribunal, 356, 371-72
Israel, 330, 338
Istanbul, Turkey, 229
Italy, 5, 11, 149
    Allied occupation of, 233
    black market in, 235
    communists in, 110
    displaced persons in, 233, 237-38, 333, 334
    food shortages in, 234-37
    fraternization in, 178
    humanitarian relief in, 219, 221-22, 224, 225, 233-39
    venereal disease and prostitution in, 95, 233, 238

Jackson, Robert, 221
Janner, Barnett, 353
Japan, 20, 187, 369
Jarrell, Randall, 183
JCS 1067, 173
Jemappes, Belgium, 62
Jenkins, Hugh, 346
Jewish Agency for Palestine, 246, 314, 321, 329, 331
Jewish Chronicle, 345-46, 350-51, 359, 364
Jewish Committee for Relief Abroad, 246, 348
Jews. See also Concentration camps
    in Belgium, 61
    as displaced persons, 238, 245-46, 310-38, 340-54
    in France, 263, 267
    German feelings about, 200-202
    in Latvia, 143-44
    in Lithuania, 142, 143, 312, 329
    in Netherlands, 100
    Palestine, dream of, 5, 238, 285, 310, 311, 319, 321, 325, 328-31, 333, 339-41, 347-49, 351-54
    in Poland, 99, 141-43, 287-88, 312, 333-35, 337, 338
    in Soviet Union, 131, 142-43
    in Ukraine, 144, 146-47
Job, Gustave, 83

Job, Oscar, 83
Jodl, Alfred, 128
Johnson, Edwin C., 352
Johnston, J. A. D., 302
Johnston, Richard J. H., 191-92
Jourde, Germaine, 274
Judenburg, Austria, 337
Juno beach, 12, 23

Kacel, Boris, 143
Kaltenbrunner, Ernst, 372
Kapos, 357, 358
Karlsruhe, Germany, 192
Kato Nevrokopion, Greece, 229-30
Katyn massacre, 152
Kaválla, Greece, 230
Keitel, Wilhelm, 128, 372
Kempten, Germany, 199, 201
Kenner, Albert W., 197
Kharkov, Russia, 138, 146
Kiel Canal, 105
Kielce massacre, 338
Kiev, Russia, 135, 143, 146
Kimmel family, 270
King, William B., 227
Klausner, Abraham J., 314-19, 331, 336
Klein, Fritz, 358-60, 362-64
Klein-Koslau, East Prussia, 164
Klin, Russia, 137
Knauth, Percy, 191, 299, 300
Kohn, Alexandre, 271
Königsberg, East Prussia, 153, 166
Kopelev, Lev, 164, 165
Kovno, Lithuania, 143, 312, 313, 329
Krakow, Poland, 287
Kramer, Josef, 341, 355-56, 358-62, 364, 371
Krasnodar, Russia, 138
Kursk, Russia, 146

La Ferté, France, 43
La Gleize, Belgium, 83
La Guardia, Fiorello, 221
La Roche, Belgium, 90-91
Lambert family, 83
Lancaster bombers, 116
Landsberg, Germany, 310, 313, 315, 323, 325-32, 336, 353
Lane, John, 127
Lanzerath, Belgium, 81
Latvia, 132
    Jews in, 143-44
Le Havre, France, 50, 69
League of Nations, 339

Leavitt, Moses, 334
Lebensraum, 133, 142
Leclerc, Philippe, 42
Leeuwarden, Netherlands, 114
Legrand, Marcel, 84
Lehman, Herbert H., 218, 219, 221, 230, 247
Lehndorff, Hans Graf von, 166-67
Leiden, Netherlands, 103, 116
Leith-Ross, Sir Frederick, 217
Leningrad, Russia, 134, 135, 138, 153
Lenip, Margaret von, 111
Leopold III, King of Belgium, 64, 65
Levi, Primo, 257, 283-84, 287, 289-92, 367-68
Levine, Joseph, 334
Levy, Yvette, 307
Lévy-Hass, Hanna, 305
Lévy-Osbert, Liliane, 270
"Liberation Complex," 251, 332
Lichtheim, Fela, 305-6
Liebling, A. J., 22-23
Liège, Belgium, 61, 64, 67, 68, 73, 84, 86, 91, 92
Lienz, Austria, 260
Life magazine, 299
Lille, France, 264, 270
Lingen, Germany, 345
Lingeuville, Belgium, 81
Lion-sur-Mer, France, 28
Lipscombe, F. M., 341
Lisieux, France, 28, 37, 44
Lithuania, 132, 311
    Jews in, 142, 143, 312, 329
Lódź, Poland, 142, 287-88, 334
Logistics problems, in Belgium, 69-70, 72
Lombard, Laurent, 81
London Illustrated News, 356
Long, Tania, 202
Longues-sur-Mer, France, 28
Longuyon, France, 264
Looting, 41-42, 91-92, 255
Lorraine, 72
Losheim, Belgium, 81, 85
Lublin, Poland, 154, 288, 334
Luftwaffe, 139, 184, 187
Lüneburg, Germany, 358
Lüneburg Heath, Germany, 128
Luxembourg, 1-2
Lvov, Poland, 142-43, 154

Maas river, 102, 108, 114
Maben, Buell, 230
MacAuslan, Alan, 302

MacDonald, Charles, 74, 77, 78
Mainz, Germany, 191
Maisy, France, 28
Majdanek concentration camp, 287, 288
Malaria, 227, 228, 231, 233, 236
Malmédy, Belgium, 80, 81, 88-89
Malmédy massacre, 82-83
Manche, France, 12, 28
Mannheim, Germany, 192
Maps
    Départment of Calvados, 24
    Germany and East Prussia, 163
    Holland, 104
    Normandy 6 June-1 July 1944, 16-17
    Occupied Germany, 185
    Pursuit to the German Border 26
        August-10 September 1944, 70-71
Maréchal, Joseph, 87
Marseilles, France, 264, 271
Marshall, George, 107, 197-98, 319
Marshall Plan, 247
Martiny, Joséphine, 87
Masset, Georges, 273, 275-77
Mathis-Izikowitz, Mary-Rose, 271-72
Maubeuge, France, 264
Mauthausen concentration camp, 270,
    293, 309, 360
Mayer, Edward, 317
McBride, Horace, 327
McNarney, Joseph T., 279, 336
Mein Kampf (Hitler), 133, 313
Melchior family, 89
Menshikov, Michail, 221
Merville, France, 28
Messec, Harry, 335, 337
Metz, France, 72
Meurer, Elly, 86
Meuse river, 63, 73, 81, 85
Mézidon, France, 28, 51
Middleton, Drew, 180-81, 198
Mihailović, Draža, 239, 240
Mikołajczyk, Stanisław, 151, 155, 159
Milos island, 215
Minsk, Russia, 134, 143, 154
Mintzer, Oscar, 323-24
Mitterrand, François, 58-59, 262-63, 265
Modena, Italy, 290
Molotov, Vyacheslav, 158
Mondeville, France, 28
Mons, Belgium, 62, 67
Mont Fleury, France, 28
Montebourg, France, 28
Montenegro, 240
Montgomery, Sir Bernard Law, 72

displaced persons and, 278
food shortages and, 204, 206
German surrender and, 128
Netherlands and, 106-7, 109, 115
    in Normandy, 12, 14, 29, 31, 33
Moravia, 307
Morgan, Sir Frederick, 337-38
Morgenthau, Henry, 170-75, 318, 319
Morrell, Sydney, 242
Morris, K. W., 38
Moscow, Russia, 134-38
Mouvement National des Prisonniers
    de Guerre et Deportés (National
    Movement of Prisoners of War and
    Deportees), 262
Mulhouse, France, 264, 267
Müller, Filip, 292
Munich, Germany, 192, 199, 200, 310,
    314, 323, 325, 330
Münster, Germany, 199
Murray, James E., 352
Murrow, Edward R., 299-300
Mussert, Anton, 100

Nadich, Judah, 321
Nahon, Marco, 293
Nakomiady, Poland, 163
Namur, Belgium, 63, 91
Nancy, France, 72, 269
Nansen, Fridtjof, 223
Naples, Italy, 233, 235, 236
Napoleon Emperor, 153
National Catholic Welfare Conference,
    245, 246
National People's Liberation Army
    (ELAS) (Greece), 228
National War Fund, 244
Natzweiler concentration camp, 295, 360
Nazi Party. See Germany
Neidenburg, East Prussia, 165
Neill, George, 75-77
Netherlands, 5, 98-122, 128
    Amsterdam, 98, 103, 105, 106, 111-12,
        118-20, 122
    atrocities in, 100-101
    black market in, 102, 113, 120
    bombing of, 99, 101, 109, 110
    British government and, 102-3, 108-9
    Canadians in, 114, 117-21
    coal production in, 103, 107, 112
    collaborators in, 100
    communists in, 110
    flooding of, 101, 109, 115, 122
    food crisis in, 98, 99, 101-22, 368

Germany and, 98-102
government-in-exile, 99, 101-3, 106, 108
Hague, 98, 106, 116, 119, 122
Jews in, 100
labor for Germany from, 100, 102
resistance in, 100-102, 110, 116
Rotterdam, 98, 99, 106, 114, 116, 118-20, 122
Soviet Union and, 115, 116
starvation deaths in, 99, 106, 110-13, 120, 122
welcome to Allies in, 99, 117-18, 121
Netherlands Military Administration, 120
Neumünster, Germany, 199
New York Herald Tribune, 255
New York Times, 18, 180, 191, 198, 202, 230, 300, 354, 356
New Yorker, The, 22, 268
New Zealand, 220
Newman, Al, 299
Newman, Jean, 248
News of Germany, 203-4
Newsweek magazine, 288, 299
Nicolay family, 83
Nijmegen, Netherlands, 72, 101, 114
NKVD, 155
Nomberg-Przytyk, Sara, 293
Nordhausen concentration camp, 296
Normandy, 1-3, 6-7, 11-15, 19-23, 27-59, 69, 131
North Africa, Anglo-American landings in, 11, 217
North African soldiers, 50, 52, 54
Nuremberg, Germany, 191-92, 200, 201
Nuremberg war crimes trials, 117, 356, 357, 360, 364, 371-72

October Revolution, 136
Oder river, 126, 151, 152, 161, 165
Odessa, Ukraine, 153, 257, 264, 271
O'Dwyer, Lieutenant-Colonel, 337
Office of Foreign Relief and Rehabilitation Operations (OFRRO), 221
Office of Strategic Services (OSS), 251
Ohrdruf concentration camp, 295-96, 308
Oleiski, Jacob, 329
Olson, Sidney, 189, 300
Omaha beach, 12-13, 23, 28, 58
Operation Bagration, 153-54, 160
Operation Barbarossa, 133, 143
Operation Epsom, 31
Operation Market Garden, 72, 74, 101

Operation Overlord, 3, 7, 11-14, 19, 21, 27-29, 36, 74, 149, 152
Operation Tally Ho, 277
Operation Veritable, 114
Order Service (Netherlands), 100
Orel, Russia, 135
Orne, France, 28
Orne river, 12, 29, 35, 57
Osnabrück, Germany, 204
Ostarbeiter (eastern workers), 145
Osterode, East Prussia, 162
Ostrava, Germany, 307
Ostróda, Poland, 162
Ouistreham, France, 27-29, 45, 57
Ourthe river, 86
Overy, Richard, 138

Padover, Saul, 196
Palestine, 5, 238, 285, 310, 311, 319, 321, 325, 328-31, 333, 339-41, 347-49, 351-54
Papandreou, George, 228
Parfondruy, Belgium, 84
Paris, France, 15, 42-43, 267-70, 290
Pas-de-Calais, France, 25, 27, 28, 72
Patras, Greece, 229, 230, 232
Patton, George S., Jr., 1, 73, 203, 295-96, 299, 321
Paulus, Friedrich, 139
Pavelic, Ante, 239
Peiper, Joachim, 81, 83, 84
Pétain, Henri-Philippe, 23, 25, 265
Peter, King of Yugoslavia, 239, 240
Petrov, Yevgeny, 137
Pforzheim, Germany, 204
Phillips, Raymond, 356, 357, 361
Pierlot, Hubert, 64-67
Pillau, Germany, 165
Pinson, Koppel, 324, 325
Piraeus, Greece, 228
Plainsman, The (movie), 68
Pocket Guide to Germany (War Department), 176-78, 181, 200
Pohl, Oswald, 362
Pointe du Hoc, France, 28
Poirier, Joseph, 30, 31, 34-35
Poland, 3-4, 11
atrocities in, 142-43, 152, 157, 338
displaced persons in, 256, 272-80
Germany and, 99, 141, 150, 151
government-in-exile, 151-52, 154-55, 159
Jews in, 99, 141-43, 287-88, 312, 333-35, 337, 338

Poland, *cont.*
  postwar political turmoil in, 333
  resistance in, 62-63, 66-67, 87, 155
  Soviet Union and, 4, 132, 147, 154-56,
    158-59, 161
  territory issue at Tehran Conference,
    150-53
  UNRRA in, 219
  Warsaw, 134, 142, 154, 155
  Warsaw Rising, 156-58
Polish-Americans, 244
Polish Committee of National Libera-
  tion, 155
Polish Jewish Restitution Committee,
  323
Pomerania, 128, 161, 167
Popular Front (France), 2
Port-en-Bessin, France, 28
Potsdam Conference of 1945, 202, 203,
  234
President's War Relief Control Board,
  244
Preussisch Holland, East Prussia, 162
Prisoners, 15, 19, 38, 55, 73, 74, 80, 82,
  83, 85, 101, 134, 136, 138, 139,
  145, 154, 160, 249, 250, 258-60,
  263-67
Prochnik, Poland, 164
Prostitution, 252
  in Belgium, 94, 95
  in France, 55-56
  in Germany, 197
  in Italy, 95, 233, 238
"Psychological Problems of Displaced
  Persons," 251-52
Pucheu, Pierre, 262
Pyle, Ernie, 19-21, 23, 57, 74

Quaregnon, Belgium, 62
Quebec Conference of 1943, 149, 172
Quevaucamps, Belgium, 62-63

Racial prejudice, 50-55
Radom, Poland, 334
RAMPs (recovered Allied military personnel), 250
Rape
  in Belgium, 92
  in France, 53-55
  in Germany, 160, 162-169, 194-195
  by Red Army, 160, 162-169
  by U.S. soldiers, 53-55, 92, 194-195
Rauter, Hanns Albin, 100, 101

Ravensbrück concentration camp,
  268-71, 288, 306, 307, 360
Reading, Marchioness of, 349-51
Red Army, 4, 11, 126-28, 132, 134, 136,
  138, 143-47, 153-58, 160-69, 240,
  258, 288, 370
Red Ball Express, 50, 51
Red Cross, 101, 105, 111, 115, 119, 120,
  238, 246, 265, 271, 277, 317
Red Star newspaper, 128, 131, 135,
  140-41, 160
Rees, Netherlands, 114
Refugee Relief Committee, 246
Refugees. *See also* Displaced persons
    (DPs)
  Belgian, 81, 86, 97
  French, 33, 40-41, 44, 57
  German, 128, 162-63, 165-67, 192
  Greek, 226-27
  Soviet, 135
Relève (relief) scheme, 265
Renardmont, Belgium, 84
Renier, Anny, 89
Renier, Maria, 89
Reparations, 172, 175, 202
Resistance groups
  Belgian, 62-63, 66-67, 87
  Dutch, 100-102, 110, 116
  French, 25, 27, 28, 48, 59, 262-67, 269
  German, 125
  Greek, 228-29, 369
  Polish, 62-63, 66-67, 87, 155
  Yugoslav, 369
Responsibility, denial of, 180-82, 194,
  200-202
Reza Shah Pahlavi, Mohammed, 148
Rhine river, 69, 72, 101, 102, 105, 108,
  109, 114, 115, 126, 180, 189, 191,
  253
Rhineland, 1, 106, 172, 178, 189
Rhön mountains, 273
Ribbentrop, Joachim von, 372
Ribbentrop-Molotov Line, 152
Richards, I., 345
Rifkind, Simon, 38, 322, 335, 336, 354
Riga, Latvia, 142-44
Ritchie, Major G., 43
Rivière, Belgium, 63
Rock, Eli, 334-35
Roer river, 72, 180
Roker, L. F., 22
Romania, 4, 133, 147, 154, 159, 240, 311,
  319, 334

Rome, Italy, 11, 234, 235
Rooks, Lowell W., 221
Roosevelt, Franklin D., 129, 147, 241
   death of, 267
   Four Freedoms of, 7, 75, 218
   German occupation policy and,
      170-76
   Netherlands and, 106-8, 110-11
   at Tehran Conference, 148-50, 152-53
   UNRRA and, 217-18
   at Yalta Conference, 174-75
Rosenberg, Alfred, 372
Rosenman, Sam, 354
Rosensaft, Hadassah (Ada Bimko), 306,
   361, 364
Rosensaft, Josef, 347, 354, 361
Rostov, Russia, 138
Rötgen, Germany, 180
Rotterdam, Netherlands, 98, 99, 106,
   114, 116, 118-20, 122
Rouen, France, 27
Royal Air Force (RAF), 28, 29, 33, 35, 60,
   85, 184, 186-89, 191
Royal Army Medical Corps (RAMC), 302
Rozenblum, Nathan, 307
Rubin, Yvette, 248
Ruhr, 109, 126, 172, 183, 190, 191, 205
Rundstedt, Gerd von, 25
Rusinek, Zygmunt, 274

Saar basin, 72, 172
Sachsenhausen concentration camp, 360
Sainlez, Belgium, 89-90
Saint-Aubin, France, 28
Saint-Lô, France, 15, 20, 29, 38, 50
St. Louis Star-Times, 205
Sainte-Mère-Eglise, France, 45
Saint Ottilien monastery, Schwabhausen,
   Germany, 312-14, 317, 323, 330
Saint-Pierre-du-Mont, France, 28
Saint Vith, Belgium, 85-86
Salm river, 85, 86
Salonika, Greece, 229, 230
Salvation Army, 120
Sandbostel concentration camp, 303
Sardinia, 233
Saturday Evening Post, 190
Sauckel, Fritz, 26, 145
Save the Children, 120
Sayre, Francis B., 218, 221, 247
Scheldt estuary, 69, 72, 114
Schleiter, Josephine, 162-63
Schmidt, Ilse, 198

Schwabhausen, Germany, 312
Schwandorf, Germany, 334
Schwartz, Anna, 166
Schwartz, Joseph, 319-21
Schwebel, Ernst, 116
Scobie, Ronald, 228
Segalson, Moses, 329
Seine-Maritime, France, 28
Seine river, 15, 42, 61, 69
Selborne, Lord, 103
Serbia, 239, 240
Sérrai, Greece, 229
Sevastopol, Russia, 138, 176
Sexual violence. See Rape
Seyss-Inquart, Arthur, 99-100, 102,
   114-17, 372
Shakespeare, William, 140
She'erit Hapleitah (surviving remnant),
   312
Shils, Edward A., 251
Siberia, 132, 151, 166
Sicily, 233
Siegfried Line, 15, 63, 69, 98, 131
Sikorski, Władysław, 151, 152
Silesia, 128, 161, 167, 290, 294
Sington, Derek, 301, 303, 345, 346, 347,
   361
Smith, H. A., 361-62
Smith, Marcus, 299
Smith, Walter Bedell, 116, 117, 189, 330,
   336
Smolensk, Russia, 134
Sobibór concentration camp, 287
Solzhenitsyn, Aleksandr, 260
South Africa, 220
Sovet, Belgium, 63
Soviet 60th Army, 283
Soviet 3rd Belorussian Front, 166
Soviet Union, 2-4, 369
   atrocities in, 137
   casualties, 131-32, 136, 138, 139
   coal production in, 138
   displaced persons in, 254, 257-61
   food shortages, 138, 146
   Germany and, 4, 11, 126-28, 131-38,
      141-46, 153-54, 160-68, 260
   Jews in, 131, 142-43
   labor for Germany from, 132, 145
   Leningrad, 134, 135, 138, 153
   liberation of concentration camps,
      283, 288-89, 291-92, 307
   Moscow, 134-38
   Netherlands and, 115, 116

Soviet Union, *cont.*
  Poland and, 4, 132, 147, 154-56,
    158-59, 161
  Red Army, 4, 11, 126-28, 132, 134,
    136, 138, 143-47, 153-58, 160-69,
    240, 258, 288, 370
  scorched-earth policy of, 136
  Stalingrad, 11, 138-41
  Stalinist rule in, 132
Spanish Civil War, 224
Speer, Albert, 25
Spender, Stephen, 182-83
Srole, Leo, 328, 336
SS Panzer Grenadiers, 63
Stahel, Rainer, 156
Stalin, Josef, 129, 260
  dictatorship of, 132-33
  German invasion and, 134-36, 138,
    140
  German surrender and, 128
  "percentages" conversation with
    Churchill, 158-59
  Polish question and, 4, 151-53, 158-59
  at Tehran Conference, 148-53, 159
  Warsaw Rising and, 157-58
  at Yalta Conference, 174-75
Stalingrad, Russia, 11, 138-41, 217
Stars and Stripes, 195-96
State, U.S. Department of, 173, 174, 219,
  221, 247, 318
Stavelot, Belgium, 81-85
Stettinius, Edward, Jr., 174
Stimson, Henry, 171-73, 319
Stolberg, Germany, 180
Stoumont, Belgium, 83
Stourdze, Marcel, 293
Strasbourg, France, 72, 264
Stratton, W. H., 337
Student Peace Service, 224
Stuttgart, Germany, 192
Stuttgarter Zeitung, 207
Stutthof concentration camp, 292
Submarines, 166
Susloparov, Ivan, 116
Sweden, 103-5, 271
Sword beach, 12, 23

Taft, Robert, 352
Tchaikovsky, Pyotr Ilich, 137
Tehran Conference of 1943, 148-53, 159
Templer, G. W. R., 349-50
Teutonic Knights, 127, 166
Theresienstadt concentration camp, 309,
  314

Thiele, Hannelore, 168
Thury-Harcourt, France, 29
Tilly-sur-Seulles, France, 14, 29, 31, 37, 44
Time magazine, 127, 189, 191, 198, 299,
  300
Times of London, 118, 189-91, 206, 351,
  359, 364
Tito, Marshal (Josip Broz), 239-41
Todt Organization, 25
Torgau, Germany, 126
Tousley, Harry, 46
Trager, David, 329
Treasury, U.S. Department of, 173
Treblinka concentration camp, 287
Trench foot, 76
Trobe, Jacob, 335
Trofaiach, Austria, 337
Trois Ponts, Belgium, 82, 84
Trouville, France, 51
Truman, Harry, 318-22, 333, 351-52, 354
Tuberculosis, 228, 234, 236, 341, 343
Turkey, 149
Typhoid, 106, 113
Typhus, 101, 228, 232, 240, 263, 301,
  341, 343, 344

Ukraine, 4, 131, 142, 151, 153
  German invasion and occupation of,
    133-36, 138
  Jews in, 144, 146-47
  labor for Germany from, 145
  Stalinist rule in, 132
  UNRRA in, 219
Unitarian Service Committee (USC),
  235-36, 245
United Nations, 149, 175
United Nations Relief and Rehabilitation
  Administration (UNRRA), 213,
  215-48
  Allied armies and, 216, 218, 219, 223,
    275-76
  Balkan Mission, 226
  charter of, 217, 219
  displaced persons and, 251-53, 255,
    272-80, 318-20, 323-25, 328, 333,
    335, 337, 346
  Eisenhower and, 218-19
  founding of, 215-16
  funding of, 212, 220
  in Germany, 219, 221, 222, 225, 238,
    250-55, 272-77, 279-80, 315, 316
  in Greece, 215, 219, 221-22, 225,
    227-33
  in Italy, 219, 221-22, 224, 225, 233-39

leaders of, 218, 221
staff of, 216-17, 221-25, 234
success of, 216-17, 225, 247-48
training of workers, 217, 219, 222, 223, 225
voluntary relief organizations and, 216, 243-46
in Yugoslavia, 219, 221-22, 224, 225, 239, 241-43
United Nations War Crimes Tribunal, 356
United Palestine Appeal, 245
UNRRA. *See* United Nations Relief and Rehabilitation Administration (UNRRA)
Unzer Sztyme (Our Voice) newspaper, 347
U.S. Army Air Forces (USAAF), 187, 188
U.S. Army Judge Advocate General (JAG), 194-95
U.S. Army VII Corps, 14, 45, 69, 73, 180, 189
U.S. Army XII Corps, 191
U.S. Eighth Air Force, 28, 29, 35, 187
U.S. 82nd Airborne, 12, 72, 74
U.S. 84th Infantry Division Airborne, 76, 98
U.S. 89th Infantry Division, 296
U.S. First Army, 1, 15
U.S. 4th Armored Division, 89, 296
U.S. 4th Infantry Division, 73, 76
U.S. Ninth Air Force, 28, 35, 85, 87
U.S. 99th Infantry Division, 73, 75, 82
U.S. 101st Airborne Division, 12, 41, 45, 72, 73, 74, 77
U.S. 106th Infantry Division, 73, 85
U.S. 2nd Infantry Division, 74
U.S. 7th Armored Division, 73, 85
U.S. 7th Army, 299
U.S. 76th Infantry Division, 6
U.S. Strategic Bombing Survey, 187-88, 199, 200
U.S. 10th Armored Division, 73
U.S. Third Army, 2, 15, 73, 89, 203, 274, 276, 277, 320, 322
U.S. 30th Infantry Division, 83
U.S. 12th Army Group, 73, 180
U.S. 24th Cavalry Reconnaissance Squadron, 90
U.S. 28th Division, 73, 75
U.S. 285th Field Artillery Observation Battalion, 82
U.S. 298th Combat Engineers, 91
USO, 192, 244

USSR. *See* Soviet Union
Ustaše movement, 239, 241
Utah beach, 12
Utrecht, Netherlands, 118, 121

V-1 and V-2 rockets, 68, 186
Vaad Hahatzala, 246
Valenciennes, France, 62
Valognes, France, 29
van der Zee, Henri, 113-14
van Zile Hyde, H., 242
Vel d'Hiv roundup, Paris, 290
Venereal disease (VD)
    in Belgium, 93-97
    in Germany, 197
    in Greece, 228
    in Italy, 95, 233, 238
Verviers, Belgium, 95-96
Vichy government, 23, 25, 26, 46, 262, 265, 267, 371
Vielsalm, Belgium, 86
Vierville, France, 13
Villedieu, France, 38
Villers-Bocage, France, 14, 29, 31, 37-38
Villers-le-Sec, France, 29
Vilna, Lithuania, 143
Vilnius, Lithuania, 154
Vinnhorst, Germany, 353
Vire, France, 29, 44, 51
Virgili, Fabrice, 49
Vistula river, 126, 154, 156, 157, 161
Volga river, 11, 134, 138, 139
Volkenrath, Elisabeth, 358-60, 364
Volterra, Mario, 235
Voluntary relief organizations, 216, 243-46
Von dem Bach, Erich, 157
Voronezh, Russia, 138
Vosges mountains, 72

Waal river, 72, 102, 108
Wageningen, Belgium, 117
Walcheren Island, 69, 72
Wallace, R. J., 276
Wallis, Marie Pope, 224-25
Walton, William, 127
"Wandering Jew, The" exhibit, Deutsches Museum, Munich, 315, 318
War, U.S. Department of, 53-54, 94, 105, 171, 173, 176
War correspondents, 19-21, 74, 137, 189-92, 198, 288, 298-300
War crimes trials, 117, 192, 202, 355-65, 371-72

War Prisoners Aid, 244
Warburg, Edward, 354
Warburg, Felix M., 316
Warhaftig, Zorach, 323, 324, 330
Warnant, Belgium, 63
Warsaw, Poland, 134, 142, 154, 155
Warsaw Rising, 156-58
Webster, David Kenyon, 41
Weisskirchen, Germany, 307
Weizmann, Chaim, 351, 353
Werth, Alexander, 138, 139
Wesel, Netherlands, 114
West Germany, 172, 370-72
West Wall, 63, 180
White, Arthur A., 331
White, J. Y., 34
White Paper on Palestine of 1939, 352, 353
Whiting, J. H., 275
Wiesbaden, Germany, 255
Wiesel, Eli, 293, 308-9
Wildflecken Camp, Bavaria, 272-77, 279-80
Wilhelm II, Kaiser, 177
Wilhelmina, Queen of the Netherlands, 64, 99, 102, 106
Wilson, Francesca, 222-23
Wilson, George, 76, 77
Winkler, Gerlinde, 164
Winwood, T. C. M., 362, 363
Winzer, Germany, 314

Witten, Germany, 199
Wolfsschanze, East Prussia, 127
World Jewish Congress, 336, 349, 351, 359, 361
World ORT Union, 246, 329
World Student Relief, 246
World Zionist Conference, 351
Wormser-Migot, Olga, 268
Wuppertal, Germany, 191
Wurst, Spencer, 74
Wurzburg, Germany, 204

Yalta Conference of 1945, 174-75, 250, 259
YMCA/YWCA, 245, 246
Youth of soldiers, 74-75
Yugoslavia, 4, 147, 154, 159, 212, 219
    civil war in, 239-41
    communists in, 239-41
    food shortages in, 240
    German invasion of, 239
    humanitarian relief in, 219, 221-22, 224, 225, 239, 241-43
    resistance in, 369

Zaun, Inge, 168
Zeilsheim, Germany, 310, 330, 336
Zhukov, Georgi, 128, 135, 139, 140, 161
Zionism, 329, 352
Zuid-Holland, 116
Zutphen, Netherlands, 114

About the Author

WILLIAM I. HITCHCOCK is Professor of History at Temple University in Philadelphia. He was born in Fukuoka, Japan, in 1965, and has lived in Tokyo, Tel Aviv, Paris, Brussels, Washington, Boston, and New Haven. He received his B.A. from Kenyon College in 1986, where he studied history and French literature, and earned his Ph.D. in history from Yale University in 1994. He taught at Yale for six years and won a teaching prize there. He has also taught at Wellesley College. Hitchcock is the author of *France Restored: Cold War Diplomacy and the Quest for Leadership in Europe 1945–1954* (Chapel Hill: University of North Carolina Press, 1998); and *The Struggle for Europe: The Turbulent History of a Divided Continent, 1945–Present* (New York: Doubleday, 2003). With Paul Kennedy, he co-edited *From War to Peace: Altered Strategic Landscapes in the Twentieth Century* (New Haven: Yale University Press, 2000). He is married to the historian Elizabeth R. Varon.